ASCENT®
CENTER FOR TECHNICAL KNOWLEDGE

CATIA V5-6R2017:
Advanced Surface Design

Learning Guide
1st Edition

ASCENT - Center for Technical Knowledge®
CATIA V5-6R2017: Advanced Surface Design
1st Edition

Prepared and produced by:

ASCENT Center for Technical Knowledge
630 Peter Jefferson Parkway, Suite 175
Charlottesville, VA 22911

866-527-2368
www.ASCENTed.com

Lead Contributor: Scott Hendren

ASCENT - Center for Technical Knowledge is a division of Rand Worldwide, Inc., providing custom developed knowledge products and services for leading engineering software applications. ASCENT is focused on specializing in the creation of education programs that incorporate the best of classroom learning and technology-based training offerings.

We welcome any comments you may have regarding this learning guide, or any of our products. To contact us please email: feedback@ASCENTed.com.

Contents

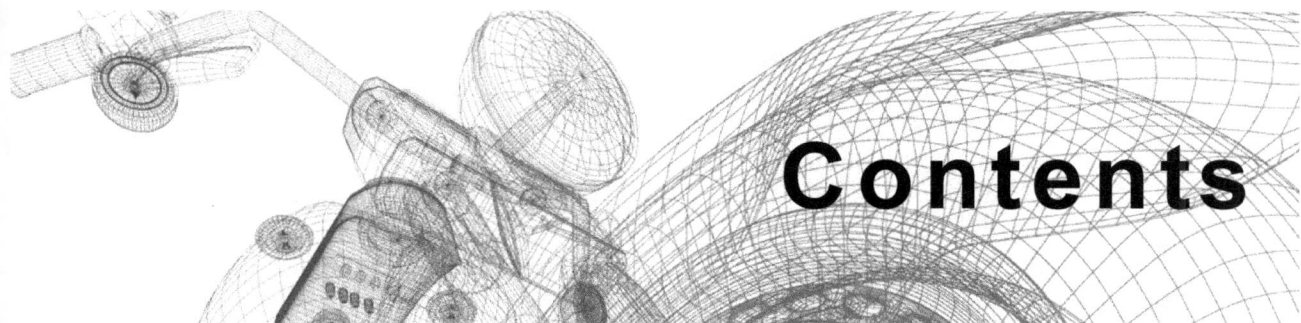

Preface

The *CATIA V5-6R2017: Advanced Surface Design* learning guide expands on the knowledge learned in the CATIA: Introduction to Surface Design learning guide by covering advanced curve and surface topics found in the Generative Shape Design Workbench. Topics include: advanced curve construction, advanced swept, blend and offset surface construction, complex fillet creation, and the use of laws. Curve and surface analysis are introduced to validate the student's geometry. Tools and methods for rebuilding geometry are also discussed. As with the *CATIA: Introduction to Surface Design* learning guide, meeting model specifications (such as continuity settings) remains forefront in introducing tools and methodologies.

Topics Covered

- Surface Design Overview

- Advanced Wireframe Elements

- Curve Analysis and Repair

- Swept Surfaces

- Blend Surfaces

- Adaptive Sweep

- Laws

- Advanced Surface Fillets

- Alternative Filleting Methods

- Duplication Tools

- Knowledge Templates

- Surface Analysis and Repair

- Offset Surfaces

- Project Exercises

Note on Software Setup

This learning guide assumes a standard installation of the software using the default preferences during installation. Lectures and practices use the standard software templates and default options for the Content Libraries.

This guide was developed against CATIA V5-6R2017, Service Pack 1.

Lead Contributor: Scott Hendren

Scott Hendren has been a trainer and curriculum developer in the PLM industry for over 20 years, with experience on multiple CAD systems, including Pro/ENGINEER, Creo Parametric, and CATIA. Trained in Instructional Design, Scott uses his skills to develop instructor-led and web-based training products.

Scott has held training and development positions with several high profile PLM companies, and has been with the Ascent team since 2013.

Scott holds a Bachelor of Mechanical Engineering Degree as well as a Bachelor of Science in Mathematics from Dalhousie University, Nova Scotia, Canada.

Scott Hendren has been the Lead Contributor for *CATIA: Advanced Surface Design* since 2013.

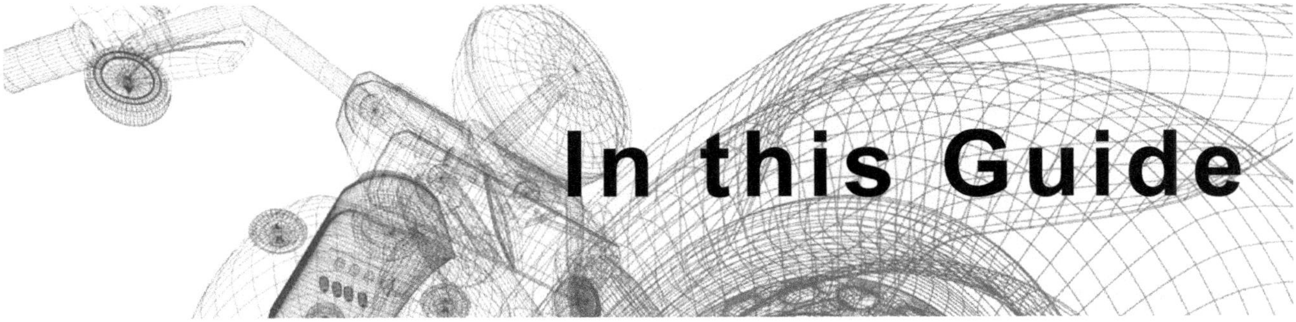

In this Guide

The following images highlight some of the features that can be found in this Learning Guide.

Practice Files

To download the practice files for this student guide, use the following steps

1. Type the URL shown below into the address bar of your Internet browser. The URL must be typed **exactly as shown**. If you are using an ASCENT ebook, you can click on the link to download the file.

Address bar

http://www.ASCENTed.com/getfile?id=xxxxxxxx

File Edit View Favorites Tools Help

2. Press <Enter> to download the .ZIP file that contains the Practice Files
3. Once the download is complete, unzip the file to a local folder. The unzipped file contains an .EXE file
4. Double-click on the .EXE file and follow the instructions to automatically install the Practice Files on the C:\ drive of your computer

   Do not change the location in which the Practice Files folder is installed. Doing so can cause errors when completing the practices in this student guide.

http://www.ASCENTed.com/getfile?id=xxxxxxxx

Stay Informed!
Interested in receiving information about upcoming promotional offers, educational events, invitations to complimentary webcasts, and discounts? If so, please visit:
www.ASCENTed.com/updates/

Help us improve our product by completing the following survey:
www.ASCENTed.com/feedback
You can also contact us at: *feedback@ASCENTed.com*

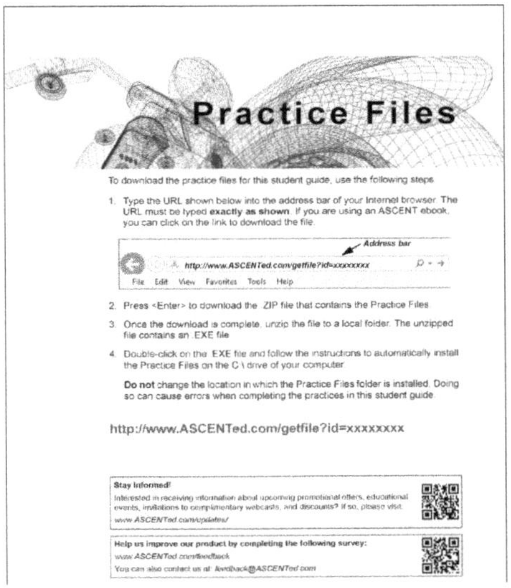

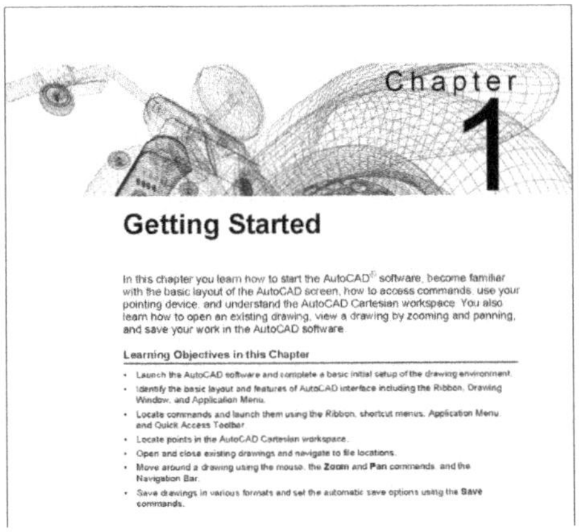

FTP link for practice files

Practice Files

The Practice Files page tells you how to download and install the practice files that are provided with this learning guide.

Chapter 1

Getting Started

In this chapter you learn how to start the AutoCAD® software, become familiar with the basic layout of the AutoCAD screen, how to access commands, use your pointing device, and understand the AutoCAD Cartesian workspace. You also learn how to open an existing drawing, view a drawing by zooming and panning, and save your work in the AutoCAD software.

Learning Objectives in this Chapter

- Launch the AutoCAD software and complete a basic initial setup of the drawing environment.
- Identify the basic layout and features of AutoCAD interface including the Ribbon, Drawing Window, and Application Menu.
- Locate commands and launch them using the Ribbon, shortcut menus, Application Menu and Quick Access Toolbar.
- Locate points in the AutoCAD Cartesian workspace.
- Open and close existing drawings and navigate to file locations.
- Move around a drawing using the mouse, the **Zoom** and **Pan** commands, and the Navigation Bar.
- Save drawings in various formats and set the automatic save options using the **Save** commands.

Learning Objectives for the chapter

Chapters

Each chapter begins with a brief introduction and a list of the chapter's Learning Objectives.

Side notes

Side notes are hints or additional information for the current topic.

Instructional Content

Each chapter is split into a series of sections of instructional content on specific topics. These lectures include the descriptions, step-by-step procedures, figures, hints, and information you need to achieve the chapter's Learning Objectives.

1.3 Working with Commands

Starting Commands

The main way to access commands in the AutoCAD software is to use the Ribbon. Several of the file commands are available in the Quick Access Toolbar or in the Application Menu. Some commands are available in the Status Bar or through shortcut menus. There are additional access methods, such as Tool Palettes. The names of all of the commands can also be typed in the Command Line. A table is included to help you to identify the various methods of accessing the commands.

When typing the name of a command in either the Command Line or Dynamic Input, the **AutoComplete** option automatically completes the entry when you pause as you type. It also supports mid-string search by displaying all of the commands that contain the word that you typed, as shown in Figure 1-12. You can then scroll through the list and select a command.

Figure 1-12

You can also click (Customize) *to display the Input Settings for the AutoComplete feature*

To set specific options for the **AutoComplete** feature, right-click on the Command Line, expand Input Settings, and select from the various options, such as the ability to search for system variables or to set the delay response time, as shown in Figure 1-13.

Figure 1-13

If you need to stop a command, press <Esc> to cancel. You might need to press <Esc> more than once.

As you work in the AutoCAD software, the software prompts you for the information that is required to complete each command. These prompts are displayed in the drawing window near the cursor and in the Command Line. It is crucial that you read the command prompts as you work, as shown in Figure 1-14.

© 2015 ASCENT - Center for Technical Knowledge®   1-9

Practice Objectives

Practices

Practices enable you to use the software to perform a hands-on review of a topic.

Some practices require you to use prepared practice files, which can be downloaded from the link found on the Practice Files page.

Practice 1c   Saving a Drawing File

Practice Objectives

• Open and save a drawing.
• Modify the **Automatic Saves** option.

Estimated time for completion: under 5 minutes

In this practice you will open a drawing, save it, and modify the **Automatic saves** option, as shown in Figure 1-51.

Figure 1-51

1. Open **Building Valley-M.dwg** from your class files folder.

2. In the Quick Access Toolbar, click (Save). In the Command Line, _QSAVE displays indicating that the AutoCAD software has performed a quick save.

3. In the Application Menu, click to open the Options dialog box.

4. In the Open and Save tab, change the time for Automatic save to 15 minutes.

Practice Files

To download the practice files for this learning guide, use the following steps:

1. Type the URL shown below into the address bar of your Internet browser. The URL must be typed **exactly as shown**. If you are using an ASCENT ebook, you can click on the link to download the file.

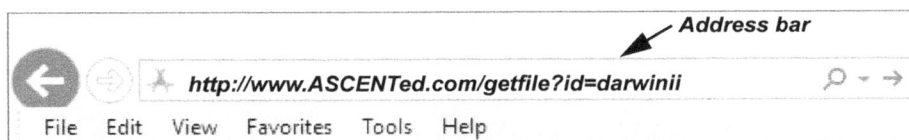

Address bar

http://www.ASCENTed.com/getfile?id=darwinii

File   Edit   View   Favorites   Tools   Help

2. Press <Enter> to download the .ZIP file that contains the Practice Files.

3. Once the download is complete, unzip the file to a local folder. The unzipped file contains an .EXE file.

4. Double-click on the .EXE file and follow the instructions to automatically install the Practice Files on the C:\ drive of your computer.

    Do not change the location in which the Practice Files folder is installed. Doing so can cause errors when completing the practices in this learning guide.

http://www.ASCENTed.com/getfile?id=darwinii

Stay Informed!

Interested in receiving information about upcoming promotional offers, educational events, invitations to complimentary webcasts, and discounts? If so, please visit:

www.ASCENTed.com/updates/

Help us improve our product by completing the following survey:

www.ASCENTed.com/feedback

You can also contact us at: *feedback@ASCENTed.com*

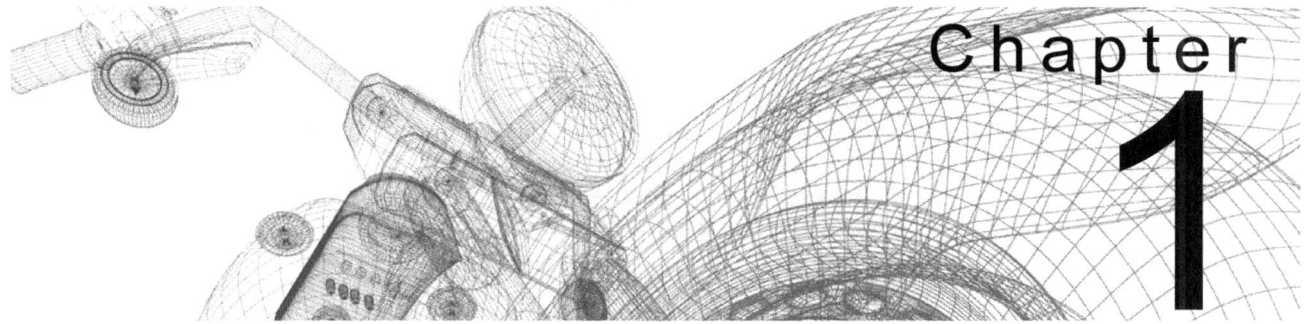

Surface Design Overview

This chapter serves as an overview of wireframe and surface design fundamentals and the typical surface design process.

Learning Objectives in this Chapter

- Recognize the surfacing tools in CATIA V5.
- Become familiar with the Generative Shape Design workbench.
- Review the surface design process.
- Review the concept of design intent as it relates to surface design.
- Review the organization of the Specification Tree.

1.1 Surfacing Tools in CATIA V5

Surface features introduce additional flexibility to a model. Surfaces can be used to define a complete part or to integrate a complex shape into the solid part (in the Part Design workbench). As learned previously, many parts can be designed directly using solid geometry. However, when shapes become more complex, surface shapes must often be used.

CATIA has several workbenches available to create surface geometry. The primary workbench is Generative Shape Design (GSD).

The GSD workbench contains the required tools for wireframe and surface design. Other surfacing workbenches available in CATIA are shown in Figure 1–1.

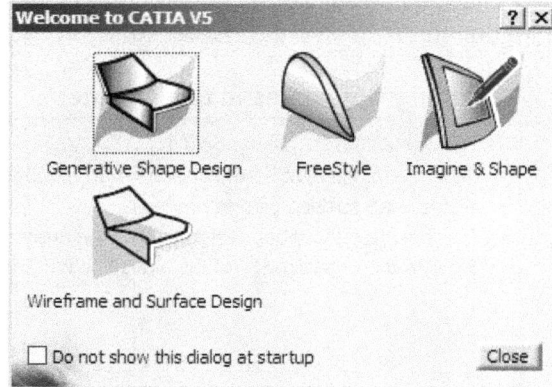

Figure 1–1

The Wireframe and Surface Design workbench has basic wireframe and surfacing capabilities.

The Freestyle workbench provides design tools for an Industrial Designer. Non-parametric wireframe and surface geometry can be quickly developed and optimized around conceptual drawings and models.

The Imagine & Shape workbench contains non-parametric surface creation tools. The surfaces are NURBS based, enabling pushing and pulling on a mesh. Organic and freeform type shapes can easily be created.

1.2 Generative Shape Design Workbench

Access the GSD Workbench

Until now, you normally worked in the Mechanical Design area of CATIA to develop part and surface models. Solid geometry was created in the Part Design workbench. To access the advanced surfacing functionality in CATIA, you must use the GSD workbench. To access this workbench, select **Start>Shape> Generative Shape Design**. The workbench symbol changes to

.

GSD User Interface

The interface for the GSD workbench is similar to the Part Design workbench. The primary difference is that the toolbar options change to GSD-specific tools, as shown in Figure 1–2.

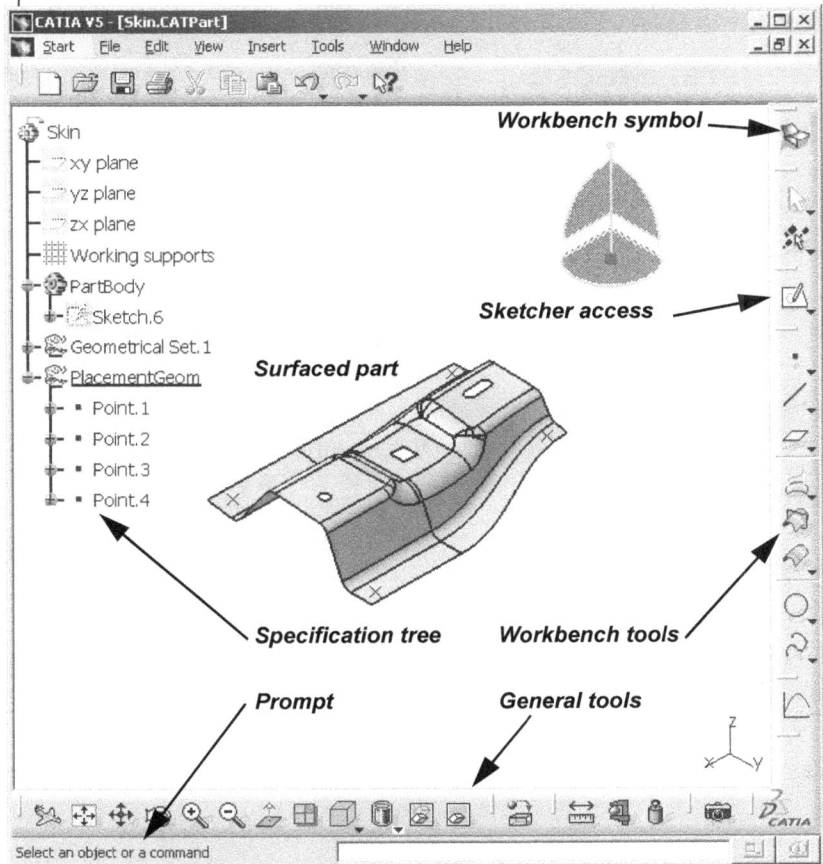

Figure 1–2

1.3 Surface Design Review

Designing surface features differs slightly from designing solid features in CATIA. With solid modeling, you can often visualize the final shape of a feature and create the geometry with individual construction features (e.g., Pad, Pocket, Fillet, or Hole). With surfaces, you must frequently create reference geometry (e.g., points and curves) before creating a single surface feature. Planning ahead is essential to achieving the required results when designing surfaces.

When creating solid features, all faces of the feature must be defined in one step. The intersections of solid features are immediately calculated and consumed in the model. With surfaces, the contours of the model can be individually created as separate features. These multiple surfaces can then be joined to generate a final solid feature. As a result, simple surfaces have the benefit of being able to yield complex results.

General StepsG eneral Steps

Use the following general steps to create a model from surface features:

1. Create wireframe geometry.
2. Create surface geometry.
3. Perform surface operations.
4. Create solid geometry.

Step 1 - Create wireframe geometry.

Wireframe geometry is the backbone on which the surface features of the model are created. You can use wireframe features to define construction elements, intersections, and common boundaries of the surfaces that define the shape of the model. Wireframe geometry can consist of simple features, such as sketches, points, lines, and planes, as well as more complex geometry, such as splines or helixes.

Figure 1–3 shows an example of a group of wireframe features that are used to develop a surface model.

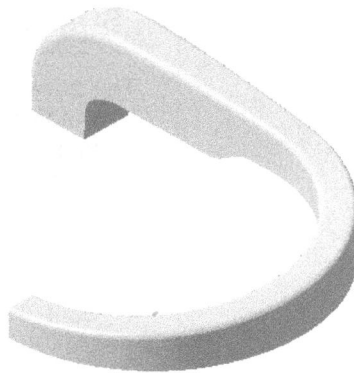

- Sketch.3
- Line.6
- Line.7
- Connect.5
- Connect.6
- Join.5
- Sweep.1
- Sweep.2
- Sweep.3
- Join.6
- Join.7
- Sweep.4
- Join.8

Figure 1–3

Step 2 - Create surface geometry.

Once the wireframe geometry has been created, surface features can be created to define the internal and external boundaries of the model. Surface features can be created independent from the rest of the model or by using existing wireframe and surface geometry as a reference. Common surface types include:

- Extruded

- Revolved

- Spherical

- Offset

The boundaries of the model shown in are completely defined. Although the surfaces appear to form a closed shape, they still need to be joined before making the solid model.

Figure 1–4

Step 3 - Perform surface operations.

The advantage of using surface features is being able to control how individual surface features connect and interact with other parts of the model. Surface operations are used to control this interaction by enabling you to manipulate existing surface features. Common ways to manipulate surfaces include:

- Join
- Split
- Trim
- Extract
- Transform

The model shown in Figure 1–5 uses the **Join** option to define the resulting surface shape.

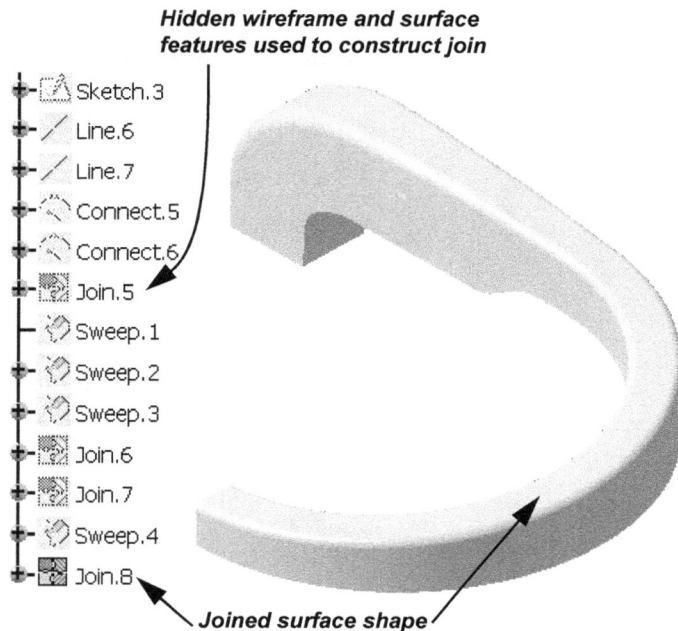

Figure 1–5

Step 4 - Create solid geometry.

When you finish creating surface features, you are ready to create solid geometry. At this point, your model contains a surface representation of the 3D model. This can be a closed surface or an open surface depending on your design intent.

If the mass properties of your model are required or you intend on performing additional solid modeling, you must create solid geometry from the surfaces. You must take the model back to the Part Design workbench and use the Surface-Based Features toolbar options to create solid geometry from the skin. These options include **Close Surface**, **Thick Surface**, **Split**, and **Sew**.

The solid geometry is added to the PartBody, as shown in Figure 1–6.

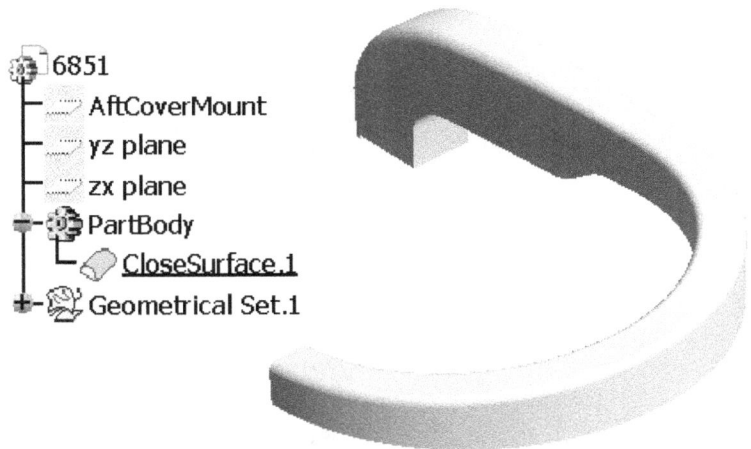

Figure 1–6

1.4 Design Intent

The key to building parametric, feature-based, surface models is to construct them so that their behavior is flexible and predictable. This process is known as capturing design intent.

You should already be familiar with several methods of capturing the design intent with a solid part model. These methods are applicable to the creation of surface features, which include the following:

When designing surfaces. decisions should always be made to drive the design intent of the finished model.

- Dimension sections and features so that your model updates based on your design intent.

- Select **Depth** options for your features to drive your design intent.

- When applicable, use symmetry conditions to drive the design intent.

Surface Modeling Methods

Surface features introduce additional flexibility into the model because of the different ways in which a surface model can be created. Modeling methods include the following:

- Boundary

- Slab

- Hybrid

Boundary

The geometry of a model can be defined by a series of curves, known as a curve network. The curve network is the backbone on which many surfaces are created. It can be used to define the intersections or common boundaries of surfaces that define the shape of the model. A curve network is used to create the model shown in Figure 1–7.

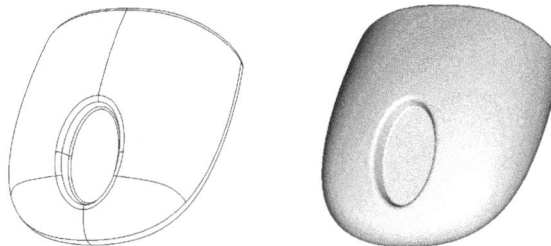

Figure 1–7

The advantages of boundary modeling are:

- Enables precise control over shape and continuity.

- More complex shapes can be created from the curve network.

The disadvantages of boundary modeling are:

- Longer setup time for required reference geometry.

- Can be time consuming to update required design changes.

Slab

Models can be defined by creating simple surfaces. Once these surfaces have been created, they can be trimmed, split, or joined to create the required shape. This method of construction is frequently used when the surface geometry can easily be broken into simple geometric shapes. These surfaces are typically called Slab or Blocked surfaces. Simple slab surfaces are shown in Figure 1–8. A more complex example is shown in Figure 1–9.

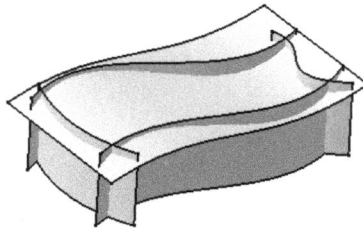

Figure 1–8

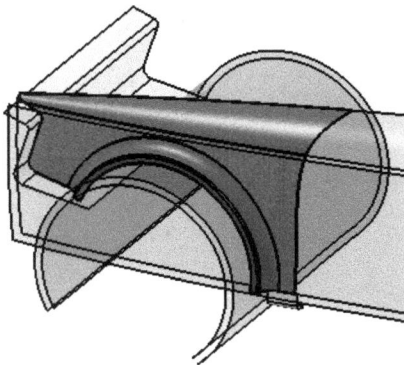

Figure 1–9

The advantages of slab modeling are:

- Simple surfaces take less time to create than a network of curves.

- Slab surfacing is easier to make design changes to downstream, than curve networks.

The disadvantages of slab modeling are:

- The order in which the surface operations is performed can create undesired results.

- Cannot always capture the design intent with simple surfacing techniques.

Hybrid

Models can be defined by combining the boundary and slab surface methods. This is the most common method of creating surface models in CATIA. Slab surfaces are generally used to start the model and curve networks are generated, as required, to complete the geometry. Three simple, extruded, slab surfaces and a curve network are shown in Figure 1–10. This example shows the two techniques used to generate the required geometry.

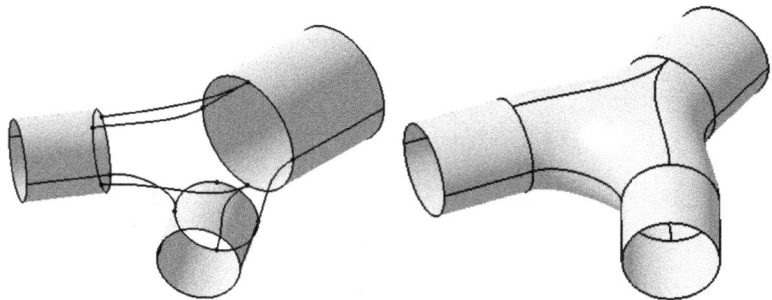

Figure 1–10

Boundary Representations

A boundary representation refers to the selection of any sub-element when defining references for a feature. This means that a feature in the specification tree is not directly referenced. Instead an entity belonging to a feature, such as the edge or vertex of a surface, is selected. Whenever a boundary representation is selected, CATIA reports the reference using **<feature>\<sub-element>**. For example, **Sweep.1\Edge.1** is shown in Figure 1–11.

On curve point created referencing a Boundary Representation

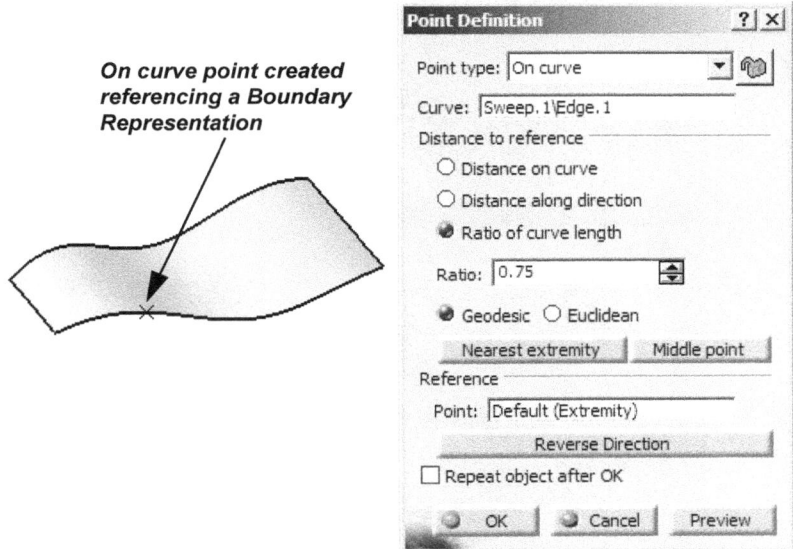

Figure 1–11

Selecting a boundary representation makes the model less stable. Modifications to features can cause the deletion of a sub-element, resulting in errors. The best practice is to reference non-boundary representations, also known as explicit elements. These display directly in the specification tree. Referencing explicit elements promotes a more stable model that you have more control over.

Recommended practices

- Create Extract and Boundary curves instead of directly referencing an edge.

- Use Sketch Profiles and Sketch Outputs when a sketch element needs to be referenced.

- Create points manually instead of selecting a vertex.

- Use the **Replace** tool when design modifications are required.

- Use contextual menus to easily create correct reference geometry as shown in Figure 1–12.

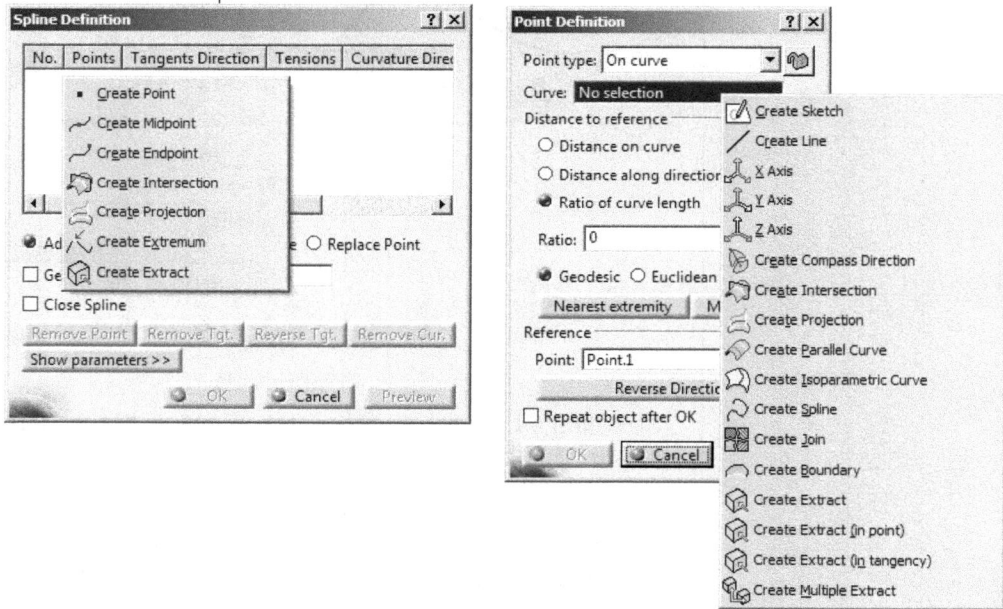

Figure 1–12

1.5 Tree Organization

The specification tree can become very long and messy in large models. You should already be familiar with some techniques to organize the tree, including inserting and changing geometrical sets to help separate and order like elements. Renaming features and geometrical sets also makes updating and investigating a model easier. The **Autosort** command is also helpful in managing the feature order in a geometrical set. Other tools exist to help organize the specification tree.

Groups

Groups enable you to control the display of features in the specification tree and can be used as a filter. Groups are created from an existing geometrical set. Features from that geometrical set are added to the group. When the Group is collapsed, only features added to the group are shown in the specification tree. When the Group is expanded, all features from the geometrical set display as shown in Figure 1–13.

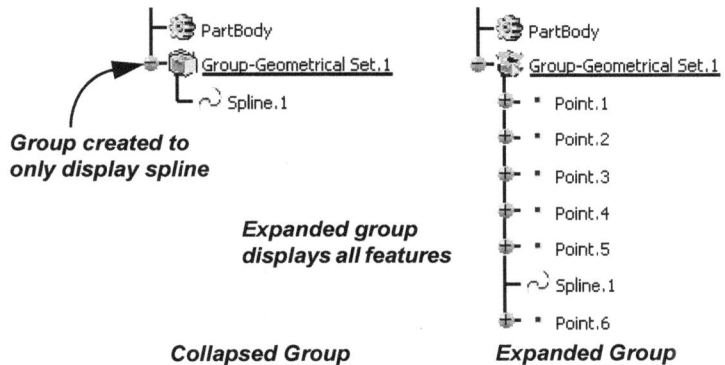

Figure 1–13

How To: Create a Group

1. Right-click on a geometrical set from which to create the group.
2. Select **Geometrical Set.# object>Create Group** in the contextual menu.
3. Enter a name for the group.
4. Select features from the geometrical set to place in the group. Any added feature is shown in the group when collapsed in the tree. All other features of the geometrical set are not shown in the specification tree.
5. Click **OK** to complete the creation of the group.

To collapse or expand a group, right-click the group in the specification tree and select **Geometrical Set.# object>Expand Group** or **Geometrical Set.# object>Collapse Group.**

Grouping is a very useful option. With Groups, insignificant construction or reference elements can be hidden in the specification tree. This makes the specification tree very concise and easy to review, which improves the effectiveness of the editing process.

If a group was the active geometrical set, any new feature added to the model would not be displayed in the specification tree until the group was expanded. For example, a point is added to the model, but not as an input to Group-Geometrical Set.1. The point is not displayed unless the group node is expanded.

There is an option that enables you to automatically add new features as input to the active group. To activate this option, select **Tools>Options>Shape>Generative Shape Design**, select the General tab, and enable the **Integration of created feature as group inputs** option, as shown in Figure 1–14.

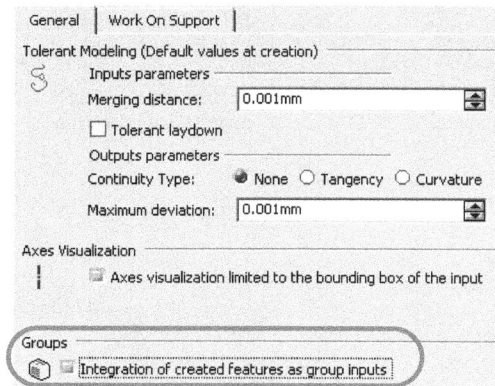

Figure 1–14

All new features are now added to the active group. Features can be removed from the group by right-clicking on the group node and selecting **Edit Group**. This only applies to features created in the Generative Shape Design workbench.

AutoSort

AutoSort is a command that organizes the features in a geometrical set. When **AutoSort** is performed on a geometrical set, the features are reordered by the order in which CATIA updates the features.

How To: Use the AutoSort Command

1. Select a geometrical set, as shown in Figure 1–15.

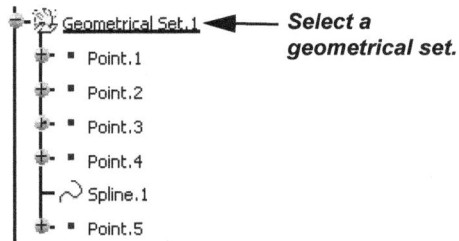

Figure 1–15

2. Right-click and select **Geometrical Set.# object>Autosort**, as shown in Figure 1–16.

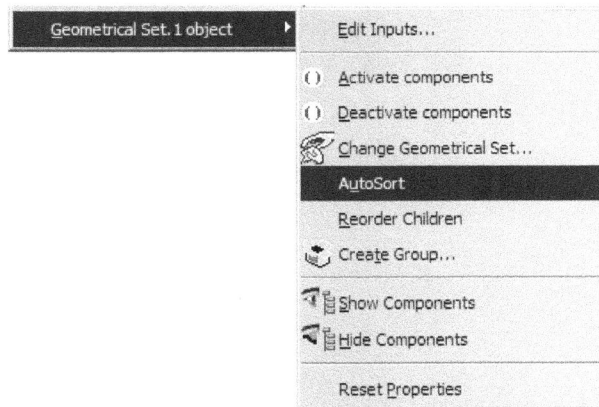

Figure 1–16

3. The result displays as shown in Figure 1–17. **Spline.1** was moved below **Point.5**. This is because **Point.5** was used to create **Spline.1**.

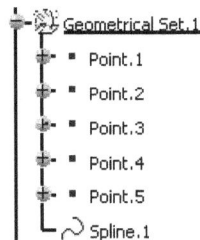

Figure 1–17

Mask

The ability to create a mask was added to the R16 version of the Generative Shape Design workbench. A mask is used to simplify the display of a part model.

⊡ (Mask) has been added to the Tools toolbar, as shown in Figure 1–18.

Figure 1–18

Alternatively, select **Tools>Mask** in the menu bar, as shown in Figure 1–19.

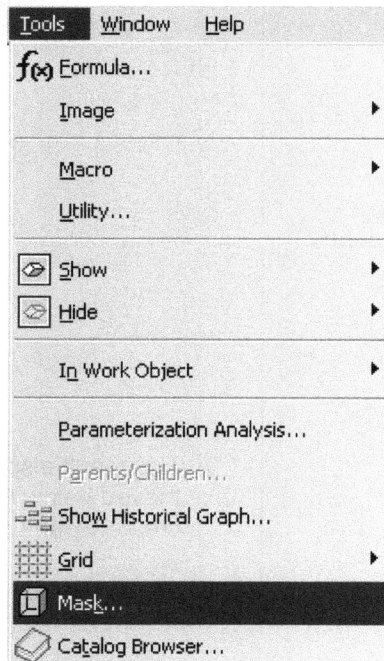

Figure 1–19

CATIA displays a bounding box around the part when a mask is created, as shown in Figure 1–20. The box has six sides, each of which has a green dot. The dot represents a handle that can be moved by selecting and dragging it with the cursor.

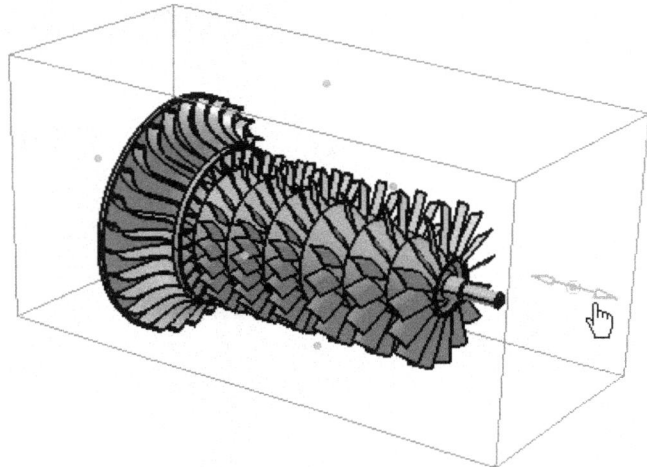

Figure 1–20

The part updates to exclude any surface or reference geometry that is completely outside of the bounding box, as shown in Figure 1–21.

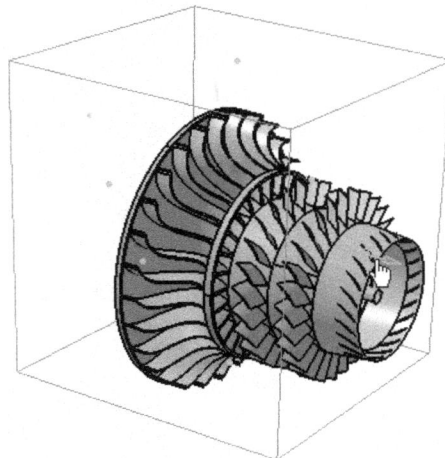

Figure 1–21

You can place the bounding box using the **Coordinates** or **Position & Dimensions** option in the **Mask Type** menu, as shown in Figure 1–22. With the **Coordinates** option, you place the box relative to selected points or vertices from the model.

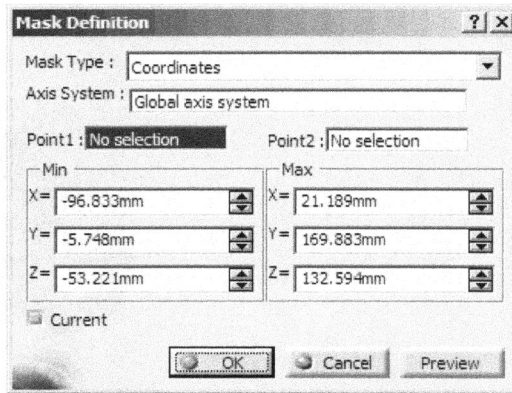

Figure 1–22

You can create multiple masks for a single part. CATIA lists all masks under the Masks node of the specification tree, as shown in Figure 1–23.

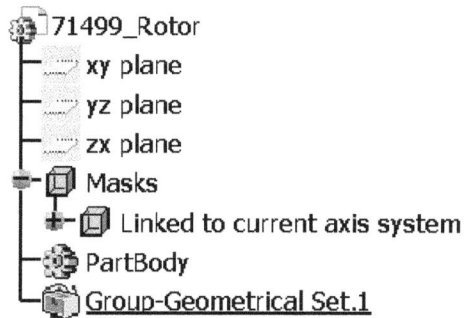

Figure 1–23

Only one mask can be active at a time. The symbol of an active mask displays in red. The active mask is circled in Figure 1–24.

The symbol of an active mask displays in red and is visible in CATIA.

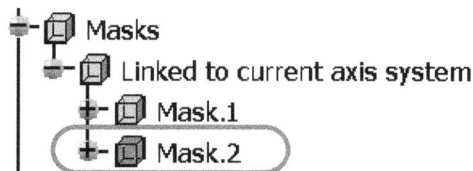

Figure 1–24

Practice 1a

Hybrid Surface Modeling

Practice Objectives

- Investigate curve tangency conditions.
- Create a curve with tangency.
- Create a surface from curves.
- Define tangency conditions for a surface.
- Organize surface data.
- Create a solid from surfaces.

In this practice, you will investigate tangency conditions of curves and surfaces. The Boundary method of surfacing will be used. The slab method of modeling produced the surfaces provided for you to start with. You will work through a typical surface-based modeling process, from wireframe to the creation of solid geometry from a surface.

The completed model is shown in Figure 1–25.

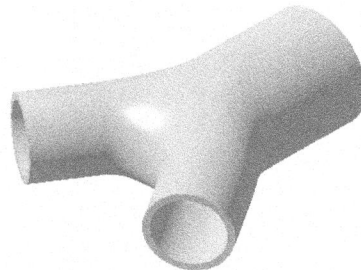

Figure 1–25

Task 1 - Open a part file.

1. Open **Y_Pipe.CATPart**. The model displays as shown in Figure 1–26.

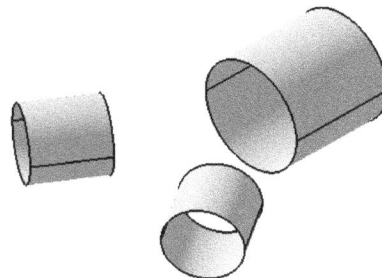

Figure 1–26

---

2. In the specification tree, note that the geometry has been organized into geometrical sets. Also note that **NewSurfaces** is the work object as shown in Figure 1–27.

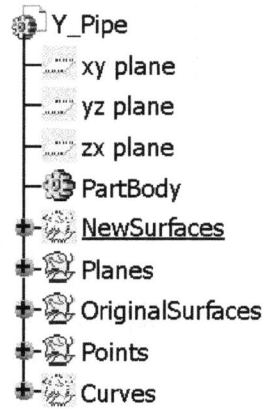

Y_Pipe
— xy plane
— yz plane
— zx plane
— PartBody
— NewSurfaces
— Planes
— OriginalSurfaces
— Points
— Curves

Figure 1–27

Task 2 - Change the display of bodies.

1. Hide the **OriginalSurfaces** geometrical set.

2. Show the **Curves** geometrical set. The specification tree will display as shown in Figure 1–28.

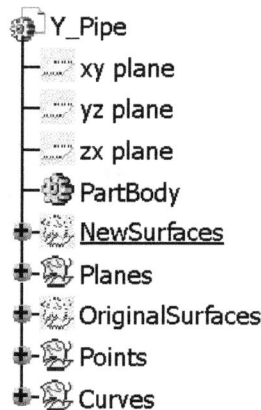

Y_Pipe
— xy plane
— yz plane
— zx plane
— PartBody
— NewSurfaces
— Planes
— OriginalSurfaces
— Points
— Curves

Figure 1–28

The model displays as shown in Figure 1–29.

Design Considerations

The visible geometry can be referred to as a curve network. Creating a curve network provides a wireframe structure that permits the creation of surface features.

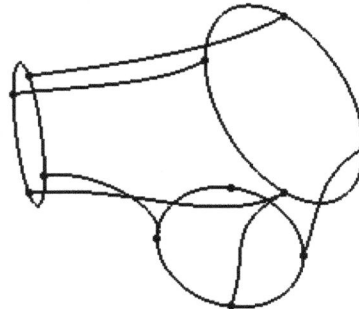

Figure 1–29

3. Show **OriginalSurfaces** as shown in Figure 1–30.

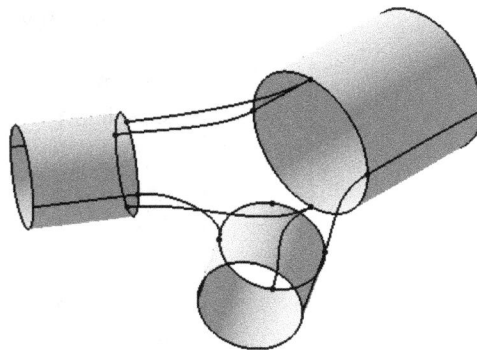

Figure 1–30

4. Show **NewSurfaces** as shown in Figure 1–31.

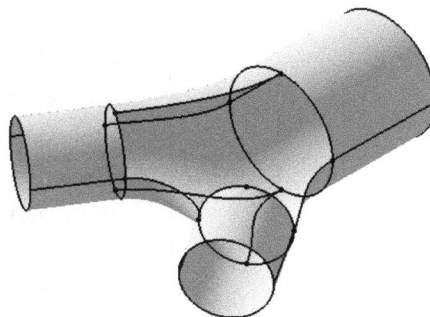

Figure 1–31

Design Considerations

Currently, the **NewSurfaces** geometrical set contains four fill surfaces. Later in the practice, you will develop additional surfaces to create a complete skin for the Y-Pipe.

5. Hide **NewSurfaces**.

6. Hide **OriginalSurfaces**, as shown in Figure 1–32.

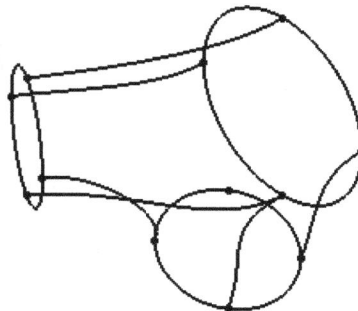

Figure 1–32

7. Hide the appropriate curves so that only the seven shown in Figure 1–33 are visible.

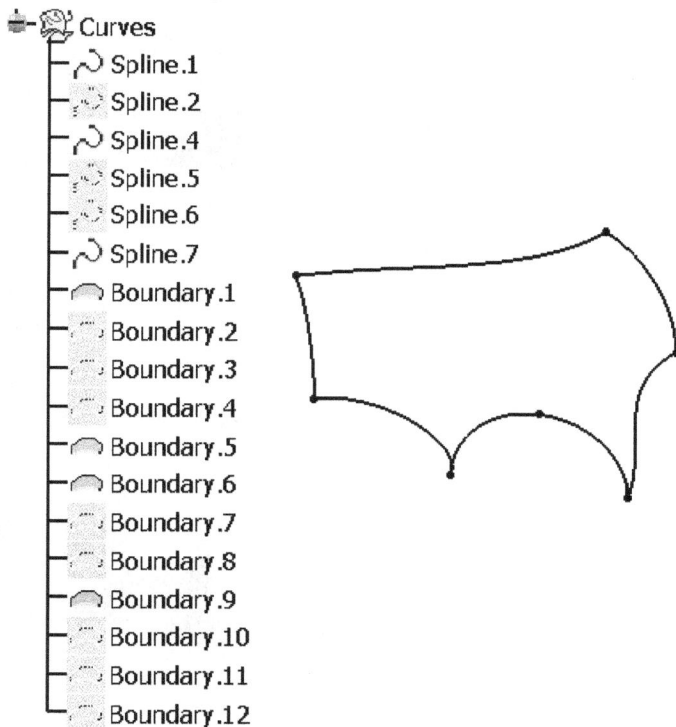

Figure 1–33

Task 3 - Investigate tangency options for a curve.

1. Select the **yz plane** in the specification tree and show it.

2. Edit the curve shown in Figure 1–34.

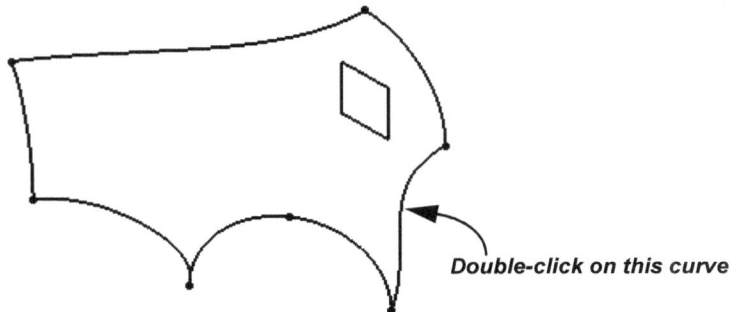

Double-click on this curve

Figure 1–34

3. The curve is a spline curve with a tangency condition applied to both ends. This is shown in the *Tangents Direction* column, as shown in Figure 1–35.

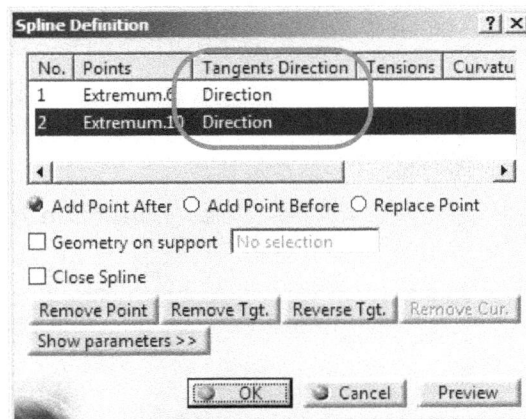

Figure 1–35

4. Click **Show parameters** to view the tangency references.

5. Select **Extremum.6** in the *Points* column in the Spline definition dialog box, as shown in Figure 1–36.

Design Considerations

For this end of the curve, a plane is used to defined tangency. If a plane is used as a Tangents Dir reference, the curve is normal to the selected plane at that end.

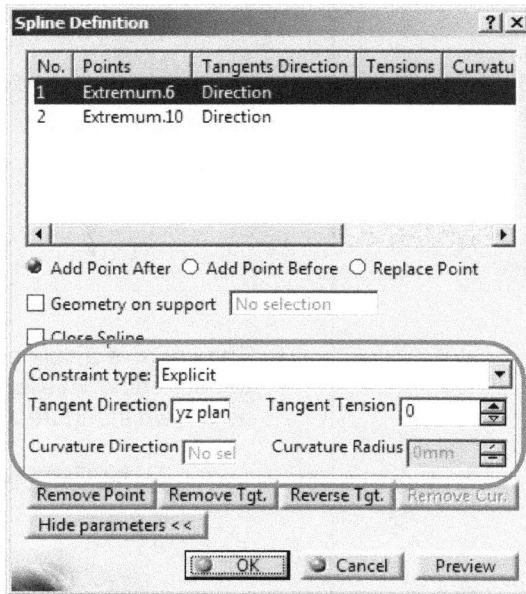

Figure 1–36

6. Select **Extremum.10** in the *Points* column.

7. Right-click on **Plane.3** in the *Tangents Direction* field and select **Hide/Show**, as shown in Figure 1–37.

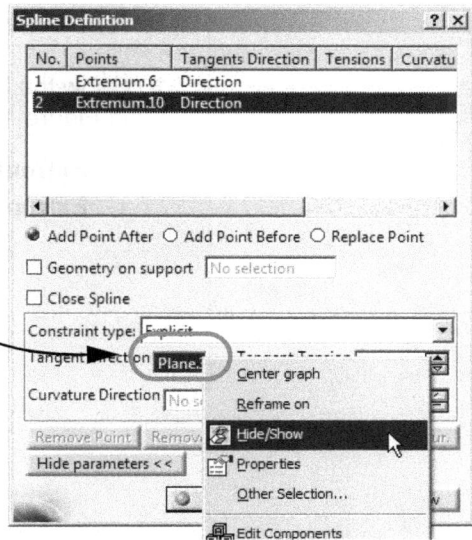

Right-click in Tangent Direction field

Figure 1–37

8. Click **OK**.

9. Ensure that the two reference planes are visible in the model, as shown in Figure 1–38.

These two reference planes should be visible.

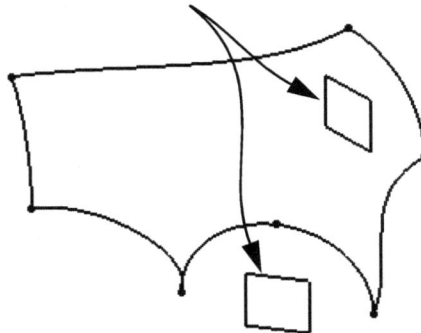

Figure 1–38

Task 4 - Create a spline curve with tangency.

1. Show the following from the Points geometrical set, as shown in Figure 1–39:

   - **Extremum.1**
   - **Extremum.8**

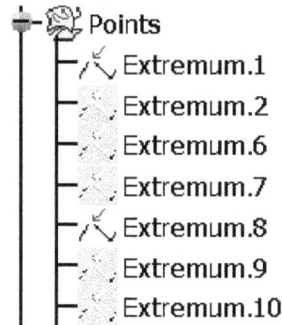

Figure 1–39

2. Show the **NewSurfaces** geometrical set.

3. Ensure that **Curves** is the active work object. The specification tree and model display as shown in Figure 1–40.

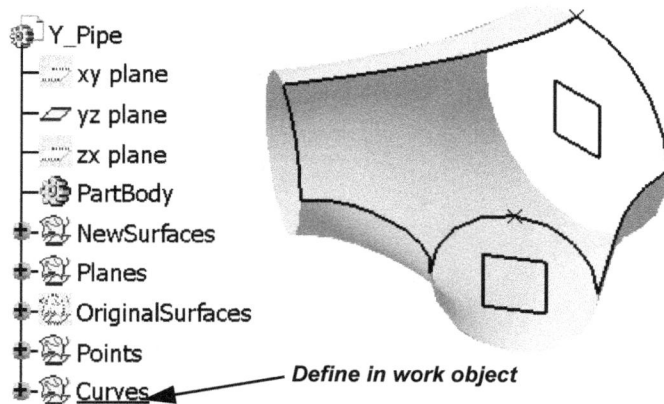

Figure 1–40

4. Click [icon] (Spline) and select the two Extremum points that have been shown.

5. Select the appropriate reference planes to define tangency for each of the two points, as shown in Figure 1–41.

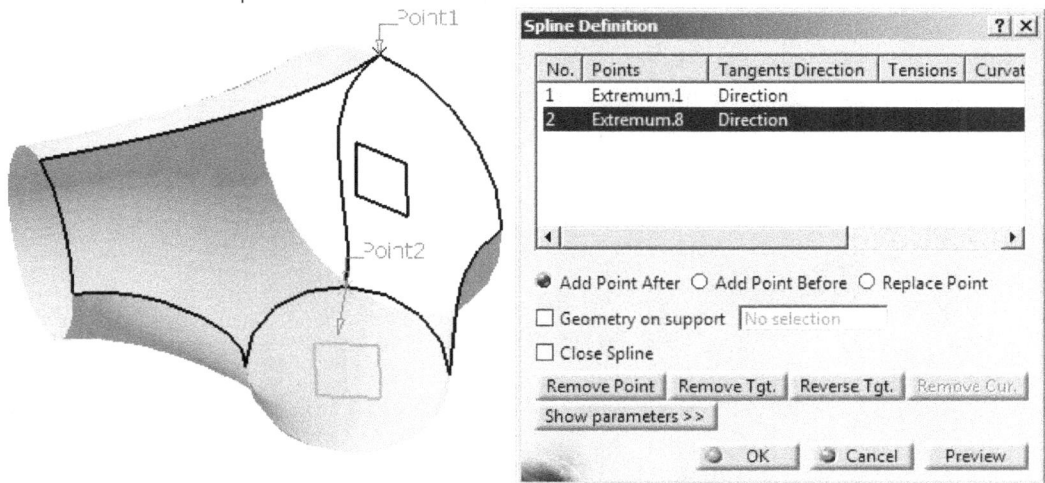

Spline Definition

No.	Points	Tangents Direction	Tensions	Curvat
1	Extremum.1	Direction		
2	Extremum.8	Direction		

● Add Point After ○ Add Point Before ○ Replace Point

☐ Geometry on support [No selection]

☐ Close Spline

[Remove Point] [Remove Tgt.] [Reverse Tgt.] [Remove Cur.]

[Show parameters >>]

[OK] [Cancel] [Preview]

Figure 1–41

6. Click **OK**.

Task 5 - Create a surface from curves.

---

1. Define **NewSurfaces** to be the work object, as shown in Figure 1–42.

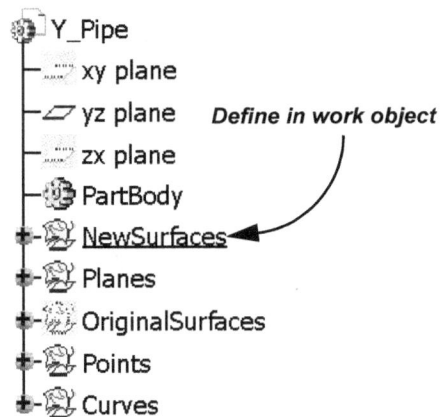

Y_Pipe
— xy plane
— yz plane   *Define in work object*
— zx plane
— PartBody
— NewSurfaces ◀
— Planes
— OriginalSurfaces
— Points
— Curves

Figure 1–42

2. Click (Fill) and select the four boundary curves shown in Figure 1–43.

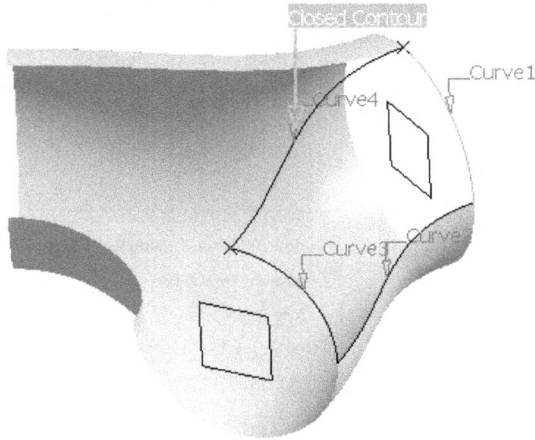

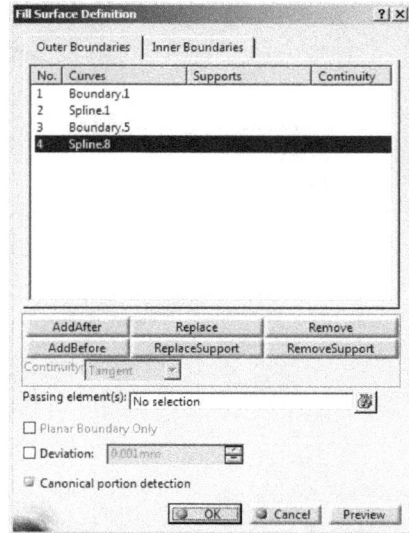

Figure 1–43

3. Show **OriginalSurfaces**.

4. Define the support for the three fill boundaries, as shown in Figure 1–44.

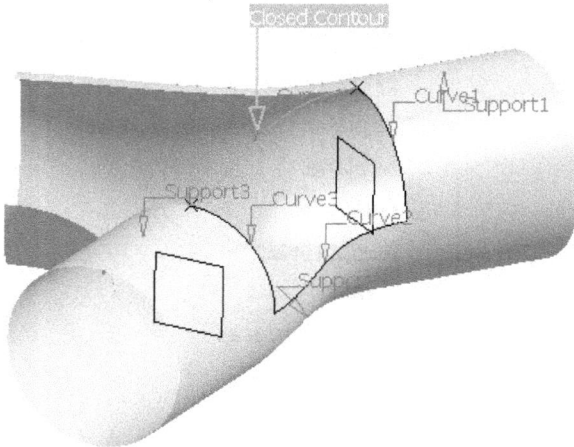

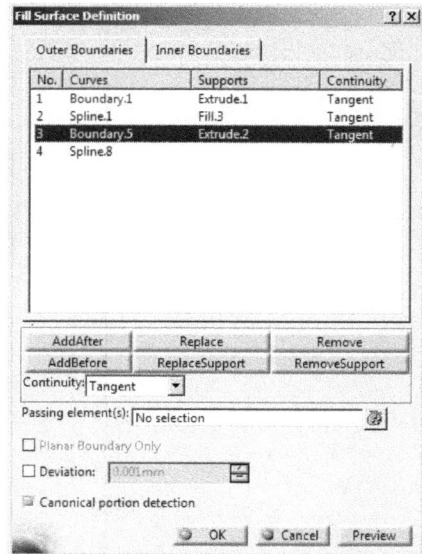

Figure 1–44

5. Hide the yz plane and **Plane.3**.

6. Complete the fill surface. The model displays as shown in Figure 1–45.

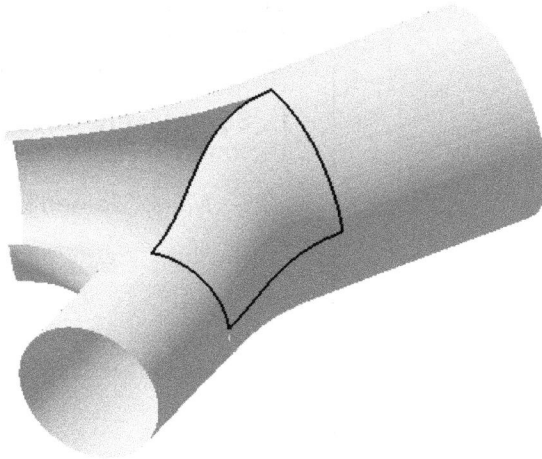

Figure 1–45

7. Create another fill surface using the five boundaries shown in Figure 1–46. Ensure that the adjacent surfaces are selected as support references. Define **Tangent** as the continuity type.

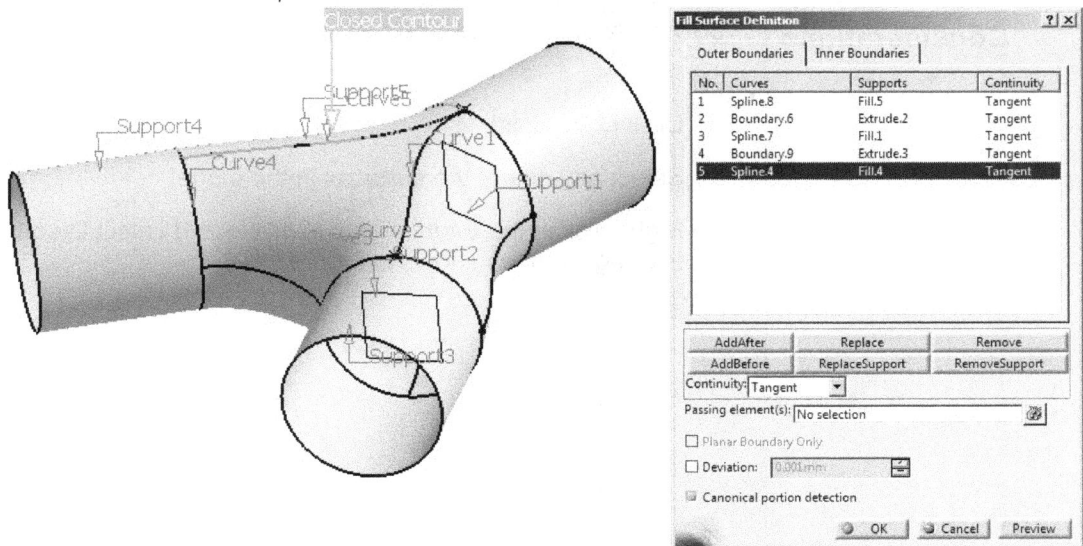

Figure 1–46

8. Complete the fill surface.

Task 6 - Create a single surface feature.

Design Considerations

Since your goal is to create solid geometry from a surface model, all surfaces (extrude and fill) need to behave as a single element for a thick surface feature creation to be successful. To help keep the geometry organized, you will insert a new geometrical set to hold the Join feature that will be created in this task.

1. Select **Insert>Geometrical Set** and enter the following as shown in Figure 1–47:

    - *Name:* **JoinedSurfaces**

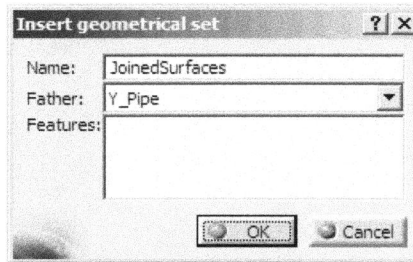

Figure 1–47

2. Click **OK**.

Design Considerations

The new geometrical set is positioned directly beneath the previously activated geometrical set.

3. Click (Join).

4. Select any one of the surfaces in the model.

5. Right-click in the *Elements to Join* field and select **Distance Propagation**, as shown in Figure 1–48.

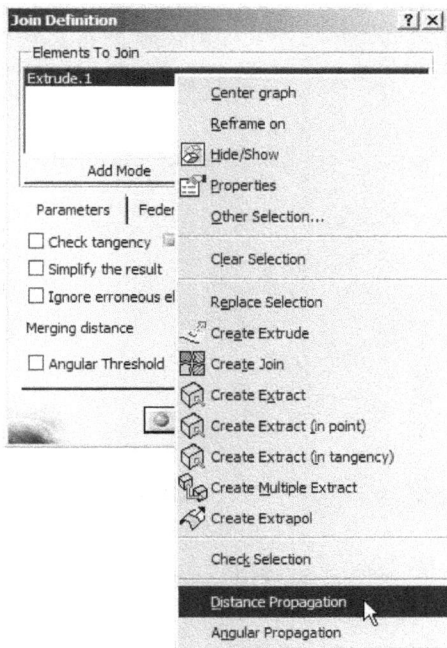

Figure 1–48

Design Considerations

This propagation tool enables the system to automatically select all surfaces that have boundaries that are within the Merging distance parameter value.

All nine surfaces should be listed in the Join dialog box, as shown in Figure 1–49. (Listing order might be different in your model.)

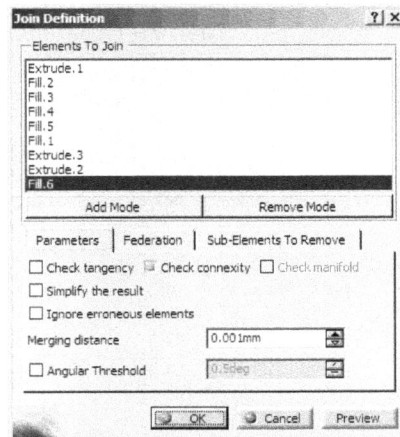

Figure 1–49

6. Click **OK**. The join is added to the JoinedSurfaces body as shown in Figure 1–50.

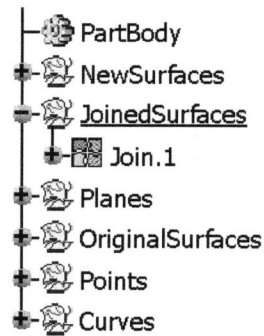

- PartBody
- NewSurfaces
- JoinedSurfaces
  - Join.1
- Planes
- OriginalSurfaces
- Points
- Curves

Figure 1–50

7. Hide all geometrical sets except for **JoinedSurfaces** as shown in Figure 1–51.

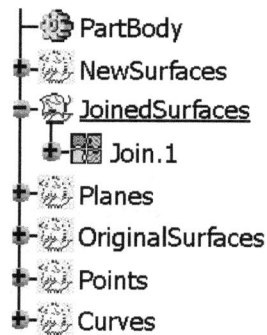

- PartBody
- NewSurfaces
- JoinedSurfaces
  - Join.1
- Planes
- OriginalSurfaces
- Points
- Curves

Figure 1–51

Task 7 - Create solid geometry.

1. Activate the Part Design workbench.

2. Define the PartBody to be the work object.

3. Use (Thick Surface) to create a **2mm** thick solid from **Join.1** in the direction shown in Figure 1–52.

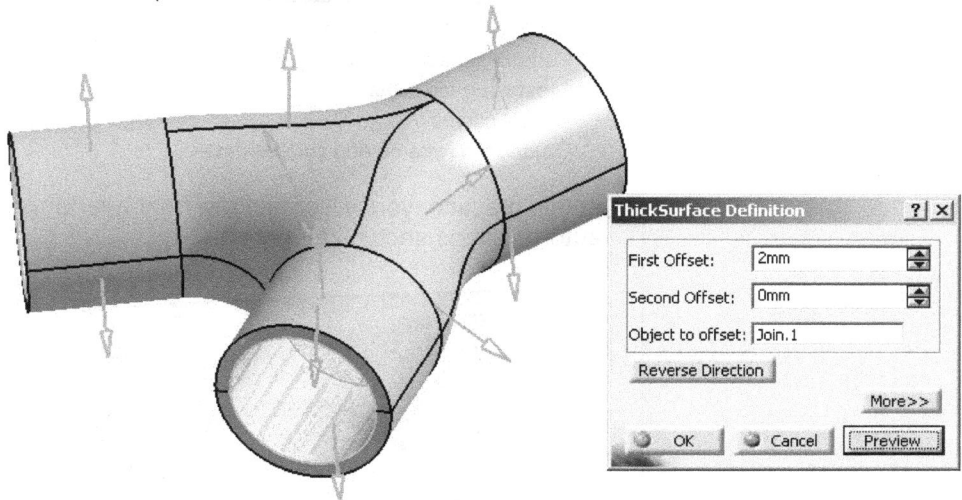

Figure 1–52

4. Select **Tools>Hide>All Geometrical Sets** to hide all wireframe and surface geometry that is still shown. The completed model displays as shown in Figure 1–53.

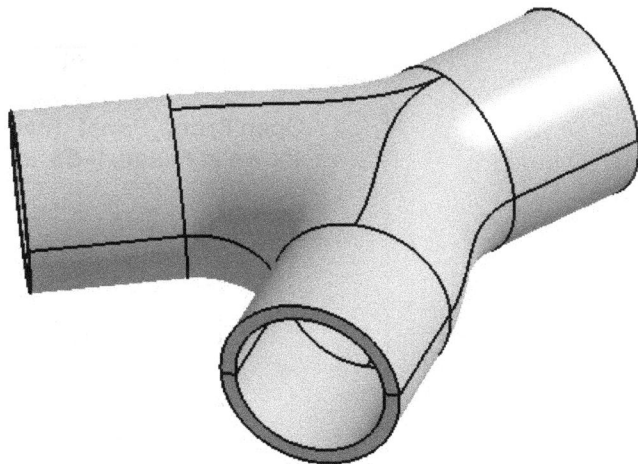

Figure 1–53

5. Save the file and close the window.

Practice 1b

Front Quarter Panel

Practice Objectives

- Use Slab surface modeling techniques.
- Perform surface operations.
- Create surface fillets.
- Project curves.
- Organize wireframe and surface data.

In this practice, you will create the front quarter panel of an automobile as shown in Figure 1–54.

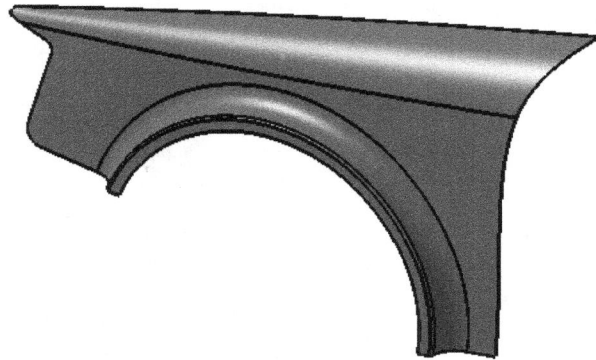

Figure 1–54

Task 1 - Open a part file.

1. Open **Front_Panel_Start.CATPart**. The model displays as shown in Figure 1–55.

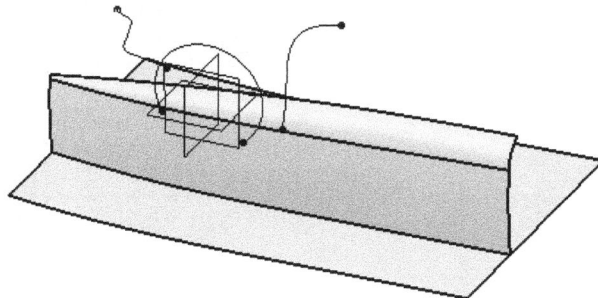

Figure 1–55

2. Ensure that the model units are set to **mm**.

3. Hide the following elements:

- **Base**
- **1/4 Panel - Door Profile**
- **Front Project Sketch**

Task 2 - Create wheel surfaces.

1. Create an extruded surface using the following specifications:

- *Profile:* **Wheel Well Sketch**
- *Direction:* **ZX plane**
- *Limit 1:* **1010mm**
- Ensure that the direction of the extrude is created towards the existing surfaces.

2. Rename the completed extrude as **Wheel Extrude**. The model displays as shown in Figure 1–56.

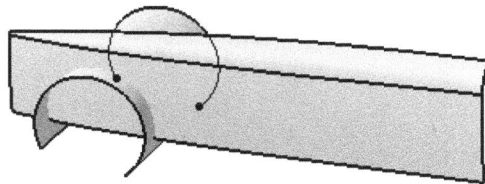

Figure 1–56

3. Hide **Wheel Well Sketch**.

4. Create an offset surface using the following specifications:

- *Surface:* **Swept Surface.1**
- *Offset:* **45mm**

The Offset direction displays as shown in Figure 1–57.

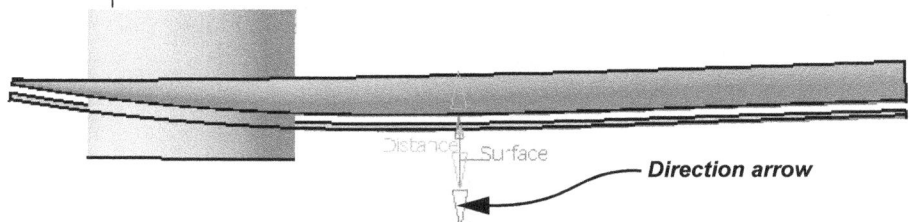

Distance Surface

— *Direction arrow*

Figure 1–57

(Extrude) is located in the Surface toolbar.

(Offset) displays in the Surfaces toolbar.

5. Rename the completed offset surface as **Body Offset**. The model displays as shown in Figure 1–58.

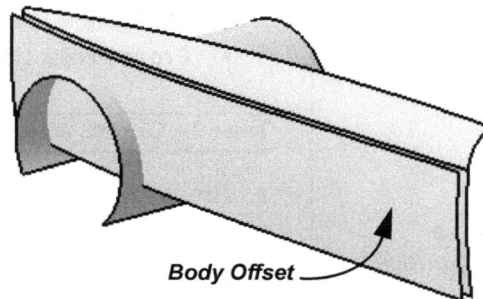

Body Offset

Figure 1–58

6. Create another offset surface using the following specifications:

- *Surface:* **Wheel Extrude**
- *Offset:* **25mm**

The offset direction needs to point outside of the Wheel Extrude surface.

7. Rename the completed offset surface as **Wheel Offset**. The model displays as shown in Figure 1–59.

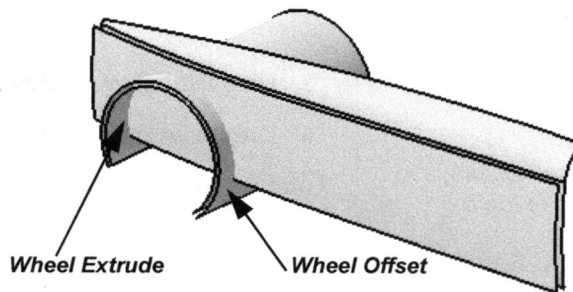

Wheel Extrude   Wheel Offset

Figure 1–59

Click **Other side** to toggle which portion of the surface is kept in the **Split** operation.

Task 3 - Split surfaces.

1. Hide **Body Offset**.

2. Click [icon] (Split). Select **Wheel Offset** as the element to cut. The cutting elements are **Body Offset**, **Swept Surface.1**, and **Base**. The completed split displays as shown in Figure 1–60.

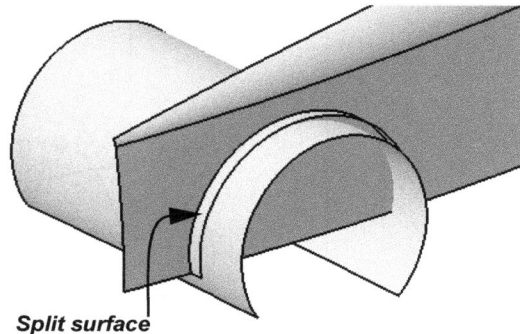

Split surface

Figure 1–60

3. Rename the split as **Wheel Outside Split**.

4. Split **Wheel Extrude**. The cutting elements will be **Body Offset**, **Swept Surface.1**, and **Base**. The completed split displays as shown in Figure 1–61.

5. Rename the split as **Wheel Inside Split**.

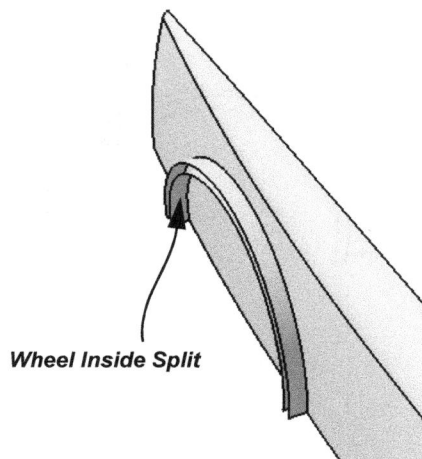

Wheel Inside Split

Figure 1–61

6. Show **Body Offset** and **Base**.

7. Split **Body Offset**. The cutting elements will be **Wheel Outside Split**, **Wheel Inside Split**, and **Base**. The completed split displays as shown in Figure 1–62.

8. Rename the split as **Wheel Front Split**.

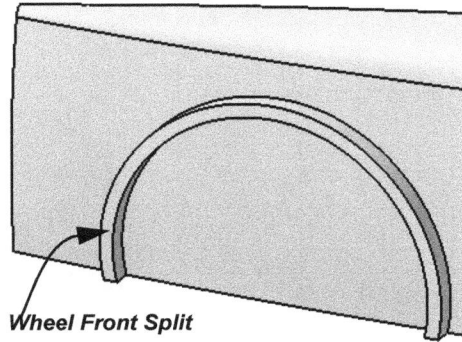

Wheel Front Split

Figure 1–62

9. If not already done, hide **Body Offset**, **Base**, and **Wheel Inside Split**.

10. Split **Swept Surface.1**. The cutting element is **Wheel Outside Split**. The completed split displays as shown in Figure 1–63.

11. Rename the split as **Body Split**.

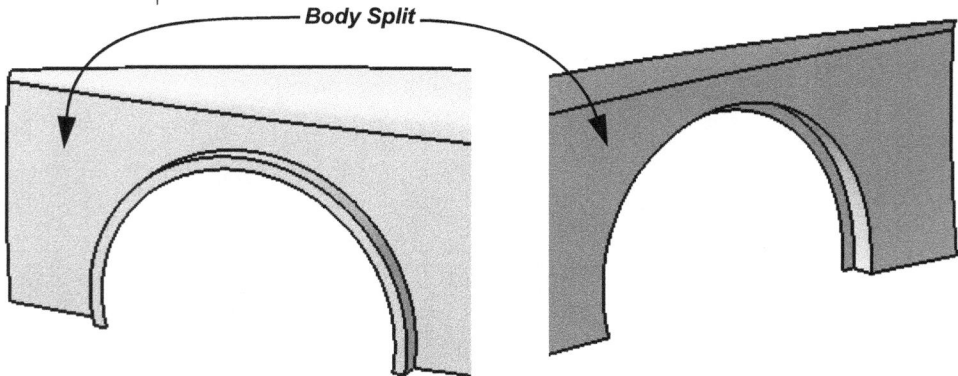

Body Split

Figure 1–63

Task 4 - Use Project curves to split.

1. Join **Swept Surface.2**, **Wheel Outside Split**, **Wheel Front Split**, and **Body Split**.

2. Rename the Join as **Surface Join**.

3. Show **1/4 Panel - Door Profile** and **Front Project Sketch**.

4. Create a projected curve using the following specifications:

   - *Projection type:* **Along a direction**
   - *Projected:* **1/4 Panel - Door Profile**
   - *Support:* **Surface Join**
   - *Direction:* **Y-Component** or the **ZX-plane**

5. Rename the completed project as **Projected Door Curve**. The model displays as shown in Figure 1–64.

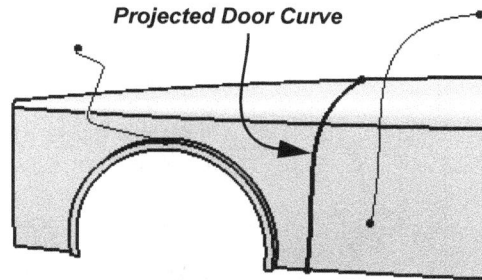

Projected Door Curve

Figure 1–64

6. Repeat Step 4 using **Front Project Sketch**. Rename the projected curve as **Projected Front Curve**. The model displays as shown in Figure 1–65.

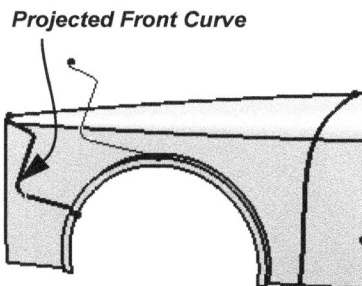

Projected Front Curve

Figure 1–65

7. Hide **1/4 Panel - Door Profile** and **Front Project Sketch**.

8. Split **Surface Join** using **Projected Door Curve** and **Projected Front Curve** as the cutting elements. The completed split displays as shown in Figure 1–66.

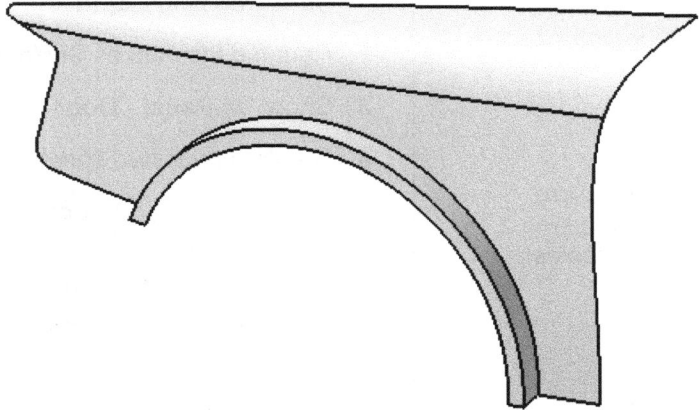

Figure 1–66

9. Using the graphic properties, color the surfaces gray.

10. Save the model.

*If a color does not display in the list, select **More Colors**.*

11. Using the **Edge Fillet** tool place fillets on the edges of the wheel well as shown in Figure 1–67.

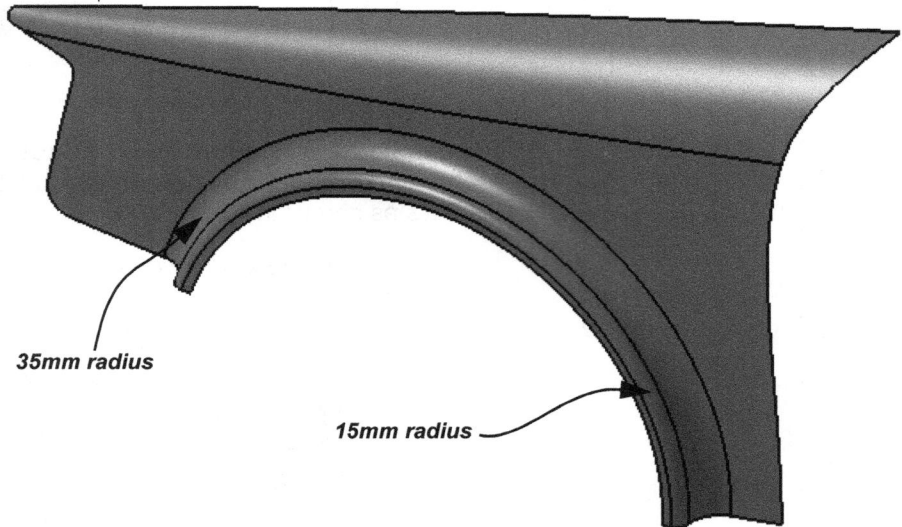

35mm radius

15mm radius

Figure 1–67

Task 5 - Organize the specification tree.

1. Right-click on **Geometrical Set.1** and select **Geometrical Set.1 object>Create Group.** The Group dialog box opens, as shown in Figure 1–68.

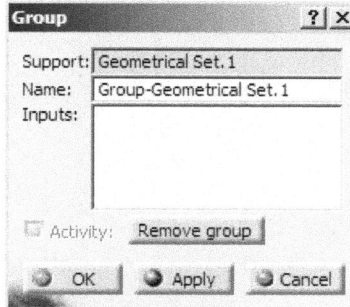

Figure 1–68

2. Select **Wheel Extrude** in the specification tree and every feature after it, as shown in Figure 1–69.

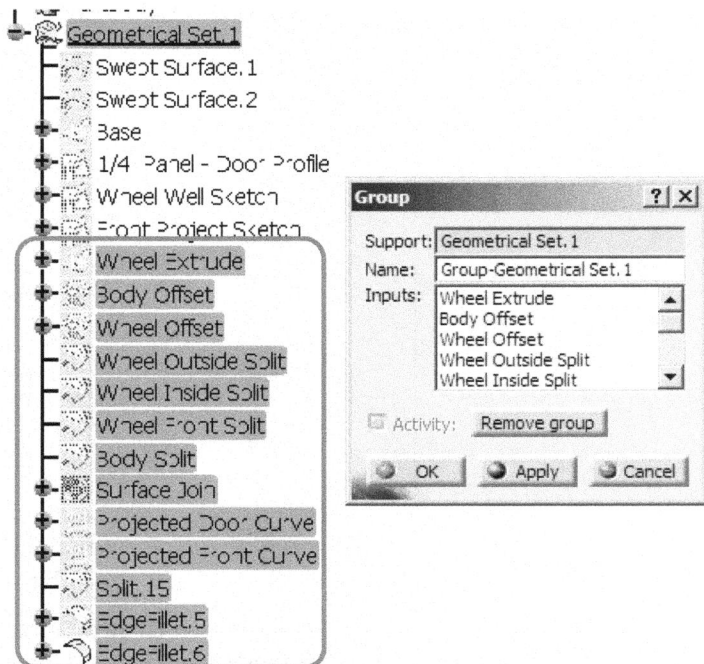

Figure 1–69

3. Click **OK** in the Group dialog box. The specification tree displays as shown in Figure 1–70. Note that only the selected features display in the group. This tool simplifies the specification tree.

Figure 1–70

4. The wireframe and surfaces not in the group can be shown by right-clicking on **Group-Geometrical Set.1** and selecting **Geometrical Set.1 object>Expand Group**. The specification tree displays as shown in Figure 1–71.

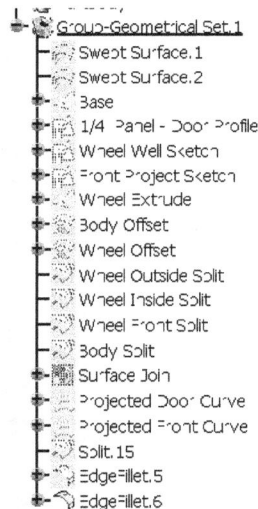

Figure 1–71

5. Right-click on **Group-Geometrical Set.1** and select **Geometrical Set.1 object>Collapse Group.** The specification tree only displays the features placed in the group.

6. Save the model and close the file.

Practice 1c

Using a Mask

Practice Objective

- Create masks for a part file.

In this practice, you will open a part that contains imported surface data. You use the mask functionality to create two mask states of the model. The third and final mask that you create will be used to return the model to a state that displays all geometry in the part.

Task 1 - Open a part file.

1. Open **71499_Rotor.CATPart**. The model displays as shown in Figure 1–72.

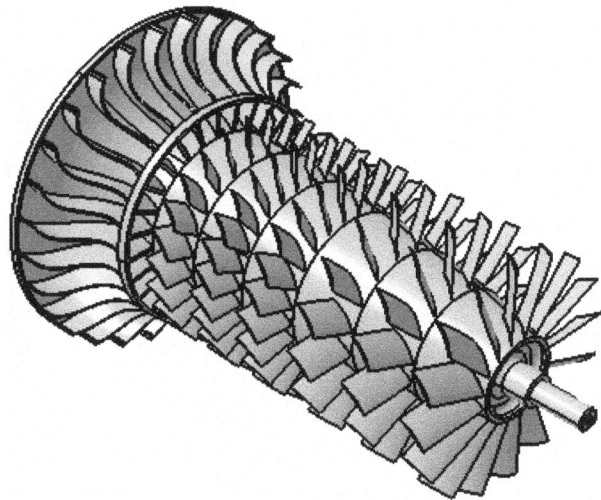

Figure 1–72

Task 2 - Create a mask.

1. Click ▢ (Mask) in the Tools toolbar, as shown in Figure 1–73.

Figure 1–73

2. A bounding box displays around the model. Each side of the box has a green handle, as shown in Figure 1–74.

Your bounding box could have a different orientation then the one shown. The bounding box displays relative to the orientation of the model.

Green handles on each side of the box

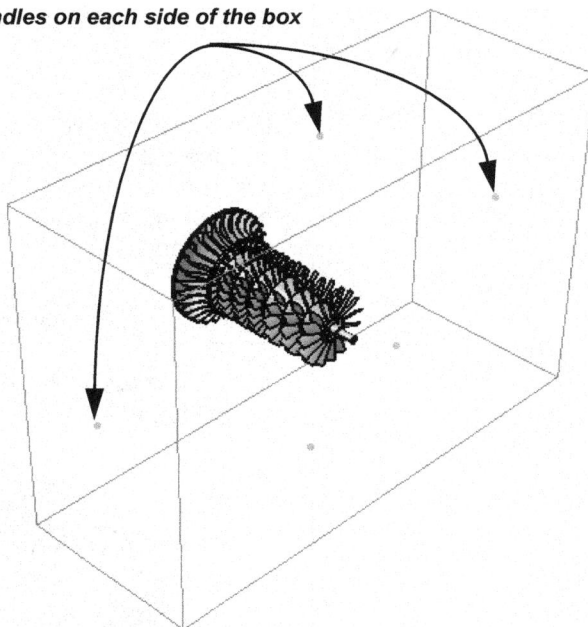

Figure 1–74

3. Use the cursor to select the handle shown in Figure 1–75.

Select this handle

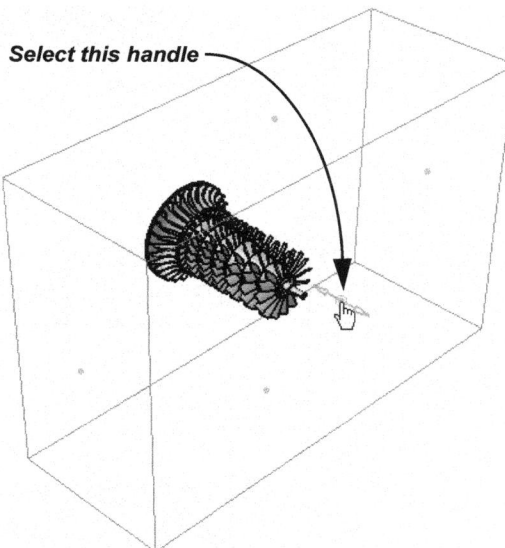

Figure 1–75

4. Drag the handle to the location shown in Figure 1–76.

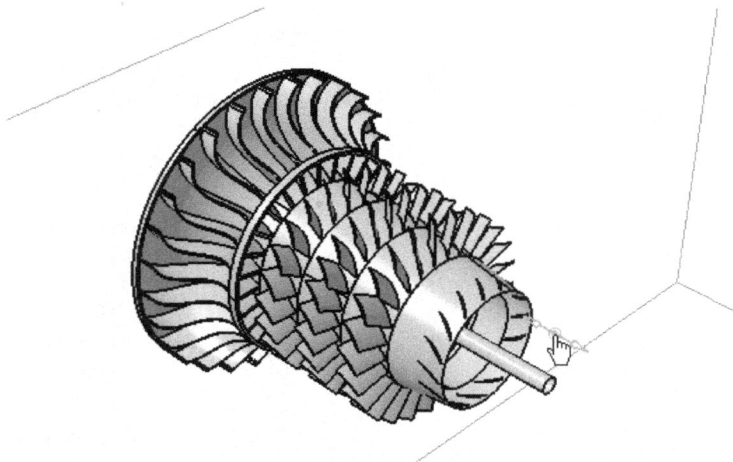

Figure 1–76

5. Click **OK**. Note that **Mask.1** has been added to the specification tree.

Task 3 - Create a second mask.

1. Create another mask that results in the display shown in Figure 1–77.

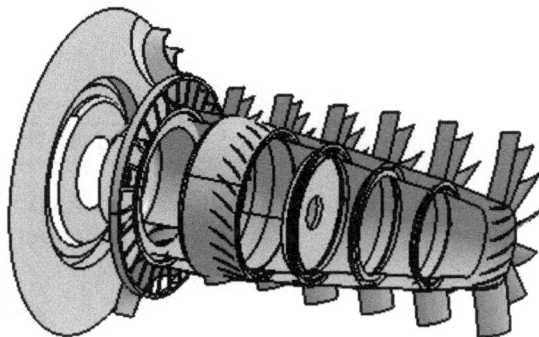

Figure 1–77

2. Click **OK** to complete the second mask.

Task 4 - Set a mask to be current.

1. Right-click on **Mask.1** and select **Mask.1 object>Set As Current**. An active mask is indicated with a red icon, as shown in Figure 1–78.

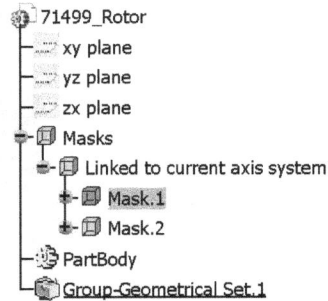

Figure 1–78

The model display updates as shown in Figure 1–79.

Figure 1–79

Task 5 - Set a mask to not be current.

1. Right-click on **Mask.1** and select **Mask.1 object>Set As Not Current**. The model displays as shown in Figure 1–80.

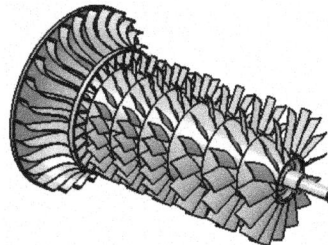

Figure 1–80

2. Save the model and close the file.

Advanced Wireframe Elements

Wireframe features form the foundation for future surface elements. This chapter discusses how to create advanced wireframe geometry, such as reference, projected, and curve geometry. The wireframe geometry can then be used to create more complex surface features.

Learning Objectives in this Chapter

- Recognize the Wireframe tools in the Generative Shape Design workbench.
- Learn how to use the Reference Geometry creation tools.
- Create Projected and Offset geometry.
- Learn how to use the curve geometry creation tools.
- Create Circle-Conic geometry.
- Learn how to use the Trim (Pieces) tool.
- Create Multi-Extract Elements.
- Learn how to use the Extrapolate operation.

2.1 Generative Shape Design Workbench

The Generative Shape Design (GSD) workbench has various wireframe types available in the Wireframe toolbar as shown in Figure 2–1.

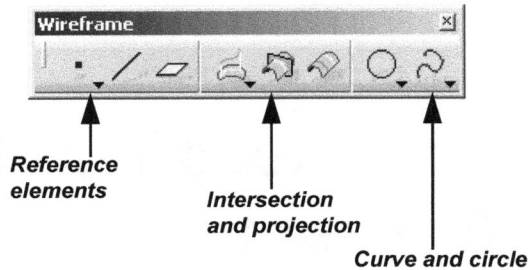

Reference elements

Intersection and projection

Curve and circle

Figure 2–1

These options enable you to create the following types of wireframe geometry:

- **Reference geometry** (points, lines, and planes)

- **Projected geometry** (curves by projection and intersection)

- **Curve geometry** (circles, splines, spirals, etc.)

2.2 Reference Geometry

Reference geometry can include points, lines, and planes. When working in the Generative Shape Design workbench (GSD), the **Extremum** and **ExtremumPolar** icons are available in the Points toolbar, as shown in Figure 2–2.

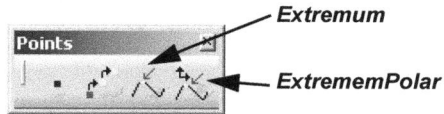

Figure 2–2

*There is no difference between the **Line** and **Plane** creation tools in the Wireframe and Surface workbench and the Generative Shape Design workbench.*

Extremum

An Extremum element can be a point or an edge of a face. It is created at the maximum or minimum extreme location of a Curve, Surface, or Pad feature.

An Extremum wireframe element helps capture design intent by ensuring that geometry maintains a maximum or minimum condition. The points shown in Figure 2–3 are created as Extremum elements with the locations defined as maximum.

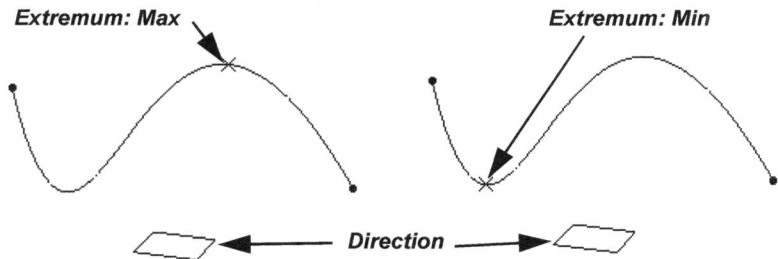

Figure 2–3

How To: Create an Extremum Element

1. Click [image: Extremum icon] (Extremum) in the Points toolbar. The Extremum Definition dialog box opens as shown in Figure 2–4.

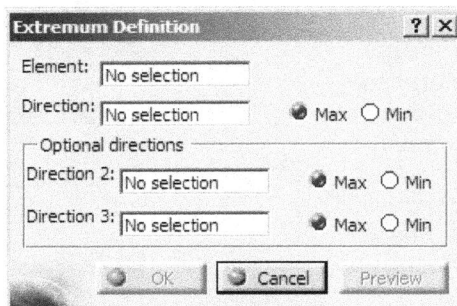

Figure 2–4

2. Select an element and define a direction.
3. Specify a **Max** or **Min** condition, as shown in Figure 2–5.

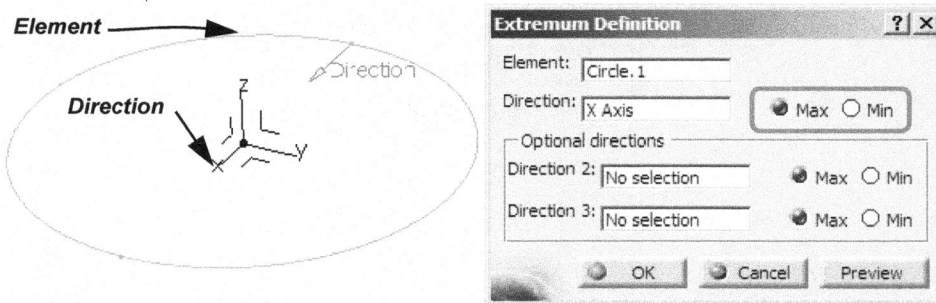

Figure 2–5

4. Complete the Extremum feature. If Max was the set condition, the model displays as shown on the left in Figure 2–6.

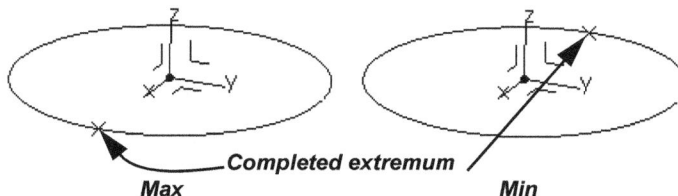

Figure 2–6

Additional directions can be selected, as shown in Figure 2–7. Each direction can be specified as a Max or Min condition.

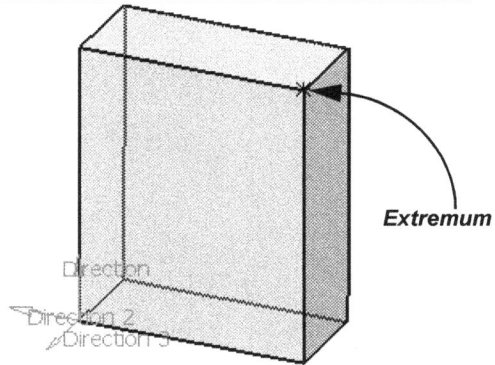

Figure 2–7

ExtremumPolar

An ExtremumPolar element can be created at either the maximum or minimum extreme location or at a maximum or minimum angle to a reference a contour or curve.

An ExtremumPolar element helps capture design intent by ensuring that geometry maintains a maximum or minimum condition relative to an origin.

How To: Create an ExtremumPolar Element

1. Click [icon] (ExtremumPolar) in the Points toolbar. The Polar Extremum Definition dialog box opens as shown in Figure 2–8.

Figure 2–8

2. Select a contour as shown in Figure 2–9.

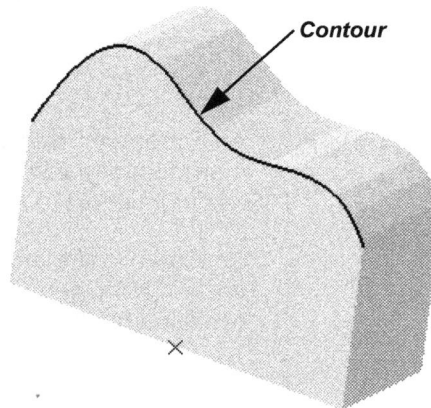

Figure 2–9

3. Select a support as shown in Figure 2–10.

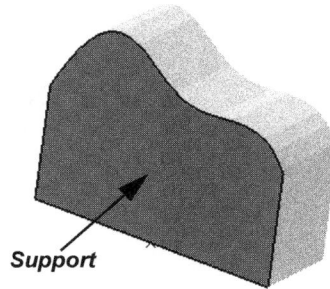

Figure 2–10

4. Select an origin and a reference from which to measure the angle, as shown in Figure 2–11.

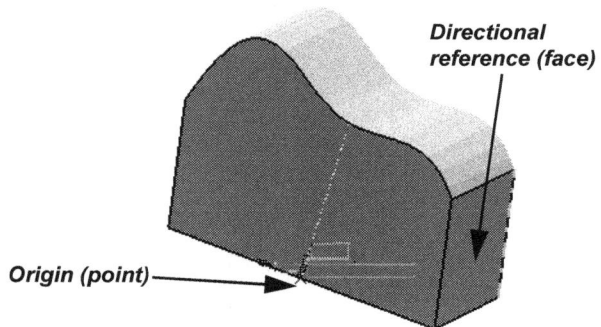

Figure 2–11

5. Click **OK** to complete the feature. An ExtremumPolar wireframe element with a Min radius condition is shown in Figure 2–12.

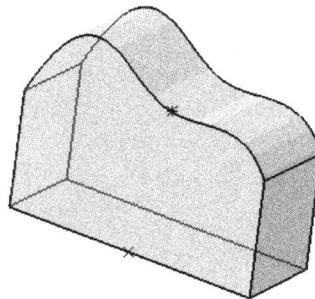

Figure 2–12

An example of an ExtremumPolar feature in the Max and Min radius conditions is shown in Figure 2–13.

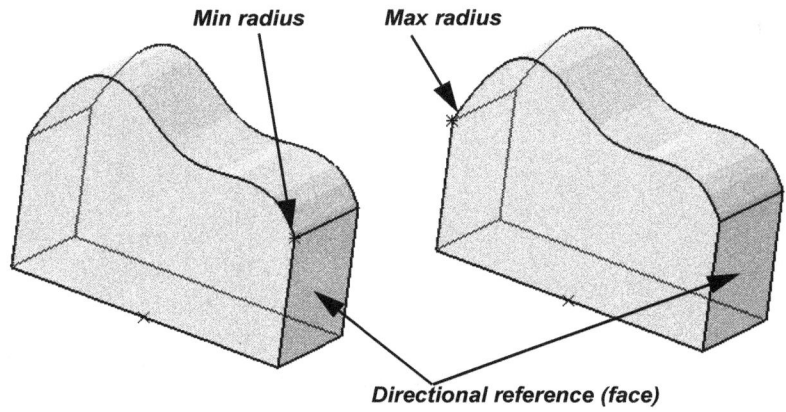

Figure 2–13

2.3 Projected Geometry

The Project-Combine flyout toolbar displays under the **Project** icon. When working in the Generative Shape Design workbench, the **Combine, ReflectLine** and **Silhouette** icons are available in this toolbar, as shown in Figure 2–14.

Figure 2–14

Combine

A Combine element enables the creation of a curve that lies on the intersection of the projection of two curves or sketches. Each curve or sketch is created independent of the other and can be projected normal to or along a specified direction. This method is analogous to creating two extruded surfaces and creating a curve using the intersection element.

A Combine element can be used to define a 3D curve with only 2D information about the curve.

How To: Create a Combine Element

1. Click (Combine). The Combine Definition dialog box opens, as shown in Figure 2–15.

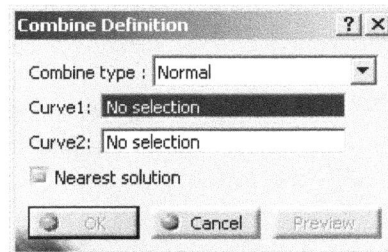

Figure 2–15

2. Set the *Combine type* to **Normal** or **Along Directions** and select two curves to define the combine element. Figure 2–16 shows two curves selected to define a Combine element.

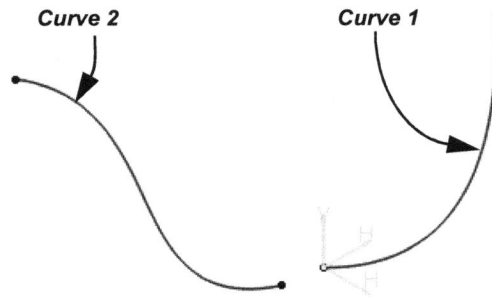

Curve 2   **Curve 1**

Figure 2–16

Figure 2–17 shows the imaginary extruded surfaces. The resulting intersection defines the location of the Combine element.

Combine curve created at the intersection of imaginary extruded surfaces

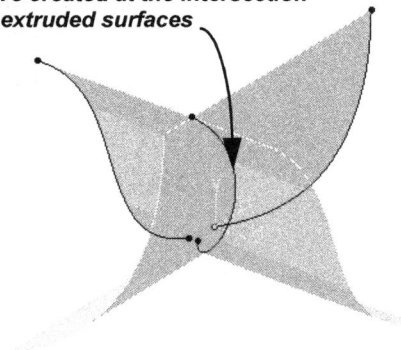

Figure 2–17

3. Click **OK** to complete the Combine element. Figure 2–18 shows a **Normal** Combine element created from two curves.

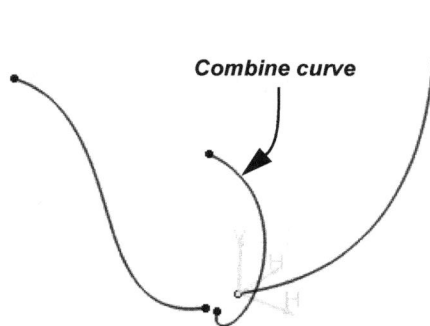

Combine curve

Figure 2–18

If the **Along directions** Combine type is specified, references must be selected for each curve. Planar references denote normal projection, as shown in Figure 2–19.

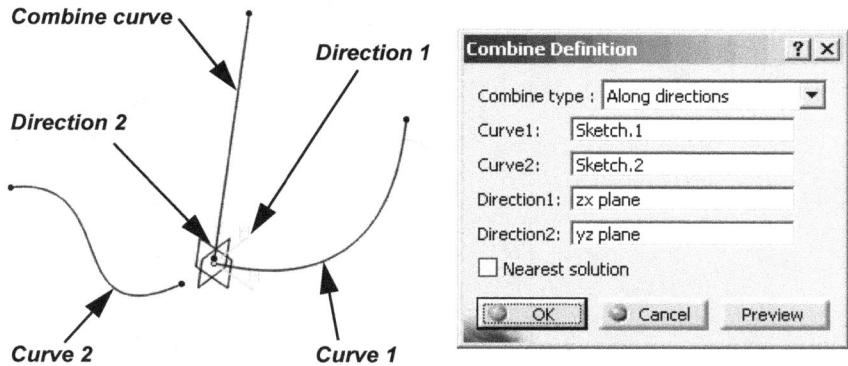

Figure 2–19

ReflectLine

A ReflectLine is a curve created through a series of points that meet specific angle, direction, and reference conditions as shown in Figure 2–20.

A Reflect Line can be defined as a Cylindrical type or a Conical type. This section demonstrates the differences between the two ReflectLine types and the various options that define the feature.

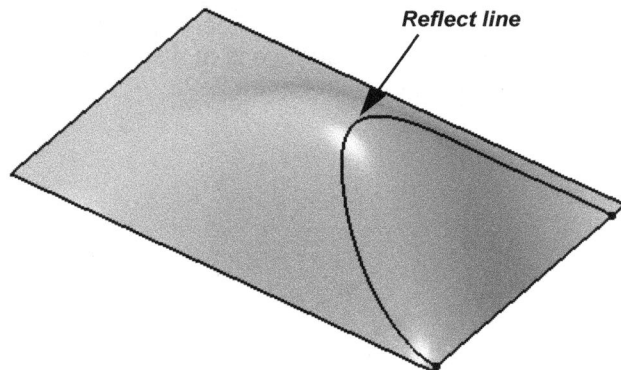

Figure 2–20

How To: Create a ReflectLine

1. Click [⟋] (Reflect Line). The Reflect Line Definition dialog box opens as shown in Figure 2–21.

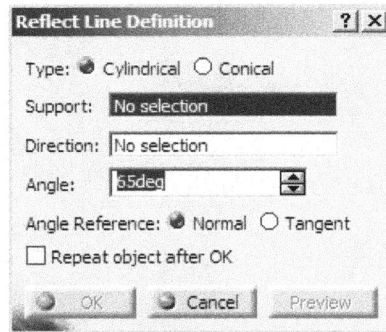

Figure 2–21

2. Specify the Cylindrical or Conical type.
3. Specify a Support surface. This is the surface that the curve lies on.
4. Specify a direction/origin reference.
5. Enter an Angle.
6. Specify the Angle Reference **Normal** or **Tangent**.
7. Click **OK** to complete the ReflectLine feature.

Cylindrical ReflectLine (Normal)

A normal cylindrical ReflectLine is a curve created through a series of points, where the surface normal at a point on the surface is at a specified angle to a direction reference as shown in Figure 2–22.

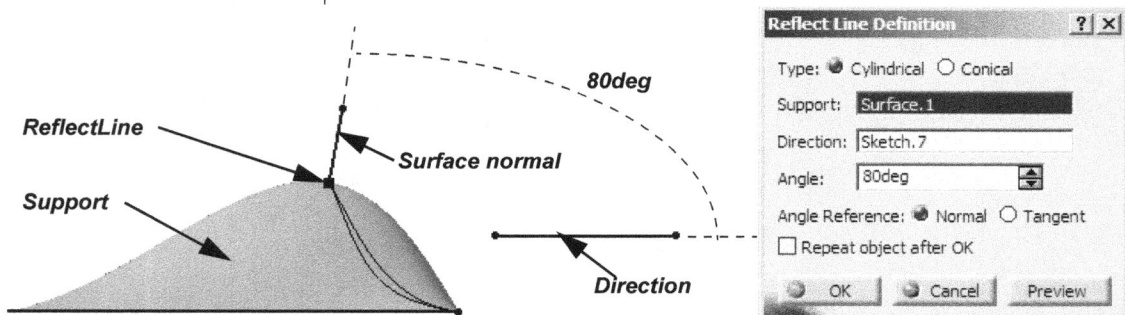

Figure 2–22

Cylindrical ReflectLine (Tangent)

A tangent cylindrical ReflectLine is a curve created through a series of points, where the tangent plane at a point on the surface is at a specified angle to a direction reference, as shown in Figure 2–23.

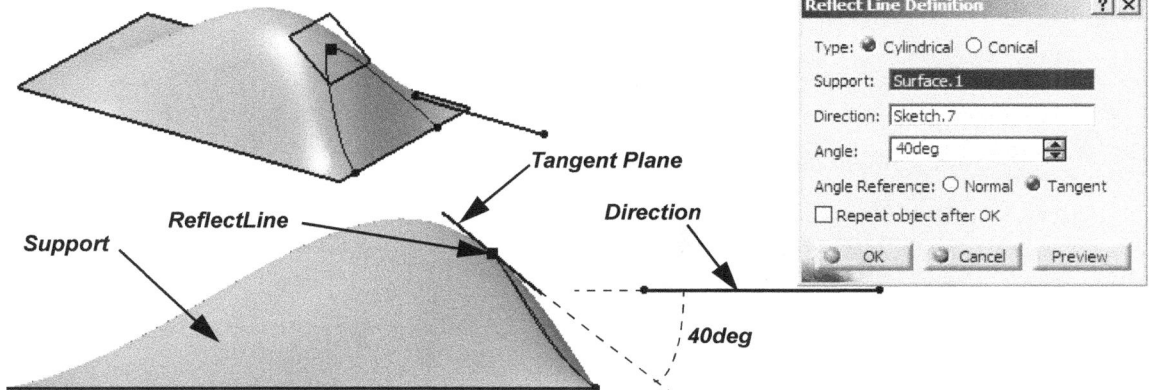

Figure 2–23

Conical ReflectLine (Normal)

A normal conical ReflectLine is a curve created through a series of points, where the surface normal is at a specified angle to a line created between the point on the surface and the origin point, as shown in Figure 2–24.

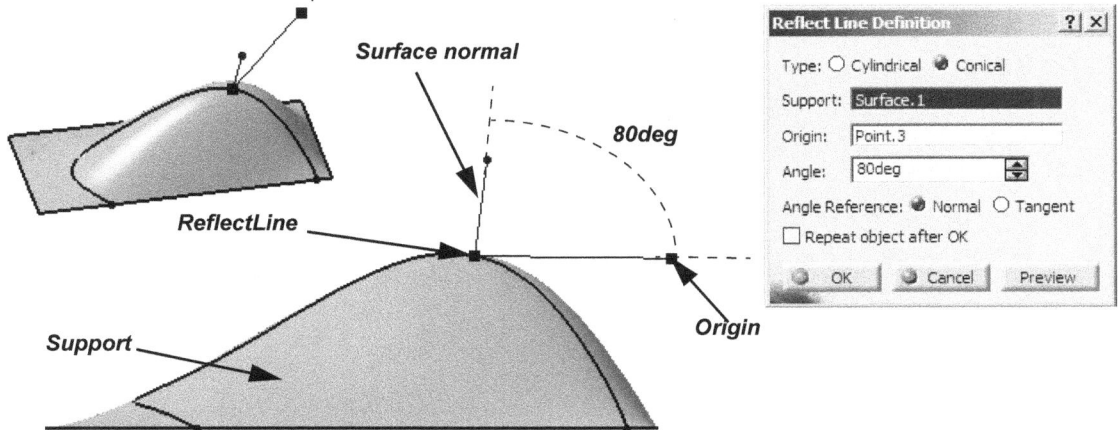

Figure 2–24

Conical ReflectLine (Tangent)

A tangent conical ReflectLine is a curve created through a series of points, where the tangent plane at a point on the surface is at a specified angle to a line created between the point on the surface and the origin point, as shown in Figure 2–25.

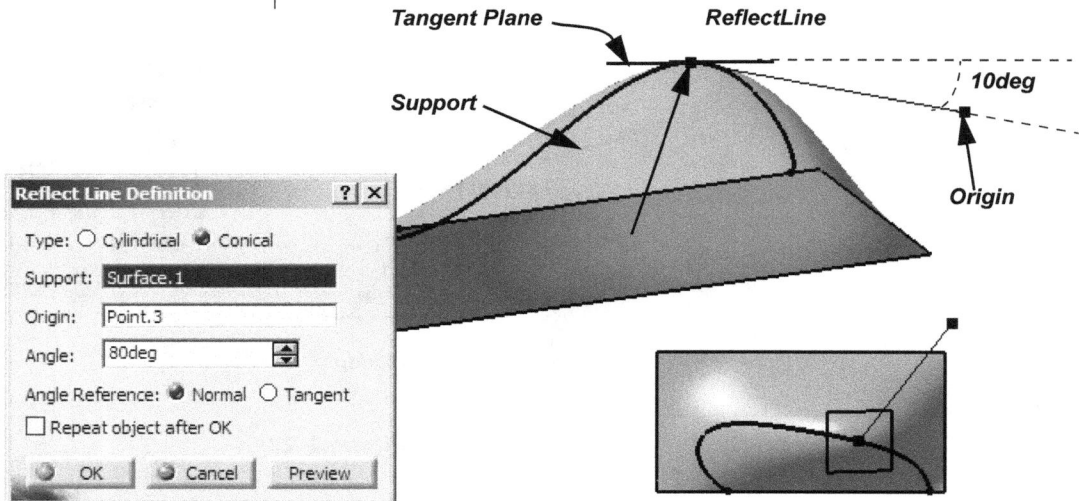

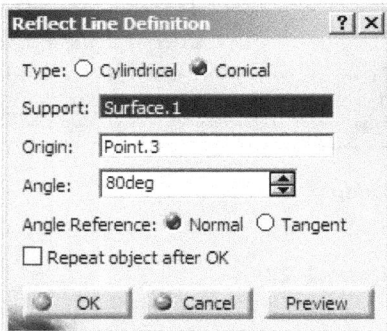

Figure 2–25

Silhouette

The silhouette command computes reflect lines and extracts edges that define the contour. It also removes non-visible areas of the contour.

How To: Create a Silhouette Element

1. Click 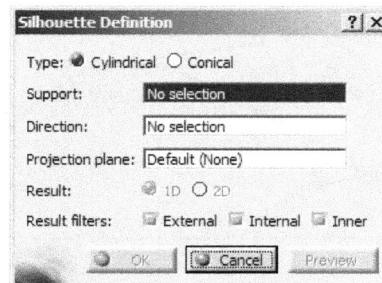 (Silhouette). The Silhouette Definition dialog box opens, as shown in Figure 2–26.

Figure 2–26

2. Select the Type as **Cylindrical** or **Conical**, where Cylindrical corresponds to the silhouette with an infinite light source and Conical with a finite point light source.

3. Select the **Support** surface.
4. Select an axis for the **Direction** if using Cylindrical, or point to the **Origin** if using Conical.
5. Select the **Projection Plane** on which the silhouette will be projected.

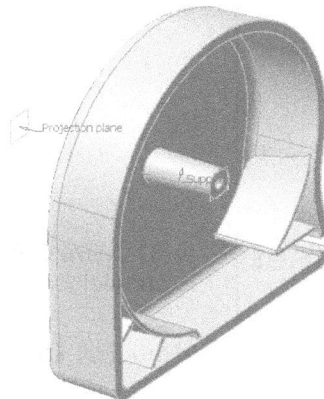

Figure 2–27

6. Select **1D** or **2D** if creating a Cylindrical silhouette.
7. Set the Result filters to **External**, **Internal**, or **Inner**, where:
   - External keeps external silhouette edges.
   - Internal keeps internal silhouette edges.
   - Inner keeps silhouette edges not otherwise defined as External or Internal.
8. Click **OK** to complete the silhouette. The result shown in Figure 2–28 was created using the External Result filter.

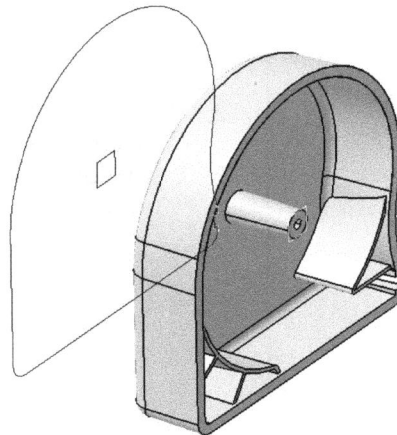

Figure 2–28

2.4 Offset Geometry

The Offset2D3D flyout toolbar displays under the **Parallel Curve** icon. When working in the Generative Shape Design workbench, the **Parallel Curve**, **Rolling Offset** and **3D Curve Offset** icons are available in the toolbar, as shown in Figure 2–29.

Figure 2–29

3D Curve Offset

A 3D Curve Offset element enables you to create a 3D curve that is parallel to a reference curve.

How To: Create a 3D Curve Offset Element

1. Click (3D Curve Offset). The 3D Curve Offset Definition dialog box opens as shown in Figure 2–30.

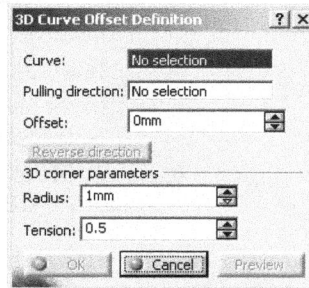

Figure 2–30

2. Select the reference curve and **Pulling direction**, as shown in Figure 2–31. Enter the *Offset* value to define the location of the offset curve.

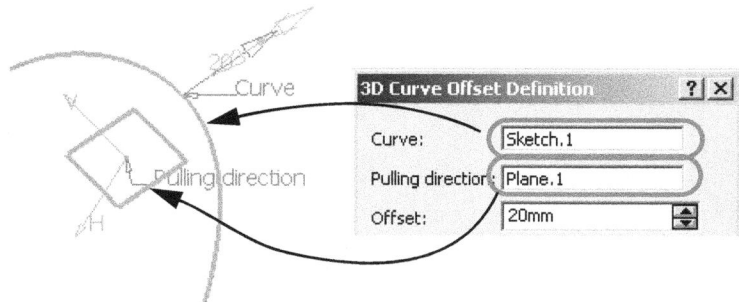

Figure 2–31

3. Specify the 3D corner parameters, as shown in Figure 2–32.

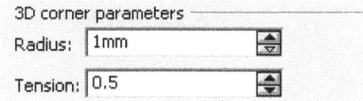

3D corner parameters
Radius: 1mm
Tension: 0.5

Figure 2–32

- **Radius:** If the defined offset value is larger than the radius of the reference curve, the radius of the offset curve decreases. This causes discontinuity. To avoid discontinuity, you must manually enter the radius of the offset curve. Note that the geometry of the offset curve might differ from the reference curve due to the radius change.
- **Tension:** Enter the tension value to define the tension of the 3D offset curve.
4. To place the Parallel curve on the other side of the reference curve, select **Reverse Direction**.
5. Click **OK** to complete the 3D Curve Offset feature.

Differences between Parallel and 3D Offset Curves

Both Parallel and 3D Offset curves create a curve offset by a specified distance. An input curve and support or direction reference are selected.

Parallel curves must lie completely on their referenced support surface. This support surface can be a planar or 3D surface.

3D Offset curves do not have to lie on the Pulling direction reference. This is because the direction is not necessarily a surface. Lines, axes, and edges are appropriate Pull direction references as well. If a surface is selected as the Pull direction reference, it must be planar.

The example shown in Figure 2–33 shows the differences between two curves that were offset by 5mm from a Boundary curve on the end of the pipe.

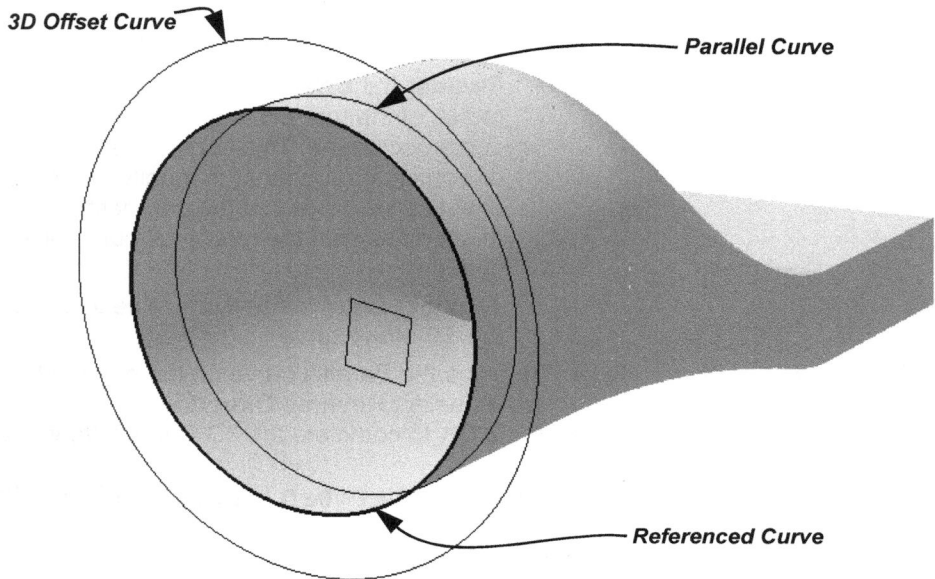

Figure 2–33

Rolling Offset

A Rolling Offset curve creates a closed loop curve that is offset on both sides of a selected curve or chain of curves.

How To: Create a Rolling Offset Curve

1. Click ⬡ (Rolling Offset) from the Curve Offsets flyout in the Wireframe toolbar. The Rolling Offset Definition dialog box opens, as shown in Figure 2–34.

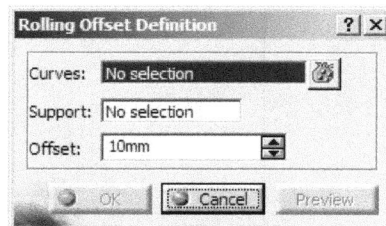

Figure 2–34

2. Select the reference curve, as shown in Figure 2–35.

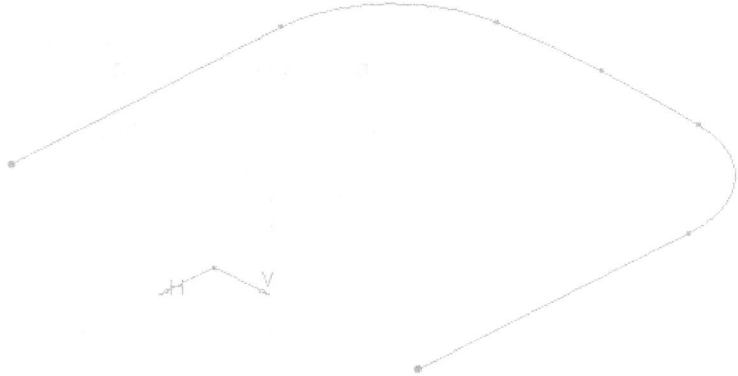

Figure 2–35

3. If the selected curves lie on a plane, the support is automatically selected. Otherwise, select the support.
4. Enter the *Offset* value and complete the feature. The result is shown in Figure 2–36.

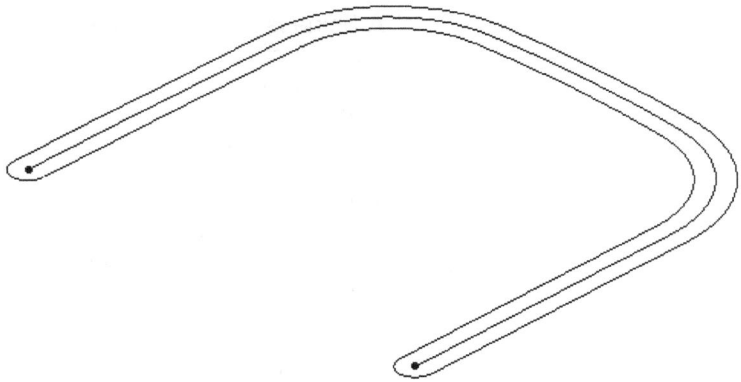

Figure 2–36

2.5 Curve Geometry

The Curves toolbar enables you to create wireframe curve elements. When working with the Generative Shape Design workbench, the [icon] (Spine), [icon] (Isoparametric Curve) and [icon] (Curve from Equations) tools are available in this toolbar, as shown in Figure 2–37. The other tools are covered in the *Introduction to Surface Design* course.

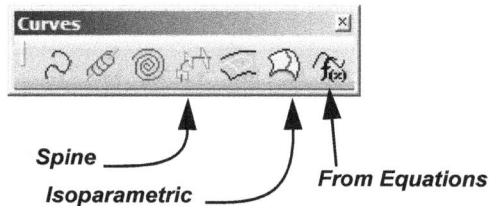

Figure 2–37

Spine

A Spine is a type of curve created based on planar or curve references. Spines are typically used as a center curve for a sweep or a spine reference for a Multi-sections feature. When referenced in a sweep or multi-sections surface, the profile for the feature remains normal to the spine curve.

There are two different ways to generate a Spine curve. The first way creates a spine curve that is normal to the selected planar references. An example of a Spine element is shown in Figure 2–38.

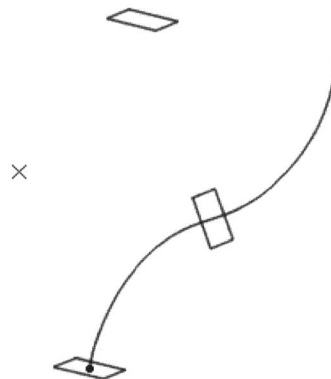

Figure 2–38

How To: Create a Spine from Planar References

1. Click [icon] (Spine) in the Curves toolbar. The Spine Curve Definition dialog box opens as shown in Figure 2–39.

Figure 2–39

2. Select the references from which the spine is computed. If Section/Plane references are selected, the spine is created normal to the references. Three reference planes, selected to create a spine curve, are shown in Figure 2–40. If curves are selected in the *Guide* field, the spine is created from the curve geometry. If the **Computed start point** option is selected, the system computes a start point.

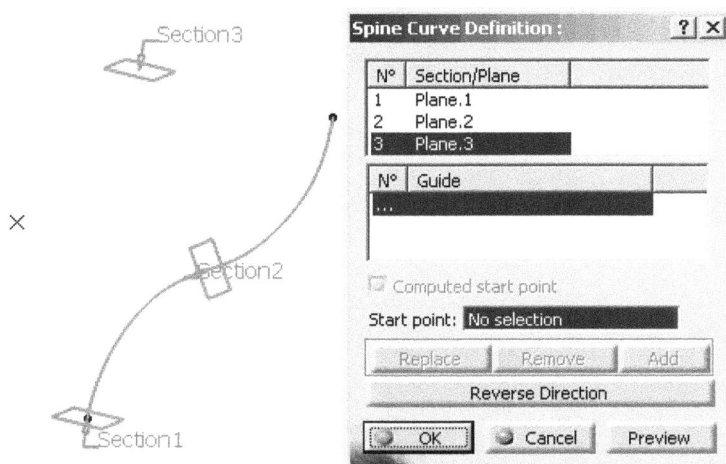

Figure 2–40

If you want to select your own start point, leave the **Computed start point** option cleared. The Spine Curve feature with a reference point specified as the start point is shown in Figure 2–41. In this case, the system projects the selected start point onto the first selected planar reference.

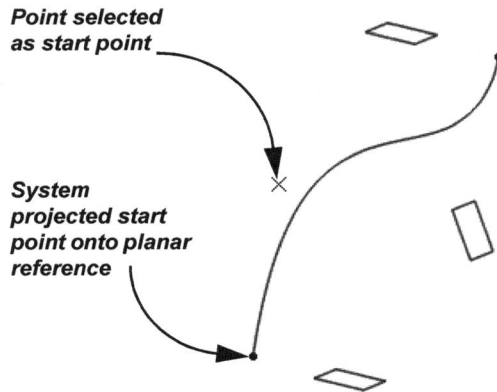

Point selected as start point

System projected start point onto planar reference

Figure 2–41

3. Click **OK** to complete the feature.

Isoparametric Curve

Typical uses of an Isoparametric curve are to create a centerline on a surface feature or for surface reconstruction of an imported surface. An Isoparametric curve is positioned by referencing a point and a line. An example of an Isoparametric curve used to find the centerline of a surface is shown in Figure 2–42.

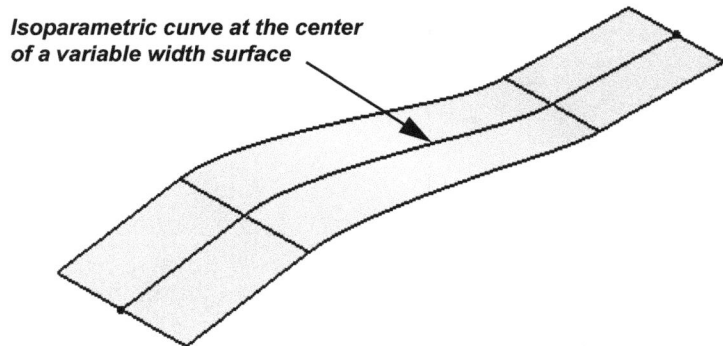

Isoparametric curve at the center of a variable width surface

Figure 2–42

How To: Create an Isoparametric Curve

1. Click ![icon] (Isoparametric Curve) in the Curves toolbar. The Isoparametric curve dialog box opens as shown in Figure 2–43.

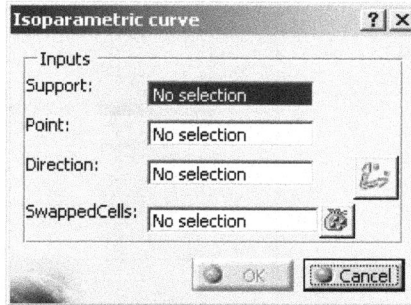

Figure 2–43

2. Select a surface. The point and line are created by the application but can be modified, as required.
3. Click **OK** to complete the feature.

Curve From Equations

The ![icon] (Curve from Equations) option enables you to create a parametric curve from three Cartesian equations. To use this option, click **Tools>Options>Infrastructure>Part Infrastructure** and ensure that **Parameters** and **Relations** are enabled in the *Display* tab.

How To: Create a Curve from Equations

1. Click ![icon] (Curve from Equations) in the Curves toolbar. The Curve from Equations Definition dialog box opens as shown in Figure 2–44.

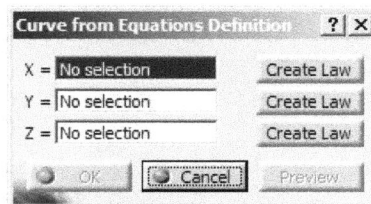

Figure 2–44

For more information on Laws, refer to Chapter 9.

2. To compute the **X** component of the curve, either click the **X** field and select an existing law or click **Create Law** to open the Law Editor dialog box, as shown in Figure 2–45.

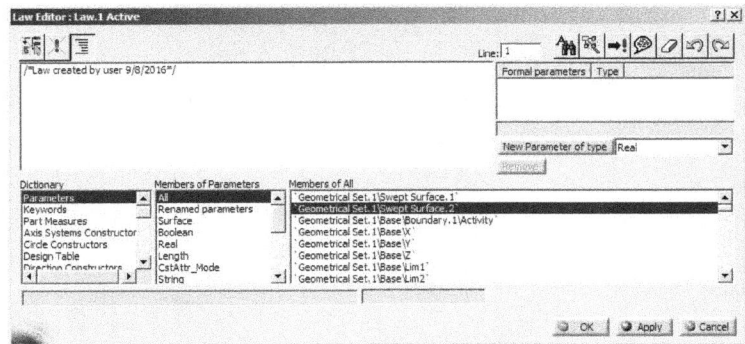

Figure 2–45

3. Repeat the previous step to select or create laws for the **Y** and **Z** components of the curve.
4. Click **OK** to create the parametric curve.

2.6 Circle-Conic Geometry

The Circle-Conic flyout toolbar is found under the **Circle** icon. When working in the Generative Shape Design workbench, the **Conic** icon is available in this toolbar, as shown in Figure 2–46.

Figure 2–46

Conic

The Conic element creates a conic curve by specifying support, parameter, and tangency conditions, as shown in Figure 2–47.

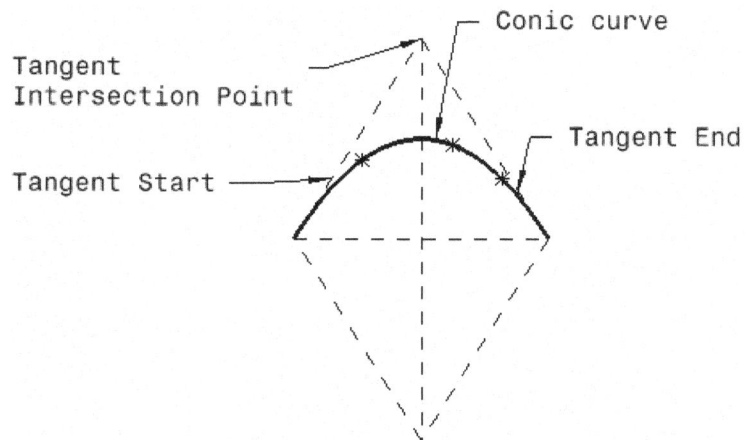

Figure 2–47

How To: Create a Conic Element

1. Click ⬚ (Conic). The Conic Definition dialog box opens as shown in Figure 2–48.

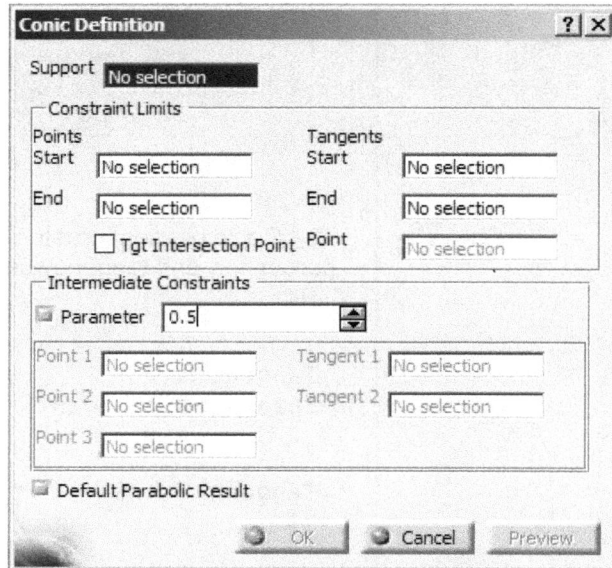

Figure 2–48

2. Specify constraint limit references. The constraint limits that are required to define a conic are shown in Figure 2–49.

- Parameter = B/A
- P = .5 = Parabola
- P > .5 = Hyperbola
- P < .5 = Ellipse

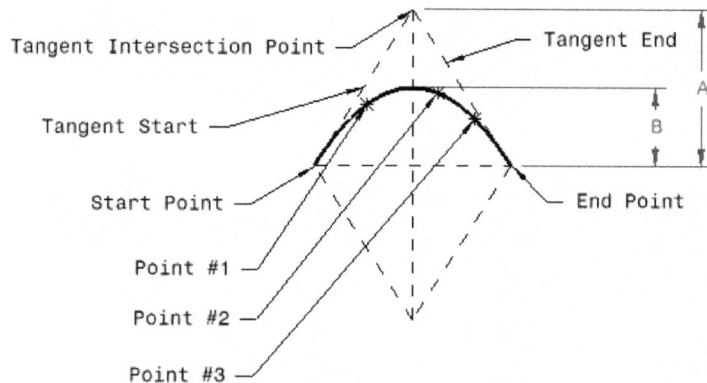

Figure 2–49

3. Define the Tangent Intersection Point, as required. The conic can be manipulated to pass through a reference point. To define the Tangent Intersection Point, select **Tgt Intersection Point** and select a point, as shown in Figure 2–50.

Tangent point

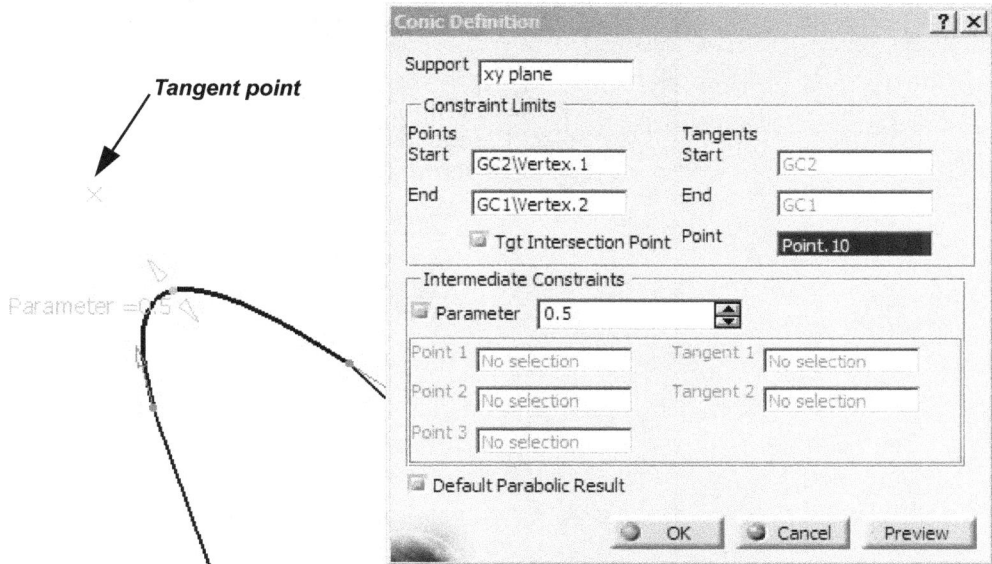

Figure 2–50

4. Set the Intermediate Constraints as required. If the **Parameter** option is cleared, intermediate points and tangency references can be selected, as shown in Figure 2–51.

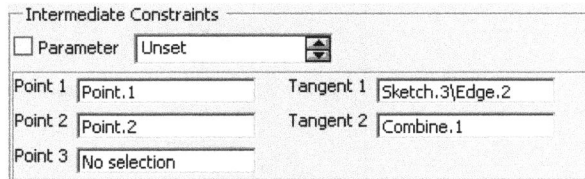

Figure 2–51

5. Click **OK** to complete the conic. A Conic Wireframe feature displays in the specification tree. The parameter value of a conic can be modified directly in the specification tree by right-clicking.

2.7 Trim (Pieces)

The Trim operation with Pieces mode trims overlapping geometry between intersecting curves.

How To: Perform a Trim Operation

1. Click ⬚ (Trim).
2. Select **Pieces** in the Mode drop-down list. The dialog box opens as shown in Figure 2–52.

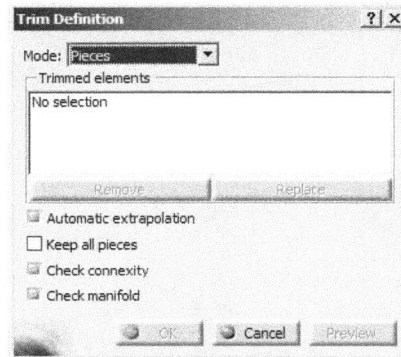

Figure 2–52

3. Select the elements to trim, as shown in Figure 2–53. The **Trim** tool keeps the sections of the curve that you click on during selection.

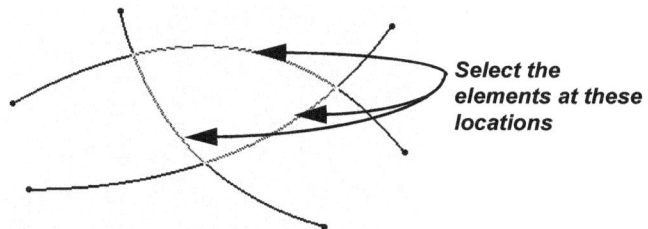

Select the elements at these locations

Figure 2–53

The result of the **Trim** operation is shown in Figure 2–54.

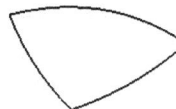

Figure 2–54

2.8 Create Multi-Extract Elements

The **Multiple Extract** tool is used to extract a group of curves or faces, while creating only one feature in the specification tree.

General Steps

Use the following general steps to perform a multi-extract:

1. Activate the **Multi-Extract** tool.
2. Select elements to extract.
3. Specify propagation type.
4. Define additional options.

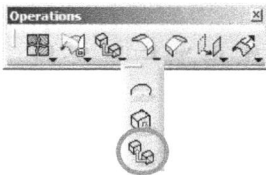

Step 1 - Activate the Multi-Extract tool.

Click (Multi-Extract) in the Extracts sub-toolbar. The Multiple Extract Definition dialog box opens as shown in Figure 2–55.

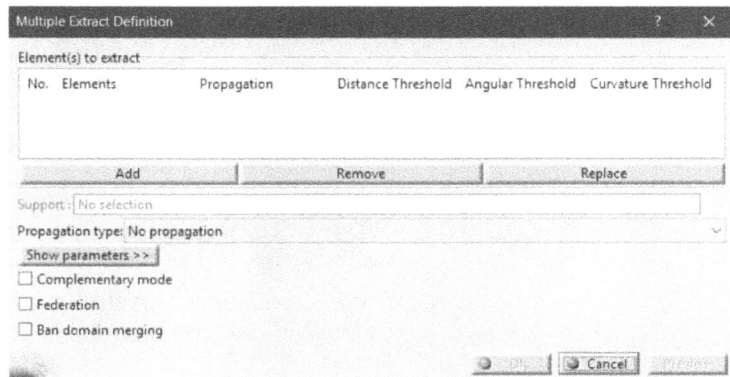

Figure 2–55

Step 2 - Select elements to extract.

Select faces or curves from the model to extract. If a face is selected, it can be a solid or non-solid surface. As each element is selected it gets added to the dialog box.

Two faces are selected for the Multi-Extract as shown in Figure 2–56. Two curves are selected for the Multi-Extract as shown in Figure 2–57.

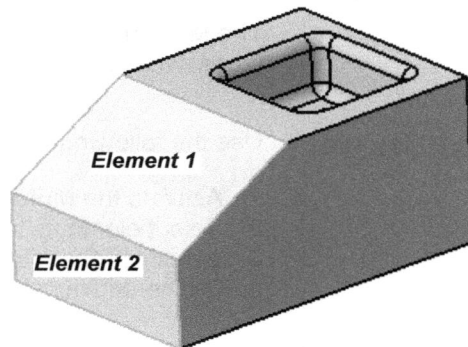

Figure 2–56

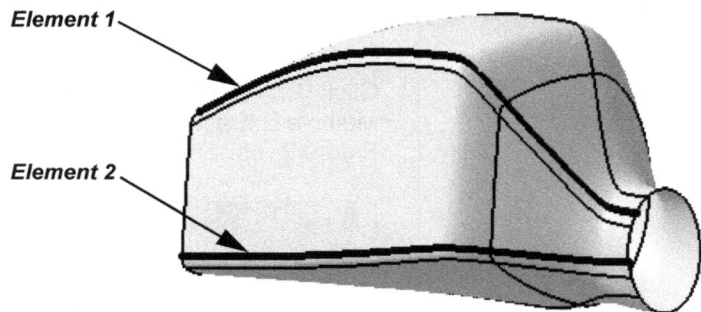

Figure 2–57

Step 3 - Specify propagation type.

For each element selected, a separate propagation type can be defined. Select the element in the list to activate it. Using the Propagation Type drop-down list, select one of the following options as shown in Figure 2–58:

- **No Propagation**

- **Point continuity**

- **Tangent continuity**

- **Curvature continuity**

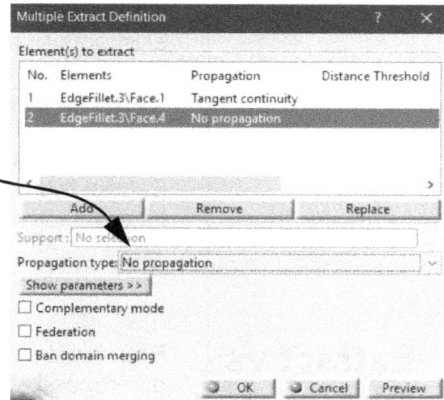

Specify propagation for each element here

Figure 2–58

Step 4 - Define additional options.

As with the **Extract** tool, the **Multi-Extract** tool has the additional functions of Complementary mode and Federation.

Select **Federation** if the resultant curve is considered a representation of all edges or curves added to the extract. Do not select **Federation** if the resultant surface is used as a collection of curves representing each individual curve or edge added to the extract.

- **Show parameters** options are only available when extracting curves. By clicking **Show parameters**, the **Distance Threshold**, **Angular Threshold**, and **Curvature Threshold** can be adjusted. These options are available when extracting edges or curves, not surfaces.

- **Distance Threshold** is a linear value between 0.001mm and 0.1mm that defines the elements that are included in the extract when point continuity is enabled.

- **Angular Threshold** is a value that defines the maximum discontinuity permitted for two tangent entities. **Angular Threshold** is available with Tangent and Curvature continuity propagation.

- **Curvature Threshold** is a ratio between 0 and 1. The ratio is derived from an equation that measure the curvature vectors of two adjacent entities. The larger the curvature threshold value, the less discontinuity is permitted. This ratio is only active to be adjusted when Curvature continuity is the selected propagation type.

When the **Ban domain merging** option is enabled, the selected elements to extract come from different domains of the same feature. The Multiple Extract feature leaves them in different domains, even if the elements are connected to one another.

With the **Ban domain merging** option cleared, the Multiple Extract feature will combine connected elements coming from different domains to a single domain.

Click **OK** to complete the **Multi-Extract**.

Extract vs Multi-Extract

Both functions enable you to extract multiple elements. The main difference between the two operations is the resultant feature. If you select two different surfaces or curves to extract, the result is two Extract features in the specification tree, as shown in Figure 2–59. Each extract then behaves on its own.

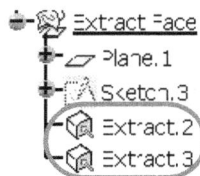

Figure 2–59

If you were to use the Multi-Extract function and select two elements, the result is one feature in the specification tree, as shown in Figure 2–60. The surfaces or curves inside the multi-extract act together.

Figure 2–60

The model displays as shown in Figure 2–61 for both situations described.

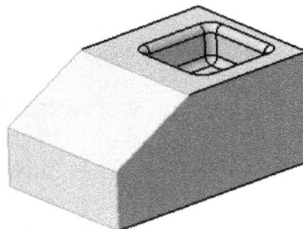

Figure 2–61

2.9 Extrapolate Operation

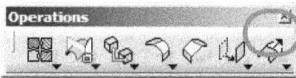

The Extrapolate operation extends a surface or curve by a specified length or up to a surface. Click [icon] (Extrapolate) to extrapolate a surface feature or curve. The Extrapolate Definition dialog box opens as shown in Figure 2–62.

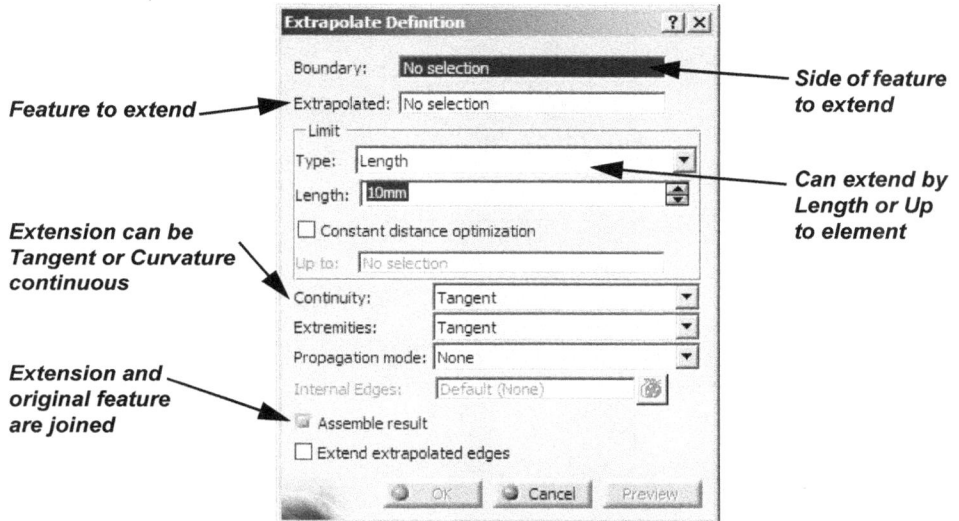

Feature to extend ——

Extension can be Tangent or Curvature continuous

Extension and original feature are joined

Side of feature to extend

Can extend by Length or Up to element

Figure 2–62

Figure 2–63 shows an example of a curve extrapolated at the selected boundary by 10mm.

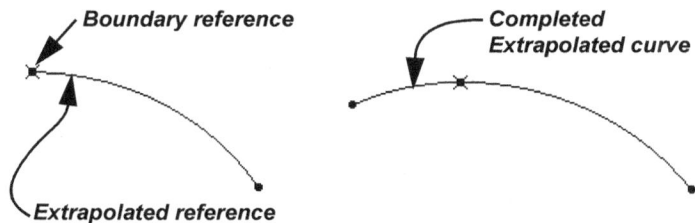

Boundary reference

Completed Extrapolated curve

Extrapolated reference

Figure 2–63

Figure 2–64 shows an example of a surface extrapolated at the selected boundary by 10 units.

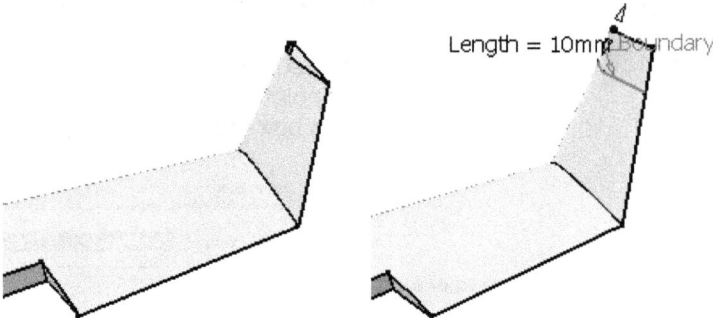

Figure 2–64

Practice 2a	# Spine Curve

Practice Objectives

- Create a spine curve.
- Use a spine curve to control a multi-sections surface.

In this practice, you will create a spine curve and edit a multi-sections surface to reference it. The multi-sections surface defines the handle of a hair dryer and the spine curve gives it shape. The completed model displays as shown in Figure 2–65.

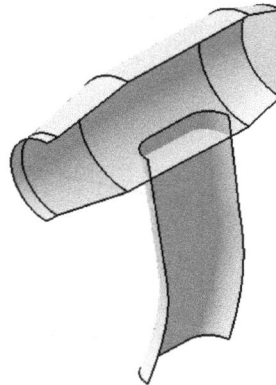

Figure 2–65

Task 1 - Open a part file.

1. Open **HairDryer_Spine.CATPart**. The model displays as shown in Figure 2–66.

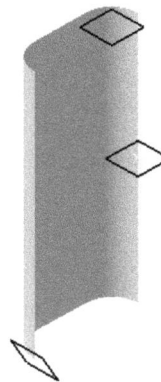

Figure 2–66

Task 2 - Create a spine curve.

1. Click ⬚ (Spine) in the Curves toolbar. Select the three planes shown in Figure 2–67.

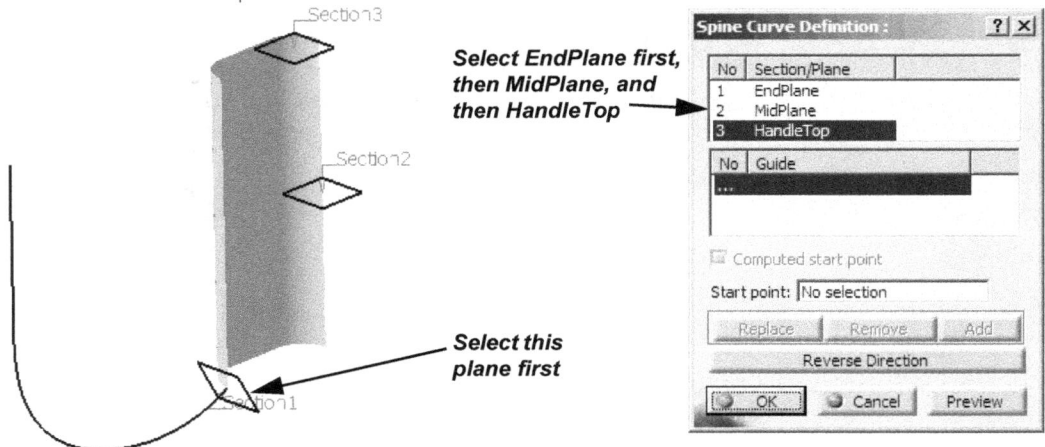

Select EndPlane first, then MidPlane, and then HandleTop ▶

Select this plane first ▶

Spine Curve Definition :

No	Section/Plane	
1	EndPlane	
2	MidPlane	
3	HandleTop	

No	Guide	
...		

☐ Computed start point

Start point: No selection

Replace | Remove | Add

Reverse Direction

OK | Cancel | Preview

Section3

Section2

Section1

Figure 2–67

2. Click **Reverse Direction**. The Spine curve displays as shown in Figure 2–68.

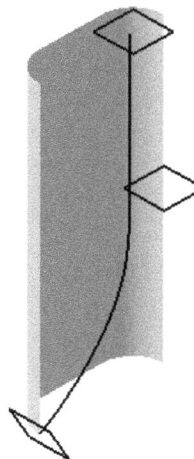

Figure 2–68

3. Click **OK**.

Task 3 - Edit the multi-sections surface.

1. Edit the **Multi-sections Surface.3** feature.

2. Select the *Spine* tab and make the following change as shown in Figure 2–69:

   - *Spine:* **Spine.1** (the spine you just created)

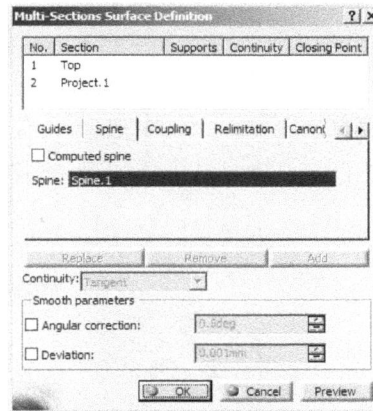

Figure 2–69

3. Click **OK**. The multi-sections surface is now controlled by the spine curve, as shown in Figure 2–70.

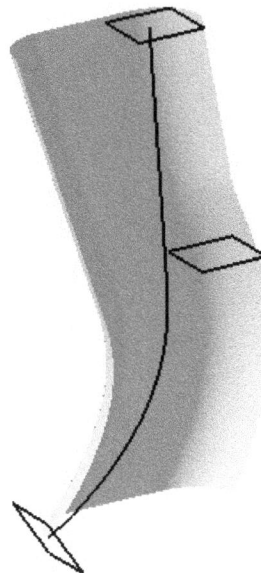

Figure 2–70

Task 4 - Edit spine reference geometry.

1. Edit the Angle parameter for the EndPlane and make the following change as shown in Figure 2–71:

    *   *Handle\EndPlane\Angle:* **50deg**

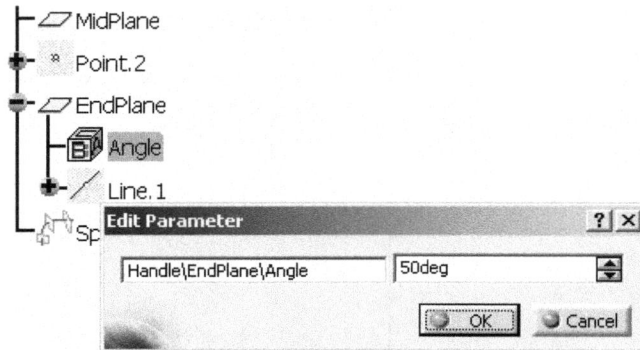

Figure 2–71

2. Click **OK**. The multi-sections surface updates as shown in Figure 2–72.

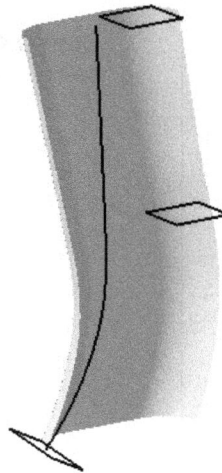

Figure 2–72

3. Use the **Tools** menu at the top and hide **All Planes** and **All Curves**.

4. Show the **Body** geometrical set. The model displays as shown in Figure 2–73.

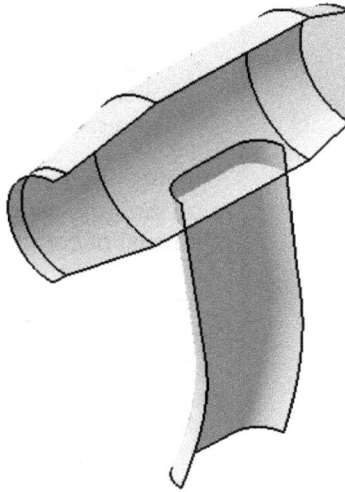

Figure 2–73

5. Save the file and close the window.

Practice 2b | Wing Surface

Practice Objectives

- Create combine curves.
- Create a spine curve.
- Use a spine during surface creation.

In this practice, you will create a reference surface required for an airplane wing. The wireframe geometry in this practice will consist of combine curves and a spine. The surface will be created using the **Sweep** command and the model will display as shown in Figure 2–74.

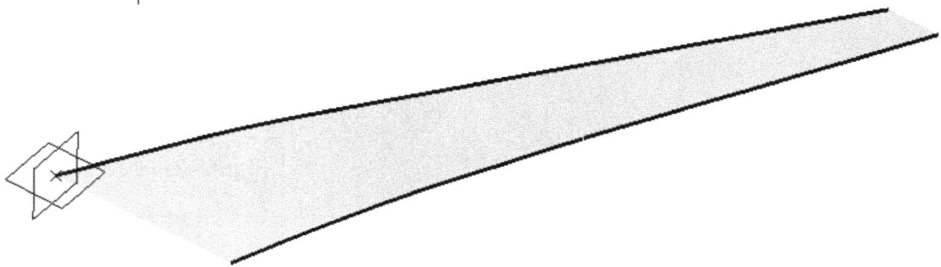

Figure 2–74

Task 1 - Open a part file.

1. Open **Combine_Start.CATPart**. The model displays as shown in Figure 2–75.

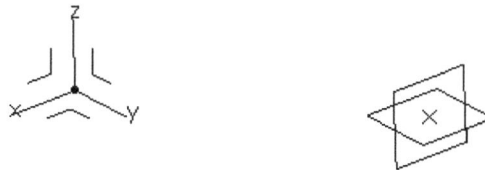

Figure 2–75

2. Ensure that the model units are set to **mm**.

Task 2 - Create sketched curves.

The sketches created in this task will be used later to create two different combine curves. Combine curves can be created from other curve types, not just sketches.

1. Create a positioned sketch using the following specifications:

    - *Sketch plane:* **Plane.2**
    - *Origin type:* **Projection Point**
    - *Origin reference:* **Point.1**

2. Sketch and constrain the geometry shown in Figure 2–76. This sketch is made up of two lines and one arc. The arc is tangent to both lines.

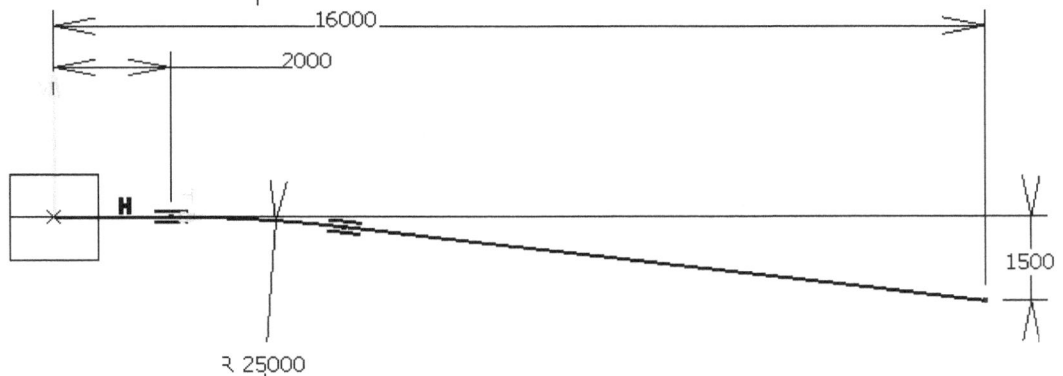

Figure 2–76

3. Exit Sketcher. If the Sketch feature is not named Sketch.1, rename it as **Sketch.1**.

4. Create another positioned sketch using the following specifications:

    - *Sketch plane:* **Plane.1**
    - *Origin type:* **Projection Point**
    - *Origin reference:* **Point.1**
    - Reverse the Vertical axis and Horizontal axis.

5. Sketch and constrain the geometry shown in Figure 2–77. This sketch is made up of one line. The 60 degree angle represents the sweep angle of the aircraft wing.

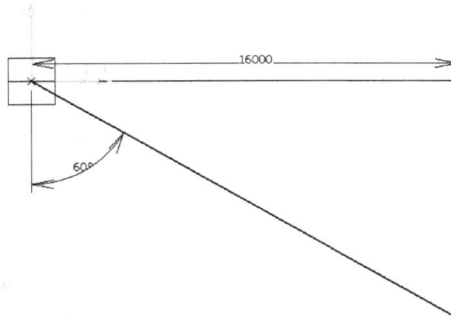

Figure 2–77

6. Exit Sketcher. Ensure that the name of the sketch is **Sketch.2**.

7. Create another positioned sketch using the following specifications:

   - *Sketch plane:* **Plane.1**
   - *Origin type:* **Projection Point**
   - *Origin reference:* **Point.1**
   - Reverse the Vertical axis and Horizontal axis.

8. Sketch and constrain the geometry as shown in Figure 2–78. The sketch consists of two lines.

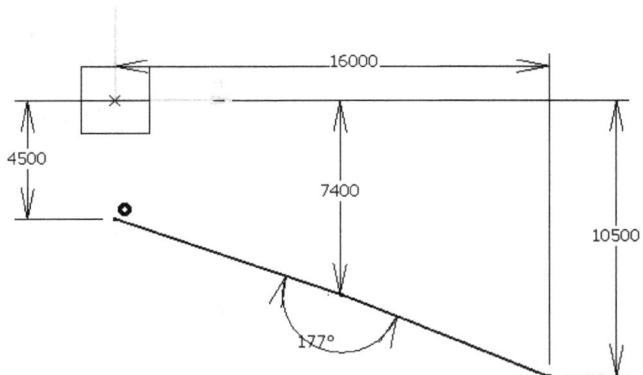

Figure 2–78

9. Exit Sketcher. Ensure that the name of the sketch is **Sketch.3**.

Task 3 - Create combine curves.

1. Click ⬜ (Combine). The Combine Definition dialog box opens as shown in Figure 2–79.

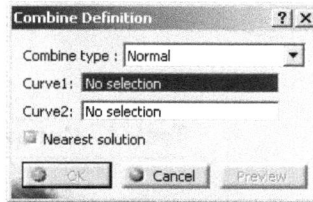

Figure 2–79

2. Ensure that the *Combine type* is set to **Normal.**

3. Select **Sketch.1** as the *Curve1* reference.

4. Select **Sketch.2** as the *Curve2* reference. The order in which the sketches are selected does not change the resulting combine curve.

5. Click **OK** in the Combine Definition dialog box. The curve displays as shown in Figure 2–80.

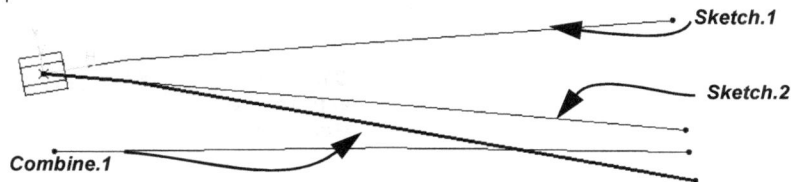

Figure 2–80

6. Hide **Sketch.2**.

7. Create another combine curve using the following specifications:

   - *Combine type:* **Normal**
   - *Curve1:* **Sketch.1**
   - *Curve2:* **Sketch.3**

8. Click **OK** in the Combine Definition dialog box.

9. Ensure that all three Sketch features in the model are hidden. The model displays as shown in Figure 2–81.

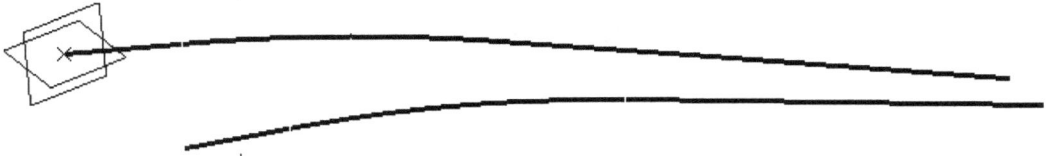

Figure 2–81

Task 4 - Complete the model.

In this task, you will create a spine curve to demonstrate its benefit when surfacing. Without the spine curve, the surface created in this task will not correctly meet the design intent.

1. Click (Spine) in the Curves toolbar. By default, the *Section/Plane* reference field is activated. Activate the *Guide* reference field, as shown in Figure 2–82.

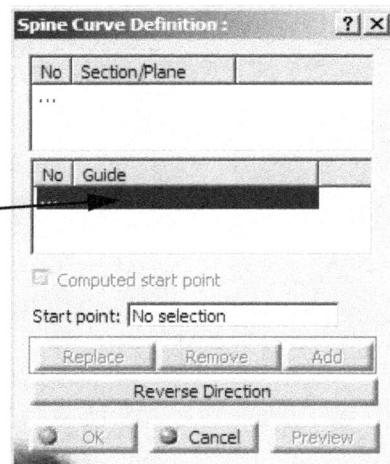

Click here to activate the Guide field.

Figure 2–82

2. Select **Combine.1** and **Combine.2**.

3. Click **OK** in the Spine Curve Definition dialog box. The model displays as shown in Figure 2–83.

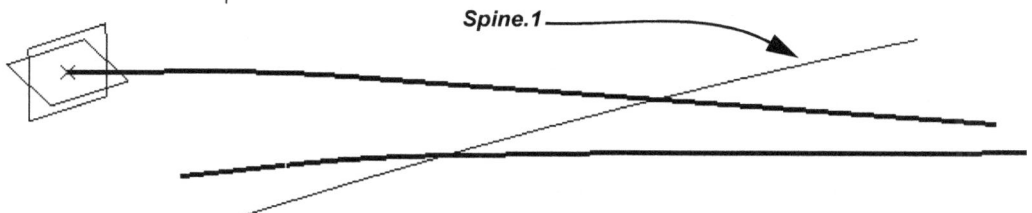

Figure 2–83

4. Click ⟲ (Sweep).

5. Select **Line** as the *Profile type*.

6. Select **Two limits** as the *Sub-type*.

7. Select **Combine.1** as *Guide curve 1*.

8. Select **Combine.2** as *Guide curve 2*. The dialog box opens as shown in Figure 2–84.

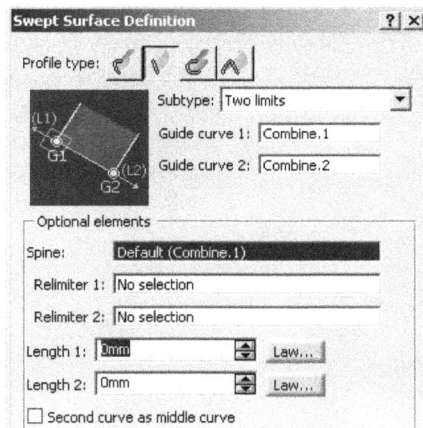

Figure 2–84

9. Click **Preview** and close the warning message that opens. The model displays as shown in Figure 2–85.

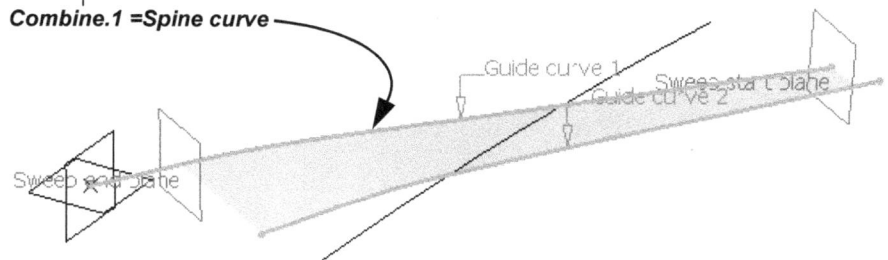

Figure 2–85

Design Considerations

The surface does not extend to the end points of both guide curves. This is because, by default the curve selected for Guide curve 1 acts as the spine curve. The spine curve dictates what the line (profile) remains normal to as it is swept along the guide curves.

10. Select **Combine.2** as the Spine reference and click **Preview**. An Update Error warning box opens as shown in Figure 2–86. This indicates that the spine curve failed because it does not have tangency continuity.

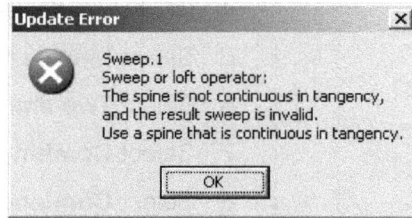

Figure 2–86

11. Click **OK** in the Update Error warning box, and close the Warnings dialog box. This error can be ignored because the selected reference does not remain upon the completion of the sweep. It has only been selected to demonstrate that a better quality curve must be used. The model displays as shown in Figure 2–87. This is not the required swept surface either.

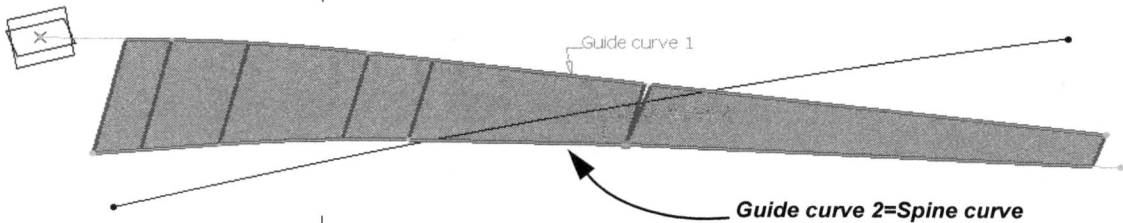

Figure 2–87

12. Select **Spine.1** as the spine curve reference.

13. Click **Preview**. The model displays as shown in Figure 2–88.

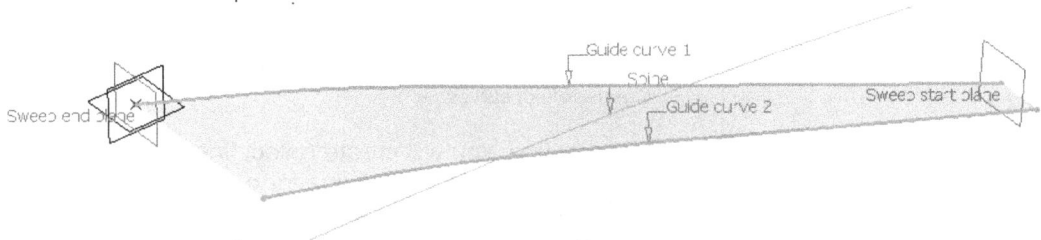

Figure 2–88

Design Considerations

The spine curve was created before the swept surface. It was calculated from **Combine.1** and **Combine.2**. This was done because the two combine curves were to be used as guide curves for the sweep. By using a Spine feature as the Spine reference in a sweep, the quality of the surface is greatly improved.

14. Click **OK** to complete the Sweep.

15. Save and close the model. The surface created advances the development of the aircraft wing model as shown in Figure 2–89.

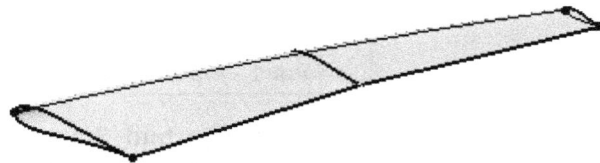

Figure 2–89

Practice 2c | Earbud Parting Line

Practice Objective

- Create reflect curves.

In this practice, you will create reflect lines and other curve geometry to find the parting line for a plastic injection molded part. The surfacing for the earbud has already been created. Once the parting lines are found, you will split the surfaces using the parting lines. The completed model is as shown in Figure 2–90.

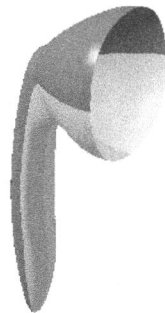

Figure 2–90

Task 1 - Open a part file.

1. Open **Earbud_Start.CATPart**. The model displays as shown in Figure 2–91. It is made up of two surfaces modeled by the industrial design department, a Fillet feature, and an extract.

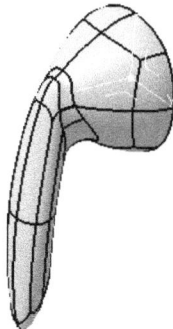

Figure 2–91

2. Ensure that the model units are set to **mm**.

Task 2 - Create reflect curves.

1. Hide **Extract.1**, and show **ID Surf2**. The model displays as shown in Figure 2–92.

Figure 2–92

2. Click (Reflect Line) in the Wireframe toolbar. The dialog box opens as shown in Figure 2–93.

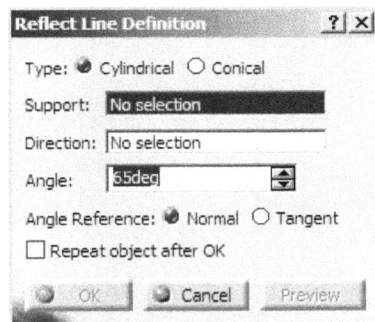

Figure 2–93

3. Ensure that **Cylindrical** is the selected type, and **Normal** is the selected Angle Reference type.

4. Select **ID Surf2** as the *Support*.

5. Select the YZ-plane or X-axis as the *Direction*.

6. Enter an *Angle* of **89.5deg**.

The line thickness of the Reflect line has been thickened to make it easier to see. This was done by adjusting the graphic properties. You do not need to do this.

7. Click **OK** to complete the Reflect Line. The model displays as shown in Figure 2–94. The reflect line represents a place on the surface where the parting line of a mold would be located.

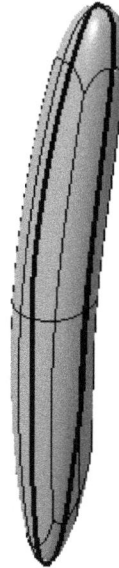

Figure 2–94

8. Hide **ID Surf2**, and show **ID Surf1**.

9. Create another reflect line using the following specifications:

- *Support:* **ID Surf1**
- *Direction:* **XY-plane** or **Z-axis**
- *Angle:* **89.5deg**
- Ensure that **Normal** is selected.

10. Click **OK** to complete the Reflect Line. The model displays as shown in Figure 2–95.

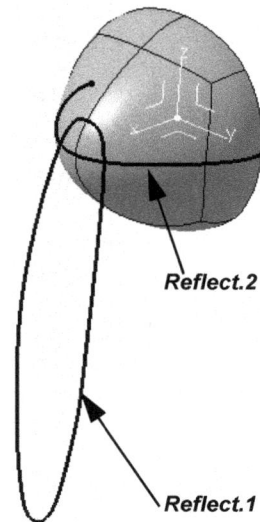

Figure 2–95

Task 3 - Create wireframe geometry from the reflect lines.

In this task, you will create more wireframe geometry, based on the reflect lines from Task 2. The display rendering was switched to **Shading** to make it easier to display the curves being created.

1. Hide **ID Surf1** and show **Extract.1**.

2. Project **Reflect line.1** onto **Extract.1** using the **Normal** Projection type.

3. Click **OK** to complete the Project.

4. Hide **Reflect line.1**. The model displays as shown in Figure 2–96.

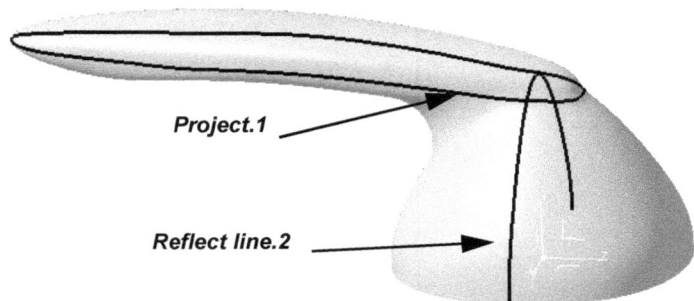

Figure 2–96

5. Project **Reflect line.2** onto **Extract.1** using the **Normal** Projection type.

6. Click **OK** to complete the Project.

7. Hide **Reflect line.2**. The model displays as shown in Figure 2–97.

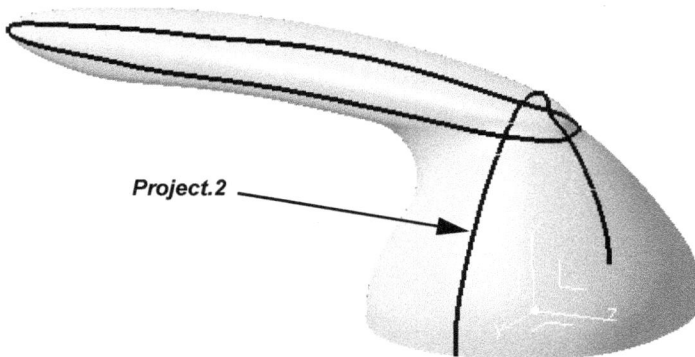

Project.2

Figure 2–97

8. Click (Split).

9. Click in the Split definition dialog box.

10. Select **Project.1** and **Project.2**. Two elements are cut in this operation.

11. Close the Elements to Cut dialog box.

12. Select the ZX-plane as the Cutting Element. A Warnings dialog box opens as shown in Figure 2–98.

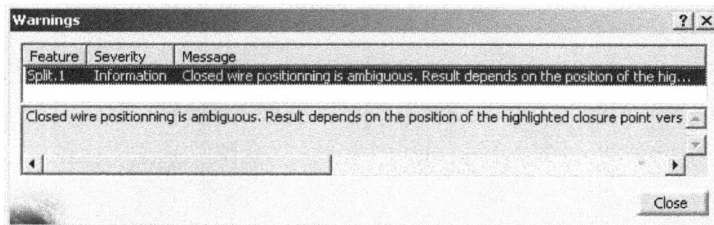

Figure 2–98

13. Close the Warnings dialog box.

It might be necessary to toggle **Other side**.

14. Click **OK** to complete the Split. Note the two split curves shown in Figure 2–99.

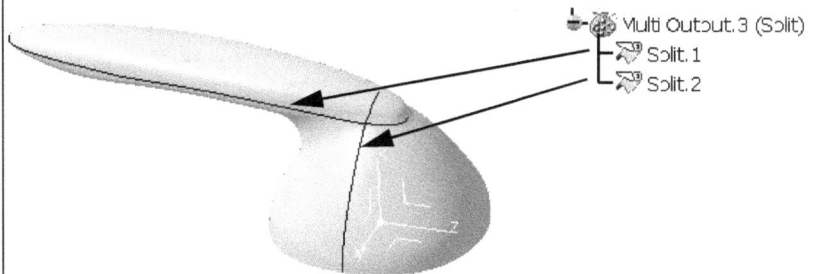

Figure 2–99

15. Create a Corner using the following specifications:

    - *Corner Type:* **Corner on Support**
    - *Element 1:* **Split.1**
    - Activate **Trim element 1**.
    - *Element 2:* **Split.2**
    - Activate **Trim element 2**.
    - *Support:* **Extract.1**
    - *Radius:* **2mm**

It might be necessary to toggle **Next Solution**.

16. Ensure that the solution matches the one in Figure 2–100.

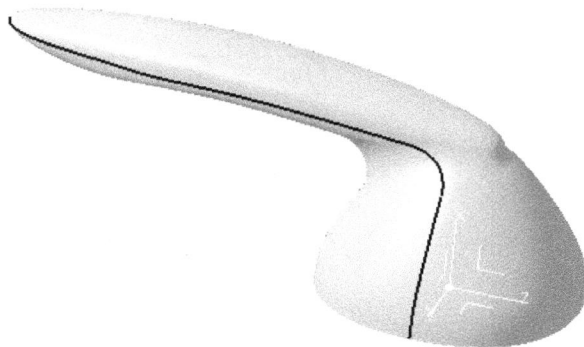

Figure 2–100

17. Click **OK** to complete the Corner.

18. Perform a **Symmetry** operation on **Corner.1** using the ZX-plane as the reference. The model displays as shown in Figure 2–101.

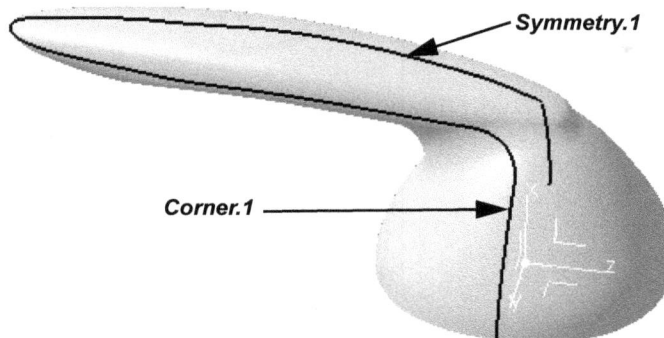

Figure 2–101

19. Join **Corner.1** and **Symmetry.1**.

Design Considerations

The joined curve represents the parting line for this earbud. It is possible that different reflect lines with a different direction reference could be created. The creation of reflect lines helps determine where the mold parting line should be located. This is also dependent on the material being used, the cost of creating the mold and part, and the aesthetics of where the parting line is located.

Task 4 - Split surfaces by parting lines.

1. Split **Extract.1** with **Join.1**. Ensure that the **Keep Both Sides** option is activated. The model displays as shown in Figure 2–102. Verify that your split names match; if not, rename them.

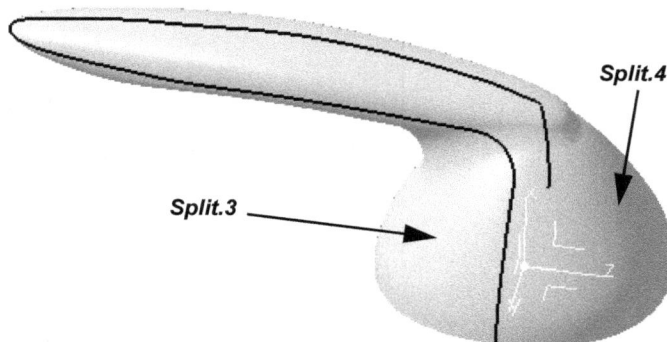

Figure 2–102

The model would be left as it currently displays. The mold created for the part would consist of two sides. In the next step, another split is created. The mold would then have three sides. These decisions are specific to each product, company, and manufacturer.

2. Create a Split using **Split.3** as the Element to Cut, and the zx plane as the cutting element. Again, ensure that the **Keep Both Sides** option is activated.

3. Upon completing the split, note that **Split.3** was hidden. This feature was consumed in the last operation.

4. Using Graphic Properties, apply different colors to **Split.4**, **Split.5**, and **Split.6**, as shown in Figure 2–103.

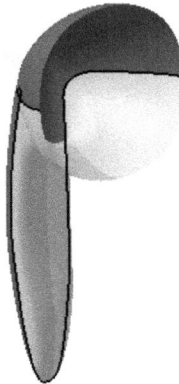

Figure 2–103

5. Save and name the model as **Earbud Parting Lines**. Close the model.

Practice 2d

(Optional) Isoparametric Curve

Practice Objective

• Create an Isoparametric curve at centerline.

In this practice, your design intent requires that a curve be created that defines the center of a variable width surface. You will create an Isoparametric curve to capture this intent. The completed model displays as shown in Figure 2–104.

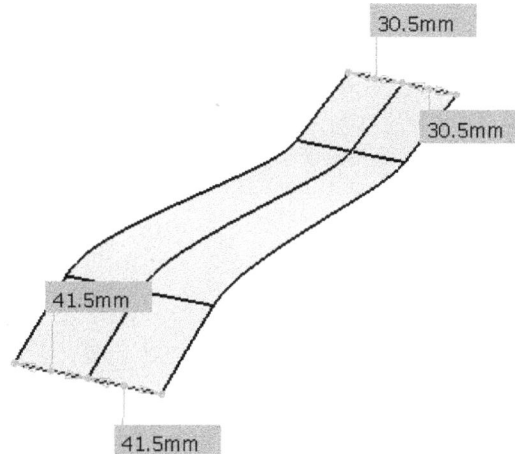

Figure 2–104

Task 1 - Open a part file.

1. Open **CenterLineCurve.CATPart**, as shown in Figure 2–105.

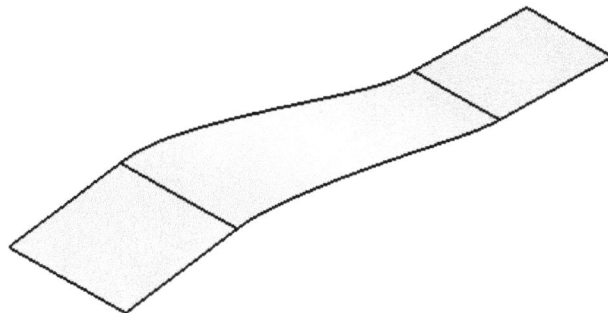

Figure 2–105

2. Click [icon] (Isoparametric curve) in the Curves toolbar, as shown in Figure 2–106.

Figure 2–106

3. Select **Surface.1** as the support. Select an approximate location on the surface that results in the curve orientation shown in Figure 2–107.

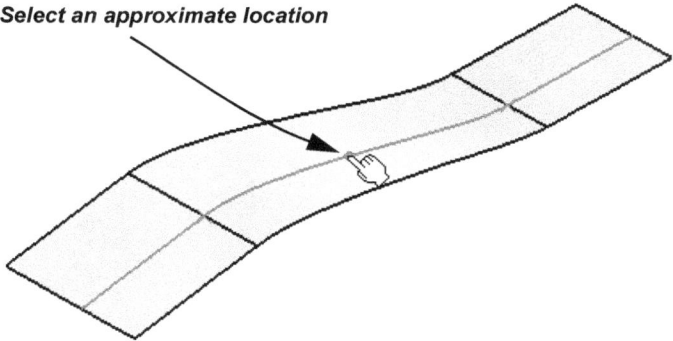

Select an approximate location

Figure 2–107

Design Considerations

The application creates a point that the Isoparametric curve passes through. The Point type used is On Surface which places the reference point in the middle of the surface. Therefore, if the Distance parameter is entered as 0, the point is positioned at the center of the selected surface.

4. Modify the position of the point by clicking [icon] in the Isoparametric curve dialog box, as shown in Figure 2–108.

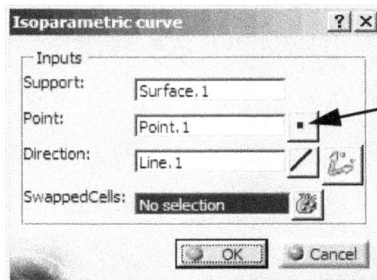

Select Point definition

Figure 2–108

5. Make the following change as shown in Figure 2–109:

  • *Distance:* **0mm**

Figure 2–109

6. Click **OK** in Point Definition and **OK** in the Isoparametric curve dialog box as shown in Figure 2–110.

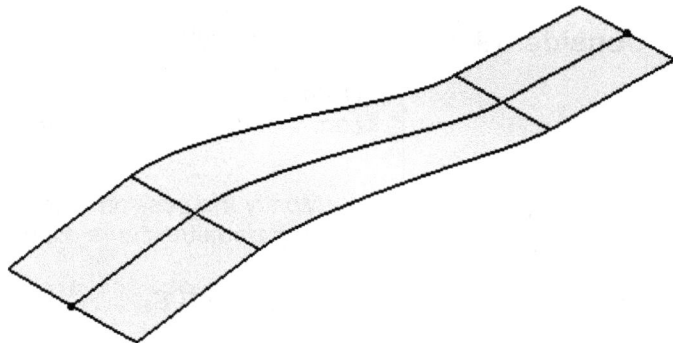

Figure 2–110

7. Measure the distances at the both ends of the Isoparametric curve to verify that it is located at the center of the surface as shown in Figure 2–111.

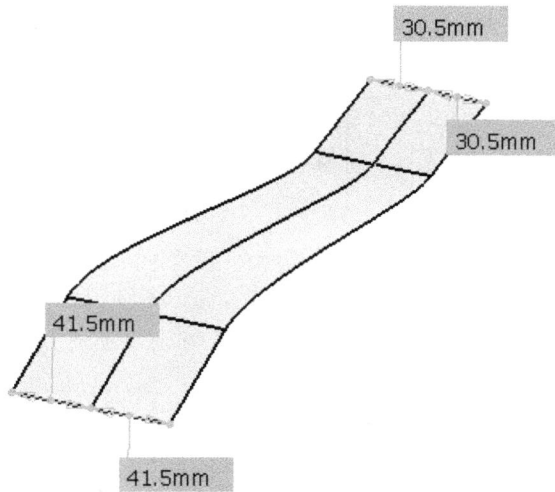

30.5mm

30.5mm

41.5mm

41.5mm

Figure 2–111

8. Save the model and close the file.

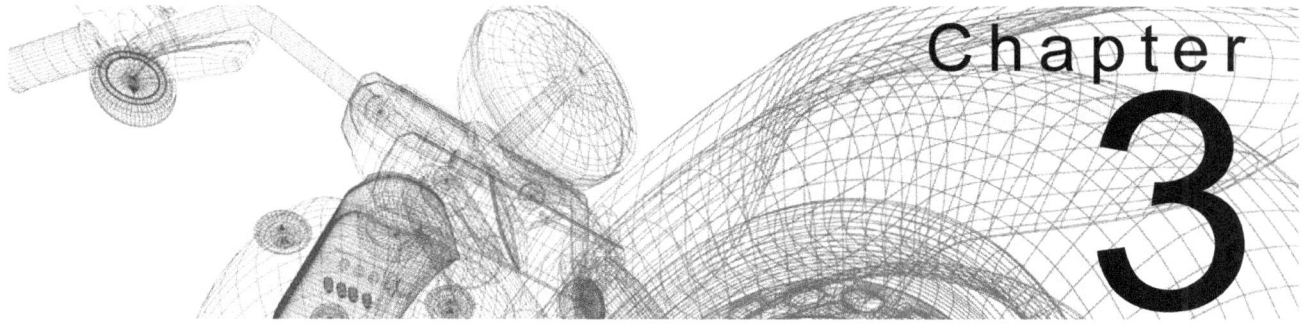

Curve Analysis and Repair

Wireframe elements and curves are used to construct surfaces. By using correct techniques to build curves, robust surfaces can be created and manipulated. However, errors can occur, resulting in undesirable geometry. CATIA provides a number of tools to identify and correct these errors.

Learning Objectives in this Chapter

- Review the terminology related to curve analysis.
- Understand how the quality of wireframe elements affects surfaces and solids that reference them.
- Use the Connect Checker Analysis tool, to analyze the connection between curves, the connection between the curve's extremity, and its projection on a curve.
- Use the Porcupine Curvature Analysis tool to analyzes the curvature of a wireframe or surface element.
- Use the Curve Smooth tool to create a Composite Curve feature if a curve analysis indicates unacceptable geometry.
- Use the Untrim Curve and Disassemble tools to manually repair curves.

3.1 Terminology Review

Curvature

The curvature of a surface or curve is equal to the inverse of the radius at any point on the surface, as shown in Figure 3–1. As the radius becomes smaller, curvature becomes greater.

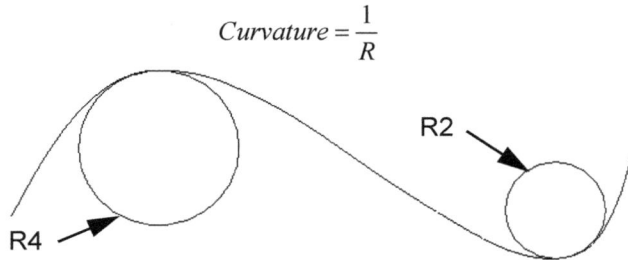

$$Curvature = \frac{1}{R}$$

R2

R4

Figure 3–1

Inflection Point

An inflection point of a curve or surface is a point at which the curvature changes from convex to concave or conversely. An inflection point is shown in Figure 3–2.

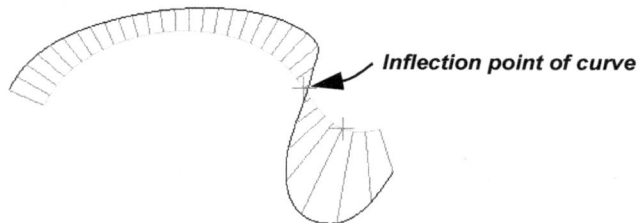

Inflection point of curve

Figure 3–2

The **Porcupine Curvature Analysis** tool can be used to detect changes in curvature. This enables you to graphically represent the degree of curvature of a selected curve and to visualize inflection points.

Degrees of Continuity

Continuity refers to how the surfaces or end points meet. The type of continuity applied between entities affects the appearance of a surface.

The geometric continuity types are described as follows:

Classification	Description
G0	The curves share a common end point but are not tangent to one another.

No Tangency

Classification	Description
G1	The curves are tangent to one another but have different curvature magnitudes at their intersection.

Entities are tangent

Classification	Description
G2	The curves are tangent and have a common curvature at their intersection. G2 continuity produces a smooth connection.

Tangent and curvature continuous

Classification	Description
G3	The curves are tangent and curvature continuous at their intersection. The rate of the curvature change also matches between the curves.

Curve 1   Curve 2

The **Connect Checker Analysis** tool can be used to analyze the connection between two or more curves.

When creating curves and surfaces in the Generative Shape Design workbench, you have the ability to apply continuity settings to the resulting feature. The available degree of continuity to apply varies between features.

Different industries and products require different continuity in their parts. For instance, exterior surfaces of an automobile have G2 or higher continuity. Glossy or shiny parts commonly have G2 continuity between surfaces. Other industries do not require G2 continuity and accept G1 continuity.

3.2 Analysis and Repair

Wireframe elements facilitate the creation of surface features, while surface features facilitate the creation of the solid features that reference them. As a result, the quality of the wireframe elements directly impacts the quality of the solid part geometry. It is important to become familiar with the errors that can occur with wireframe feature geometry and the tools required to correct the wireframe geometry.

The types of errors that can occur in curves are described as follows:

Error	Description
Inflection Point	Results in a sharp edge.
Internal Flaw	Results in a small unnecessary segment.
Tangency Discontinuity	No tangency between curves.
Curvature Discontinuity	Curves are tangent but not curvature continuous.

*The **Connect Checker Analysis** tool can also analyze the connection between surfaces, and between curves and surfaces.*

Various analysis tools are available to investigate curves and surfaces.

3.3 Analyzing Curves

With the **Connect Checker Analysis** tool, you can analyze the connection between curves, as well as the connection between the curve's extremity and its projection on a curve.

Connection Between Curves

This type of analysis enables you to check the continuity type between curves. The results for different connection types between two curves are shown in Figure 3–3.

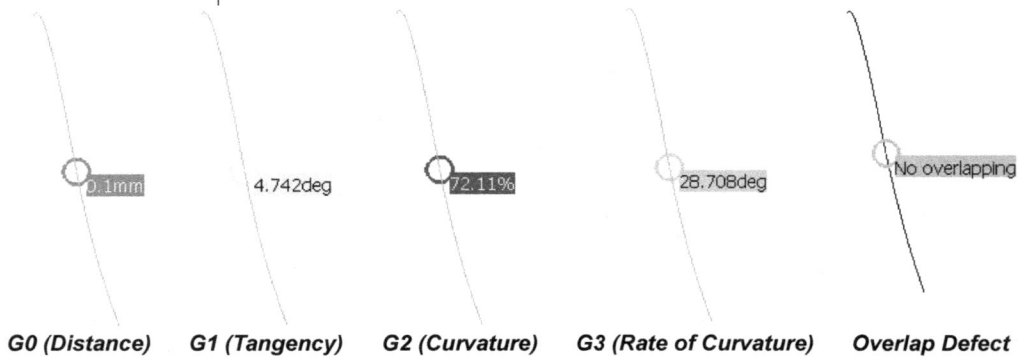

| G0 (Distance) | G1 (Tangency) | G2 (Curvature) | G3 (Rate of Curvature) | Overlap Defect |

0.1mm   4.742deg   72.11%   28.708deg   No overlapping

Figure 3–3

Projection On a Curve

The endpoint of the source curve is projected in the direction of the normal for the target curve. An example of a Projection on a curve analysis for G0 type is shown in Figure 3–4. All the continuity types described in the previous section (G0, G1, G2, G3) are available for this type of analysis.

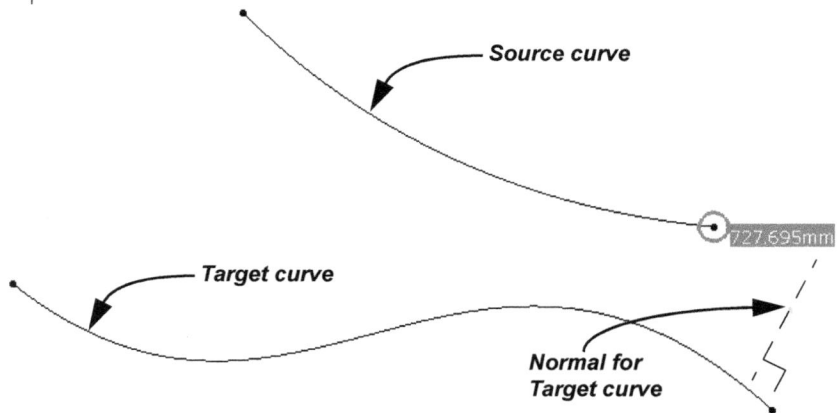

Source curve

727.695mm

Target curve

Normal for Target curve

Figure 3–4

Connection Between a Curve and a Surface

The endpoint of the curve is projected to the normal of the surface. An example of a G2 value for the **Connection between a curve and a surface** is shown in Figure 3–5. The G0, G1, and G2 continuity types described in the previous section are available for this type of analysis. The G3 and Overlap Defect options are not available for this type of analysis.

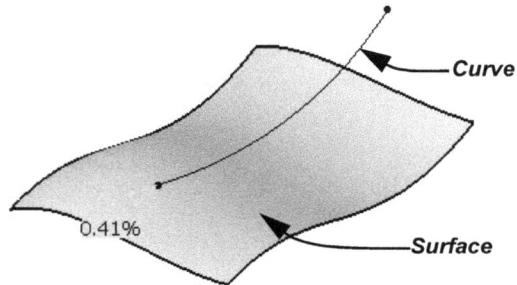

Figure 3–5

General Steps

Use the following general steps to analyze curves using **Connect Checker**:

1. Start Connect Checker Analysis.
2. Specify the type of analysis.
3. Specify the type of continuity.
4. Complete the analysis.

Step 1 - Start Connect Checker Analysis.

Click (Connect Checker Analysis) in the Analysis toolbar, and (Curve-Curve Connection) in the Connect Checker dialog box, as shown in Figure 3–6.

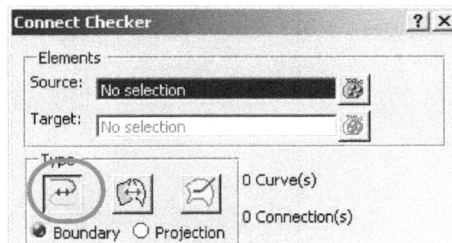

Figure 3–6

Connection Between Curves

In Boundary mode, only the Source field is activated.

Step 2 - Specify the type of analysis.

To run a **Connection between curves** analysis, select **Boundary**, as shown in Figure 3–7.

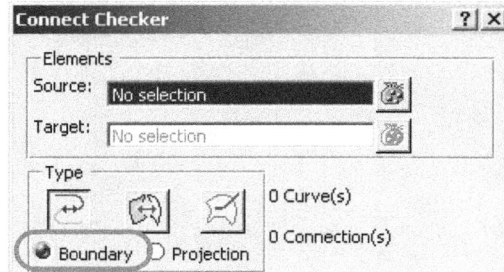

Figure 3–7

Click ⊞ (Internal Edge) to check the discontinuity condition in a curve.

Select the curve(s) to analyze from the display or specification tree. To select more than one curve, press and hold <Ctrl> and then select the curves as shown in Figure 3–8.

Set the Maximum and Minimum Gap values as required. If the existing gap between curves is not between the Maximum and Minimum Gap values, the analysis result does not display.

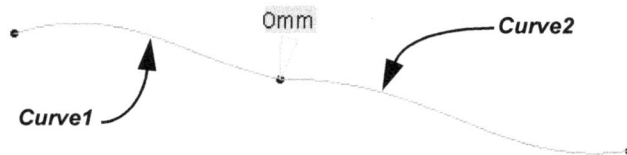

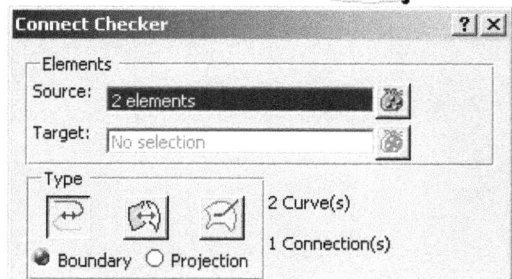

Figure 3–8

Projection on a Curve

To run a **Projection on a curve** analysis, select **Projection**, as shown in Figure 3–9.

Figure 3–9

Set the Maximum Gap value greater than the current distance value between the curves, as shown in Figure 3–10.

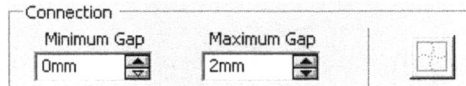

Figure 3–10

If the distance between the curves is greater than the Maximum Gap value, or the gap between the curves is smaller than the Minimum Gap value, an Information dialog box opens as shown in Figure 3–11.

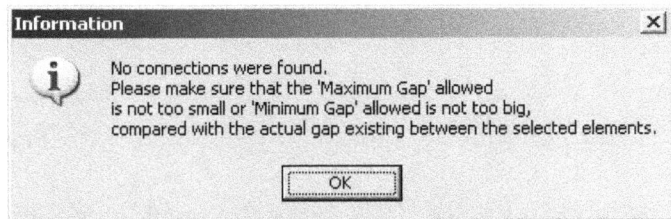

Figure 3–11

Click in the *Source* field, and select the curve(s) to be projected from the display or specification tree. To specify which curves are projected by the Source curve(s), click in the *Target* field, and select the curve(s) from the display or specification tree as shown in Figure 3–12.

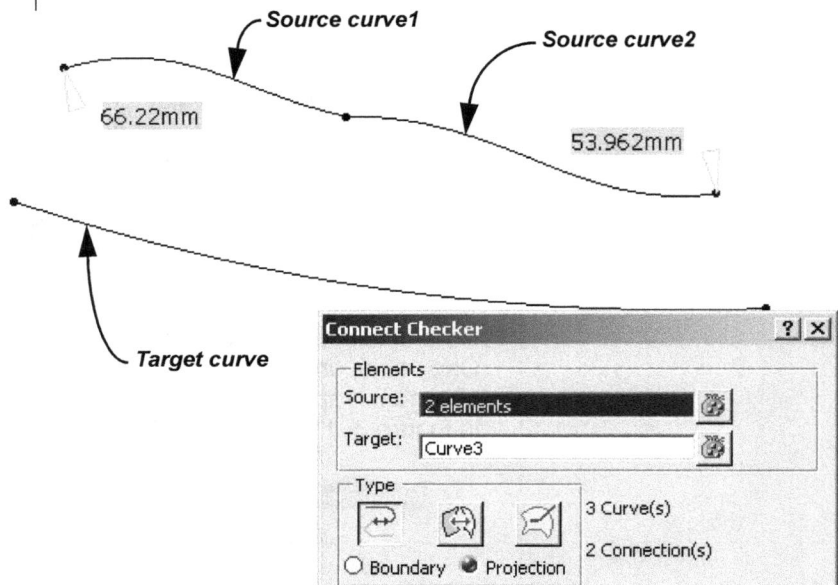

Figure 3–12

Connection Between a Curve and a Surface

To run a **Connection between a curve and a surface** analysis, click (Surface-Curve Connection), as shown in Figure 3–13.

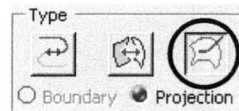

Figure 3–13

*The **Boundary** option is not available for this type of analysis.*

Set the Maximum Gap value greater than the current distance value between the curve and the surface, as shown in Figure 3–14. If the distance between the curves is greater than Maximum Gap value, or the gap between the curves is smaller than Minimum Gap value, the analysis result does not display.

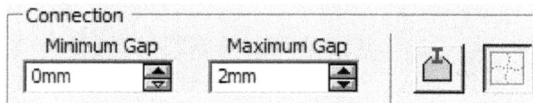

Figure 3–14

Click in the *Source* field, and select the curve(s) and surface(s) from the display or specification tree as shown in Figure 3–15.

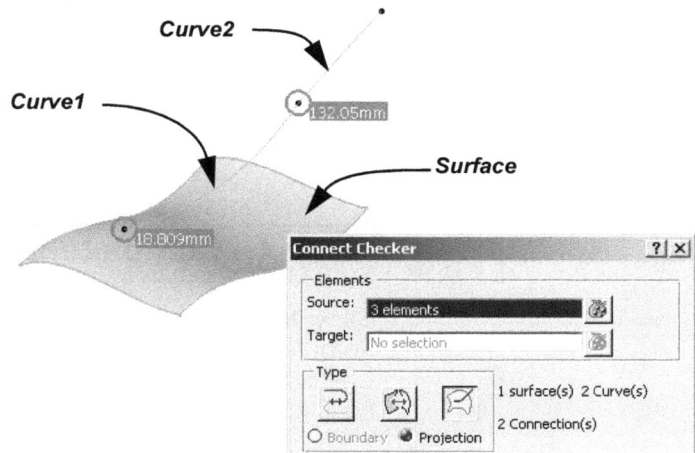

Figure 3–15

Step 3 - Specify the type of continuity.

You can check five different types of connection between curves. The connection types are described and shown below. When a different type of connection is selected, the display dynamically updates the analysis information on the model.

(Overlap Defect) is not available for the Projection analysis.

Icon	Connection Type	
	Overlap Defect	
	G0 Continuity	
	G1 Continuity	
	G2 Continuity	
	G3 Continuity	

The analysis information is also displayed in the *Max Deviation* area in the Connect Checker dialog box, as shown in Figure 3–16.

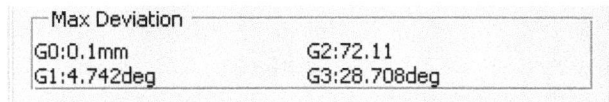

```
┌─Max Deviation ──────────────────────────────
│ G0:0.1mm              G2:72.11
│ G1:4.742deg           G3:28.708deg
```

Figure 3–16

Step 4 - Complete the analysis.

Click **OK** to complete the analysis. The system adds a Free Form Analysis node to the specification tree and a Connect Checker Analysis feature under the node, as shown in Figure 3–17.

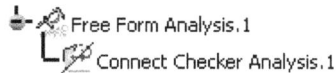

Free Form Analysis.1
Connect Checker Analysis.1

Figure 3–17

3.4 Porcupine Curvature Analysis

*The **Porcupine Curvature Analysis** tool is only available in the Generative Shape Design workbench.*

The **Porcupine Curvature Analysis** tool analyzes the curvature of a wireframe or surface element. This tool is also useful for visualizing inflection points of a curve. A Porcupine Curvature analysis is shown in Figure 3–18.

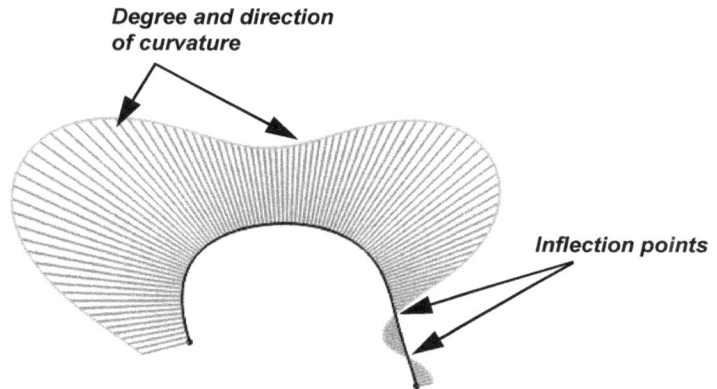

Figure 3–18

General Steps

Use the following general steps to analyze curves using Porcupine Curvature Analysis:

1. Select the curves to analyze.
2. Start the Porcupine Curvature Analysis.
3. Specify the type of analysis.
4. Specify display options.
5. Complete the analysis.

Step 1 - Select the curves to analyze.

Select two or more curves to analyze. Press and hold <Ctrl> to select multiple curves.

Step 2 - Start the Porcupine Curvature Analysis.

Click ![icon] (Porcupine Curvature Analysis) in the Analysis toolbar. The Curvature Analysis dialog box opens as shown in Figure 3–19.

If the dialog box does not display all of the options shown, click **More** *to expand it.*

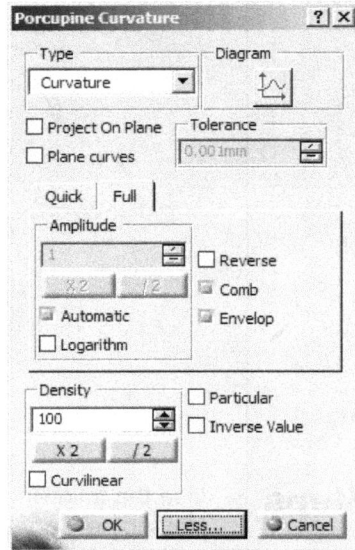

Figure 3–19

Step 3 - Specify the type of analysis.

Specify the type of analysis to perform in the Type drop-down list, as shown in Figure 3–20.

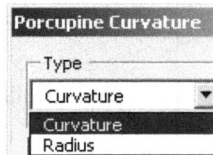

Figure 3–20

Step 4 - Specify display options.

Specify the density of the comb (porcupines) by entering a value and/or clicking **X2** or **/2** to multiply or divide the density as shown in Figure 3–21. The amplitude can be modified in the same manner if the **Automatic** option is cleared.

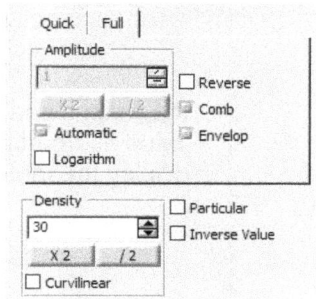

Figure 3–21

The results of applying different densities are shown in Figure 3–22.

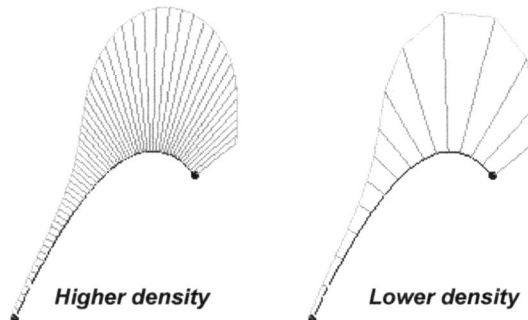

Higher density   *Lower density*

Figure 3–22

Select **Particular** to display the Max and Min values of the curvature, as shown in Figure 3–23.

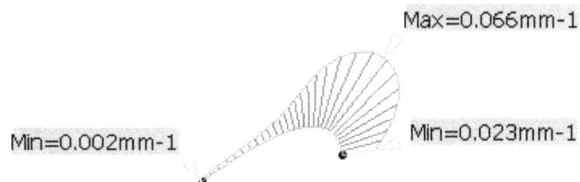

Max=0.066mm-1

Min=0.002mm-1   Min=0.023mm-1

Figure 3–23

Step 5 - Complete the analysis.

Click **OK** to complete the analysis. The Porcupine Curvature Analysis feature displays under the Free Form Analysis node in the specification tree, as shown in Figure 3–24.

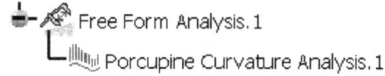

Free Form Analysis.1
Porcupine Curvature Analysis.1

Figure 3–24

If a Radius analysis is performed, the system reports the radial value at a particular point. Hold the cursor at a specific point to display the radial value, as shown in Figure 3–25.

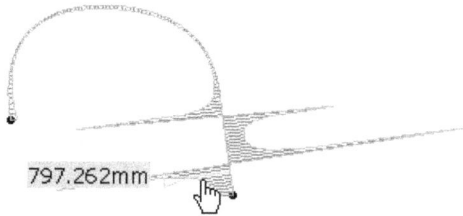

797.262mm

Figure 3–25

Graph Options

Click (Display Diagram Window) to display a graphical representation of the curvature analysis, as shown in Figure 3–26.

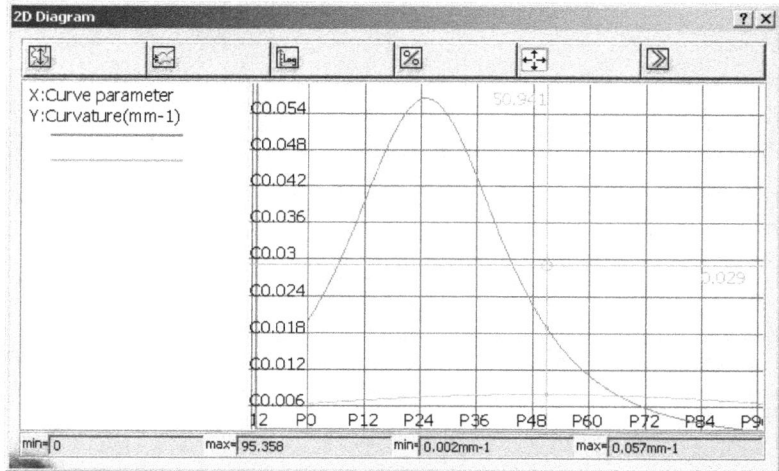

Figure 3–26

Use the icons shown in Figure 3–27 to change the display style of the graph.

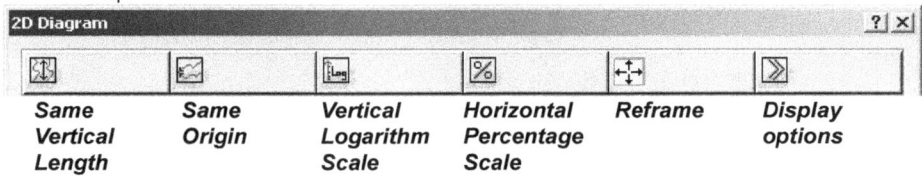

| Same Vertical Length | Same Origin | Vertical Logarithm Scale | Horizontal Percentage Scale | Reframe | Display options |

Figure 3–27

Use the cursor to drag the green cross-hairs to any point on the graph to dynamically display information about the analysis as shown in Figure 3–28. Right-click on the curve and select **Drop Marker** to create a non-associative reference point at that location on the analysis.

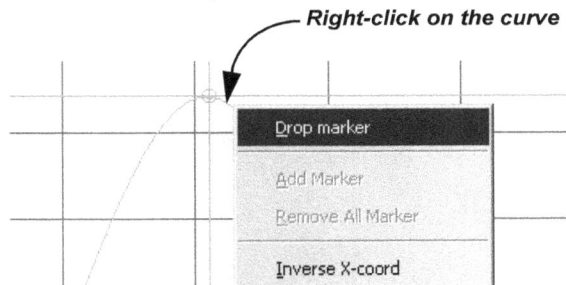

Figure 3–28

When a non-associative reference point is created, it is added to the specification tree, as shown in Figure 3–29.

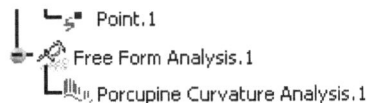

Figure 3–29

The display settings can be changed by modifying the options in the Diagram Options dialog box. You can open this dialog box by clicking ⧉ in the 2D Diagram dialog box. The Diagram Options dialog box opens as shown in Figure 3–30.

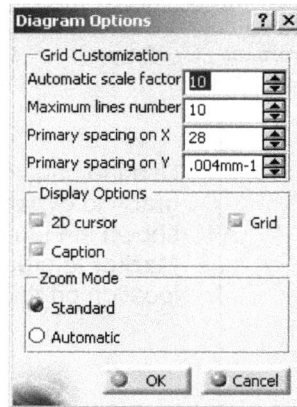

Figure 3–30

The graph is very useful for displaying a multi-curve analysis, as shown in Figure 3–31.

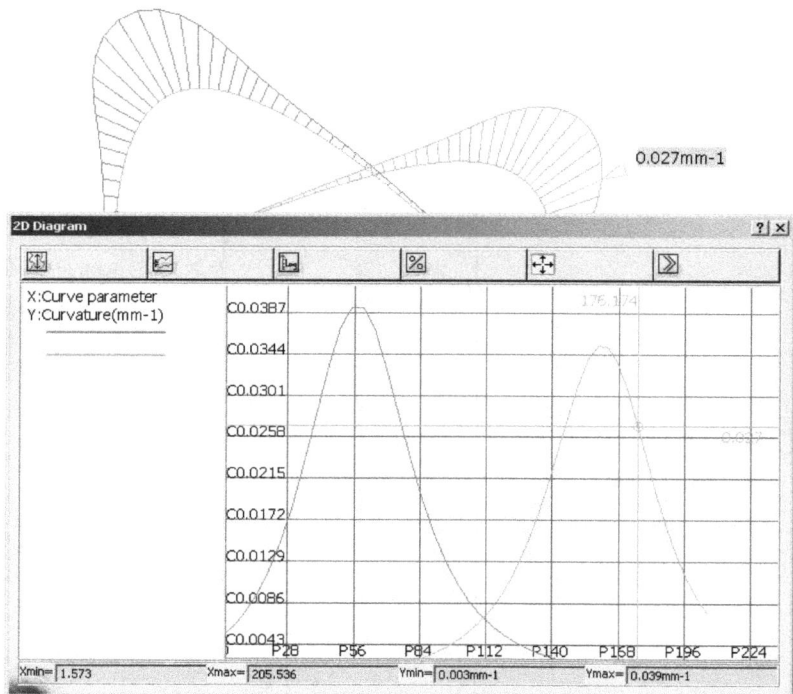

Figure 3–31

3.5 Repair Curve Geometry

If a curve analysis indicates unacceptable geometry, the **Curve Smooth** tool can be used to create a Composite Curve feature.

The **Curve Smooth** tool is accessed in the Join-Healing toolbar, as shown in Figure 3–32.

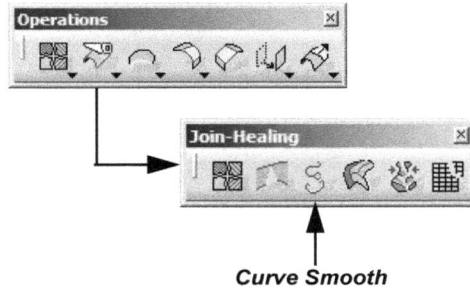

Curve Smooth

Figure 3–32

When creating a Curve Smooth feature, the system reports the discontinuity status based on the threshold values entered. The three possible color-coded states that can occur when creating a Curve Smooth feature as described as follows:

Color	Information displayed	Status
Red	In: C0, tangency discontinuous (2deg) Out: C0, tangency discontinuous (2deg)	No solution found.
Yellow	In: C0, tangency discontinuous (2deg) Out: C1, curvature discontinuous (0.452061)	Discontinuity has been improved.
Green	In: C0, tangency discontinuous (2deg) Out: vertex erased	No discontinuity, smoothing successful.

A Curvature analysis, before and after a Curve Smooth feature has been applied, is shown in Figure 3–33.

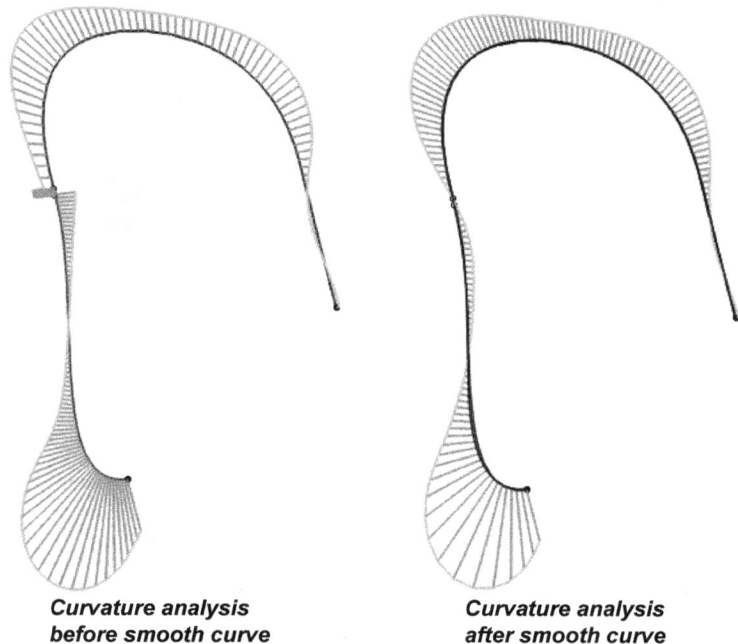

Curvature analysis before smooth curve   **Curvature analysis after smooth curve**

Figure 3–33

General Steps

Use the following general steps to create a Curve Smooth feature:

1. Start the creation of the Curve Smooth feature.
2. Specify parameter values.
3. Define additional options, as required.
4. Complete the feature.

Step 1 - Start the creation of the Curve Smooth feature.

Select a Join feature to smooth and click [S] (Smooth Curve) in the Join-Healing toolbar. The Curve Smooth Definition dialog box opens as shown in Figure 3–34.

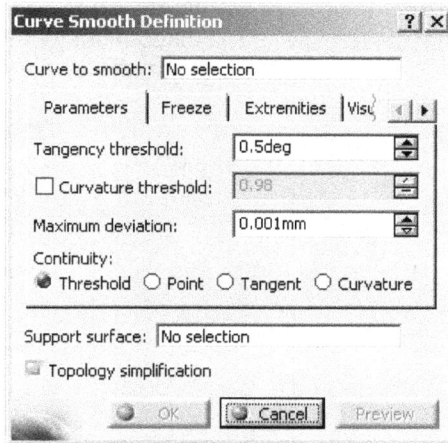

Figure 3–34

Step 2 - Specify parameter values.

Once you start the creation of the feature you can define the parameters. Using default threshold values, the status of a selected element shows that no solution is available, as shown in Figure 3–35.

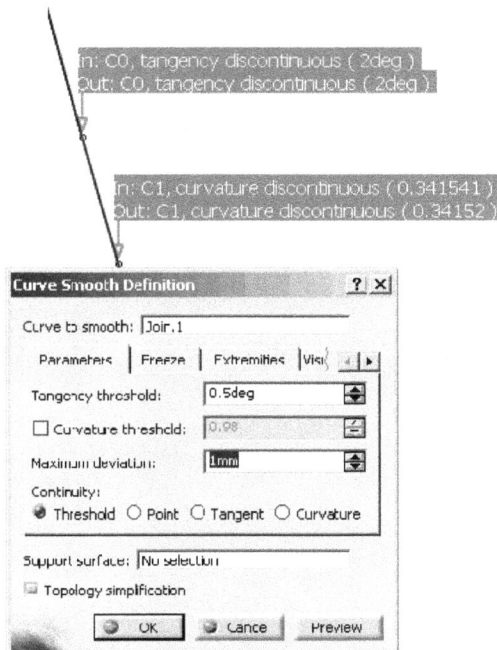

Figure 3–35

By increasing the Tangency threshold to 2.1, the status shows that discontinuity has been improved, as shown in Figure 3–36. However, the Curve Smooth feature still cannot be created.

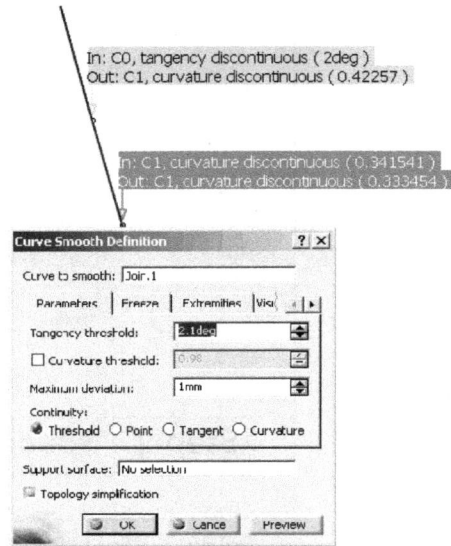

In: C0, tangency discontinuous (2deg)
Out: C1, curvature discontinuous (0.42257)

In: C1, curvature discontinuous (0.341541)
Out: C1, curvature discontinuous (0.333454)

Curve Smooth Definition

Curve to smooth: Joir.1

Parameters | Freeze | Extremities | Vis

Tangency threshold: 2.1deg

☐ Curvature threshold: 0.98

Maximum deviation: 1mm

Continuity:
⦿ Threshold ○ Point ○ Tangent ○ Curvature

Support surface: No selection

☐ Topology simplification

OK | Cance | Preview

Figure 3–36

By adding a **Curvature threshold** of 0.25, the Smooth feature can be created. The result is shown in Figure 3–37.

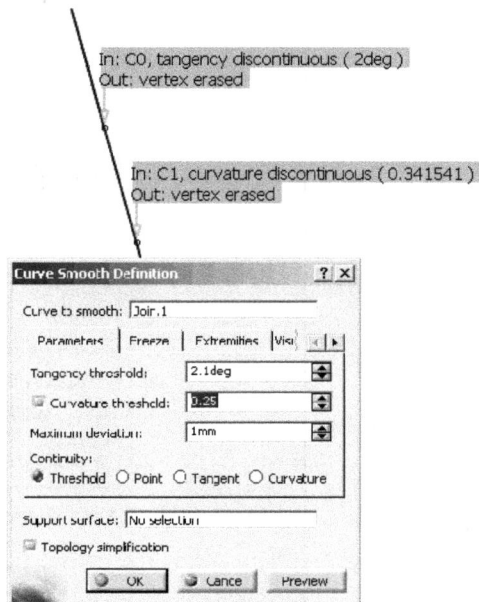

In: C0, tangency discontinuous (2deg)
Out: vertex erased

In: C1, curvature discontinuous (0.341541)
Out: vertex erased

Curve Smooth Definition

Curve to smooth: Joir.1

Parameters | Freeze | Extremities | Vis

Tangency threshold: 2.1deg

☐ Curvature threshold: 0.25

Maximum deviation: 1mm

Continuity:
⦿ Threshold ○ Point ○ Tangent ○ Curvature

Support surface: No selection

☐ Topology simplification

OK | Cance | Preview

Figure 3–37

Maximum Deviation	The Maximum deviation value is optional. This value represents the radius of an imaginary pipe that the smooth curve follows. The centerline of the pipe follows the selected element to be smoothed. Once this value has been defined, it cannot be reversed and becomes a required selection.
Support Surface	If a Surface feature is selected as the support surface, the system smooths the curve while maintaining contact with the selected support.
Topology Simplification	The **Topology simplification** option enables the system to erase points (vertices) that are no longer required to create the Curve Smooth feature. The status message indicates any erased vertices, as shown in Figure 3–38.

In: C0, tangency discontinuous (2deg)
Out: vertex erased

Vertex erased as a result
of Topology simplification

Figure 3–38

Curve Smooth	More control has been added over the continuity conditions of a smooth curve. Previously, the resulting curve would always have curvature continuity with the input curve at its end points. As a result, the output curve would have the same end points, tangency, and curvature as the input curve.

You can select the type of continuity for the output curve in the Curve Smooth Definition dialog box, as shown in Figure 3–39.

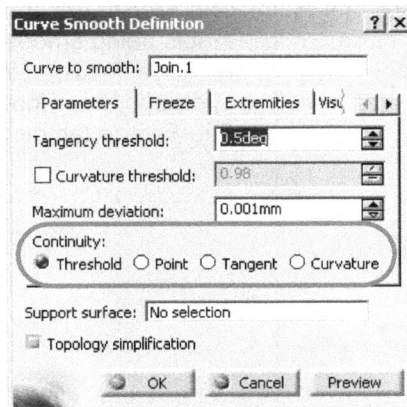

Curve Smooth Definition

Curve to smooth: Join.1

Parameters | Freeze | Extremities | Visu ◀ | ▶

Tangency threshold: 0.5deg

☐ Curvature threshold: 0.98

Maximum deviation: 0.001mm

Continuity:
◉ Threshold ○ Point ○ Tangent ○ Curvature

Support surface: No selection

☐ Topology simplification

OK | Cancel | Preview

Figure 3–39

The new **Continuity** options work in conjunction with the threshold and deviation values entered. The threshold values represent the amount of acceptable discontinuity for either tangency or curvature. If the system cannot achieve the continuity specified within the threshold and deviation values provided, the note indicates the discontinuity. The **Continuity** options are described as follows:

Option	Description
Threshold	This is the default **Continuity** option. The system attempts to optimally smooth the curve based on all threshold and deviation values entered. However, no continuity requirement is enforced on the output curve.
Point	The system attempts to make the input curve point continuous (C0) based on all threshold and deviation values entered.
Tangent	The system attempts to make the input curve tangency continuous (C1) based on the maximum deviation and (if selected) curvature threshold values entered. The tangency threshold value is ignored.
Curvature	The system attempts to make the input curve curvature continuous (C2) based on the maximum deviation value entered. The tangency and curvature threshold values are ignored.

Step 3 - Define additional options, as required.

Freeze Tab

The *Freeze* tab enables you to freeze sub-elements of a curve that is being smoothed. The sub-element(s) can be a vertex or an edge. Frozen elements are not affected by the smoothing operation; therefore, its continuity status remains unchanged. The *Freeze* tab displays as shown in Figure 3–40.

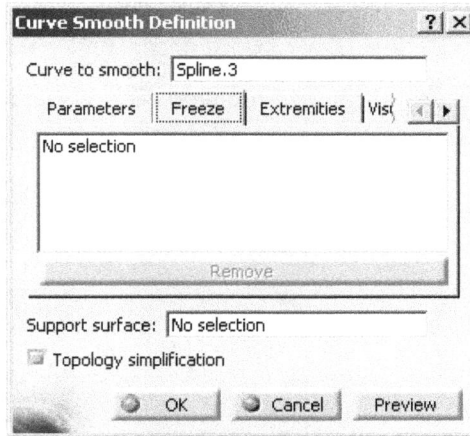

Figure 3–40

Extremities Tab

The *Extremities* tab enables you to specify continuity conditions on the curve that is being smoothed. The *Extremities* tab displays as shown in Figure 3–41.

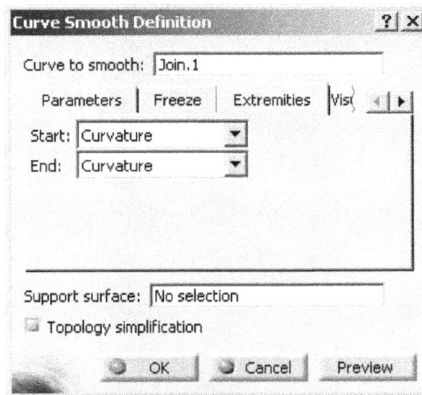

Figure 3–41

You can also select the icons at the start and end of the curve to change these options.

The three **Continuity** options available are described as follows:

Option	Description
Curvature	Input and Output curves have the same extremity points, tangency, and curvatures.
Tangency	Input and Output curves have the same extremity points and tangency. However, their curvatures can be different.
Point	Input and Output curves have the same extremity points. However, their tangency and curvatures can be different.

Visualization Tab

The *Visualization* tab enables you to simplify the display of information (messages). This option is useful when a large number of messages display and only certain messages are required. The *Visualization* tab displays as shown in Figure 3–42.

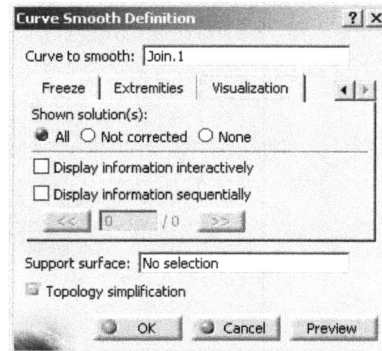

Figure 3–42

Step 4 - Complete the feature.

Select **OK** to complete the Curve Smooth feature. It displays as a feature in the specification tree, as shown in Figure 3–43.

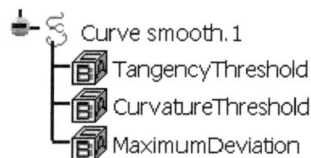

Figure 3–43

3.6 Manual Curve Repair Tools

Untrim Curve

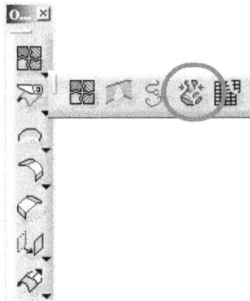

The Untrim operation restores a surface or curve that has been split. An Untrim operation should be used when it is not desirable to delete a Split feature. For example, the curve shown in Figure 3–44 has been split and a portion has been extracted and used to develop an extruded surface. To restore the original curve, an Untrim operation is performed. Deleting the Split feature would cause the extruded surface to fail.

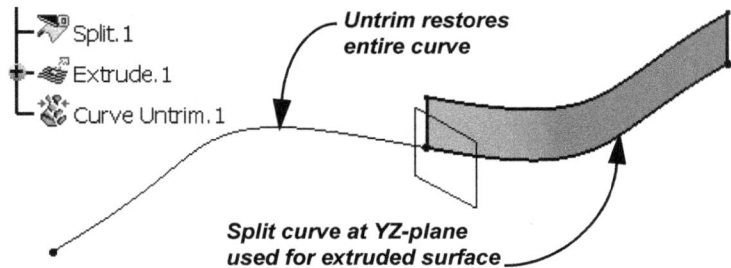

Figure 3–44

To perform an **Untrim** operation, click (Untrim) and select the element to be untrimmed. The Untrim dialog box opens as shown in Figure 3–45.

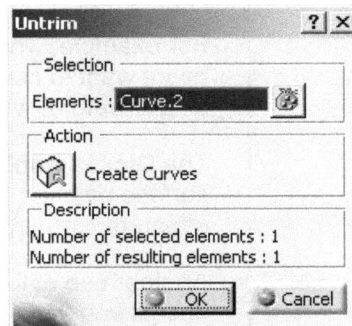

Figure 3–45

This dialog box confirms that the system has automatically located the original element and is going to restore it.

Create Curves option

If ▣ (Create Curves) is activated, this creates isolated boundary curves from the selected surface. In Figure 3–46, the Split.1 feature is untrimmed using the **Create Curves** tool. The end result for this operation is one surface and four isolated boundary curves.

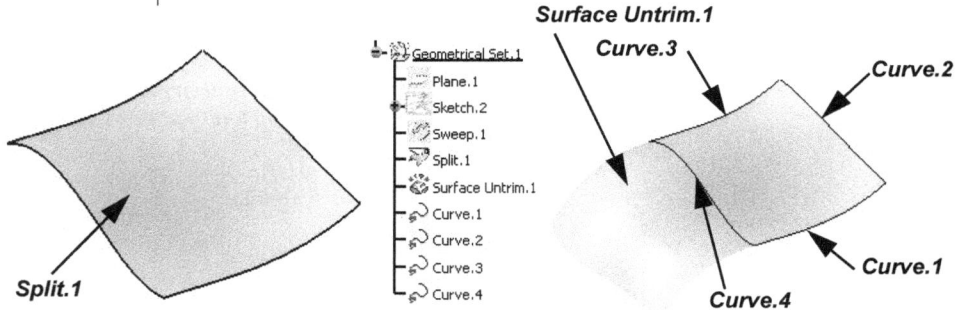

Figure 3–46

Disassemble

The **Disassemble** operation breaks a feature into separate sub-elements, creating a non-associative copy of selected surfaces and curves. A **Disassemble** operation is useful when modifications or manufacturing processes need to be performed on a model that has no specific feature information or history.

For example, when a vendor or customer transfers data, they might want to keep the history confidential and send only a single feature, which represents the skin of the model.

The **Disassemble** operation enables you to extract specific surface patches from the skin so they can be operated on as separate features.

Another use of the **Disassemble** operation is to experiment with design variations on a model without altering the original geometry. The disassembled surfaces are not associative to the referenced geometry so they can either be kept or discarded based on the results of the change.

How To: Perform a Disassemble Operation

1. Click [icon] (Disassemble). The Disassemble dialog box opens as shown in Figure 3–47.

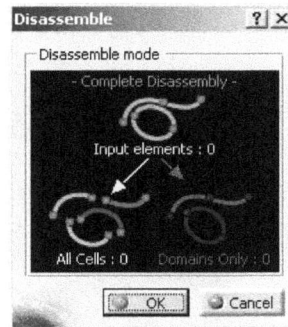

Figure 3–47

2. Select the elements to disassemble. The dialog box updates with the number of input elements and the number of elements for each type of disassembly.

   Two types of disassembly are available: **All Cells** and **Domains Only**.

   - **All Cells** divides a curve or surface into its smallest component and creates individual sub-elements for each surface or curve selected.
   - **Domains Only** creates a new datum element for each group of curves or surfaces that are connected at a point or edge.

   Figure 3–48 shows the sketch for a flange to be disassembled so that individual entities of the sketch can be selected. The Disassemble dialog box displays eighteen elements when using **All Cells** and six elements when using **Domains Only**. The six elements consist of the five circles and the outer boundary.

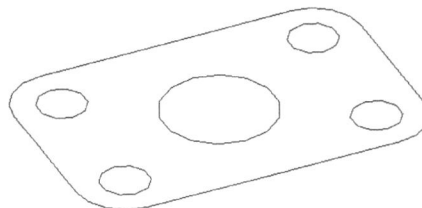

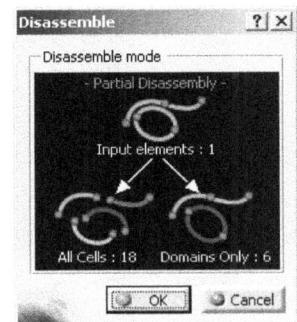

Figure 3–48

Practice 3a

Curve Analysis

Practice Objectives

- Use the Connect Checker.
- Use the Porcupine Curvature Analysis Tool.
- Repair Curves.

Task 1 - Open the part and set the standards.

1. Open **CurveAnalysis.CATPart**. The model displays as shown in Figure 3–49.

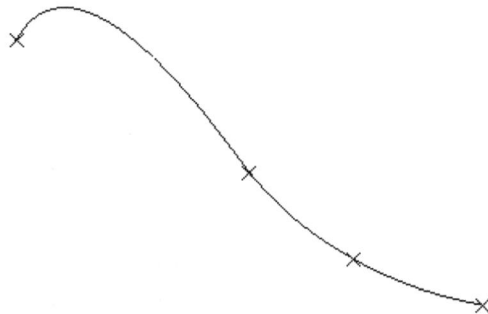

Figure 3–49

2. Display the Analysis toolbar and drag the flyout to a floating position as shown in Figure 3–50.

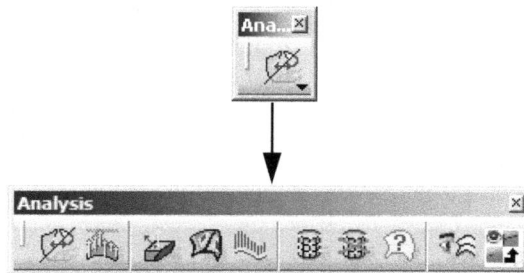

Figure 3–50

Task 2 - Analyze the curve with the Connect Checker tool.

1. Click ⬚ (Connect Checker Analysis).

2. Activate ⬚ (Curve-Curve Connection) to check the connection between the two curves.

3. Ensure that the **Boundary** option is selected.

4. Click ⬚ beside the *Source* field as shown in Figure 3–51, then select the two splines in the model.

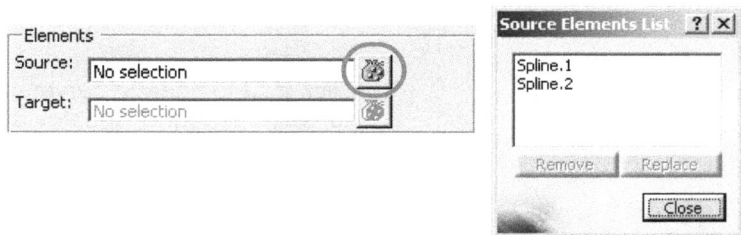

Figure 3–51

5. Close the Source Element List dialog box.

6. Click ⬚ in the *Quick* tab. Note that the corresponding G1 value displays on your model, as shown in Figure 3–52.

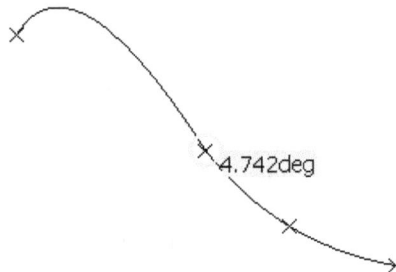

Figure 3–52

The analysis results shown in Figure 3–52 are with respect to the tangency connection check between the two curves. Although the curves appear tangent, there is a **4.742deg** discrepancy in tangency.

7. Click ⬚ to display the gap between curves. The result displays as shown in Figure 3–53. Note the discrepancy of **0.1mm** at the connection of the two curves.

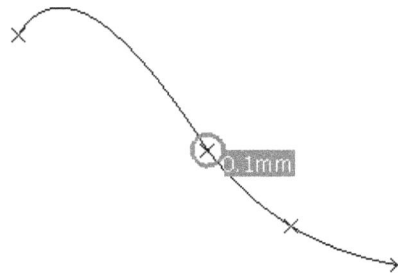

Figure 3–53

8. Click ⬚ to analyze curvature continuity between the two curves. The model updates dynamically to display the G2 value, as shown in Figure 3–54. Note the discrepancy in curvature.

Figure 3–54

9. Set the analysis back to **Distance (G0)**.

10. Click **OK** to complete the analysis. Note the addition of a Connect Checker Analysis feature under the Free Form Analysis branch in the specification tree. This analysis can be accessed in the future as required.

11. Hide **Connect Checker Analysis.1** in the specification tree.

Task 3 - Use the Porcupine Analysis tool.

1. Select the two curves and click ![icon] (Porcupine Curvature Analysis). The Curvature Analysis dialog box opens, as shown in Figure 3–55 with a plot similar to Figure 3–56.

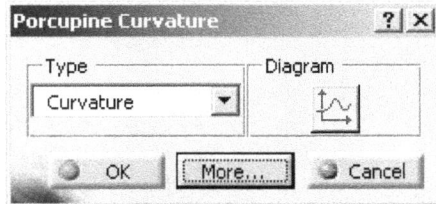

Figure 3–55

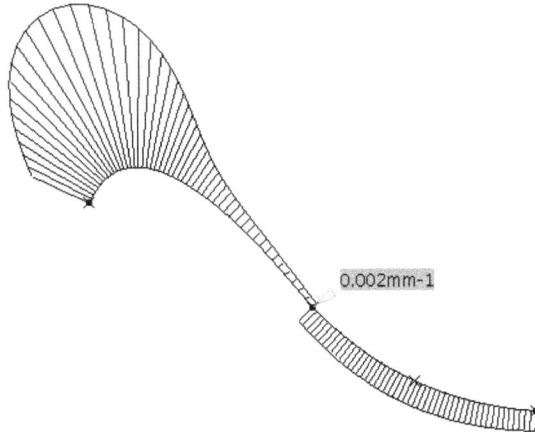

0.002mm-1

Figure 3–56

2. Click **More** to expand the Curvature Analysis dialog box. Your Curvature Analysis dialog box might already be expanded.

3. In the *Density* area shown in Figure 3–57, click **X2** to increase the number of curvature normals in the comb. Click **/2** to decrease the number.

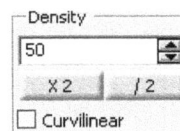

Figure 3–57

4. In the *Amplitude* area shown in Figure 3–58, clear the **Automatic** option to adjust the size of the comb. You can then manually adjust the amplitude as required.

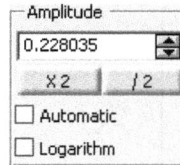

Figure 3–58

5. Activate the **Automatic** option.

6. To display specific values for minimum and maximum curvature, select **Particular** in the dialog box. A plot similar to Figure 3–59 displays.

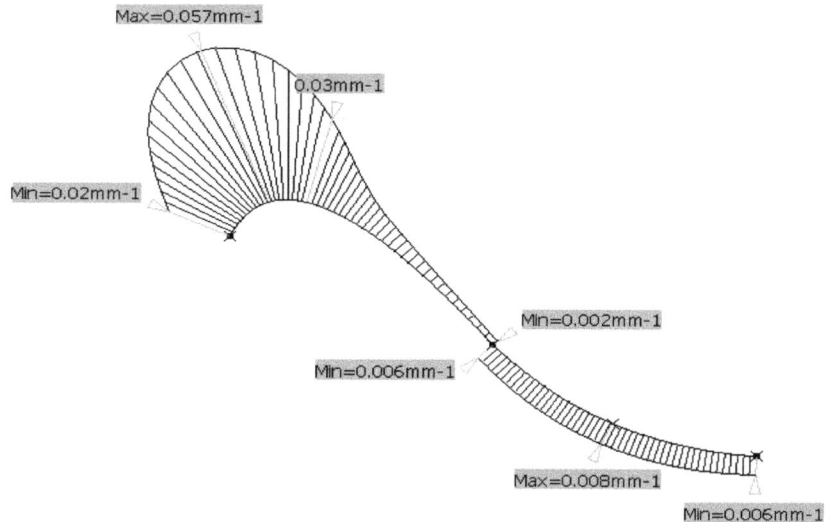

Figure 3–59

Design Considerations

Drag the cursor over the comb to display the local values. The minimum curvature values at the connection of the two curves do not match. This is another indication that there is an issue with the connection of these two curves.

7. Click (Display diagram window) to analyze the plots as a graph. Graphing the curvature enables the creation of points based on the plot.

8. With the cursor, drag the green crosshairs to the maximum Y-value on the plot. Right-click on the curve and select **Drop marker**, as shown in Figure 3–60.

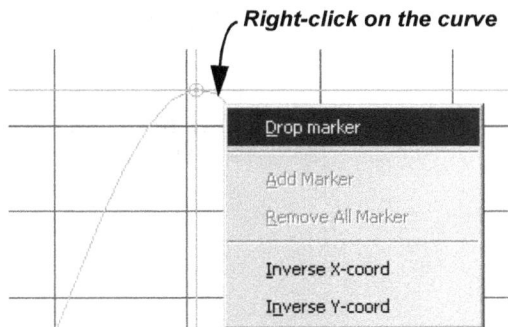

Figure 3–60

Note that a point has been added to the specification tree. The point is non-associative, as indicated by the red zig zag through the point symbol on the tree, as shown in Figure 3–61.

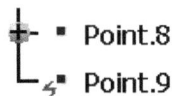

Figure 3–61

9. Close the Diagram window.

10. The **Porcupine Analysis** tool can also be used to display radius values. Select **Radius** in the Type drop-down list in the dialog box. A plot similar to Figure 3–62 displays. Drag the cursor over the plot to display the different radius values.

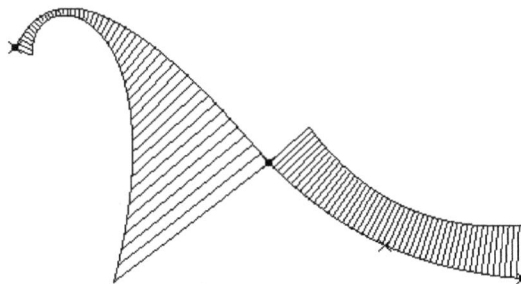

Figure 3–62

11. Click **OK** to finish the analysis.

12. Hide the feature in the specification tree to simplify the display of the model.

Task 4 - Make adjustments based on analysis results.

1. Show the **Connect Checker Analysis** feature in the specification tree.

2. Based on the detection of a **0.1mm** gap between the curves from the Connect Checker, zoom into the area to get a better view. Note that the curves are referencing different points, as shown in Figure 3–63.

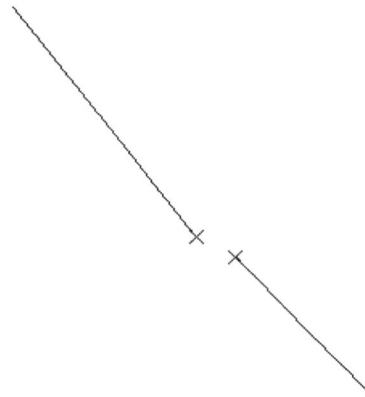

Figure 3–63

3. Edit the value of Point.4. Note the Y-value, as shown in Figure 3–64.

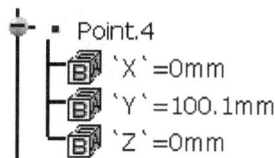

Point.4
`X`=0mm
`Y`=100.1mm
`Z`=0mm

Figure 3–64

*If the values are not visible, select **Tools> Options>Parameters and Measure**, and activate the **With value** option in the Knowledge tab.*

4. Change the point definition to:

   • Y: **100**

5. Double-click on **Connect Checker Analysis.1** to verify that a violation in distance no longer exists, but that there is still a violation in tangency, as shown in Figure 3–66. (A tangency condition has a value >=0.5deg.) If the value does not display on the model, select the *Full* tab in the dialog box as shown in Figure 3–65.

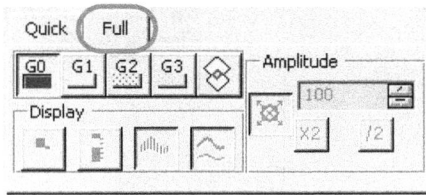

Figure 3–65

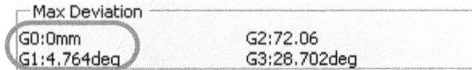

Figure 3–66

6. Click **OK**.

7. Hide the **Connect Checker Analysis** feature in the specification tree.

Task 5 - Use the Curve Smooth tool to repair the curve.

---

1. Before the **Curve Smooth** tool can be used, join the **Spline.1** and **Spline.2** curves using ▨ (Join).

▨ (Curve Smooth) can be found in the ▨ (Join) flyout.

2. Click ▨ (Curve Smooth) to open the dialog box shown in Figure 3–67.

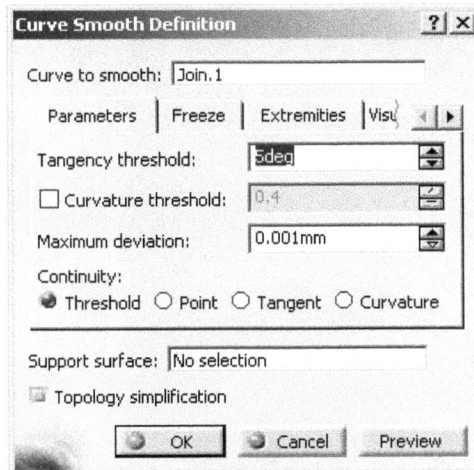

Figure 3–67

3. Select the **Join.1** feature. The model displays as shown in Figure 3–68.

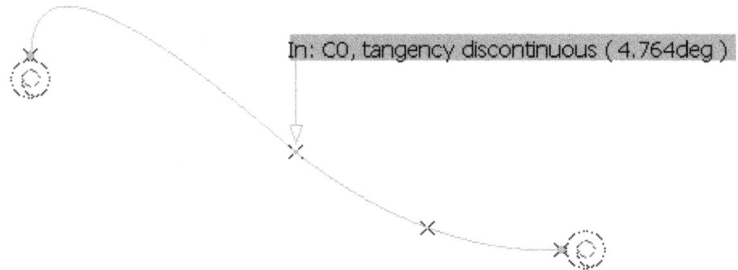

In: C0, tangency discontinuous (4.764deg)

Figure 3–68

4. Make the following change to the Curve Smooth Definition dialog box:

   • *Tangency Threshold:* **4**

5. Click **Preview**. The note displays in red.

6. Make the following change as shown in Figure 3–69:

   • *Tangency Threshold:* **5**
   • Select **Curvature threshold**.

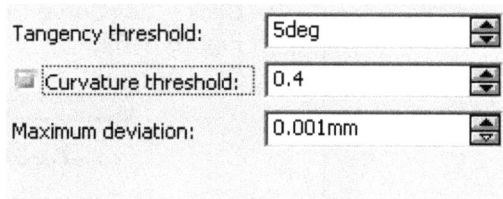

Tangency threshold:	5deg
Curvature threshold:	0.4
Maximum deviation:	0.001mm

Figure 3–69

7. Click **Preview**. The note turns green as shown in Figure 3–70. Click **OK**.

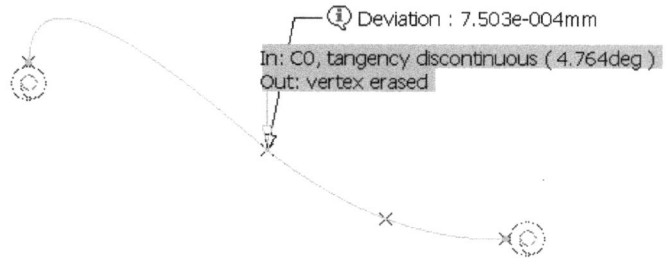

Deviation : 7.503e-004mm
In: C0, tangency discontinuous (4.764deg)
Out: vertex erased

Figure 3–70

8. Use **Connect Checker** on **Curve smooth.1** to verify that the curve has been repaired. Note that no result displays (as shown in Figure 3–71) because the smooth curve operation erased the vertex, and the curve is now a G3 curve. CATIA does not display results for a G3 single element.

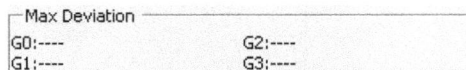

Max Deviation
G0:----   G2:----
G1:----   G3:----

Figure 3–71

*Do not open the previous Connect Checker Analysis in the specification tree to check for repairs, because it still references the **Spline.1** and **Spline.2** features rather than the **Curve Smooth.1** feature.*

Task 6 - Run a Projection on a curve type analysis.

---

1. Hide **Geometrical Set.1**, and activate **Geometrical Set.2**.

2. Click (Connect Checker Analysis).

3. Activate (Curve-Curve Connection) to check the connection between the two curves.

4. Select **Projection**.

5. Enter **25** for the *Maximum Gap*.

6. Click in the *Source* field, then select **Curve1**.

7. Click in the *Target* field, then select **Curve2**. The Connect Checker dialog box opens as shown in Figure 3–72.

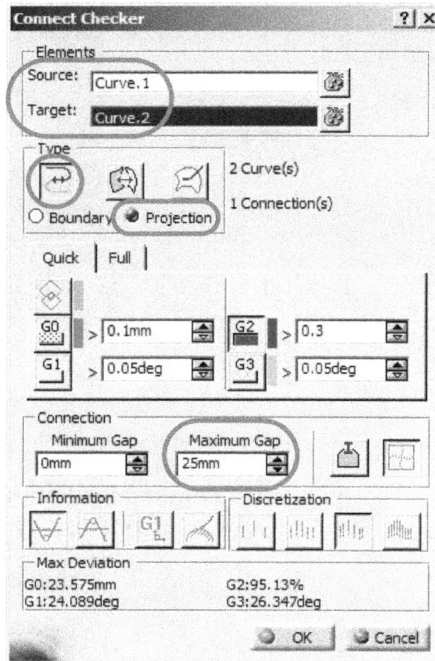

Figure 3–72

8. Click [G2] in the *Quick* tab. Note that the corresponding G2 value displays on your model, as shown in Figure 3–73.

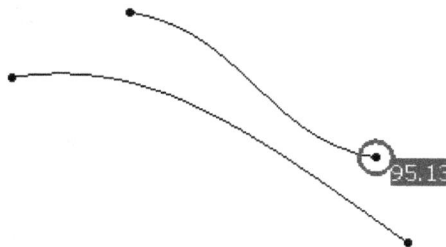

Figure 3–73

9. Click **OK** and hide the **Analysis** feature.

Task 7 - Analyze the connection between curves and a surface.

Continuity is not just a measure of smoothness between multiple curves or surfaces. Continuity can also be analyzed between a curve and a surface. In this task, you will analyze the connection between a curve and a surface.

1. Hide **Geometrical Set.2** and activate **Geometrical Set.3**.

2. Click ▨ (Connect Checker Analysis) and activate
   ▨ (Surface-Curve Connection).

3. Enter **140** for the *Maximum Gap*.

4. Click ▨ next to the *Source* field.

5. Select **Surface1**, **Curve3**, and **Line.1**, as shown in Figure 3–74.

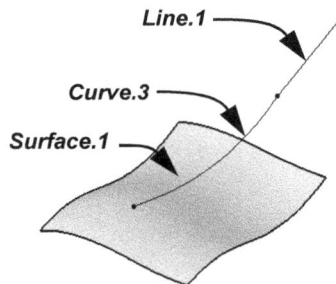

Figure 3–74

6. Close the Source Elements List dialog box. The Connect Checker dialog box opens as shown in Figure 3–75.

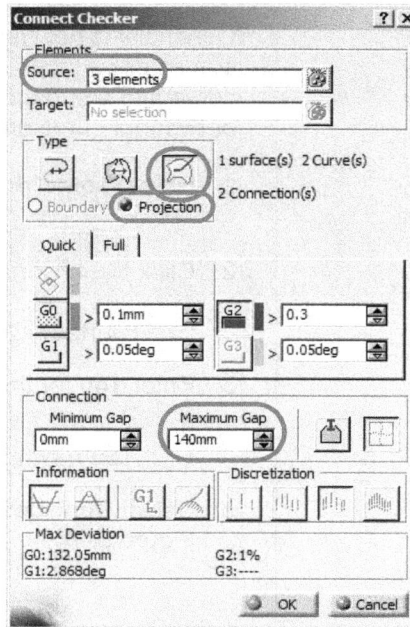

Figure 3–75

7. Click [G2]. Note that the corresponding G2 value displays on your model, as shown in Figure 3–76.

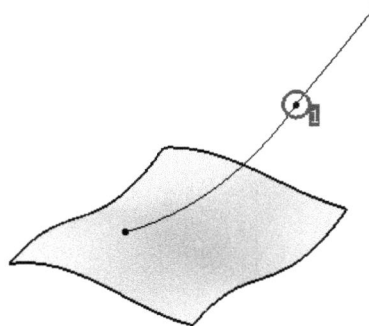

Figure 3–76

8. Click **OK** to complete the analysis.

9. Save the part and close the file.

Practice 3b

Earbud Curve Repair

Practice Objectives

- Examine and investigate curves.
- Use the Curve Smooth function.

The parting line in the headphone earbud was developed using the **Reflect Line** tool, as well as other wireframe tools. In this practice, you will examine the parting line curve and make the required repairs. The completed model is as shown in Figure 3–77.

Figure 3–77

Task 1 - Open a part file.

1. Open **Earbud-425.CATPart**. The model displays as shown in Figure 3–78.

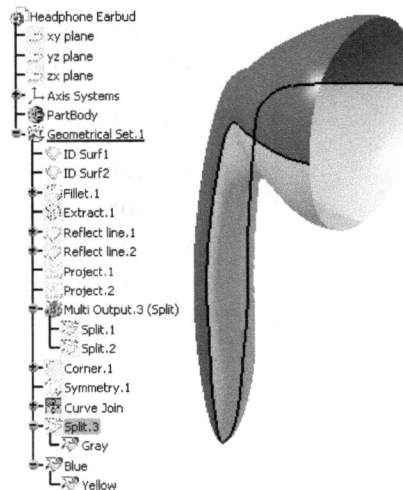

Figure 3–78

A review of the model displays as shown in Figure 3–79. Curve Join was created as the parting line for this plastic part. Curve Join splits **Extract.1** into the **Gray**, **Yellow**, and **Blue** surfaces. In this practice, you will analyze and fix any imperfections in Curve Join.

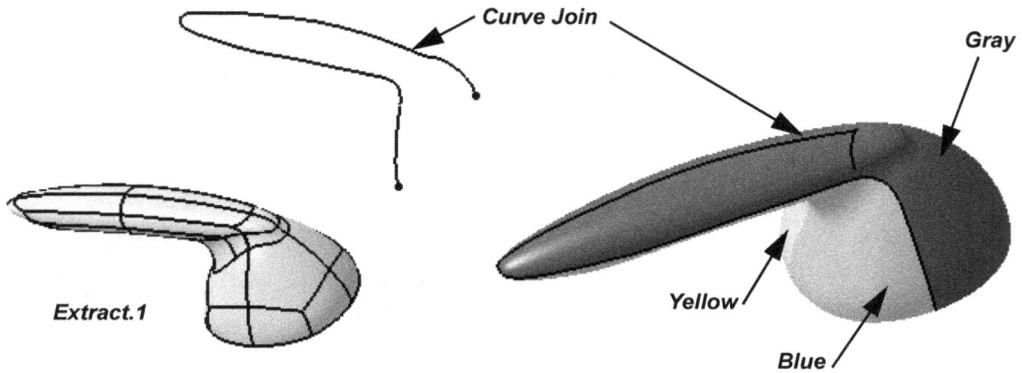

Figure 3–79

2. Ensure that the model units are set to **mm**.

Task 2 - Perform a porcupine analysis.

1. Click (Porcupine Curvature Analysis) in the Analysis toolbar.

2. Enter **200** as the Density, if the value is not already set appropriately.

3. Ensure that the following options are set:

    • **Curvature** (in the Type drop-down list)
    • **Automatic** (under Amplitude)
    • **Comb**
    • **Envelop**

The Porcupine Curvature dialog box opens as shown in Figure 3–80.

The red lines are called the Comb. The green line that follows the shape of the Comb is called the Envelop.

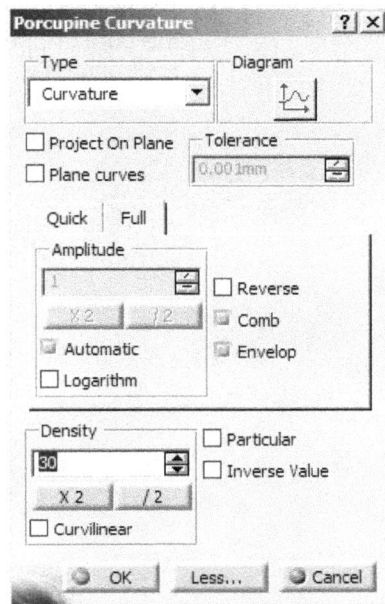

Figure 3–80

4. Select **Curve Join** in the specification tree. The porcupine curve displays on the model as shown in Figure 3–81.

It might take a very long time to get the analysis result.

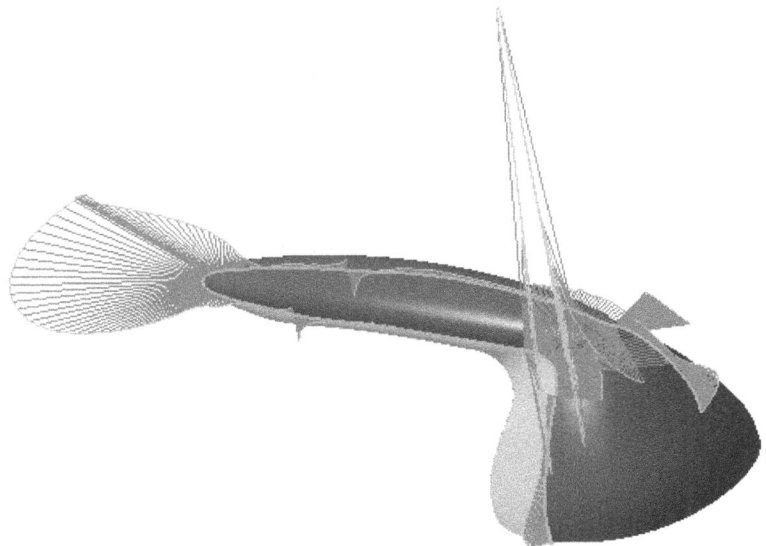

Figure 3–81

5. Zoom in on the area as shown in Figure 3–82. This area on the curve appears to be the most problematic based on the fluctuations in the Curvature Analysis.

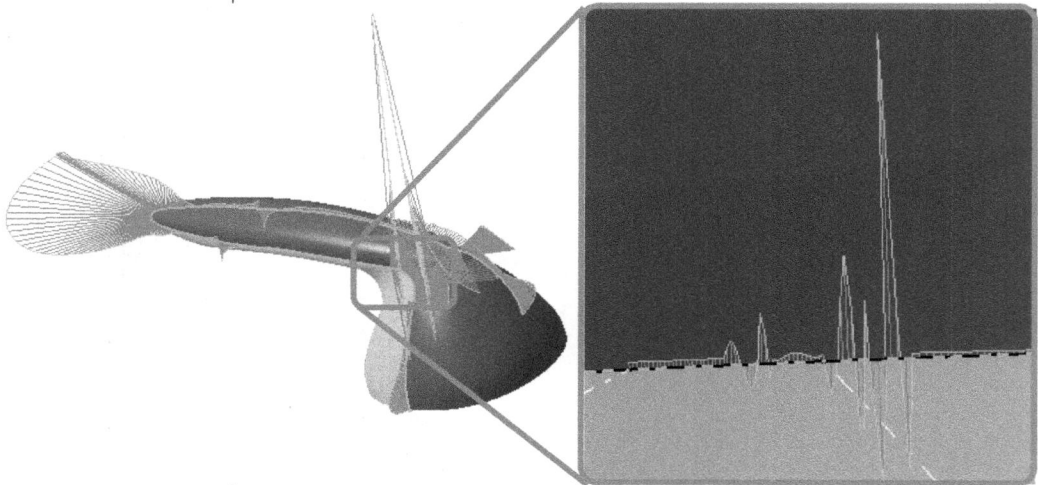

Figure 3–82

6. Leave the Porcupine Analysis dialog box open. Hide the following surfaces:

- **Gray**
- **Blue**
- **Yellow**

The model displays as shown in Figure 3–83. The red combs indicate the changes in curvature, while the green envelop indicates transition in continuity. The analysis results indicate that this curve is not curvature continuous and contains many inflection points.

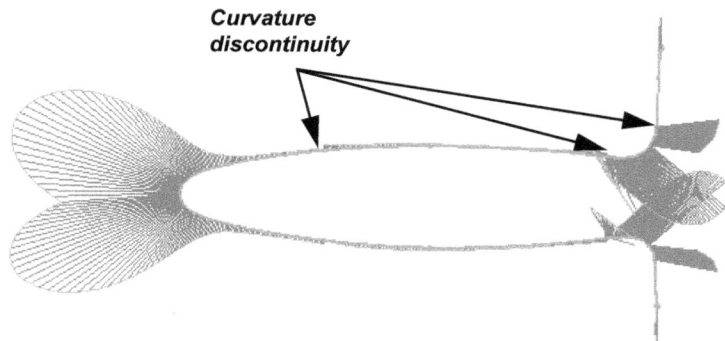

Curvature discontinuity

Figure 3–83

7. Click **OK** in the Porcupine Curvature Analysis dialog box.

8. A new branch was added to the specification tree. The Porcupine Curvature Analysis feature was added under this branch. Rename the feature as **Porcupine Curvature Analysis Before**.

9. Hide **Porcupine Curvature Analysis Before**.

Task 3 - Perform the first Curve Smooth.

1. Click ⌇ (Curve Smooth) in the Join-Healing sub-toolbar. The Curve Smooth Definition dialog box opens as shown in Figure 3–84.

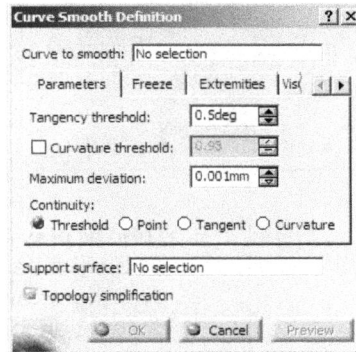

Curve Smooth Definition

Curve to smooth: No selection

Parameters | Freeze | Extremities | Vis ◄ ►

Tangency threshold: 0.5deg

☐ Curvature threshold: 0.93

Maximum deviation: 0.001mm

Continuity:
◉ Threshold ○ Point ○ Tangent ○ Curvature

Support surface: No selection

☐ Topology simplification

OK | Cancel | Preview

Figure 3–84

2. Select **Curve Join** in the specification tree. The model displays as shown in Figure 3–85.

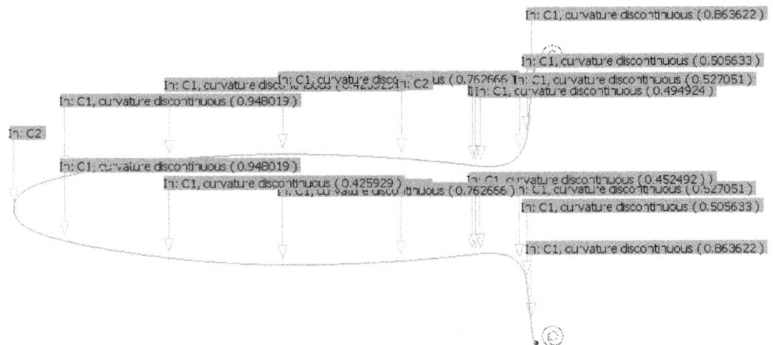

Figure 3–85

3. All problem areas are flagged, describing the issues at the indicated locations. Since there are so many problems noted it helps to clean the display. To do so, select the *Visualization* tab and select **Display information interactively**, as shown in Figure 3–86.

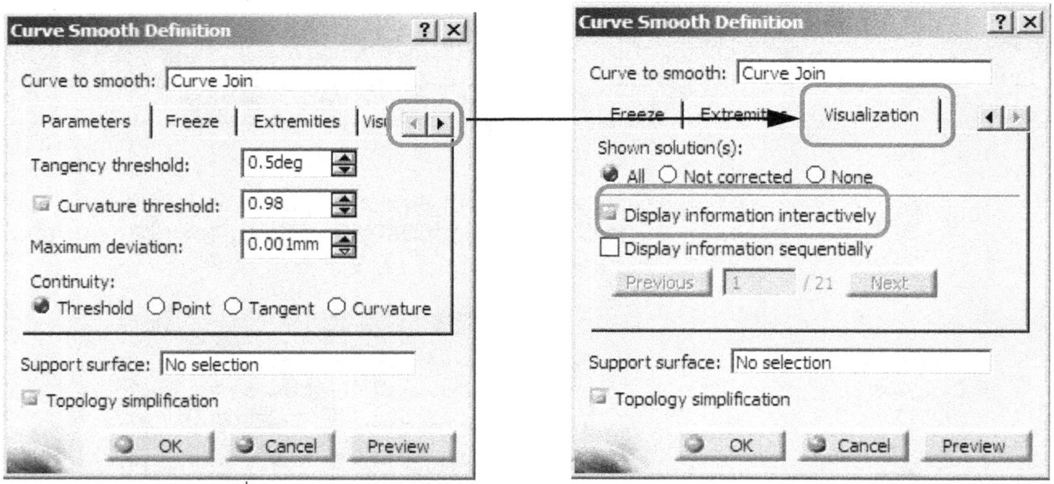

Figure 3–86

The **Display information interactively** option shows the problem areas with an arrow head. When the mouse is rolled over the arrow head icon on the model, the problem description for that location displays. This option is useful because not all problems are shown at once, which clears up the display. The model displays as shown in Figure 3–87.

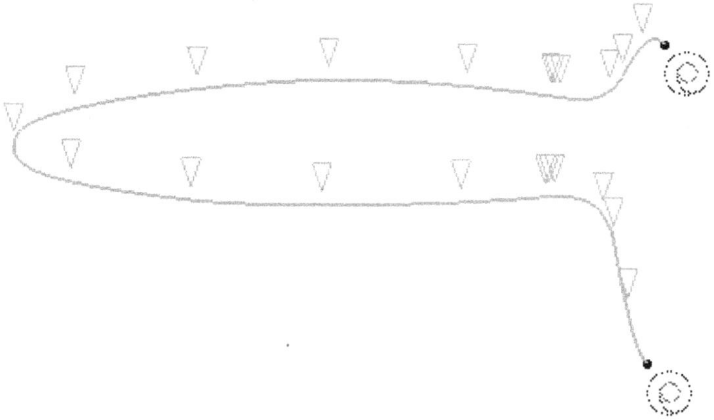

Figure 3–87

4. Hover the cursor over each arrow head to investigate the problems. The majority of the messages state curvature discontinuity. Each curvature discontinuity message displays a discontinuity number. The larger the value, the more discontinuous the curve is at that location.

5. Determine the location of the smallest curvature discontinuity value as shown in Figure 3–88.

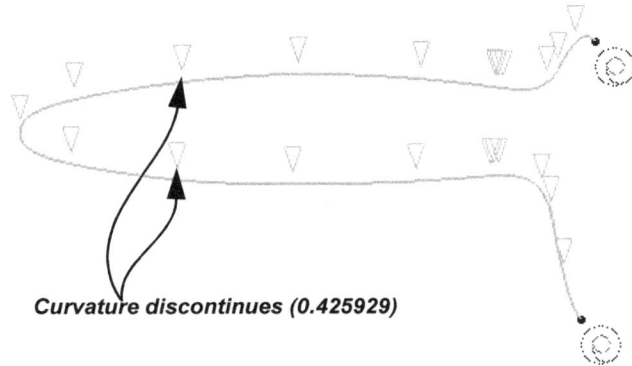

Curvature discontinues (0.425929)

Figure 3–88

Design Considerations

Multiple courses of action can be taken in the Curve Smooth Definition dialog box. For this practice a Support surface should be used. Since this curve is to be the parting line for the plastic part, it should lie on the surface of the part. To do so, this surface is selected as a support.

6. Click in the *Support surface* reference field as shown in Figure 3–89.

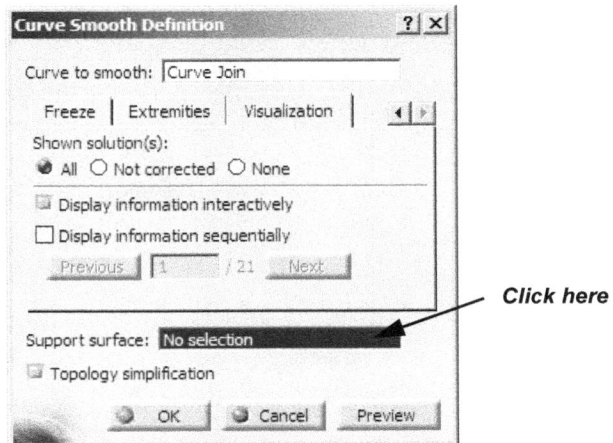

Figure 3–89

7. Select **Extract.1** as the *Support surface.*

8. Click **Preview** in the dialog box. The model displays as shown in Figure 3–90. Green indicates that the previous problem at that location was fixed. Red indicates that the problem could not be fixed with the current Curve Smooth settings.

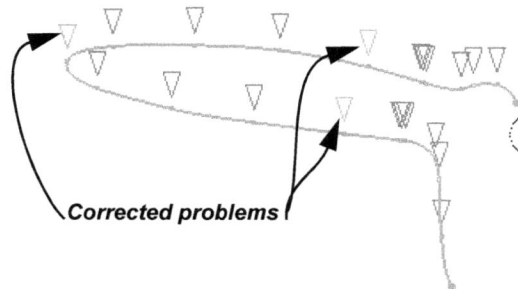

Corrected problems

Figure 3–90

9. Because there are existing problem areas that could not be fixed, further adjusting must be done. In the *Parameters* tab, select **Curvature** as shown in Figure 3–91.

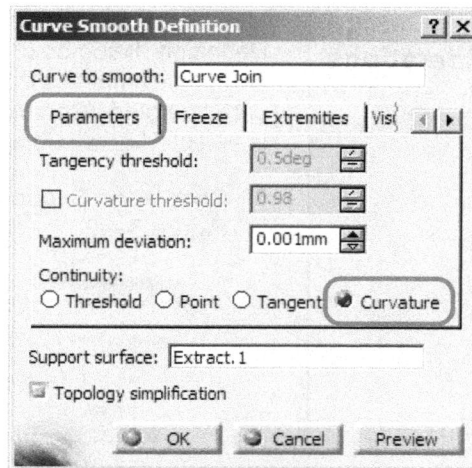

Figure 3–91

10. Click **Preview** in the dialog box. An Update Error warning box opens as shown in Figure 3–92. This means that using the **Curvature** option, the Curve Join cannot lie on the support surface and be smoothed to Curvature Continuity. Other options must be adjusted.

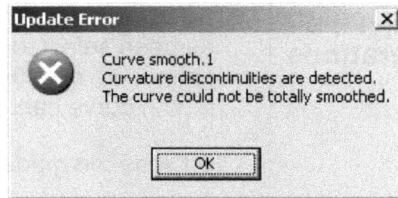

Figure 3–92

11. Enter a *Maximum deviation* value of **.1mm**. This means the curve smooth can be adjusted 0.1mm from the original curve, Curve Join.

12. Click **Preview** in the dialog box. The Update Error displays stating that the curve could not be completely smoothed.

13. Change the **Curvature** to **Threshold** option.

14. Select the **Curvature threshold** option. This enables you to manually enter a Curvature threshold value.

15. Enter **.4** as the **Curvature threshold.** The dialog box opens as shown in Figure 3–93.

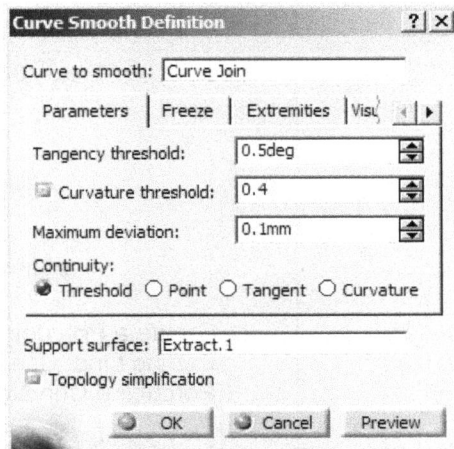

Figure 3–93

16. Preview the model, and note that there are still red locations on the curve smooth. Even after greatly adjusting values in the dialog box, Curve Join cannot be completely smoothed.

17. Cancel the Curve Smooth.

Design Considerations

The curve cannot be completely smoothed because **Extract.1** has been selected as a support. **Extract.1** is only tangent continuous, not curvature continuous. Because of this, the smooth curve cannot be entirely curvature continuous.

18. Close the model without saving any changes.

Task 4 - Open a revised version of the model.

Due to the imperfections in the model, the Industrial Designers have created a better quality surface for you to work with. They reconstructed the surfaces so that there is now curvature continuity.

1. Open **Earbud2_Start.CATPart**. The model displays as shown in Figure 3–94. A parting line has been reconstructed based on the new surface. It is your job to assess the quality of the new parting line curve.

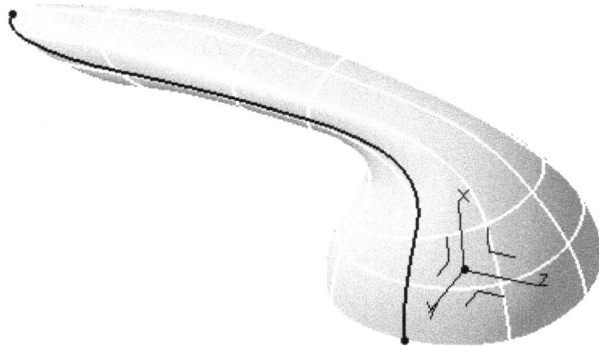

Figure 3–94

2. Create a Porcupine Curvature Analysis for the curve named Parting Line. Use the following specifications in the Porcupine Curvature dialog box:

- *Density:* **20**
- *Amplitude:* **10**
- Activate the **Comb** option.
- Activate the **Envelop** option.

3. Complete the analysis. The model displays as shown in Figure 3–95.

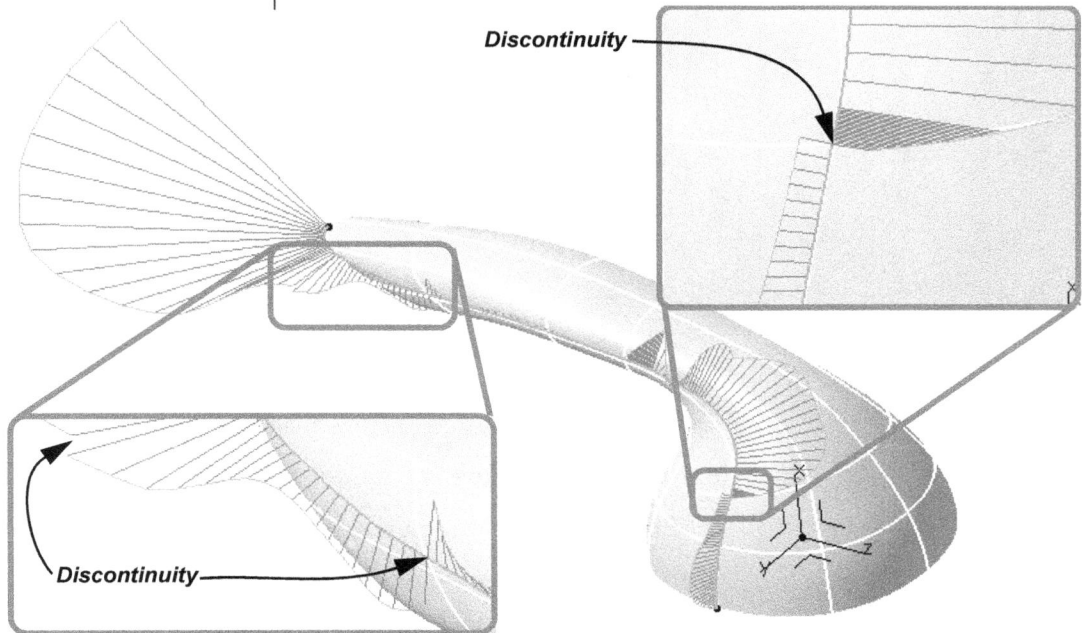

Discontinuity

Discontinuity

Figure 3–95

4. Hide **Porcupine Curvature Analysis.1**. Because of the discontinuity in the curve, adjustments need to be made.

5. Click (Curve Smooth).

6. Clear the **Display information interactively** option in the *Visualization* tab.

7. Select the **Parting Line** curve. The model now displays the problem areas as shown in Figure 3–96.

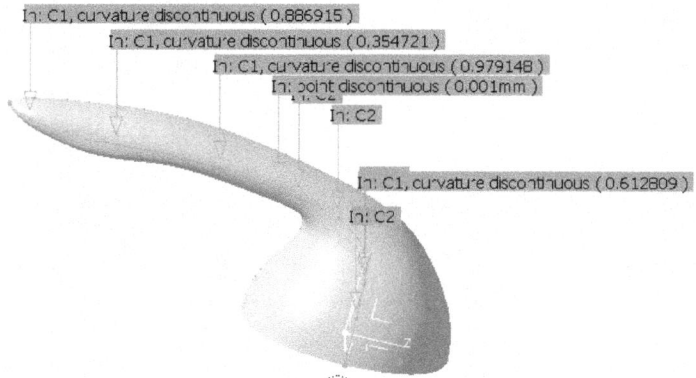

In: C1, curvature discontinuous (0.886915)
In: C1, curvature discontinuous (0.354721)
In: C1, curvature discontinuous (0.979148)
In: point discontinuous (0.001mm)
In: C2
In: C1, curvature discontinuous (0.612809)
In: C2

Figure 3–96

8. Activate **Curvature** in the *Continuity* area in the dialog box.

9. Ensure that the Maximum deviation is **.001mm**.

10. Select **ID Surf** as the Support surface.

11. Click **Preview** in the dialog box. The model displays as shown in Figure 3–97. All previous problem areas are green, indicating that the issue was corrected. Each note displays Out:C2 or
Out: Vertex erased, indicating that the curve was smoothed to Curvature Continuity and that the vertex at that location has been removed.

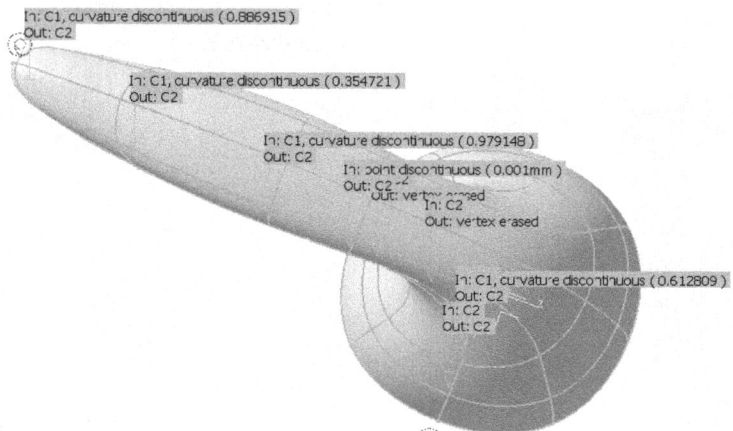

In: C1, curvature discontinuous (0.886915)
Out: C2
In: C1, curvature discontinuous (0.354721)
Out: C2
In: C1, curvature discontinuous (0.979148)
Out: C2
In: point discontinuous (0.001mm)
Out: C2
Out: vertex erased
In: C2
Out: vertex erased
In: C1, curvature discontinuous (0.612809)
Out: C2
In: C2
Out: C2

Figure 3–97

12. Complete the Curve Smooth. Because the support surface was of good quality, the Curve Smooth could easily smooth out imperfections in creating a Curvature Continuous curve. Remember that a bad quality support surface was the problem with the original Curve Smooth attempted in Task 3.

13. Perform a **Connect Checker** using the following specifications, as shown in Figure 3–98:

    • Activate (Curve-Curve Connection).

    • Select **Boundary**.

    • *G2:* **3**

    • Select **Curve Smooth.1**.

    • *Maximum Gap:* **2mm**

    • Activate (Internal Edge).

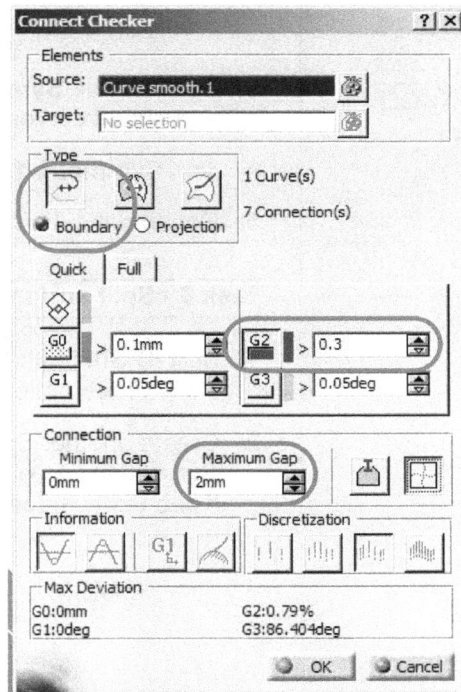

Figure 3–98

14. There are no Curvature Continuity problems greater than 3 percent. The maximum G2 value is 0.79%, as shown in Figure 3–98. Because this is such a small value, you do not further adjust any Curve Smooth parameters.

15. Complete the **Connect Checker**.

To make the model easier to visualize, the Rendering Display was set to Shading.

Task 5 - Complete the curve.

1. Use the **Symmetry** tool to mirror **Curve Smooth.1** about the zx plane.

2. Complete the Symmetry. The model displays as shown in Figure 3–99.

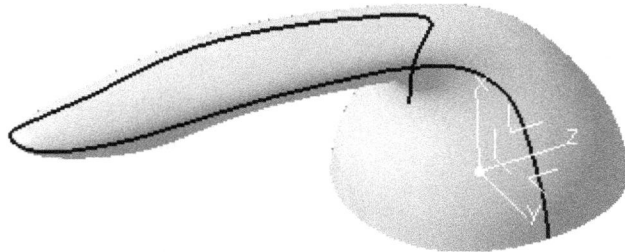

Figure 3–99

3. Because the **Symmetry** tool does not assemble the input and output curves together a **Join** operation is required.

4. Join **Symmetry.1** and **Curve Smooth.1**.

5. Rename the Join feature as **Final Parting Line**.

Task 6 - Split surfaces.

1. Split **ID Surf** with **Final Parting Line**. Verify that the **Keep Both Sides** option is activated.

2. Create another Split feature, using **Split.1** as the Element to Cut, and the zx plane as the Cutting Element. Again, use the **Keep Both Sides** option.

3. Color the split surfaces with different colors. The model displays as shown in Figure 3–100.

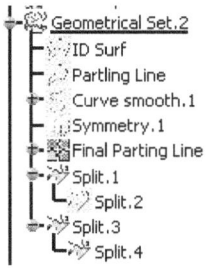

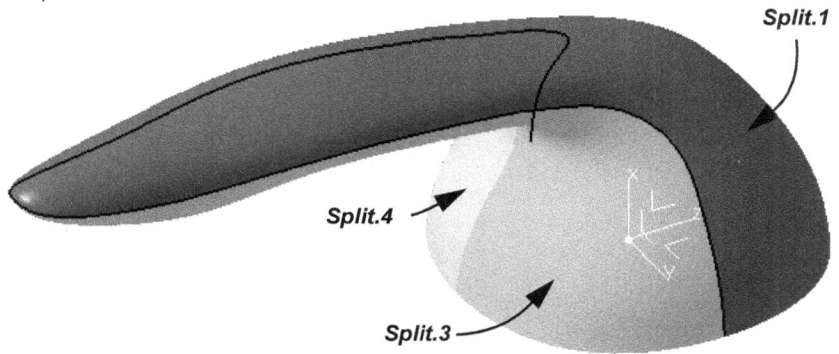

Geometrical Set.2
— ID Surf
— Partling Line
— Curve smooth.1
— Symmetry.1
— Final Parting Line
— Split.1
    └─ Split.2
— Split.3
    └─ Split.4

Figure 3–100

4. Save the model and close the file.

Practice 3c | # Known Element Method

Practice Objectives

- Disassemble curves.
- Reinforce correct non-boundary representation modeling.
- Rebuild geometry using the Known Element Method.

Although CATIA has tools to fix point, tangency, and curvature imperfections in a curve, there are other methods for reaching the same goal. The Known Element Method takes a curve and rebuilds it using points, lines, circles, and conics. No splines are used in the Known Element Method. This provides a clean and mathematically simpler way of creating curve geometry. It also reduces the occurrence of ogees in a curve. An ogee is a geometrical imperfection resulting in an unwanted inflection point on a curve. Commonly, this method is used when imported geometry is brought into CATIA. Native CATIA data is built from the imported curve to produce a better quality curve. This is then used to create surface geometry.

In this practice, you will rebuild a curve using the Known Element Method. The curve that is being rebuilt was created in an Industrial Design program. The intent of the practice is to use the existing data to build a better quality curve. The end result will be a tangency continuous curve consisting of lines, circles and conics. The final curve will display as shown in Figure 3–101.

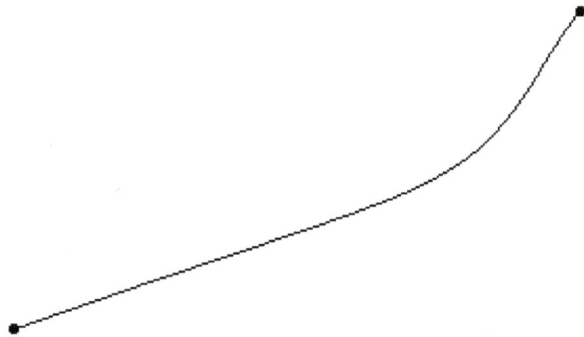

Figure 3–101

Task 1 - Open a part file.

1. Open **Known_Element_Method.CATPart**. The model displays as shown in Figure 3–102. The only feature in the specification tree is named Imported Curve. Because this curve was generated in an industrial design program and copied into the current part, it has no history or associativity.

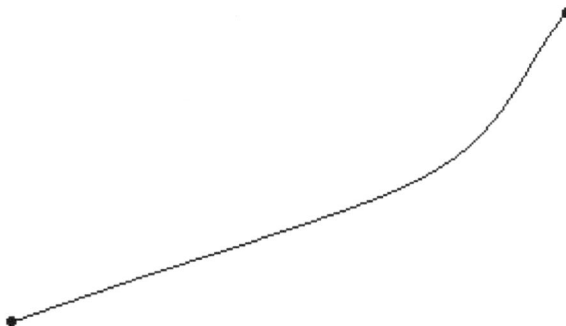

Figure 3–102

2. Create a Geometrical Set named **Rebuild1**.

Task 2 - Create reference geometry.

1. Project Imported Curve onto the zx plane of the Absolute Axis System. Use a normal projection type.

2. Click 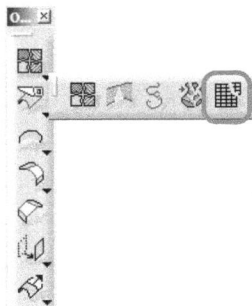 (Disassemble). The Disassemble dialog box opens as shown in Figure 3–103.

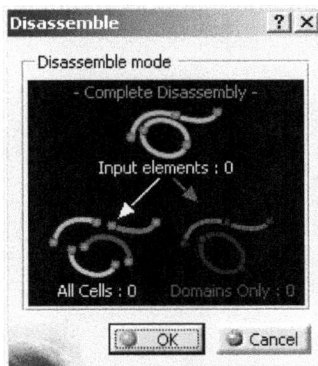

Figure 3–103

3. Select **Project.1**.

4. Complete the Disassemble and 11 isolated curves are added to the model.

Design Considerations

Disassembling a curve can aid in building reference geometry by enabling smaller curve elements to be used instead of one large curve. Because Imported Curve was pasted into CATIA without any history, there is no way to see how it was created. In the following steps, the **Disassemble** tool will help create points that will be used in reconstructing the curve.

5. Hide **Project.1** and **Imported Curve**. The model displays as shown in Figure 3–104.

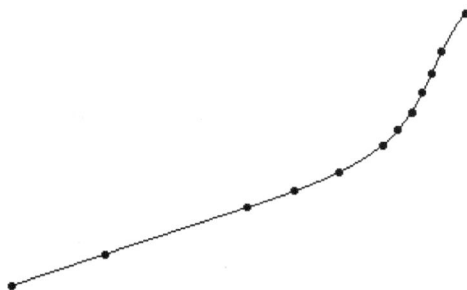

Figure 3–104

6. Rename the Disassemble features, as shown in Figure 3–105. This makes them easier to identify during the practice.

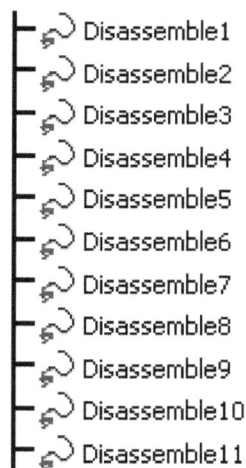

Disassemble1
Disassemble2
Disassemble3
Disassemble4
Disassemble5
Disassemble6
Disassemble7
Disassemble8
Disassemble9
Disassemble10
Disassemble11

Figure 3–105

7. At each location listed in Figure 3–106, create a point by using **On Curve** as the type and selecting a disassembled curve. Each point is located at an end point of a disassemble curve.

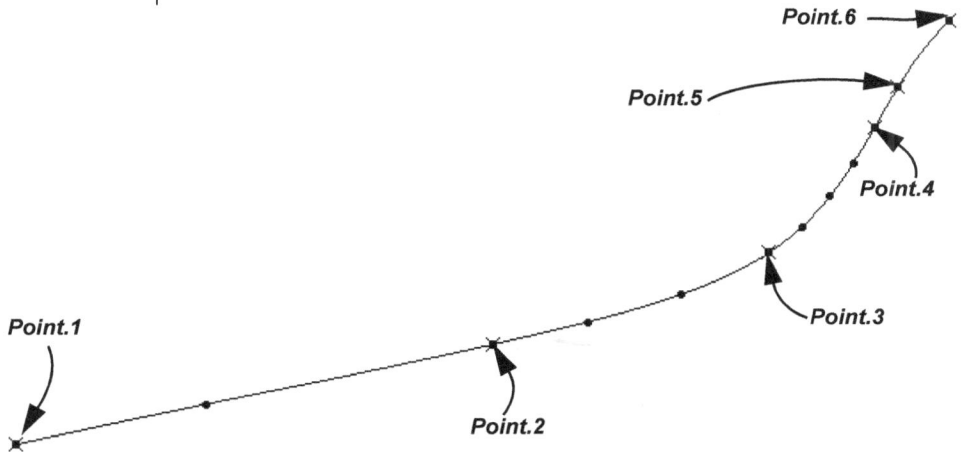

Point.1

Point.2

Point.6

Point.5

Point.4

Point.3

Figure 3–106

8. Hide all of the **Disassemble** curves.

Task 3 - Create wireframe from reference geometry.

Do not use the vertices of the Disassemble curves to create the line as this would create a Boundary Representation.

1. Create a point-point line using the points shown in Figure 3–107. Ensure that the zx plane of the Absolute Axis is used as the Support.

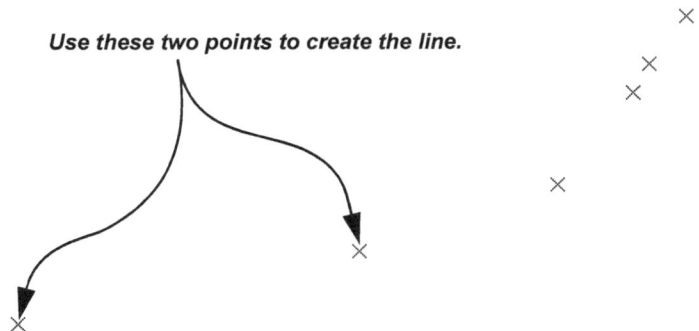

Use these two points to create the line.

Figure 3–107

2. Ensure that the name of the newly created Line feature is **Line.1**.

3. Create another point-point line using the points shown in Figure 3–108. Use the zx plane of the Absolute Axis as the Support.

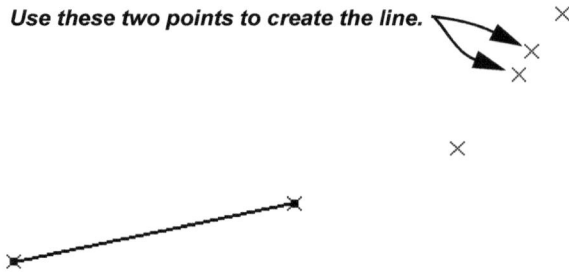

Use these two points to create the line.

Figure 3–108

4. Ensure that the name of the newly created Line feature is **Line.2**.

5. Create an Intersect feature using **Line.1** and **Line.2**. Activate the **Extend linear supports for intersection** option for the First and Second Elements. The resulting intersection point displays as shown in Figure 3–109.

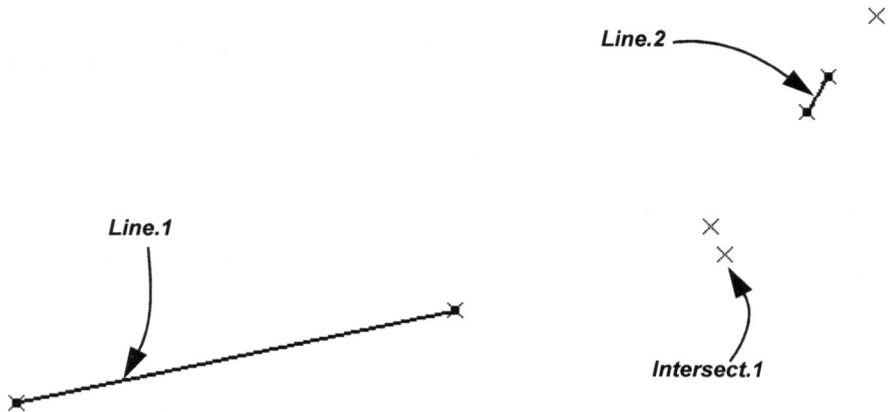

Line.2

Line.1

Intersect.1

Figure 3–109

6. Click ⌐ (Conic). The Conic Definition dialog box opens as shown in Figure 3–110.

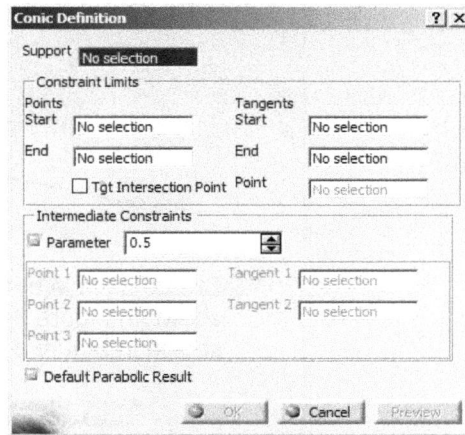

Figure 3–110

7. Select the **zx plane** of the Absolute Axis as the *Support*.

8. Activate the **Tgt Intersection Point** option.

9. Clear the **Parameter** option.

10. Select the points, as shown in Figure 3–111. The names of the points match the names of the references required in the dialog box.

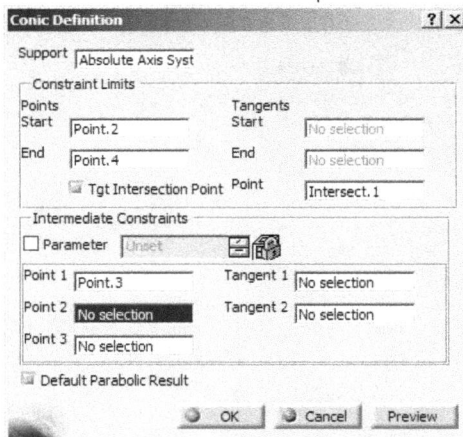

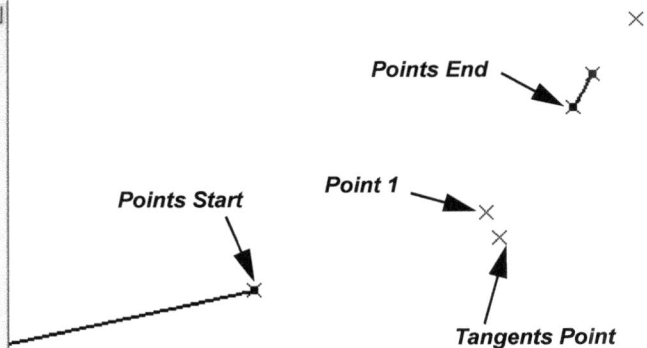

Figure 3–111

11. Complete the conic. The model displays as shown in Figure 3–112.

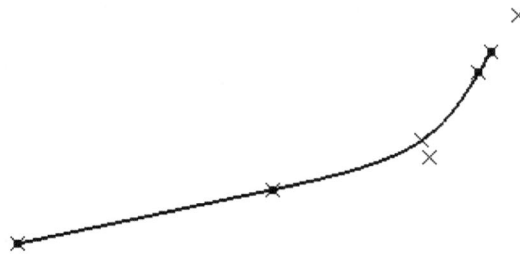

Figure 3–112

12. Create a circle by using a Bitangent and point circle type as shown in Figure 3–113. Select the appropriate references, as shown in Figure 3–114.

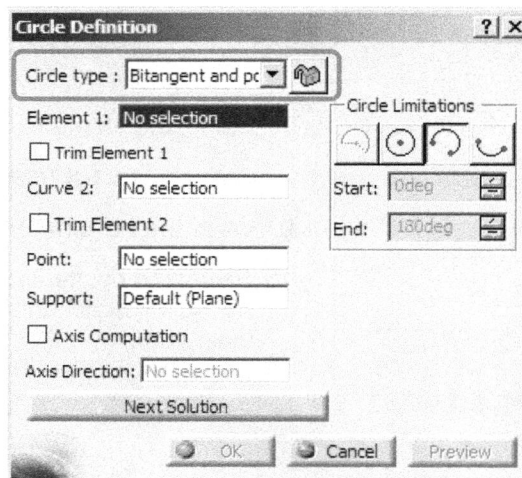

Figure 3–113

- Refer to Figure 3–106 for point names.

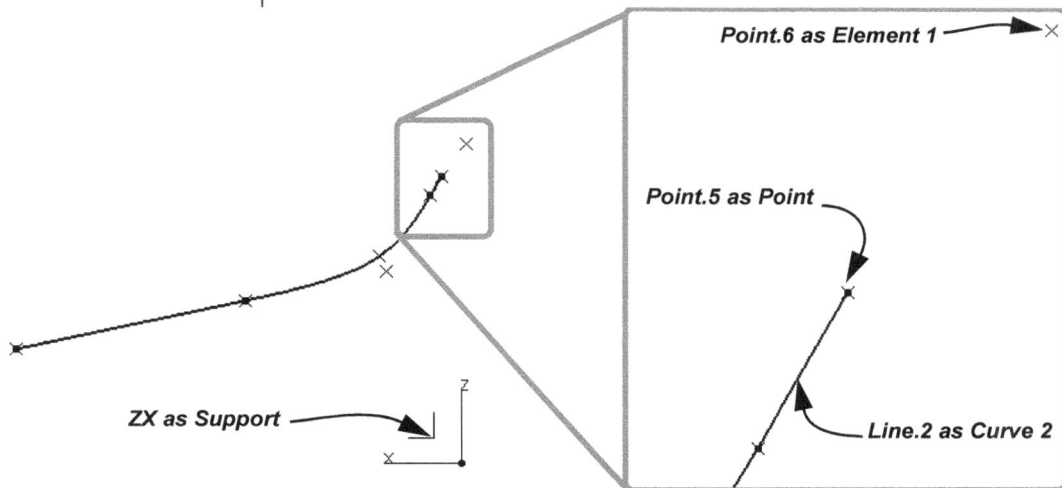

Point.6 as Element 1

Point.5 as Point

ZX as Support

Line.2 as Curve 2

Figure 3–114

13. Complete the circle. The model displays as shown in Figure 3–115.

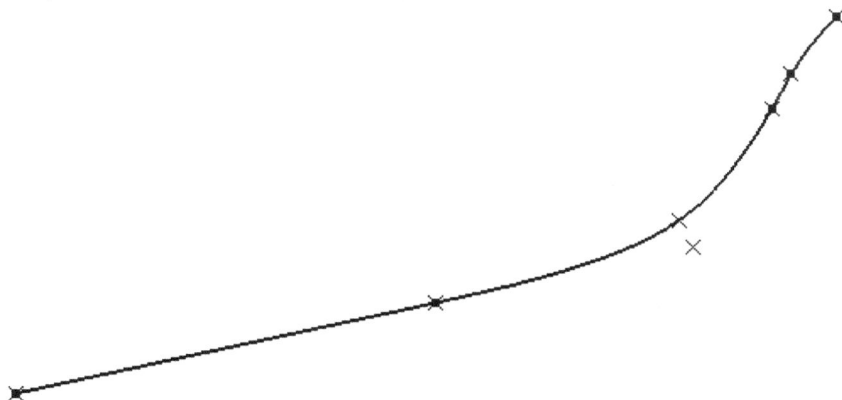

Figure 3–115

14. Join **Line.1**, **Line.2**, **Conic.1**, and **Circle.1**.

15. Hide the **Rebuild1** geometrical set.

Task 4 - Create reference geometry.

In this task, you will project the Imported Curve onto a plane and rebuild it. First, you must set up the reference geometry.

1. Create a new geometrical set named **Rebuild2**.

2. Project Imported Curve onto the xy plane of the Absolute Axis using **Normal** as the projection type.

3. Disassemble the projected curve. The operation results in 11 disassemble curves.

*To orient the model as shown in Figure 3–116, select **Z** on the compass.*

4. Rename each one Disassemble12 as **Disassemble22**, as shown in Figure 3–116. Before renaming, note the orientation of the model from the compass.

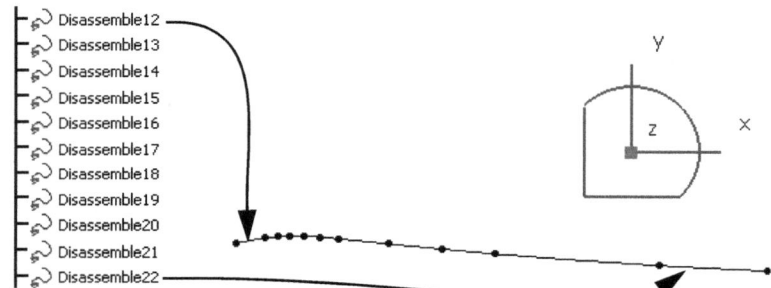

Figure 3–116

5. Hide **Project.2**.

6. At each location listed in Figure 3–117, create a point using **On Curve** as the type and selecting a disassembled curve. All points are created at the end points of the disassemble curves.

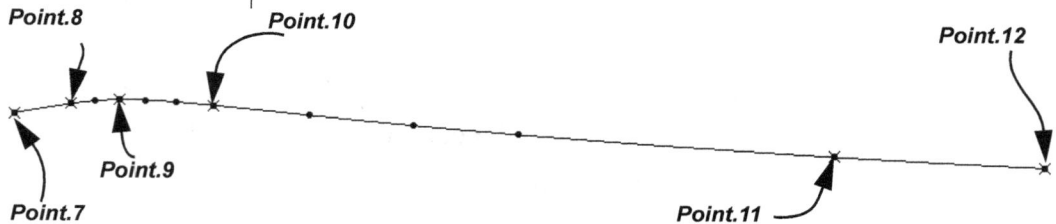

Figure 3–117

7. Hide all **Disassemble** curves.

Task 5 - Create wireframe from reference geometry.

1. Create a circle using three points as the circle type. Use **Point.10**, **Point.11**, and **Point.12** as the three points. The completed circle displays as shown in Figure 3–118.

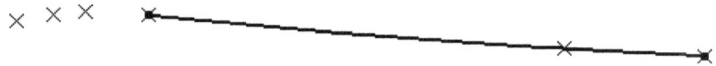

Figure 3–118

2. Create a line using point-point as the line type. Select **Point.7** and **Point.8** as the two point references. Use the xy plane of the Absolute Axis as the support. The completed line displays as shown in Figure 3–119.

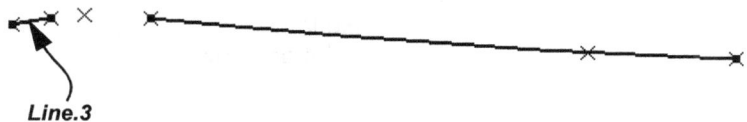

Figure 3–119

3. Hide **Point.9**.

4. Create a line using tangent to curve as the line type. Select **Line.3** as the *Curve reference*, and **Point.8** as *Element 2*. Enter an *End* value of **50mm**. The completed line displays as shown in Figure 3–120.

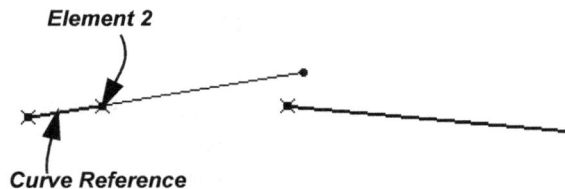

Figure 3–120

5. Rename the line as **Tangent Line1**.

6. Create another line using tangent to curve as the line type. Select **Circle.2** as the *Curve reference* and **Point.10** as *Element 2*. Enter an *End* value of **50mm**. The completed line displays as shown in Figure 3–121.

You might need to reverse direction to achieve the same result.

7. Rename the line as **Tangent Line2**.

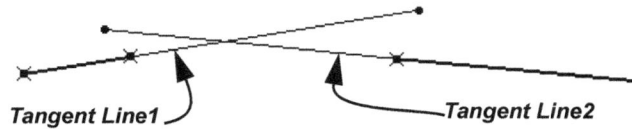

Figure 3–121

8. Create an intersection between **Tangent Line1** and **Tangent Line2**.

9. Rename the intersection point as **Point.13**. The result is a point as shown in Figure 3–122.

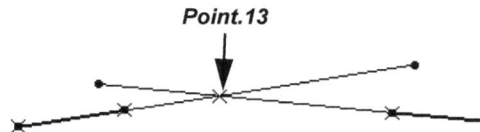

Figure 3–122

10. Hide **Tangent Line1** and **Tangent Line2**.

11. Show **Point.9**.

12. Create a conic using the following specifications as shown in Figure 3–123:

   - *Support:* **Absolute Axis XY Plane**
   - *Points Start:* **Point.10**
   - *Points End:* **Point.8**
   - Activate the **Tgt Intersection Point** option.
   - *Tangents Point:* **Point.13**
   - Clear the **Parameter** option.
   - *Point 1:* **Point.9**

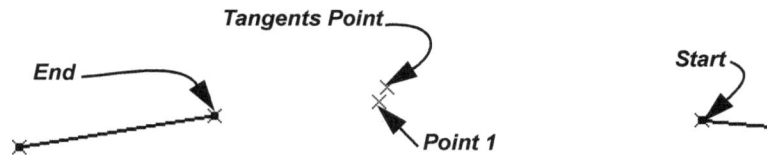

Figure 3–123

13. Complete the conic. The feature displays as shown in Figure 3–124.

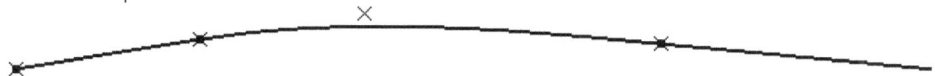

Figure 3–124

14. Join the conic, circle, and line that were created in this task.

15. Hide all points. The model displays as shown in Figure 3–125.

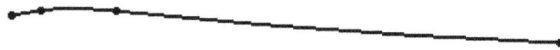

Figure 3–125

Task 6 - Complete rebuilding the curve.

Two curves have been rebuilt using Lines, Circles, and Conics. These are the only types of features permitted using the Known Element Method. In this task, the two rebuilt curves are combined to form the final curve.

1. Define Input as the active work object.

2. Show **Join.1** and **Imported Curve**. The model displays as shown in Figure 3–126.

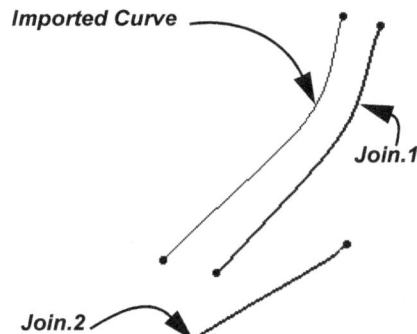

Imported Curve

Join.1

Join.2

Figure 3–126

Design Considerations

By projecting Imported Curve onto two different planes, each individual project can be disassembled and rebuilt. This enables the identification of lines, circles, and conic elements. This identification is a visual approximation. An element type should be selected to closely resemble the area of the curve that is being rebuilt. By rebuilding a planar curve, such as the disassembled projection, the end result can later be recombined to become a 3D curve.

3. Combine **Join.1** and **Join.2** using **Normal** as the combine type.

4. Hide **Join.1** and **Join.2**. The model displays as shown in Figure 3–127. The combine curve represents the final rebuilt curve.

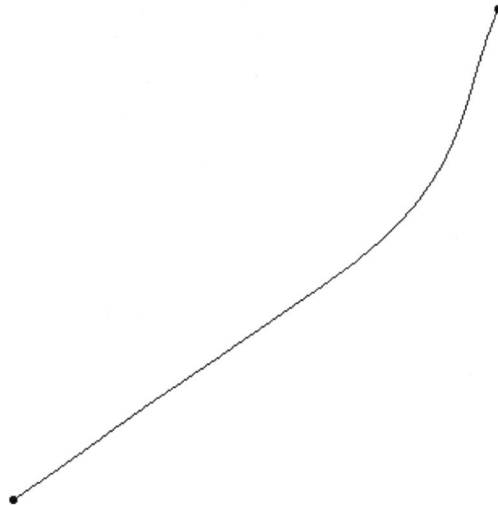

Figure 3–127

5. Show **Imported Curve**. Compare Imported Curve to **Combine.1**. The rebuilt curve, **Combine.1** is a very close representation of Imported Curve. If the design intent requires a closer representation, different lines, circles, and conics can be defined.

6. Save the model and close the file.

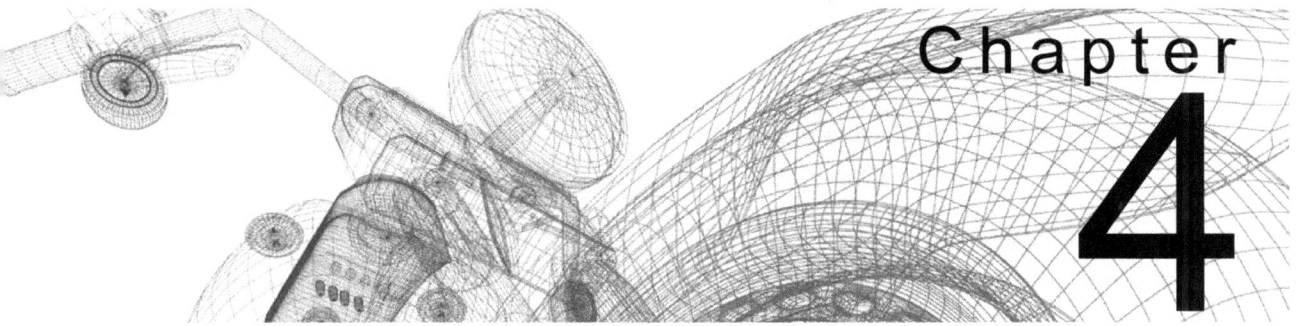

Blend Surfaces

This chapter goes into depth regarding the options in the Blend dialog box. These include trim supports, creating coupling curves, coupling types, and continuity settings.

Learning Objectives in this Chapter

- Create surfaces that transitions between two curves.
- Understand the optional blend elements.

4.1 Blended Surfaces Overview

Blended surfaces create a surface that transitions between two curves. Blend surfaces provide tools to enforce point, tangent, or curvature continuity. It is one of only a few surface based features able to provide curvature continuity.

This chapter focuses on more advanced options that provide more control over the shape of the feature.

How To: Create a Blended Surface

1. Start the creation of the blended surface by clicking

    (Blend).
2. Define the curves to blend. The first and second curve are selected, as shown in Figure 4–1.

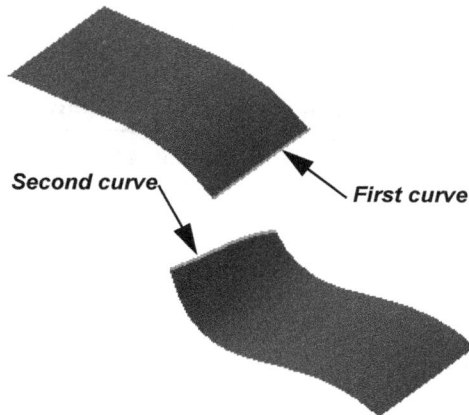

Second curve

First curve

Figure 4–1

3. Define support surfaces as required. The support surfaces are used as a reference for the imposed continuity condition.
4. Specify the continuity conditions: **Point**, **Tangent**, or **Curvature Continuity**.
5. Specify optional conditions, which include:
   - Continuity type
   - Trim supports
   - Tension
   - Modifying closing points
   - Coupling
   - Developable

6. Complete the feature as shown in Figure 4–2.

Figure 4–2

4.2 Optional Blend Elements

Trim Supports

The support surface can be trimmed to the blended surface automatically by selecting the **Trim first support** and **Trim second support** options as shown in Figure 4–3 and Figure 4–4.

The Tangent Borders drop-down lists apply the continuity setting at the start, end, both, or neither end(s) of the curve.

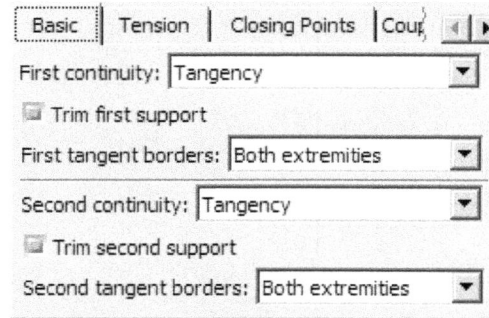

Figure 4–3

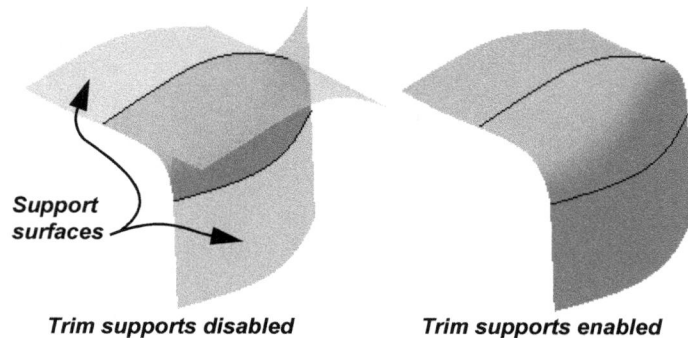

Support surfaces

Trim supports disabled   *Trim supports enabled*

Figure 4–4

Tangent Borders

Each curve has an option for tangent borders in the *Basic* tab as shown in Figure 4–5.

Tangent borders

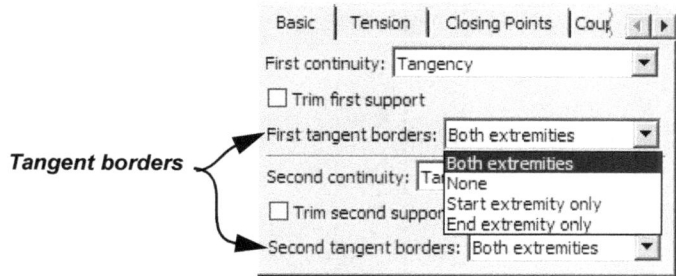

Figure 4–5

This option dictates the continuity of the blend boundary to the support boundary. Each curve in the blend has a start and end location as shown in Figure 4–6. The continuity setting can apply to the following:

- Both extremities

- None

- Start extremity only

- End extremity only

Second curve- End extremity   **First curve- End extremity**

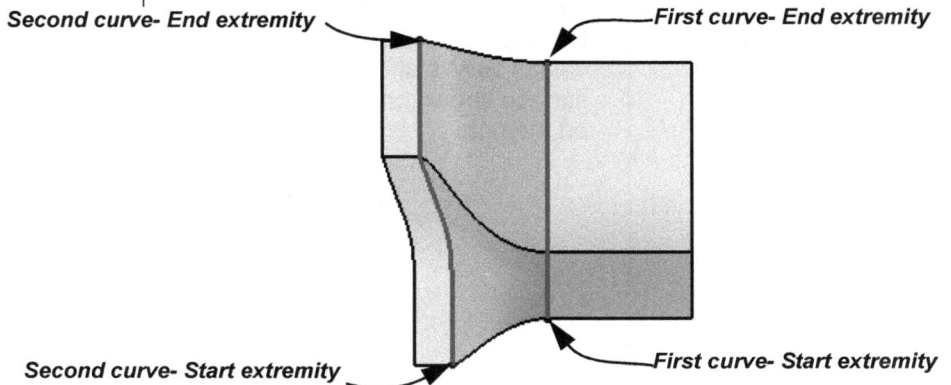

Second curve- Start extremity   **First curve- Start extremity**

Figure 4–6

When the Blend dialog box is open the start and end extremities are noted with red arrows as shown in Figure 4–7.

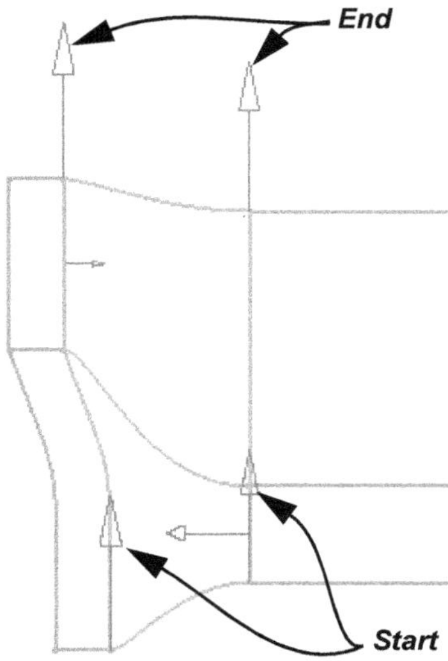

Figure 4–7

Tension

The *Tension* tab displays as shown in Figure 4–8. Tension determines how much the shape of the blended surface can change to maintain the continuity settings defined in the *Basic* tab. The tension can be constant or vary linearly from the start to the end of the curve. An example of how increased tension values vary is shown in Figure 4–9. The curvature continuous surface shown on the left is used to produce the surface shown on the right.

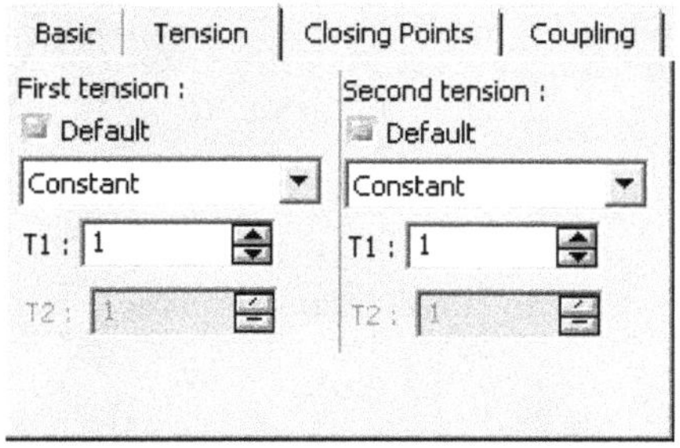

Figure 4–8

An example of how increased tension values vary is shown in Figure 4–9.

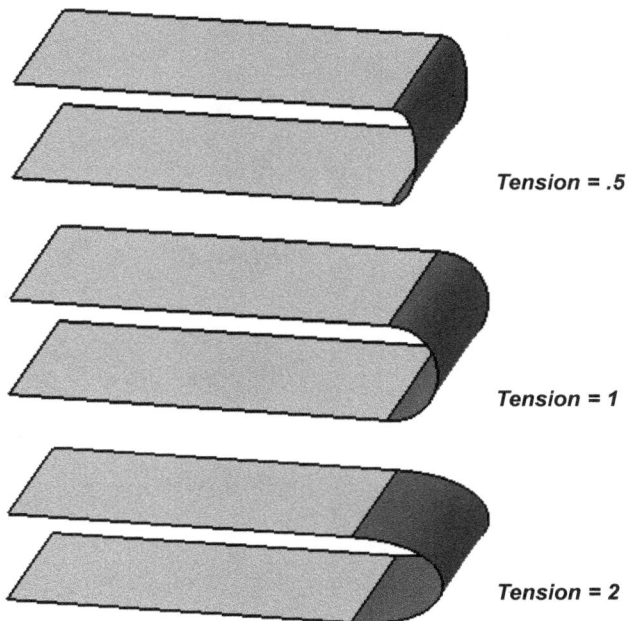

Tension = .5

Tension = 1

Tension = 2

Figure 4–9

Coupling

The **Coupling** option is used to define the transitions between the two curves of the blended surface. The *Coupling / Spine* tab displays as shown in Figure 4–10.

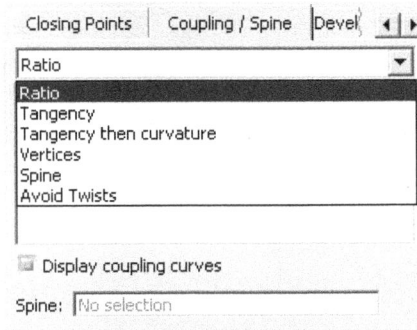

Figure 4–10

The following **Coupling** options are demonstrated using the references shown in Figure 4–11. The first and second curve have an equal number of vertices in each section. The First and Second continuity were set to tangency.

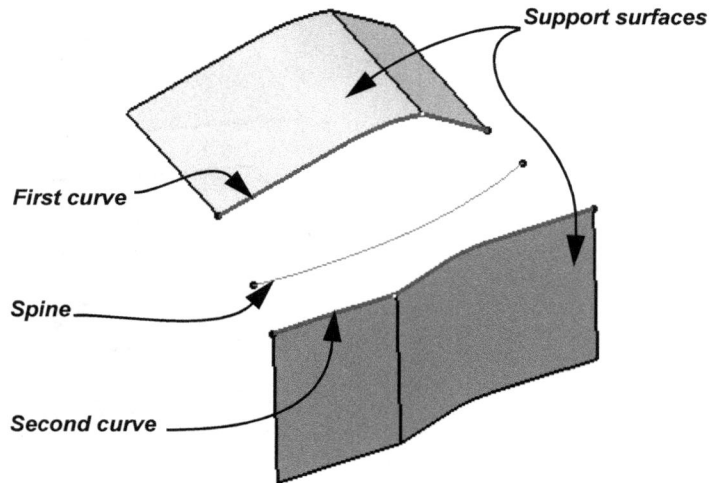

Support surfaces

First curve

Spine

Second curve

Figure 4–11

Ratio

Ratio is the default **Coupling** option. Coupling is computed by the percentage length of each vertice along each curve.

This option is recommended when non-equal numbers of vertices are present in the sketch sections.

In the example in Figure 4–12, each curve has three vertices. The end points of each curve are coupled together. The middle vertices couple to a location at the same percentage length along the curve.

First curve
vertices

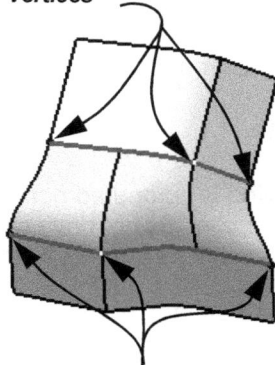

Second curve
vertices

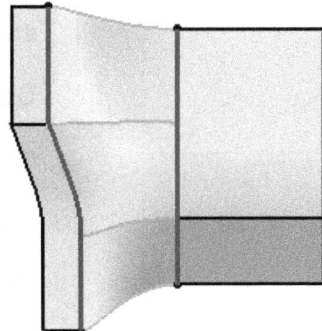

View from Z-axis

Figure 4–12

Tangency

If the blend sections have the same number of tangency discontinuity points, these points are coupled together between sections.

The blend using **Tangency coupling** is shown in Figure 4–13.

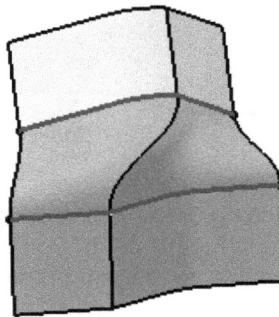

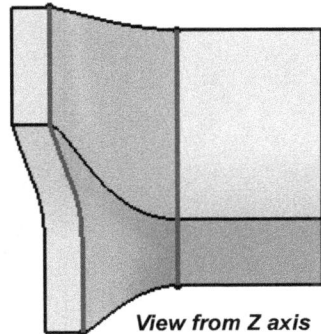

View from Z axis

Figure 4–13

Tangency then Curvature

If the blend sections have the same number of tangency and curvature discontinuity points, tangency discontinuity points are coupled together between sections, and then curvature discontinuity points are coupled together between sections.

Vertices

If the sections have the same number of vertices, these points are coupled together between sections.

Spine

Coupling is computed normal to the selected spine reference. The sections do not have to have the same number of vertices. If a spine is not selected, the first curve is used.

Imagine a plane normal to the spine at an arbitrary point along the spine. Where that plane intersects with First curve and Second curve, those locations are coupled in the blend.

A blend using the **Spine Coupling** option is shown in Figure 4–14.

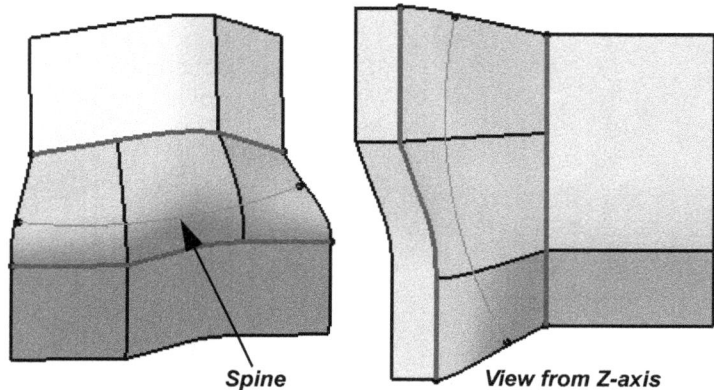

Spine　　*View from Z-axis*

Figure 4–14

Depending on the spine selected, a warning might display as shown in Figure 4–15. Sometimes it is not possible for the blend to maintain its tangent border continuity condition and remain normal to the selected spine curve. The feature can still be created, but CATIA gives a warning saying that the Blend feature is no longer in accordance with the tangent border continuity setting. The **Spine Coupling** overrides the continuity in this case.

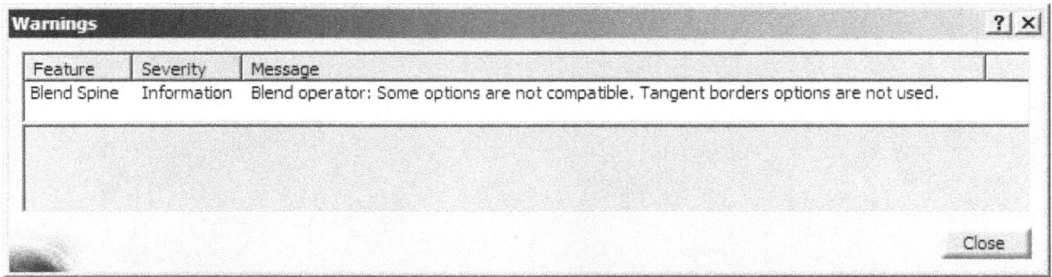

Feature	Severity	Message
Blend Spine	Information	Blend operator: Some options are not compatible. Tangent borders options are not used.

Figure 4–15

Avoid Twists

Coupling curves are created automatically to avoid twisted geometry. Manual coupling is not available when this option is selected. The Avoid Twists coupling type only works when the point continuity is selected from the *Basic* tab.

A comparison of three different **Coupling** options is shown in Figure 4–16.

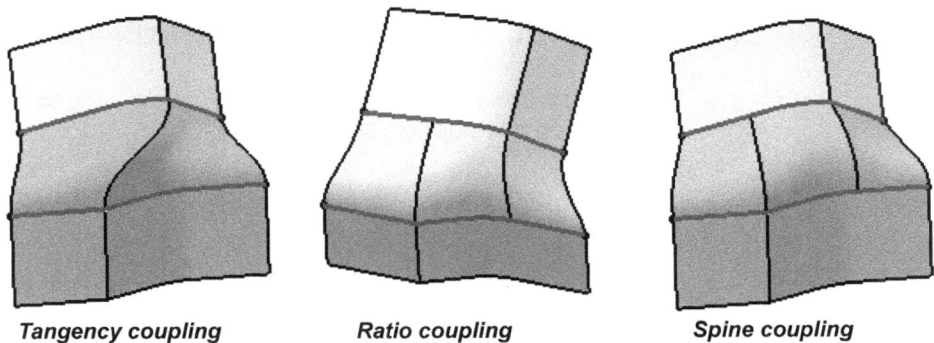

Tangency coupling   *Ratio coupling*   *Spine coupling*

Figure 4–16

Developable

Definition: Ruled Developable Surface

A ruled developable surface is a surface where a straight line lies at every point on the surface. This can be thought of as a straight line "sweeping" through space forming the surface. A ruled developable surface has a Gaussian maximum curvature of zero. A ruled developable surface can also be flattened without distortion.

Common examples of ruled surfaces are shown in Figure 4–17.

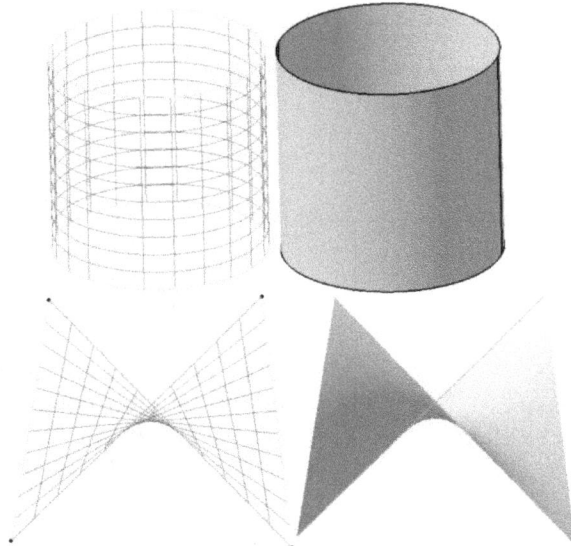

Figure 4–17

Creating a Ruled Developable Blend Surface

This functionality enables you to create a blend surface that is a ruled developable surface.

How To: Create a Ruled Developable Blend

1. Click ⬓ (Blend) to open the Blend Definition dialog box.
2. Select a curve from the model as the First curve reference.
3. Select a curve from the model as the Second curve reference as shown in Figure 4–18. Do not specify any support surfaces.

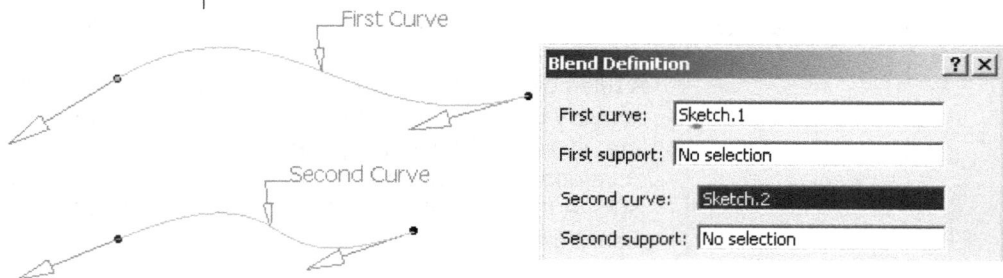

Figure 4–18

4. Ensure that the coupling is set to **Ratio**.
5. Select the *Developable* tab.
6. Select **Create a ruled developable surface**, as shown in Figure 4–19.

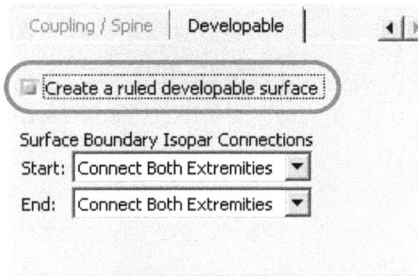

Figure 4–19

7. Optionally, you can adjust the Surface Boundary Isopar Connections. The Start drop-down list, as shown in Figure 4–20, represents the start or beginning of the resultant Blend surface.

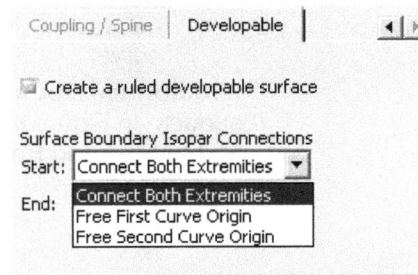

Figure 4–20

- **Connect Both Extremities:** Connects the end point of the First curve to the end point of the Second curve.
- **Free First Curve Origin:** The Blend surface does not necessarily have to begin at the start point of the First curve.
- **Free Second Curve Origin:** The Blend surface does not necessarily have to begin at the start point of the Second curve.

The End drop-down list, as shown in Figure 4–21, represents the start or beginning of the resultant Blend surface.

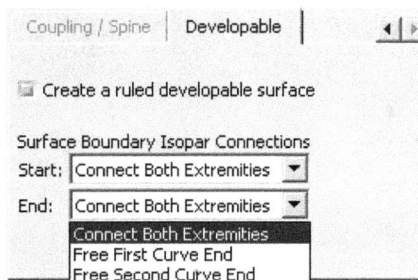

Figure 4–21

- **Connect Both Extremities:** Connects the end point of the First curve to the endpoint of the Second curve.
- **Free First Curve End:** The Blend surface does not necessarily have to stop at the end point of the First curve.
- **Free Second Curve End:** The Blend surface does not necessarily have to stop at the end point of the Second curve.

The **Surface Boundary Isopar Connection** options relimit the surface. In Figure 4–22, **Connect Both Extremities** is selected for the Start and End connections.

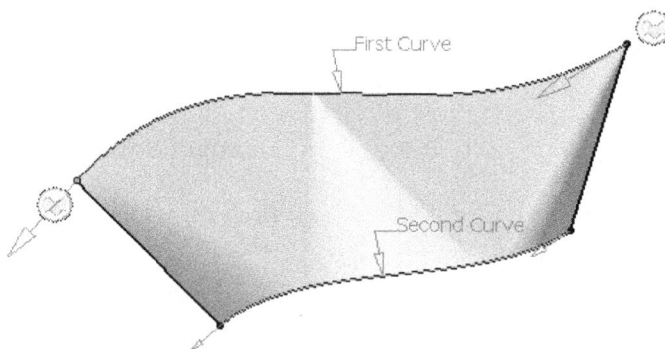

Figure 4–22

When one or more of the **Free Curve** options are used, the entire curve(s) is not used in the Blend, as shown in Figure 4–23. Note that the surface does not begin and end at the end points of the Second Curve.

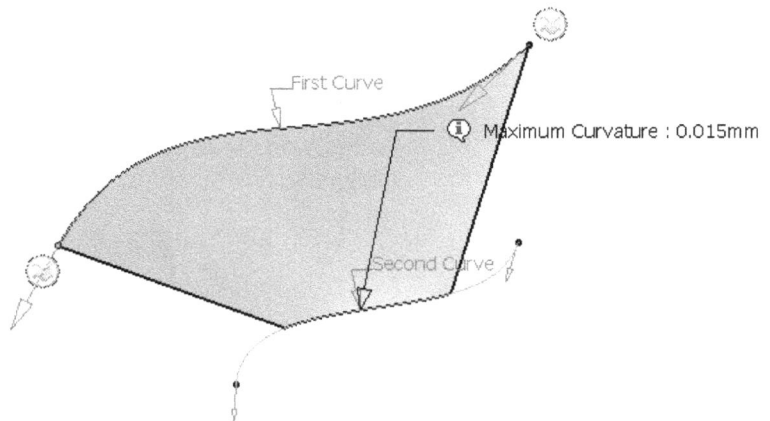

First Curve

ⓘ Maximum Curvature : 0.015mm

Second Curve

Figure 4–23

8. Complete the Blend surface. The resultant surface is a ruled developable surface.

Practice 4a

Simple Blend

Practice Objectives

- Use different tangent border options.
- Blend surface with spine coupling.

In this practice, you will create a blend between two extruded surfaces. A variety of blend attributes will be used demonstrate the effects on the resultant surface. The completed model displays as shown in Figure 4–24.

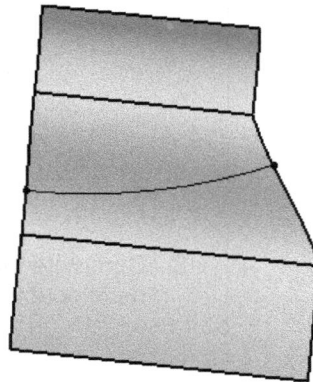

Figure 4–24

Task 1 - Open a part file.

1. Open **Simple_Blend_Start.CATPart**. The model displays as shown in Figure 4–25.

Figure 4–25

Task 2 - Create extruded surfaces.

1. Create an extruded surface using the following specifications:

    - *Profile:* **Sketch.1**
    - *Direction:* **yz plane**
    - *Limit 1:* **184mm**
    - *Limit 2:* **68mm**

    To ensure correct orientation of the extruded surface, **Limit 1** points in the positive X-direction, while **Limit 2** points in the negative X-direction. If this is not the case, reverse the direction of feature creation. The completed extrude displays as shown in Figure 4–26.

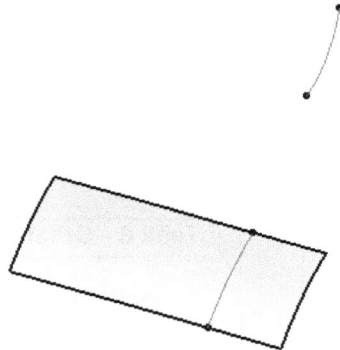

Figure 4–26

2. Create another extruded surface using the following specifications:

    - *Profile:* **Sketch.2**
    - *Direction:* **yz plane**
    - *Limit 1:* **184mm**
    - *Limit 2:* **0mm**

Similar to creating **Extrude.1**, **Limit 1** points in the negative X-direction. Reverse the direction of feature creation as required. The completed extrude displays as shown in Figure 4–27.

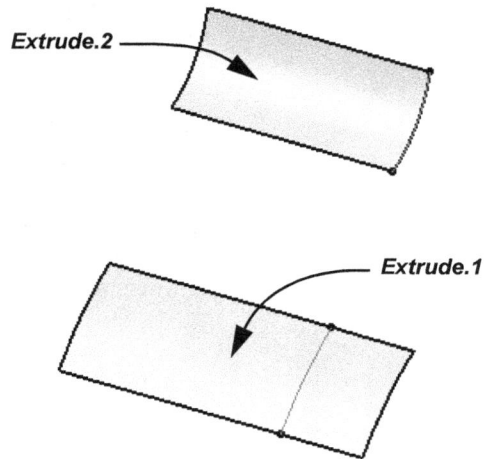

Extrude.2

Extrude.1

Figure 4–27

Task 3 - Create curves for blend.

1. Hide **Sketch.1** and **Sketch.2**.

2. Extract the edges as shown in Figure 4–28.

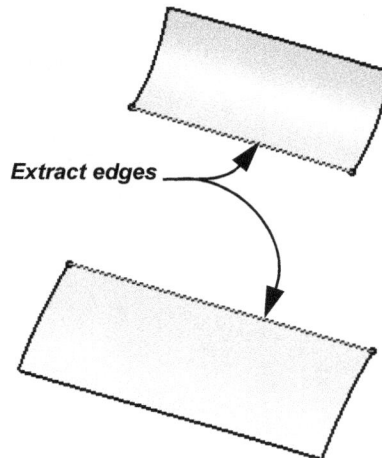

Extract edges

Figure 4–28

3. Rename the features, as shown in Figure 4–29. The extracted curves are used in a blend created in the next task.

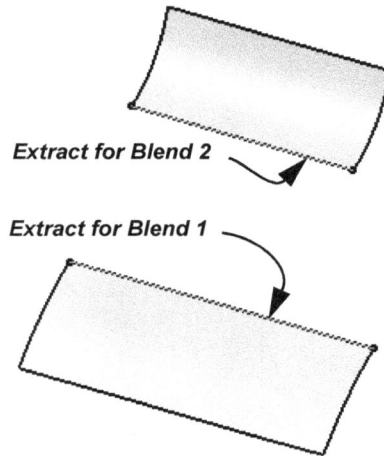

Extract for Blend 2

Extract for Blend 1

Figure 4–29

4. Create a spine curve using the two newly created extracted curves. The completed spine displays as shown in Figure 4–30.

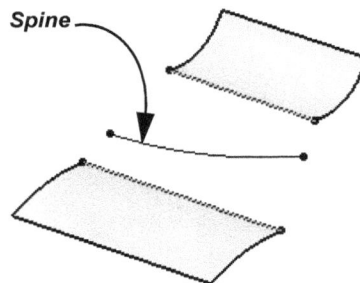

Spine

Figure 4–30

5. Hide **Spine.1**.

Task 4 - Create a blend surface.

1. Click (Blend).

2. Select **Extract for Blend 1** as the first curve reference.

3. Select **Extrude.1** as the first support.

4. Select **Extract for Blend 2** as the second curve reference.

5. Select **Extrude.2** as the second support. The model displays as shown in Figure 4–31.

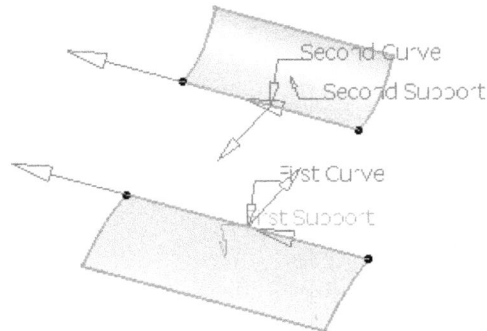

Figure 4–31

6. In the *Basic* tab, ensure that the first and second continuity options are set to **Tangency**, as shown in Figure 4–32.

7. By default, **Both extremities** is selected in the First and Second tangent borders drop-down list, as shown in Figure 4–32. This means that the start and end boundaries of the blend are tangent to the support surface boundaries.

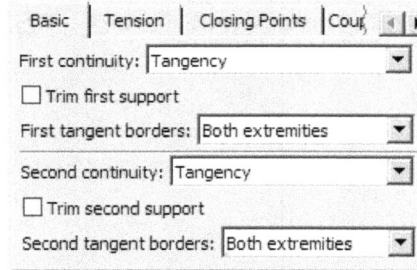

Figure 4–32

8. Preview the blend. The model displays as shown in Figure 4–33. The start and end extremities for the first and second curve of the blend are tangent to the support surfaces.

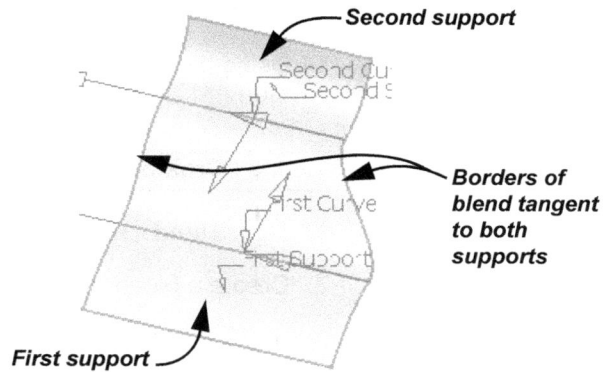

Figure 4–33

9. Select **End extremity only** in the First tangent borders drop-down list.

10. Preview the blend. The model displays as shown in Figure 4–34. The Start extremity of the first curve is not tangent to the border of the first support.

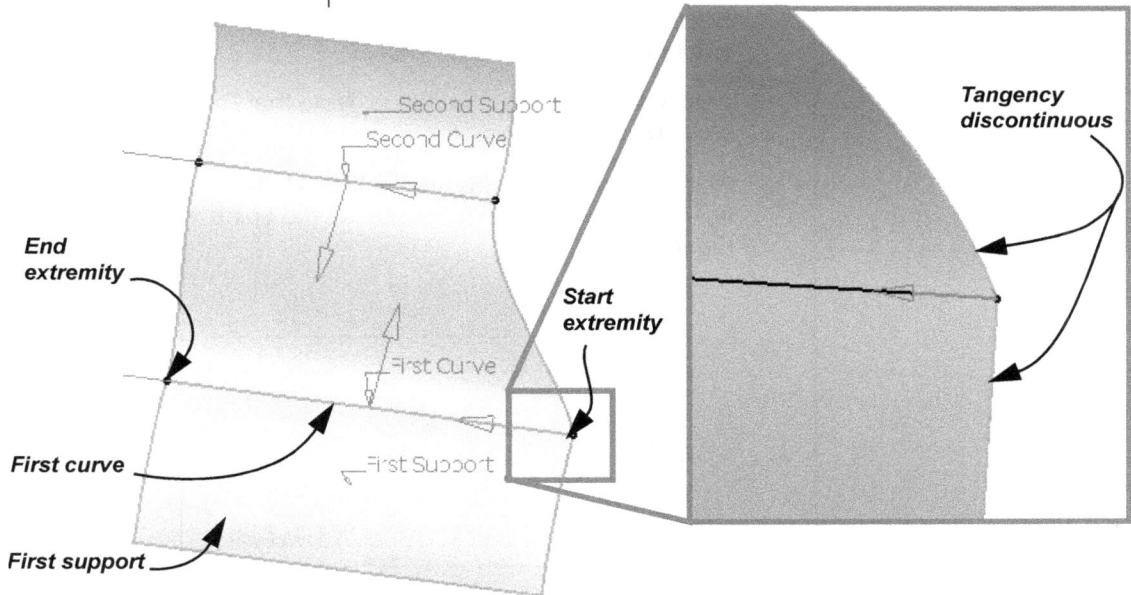

Figure 4–34

11. Return the **First tangent borders** option to **Both extremities**.

12. Complete the blend.

13. Rename the feature as **Blend - ratio coupling**.

14. Using the graphic properties, color the newly created blend blue.

Task 5 - Create a second blend.

---

1. Hide **Blend - ratio coupling**, then show **Spine.1**.

2. Create a blend using the following specifications:

   - *First curve:* **Extract for Blend 1**
   - *First support:* **Extrude.1**
   - *Second curve:* **Extract for Blend 2**
   - *Second support:* **Extrude.2**

   After the selection of the references, leave the Blend Definition dialog box open.

3. In the *Basic* tab, ensure that the First and Second continuity are set to **Tangency**.

4. Set the First and Second tangent borders to **Both extremities** if not already done.

5. Select the *Coupling / Spine* tab. Note that **Ratio** is the default coupling option.

6. Select **Spine** in the drop-down list. CATIA automatically selects the first curve reference as the spine, as shown in Figure 4–35.

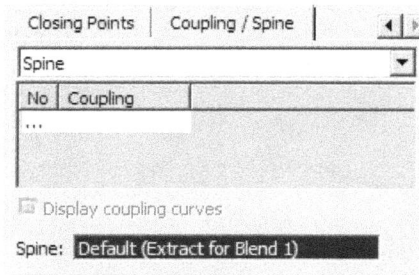

Figure 4–35

7. Select **Spine.1** as the spine reference. This spine curve dictates how the blend is coupled.

8. Preview the blend.

9. The following Warning dialog box opens as shown in Figure 4–36. Remember that the tangent border setting was set to both extremities, meaning that at the start and ends of the blend, the boundaries are tangent to the support boundaries. This warning says that with the selected spine for spine coupling, the tangency borders setting cannot be fulfilled.

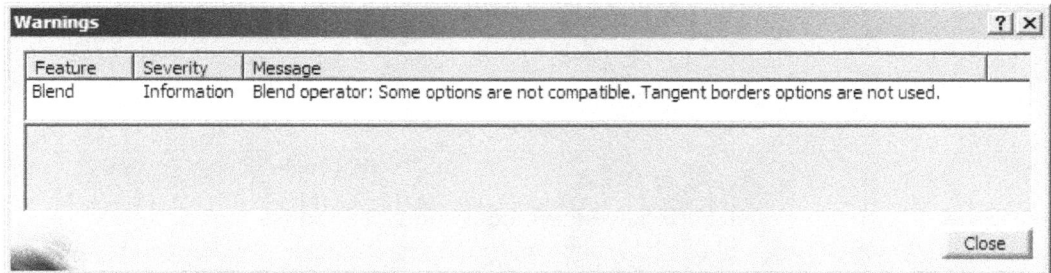

Feature	Severity	Message
Blend	Information	Blend operator: Some options are not compatible. Tangent borders options are not used.

Figure 4–36

10. Close the Warning dialog box. The model displays as shown in Figure 4–37. The blend borders are no longer tangent to the support borders.

Figure 4–37 has been altered to clean up the display.

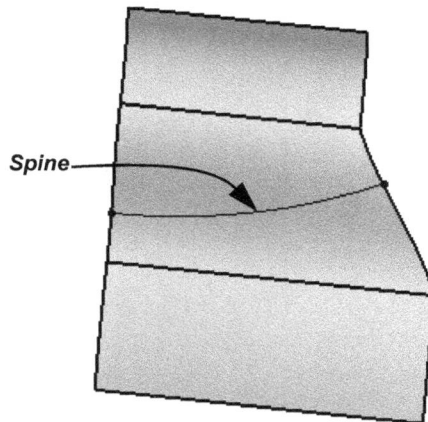

Figure 4–37

11. Complete the blend.

12. Rename the feature as **Blend - Spine coupling**.

13. Using the graphic properties color the blend green.

14. A comparison between the two blend surfaces created in the practice is shown in Figure 4–38.

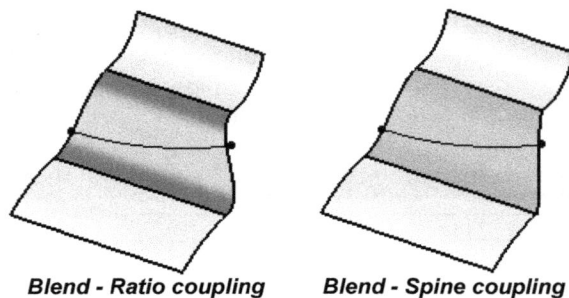

Blend - Ratio coupling   **Blend - Spine coupling**

Figure 4–38

15. Save the model and close the file.

Practice 4b | Diablo

Practice Objective

- Create a complex blend.

A diablo is a small area of flat geometry amongst curved and more complex geometry. The purpose of the flat surface is to help fasten the part when assembled. A blend will be used to transition from the curved surfaces to a flat surface in the model. The completed model will display as shown in Figure 4–39.

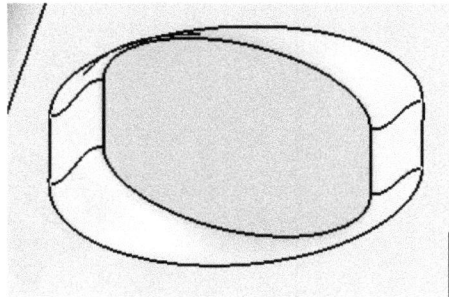

Figure 4–39

Task 6 - Open a part file.

1. Open **Diablo_Blend_Start.CATPart**. The model displays as shown in Figure 4–40. It does not have any flat surfaces.

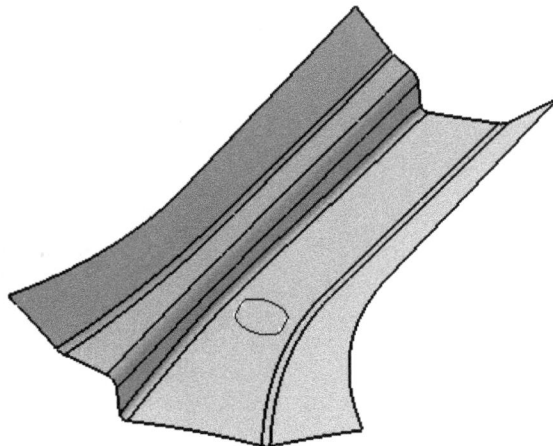

Figure 4–40

Task 7 - Create reference geometry for blend.

A flat surface must be built to meet the design intent. In this task a sketch will be used to create a surface and wireframe elements.

1. Create a fill surface using **Sketch.5**. No support surfaces are required. The completed fill displays as shown in Figure 4–41.

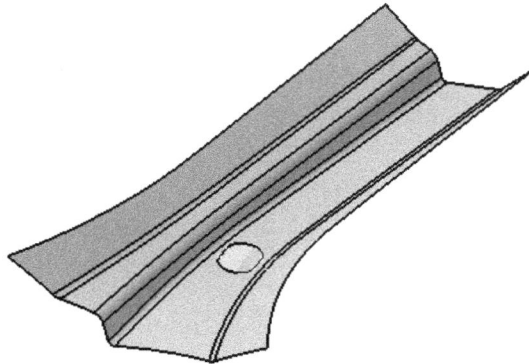

Figure 4–41

This fill surface serves as a flat area on the part. When assembling this part, a fastener is placed in the flat area of the part.

2. Project **Sketch.5** onto **EdgeFillet.2** using **Along a direction** as the projection type. Select the Z Component as the direction reference. The completed project curve displays as shown in Figure 4–42.

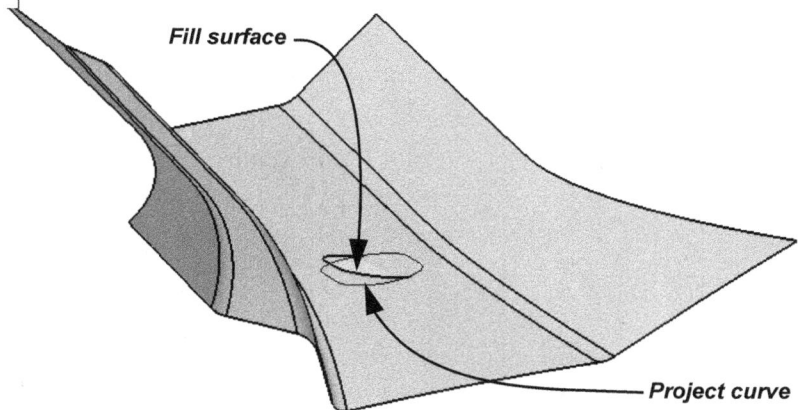

Fill surface

Project curve

Figure 4–42

3. Create a Parallel curve using the following specifications:

   - *Curve:* **Project.1**
   - *Support:* **EdgeFillet.2**
   - *Constant:* **2mm**

   Ensure that the arrow representing the offset points to the outside of **Project.1**. The completed curve displays as shown in Figure 4–43. This parallel curve serves as a curve reference in a future blend operation.

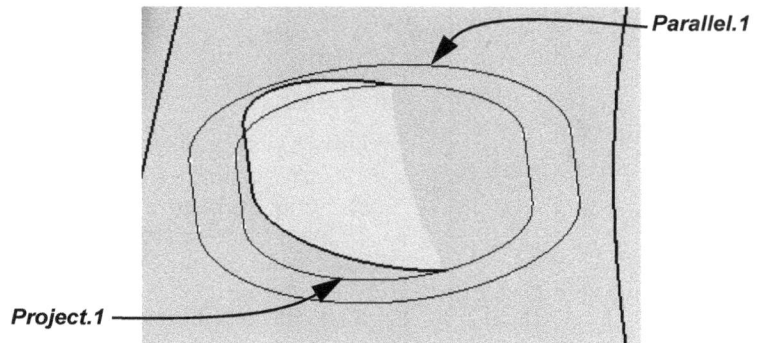

Figure 4–43

Task 8 - Create a blend.

In this task, a blend will be created between **Sketch.5** and **Parallel.1**.

1. Hide **Project.1**. This curve is no longer used. However, because it is referenced by **Parallel.1** it cannot be deleted.

2. Create a blend using the following specifications:

   - *First curve:* **Sketch.5**
   - *First support:* **Fill.1**
   - *Second curve:* **Parallel.1**
   - *Second support:* **EdgeFillet.2**

3. In the *Basic* tab, ensure that **Trim first support** and **Trim second support** are selected.

4. Select **Tangency then Curvature** in the drop-down list in the *Coupling* tab.

5. Complete the Blend feature.

6. Hide **Parallel.1**.

7. The model displays as shown in Figure 4–44.

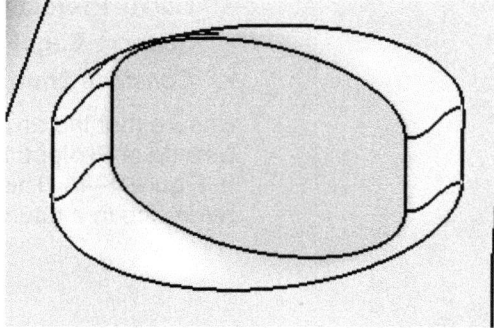

Figure 4–44

If the blend does not display as shown in the image, examine the arrows in the Blend feature. Remember that the arrows can only be seen when editing the feature. One set of arrows dictates tangency direction. The other set dictates the order in which the coupling is created.

8. Save the model and close the file.

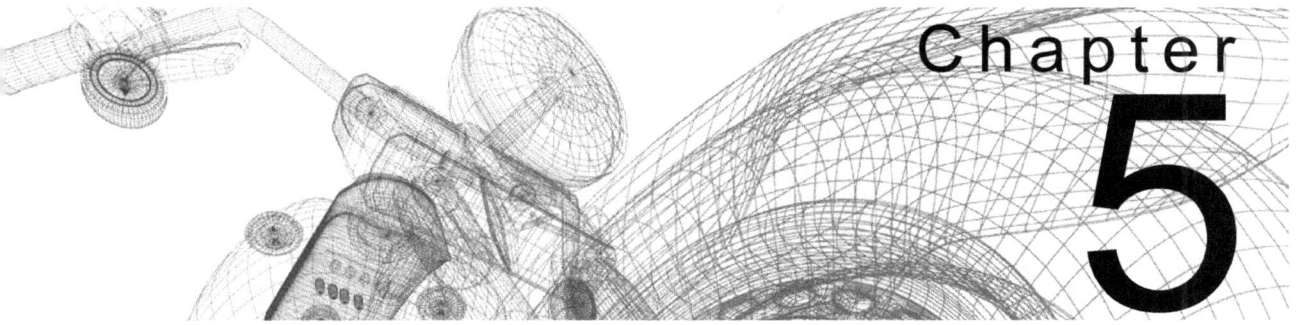

Adaptive Sweeps

The Adaptive Sweep tool creates surface geometry based on a profile whose dimensions can be adjusted as it sweeps along a guide curve. This feature enables greater control over the profile than a regular swept surface.

Learning Objective in this Chapter

- Understand the creation and elements required to create an Adaptive Sweep.

5.1 Adaptive Sweep

The Adaptive Swept surface feature is similar to an Explicit profile swept surface. The feature sweeps a profile along the length of a guide curve to define the surface geometry. The adaptive surface enables you to define unique dimensional values for the profile at any position along the length of the guide curve. An example is shown in Figure 5–1.

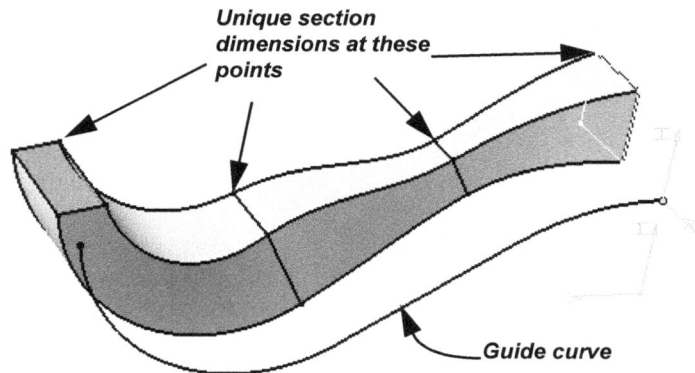

Unique section dimensions at these points

Guide curve

Figure 5–1

General Steps

Use the following steps to create an Adaptive Sweep surface:

1. Start the creation of the Adaptive Sweep feature.
2. Select a guiding curve.
3. Select or create a sketch.
4. Control the section dimensions.
5. Specify optional elements.
6. Complete the feature.

Step 1 - Start the creation of the Adaptive Sweep feature.

Click (Adaptive Sweep) in the Surfaces toolbar. The Adaptive Sweep dialog box opens as shown in Figure 5–2.

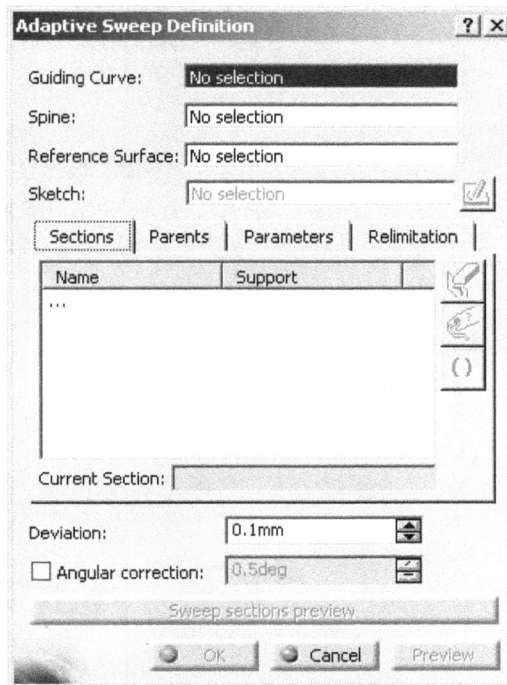

Figure 5–2

Step 2 - Select a guiding curve.

Similar to a conventional swept surface, the guiding curve determines the path that the sketch is swept along. The section of an Adaptive sweep must be perpendicular to the guiding curve at all points. The curve can be an existing wireframe element, sketch, or edge. Alternatively, the curve can be created on the fly.

The Reference Surface is an optional element that defines the axis system in which the adaptive surface is created.

Step 3 - Select or create a sketch.

The sketch is swept along the guiding curve and determines the shape of the resulting surface. If a sketch is already created, it can be selected from the model or specification tree.

To create a sketch, right-click in the *Sketch* field in the Adaptive Sweep dialog box and select **Create Sketch**. The Sketch Creation for Adaptive Sweep dialog box opens as shown in Figure 5–3.

Figure 5–3

Select a point to determine the support plane. The support plane for the sketch is selected as a plane perpendicular to the guiding curve at the selected point. Additionally, geometry can be selected as construction elements for the sketch. The construction elements are created by intersecting the selected entities with the sketch support. The sketch plane orients accordingly and the section can be created.

If the sketch is made coincident to any existing curves, they act as guide curves and control the shape of the swept surface. An example is shown in , where the section is coincident with the guide curve.

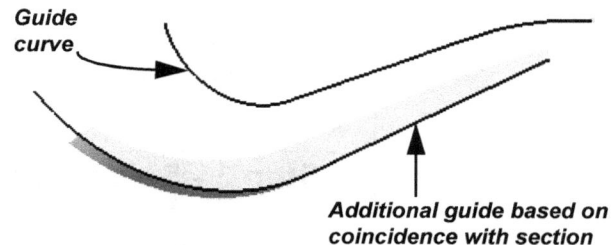

Figure 5–4

Step 4 - Control the section dimensions.

The power of the **Adaptive Sweep** comes from its ability to modify the value of section dimensions at any point along the length of the guiding curve. To control the section dimensions, select the *Parents* tab and select points on the guiding curve at which the section dimensions are to be modified. The section displays at each point as it is selected, as shown in Figure 5–5.

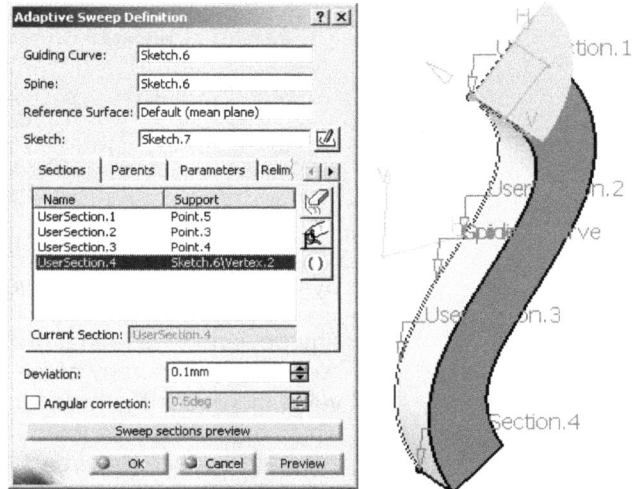

Figure 5–5

Select the *Parameters* tab, as shown in Figure 5–6.

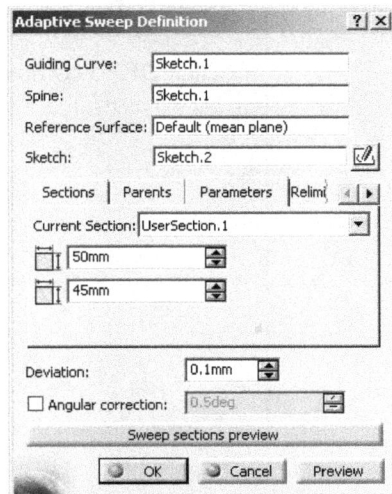

Figure 5–6

Select a section in the drop-down list and enter new dimensional values. This can also be done by modifying the dimensions on the model.

Step 5 - Specify optional elements.

The **Spine** option can be used to specify a spine, as shown in Figure 5–7.

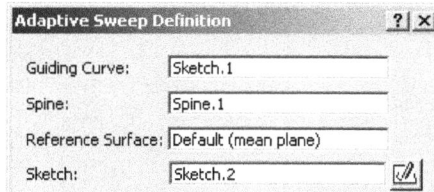

Figure 5–7

By default, the guiding curve is selected as the spine.

The deviation value that displays at the bottom of each tab controls the accuracy of the adaptive sweep surface. A lower value increases the number of points along the guiding curve at which the surface geometry is calculated. This creates a more accurate surface feature while increasing calculation and update time.

Step 6 - Complete the feature.

Click **OK** to complete the feature.

Practice 5a	# Adaptive Sweep Surfaces I

Practice Objective

* Create adaptive sweep surfaces with defined sections.

In this practice, you will use features to create an adaptive sweep. The design intent is for the funnel to taper inward from the intake to the outlet at the end of the guide curve. You will create several points along the guide curve and modify the section properties of the adaptive sweep at each point. The completed model displays as shown in Figure 5–8.

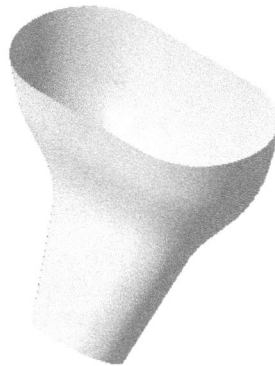

Figure 5–8

Your task is to create the surfaces that define an angled funnel. You will start with a sketch that defines the section of the intake and a guide curve that defines the direction of the funnel, as shown in Figure 5–9.

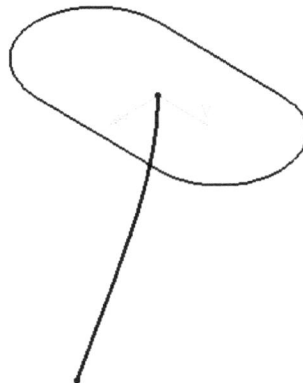

Figure 5–9

Task 1 - Open the part file containing the profile and guide curve.

1. Open **AdaptSweep1.CATPart**.

2. Double-click on the Profile sketch under the PartBody and view the existing dimensions (these are later modified at sections along the sweep).

3. Exit the Sketcher workbench.

Task 2 - Create an Adaptive Sweep feature with the profile and guide curve.

1. Click ![icon] (Adaptive Sweep).

2. Select the following:

   • *Guiding Curve:* **Guide**
   • *Sketch:* **Profile**

   The dialog box opens as shown in Figure 5–10. Only one section is defined in the *Sections* tab. This section is located at the start of the guiding curve where it meets the sketch.

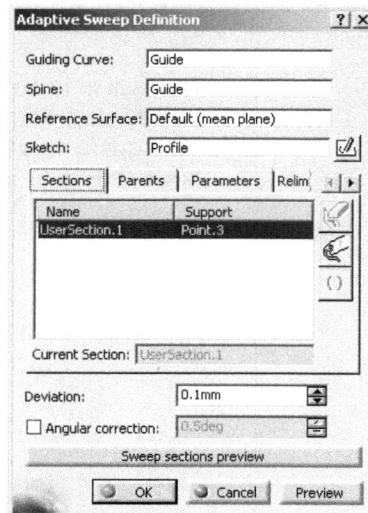

Figure 5–10

3. Click **OK**. The feature displays as shown in Figure 5–11.

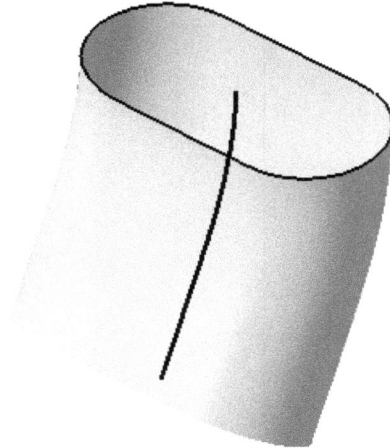

Figure 5–11

Note that without defining any additional sections, the adaptive sweep is the same as an explicit-type sweep along a guide curve.

Task 3 - Create points to define sections along the adaptive sweep.

To modify the section properties along the adaptive sweep, you will create several points along the guide curve that will be used to define sections.

1. Hide **Adaptive sweep.1**.

2. Double-click on (Point) to create multiple points.

3. Define the first point as follows:

    • *Point type:* **On Curve**
    • *Curve:* **Guide**
    • Select **Ratio of curve length**.
    • *Ratio:* **0.2**

4. Click **OK**.

5. Create another point on the Guide curve at a *Ratio* of **0.6**. The two points display as shown in Figure 5–12.

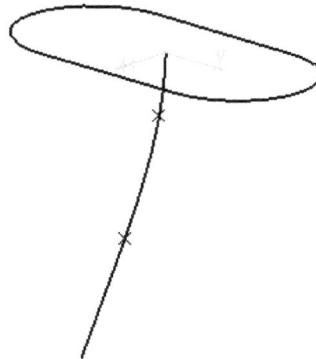

Figure 5–12

6. Click ▪ (Point) to deactivate the **Point** tool.

Task 4 - Create sections using the defined points.

1. Show **Adaptive sweep.1**.

2. Double-click on **Adaptive sweep.1**.

3. Select the point you created at ratio 0.2 (a new section is created in the *Sections*).

4. Select the point you created at ratio 0.6.

5. Select the end point of the Guide curve to add sections at those points as shown in Figure 5–13.

Select the point at 0.6 and the end point of Guide curve

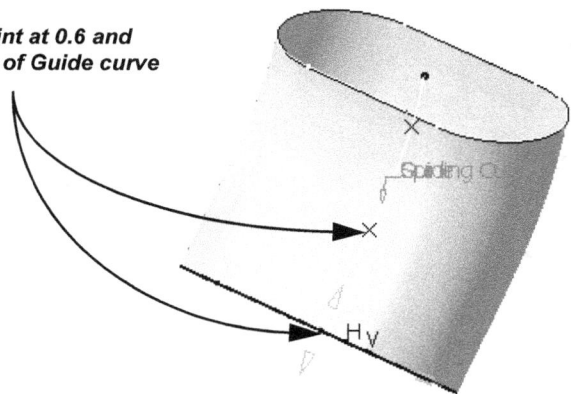

Figure 5–13

The dialog box opens as shown in Figure 5–14.

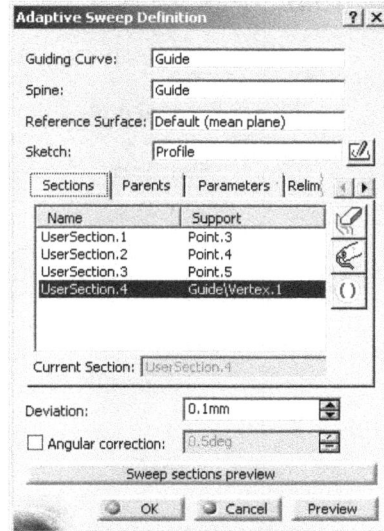

Figure 5–14

Task 5 - Modify the properties of the sections.

At each defined section, the dimensions in the sketch can be modified to capture the design intent.

1. Select the *Parameters* tab.

2. Select **UserSection.2** in the Current Section drop-down list, as shown in Figure 5–15.

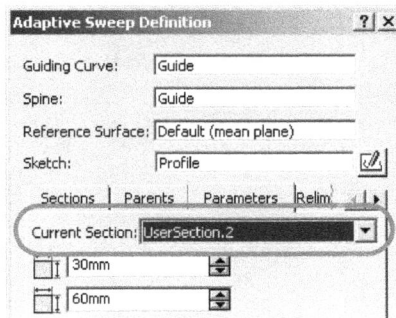

Figure 5–15

Design Considerations

The first dimension (30mm) represents the radius of the Profile arc, and the second dimension (60mm) represents the length of the Profile side. The dimensional changes for each new section are described in the following table.

3. Make the following changes:

Section	Was 30	Was 60
UserSection.2	28	55
UserSection.3	15	30
UserSection.4	15	10

4. Click **OK**. The model displays as shown in Figure 5–16.

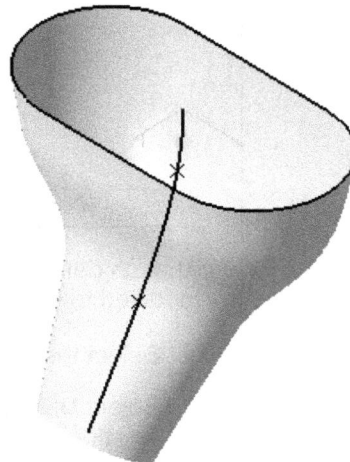

Figure 5–16

5. Save the file and close the window.

Practice 5b

Adaptive Sweep Surfaces II

Practice Objective

*   Create adaptive sweep surfaces that follow path surfaces.

In this practice, you will create another funnel using a guide curve and a top profile. Instead of defining several sections and modifying the section properties, you are given an additional guiding curve that the surface must follow along its length. This can be accomplished with an Adaptive Sweep surface feature. The design intent requires the surface to be symmetrical in the Y-direction. The completed model displays as shown in Figure 5–17.

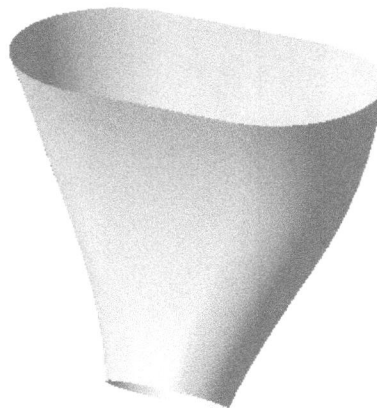

Figure 5–17

Task 1 - Open the part file containing the profile and guide curve.

1. Open **AdaptSweep2.CATPart**.

Task 2 - Import the path curve.

1. Open **Path.CATPart**. The path curve is defined by a spline named Path.

2. Copy **Geometrical Set.1** from the specification tree.

3. Activate the **AdaptSweep2.CATPart** window.

4. Paste into **Geometrical Set.1**.

Task 3 - Mirror the path curve to create a symmetric copy.

The Profile sketch will be constrained to both copies of the curve to maintain symmetry when the adaptive sweep surface is created.

1. Click ▢ (Symmetry).

2. Select the following:

   • *Element:* **Path**
   • *Reference:* **zx plane**

3. Click **OK**. The model displays as shown in Figure 5–18.

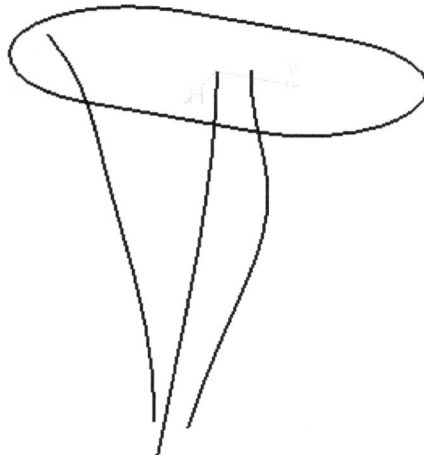

Figure 5–18

Task 4 - Constrain the sketch to the path curves.

Two vertices of the section must be constrained to the imported paths. Intersect 3D elements will be used to capture design intent.

1. Edit the Profile sketch.

2. Click ▣ (Intersect 3D Elements).

3. Select one of the path curves. A point is created representing the intersection of the path curve and the sketch plane.

4. Repeat to create an intersection point for the other path curve.

5. Constrain the vertex and the intersection shown in Figure 5–19 to be coincident.

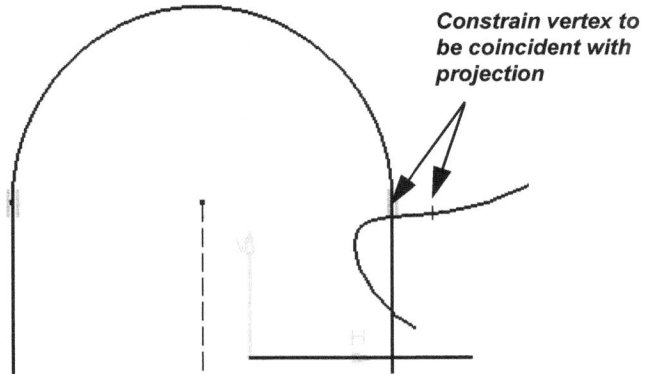

Constrain vertex to be coincident with projection

Figure 5–19

6. Constrain the vertex and intersection shown in Figure 5–20 to be coincident.

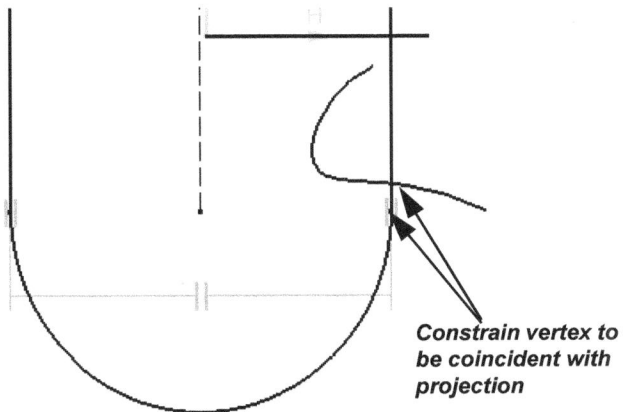

The specification tree can be used to select the intersection point if you cannot select it in the geometry.

Constrain vertex to be coincident with projection

Figure 5–20

7. Exit the Sketcher workbench.

Task 5 - Create an Adaptive Sweep feature with the profile and guide curve.

1. Click ▨ (Adaptive Sweep).

2. Select the following:

   - *Guiding Curve:* **Guide**
   - *Sketch:* **Profile**

3. Click **OK**. The Adaptive Sweep feature automatically follows the two Path curves (due to the coincidence constraints). The model displays as shown in Figure 5–21.

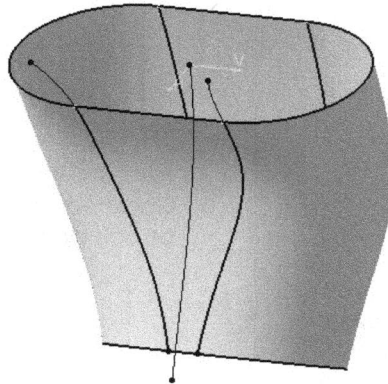

Figure 5–21

4. Save the file and close the window.

Practice 5c

Rear View Mirror

Practice Objectives

- Create an Adaptive Sweep surface feature.
- Create a Fill surface feature.

In this practice, you will create the surfaces for the casing of a rear view mirror using adaptive sweep and fill features. The base geometry of the profile is provided. The completed model displays as shown in Figure 5–22.

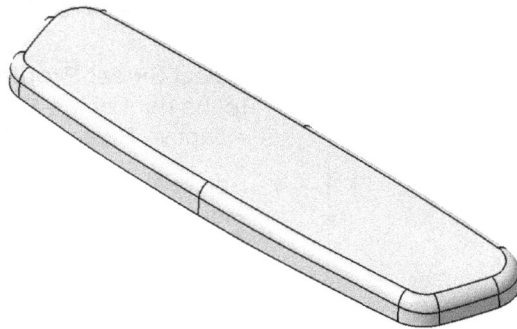

Figure 5–22

Task 1 - Open a part file.

1. Open **RearViewMirror.CATPart**. The model displays as shown in Figure 5–23.

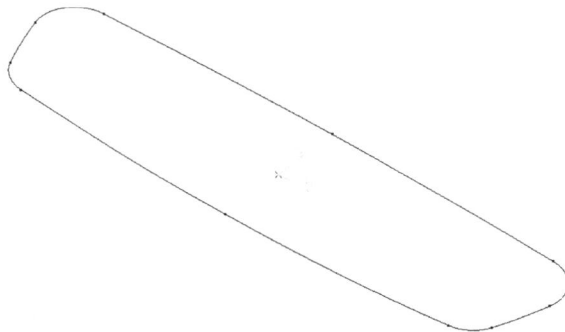

Figure 5–23

2. Ensure that model units are set to **mm**.

Task 2 - Create an Adaptive Sweep surface feature.

In this task, the profile to be swept is created contextually in the Adaptive Sweep Definition dialog box. Using this sketched profile, the side surface of the rear view mirror cover will be created and controlled by an Adaptive Sweep feature that follows the SweepProfile curve.

1. Ensure that the **Side Profile** geometrical set is active.

2. Click 🔧 (Adaptive Sweep) to open the Adaptive Sweep Definition dialog box.

3. Select **SweepProfile** as the *Guiding Curve*. Click 🖉 located to the right of the *Sketch* field to open the Sketch Creation for Adaptive Sweep dialog box.

4. Select the point named **AdaptiveSweepPoint** as shown in Figure 5–24 as the optional construction element and click **OK** to enter the Sketcher workbench.

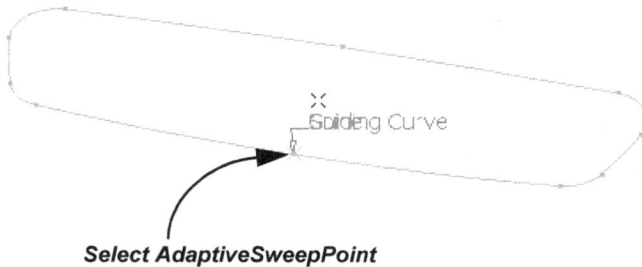

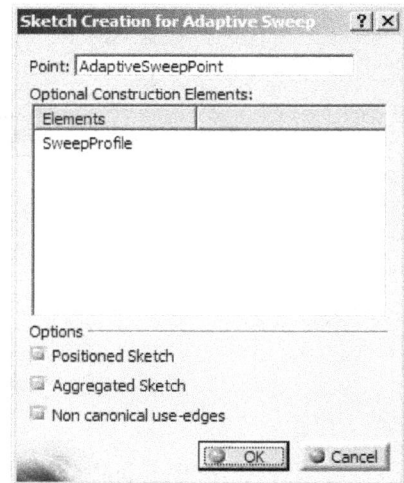

Select AdaptiveSweepPoint

Figure 5–24

Design Considerations

Using **Sketch Creation for Adaptive Sweep** is advantageous because it ensures that the swept sketch remains normal to the sweep profile, regardless of the profile orientation. Also, creating a sketch using this tool is faster than manually creating a positioned sketch, and the resultant sketch is aggregated (embedded) under the main Adaptive Sweep feature node, helping to reduce the visible feature count in the specification tree.

5. Create the geometry and constraints shown in Figure 5–25 in the Sketcher workbench.

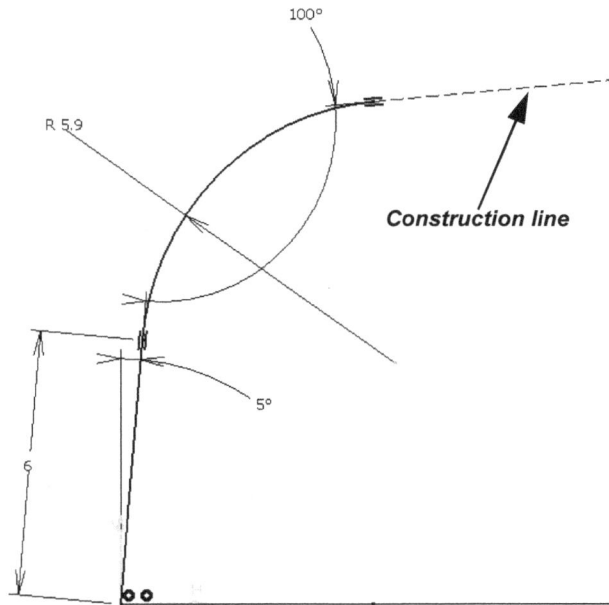

Figure 5–25

6. Exit the Sketcher workbench.

7. In the Adaptive Sweep Definition dialog box, select the vertices in the SweepProfile sketch to create new sections as shown in Figure 5–26.

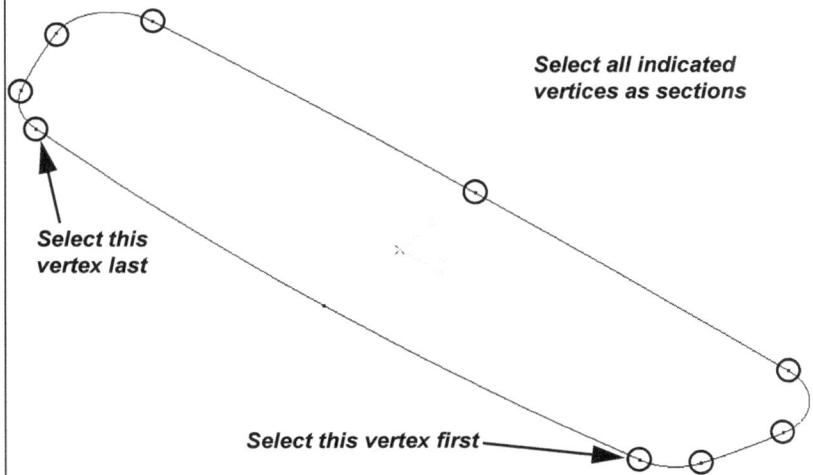

Figure 5–26

**Design
Considerations**

Sections of an Adaptive Sweep surface feature are defined by points along the guide curve. There is no minimum requirement or maximum allowance of cross-sections. The constraint parameters of the swept profile sketch (and thus the shape of the sweep) can be modified at each section in the Adaptive Sweep Definition dialog box.

The Adaptive Sweep Definition dialog box opens as shown in Figure 5–27.

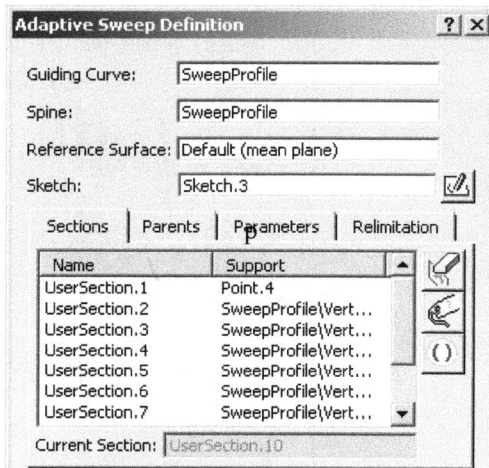

Figure 5–27

8. Select the *Parameters* tab in the Adaptive Sweep Definition dialog box as shown in Figure 5–28. Modify the 6mm value for each section. Depending on the dimension creation order, the 6mm value might display in a different row in the dialog box.

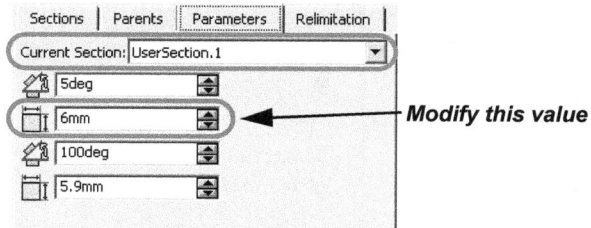

Figure 5–28

Select each section in the Current Section drop-down list and replace the value shown in Figure 5–28 with the values provided as follows:

UserSection.#	Value
1, 6	8mm
2, 5, 7, 10	7mm
3, 4, 8, 9	6mm

9. Select the *Relimitation* tab. Clear the **Relimited on start section** and **Relimited on end section** options.

Traditionally, adaptive sweep surface guide curves are open profiles. By default, the Adaptive Sweep function automatically computes and attaches relimitation planes normal to the curve at the end points of an open profile. Because SweepProfile is a closed profile, both the **Start** and **End Relimitation** options must be disabled; if they remain enabled, CATIA computes the default start and end planes, producing a gap in the swept surface.

10. Click **OK** to complete the Adaptive Sweep surface feature.

11. Rename the Adaptive Sweep feature as **SideSurf** and hide **SweepProfile**. The model displays as shown in Figure 5–29.

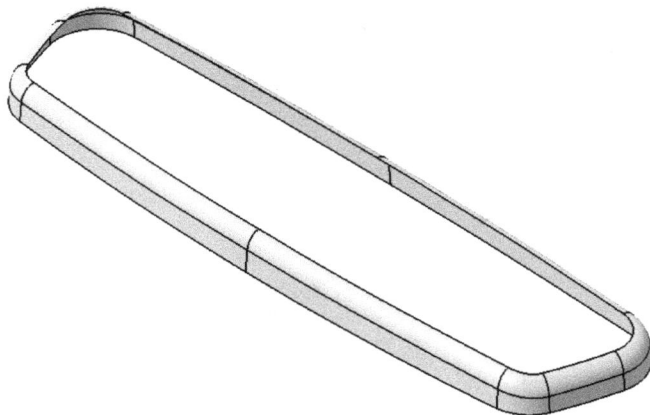

Figure 5–29

Task 3 - Create a Fill Surface feature.

To completely seal the rear view mirror cover, a Fill feature is added to the adaptive sweep created in Task 2. Supports are used to enforce curvature continuity in the surface, which ensures that the part will be manufacturable.

1. Extract the edge shown in Figure 5–30. Use the **Point continuity** propagation type.

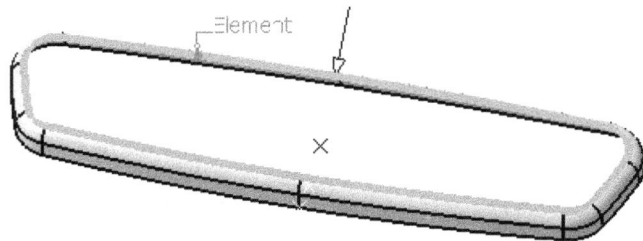

Figure 5–30

2. Click (Fill) to open the Fill Surface Definition dialog box.

3. Select the extracted curve created in Step 1 as the curve reference.

4. Select **SideSurf** as the support as shown in Figure 5–31.

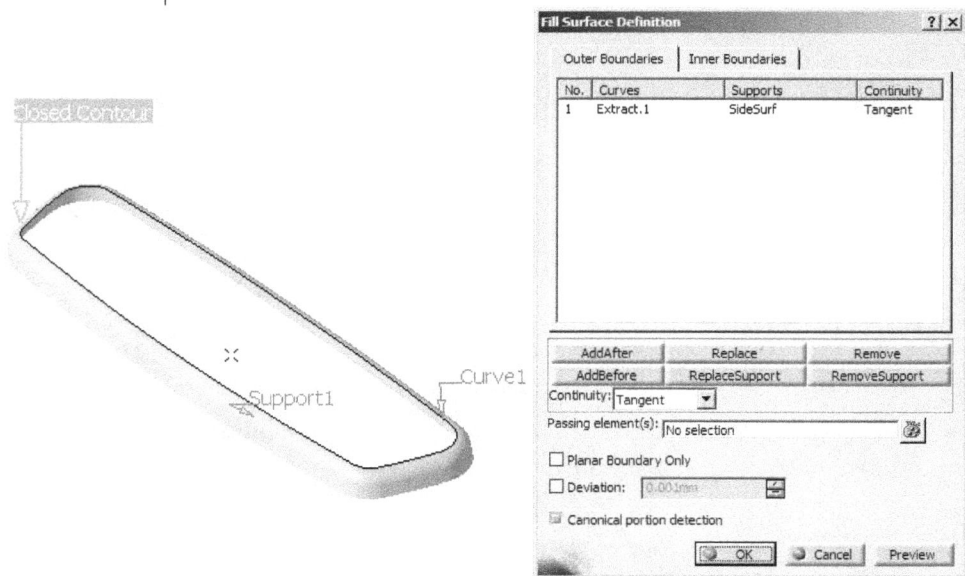

Figure 5–31

5. Click **OK** to complete the Fill surface feature.

6. Rename the fill surface as **TopFill**.

Task 4 - Create a Join feature.

To prepare the part for downstream operations, such as Fill or Shell features, all of the surfaces comprising the rear view mirror cover are joined to form a single entity.

1. Create a join feature using the **TopFill** and **SideSurf** surfaces.

2. Rename the Join feature as **RearViewMirrorSurf**. The completed model displays as shown in Figure 5–32.

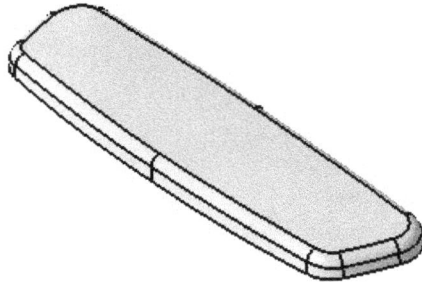

Figure 5–32

3. Save and close the file.

Practice 5d | Air Intake Tube

Practice Objectives

- Create an Adaptive Sweep surface feature.
- Create a Fill surface feature.

In this practice, you will create an air intake tube using the provided Tube Center curve and **Adaptive Sweep** command in the Surfaces toolbar. The Tube must past through the heat box and maintain a minimum clearance from the box of 1mm. The inside cross-section area of the Tube must be in a range of between **1200mm^2** to **1300mm^2**. The completed model displays as shown in Figure 5–33.

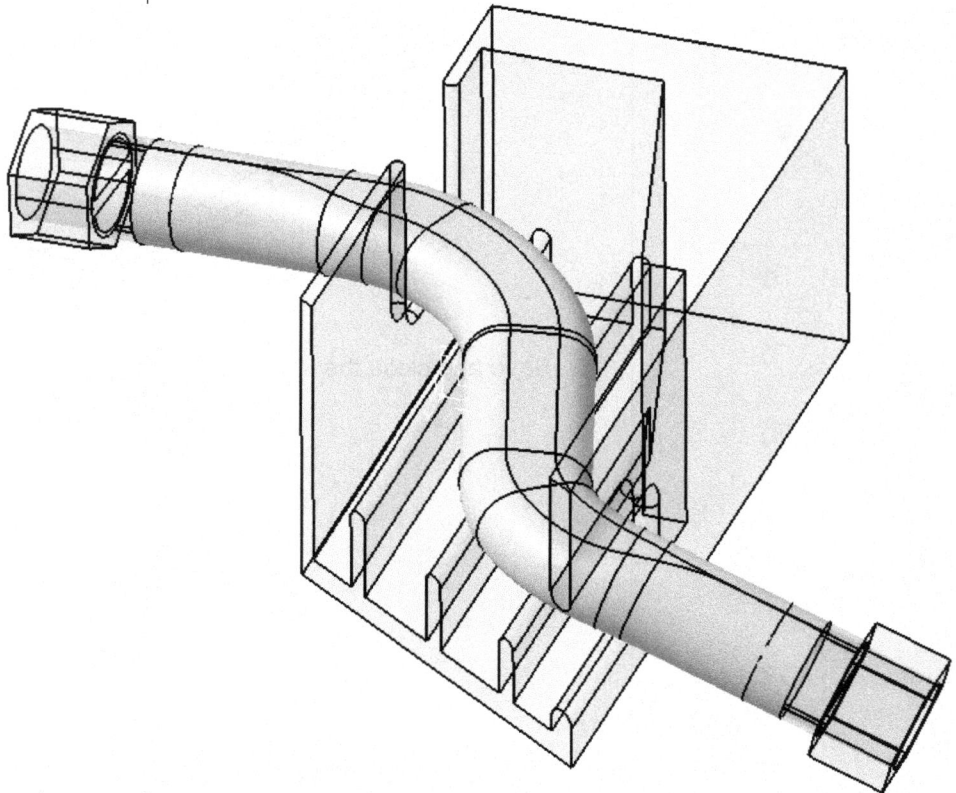

Figure 5–33

Task 1 - Open an assembly file.

1. Open **Tube-Box.CATProduct**. The assembly displays as shown in Figure 5–34.

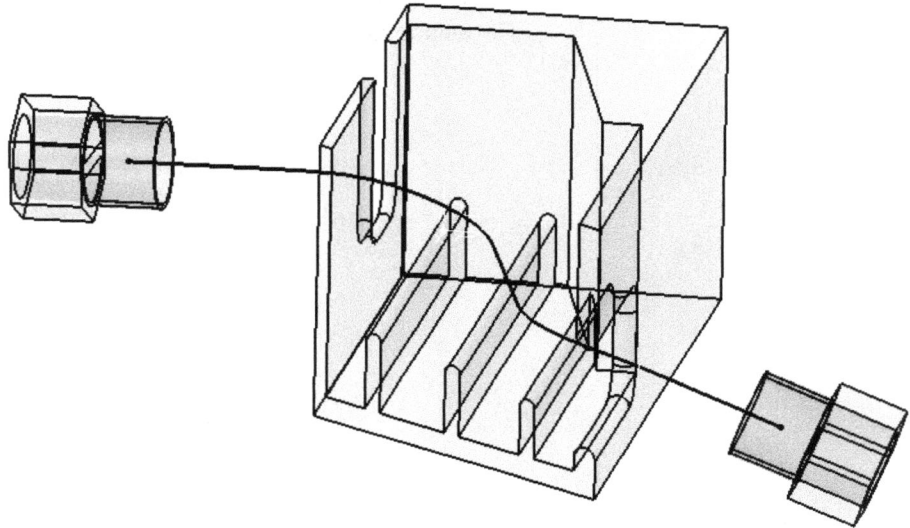

Figure 5–34

2. Ensure that the model units are set to millimeters (mm).

3. Hide the following parts:

   - **Heat Box**
   - **Input-Side**
   - **Output-Side**

4. Expand the specification tree under the part named Intake Tube. Double-click on **Geometrical Set.1** to activate the Intake Tube part.

5. Ensure that the active workbench is Generative Shape Design.

Task 2 - Create points.

In this task you will create points along the length of Tube Center. These will control the location where the adaptive sweep will be modified later in the practice.

1. Click [icon] (Points and Planes Repetition) in the Wireframe toolbar.

2. Set the number of instances to **3**.

3. Select the **Tube Center** curve. The Points & Planes Repetition dialog box opens as shown in Figure 5–35.

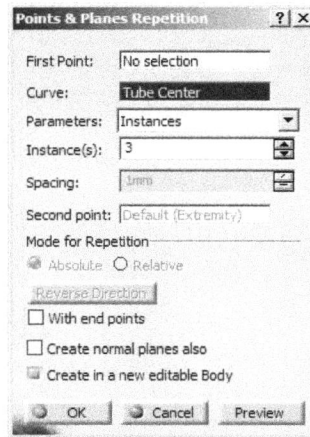

Figure 5–35

4. Click **OK** to complete the feature.

Task 3 - Create adaptive sweep surface.

1. Click [icon] (Adaptive Sweep) in the Surfaces toolbar.

2. Select **Tube Center** as the *Guiding Curve*.

3. Click [icon] in the Adaptive Sweep Definition dialog box as shown in Figure 5–36.

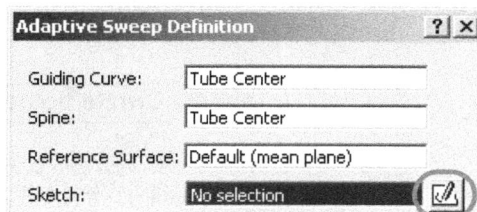

Figure 5–36

*The selected point is the
end point in the positive
Y-direction.*

4. The Sketch Creation for Adaptive Sweep dialog box opens.
   Select the end point, as shown in Figure 5–37. The selection
   of this point indicates to CATIA that the sketch will be created
   using that point as the origin. The sketch plane will be normal
   to Tube Center (the guide curve).

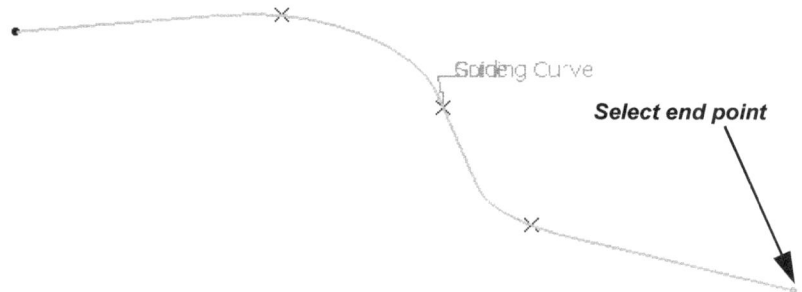

Guiding Curve

Select end point

Figure 5–37

5. Click **OK** in the Sketch Creation for Adaptive Sweep dialog
   box. CATIA automatically takes you into the Sketcher
   workbench.

6. From inside the sketcher, create an elongated hole with the
   dimensions shown in Figure 5–38.

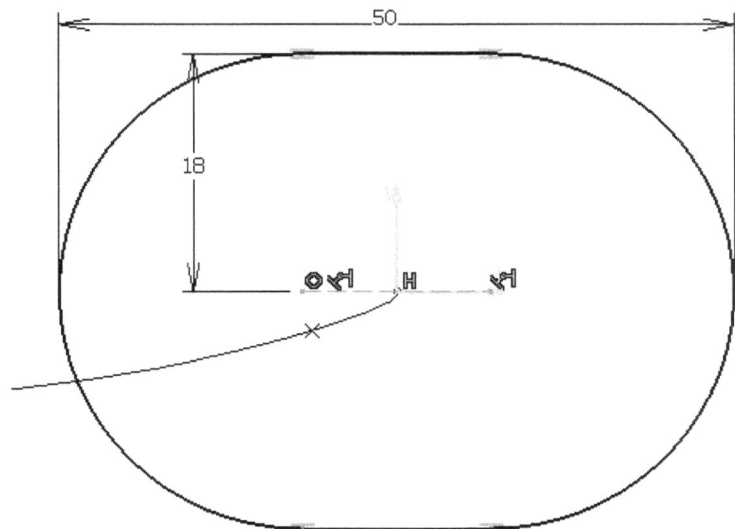

50

18

H

Figure 5–38

7. Expand the specification tree as shown in Figure 5–39. Create an Equidistant constraint using the center points of the arcs and **Mark.1** in the specification tree. Ensure that the center points of the arcs are coincident with **Mark.1**.

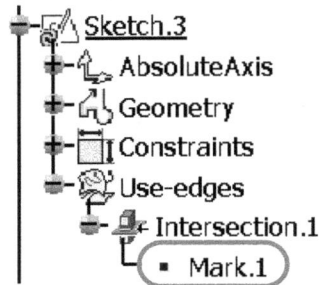

Figure 5–39

8. Change the *50mm* dimension to **40**.

9. Change the *18mm* dimension to **19.9**. The sketch displays as shown in Figure 5–40.

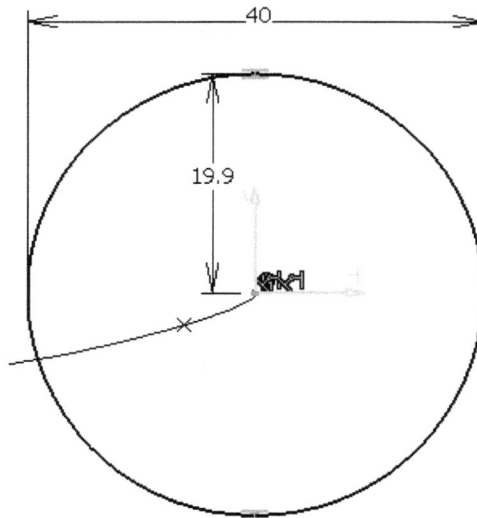

Figure 5–40

10. Click [⬆] to exit Sketcher.

Task 4 - Continue creating the Adaptive Sweep.

1. Select the points, as shown in Figure 5–41. These represent locations along Tube Center where the sketched profile can be modified.

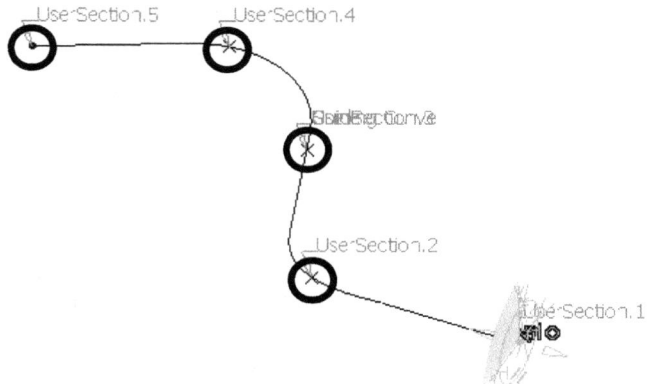

Figure 5–41

2. Select the *Parameters* tab. Select **UserSection.2** in the Current Selection drop-down list, as shown in Figure 5–42.

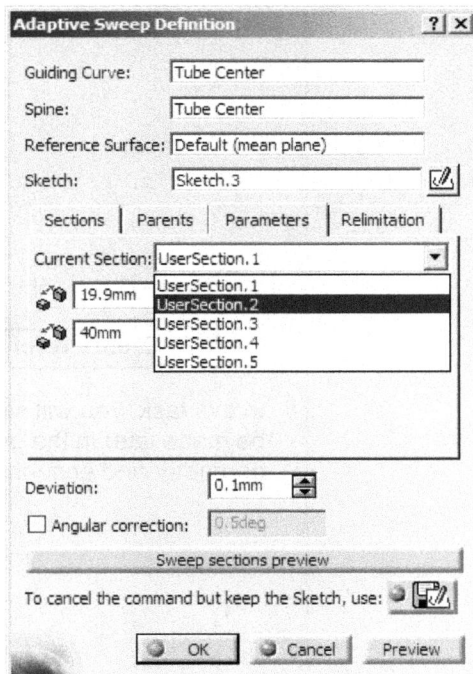

Figure 5–42

3. Change *19.9mm* to **15mm**.

4. Change *40mm* to **50mm**.

5. Select **UserSection.3** in the drop-down list and adjust the dimensions as follows:

   - Change *19.9mm* to **15mm**.
   - Change *40mm* to **51mm**.

6. Select **UserSection.4** in the drop-down list and adjust the dimensions as follows:

   - Change *19.9mm* to **16mm**.
   - Change *40mm* to **48mm**.

7. Click **OK** to complete the Adaptive Sweep. The model displays as shown in Figure 5–43.

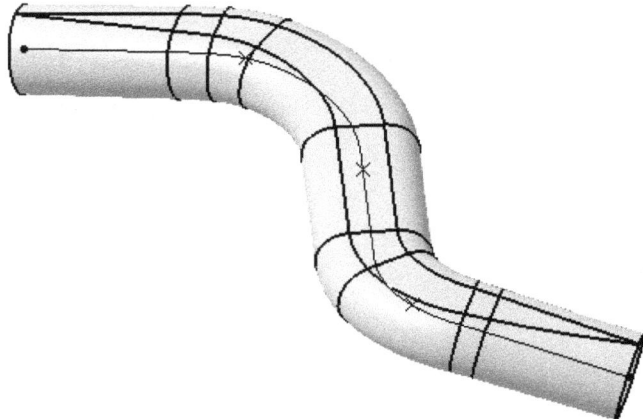

Figure 5–43

Task 5 - Create reference geometry.

In this task, you will set up the model for measurements that will be made later in the practice. This will include creating reference geometry and ensuring that correct options are set.

1. Before measuring the cross-section area, ensure that the units for area are set to mm². Select **Tools>Options> General>Parameters and Measure>Units**, as shown in Figure 5–44.

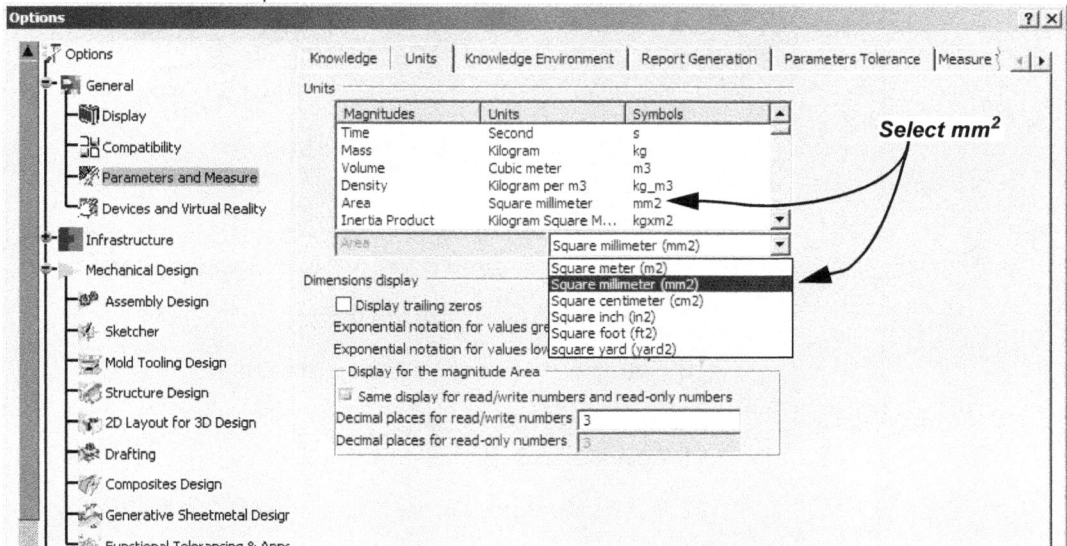

Figure 5–44

2. Select the *Measure Tools* tab. Ensure that **Automatic Update in part** option is selected. Click **OK** to exit the Options dialog box.

3. Reference geometry needs to be set up before taking any measurements. Click [icon] in the Wireframe toolbar.

4. Select **On Curve** in the Point type drop-down list.

   - *Curve:* **Tube Center**
   - Select **Distance on curve**.
   - *Length:* **50mm**
   - Select **Geodesic**.

5. Rename the newly created point as **Measure Point**.

6. Create a plane normal to Tube Center located at Measure Point.

7. Rename the newly created plane as **Measure Plane**. The model displays as shown in Figure 5–45.

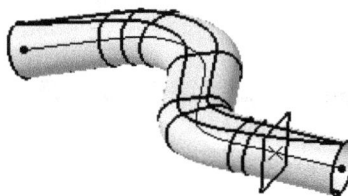

Figure 5–45

8. Click in the Wireframe toolbar. Create the Intersection between **Adaptive Sweep.1** and Measure Plane.

9. Click **OK** to complete the feature.

10. Rename *Intersect.1* as **Measure Curve**.

11. Activate .

12. Select **Measure Curve** and complete the feature.

13. Rename Fill.1 as **Area Surface**. The specification tree displays as shown in Figure 5–46.

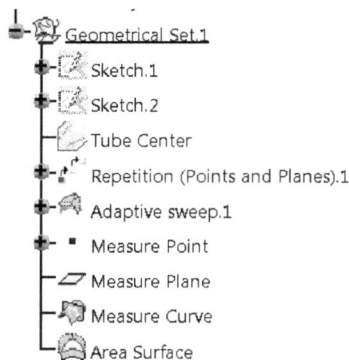

Figure 5–46

Task 6 - Create and inspect measurements.

Part of the design intent for the Intake Tube was that it maintained an area between **1200mm^2 - 1300mm^2**. In this task you will ensure that this goal is met.

1. Click in the Measure toolbar.

2. Select **Area Surface**. Ensure the **Keep Measure** option is selected. The model displays as shown in Figure 5–47.

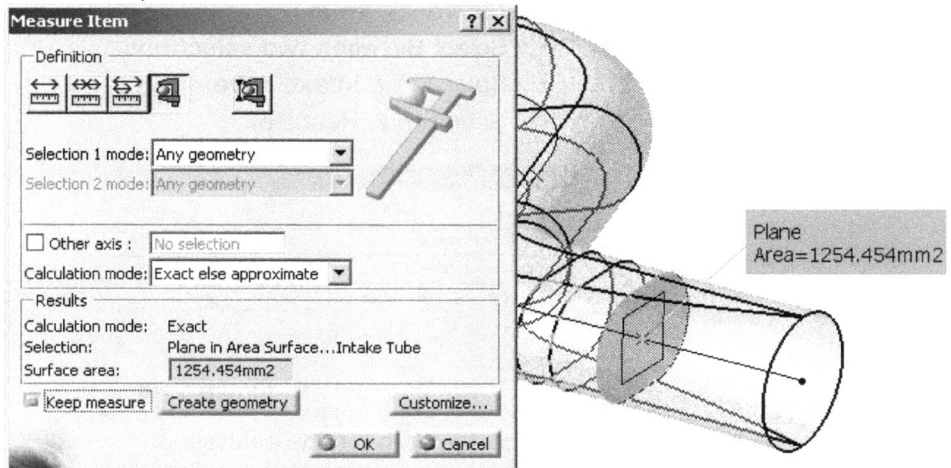

Figure 5–47

3. Click **OK** to store the measure in the part.

4. Modify Measure Point. Change the length value and the Area measure updates.

5. Repeat Step 4 by entering different length values for the location of Measure Point. Note that at various locations along Tube Center, the area is above $1300mm^2$.

Task 7 - Run a Clash analysis.

1. Another aspect of the design intent involved the Air Intake Tube maintaining a 1mm or larger clearance from the Heat Box. To check this condition, double-click on Tube-Box, the top level of the assembly.

2. Ensure that you are in the Assembly Design workbench.

3. Show the following parts:

   • **Input-Side**
   • **Output-Side**
   • **Heat Box**

4. Select **Analyze>Clash**.

5. Create the Clash analysis with the following criteria. The dialog box opens as shown in Figure 5–48.

   - *Type:* **Clearance + Contact + Clash**
   - *Clearance:* **1mm**
   - Select **Between two selections**.
   - *Selection 1:* **Intake Tube**
   - *Selection 2:* **Heat Box**

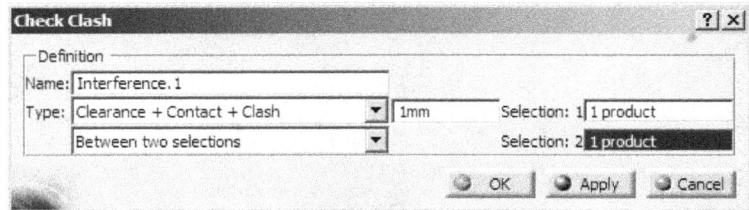

Figure 5–48

6. Click **Apply** to run the analysis.

7. One clearance issue was detected, as shown in Figure 5–49. Click **OK** to complete the analysis.

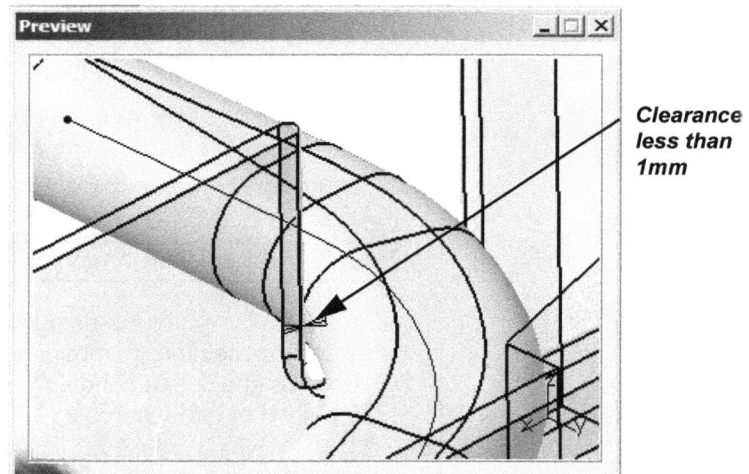

Clearance less than 1mm

Figure 5–49

8. Select **File>Save Management**.

9. Select **Intake-Tube.CATPart** and save as, using the new name **Intake-Tube Completed.CATPart**.

Task 8 - (Optional) Edit the Adaptive Sweep.

The last two tasks have proven that the Air Intake Tube does not meet the design intent. There is a clearance problem and the area requirements are not met.

1. Activate the Intake Tube part, and make the required changes to **Adaptive Sweep.1**.

2. Check that the area and clearance requirements have been met.

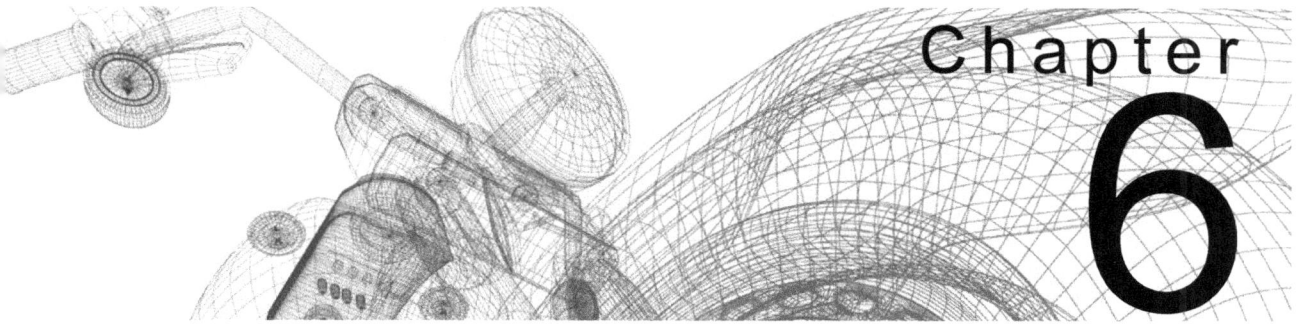

Additional Sweep Types

This chapter discusses additional profile types and sub-types available for a swept surface.

Learning Objectives in this Chapter

- Investigate additional types of surfaces.
- Understand the Line Profile, the Circle Profile, and the Conic Profile.

6.1 Swept Surface Types

This chapter broadens the discussion of sweep types. A table is shown in describing every sweep sub-type. The next three sections of this chapter describe the common line, circle, and conic sweep sub-types.

Profile Type	Sub-type	Description
Explicit		Profile is explicitly defined by selecting a curve from the model.
	With reference surface	The surface is defined by selecting a guide curve for the profile. An angle with respect to a reference surface is also specified.
	With two guide curves	The surface is defined by two guide curves.
	With pulling direction	The surface is defined by a guide curve and a pulling direction for the profile.
Line		The profile is defined by a straight line. The following sub-types determine how the line is generated.
	Two Limits	Each end of the line is defined by a guide curve.
	Limit and middle	One end of the line is defined by one of the guide curves. The other guide curve defines the midpoint of the line.

Profile Type	Sub-type		Description
	With reference surface		Line is defined by specifying a length and angle with respect to a reference surface.
	With reference curve		Line is defined by specifying a length and angle with respect to a reference curve.
	With tangency surface		Line is defined by specifying the guide curve and a reference surface it is to be tangent to.
	With draft direction		Line is defined by specifying a length and angle with respect to a draft direction.
	With two tangency surfaces		Line is defined by specifying two reference surfaces it is to be tangent to.
Circle			Profile is defined by arc or circle. The following sub-types determine how the arc or circle is generated.
	Three guides		The profile curve is an arc. The start, end, and radius of the arc are defined by three guide curves.
	Two guides and radius		The profile curve is a circle. Two guide curves define the start and end of the circle. The radius of the circle is entered.

Profile Type	Sub-type	Description
Center and two angles		The profile is an arc. The center and radius of the arc are defined by two guide curves. The arc angle is entered by defining two angles.
Center and radius		The profile is a circle. The center of the circle is defined by a guide curve and the radius is entered.
Two guides and tangency surface		The profile is an arc. The start and end of the arc are defined by guide curves. The radius is defined by selecting a tangency surface.
One guide and tangency surface		The profile is an arc. The start of the arc is defined by a guide curve. The end of the arc is defined by the radius and a tangency surface. The radius of the arc is entered.
Limit curve and tangency surface		The profile is an arc. The limit curve lies on the tangency surface. The radius of the arc is entered. The start of the arc is dictated by Angle 1. The end of the arc is dictated by Angle 2. This sub-type is new to R17.
Conic		The profile is defined by a conic. The following sub-types determine how the conic is generated.
Two guide curves		Each side of the conic is defined by a guide curve and a tangency surface. The shape factor of the conic is determined by entering a conic parameter.
Three guide curves		Each side of the conic is defined by a guide curve and a tangency surface. The shape factor of the conic is defined by a third guide curve.

Profile Type	Sub-type	Description
Four guide curves	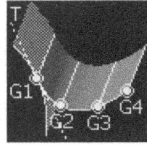	One side of the conic is defined by a guide curve and a tangency surface. The other side is defined by two guide curves. A fourth guide curve determines the conic shape factor.
Five guide curves	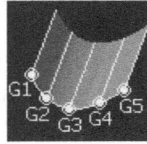	Each side of the conic is defined by two guide curves. A fifth guide curve determines the conic shape factor.

6.2 Line Profile

Two Limits

The Two limits line profile defines each end of a line using a guide curve. With this type of swept feature, you can specify a length for the profile and change the sub-type.

Length Options

The profile of the surface can be extended beyond the guide curves by specifying a value for *Length 1* or *Length 2*, as shown in Figure 6–1. A negative value can be entered to limit the profile to a distance inside the guide curves.

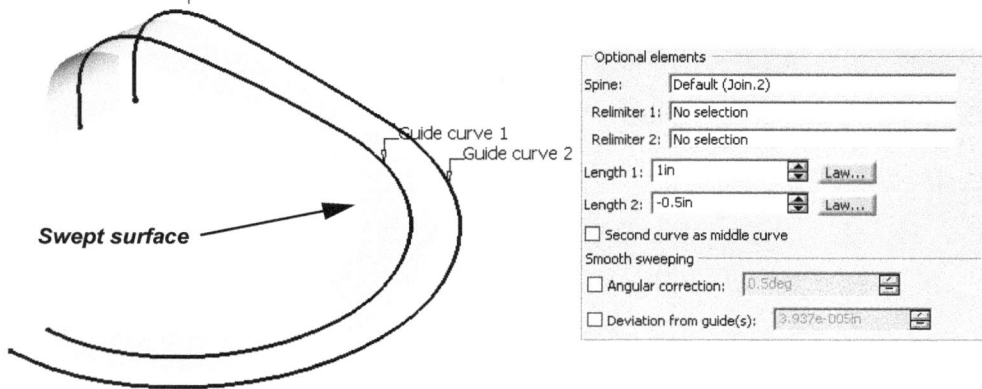

Figure 6–1

Second Curve As Middle Curve

The **Second curve as middle curve** option changes the sub-type from **Two limits** to **Limit and middle**. This is similar to the **Mirrored Extent** option for pad creation in the Part Design workbench. Guide curve 2 becomes the middle curve about which the profile of the surface is mirrored. An example is shown in Figure 6–2.

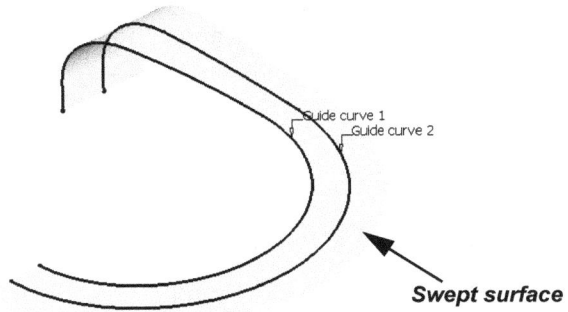

Figure 6–2

With Draft Direction

The With draft direction is a unique type of Line Profile swept surface because it uses elements that are not common with any other type of swept surface. The options for this type of surface display as shown in Figure 6–3.

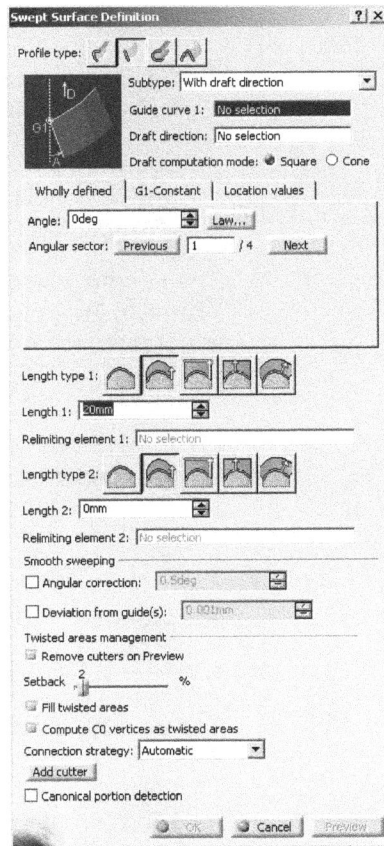

Figure 6–3

The surface is generated by sweeping a line along a guiding curve at an angle to the draft direction. The draft direction can be a planar surface or edge. In the example shown in Figure 6–4, the surface is drafted by 30 degrees from the YZ-plane (or in the X-direction).

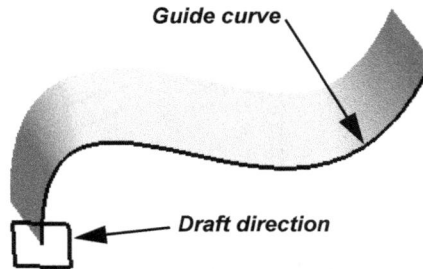

Figure 6–4

The angle can be specified using the following values:

- **Wholly defined** keeps the draft angle constant for the swept surface.

- **G1-Constant** enables you to specify a different draft angle for each non-tangent segment of the guide curve.

- **Location values** enables you to specify the draft angle at specific points on the guide curve. The points can be vertices on the guide curve or reference points.

The Length type can be specified as **From Curve**, **Standard**, **From/Up To**, or **From Extremum**. The length can be specified in either direction from the guide curve.

- (From Curve) defines the surface with zero length in the specified direction.

- (Standard) defines the length by the value entered.

- (From/Up To) defines the length by selecting a relimiting element that defines the end point of the line. The relimiting element can be a point, curve, or plane.

- (From Extremum) defines the length by an extremum plane.

- (Along surface) defines the length along a direction.

With Tangency Surface

The line profile with tangency surface sub-type enforces tangency continuity to a reference surface. The length of the line is generated by the selected guide curve and the tangency surface.

The necessary references required to complete this sweep type are shown in Figure 6–5.

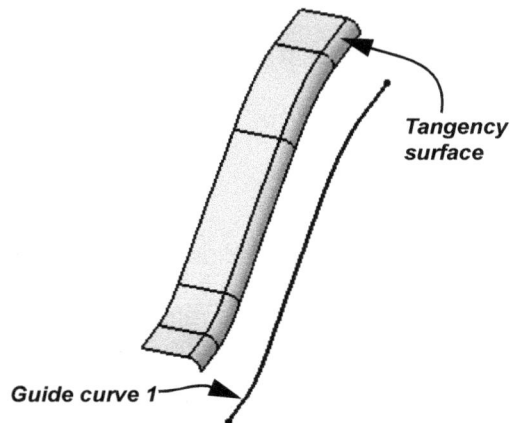

Tangency surface

Guide curve 1

Figure 6–5

The completed line sweep using with tangency surface is shown in Figure 6–6.

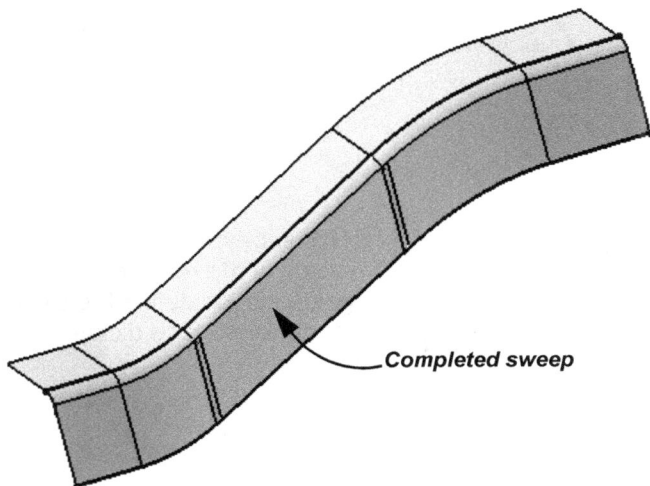

Completed sweep

Figure 6–6

6.3 Circle Profile

Center and Two Angles

When creating a swept surface using the Center and two angles circle profile, by default, the radius of the circle follows the shape of the reference curve, as shown in Figure 6–7.

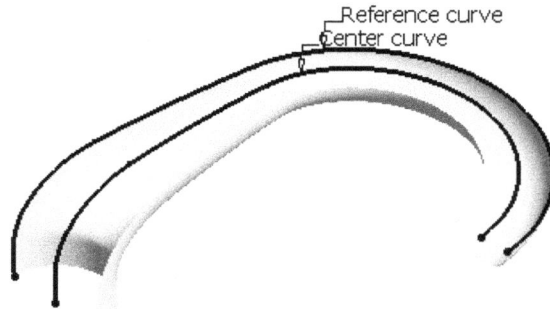

Figure 6–7

The radius can be fixed by selecting **Use fixed radius** and entering a fixed radius, as shown in Figure 6–8. The surface uses the reference curve to locate the angles of the circle; however, the radius is driven by the value entered.

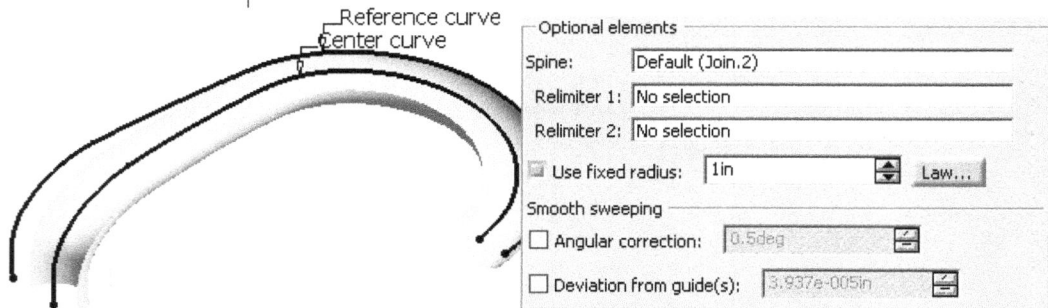

Figure 6–8

Two Guides and Tangency Surface

This sub-type of the circle profile sweep is useful when the radius of the required sweep is not known. In this case, two guide curves define the extremities of the arc shape, while a tangency surface dictates the continuity.

The three necessary elements required to complete the sweep are shown in Figure 6–9.

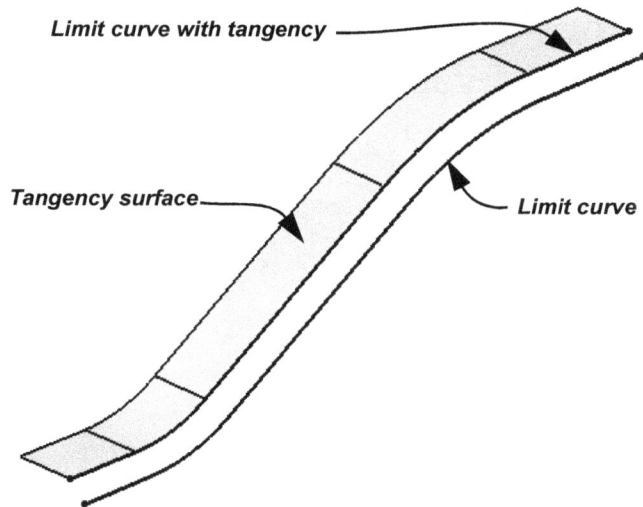

Figure 6–9

By default, CATIA uses the Limit curve with tangency reference as the spine. As with all other sweep types, a different reference can be selected for the spine.

The completed circle sweep - two guides and tangency surface sub-type is shown in Figure 6–10.

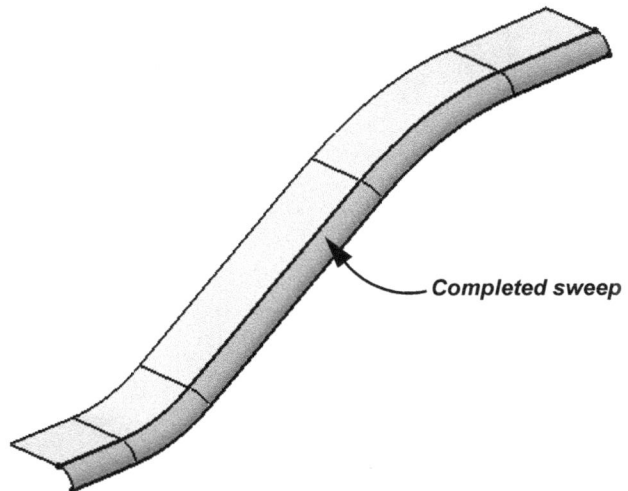

Figure 6–10

6.4 Conic Profile

Two Guide Curves

The guide curves in a Two guide curve conic profile define the extremities of the conic shape. Two tangency surfaces must also be selected. Each guide curve must lie on the selected tangency reference surface.

Optionally, an angle can be specified measuring from the tangency surface. A parameter value can be adjusted between 0 and 1 defining the rho value of the conic. By default, this value is set to **.5**. The dialog box opens as shown in Figure 6–11.

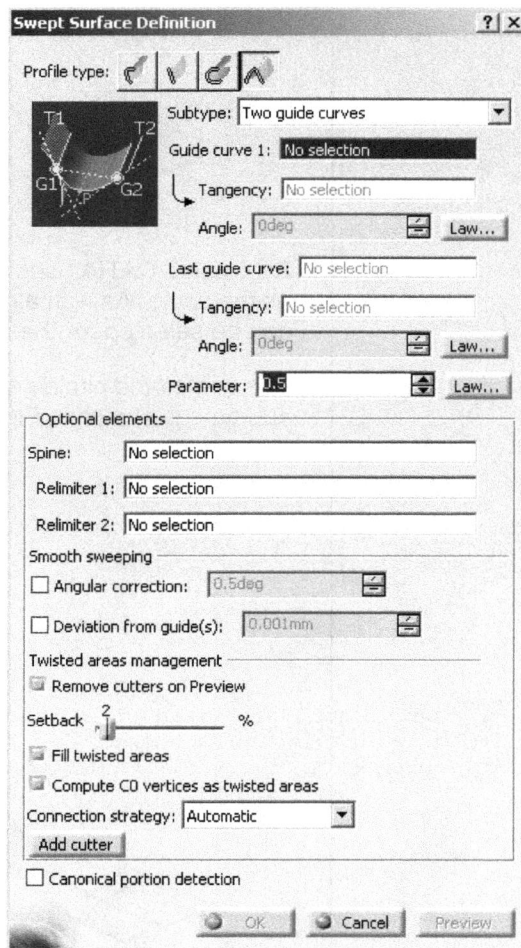

Figure 6–11

The necessary references to complete a conic profile using two guide curves is shown in Figure 6–12.

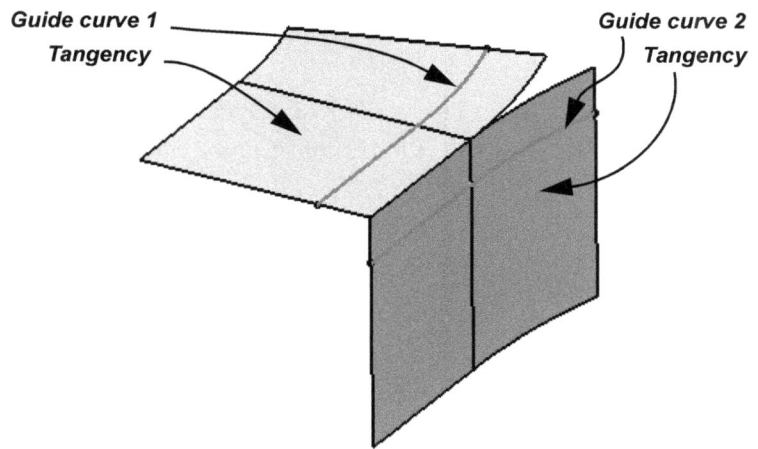

Figure 6–12

The completed conic sweep displays as shown in Figure 6–13.

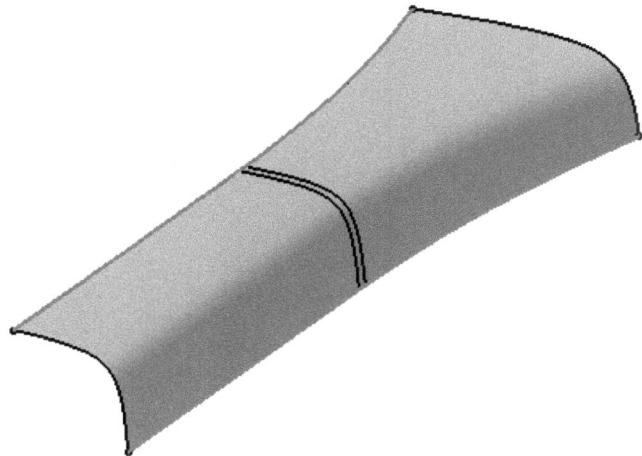

Figure 6–13

Five Guide Curves

When using the five guide curves sub-type, the shape of the conic is defined completely by the selected curves. There are no angles, tangency surfaces, or parameter values to influence the shape as in the other conic sub-types.

An example of the references for a five guide curve sub-type of a conic sweep is shown in Figure 6–14.

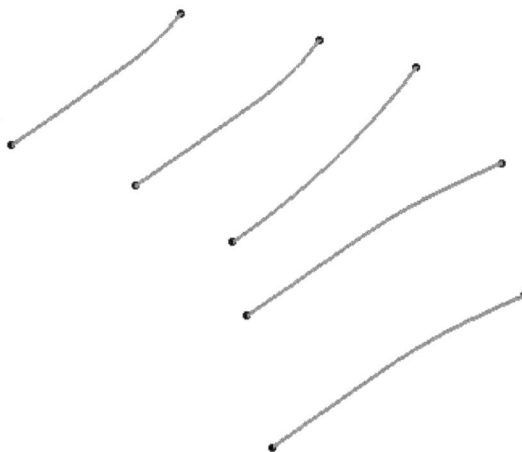

Figure 6–14

The completed conic sweep displays as shown in Figure 6–15.

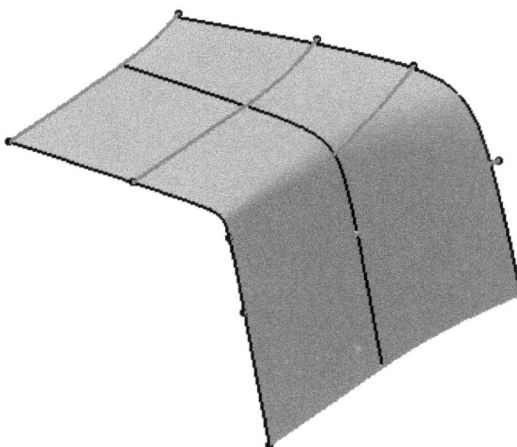

Figure 6–15

Practice 6a

Remote Control Sweeps

Practice Objectives

- Create a circle sweep.
- Create an explicit sweep.

In this practice, you will create two types of swept surfaces. The sketches and curves have been created for you and are listed under the wireframe body. The completed model displays as shown in Figure 6–16.

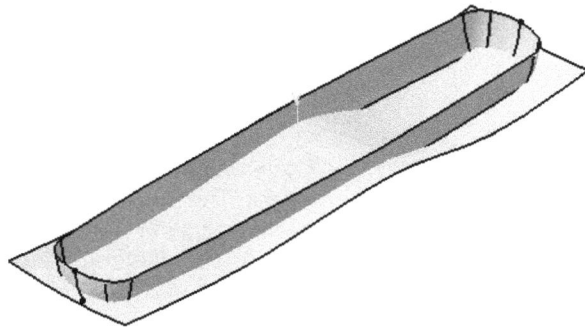

Figure 6–16

Task 1 - Open a part file.

1. Open **RemoteControl_Sweep.CATPart**. The model displays as shown in Figure 6–17.

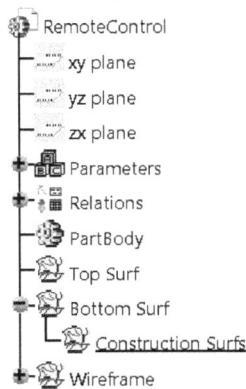

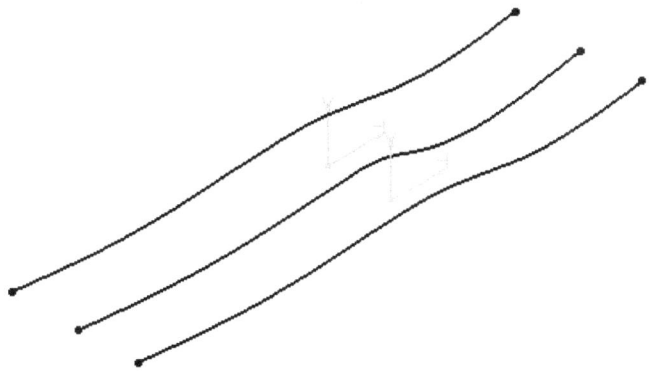

Figure 6–17

2. Expand the **Wireframe**, **Sketches**, and **Curves** geometrical sets in the specification tree, as shown in Figure 6–18.

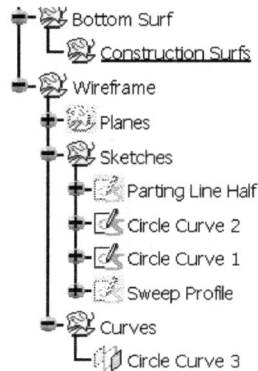

Figure 6–18

Design Considerations

The Construction Surfs body has been defined as the work object. The swept surfaces in this practice will be created in this geometrical set. You will use sketches and a curve to create the sweep. The sketches and curve have been organized under the Wireframe body and renamed so that they can be easily identified.

Task 2 - Create a circle sweep.

1. Click (Swept Surface) and define the sweep as follows and as shown in Figure 6–19:

- *Profile type:* (Circle)
- *Sub-type:* **Three guides**
- *Guide curve 1:* **Circle Curve 1**
- *Guide curve 2:* **Circle Curve 2**
- *Guide curve 3:* **Circle Curve 3**

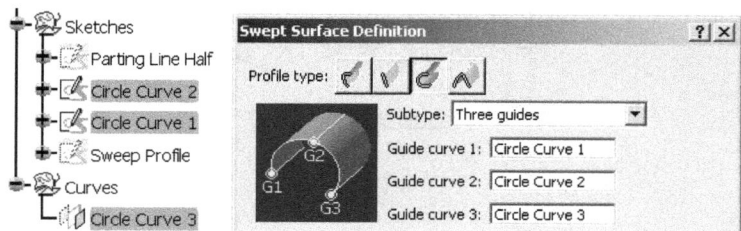

Figure 6–19

2. Click **Preview**. Close the Warning message box that opens. The circle sweep displays as shown in Figure 6–20.

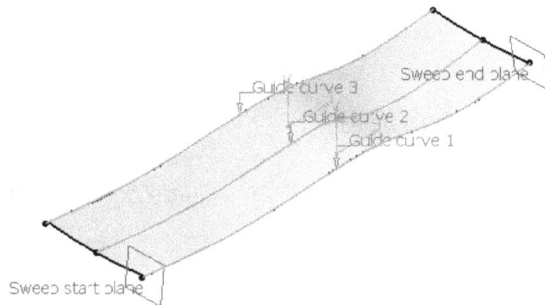

Figure 6–20

3. Click **OK**.

Task 3 - Create an explicit sweep.

1. Hide the following elements:

- **Circle Curve 1**
- **Circle Curve 2**
- **Circle Curve 3**

2. Show the following elements in the **Sketches** geometrical set as shown in Figure 6–21:

- **Parting Line Half**
- **Sweep Profile**

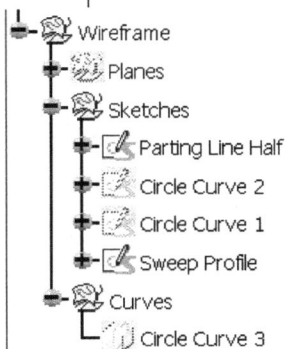

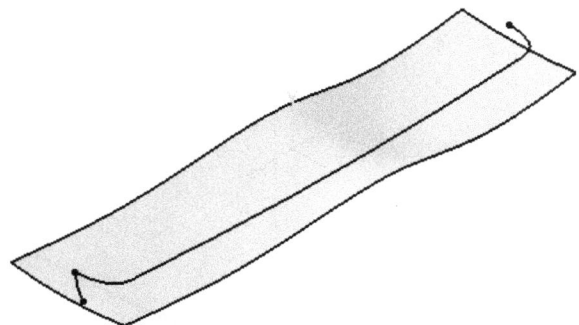

Figure 6–21

3. Click ![icon] and define the sweep as follows and as shown in Figure 6–22:

- *Profile type:* ![icon] (Explicit)
- *Sub-type:* **With reference surface**
- *Profile:* **Sweep Profile**
- *Guide curve:* **Parting Line Half**

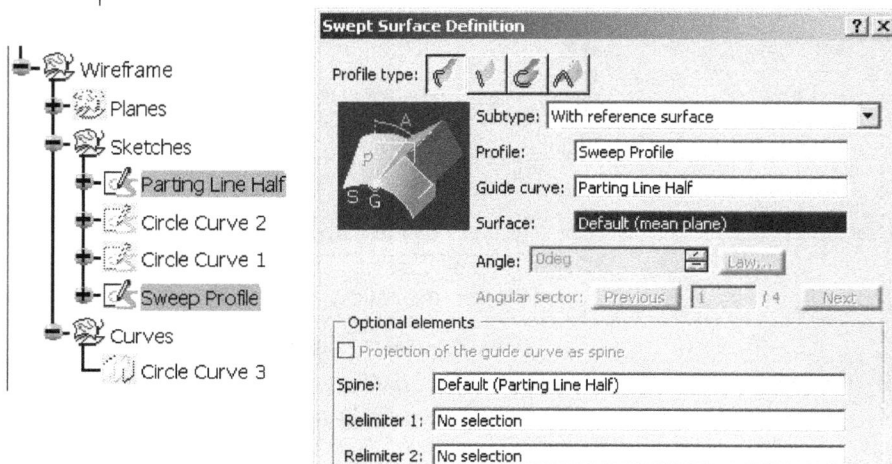

Figure 6–22

4. Complete the sweep.

5. Hide **Parting Line Half** and **Sweep Profile**. The model displays as shown in Figure 6–23.

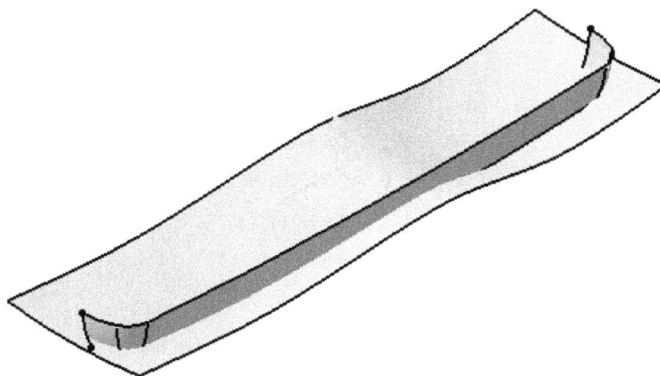

Figure 6–23

6. Click ![Symmetry icon] (Symmetry) and reference the zx plane to create the opposite side of the bottom surface on the remote control as shown in Figure 6–24.

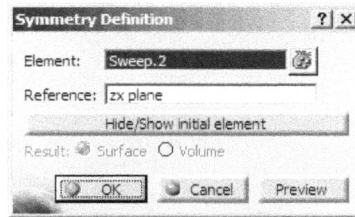

Symmetry Definition

Element: Sweep.2

Reference: zx plane

Hide/Show initial element

Result: ⦿ Surface ○ Volume

OK   Cancel   Preview

Figure 6–24

7. Complete the Symmetry. The model displays as shown in Figure 6–25.

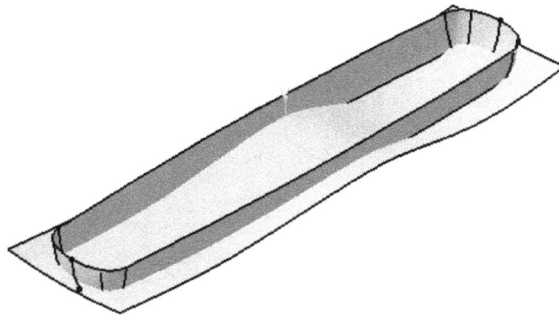

Figure 6–25

8. Create a Join feature with **Sweep.2** and **Symmetry.2**. The **Construction Surfs** geometrical set displays as shown in Figure 6–26.

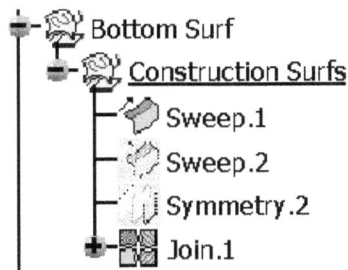

Bottom Surf
Construction Surfs
Sweep.1
Sweep.2
Symmetry.2
Join.1

Figure 6–26

9. Save the model and close the file.

Practice 6b | Helix Sweep

Practice Objectives

- Create a Line sweep.
- Create a Conic sweep.

Using various swept surfaces and wireframe geometry, you will create the geometry shown in Figure 6–27. You will create two line sweeps and one conic sweep to remove geometry from the solid. Reference geometry and a solid have already been created.

Figure 6–27

Task 1 - Open a part file.

1. Open **Helix_Sweep_Start.CATPart**. The model displays as shown in Figure 6–28. A part body exists with a Pad feature. A geometrical set also has various wireframe elements. These will be used as reference for further geometry creation.

Figure 6–28

2. Zoom in on the bottom of the cylinder. The model displays as shown in Figure 6–29. Note that an inner and outter circle are created and there are three points. These will be used to build a wireframe in the next task.

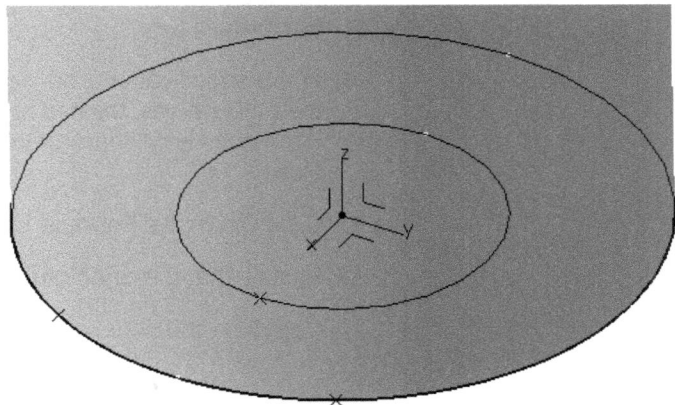

Figure 6–29

3. Besides existing geometry, there are existing parameters created as shown in Figure 6–30. These will be used later to drive multiple dimensions.

Figure 6–30

4. Hide the **Part Body**. The geometry here will not be used until the end of the practice.

*Select **Tools>Options>Infrastructure>Part Infrastructure>Display** and ensure that the Parameters option is selected.*

Task 2 - Create helix curves.

1. Ensure that the **Wireframe** geometrical set is defined as the active work object.

2. Click (Helix).

3. Select **Height and Pitch** as the *Helix Type*.

4. Select **Point.2** as the *Starting Point* reference.

5. Select the Z-axis as the *Axis* reference.

6. Right-click in the *Pitch reference* field and select **Edit Formula**.

7. In the specification tree, select the parameter named **Pitch**.

8. Click **OK** in the Formula Editor dialog box.

9. Right-click in the *Height reference* field and select **Edit Formula**.

10. In the specification tree, select the **Height** parameter. All of the helix curves created in this practice will be driven by the Pitch and Height parameters. This makes updating the model easier.

11. Click **OK** in the Formula Editor dialog box.

12. Ensure that the orientation is set to **Counterclockwise**.

13. Complete the helix.

14. Using Steps 2-10, create two more helix curves using **Point.3** and **Point.1** as the respective start points. All other references will be the same.

15. The completed helix curves display as shown in Figure 6–31. Ensure the names of each helix curve matches that of Figure 6–31.

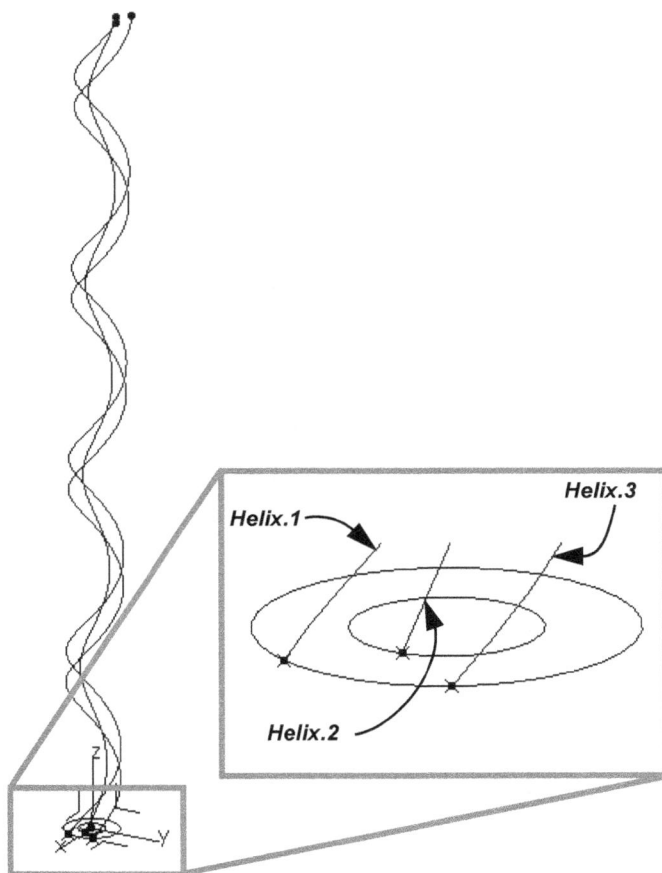

Figure 6–31

Task 3 - Create two line sweeps.

1. Create a sweep using the following specifications:

   - *Profile type:* **Line**
   - *Sub-type:* **Two limits**
   - *Guide curve 1:* **Helix.1**
   - *Guide curve 2:* **Helix 2**
   - *Spine:* **Z-axis**
   - *Length 1:* **0mm**
   - *Length 2:* **0mm**

The completed sweep displays as shown in Figure 6–32.

Figure 6–32

2. Create another sweep using the following specifications:

   - *Profile type:* **Line**
   - *Sub-type:* **Two limits**
   - *Guide curve 1:* **Helix.2**
   - *Guide curve 2:* **Helix 3**
   - *Spine:* **Z-axis**
   - *Length 1:* **0mm**
   - *Length 2:* **0mm**

The completed sweep displays as shown in Figure 6–33.

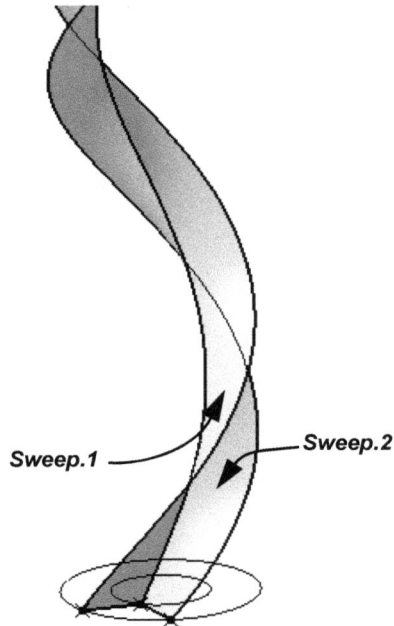

Figure 6–33

The swept surfaces in this task will be used as future references for wireframe and surface creation.

Task 4 - Create wireframe for the conic sweep.

In this task, you will create a wireframe to support two more helix curves.

1. Extract the edges shown in Figure 6–34. Also ensure that the names of the curves are as shown in Figure 6–34. These extracted curves will be used as reference for two of the curve points.

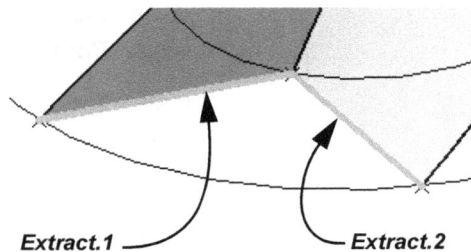

Figure 6–34

2. Create an **On Curve** type point using the following specifications:

- *Curve:* **Extract.1**
- *Ratio:* **.25**
- *Point:* **Point.3**

3. The dialog box opens as shown in Figure 6–35. Complete the point.

You might need to reverse direction to achieve the required result.

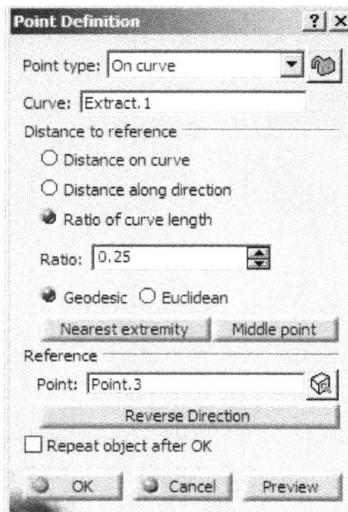

Figure 6–35

4. If not already done, rename the point as **Point.4**.

5. Create another **On Curve** type point using the following specifications:

- *Curve:* **Extract.2**
- *Ratio:* **.25**
- *Point:* **Point.3**

6. Complete the point. If not already done, rename the point as **Point.5**.

7. Create a helix using the following specifications:

- *Helix Type:* **Height and Pitch**
- *Starting Point:* **Point.4**
- *Axis:* **Z-Axis**

Refer to Task 2 for detailed steps on creating a formula using an existing parameter.

- *Pitch:* Create a formula equal to the parameter named Pitch.
- *Height:* Create a formula equal to the parameter named Height.

8. Complete the helix. Ensure that the name of the feature is **Helix.4**.

9. Create another helix using **Point.5** as the start point. All other references are the same as in the previous helix.

10. Ensure that the name of the helix is **Helix.5** as shown in Figure 6–36. The two helix curves from this task will be used as guide curves when creating a sweep in the next task.

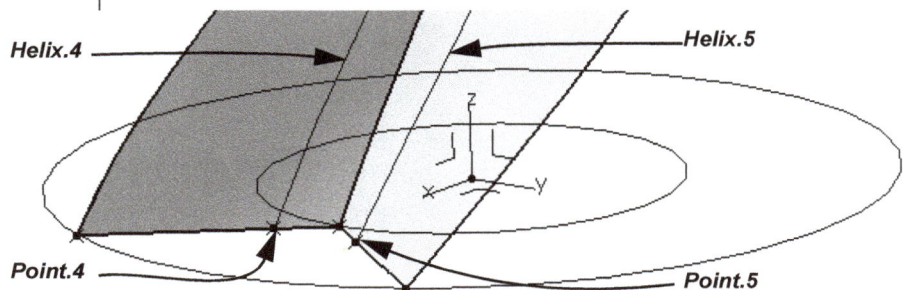

Figure 6–36

Task 5 - Create a conic sweep.

1. Create a new geometrical set named **Surfaces**.

2. The two line sweeps are located in the **Wireframe** geometrical set. Move them to the new **Surfaces** geometrical set.

3. Create a sweep using the following specifications:

- *Profile type:* **Conic**
- *Sub-type:* **Two guides curves**
- *Guide curve 1:* **Helix.4**
- *Tangency:* **Sweep.1**
- *Last guide curve:* **Helix.5**
- *Tangency:* **Sweep.2**
- *Spine:* **Z Axis**
- *Relimiter 1:* **xy plane**

The dialog box opens as shown in Figure 6–37.

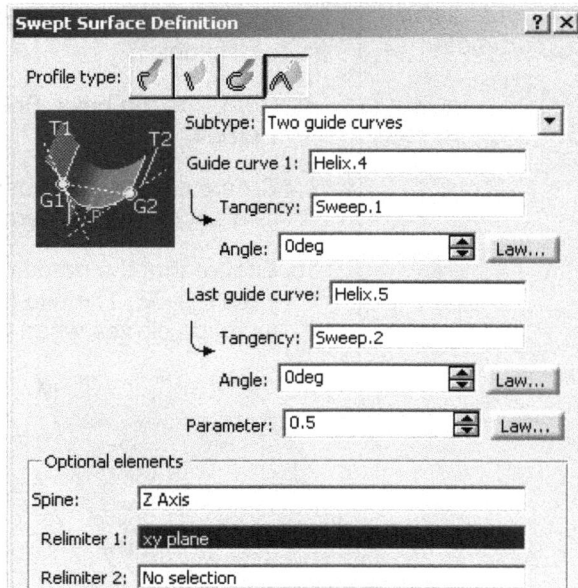

Figure 6–37

4. Complete the sweep. The model displays as shown in Figure 6–38.

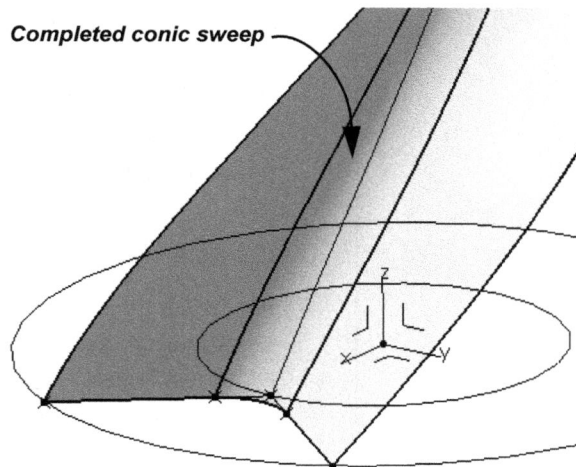

Completed conic sweep

Figure 6–38

Task 6 - (Optional) Complete the model.

1. Use the **Split** tool to remove the unwanted portions of the surfaces shown in Figure 6–39.

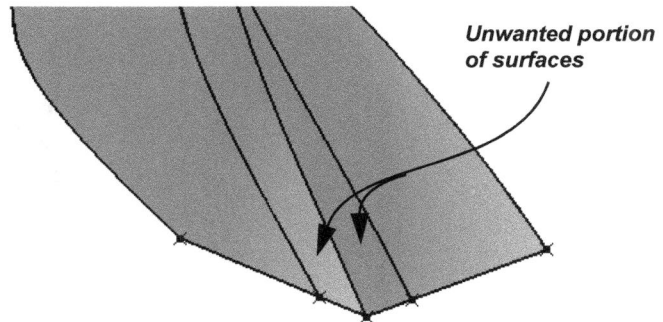

Unwanted portion of surfaces

Figure 6–39

2. Ensure the three surfaces are joined together. The completed operation displays as shown in Figure 6–40. Wireframe elements have been hidden in this picture to be able to see the surfaces more easily.

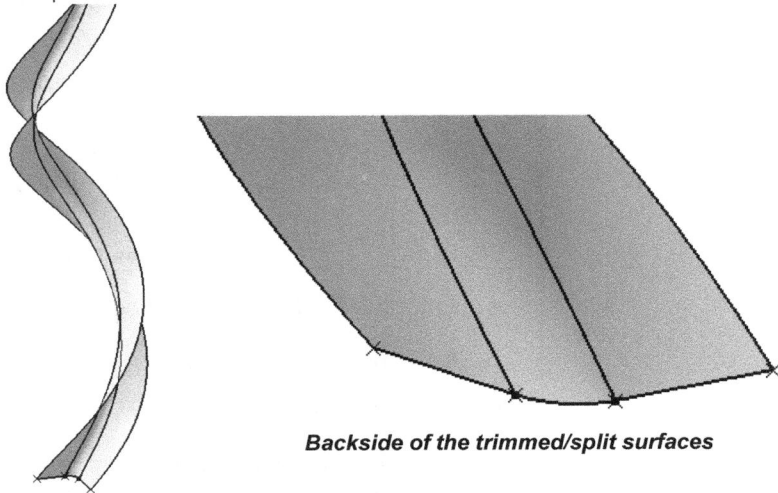

Backside of the trimmed/split surfaces

Figure 6–40

3. Use the **Rotate** tool to move the joined surface 180 degrees about the Z-axis as shown in Figure 6–41

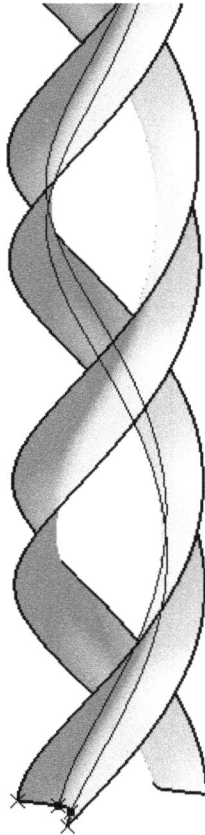

Figure 6–41

4. Enter the Part Design workbench.

5. **Activate the PartBody**.

6. Hide all wireframe geometry.

7. Create a split using the joined surface as the splitting element. Ensure that the arrows point towards the inside of the model. These arrows dictate the solid to be kept. Zoom out on the model if the arrows are not shown.

8. Create another split using the rotated surface as the splitting element. Again, ensure that the arrows point towards the inside of the model.

    The completed model displays as shown in Figure 6–42.

Figure 6–42

9. Save the model and close the file.

Practice 6c | Exhaust Diffuser 1

Practice Objectives

- Create an Extruded surface.
- Create a Swept surface.
- Create a Fill surface.

In this practice, you will create the surfaces for a diffuser housing using Sweep and Fill features. The base geometry of the profile is provided. The completed model displays as shown in Figure 6–43.

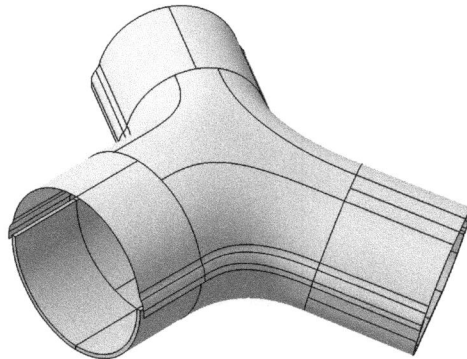

Figure 6–43

Task 1 - Open a part file.

1. Open **ExhaustDiffuser.CATPart**. The model displays as shown in Figure 6–44.

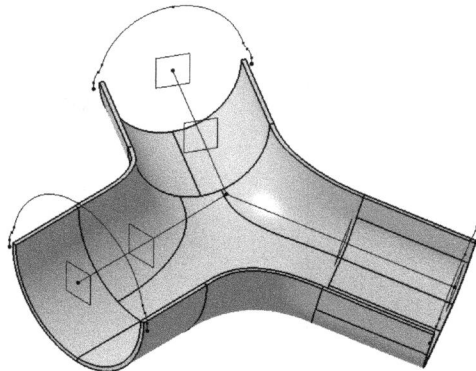

Figure 6–44

2. Set units to **mm**.

Task 2 - Create Extrude surface features.

In this task, the base surface geometry will be created. At the end of this task, the model displays as shown in Figure 6–45.

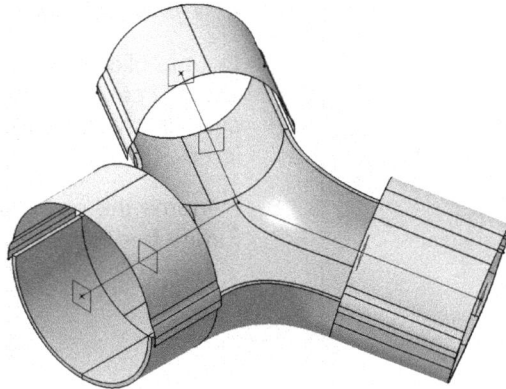

Figure 6–45

1. Activate the **TopSurf** geometrical set.

2. Double-click on (Extrude) to open the Extruded Surface Definition dialog box. Make the following selections:

   - *Profile:* **Sketch.1**
   - *Direction:* **Plane.2**
   - *Limit 1 Type:* **Up-to element**
   - *Up-to element:* **Plane.4**

3. Complete the Extrude feature. A new Extrude dialog box opens.

4. Use the following references to define the extrude:

   - *Profile:* **Sketch.2**
   - *Direction:* **Plane.3**
   - *Limit 1 Type:* **Up-to element**
   - *Up-to element:* **Plane.5**

5. Complete the Extrude feature. A new Extrude dialog box opens.

6. Use the following references to define the last extrude:

- *Profile:* **Sketch.3**
- *Direction:* **Plane.1**
- *Limit 1 Type:* **Up-to element**
- *Up-to element:* **Plane.6**

7. Double-clicking on an icon enables the selected feature to be created continuously. To finish the repetition of extruded surface creation, close the dialog box or select the feature icon.

8. Rename the newly created extruded surfaces, as shown in Figure 6–46.

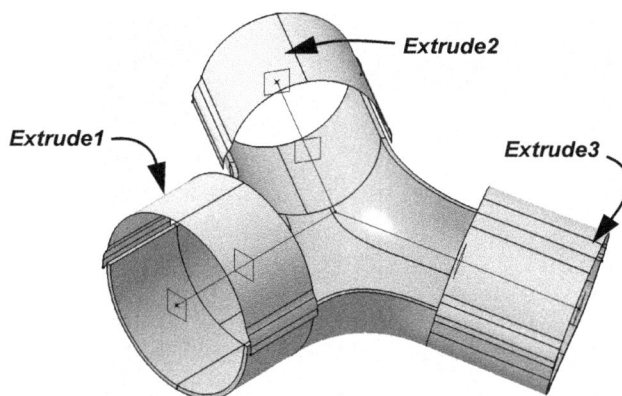

Figure 6–46

Task 3 - Create connect curves between the extruded surfaces.

---

1. Hide the following elements:

- **Part Body**
- **Group-Base Profiles**

2. Extract the eight edges highlighted in Figure 6–47.

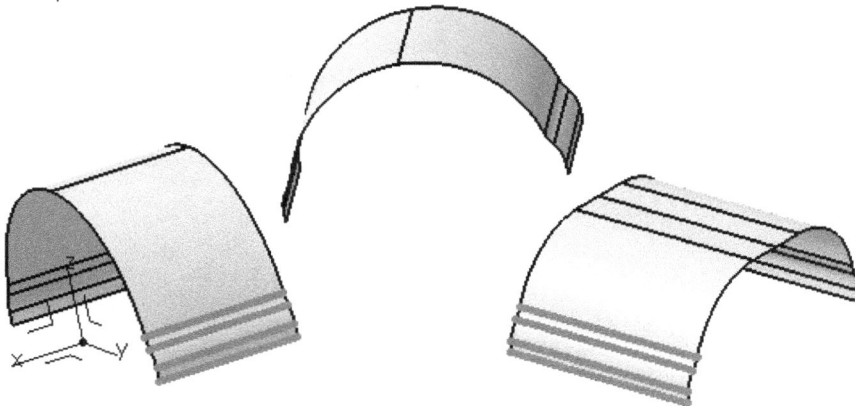

Figure 6–47

3. Hide the following elements:

   - **Extrude1**
   - **Extrude2**
   - **Extrude3**

4. This ensures that no sub-elements are selected from these surfaces during wireframe creation in this task. The model displays as shown in Figure 6–48. Ensure that the names of the extract curves match those shown.

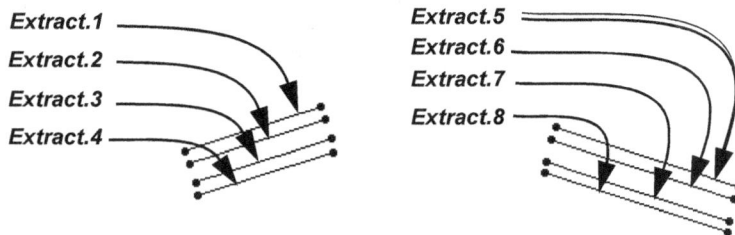

Figure 6–48

5. Click ⬓ (Connect Curve). The Connect Curve Definition dialog box opens. In the First Curve area in the dialog box, right-click in the *Point* reference field and select **Create Endpoint**, as shown in Figure 6–49. This enables an on-curve type point to be created on the fly.

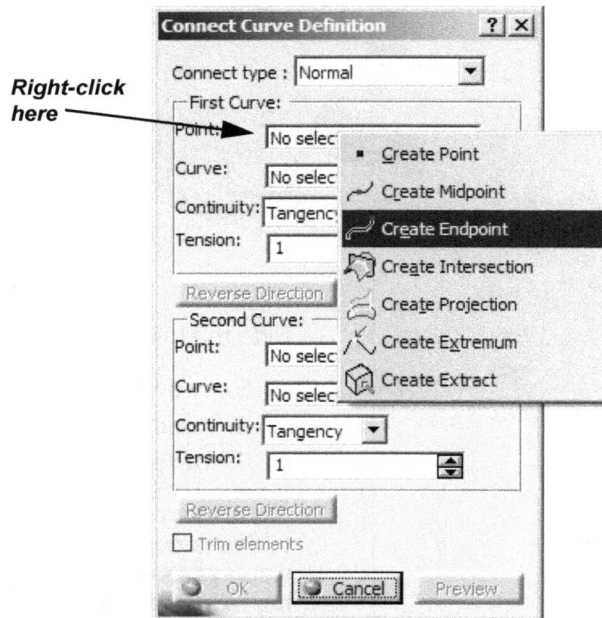

Figure 6–49

6. Select the end point from Extract.8, as shown in Figure 6–50.

Figure 6–50

7. Because the selected end point from step 7 lies on **Extract.8**, the curve reference automatically selects **Extract.8**.

8. Select **Curvature** in the First Curve Continuity drop-down list.

9. In the Second Curve area in the dialog box, right-click in the *Point* reference field and select **Create Endpoint**.

10. Select the point shown in Figure 6–51.

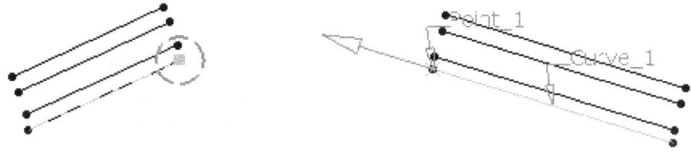

Figure 6–51

Flip continuity arrows as required.

11. Select **Curvature** in the Second Curve Continuity drop-down list.

12. Complete the connect curve. The model displays as shown in Figure 6–52.

Figure 6–52

13. Repeat steps 5-13 using the remaining extracted curves so that the model displays as shown in Figure 6–53.

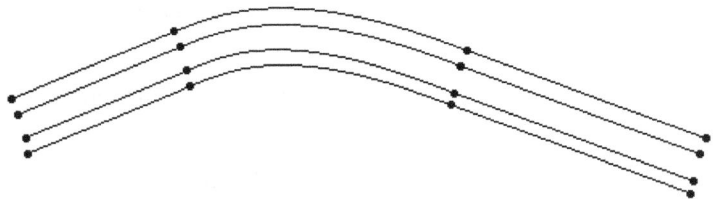

Figure 6–53

14. Rename the connect curves, as shown in Figure 6–54.

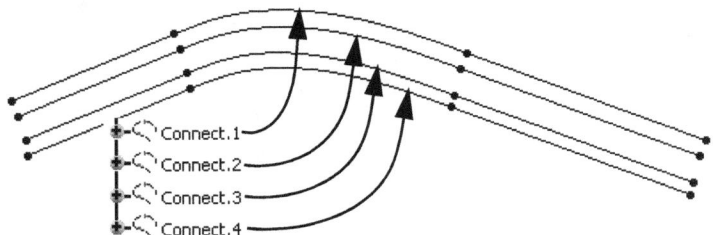

Figure 6–54

15. Show **Extrude.1**, **Extrude.2**, and **Extrude.3**.

16. Save the model and keep the file open.

Task 4 - Create sweep surfaces.

With wireframe geometry established, the surfaces connecting each lower segment of the diffuser can be constructed using sweep and fill surfaces. At the end of this task, the model displays as shown in Figure 6–55.

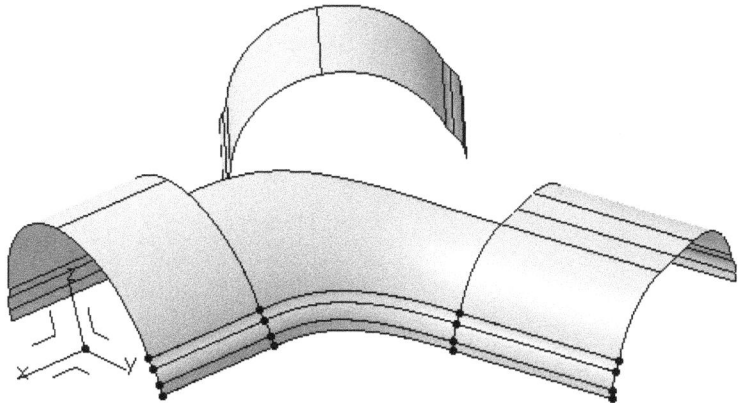

Figure 6–55

1. Click ✍ (Sweep) to open the Swept Surface Definition dialog box.

2. Select **Line** as the *Profile type* and **Two limits** as the *Sub-type*.

3. Make the selections shown in Figure 6–56.

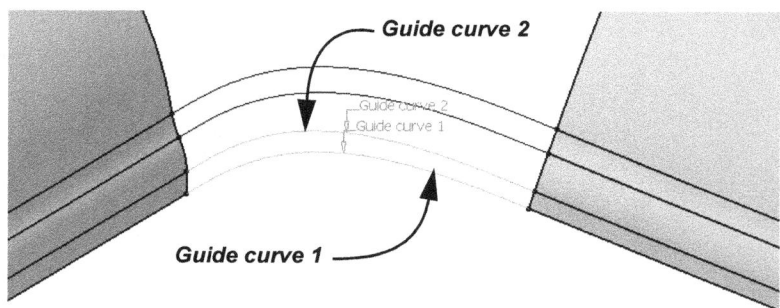

Figure 6–56

4. Enter a *Length 1* value of **0mm**.

5. Ensure *Length 2* equals **0mm**. It might already be set to this value.

6. Complete the line sweep. The model displays as shown in Figure 6–57.

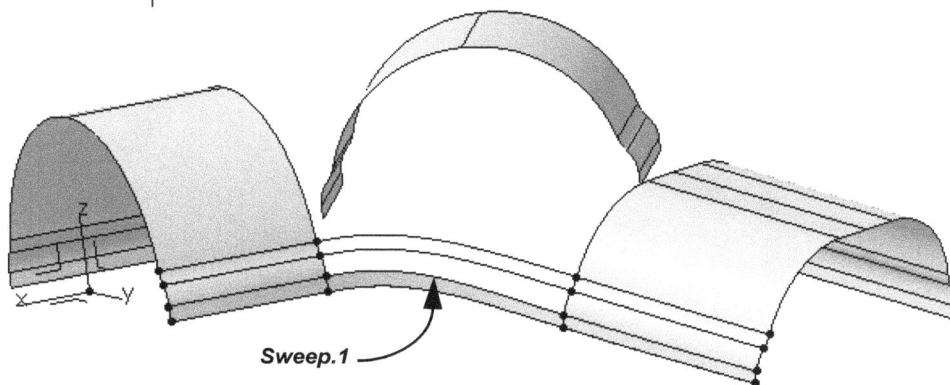

Figure 6–57

7. Click (Sweep) to open the Swept Surface Definition dialog box.

8. Select **Circle** as the *Profile type*.

9. Select **Two guides and radius** as the *Sub-type*.

10. Make the selections shown in Figure 6–58.

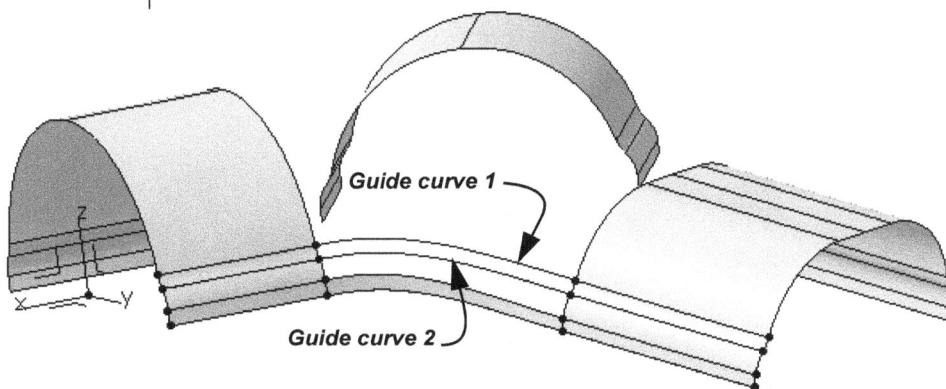

Figure 6–58

11. Enter a radius value of **8mm**. This radius value matches that of the adjacent extruded surfaces.

12. Select the solution that matches the one in Figure 6–59.

Sweep.2

Figure 6–59

13. Create a sweep using the following specifications as shown in Figure 6–60:

- *Profile type:* **Circle**
- *Sub-type:* **Two guides and tangency surface**
- *Limit curve with tangency:* **Connect.2**
- *Tangency surface:* **Sweep.2**
- *Limit curve:* **Connect.3**
- *Spine:* **Default** (Connect.2)
- *Solution(s):* Select the solution that matches the one in Figure 6–61.

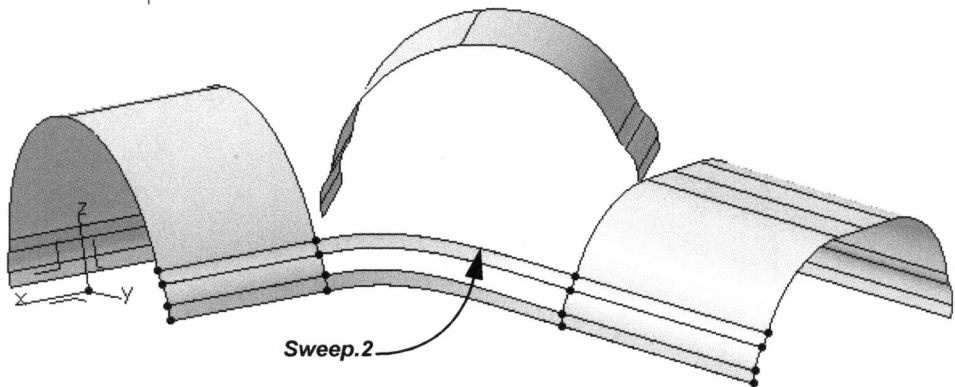

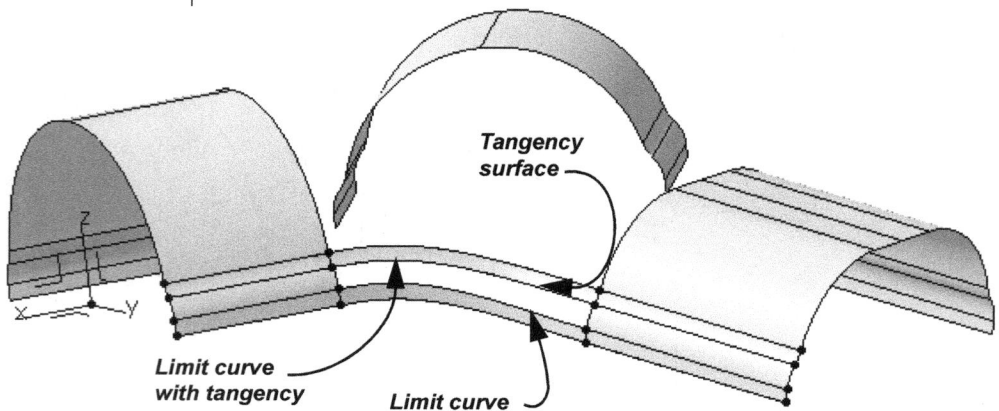

Tangency surface

Limit curve with tangency

Limit curve

Figure 6–60

The model displays as shown in Figure 6–61.

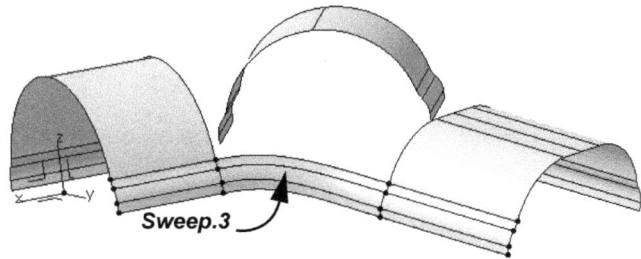

Figure 6–61

Task 5 - Create point and spline reference geometry.

Additional wireframe geometry must be created to support the last sweep feature. To maintain continuity for smooth airflow, splines will control the part geometry. At the end of this task, the model displays as shown in Figure 6–62.

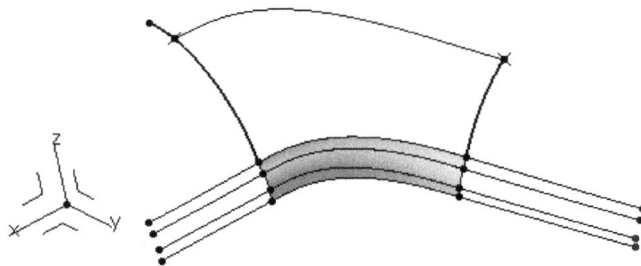

Figure 6–62

1. Extract the two edges shown in Figure 6–63.

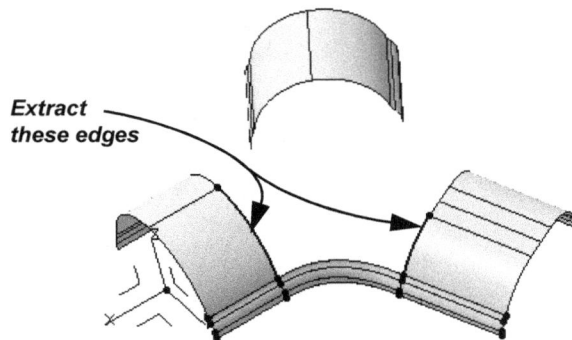

Figure 6–63

2. Hide the following elements:

    • **Extrude1**
    • **Extrude2**
    • **Extrude3**

3. Create the on-curve points, as shown in Figure 6–64.

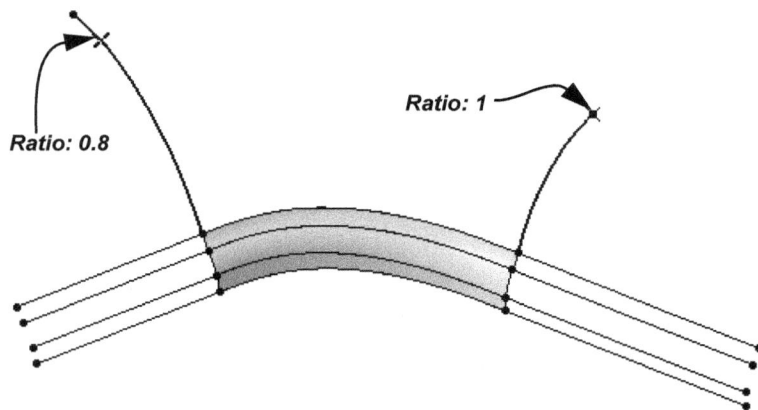

Figure 6–64

4. Show **Group-Base Profiles**.

5. Create a curvature continuous spline using the references shown in Figure 6–65. The spline is created between two points.

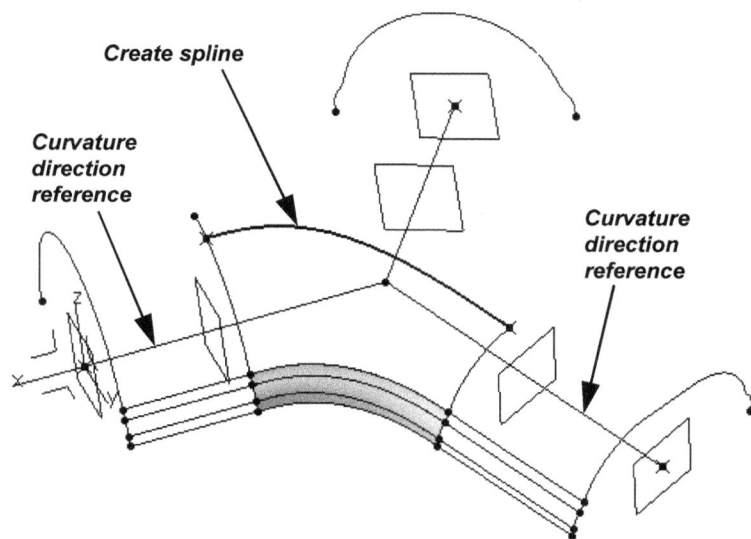

Figure 6–65

The Spline Definition dialog box opens as shown in Figure 6–66. The names of the points shown in Figure 6–66 might differ from the names of your points.

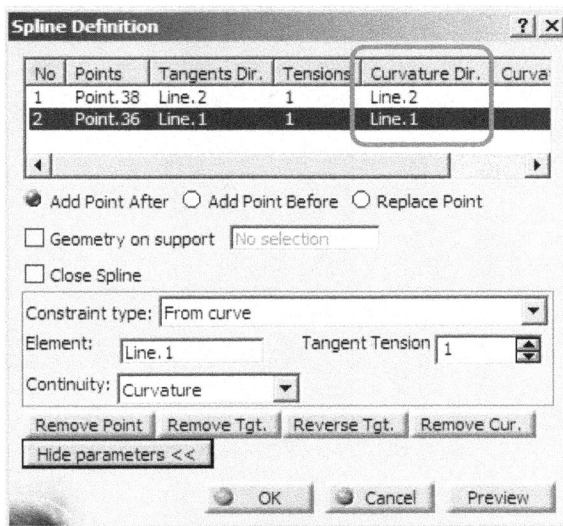

Figure 6–66

6. Complete the Spline feature.

7. Rename the spline as **Limit Spline**.

Task 6 - Create the final sweep surface.

Using the wireframe created in previous steps of the practice, the last sweep surface can be created.

1. Hide **Group-Base Profiles**.

2. Create a sweep using the following specifications:

   - *Profile type:* **Circle**
   - *Sub-type:* **Two guides and tangency surface**
   - *Limit curve with tangency:* **Connect.1**
   - *Tangency surface:* **Sweep.2**
   - *Limit curve:* **Limit Spline**
   - *Spine:* **Default (Connect.1)**

- *Solution(s):* Select the solution matches the one in Figure 6–68.

The reference elements display as shown Figure 6–67.

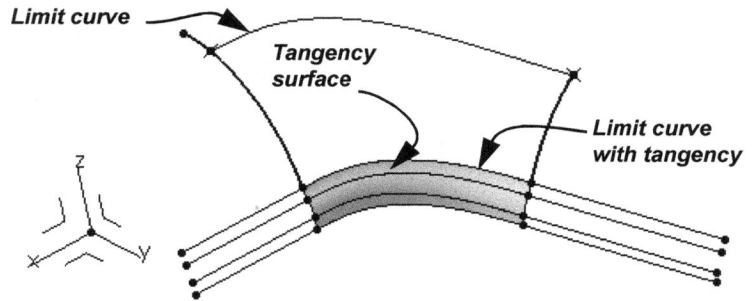

Figure 6–67

The completed sweep displays as shown in Figure 6–68.

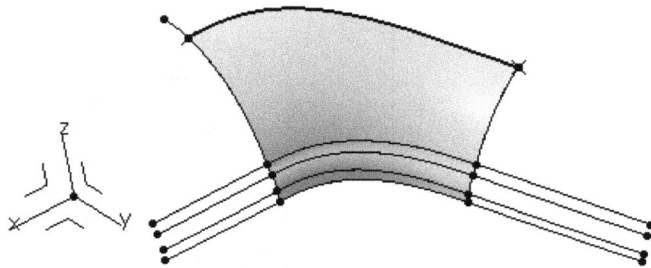

Figure 6–68

3. Show the following elements:

   - **Extrude1**
   - **Extrude2**
   - **Extrude3**

4. The completed model displays as shown in Figure 6–69. Save the model and close the file.

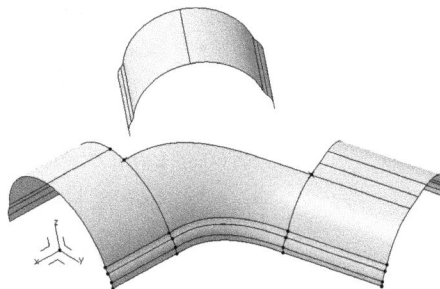

Figure 6–69

Chapter 7

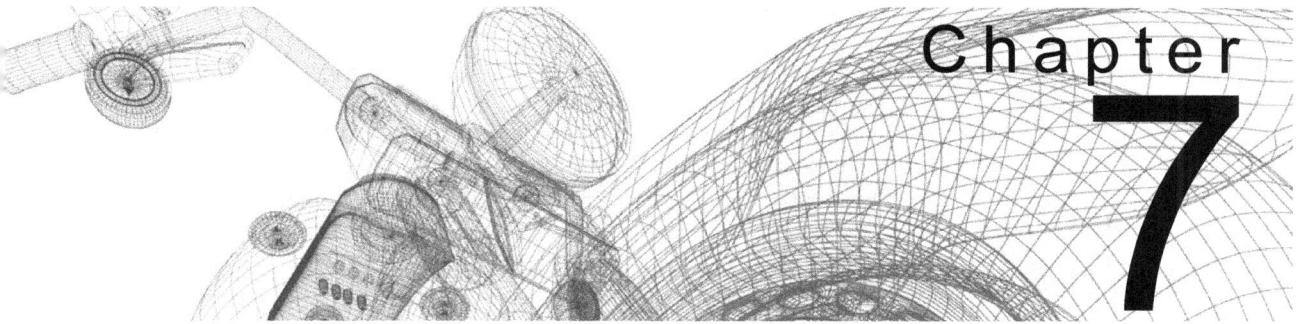

Optional Elements - Sweeps

In this chapter, optional elements are discussed. Some optional elements are unique to the explicit profile and enable more control over the swept surface.

Learning Objectives in this Chapter

- Apply optional Sweep elements.
- Apply optional Explicit Sweep elements.

7.1 Sweep Optional Elements

Swept surface options enable you to use a variety of reference geometry to further control the swept feature. Regardless of the profile type, these optional elements are available. This section provides a brief overview of creating a swept surface. It also introduces the optional elements available for Sweeps.

General Steps

Use the following general steps to create an advanced Swept Surface feature:

1. Start the creation of a Swept Surface.
2. Select curve geometry to define the sweep.
3. Specify optional elements.
4. Complete the feature.

> **Step 1 - Start the creation of a Swept Surface.**

To start the creation of a Swept Surface feature, click (Sweep) in the Surfaces toolbar. The Swept Definition dialog box opens as shown in Figure 7–1.

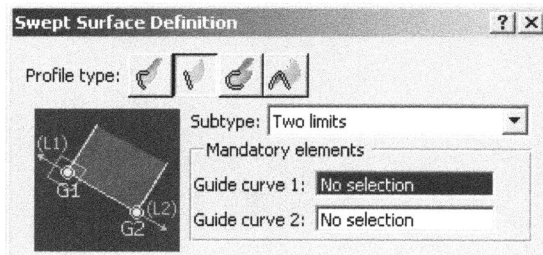

Figure 7–1

Select a Profile type at the top of the dialog box and a sub-type (as required).

The options available for a swept surface depend on the Profile type and sub-type selected. This chapter focuses on the options available for Explicit profile types. The different types of Explicit Sweeps are described as follows:

Profile type	Sub-type		Description
Explicit			Profile is explicitly defined by selecting a curve from the model.
	With reference surface		The surface is defined by selecting a guide curve for the profile. An angle is also specified with respect to a reference surface.
	With two guide curves		The surface is defined by two guide curves.
	With pulling direction		The surface is defined by a guide curve and a pulling direction for the profile.

Step 2 - Select curve geometry to define the sweep.

Depending on the selections made in Step 1, the sweep definition might require the selection of a variety of reference geometry. This can include reference points, lines or planes, surfaces or faces, or other wireframe elements. For example, an Explicit profile requires the selection of a profile curve and guide curve.

Step 3 - Specify optional elements.

Use the optional elements in the Swept Surface Definition dialog box to further define the shape of the swept surface. The optional elements available depend on the selections made in Step 1.

These options include:

- Spine

- Relimiter 1/Relimiter 2

- Smooth Sweeping

- Solutions

- Twisted areas management

- Canonical portion detection

Step 4 - Complete the feature.

Click **OK** to complete the feature.

The following sections discuss the optional attributes available for swept surfaces. The optional elements are shown in Figure 7–2.

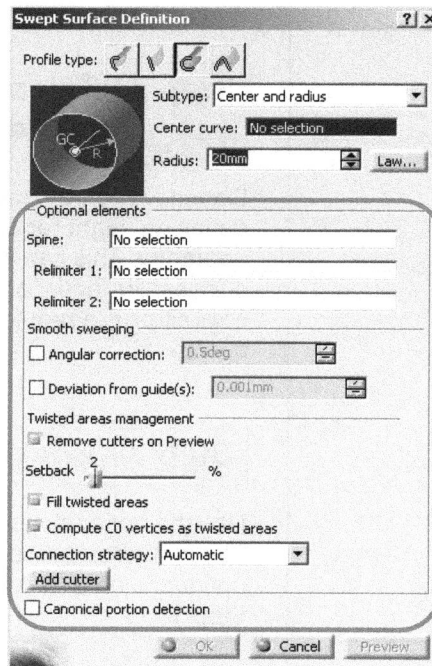

Figure 7–2

Spine

Keeps the cross-section of the swept surface normal to the spine. CATIA uses the guide curve (or guide curve 1 if there is more than one guide) as the default spine. To define a spine, select an edge, curve, or sketch. If the spine has any discontinuities, the sweep also finds them.

For a sweep using the default spine, the guide curve is shown in Figure 7–3.

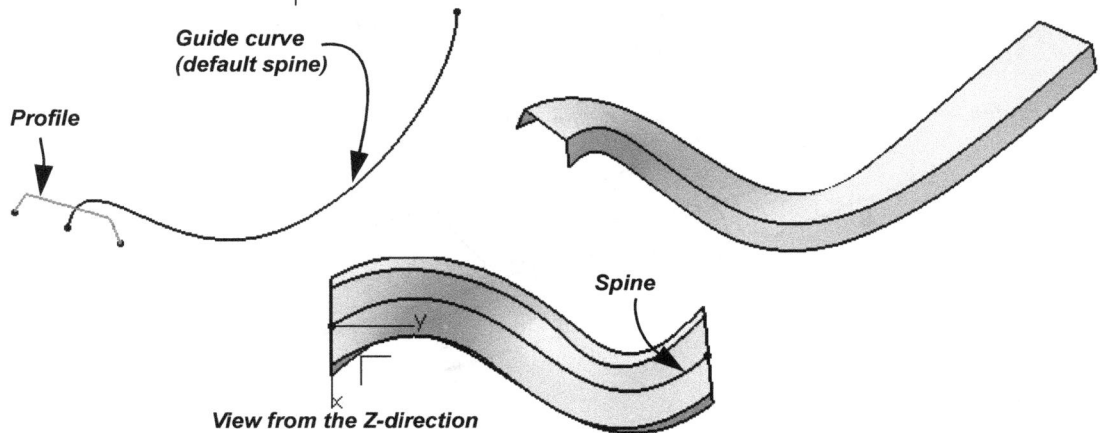

Figure 7–3

A sweep using the Y-axis as the spine is shown in Figure 7–4. The profile and guide curve from Figure 7–3 are used.

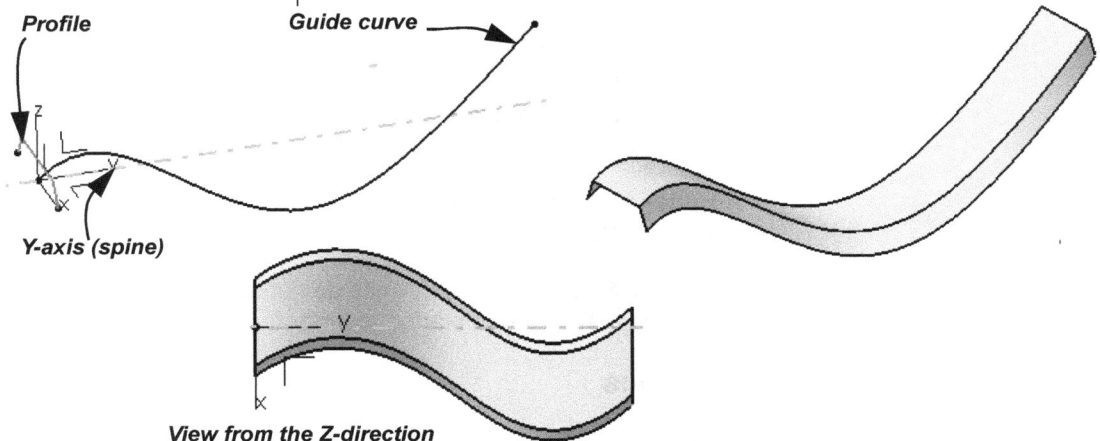

Figure 7–4

Relimiter 1 & 2

Defines the start (Relimiter 1) and end (Relimiter 2) of the swept surface using a reference plane, surface, or face. If the sweep only uses one guide curve, a point can be selected as a Relimiter reference.

The example below shows an explicit profile sweep using With Two Guide Curves as the sub-type. A plane was selected as the Relimiter 2 reference as shown in Figure 7–5. Because a reference was not selected for Relimiter 1, the Sweep is started at the extremities of the guide curves and continues until it intersects the plane.

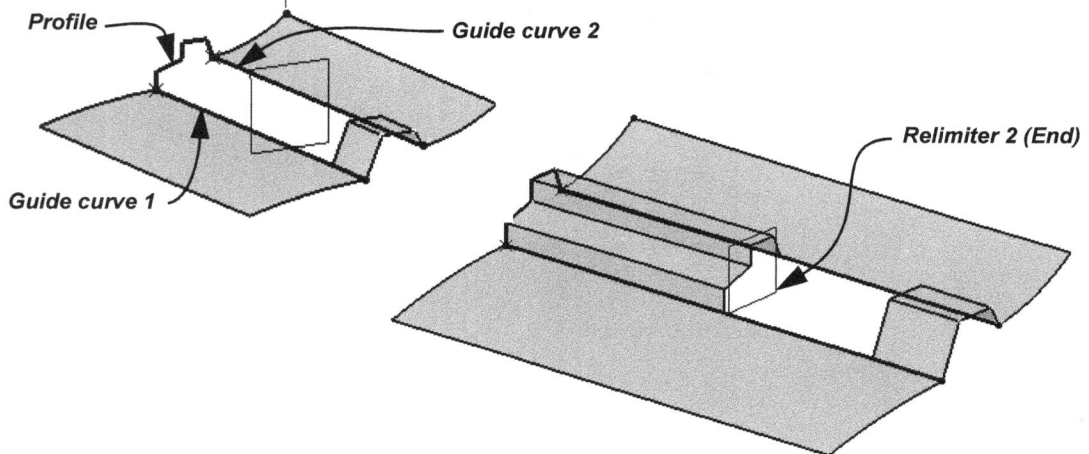

Figure 7–5

Smooth Sweeping

Determines the smoothness of the swept surface. Two parameters can effect the smoothness of the swept surface.

Angular Correction smooths any portion of the surface with an angular deviation less than the value specified in degrees.

Deviation from guide(s) permits deviation from the guide curves by a specified distance to smooth the swept surface.

Solutions

Enables you to toggle between the available solutions (if more than one exists) to select the required swept surface.

Twisted areas management

The Twisted areas management is an optional element to remove erroneous or twisted geometry from the preview display of a sweep. The erroneous portions of the swept surface can be removed automatically by CATIA or by manual definition. If manual definition is preferred, cutters can be positioned along the sweep to denote the areas of the sweep to be removed.

How To: Automatically Remove Twisted Geometry from a Sweep

1. Define all sweep elements, such as profile type, sub-type, guide curve(s), etc.
2. Clear the **Remove cutters on Preview** and **Fill twisted areas** options in the Sweep Definition dialog box, as shown in Figure 7–6.

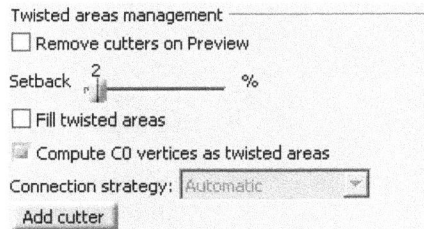

Figure 7–6

3. Click **Preview** in the Swept Surface Definition dialog box. An Update Error message box opens indicating that there are twisted areas for this operation, as shown in Figure 7–7.

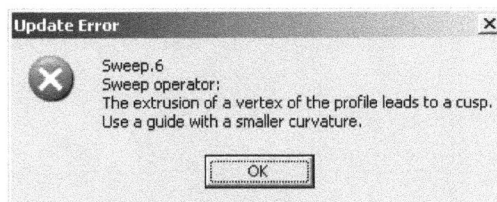

Figure 7–7

4. Close the Update Error dialog box and click **Preview**. The swept geometry displays as shown in Figure 7–8. CATIA automatically removed the twisted portion of the sweep. Other portions of the previewed sweep are self-intersecting.

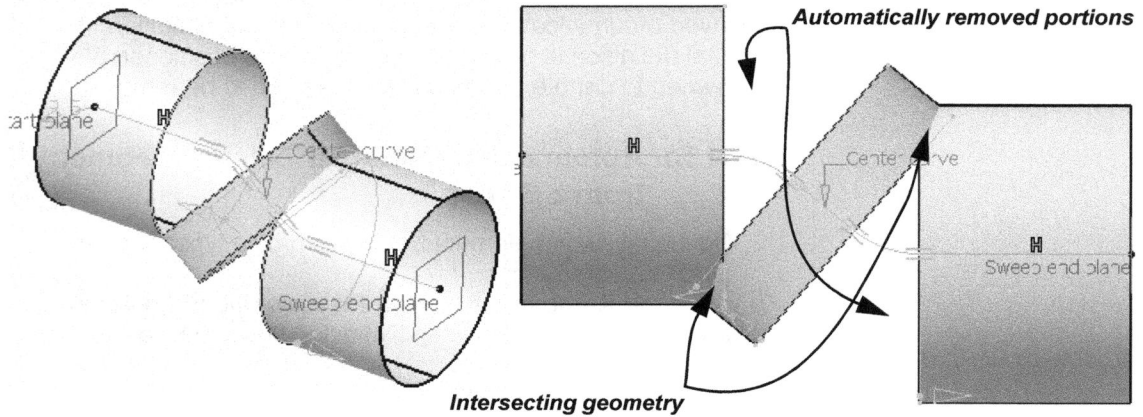

Automatically removed portions

Intersecting geometry

Figure 7–8

5. Complete the sweep feature.
6. Use **Multi-Result Management** as required to determine whether all sub-elements of the sweep are to be kept or not, as shown in Figure 7–9. In this example, the sweep is made of three surfaces; therefore, the Multi-Result Management dialog box opens.

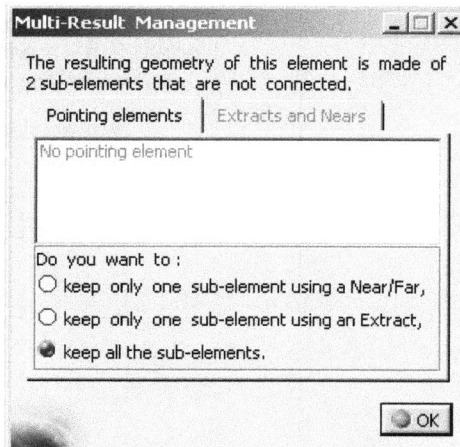

Figure 7–9

7. Build the remaining portions of the surfaces using wireframe and surfacing tools. Operation tools, such as **Split** or **Trim** might need to be used for any overlapping pieces of the swept surface.

How To: Manually Define the Portions of the Swept Surface to be Removed

1. Define all sweep elements, such as the profile type, sub-type, guide curve(s), etc.
2. Make the selections for the **Remove cutters on Preview** and **Fill twisted areas** options, as shown in Figure 7–10.

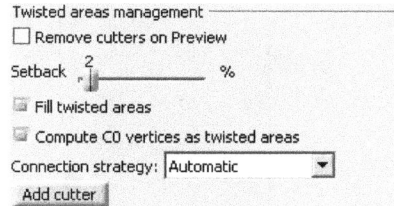

Figure 7–10

3. Click **Preview** in the Swept Surface Definition dialog box. An Error message dialog box opens as shown in Figure 7–11. It states that the swept surface is self-intersecting. This error also means that CATIA was not able to fill the twisted areas.

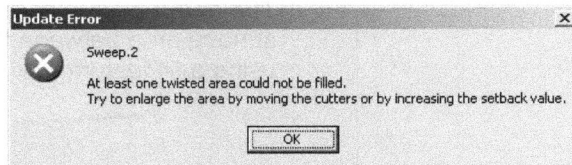

Figure 7–11

4. Click **OK** in the Update Error dialog box and close the Warning message. The model displays as shown in Figure 7–12. The cutters display with the preview of the sweep.

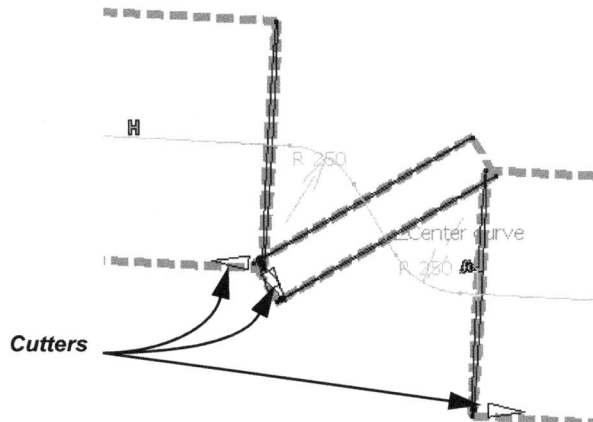

Figure 7–12

Another method to relocate the cutters is to drag the Setback slider in the Swept Surface Definition dialog box.

5. Click and drag on the green cutters to define the portions of the sweep to remove, as shown in Figure 7–13.

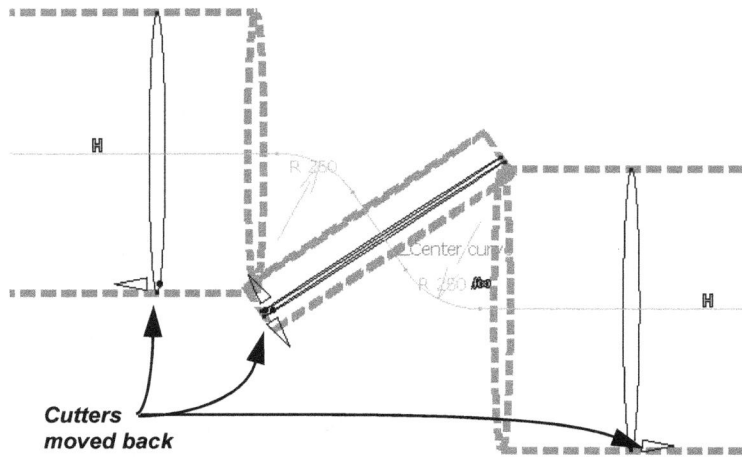

Figure 7–13

6. Click **Preview** in the Swept Surface Definition dialog box. The swept geometry displays as shown in Figure 7–14. The surface area between the cutters is created automatically using a fill feature.

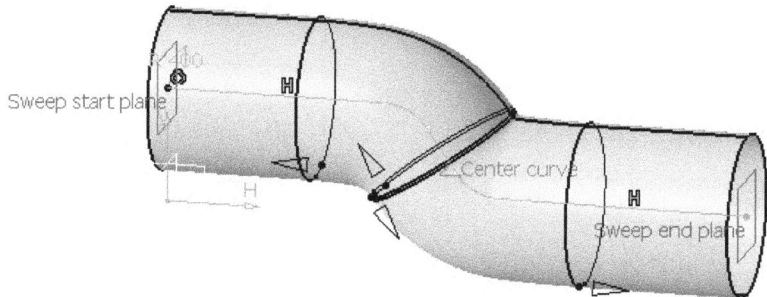

Figure 7–14

7. You can create additional cutters, if required. Click **Add cutter**.
8. Select a location on the guide curve to place the cutter, as shown in Figure 7–15. These cutters can then be clicked and dragged to form a new fill area. (The fill is created when you click **Preview**.)

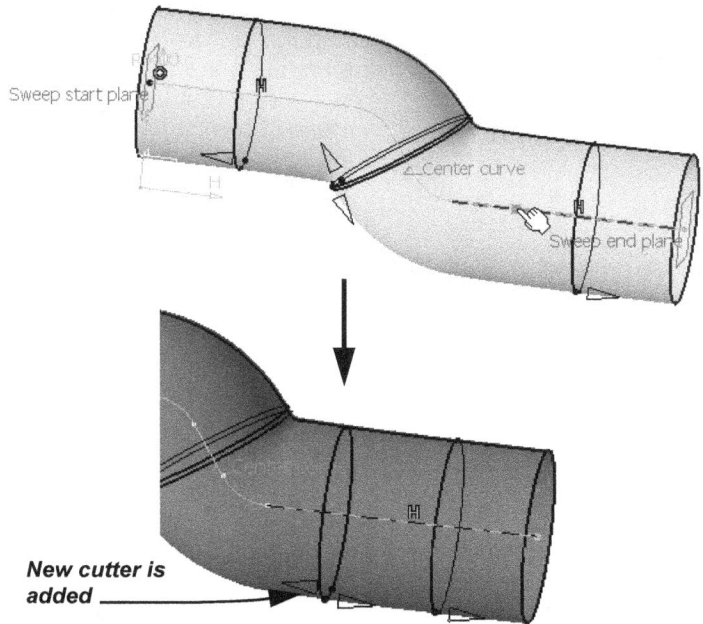

Figure 7–15

9. Complete the sweep feature using Multi-Result Management. Here, you can determine which portions of the sweep to keep. Figure 7–16 shows portions of the sweep that have been kept.

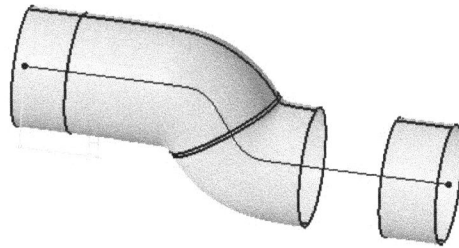

Figure 7–16

Canonical portion detection

Except for the Explicit sweep type, the bottom area of the Swept Surface Definition dialog box contains the **Canonical portion detection** option, as shown in Figure 7–17.

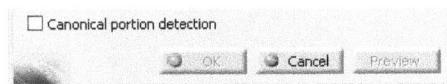

Figure 7–17

By default, the **Canonical portion detection** option is disabled. When this option is enabled, the system detects planar faces of the resulting swept surface so that they can be used for downstream features. For example, the surface of the line swept surface shown in Figure 7–18 can be selected as a sketch support to define the profile for another feature. If the **Canonical portion detection** option is disabled, the face cannot be selected as a planar reference, regardless of its curvature.

Face can be selected as a sketch support

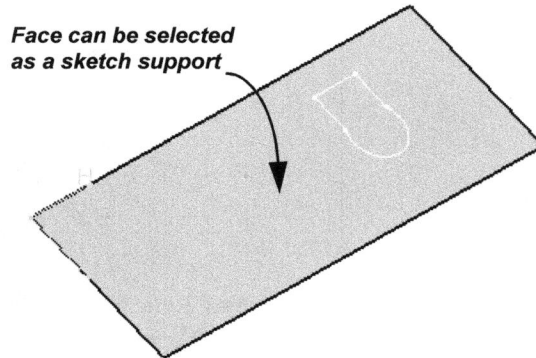

Figure 7–18

7.2 Explicit Sweep Optional Elements

There are optional elements unique to the Explicit profile type. These options are not required to complete an Explicit Sweep, but can help to further control the surface being built. This section discusses using anchor points and positioning the profile.

Anchor Points

Anchor points are available on an Explicit Sweep using With Two Guide Curves as the sub-type. Anchor points are vertices or points that indicate where each guide curve intersects the profile or profile plane. Anchor points do not have to be located on the profile itself. They are used to orient the profile to the guide curves. As the surface is swept along the two guide curves, the anchor points always remain in contact with the guides.

There are two anchoring types available to define Anchor Points.

- Two Points

- Point and direction

Anchor type: Two Points

The Two Points anchoring type takes the profile and fits it to both guide curves to form the swept surface. The points selected as anchors remain coincident with the selected guide curves.

How To: Manually Define Anchor Points using Two Points Anchoring Type

1. Define the Explicit Sweep's profile and two guide curves, as shown in Figure 7–19.

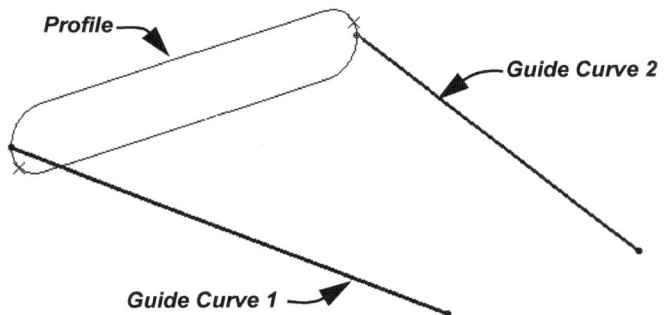

Figure 7–19

2. Select **Two Points** in the Anchoring type drop-down list, as shown in Figure 7–20.

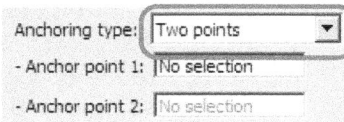

Anchoring type: | Two points ▼ |
- Anchor point 1: | No selection |
- Anchor point 2: | No selection |

Figure 7–20

3. Select a point for the Anchor point 1 reference. This becomes coincident with Guide Curve 1 on the swept surface.
4. Select a point for the Anchor point 2 reference. This becomes coincident with Guide Curve 2 on the swept surface.
5. Click **OK** to complete the sweep. The model displays as shown in Figure 7–21. The profile adjusts so that the anchor points intersect the guide curves.

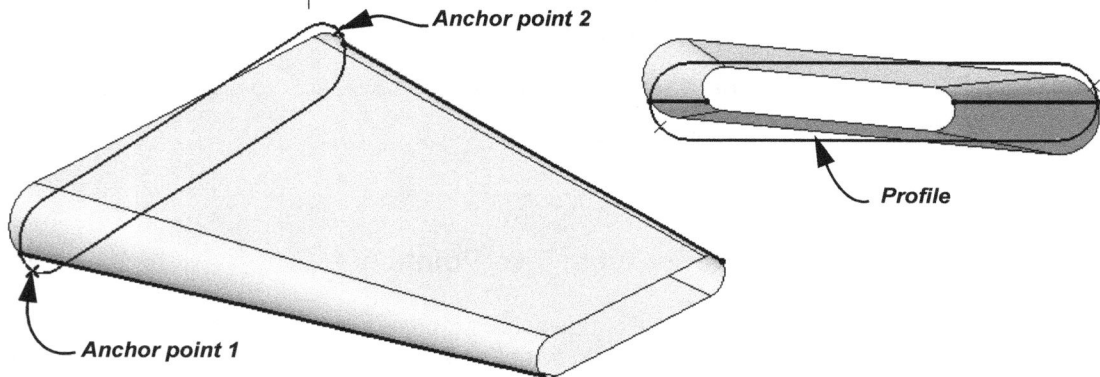

Anchor point 2

Profile

Anchor point 1

Figure 7–21

Anchor type: Point and direction

With the Point and direction Anchoring type, the location of the profile is defined by selecting a point and the orientation of the profile is determined by defining a direction. The selected point remains coincident with Guide Curve 1 throughout the sweep. The direction (defined by a line, linear edge, or plane) is made coincident with a vector that connects two corresponding points on each guide curve at any position along the length of the sweep. As this vector changes orientation throughout the sweep, the profile rotates about Guide Curve 1 to match. With this type of sweep, Guide Curve 2 does not control the shape of the section (i.e., the profile does not remain coincident with Guide Curve 2). It is only used as an orientation reference for the profile.

How To: Use the Point and Direction Anchoring Type

1. Define the Explicit Sweep's profile and two guide curves as shown in Figure 7–22.

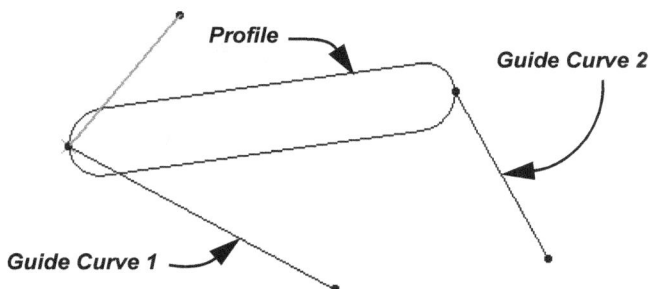

Figure 7–22

2. Select **Point and direction** in the Anchoring type drop-down list, as shown in Figure 7–23.

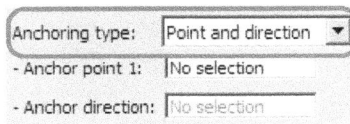

Figure 7–23

3. Select a point or vertex for the **Anchor point 1** reference. This point becomes coincident with **Guide Curve 1**. The profile rotates about this anchor point.
4. Select a reference to generate a direction vector. This could be a line, edge, plane, surface, or axis. This is referred to as the user direction.

   Anchor point 1 and Anchor direction are shown in Figure 7–24. The Anchor direction is referred to as the user direction vector.

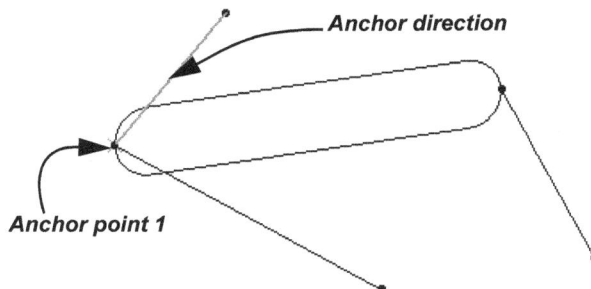

Figure 7–24

An imaginary line is calculated between the end points of Guide Curve 1 and Guide Curve 2, forming the dotted line shown in Figure 7–25. This line is called the computed direction. CATIA shows the computed direction in blue before you manually select an anchor point and anchor direction.

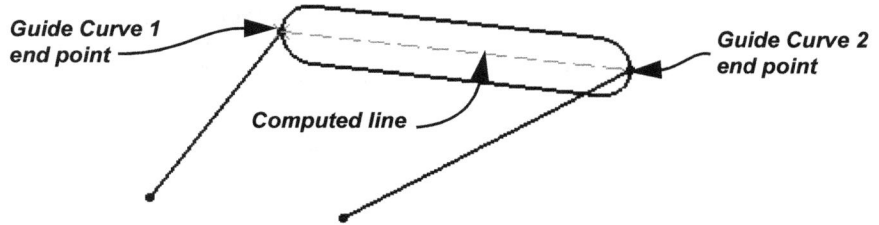

Figure 7–25

The angle between the user direction vector and the computed line determines the rotation of the profile about the anchor point. The direction vector is rotated along with the profile until it is aligned with the computed direction. This process is broken down to help you better understand how the profile gets reoriented as shown in Figure 7–26.

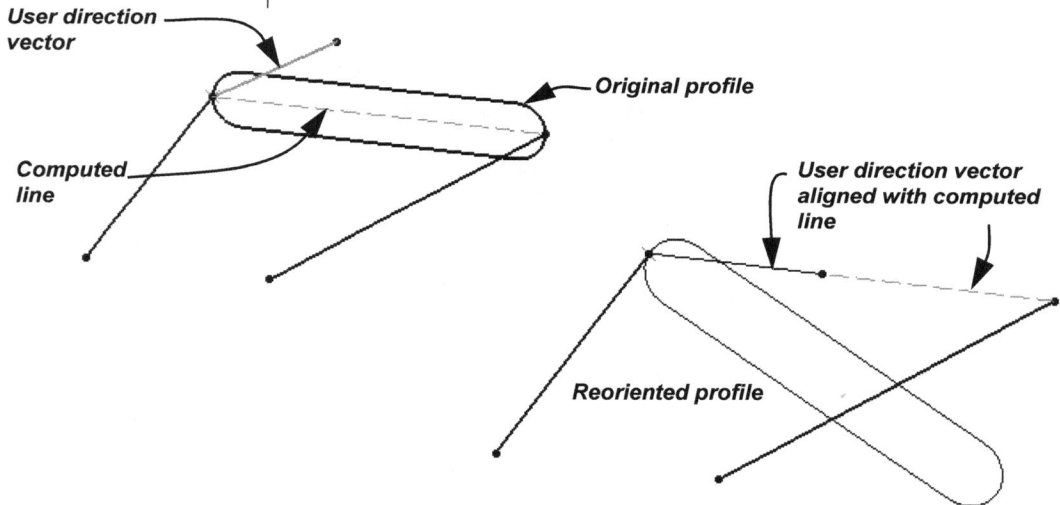

Figure 7–26

5. Click **OK** to complete the sweep. The model displays as shown in Figure 7–27.

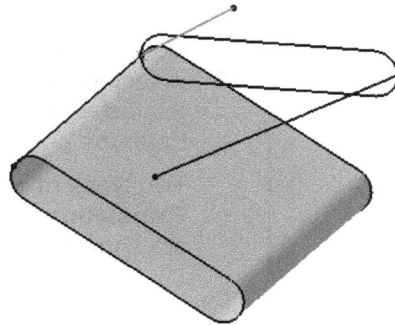

Figure 7–27

Position Profile

The **Position profile** option enables you to modify the location of the profile with respect to the guide curve. The default location of the profile is defined during its creation.

Explicit Sweeps using **With Reference Surface** or **With Pulling Direction** as the sub-type can adjust the position by translating or rotating the profile. Explicit Sweeps using **With Two Guide Curves** as the sub-type have only options to invert the profile.

How To: Reposition the Profile

These operations are performed with respect to the profiles anchor elements.

1. Select **Position profile** and click **Show parameters**. The dialog box updates, as shown in Figure 7–28.

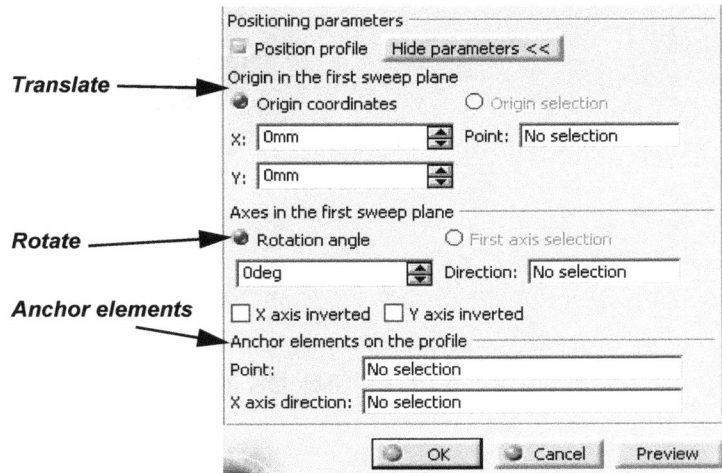

Figure 7–28

2. Select an anchor point on the profile. This point determines how the positioning parameters affect the profile. If the intersection of the profile and the guide curve are selected and no parameters are entered, the profile remains unchanged.
3. Select the X-axis direction. This determines how the profile is rotated about the anchor point.
4. Enter the positioning parameters.

   Two types of positioning can be performed on the profile: **Translation** and **Rotation**. Examples of profile repositioning are shown in Figure 7–29.

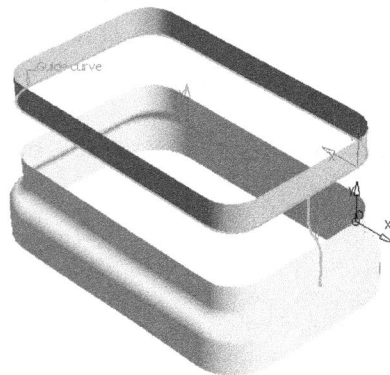

Translated in the Y-direction

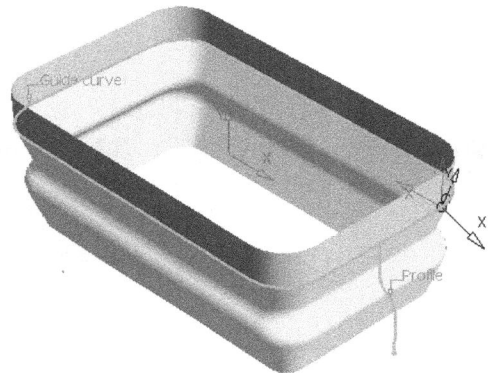

Rotated by 20 degrees

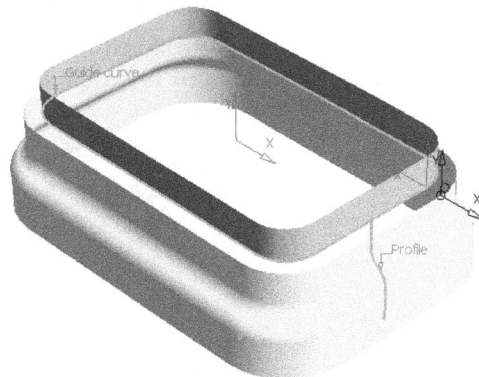

Translated in the X-direction

Figure 7–29

5. Click **OK** to complete the feature.

Practice 7a

Explicit Swept Surface

Practice Objective

- Use anchor points with an Explicit Sweep.

In this practice, you will create a simple explicit swept surface. The sub-type for this surface will be **With Two Guide Curves**. This will enable you to explore using the different anchor point types. The completed model displays as shown in Figure 7–30.

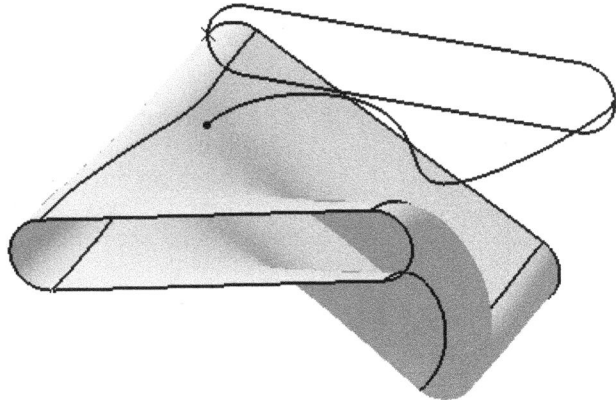

Figure 7–30

Task 1 - Open a part file and create reference geometry.

1. Open **Anchor_Points_Start.CATPart**. The part displays as shown in Figure 7–31.

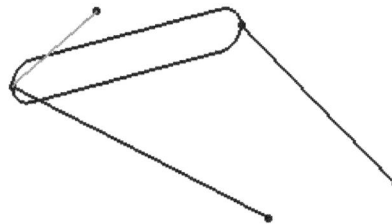

Figure 7–31

2. Create an Extremum point using the X-axis. The element should be **Elongated Hole**. The completed point displays as shown in Figure 7–32. This point is a reference for creating other points.

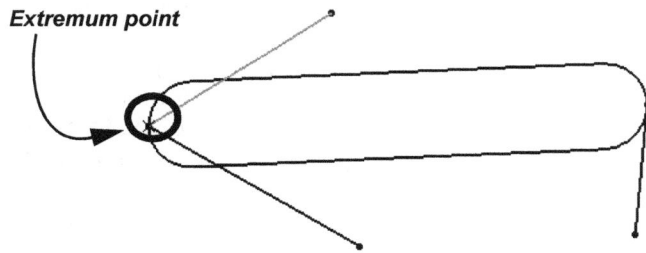

Extremum point

Figure 7–32

3. Create an on-curve point located on the sketch named **Elongated Hole**. Use **Extremum.1** as the reference point. The direction arrow should point down (the negative Z-direction). Enter a ratio of **.03**. The completed point displays as shown in Figure 7–33.

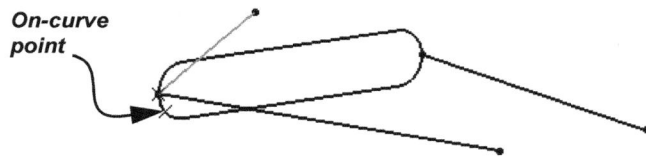

On-curve point

Figure 7–33

4. Rename the point as **Point - anchor 1**.

5. Create another on-curve point located on the sketch named **Elongated Hole**. Use **Extremum.1** as the reference point. The direction arrow should point down (the negative Z-direction). Enter a ratio of **.53**. The completed point displays as shown in Figure 7–34.

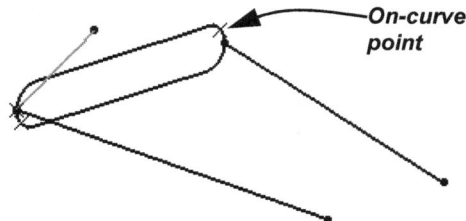

On-curve point

Figure 7–34

6. Rename the point as **Point - anchor 2**.

7. Click ⬚ (Spine).

8. Activate the *Guide* reference field as shown in Figure 7–35.

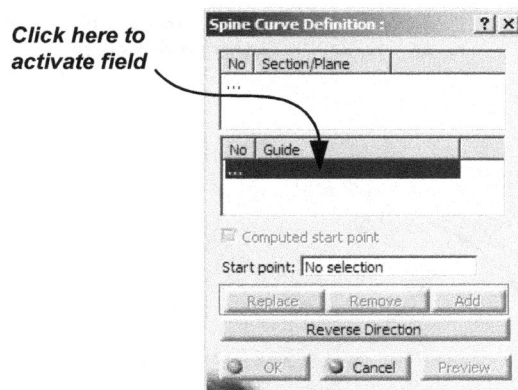

Click here to
activate field

Spine Curve Definition :   **? X**

No	Section/Plane	
...		

No	Guide	
...		

☐ Computed start point

Start point: No selection

Replace	Remove	Add

Reverse Direction

● OK	● Cancel	Preview

Figure 7–35

9. Select **GC1** and **GC2**.

10. Complete the spine. The curve displays as shown in Figure 7–36.

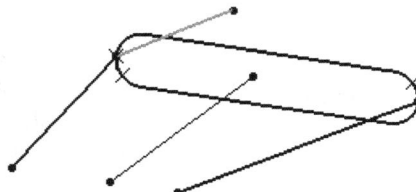

Figure 7–36

Task 2 - Create a swept surface.

---

1. Click ⬚ (Sweep). Ensure that the profile type is **Explicit**, and the sub-type is **With two guide curves**.

2. Select the **Elongated Hole** sketch as the profile.

3. Select **GC1** as the *Guide Curve 1* reference.

4. Select **GC2** as the *Guide Curve 2* reference.

5. The default spine reference is shown in Figure 7–37. GC1, the *Guide Curve 1* reference, is used as the default Spine. Click **Preview** in the Swept Surface Definition dialog box and close the Warning message box that opens.

6. The preview shows a gap between the profile and the start of the swept surface as shown in Figure 7–37.

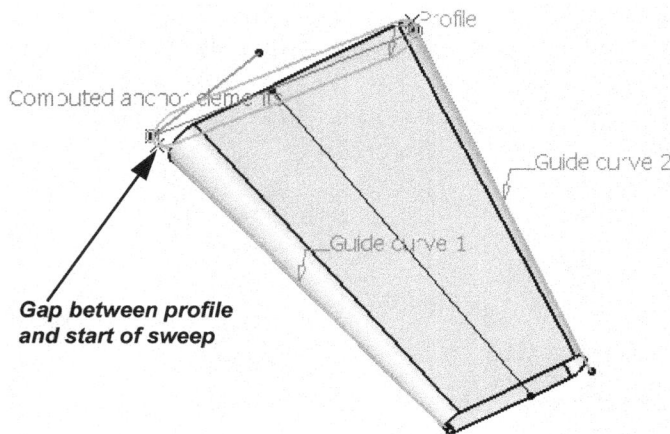

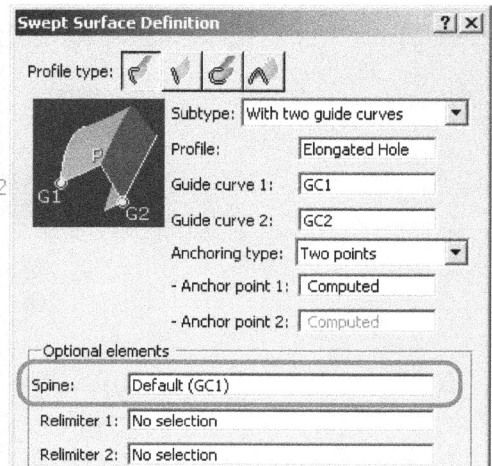

Figure 7–37

Design Considerations

The gap exists in the preview of the sweep because the profile is trying to stay normal to the spine. The spine is currently defined as the default (GC1). The default spine in this situation does not meet the design intent, which is to have the sweep created between the extremities of each guide curve. A different spine reference must be used.

7. Select **Spine.1** as the spine reference.

8. Preview the sweep again. The model displays as shown in Figure 7–38. You have met the design intent by using **Spine.1** as the spine reference. The surface is swept between the extremities of each guide curve.

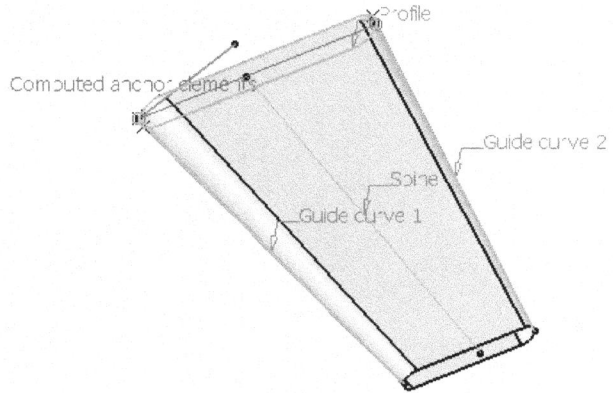

Figure 7–38

9. In the specification tree, hide **Sweep.1**. By hiding the previewed sweep, it is easier to see curves and points being defined in the sweep.

10. In the Sweep dialog box, select **Two points** in the Anchoring type drop-down list. The *Anchor point 1* and *Anchor point 2* reference fields display **Computed**. CATIA calculated default points on the profile or profile plane to use as references. The computed points are annotated in blue on the model, as shown in Figure 7–39.

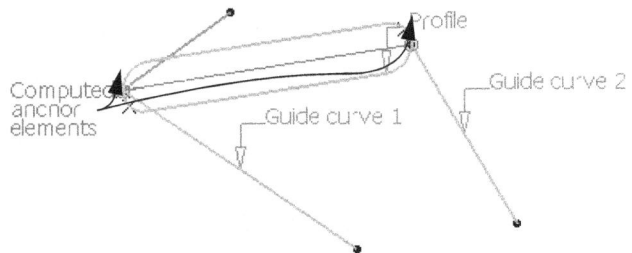

Figure 7–39

11. Activate the *Anchor point 1* reference field, and select **Point - anchor 1**.

12. Select **Point - anchor 2** for the *Anchor point 2* reference.

13. Click **Preview** in the Swept Surface Definition dialog box. The model displays as shown in Figure 7–40. The profile was reoriented so that the two anchor points are coincident with the guide curves.

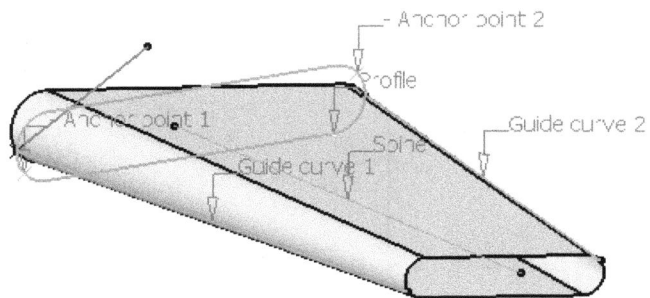

Figure 7–40

14. Complete the sweep. Rename the feature as **Sweep - Anchor Two Points**.

15. Show **Sweep Anchor Two Points**.

16. The model displays as shown in Figure 7–41. The two anchor points remain coincident with the guide curves as the profile is swept.

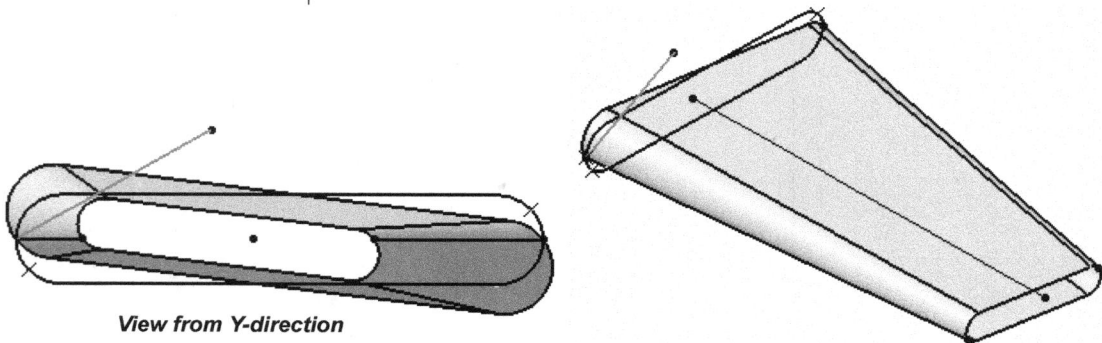

View from Y-direction

Figure 7–41

17. Hide **Sweep - Anchor Two Points**, **Point - anchor 1**, and **Point - anchor 2**.

Task 3 - Create a sweep using different optional elements.

---

1. Create an explicit sweep using **With two guide curves** as the *Sub-type*.

2. Select the **Elongated Hole** sketch as the profile.

3. Select **GC1** as the *Guide Curve 1* reference.

4. Select **GC2** as the *Guide Curve 2* reference.

5. Select **Spine.1** as the spine reference.

6. Select **Point and direction** in the Anchoring type drop-down list. The model displays as shown in Figure 7–42. The blue line connecting the end points of *Guide Curve 1* and *Guide Curve 2* is the computed anchor direction.

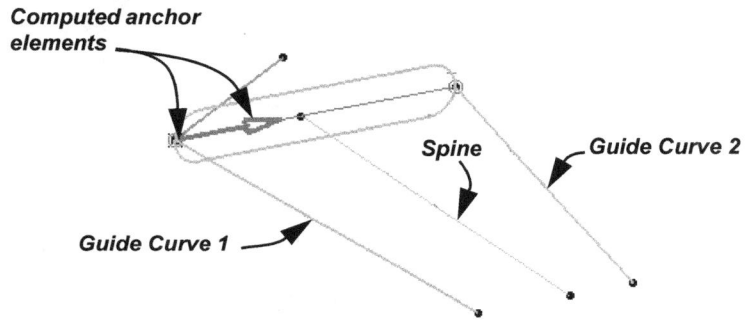

Figure 7–42

7. As the *Anchor Point 1* reference, select **Extremum.1**. Note that the blue arrow and computed direction are no longer shown.

8. For the Anchor direction, select **Line.1**. A green arrow displays pointing in the direction vector, based on the selected **Line.1** reference. The model displays as shown in Figure 7–43.

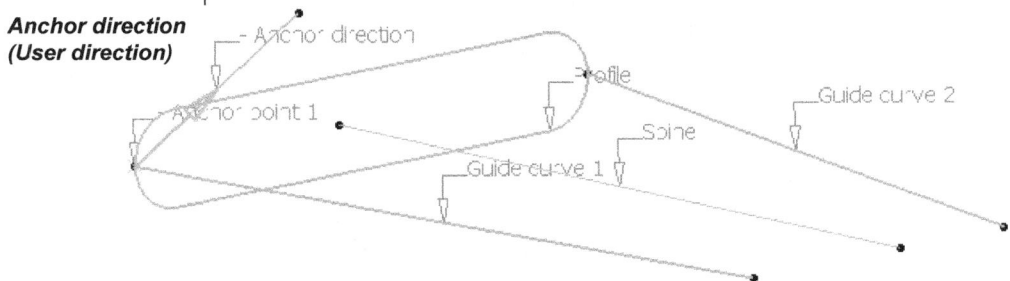

Figure 7–43

Design Considerations

The angle between the computed anchor direction and the user selected anchor direction is 30 degrees. (Between the previously shown blue arrow and currently shown green arrow.) Therefore, the profile will rotate 30 degrees. The profile rotates about **Anchor Point 1**.

9. Preview the sweep. The model displays as shown in Figure 7–44. Note that with the point and direction anchor type, the swept surface does not remain coincident to Guide Curve 2.

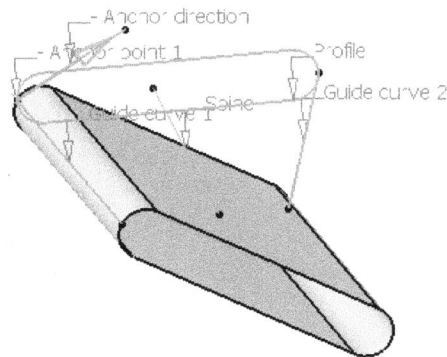

Figure 7–44

10. Complete the feature. Rename the sweep as **Sweep - Anchor Point Direction**.

11. Show **Spline.1**. This curve is used to modify the newly created sweep.

12. Hide **GC2**.

13. Edit **Sweep - Anchor Point direction**.

14. Select **Spline.1** as the *Guide Curve 2* reference.

15. Click **OK** in the Sweep dialog box. The model displays as shown in Figure 7–45. The swept surface updates showing the curvature of *Guide Curve 2* affecting the shape of the sweep.

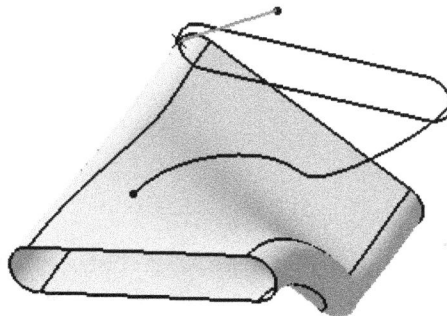

Figure 7–45

16. Save the model.

Task 4 - (Optional) Edit Sweep - Anchor Point Direction

1. Edit **Sweep - Anchor Point Direction** so that the model displays as shown in Figure 7–46. The sweep is 90 degrees from the original profile.

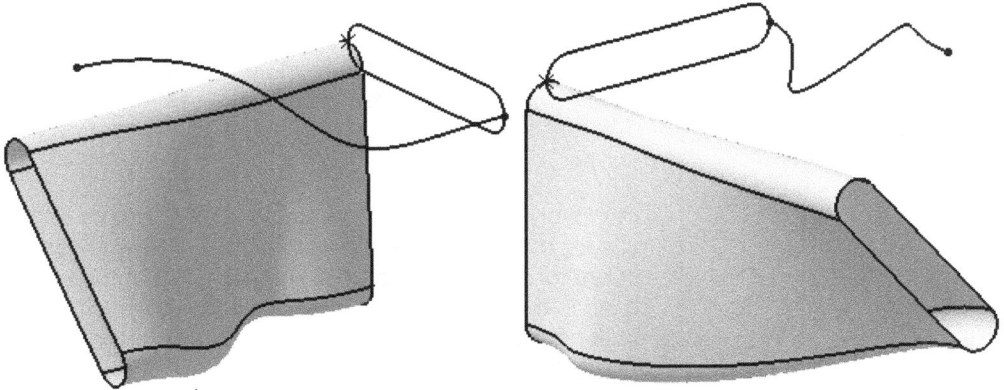

Figure 7–46

2. Save the model and close the file.

Practice 7b | Using Spines to Build Surfaces

Practice Objective

- Create swept surfaces using spine curves.

By default, the first guide curve you select for a swept surface becomes the default spine curve. Some surfaces are generated correctly from their profiles, guide curves, references, and default spines. However, many surfaces need the input of a different spine curve that can help to better define the surface shape.

In this practice, you will create several surfaces using spine curves to correctly define their shape. You will also build a spine curve to use for surface development. All of the surfaces you build in the practice are Sweeps and will need spine curves to be built correctly. The completed model displays as shown in Figure 7–47.

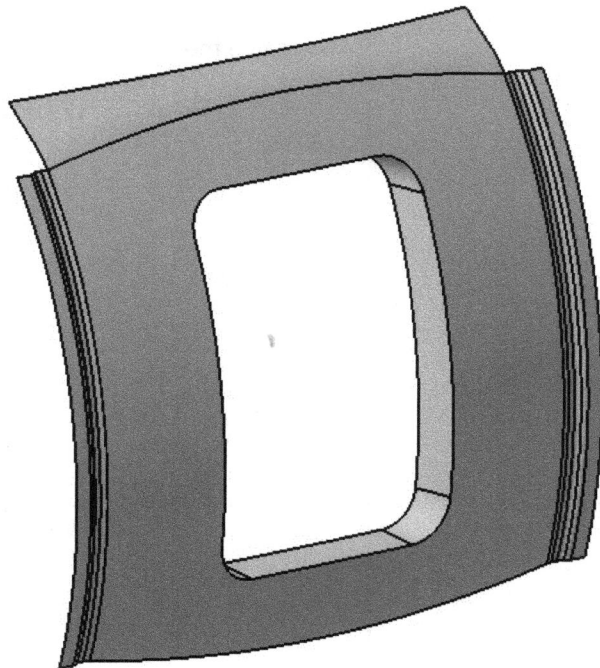

Figure 7–47

Task 1 - Open a part file.

1. Open **UsingSpines_Start.CATPart**. The part displays as shown in Figure 7–48.

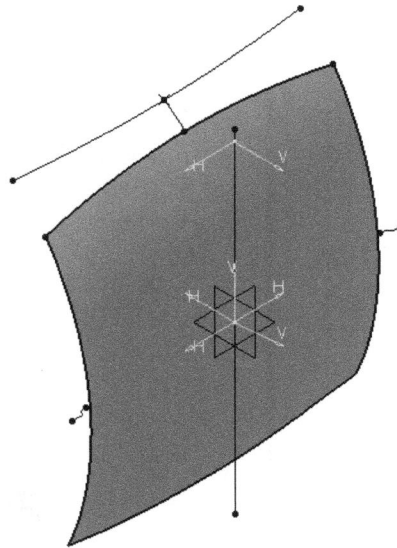

Figure 7–48

2. Use the specification tree to examine the existing features in the model.

Task 2 - Create a flanged side surface with the existing wireframe.

1. Define the **SideFlangeSurfs** geometrical set as the Work Object.

2. Click (Sweep).

3. Create the swept surface using the follow specifications as shown in Figure 7–49:

- *Profile type:* ▱ (Explicit)
- *Sub-type:* **With reference surface**
- *Profile:* **SideFlange1 Profile**
- *Guide curve:* **SideFlange1Guide**
- *Surface:* **BaseSurf**
- *Angle:* **0deg**
- *Angular sector:* **1**
- *Spine:* Keep the default spine setting

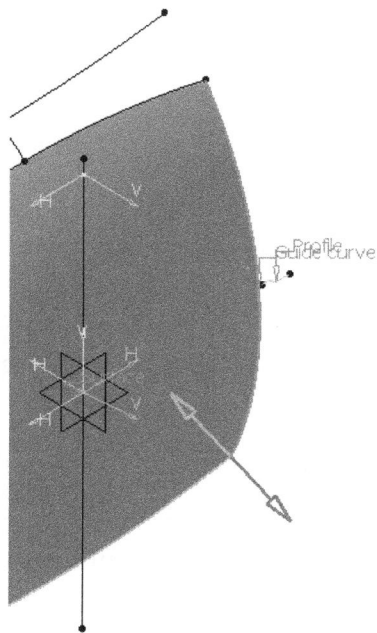

Figure 7–49

4. Click **OK** to complete the swept surface. It displays as shown in Figure 7–50.

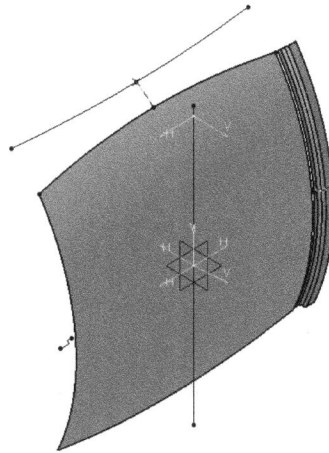

Figure 7–50

5. Rename the sweep surface as **SideFlange1**.

Task 3 - Examine the sweep and define a proper spine with which to sweep the surface.

The swept surface created in the last task used the default spine to determine the shape of the surface. You will now examine the effects of using a proper spine to build the correct surface shape.

1. Click ⊟ (Right View) and zoom into the top right corner of the surface geometry as shown in Figure 7–51.

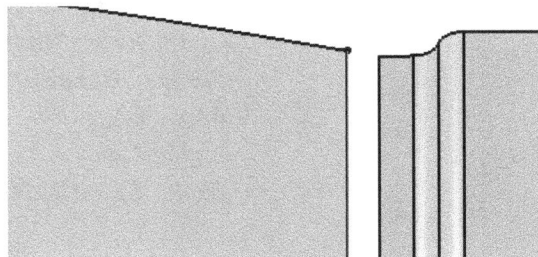

Figure 7–51

2. Edit **SideFlange1**.

3. Change the default Spine to **Spine SideFlanges1 & 2** by selecting it from the specification tree. The surface color will turn red as it is being modified.

4. Click **Preview**. The model displays as shown in Figure 7–52. Note the difference in the swept surface when using the new spine.

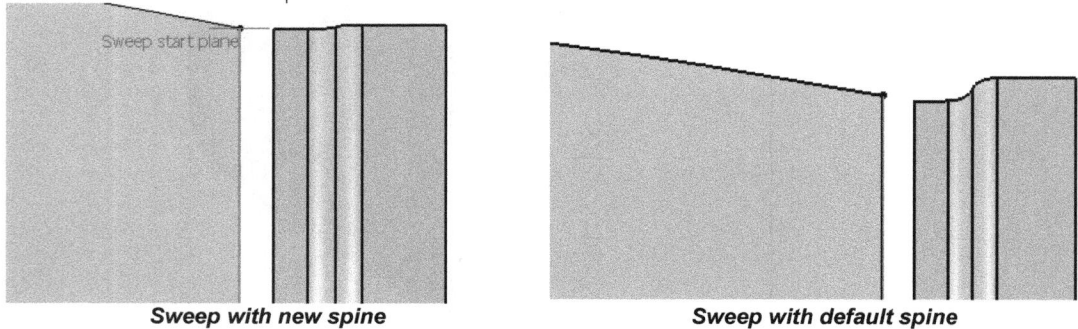

Sweep with new spine

Sweep with default spine

Figure 7–52

5. Click **OK** to complete the swept surface modification.

Task 4 - Create the other flanged side surface with the existing wireframe.

1. Click (Sweep) and define the sweep with the following settings:

- *Profile type:* (Explicit)
- *Sub-type:* **With reference surface**
- *Profile:* **SideFlange2 Profile**
- *Guide curve:* **SideFlange2Guide**
- *Surface:* **BaseSurf**
- *Angle:* **0deg**
- *Angular sector:* **1**
- *Spine:* **Spine SideFlanges1 & 2**

2. Click **OK** to complete the swept surface. The model displays as shown in Figure 7–53.

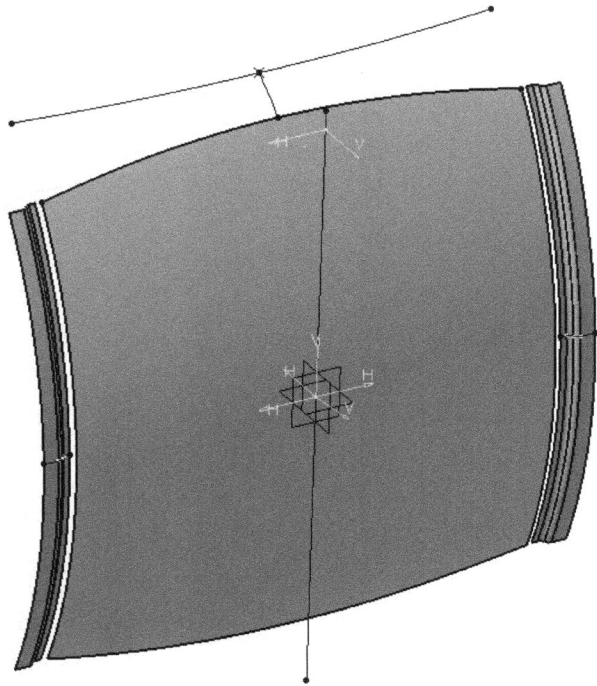

Figure 7–53

3. Rename the sweep as **SideFlange2**.

4. Hide the Construction geometrical set that displays immediately under the **SideFlangeSurfs** geometrical set as shown in Figure 7–54.

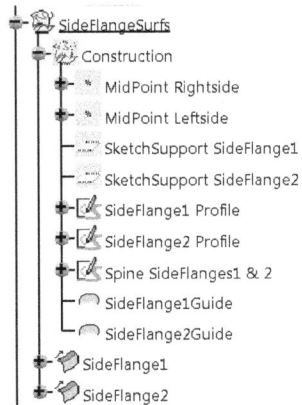

Figure 7–54

Task 5 - Create blended surfaces on the SideFlange surfaces.

1. Extract the two curves shown in Figure 7–55. They will be used to create a Blend surface in the next step.

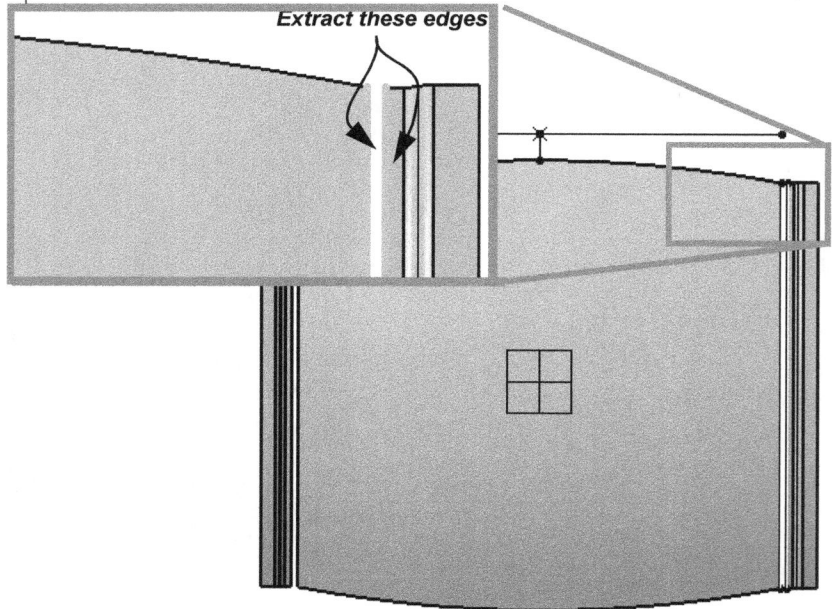

Figure 7–55

2. Rename the extracted curves, as shown in Figure 7–56.

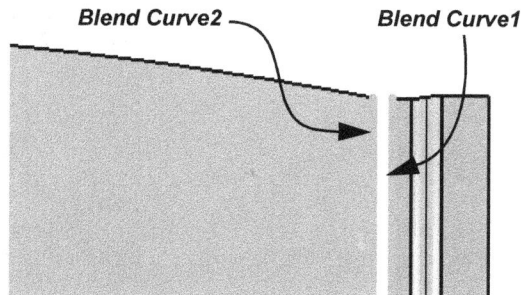

Figure 7–56

3. Click ⬙ (Blend) to create a blended surface between SideFlange1 and BaseSurf as follows:

- *First curve:* **Blend Curve1**
- *First support:* **SideFlange1**

- *Second curve:* **Blend Curve2**
- *Second support:* **BaseSurf**
- Select **Trim First support**.

The dialog box and surfaces display as shown in Figure 7–57.

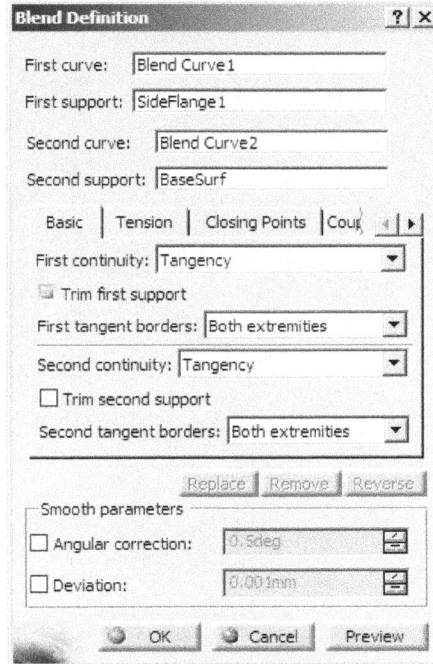

Figure 7–57

4. Click **OK** to complete the blend surface. The model displays as shown in Figure 7–58.

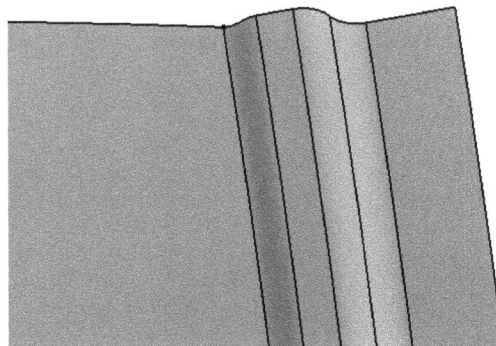

Figure 7–58

5. Rename the blend as **SideFlange1 Blended**.

6. Repeat the process shown in Steps 1-5 to create a Blend surface between **SideFlange2** and **BaseSurf**.

7. Complete the Blend surface and rename it as **SideFlange2 Blended**. The model displays as shown in Figure 7–59.

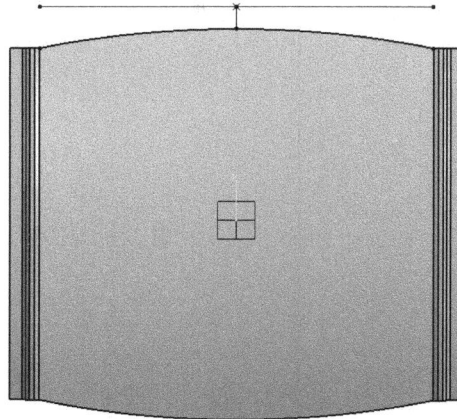

Figure 7–59

8. Hide the extracted curves that you created for the blend features.

Task 6 - Create a spine curve for the top flanged surface.

To build the TopFlangeSurface, a spine curve will be constructed. This will provide a better shape for the swept surface.

1. Define the active work object as the **Construction** geometrical set located under the **TopFlangeSurf** geometrical set.

2. Click (Spine) and click in the *Guide* field, as shown in Figure 7–60.

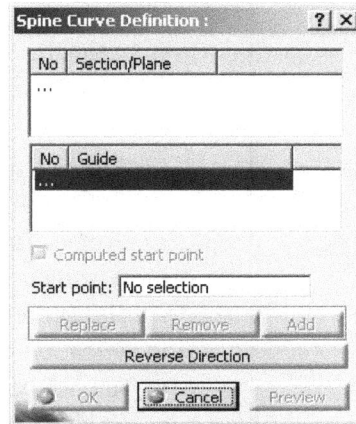

Figure 7–60

3. Select **TopFlange Guide1** and **TopFlange Guide2**, as shown in Figure 7–61.

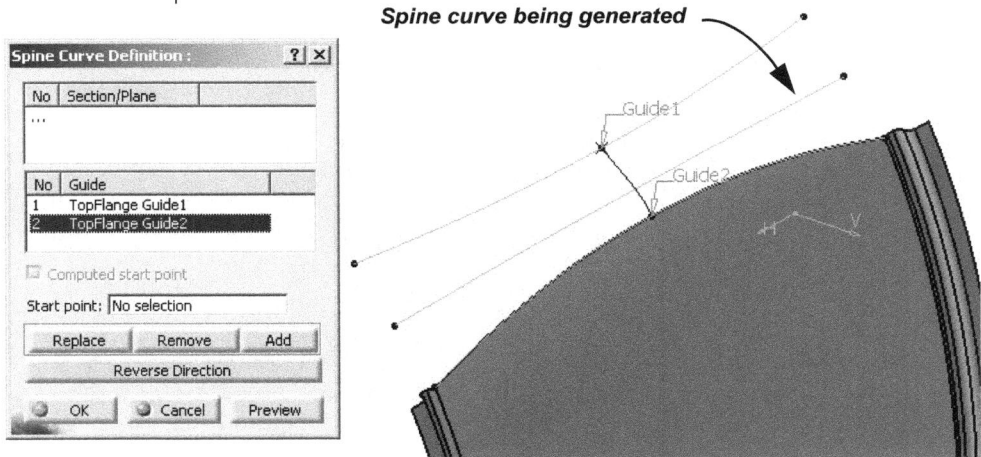

Figure 7–61

4. Click **OK** to complete the spine curve. The **Spine Curve** tool has a unique ability to create a spine curve from existing guide curves.

5. Rename the spine to **TopFlange Spine**.

Task 7 - Create the top flanged surface.

1. Define the **TopFlangeSurf** geometrical set as the active Work Object.

2. Click ![Sweep] (Sweep) and define the sweep as follows:

   - *Profile type:* ![icon] (Explicit)
   - *Sub-type:* **With two guide curves**
   - *Profile:* **TopFlange Profile**
   - *Guide curve 1:* **TopFlange Guide1**
   - *Guide curve 2:* **TopFlange Guide2**
   - *Anchoring type:* **Two points**
   - *Anchor point 1:* **Computed**
   - *Spine:* **TopFlange Spine**

3. Click **OK** to complete the swept surface. The swept surface displays as shown in Figure 7–62.

4. Rename the sweep surface as **TopFlange**.

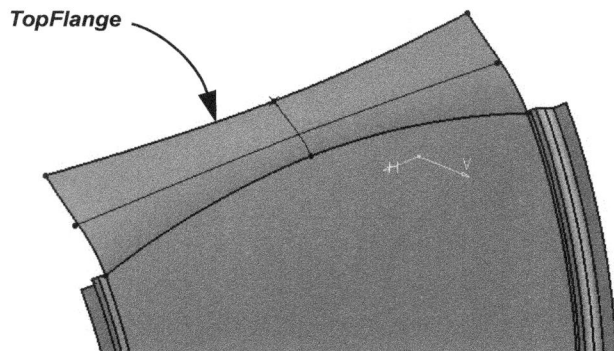

TopFlange

Figure 7–62

5. Hide the **Construction** geometrical set that appears immediately under the **TopFlangeSurf** geometrical set in the specification tree.

Task 8 - Create the wireframe for the cutout surface.

In this task, you will construct the wireframe needed for building surfaces in later tasks.

1. Define the active Work Object as the **Construction** geometrical set located immediately under the **CutoutSurf** geometrical set in the specification tree.

2. Create a reference plane using the following:

   - *Plane type:* **Offset from plane**
   - *Reference:* **ZX-plane**
   - *Offset:* **150mm**

3. Rename the plane to **SketchSupport Cutout Spine**.

4. Using the plane just created, sketch the closed section shown in Figure 7–63. This profile will serve as the spine for the cutout surface you will create later. You will also use this curve to make the guide curve for the cutout surface.

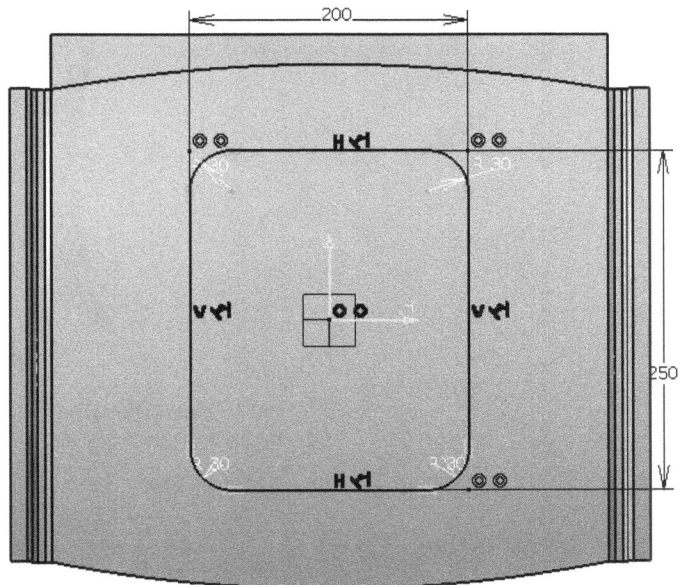

All radii are 30mm

Figure 7–63

5. Rename the sketch as **Cutout Spine**.

6. Click ⬜ (Project) and select the following:

   - *Projection type:* **Along a direction**
   - *Projected:* **Cutout Spine**
   - *Support:* **BaseSurf**
   - *Direction:* **zx plane**

7. Rename the projected curve to **Cutout Guide**. The model displays as shown in Figure 7–64.

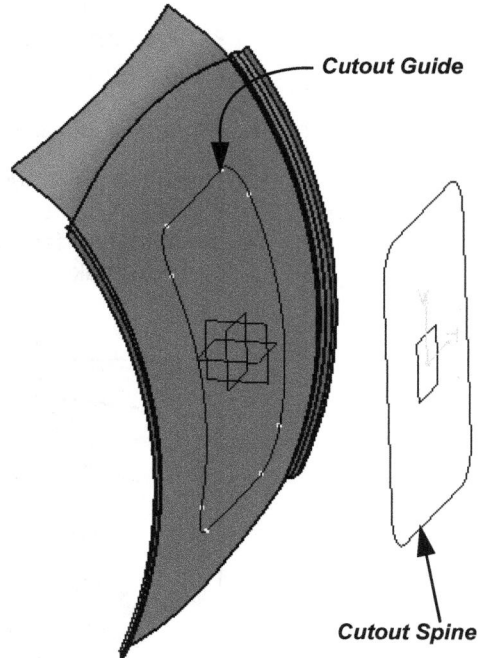

Figure 7–64

8. Hide the **SketchSupport Cutout Spine** feature as you will not need to use it again.

9. Save the model.

Task 9 - Create the cutout of the BaseSurf.

In this task, another swept surface with a spine will define the cutout flange shape. However, for clarity you will first need to split the BaseSurf to create the opening that the cutout flange surface will be swept along.

1. Make the **BaseSurf** geometrical set the Work Object.

2. Click ![Split icon] (Split).

3. Use the following specifications to define the Split:

   - *Element to cut:* **BaseSurf**
   - *Cutting elements:* **Cutout Guide**

   The model and Split Definition dialog box appear as shown in Figure 7–65. If required, select the **Other side** button to remove only the part of the BaseSurf on the interior of the Cutout Guide.

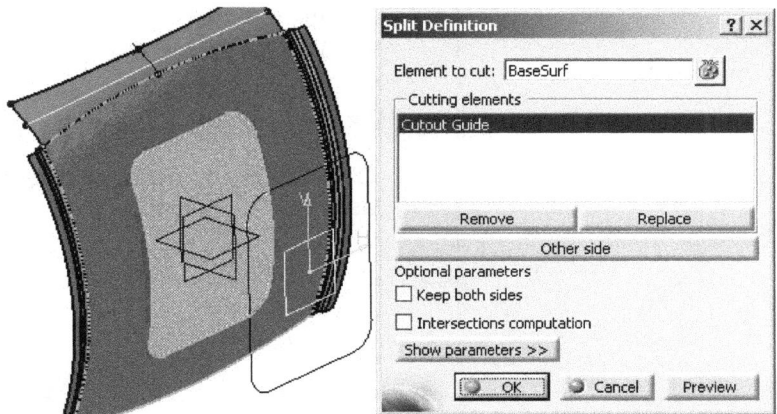

Figure 7–65

4. Complete the split operation and rename it as **BaseSurf with Cutout**. The model displays as shown in Figure 7–66.

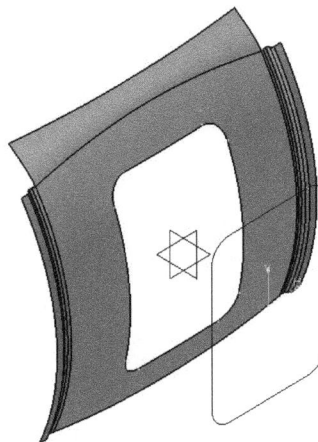

Figure 7–66

Task 10 - Create the swept flange surface.

1. Make the **CutoutSurf** geometrical set the Work Object.

2. Create a sweep and define the surface as follows:

   - *Profile type:* (Line)
   - *Sub-type:* **With reference surface**
   - *Guide curve 1:* **Cutout Guide**
   - *Reference surface:* **zxplane**
   - *Angle:* **85deg**
   - *Angular sector:* **4**
   - *Length 1:* **40mm**
   - *Spine:* Keep the default spine setting

3. Click **OK** to complete the swept surface. The model displays as shown in Figure 7–67.

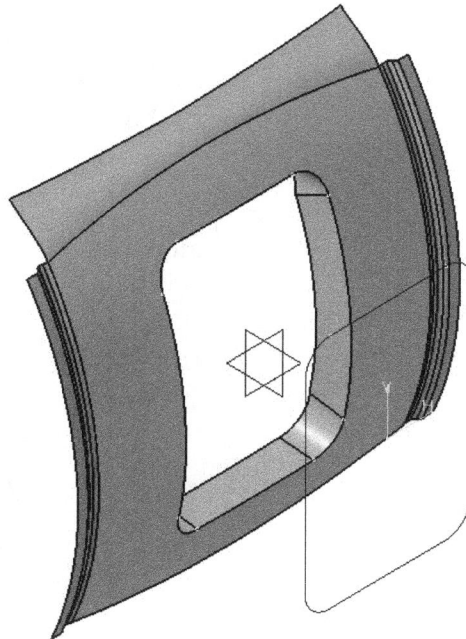

Figure 7–67

4. Rename the sweep surface as **Cutout**.

Task 11 - Examine the newly created sweep geometry.

The swept surface created in the last task used the default spine to determine the shape of the surface. In this task, you will examine the effects of using a proper spine to build the correct surface shape.

1. Orient the model from the left side view, and zoom into the top of the surface geometry, as shown in Figure 7–68.

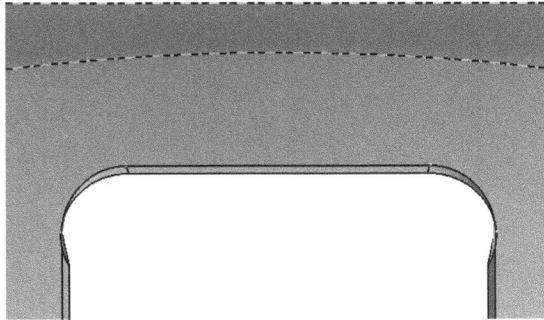

Figure 7–68

2. Double-click the sweep named Cutout.

3. Change the spine reference to **Cutout Spine**. The surface color will turn red as it is being modified.

4. Click **Preview** to visualize the change in the sweep as shown in Figure 7–69.

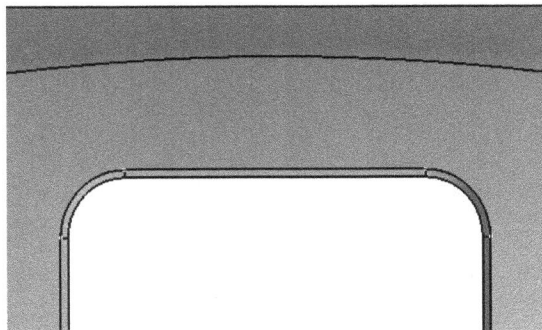

Figure 7–69

5. Click **OK** to complete the swept surface modification.

6. Hide the **Construction** geometrical set immediately under the **CutoutSurf** geometrical set in the specification tree.

Task 12 - Join surfaces.

1. Make the **FinalSurf** geometrical set the Work Object.

2. Click ▦ (Join) and select the surfaces shown in Figure 7–70.

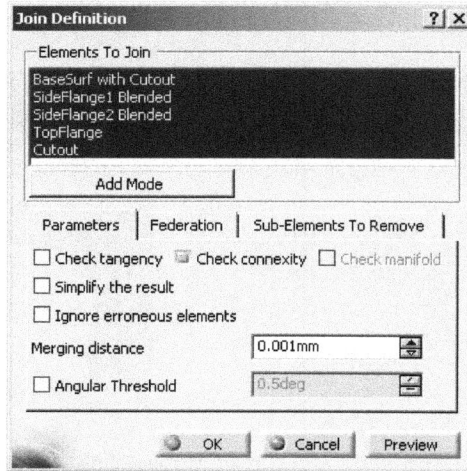

Figure 7–70

3. Rename the joined surface to **FinalSurf**. The finished model displays as shown in Figure 7–71.

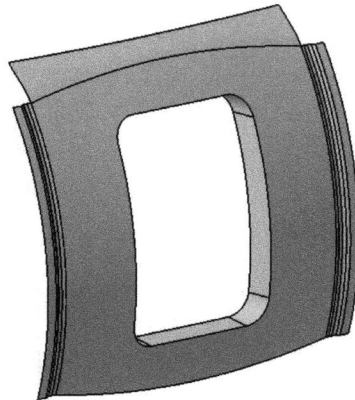

Figure 7–71

4. Save the model and close the file.

Practice 7c

Twisted Areas Management

Practice Objectives

- Manage twisted areas and cutters.
- Use Multi-Result Management to Extract the surfaces.

Swept surfaces require input elements such as guide curves, spines, lengths, and angles. These can impact whether the feature is created successfully. Sweep failures might occur when you are given a guide curve that possesses too great a curvature for the required surface. A draft angle or surface length might result in overlapping or twisted geometry. Changing the definition of the surface to avoid the failure in the first place might be acceptable in some cases. In many cases you need to manage the twisted geometry to extract the correct surface shapes that you need.

In this exercise, you will be given most of the geometry for the model. However, you will need to build some new wireframe and surface geometry that is required to finish the surface shape. The input elements for these surfaces will purposely lead to failed geometry by virtue of twisted surfaces. You will need to perform twisted surface management to finish the surface shapes with the correct input definitions. The completed model displays as shown in Figure 7–72.

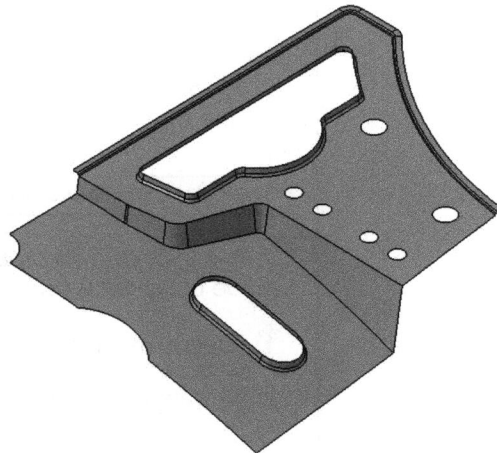

Figure 7–72

Task 1 - Open a part file.

1. Open **ManagingTwistedSurfaces.CATPart**. The part displays as shown in Figure 7–73.

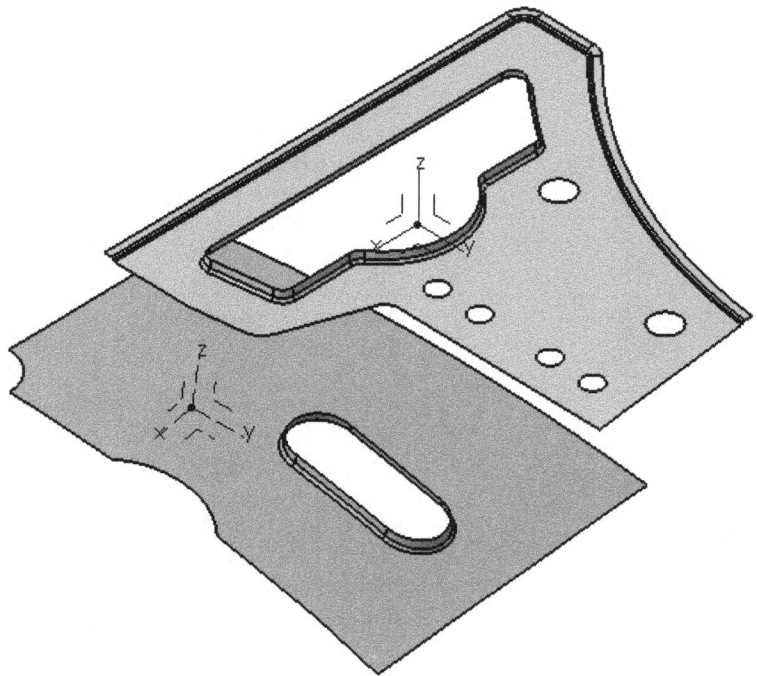

Figure 7–73

2. Use the specification tree to examine the existing features in the model.

Task 2 - Create a boundary curve.

In this task you will create a boundary curve to use as the future guide curve for a sweep.

1. Define the **Top Surface** geometrical set as the Work Object.

2. Create a Boundary curve using tangent continuity as the propagation type.

3. Select the edge shown in Figure 7–74 as the Surface edge reference.

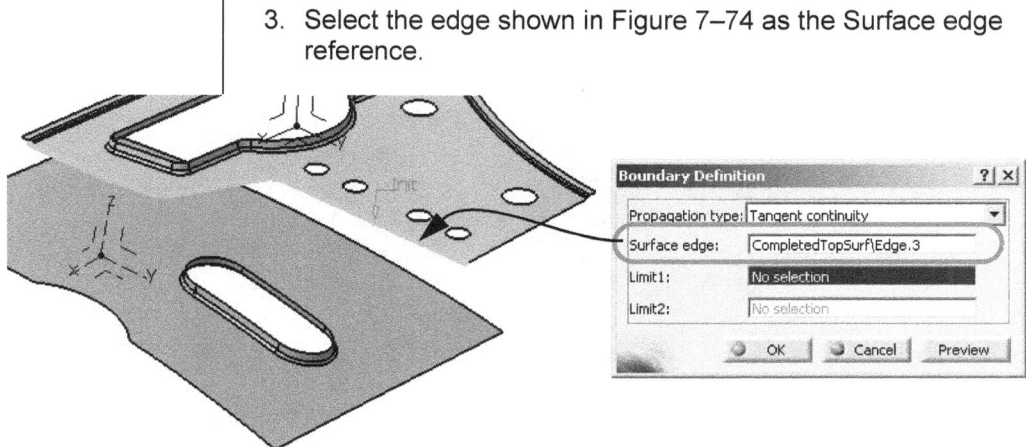

Figure 7–74

4. Complete the boundary curve.

5. Rename the feature to **JunctionGuideCurve**.

Task 3 - Create the line sweep for the junction surface.

Per the design intent, the length and angle value for the sweep are required. The resulting sweep will have twisted areas within it and will need to be managed. In this task, you will examine and move cutters to extract the proper portions of the sweep.

1. Define the **Bottom Surface** geometrical set as the Work Object.

2. Hide the **BlendedBottomSurfWithAllCutouts** feature to completely visualize the sweep surface you are about to create.

3. Create a sweep using the following specifications:

   • *Profile type:* **Line**
   • *Sub-type:* **With reference surface**
   • *Guide curve 1:* **JunctionGuideCurve**
   • *Reference surface:* **TopSurfaceAxis\XY Plane**
   • *Angle:* **80deg**
   • *Angular sector:* **4**
   • *Length 1:* **60mm**
   • *Spine:* Default (**JunctionGuideCurve**)

The model and dialog box display as shown in Figure 7–75.

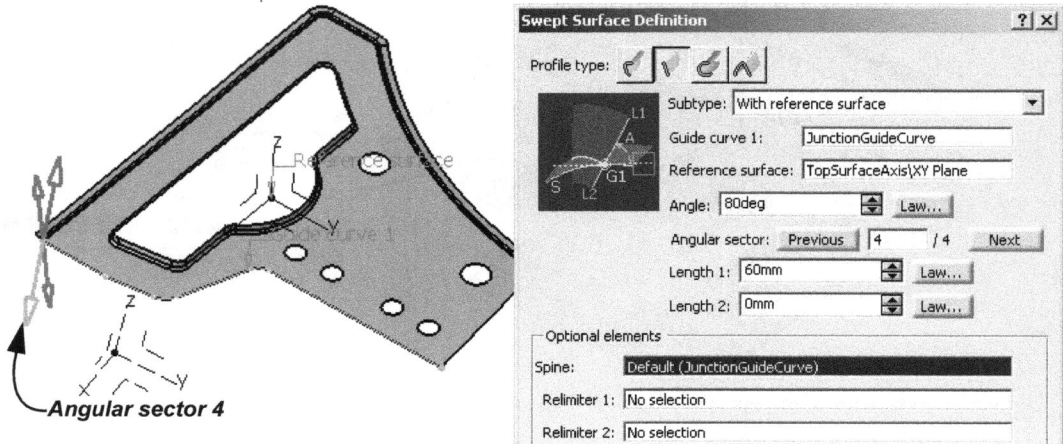

Figure 7–75

4. Ensure that the **Remove cutters on Preview** option is selected.

5. Clear the **Fill twisted areas** option.

6. Set the *Setback distance* value to **0**.

7. Preview the Sweep feature.

8. A Warning dialog box opens, as shown in Figure 7–76. This message states that the surface you are trying to build is self-intersecting or twisted. It suggests that you use a guide with a smaller curvature (i.e., a larger radius). However, per the design intent of the adjoining surface, the guide curve cannot be changed.

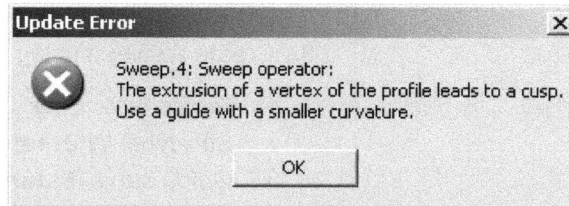

Figure 7–76

9. Click **OK** in the Update Error dialog box. The model displays as shown in Figure 7–77 with the twisted areas displayed in red.

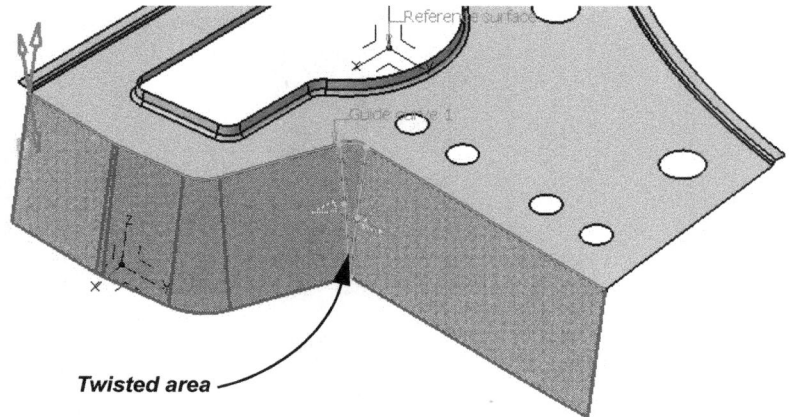

Figure 7–77

10. Zoom in on the twisted area shown in Figure 7–78.

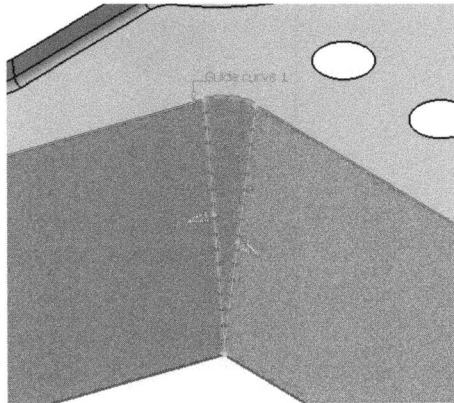

Figure 7–78

11. Use the cursor to click and drag the green cutters back, as shown in Figure 7–79. This prevents the swept surface from self-intersecting.

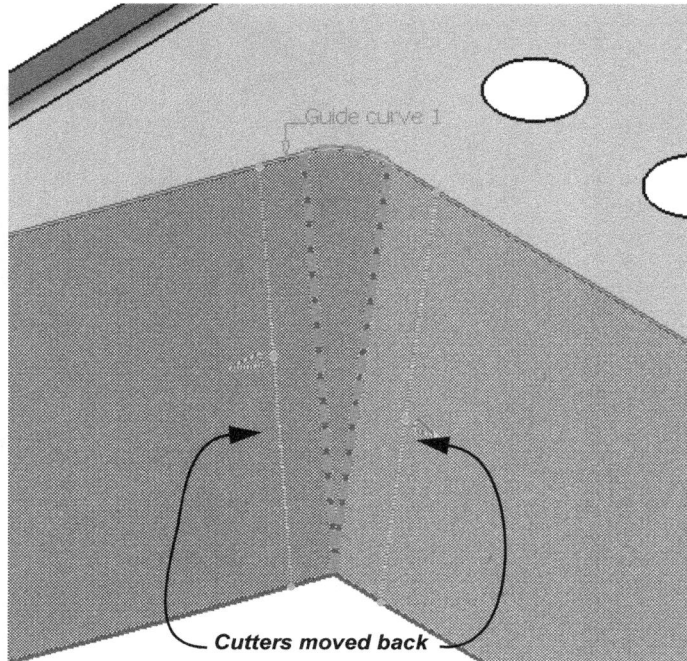

Figure 7–79

12. Clear the **Remove cutters on Preview** option as shown in Figure 7–80. This enables you to see what the swept surface will look like if the current cutter positions are used when the feature is completed.

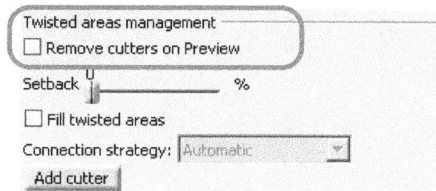

Figure 7–80

13. Click **Preview**. The model displays as shown in Figure 7–81.

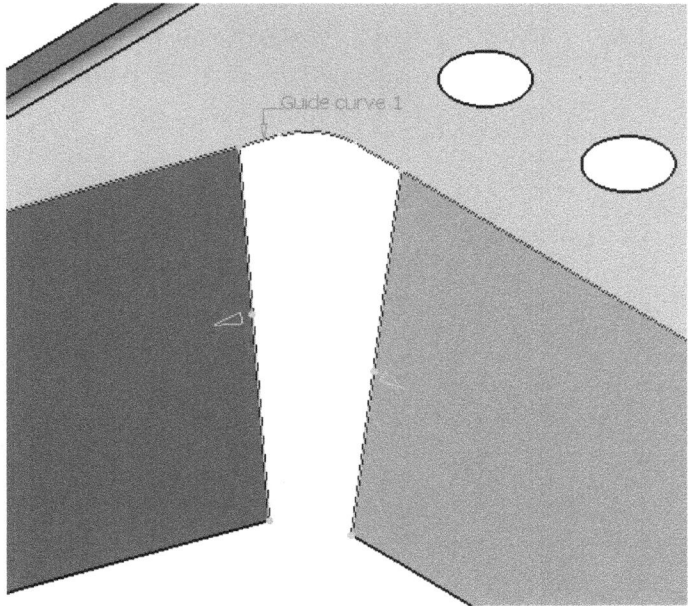

Figure 7–81

14. Select the **Fill twisted areas** option.

15. Click **Preview**. The model displays as shown in Figure 7–82. A warning appears stating that the surface has a small edge. Close this warning.

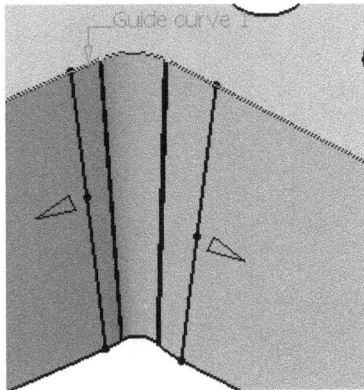

Figure 7–82

Design Considerations

In some cases, this might be the required result. However, the surfaces for this model need to be kept at their uncut lengths so that surface pieces can be extracted.

Each cutter can be reset individually.

16. To change the cutter position from its current location to the default location, right-click on the left cutter and select **Reset to initial position,** as shown in Figure 7–83.

Right-click here

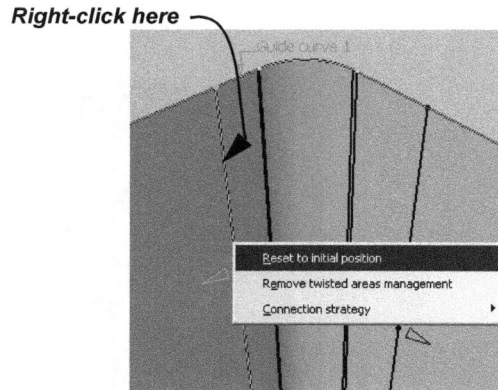

Figure 7–83

17. Repeat the same Steps for the other cutter.

18. Clear the **Fill twisted areas** option.

19. Click **OK** in the Sweep dialog box. The Multi-Result Management dialog box opens because two sub-elements were created from the sweep.

20. Select **Keep only one sub-element using an Extract** in the Multi-Result Management dialog box.

21. Click **OK** in the Multi-Result Management dialog box.

The Propagation type does not matter for this step.

22. Select the surface in the Extract Definition dialog box, as shown in Figure 7–84.

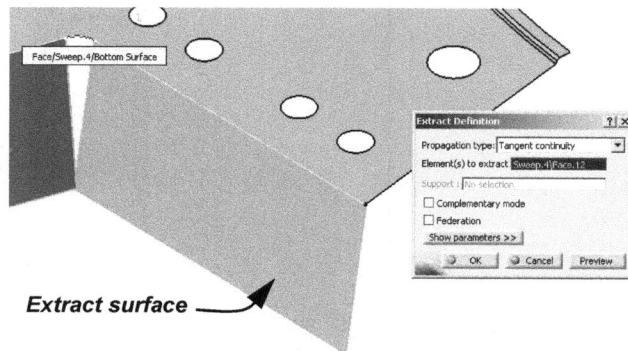

Extract surface

Figure 7–84

23. Click **OK** and rename the feature as **JunctionSurfSweep1**.

Task 4 - Extract elements for the Junction surface.

The **Multi-Result Management** tool only enables you to Extract one element at a time. In the this task, you will extract the other portion of the swept surface.

1. Double-click on **Sweep.4**.

2. Click **OK** in the Sweep Definition dialog box. The Multi-Result Management dialog box opens again.

3. Select the *Pointing* elements tab.

4. Select **Keep only one sub-element using an Extract**.

5. Click **OK** in the Multi-Result Management dialog box.

6. The Extract Definition dialog box opens. Ensure that tangent continuity is set in the Propagation type drop-down list.

7. Show **Sweep.4**.

8. Select the surface shown in Figure 7–85.

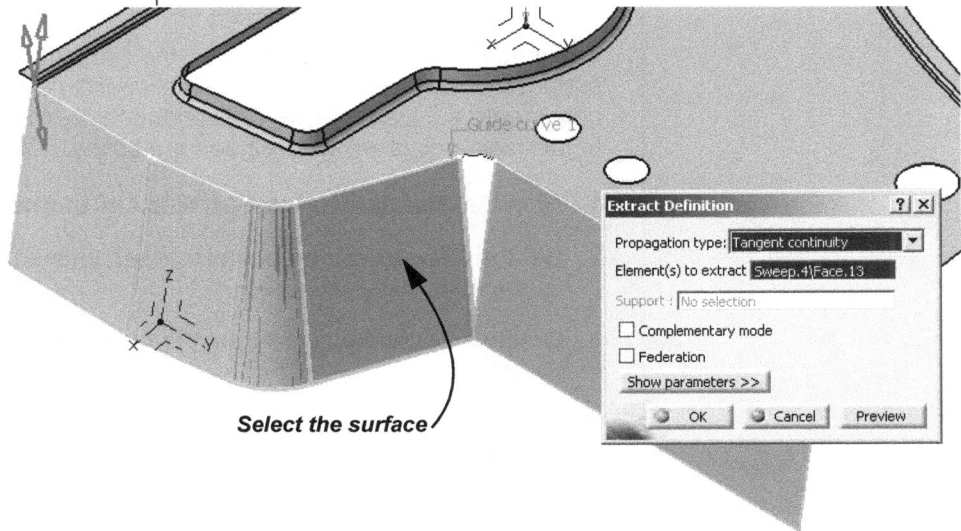

Figure 7–85

9. Complete the Extract feature.

10. Rename the extract as **JunctionSurfSweep2**.

11. Hide the **JunctionGuideCurve** feature.

12. Show the **BlendedBottomSurfWithAllCutouts** feature.

13. Rotate the model to examine the resulting surfaces. The model displays as shown in Figure 7–86.

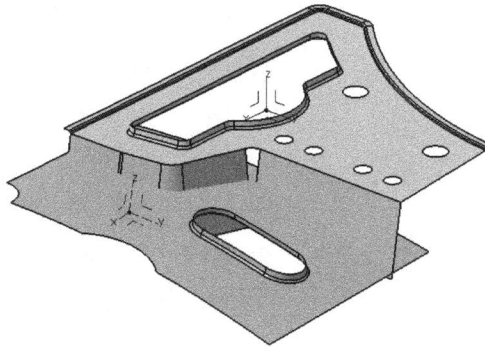

Figure 7–86

14. Save the model, but do not close the file.

Task 5 - Create reference geometry for future wireframe curves.

The model now has a gap between the two extracted, swept surfaces. You will need to build some wireframe geometry to help create a Fill surface that will bridge the two swept surfaces. In this task, points will be created for a spline.

1. Hide the **BlendedBottomSurfWithAllCutouts** feature.

2. Set the **Construction** geometrical set, located under Bottom Surface, as the work object.

3. Create a boundary curve from the edge shown in Figure 7–87.

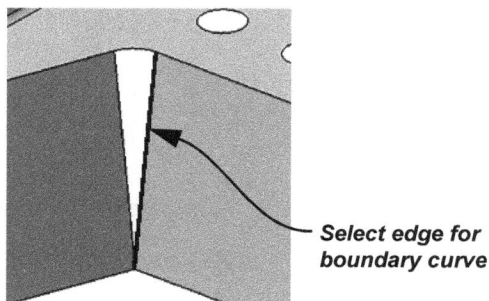

Select edge for boundary curve

Figure 7–87

4. Rename the curve as **JunctionFillCurve2**.

5. Create a point located at the midpoint of the newly created boundary curve.

6. Repeat Steps 2-5 for the entity shown in Figure 7–88. Rename the boundary curve as **JunctionFillCurve4**.

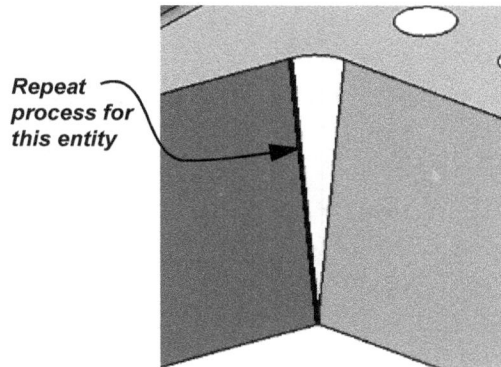

Repeat process for this entity

Figure 7–88

7. Rename the two newly created points, as shown in Figure 7–89.

MidPointJunctionSurfSweep2   *MidPointJunctionSurfSweep1*

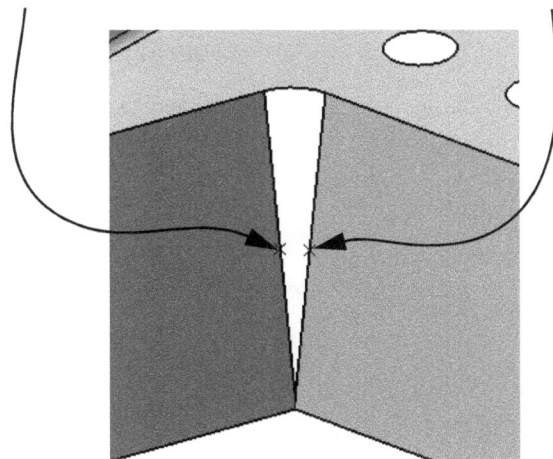

Figure 7–89

Task 6 - Create curves for a fill surface.

1. Create two boundary curves from the edges shown in
   Figure 7–90. Use **No propagation** as the propagation type.

Edges for boundary curves

Figure 7–90

2. Rename the boundary curve on the right as
   TangentDirection1. Rename the boundary curve on the left
   as **TangentDirection2**.

3. Create a spline between **MidPointJunctionSurfSweep1** and
   MidPointJunctionSurfSweep2. Use the boundary curves
   from Step 1 as appropriate tangent direction references. The
   completed spline displays as shown in Figure 7–91.

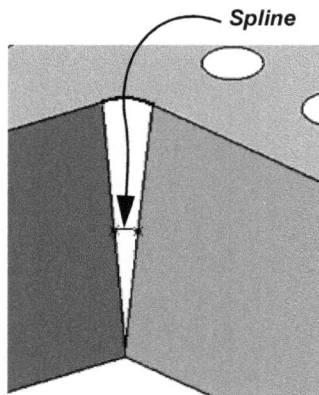

Spline

Figure 7–91

4. Rename the spline as **JunctionFillCurve1**.

5. Create another boundary curve using the edge shown in Figure 7–92. Ensure that **No propagation** is selected in the Propagation type drop-down list.

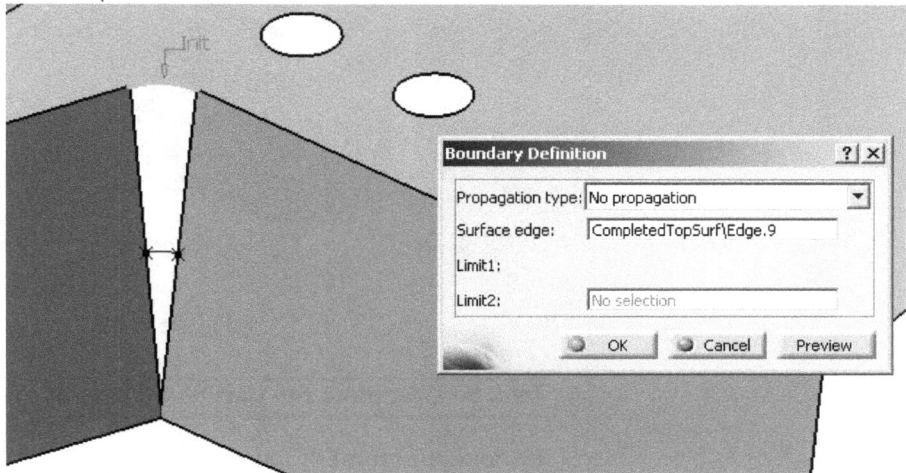

Figure 7–92

6. Rename the boundary curve as **JunctionFillCurve3**.

Task 7 - Create a fill surface between the swept surfaces.

1. Define the **Bottom Surface** geometrical set as the active work object.

2. Create a fill surface using the following curves:

   - **JunctionFillCurve1**
   - **JunctionFillCurve2**
   - **JunctionFillCurve3**
   - **JunctionFillCurve4**

3. Define **JunctionSurfSweep1** as the tangent support for **JunctionFillCurve2**.

4. Define **JuncitonSurfSweep2** as the tangent support for **JunctionFillCurve4**.

5. Complete the fill.

6. Rename the fill feature as **JunctionFill**.

7. Hide the **Construction** geometrical set. The model displays as shown in Figure 7–93.

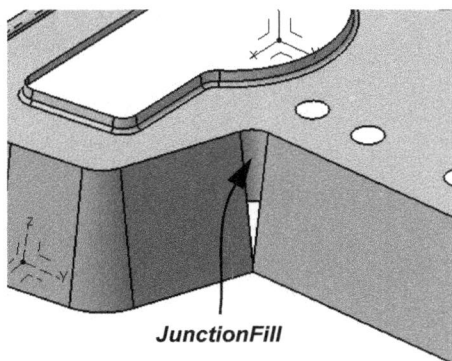

JunctionFill

Figure 7–93

Task 8 - Complete the part using operation tools.

1. Join **JunctionFill**, **JunctionSurfSweep1**, and **JunctionSurfSweep2**.

2. Rename the join as **JunctionSurf**. Now that the surface is joined together, it can be trimmed in one step.

3. Show **BlendedBottomSurfWithAllCutouts**.

4. Trim **BlendBottomSurfWithAllCutouts** and **JunctionSurf**, as shown in Figure 7–94.

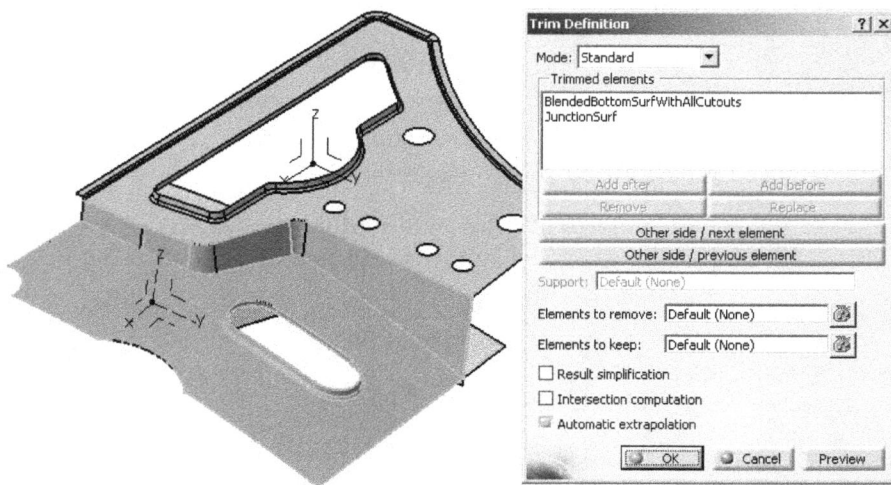

Figure 7–94

5. Rename the trimmed surface to **TrimmedBottomSurf**. The model displays as shown in Figure 7–95.

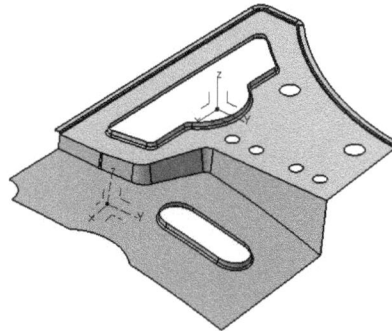

Figure 7–95

6. Define the Final Surface geometrical set as the active work object.

7. Join **CompletedTopSurf** and **TrimmedBottomSurf**.

8. Rename the join as **FinalSurf**.

9. Hide both axis systems for the model. The completed model displays as shown in Figure 7–96.

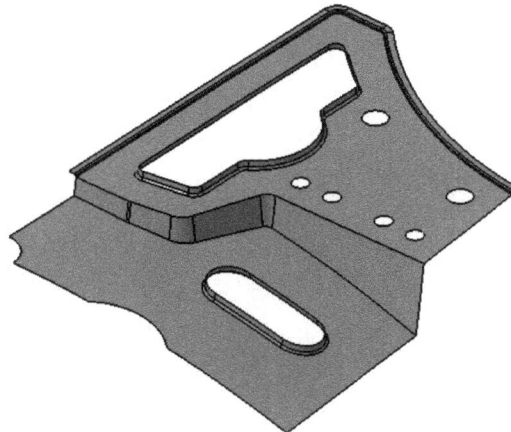

Figure 7–96

10. Save the model and close the file.

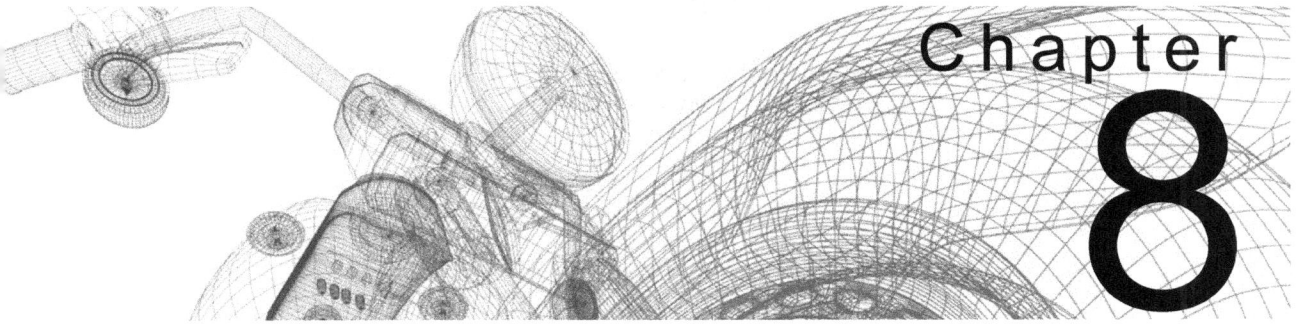

Advanced Filleting

In this chapter, advanced surface fillet options are discussed. These can help you to create more complex fillets. When the standard Generative Shape Design fillet tools do not meet the design intent, alternative methods of building a fillet are introduced. Through wireframe and surface creation, a fillet can be built manually.

Learning Objectives in this Chapter

- Review the surface fillet creation process.
- Create Chordal and Tritangent fillets.
- Learn how to use the Trim options.
- Understand fillet Orientation and Boundary Options.
- Understand alternative methods of filleting.

8.1 Surface Fillet Overview

The different surface **Fillet** tools available in the Generative Shape Design work bench are shown in Figure 8–1.

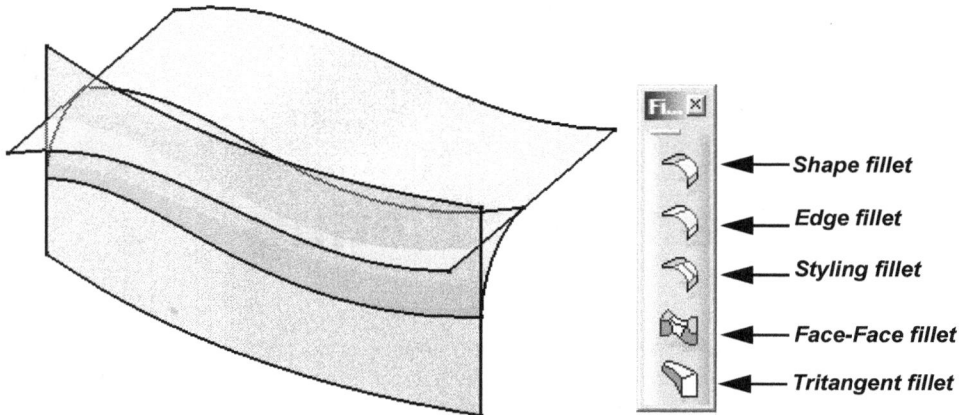

Shape fillet
Edge fillet
Styling fillet
Face-Face fillet
Tritangent fillet

Figure 8–1

How To: Create a Surface Fillet

1. Start the creation of the feature. You can create the following types of fillets:
   - Shape fillet
   - Edge fillet
     - Chordal fillet
     - Variable radius fillet
   - Styling fillet
   - Face-Face fillet
   - Tritangent fillet
2. Enter a radius value.
3. Set the extremity type:
   - **Smooth** or **Straight**
   - **Maximum** or **Minimum**
4. Trim support surfaces.
5. Set the conic option.

Styling fillet requires FS1 license.

6. Select additional reference geometry, if required. These are described as follows:

Fillet Type	Reference Geometry
Shape Fillet	Hold curve and spine.
Edge Fillet	Edges to keep, limiting element.
Variable Radius Fillet	Edges to keep, limiting element.
Face-Face Fillet	Limiting element, hold curve and spine.
Tritangent Fillet	Limiting element.

7. Complete the feature.

8.2 Chordal Fillet

The **Chordal Fillet** tool creates a fillet that is measured by a chord length, not a radius value. A cross-section of a fillet is shown in Figure 8–2. The measurements show what a chord looks like in comparison to a radius measurement.

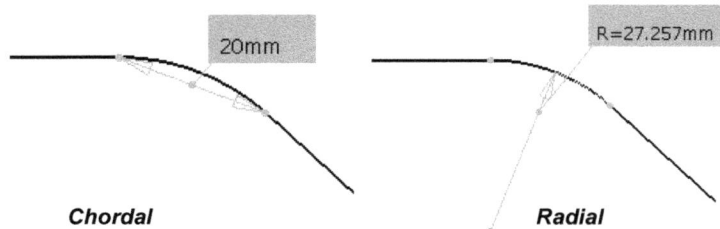

Chordal   **Radial**

Figure 8–2

How To: Create a Chordal Fillet

1. Click [icon] (Edge Fillet), then click [icon] (Chordal).
2. Select the edge(s) on which to apply the fillet. The Edge Fillet Definition dialog box displays, as shown in Figure 8–3.

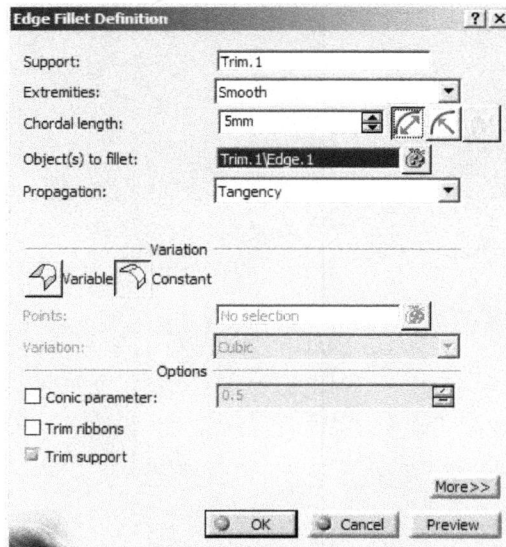

Figure 8–3

3. A constant chordal fillet can be created by entering a Chordal length. A variable chordal fillet can be created by selecting points or vertices. A different chordal length can then be defined at the location of these points, as shown in Figure 8–4. Cubic or linear variation can be specified to define how the fillet blends from one chordal length location to the next.

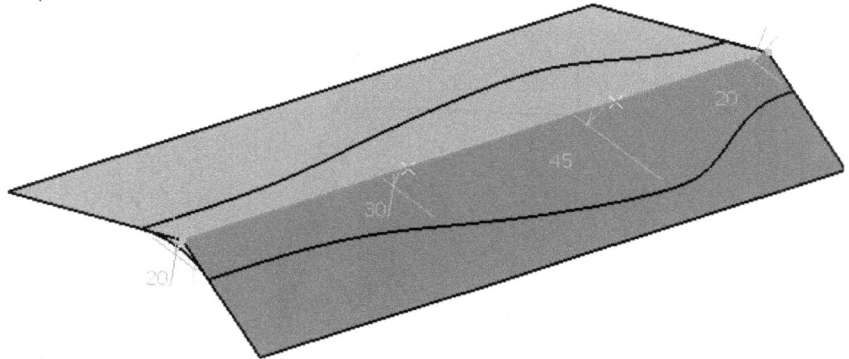

Figure 8–4

4. (Optional) Define additional fillet characteristics and parameters, as with any other fillet type.
5. Complete the Chordal Fillet.

8.3 Tritangent Fillet

A Tritangent fillet replaces a selected surface with a fillet. The fillet is tangent to the two selected surfaces bounding the removed surface. An example of a Tritangent fillet is shown in Figure 8–5.

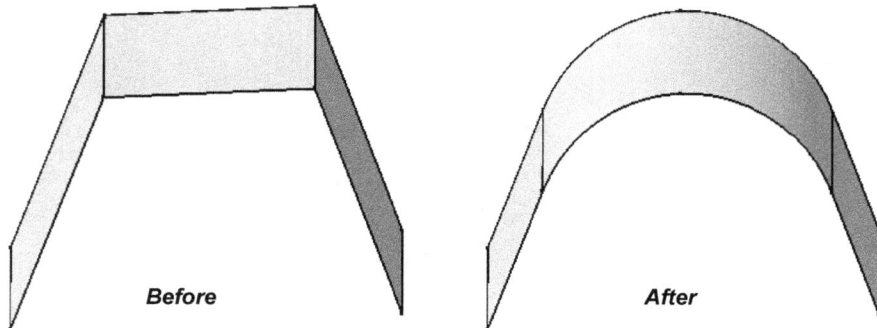

Before   *After*

Figure 8–5

To create a Tritangent fillet, click (Tritangent Fillet) and select a surface on which to apply the fillet. The Tritanget Fillet Definition dialog box opens as shown in Figure 8–6.

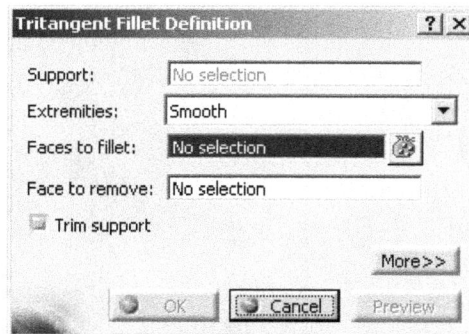

Figure 8–6

Select the two faces to fillet and one face to remove, as shown in Figure 8–7.

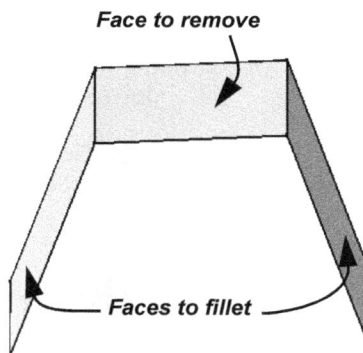

Face to remove

Faces to fillet

Figure 8–7

Optional elements can be used to further define the Tritangent fillet.

8.4 Trim Options

Trim Supports

When the two surfaces referenced in the fillet intersect each other, the surfaces can be trimmed at their intersection as shown in Figure 8–8.

All of the fillet types have the ability to trim supports. The **Trim Support** option is shown in Figure 8–9.

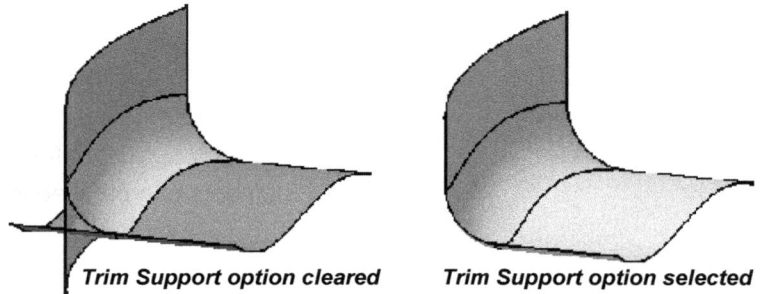

Trim Support option cleared   *Trim Support option selected*

Figure 8–8

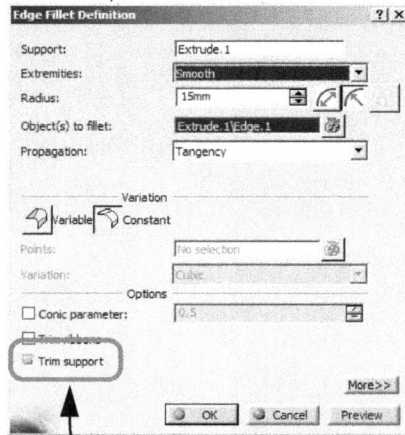

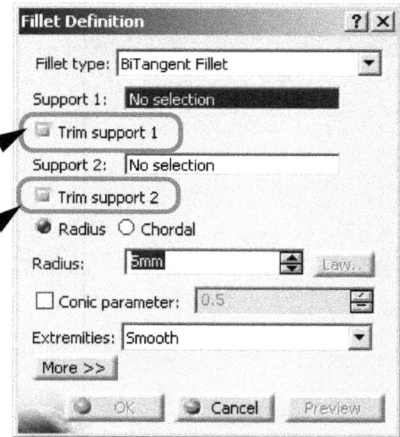

Select the Trim Support option to trim intersecting surfaces.

Figure 8–9

Trim Ribbons

If you select more than one edge to fillet and they intersect each other, you can trim them by selecting **Trim Ribbons**, as shown in Figure 8–10. This option trims the fillets where they overlap.

Select the Trim Ribbons option to trim intersecting edge fillets

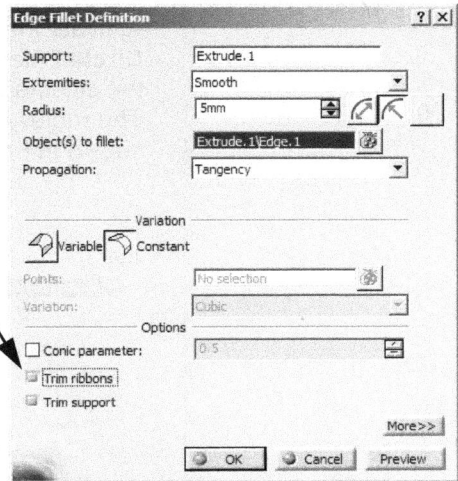

Figure 8–10

The left side of Figure 8–11 shows two edges that are filleted. The edges intersect and their geometry does not match the design intent. The two fillets are trimmed at their intersection if you select the **Trim Ribbons** option, as shown on the right side of Figure 8–11.

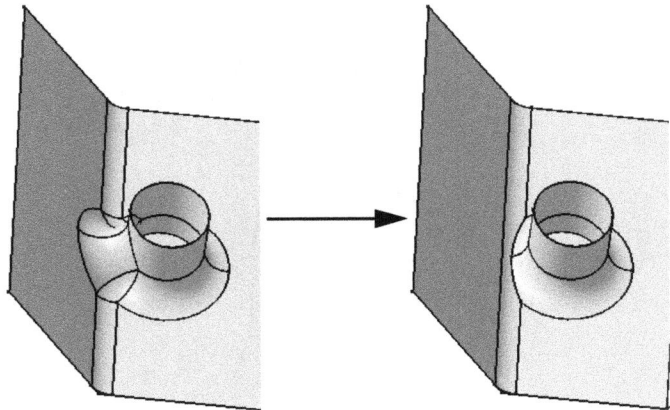

Figure 8–11

Trim ribbons is only available in the Edge Fillet Definition dialog box.

8.5 Fillet Orientation Options

Spine/Circle

Activate the 🗗 (Variable) option, click **More**, and enable the
Circle Fillet option. Select a spine as shown in Figure 8–12, and
the selected curve or edge can define the orientation of the fillet.
The radius of the fillet remains perpendicular to the spine as
shown in Figure 8–13.

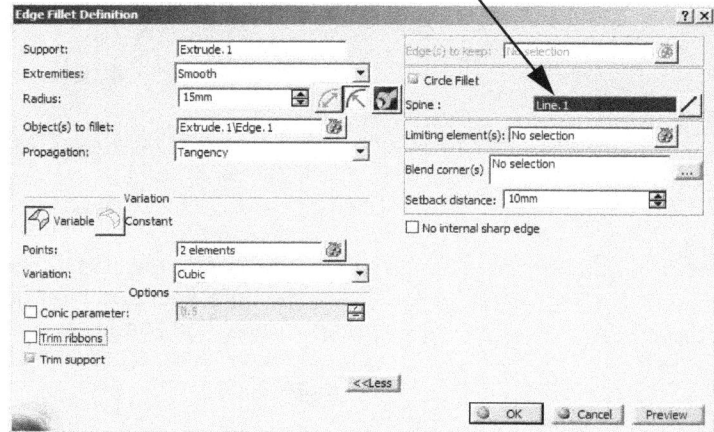

*Select a spine to use
the Circle Fillet option*

Figure 8–12

Figure 8–13 shows a variable radius fillet with and without using
the **Circle Fillet** option.

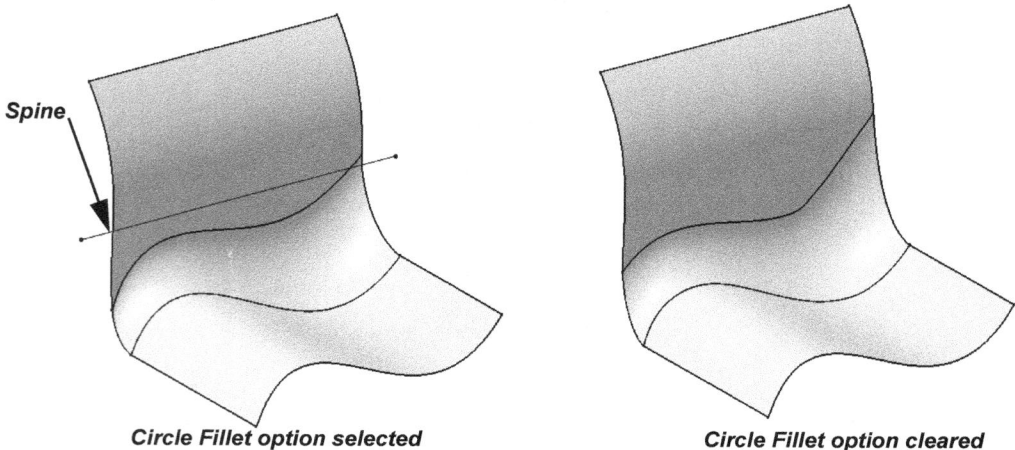

Circle Fillet option selected   *Circle Fillet option cleared*

Figure 8–13

The ability to select a spine curve is available in the following fillet tools:

- Shape Fillet
- Edge Fillet with a variable radius

Hold Curve

You can further define the fillet by selecting a Hold curve. The *Hold Curve* field enables you to select a predefined limiting curve to control the radius. You must also select a spine to control the shape of the fillet. The radius of the fillet remains perpendicular to the spine.

A hold curve is available to define in the following fillet types:

- Shape fillet
- Face-Face fillet

The Shape fillet definition dialog box and Face-Face fillet definition dialog box are shown in Figure 8–14. The *Radius* field is cleared because the Hold curve now defines the radius. The final result is shown on the right side.

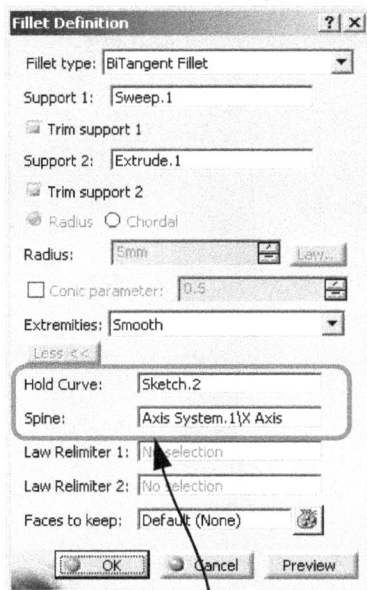

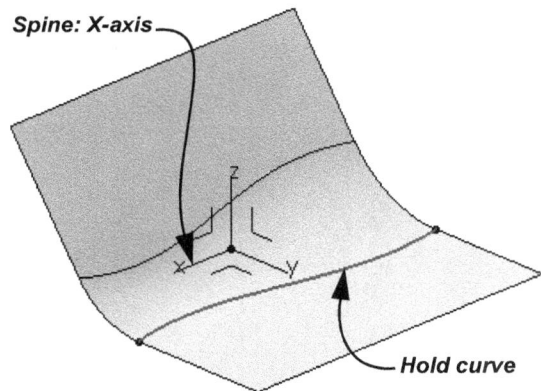

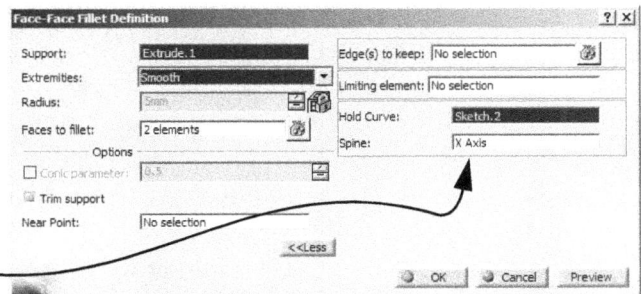

Figure 8–14

8.6 Fillet Boundary Options

Edges to Keep

Edges of the surface involved in the fillet operation can be selected to not be filleted. Select the edge using the *Edge(s) to keep* field, as shown in Figure 8–15.

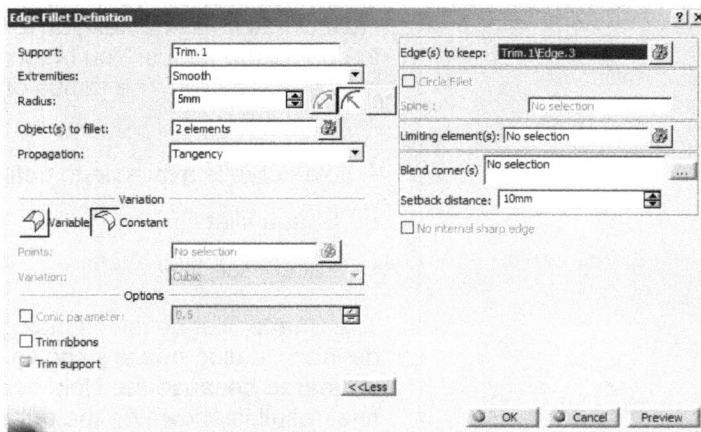

Figure 8–15

The left side of Figure 8–16 shows a fillet without any edges selected to keep; the fillet on the right side has an edge selected to keep.

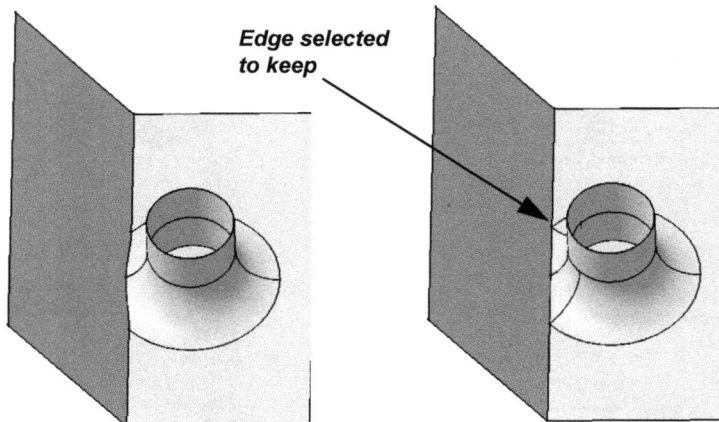

Figure 8–16

The **Edges to Keep** option is only available in the Edge Fillet dialog box.

Limiting Element

You can also limit the fillet by selecting a surface that intersects it completely. Expand the dialog box by clicking **More**. Use the *Limiting Element(s)* field to select a trimming feature. The trimming feature can be a surface, plane, or points on an edge. An arrow indicates the portion of the fillet that is created. Select this arrow direction to change its direction. An example of a fillet that has been limited by an intersecting surface is shown in Figure 8–17.

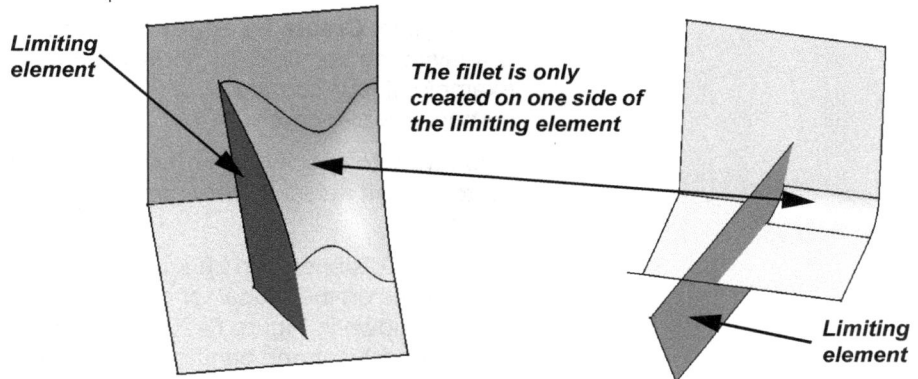

Limiting element

The fillet is only created on one side of the limiting element

Limiting element

Figure 8–17

The **Limiting Element** option is available in the following fillet tools:

- Edge Fillet (Constant, Variable, Chordal)

- Tritangent Fillet

Blend Corner

When more than two edges transition into a corner of one fillet feature, the **Blend Corner** option is available. It reshapes the way the fillet edges transition together, as shown on the right of Figure 8–18.

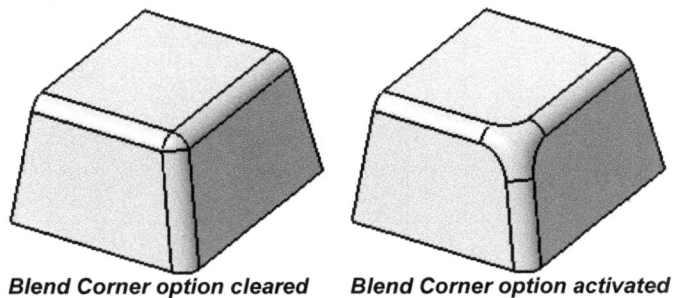

Blend Corner option cleared　　*Blend Corner option activated*

Figure 8–18

How To: Use the Blend Corner Option

1. Click **More** in the dialog box.
2. Right-click in the *Blend corner(s)* area. Two options display, as shown in Figure 8–19.

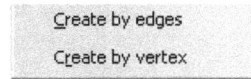

*Depending on your Service Pack, this option may display as **Create by edges or vertex**.*

Create by edges

Create by vertex

Figure 8–19

3. If you select **Create by edges**, all corners in the fillet feature display in the text field, as shown in Figure 8–20. For example, if four corners exist in the fillet feature, all four corners are blended.

   If you want to specify the corners manually, select **Create by vertex**. Then select a vertex on the model to create or add a corner.

4. A Setback distance can be specified by modifying the dimensions on the model, or changing the value in the dialog box, as shown in Figure 8–20. The setback distance defines where the fillet shape begins blending into the other fillet shapes.

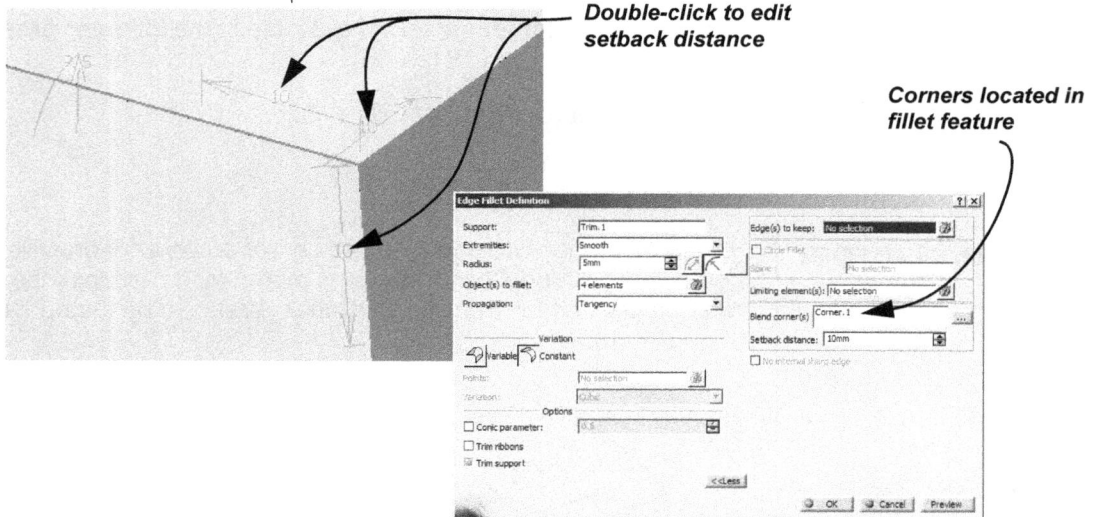

Double-click to edit setback distance

Corners located in fillet feature

Figure 8–20

8.7 Alternative Methods of Filleting

In certain circumstances, the **Filleting** tools in the Generative Shape Design workbench do not yield the required geometry. This could be because the fillet failed, or because the fillet surface generated was distorted. Alternative methods can be used to achieve the fillet geometry.

A Fillet can be created manually using the following tools:

- Sweep
- Blend
- Multi-sections Surface
- Fill

These tools create a similar profile shape to a fillet, and enable continuity to be established.

Sweeps

Using the circle or conic type profile, a fillet type surface can be created as shown in Figure 8–21. The **Sweep** is the only tool that can create a conic fillet.

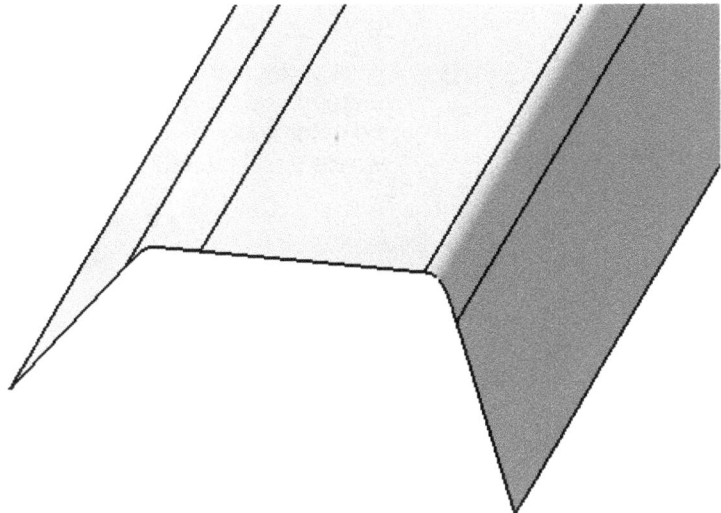

Figure 8–21

Blends

The blend surface's transition from one curve to another can create a fillet-like shape. This feature has the ability to trim supports, similar to the **Filleting** tools. The advantage of using a blend to create a fillet shape surface, is that the continuity can be set to point, tangency, or curvature. A fillet shape created from a blend is shown in Figure 8–22.

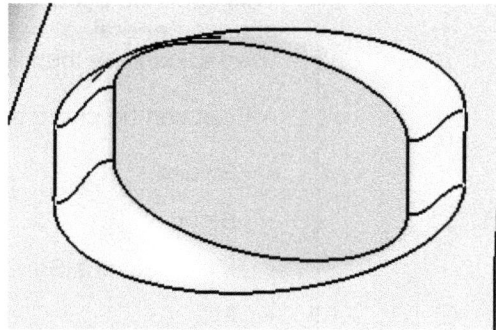

Figure 8–22

Multi-Sections Surface

While blends can only transition between two curves, the multi-sections surface enables two or more sections to be selected. This gives you the ability to provide variation to the fillet shape or size. A multi-sections surface cannot impose curvature continuity like a blend. It only has the option of creating a tangency continuous surface.

Fill

A fill surface enables a surface to be created between wireframe elements while maintaining continuity to the supports. A fill can be point, tangent, or curvature continuous. A common situation where a fill is useful is shown in Figure 8–23.

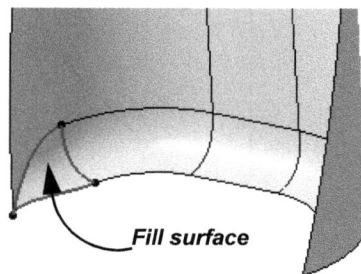

Fill surface

Figure 8–23

Practice 8a

Advanced Fillet Options

Practice Objectives

- Create a fillet using a Hold curve.
- Create a fillet with blended corners.
- Limit a fillet feature.

In this practice, you will explore the various options available when filleting. These options control the shape, and orientation of the fillet. The completed model displays as shown in Figure 8–24.

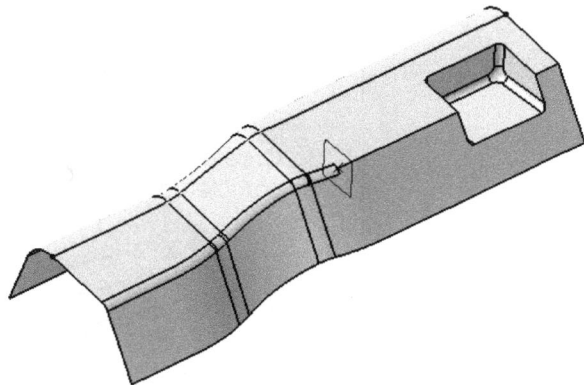

Figure 8–24

Task 1 - Open a part file.

1. Open **Adv_Fillet_Options_Start.CATPart**. The part displays as shown in Figure 8–25.

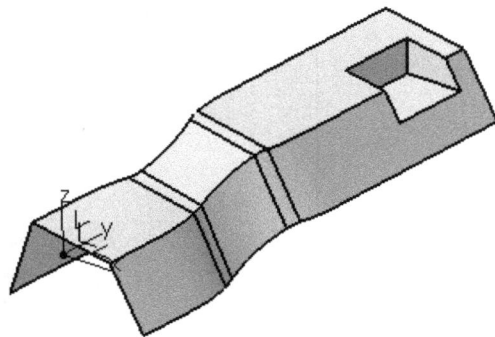

Figure 8–25

Task 2 - Create wireframe geometry.

In this task, you will create points, lines, and curves. These elements are used later by fillet features when defining additional options.

1. Create a point with the following coordinate values:

    • X = **-20mm**
    • Y = **0mm**
    • Z = **0mm**

2. Create another point with the following coordinate values:

    • X = **-20mm**
    • Y = **450mm**
    • Z = **0mm**

3. Create a line between the two newly created points. The completed line displays as shown in Figure 8–26.

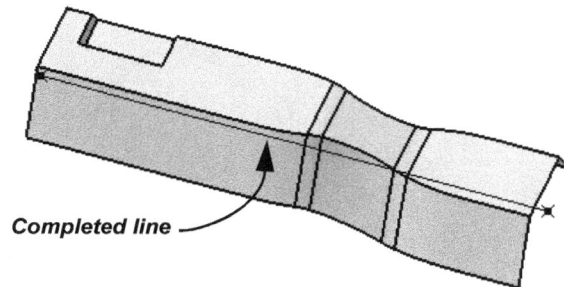

Completed line

Figure 8–26

4. Project the line onto **Trim.1**. Use the **Along a direction** projection type. Select the Z component as the direction reference as shown in Figure 8–27.

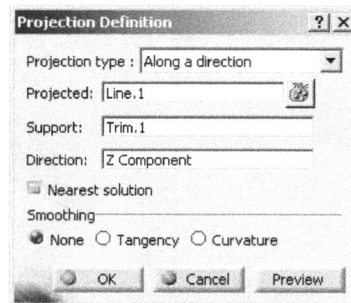

Figure 8–27

5. Complete the projection. The projected curve is used as a Hold curve for a fillet created later in the practice.

6. Hide the line, and the two point features. The model displays as shown in Figure 8–28.

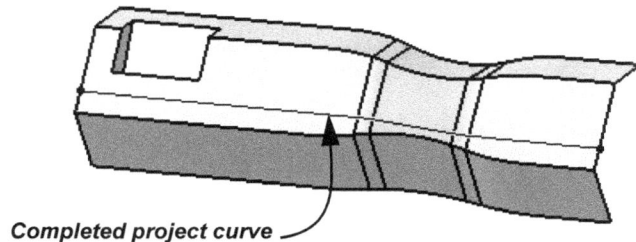

Completed project curve

Figure 8–28

7. Extract the edge shown in Figure 8–29 using the **Tangent continuity** propagation type.

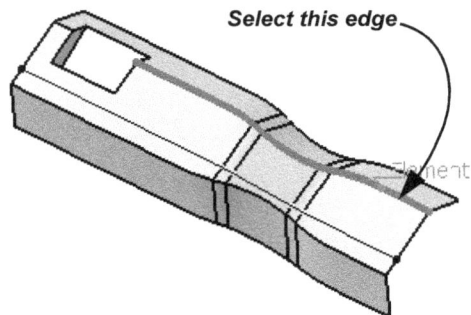

Select this edge

Figure 8–29

8. Create an **On curve** type point, located on the newly created extracted curve. Enter a distance of **230mm**. The completed point displays as shown in Figure 8–30.

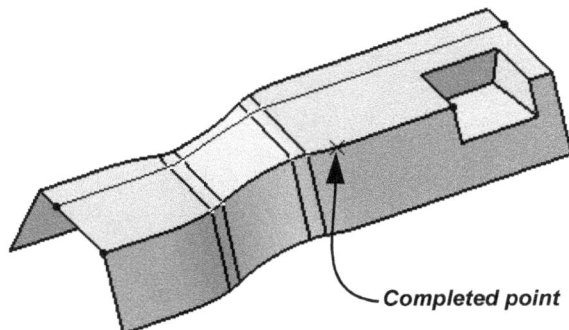

Completed point

Figure 8–30

9. Create a plane located at the newly created point as shown in Figure 8–31. The plane must be normal to the extract curve. This plane serves as an element to limit a fillet later in the practice.

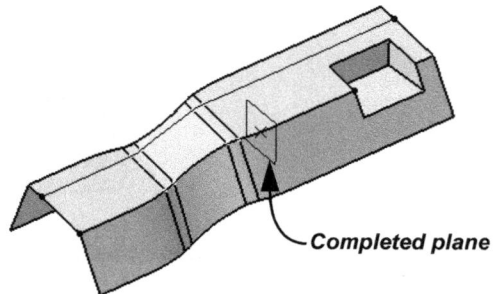

Figure 8–31

10. Hide the extract curve.

Task 3 - Create a Shape Fillet.

1. Click (Shape Fillet).

2. Select **Surface.3** as the *Support 1* reference.

3. Select **Trim.1** as the *Support 2* reference.

4. Ensure that both **Trim support** options are activated, as shown in Figure 8–32.

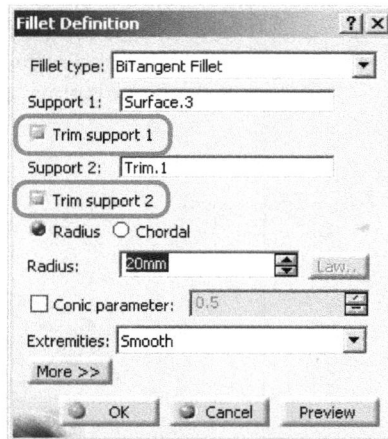

Figure 8–32

5. Enter a *Radius* value of **20mm**.

6. Ensure that the red arrows point towards the inside of the model. If not, select the arrow to flip the arrow direction.

7. Complete the Shape Fillet. The model displays as shown in Figure 8–33.

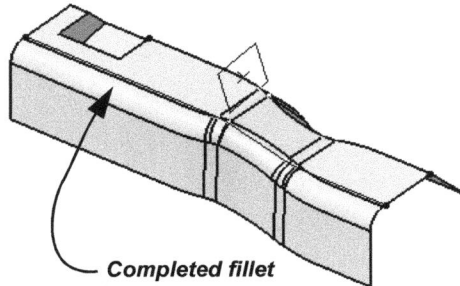

Completed fillet

Figure 8–33

8. Edit the newly created fillet, and click **More**.

9. Select the project curve as the Hold Curve reference. This curve now defines the radius of the fillet.

10. Select the Y-axis as the Spine reference. A Spine reference must be specified when a Hold curve is used.

11. Complete the Shape fillet. The model displays as shown in Figure 8–34. The shape of the fillet follows that of the project curve.

The line thickness for the project curve has been modified in this figure. It does not display this way on your model.

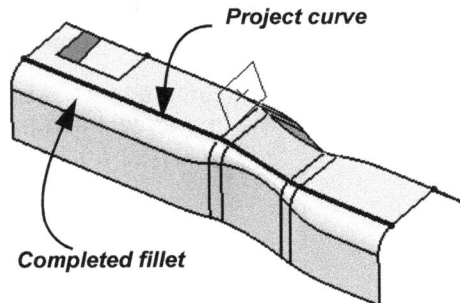

Project curve

Completed fillet

Figure 8–34

Task 4 - Create an Edge Fillet.

1. Click ⬚ (Edge Fillet).

2. Select the edge shown in Figure 8–35.

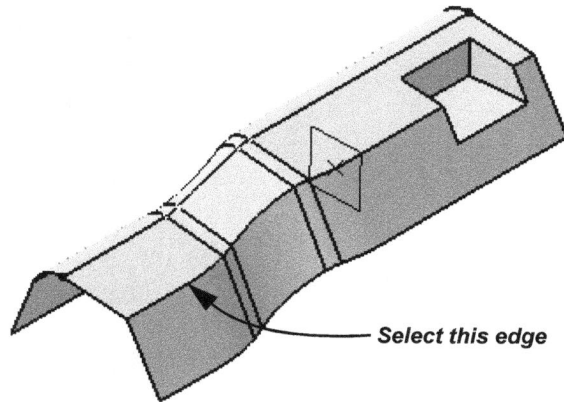

— *Select this edge*

Figure 8–35

3. Ensure that the *Selection mode* is set to **Tangency**.

4. Enter a *Radius* value of **5mm**.

5. Ensure that **Trim support** is activated.

6. Click **More** in the Edge Fillet Definition dialog box.

7. Select the plane shown in Figure 8–36 as the Limiting element reference.

8. Ensure that the arrow direction matches Figure 8–36. Select the arrow head to flip the direction as required.

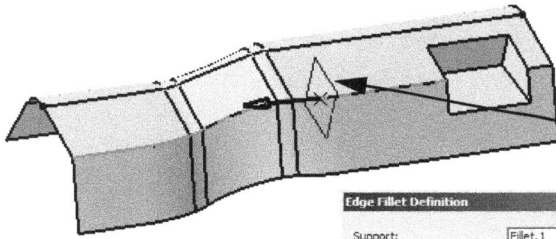

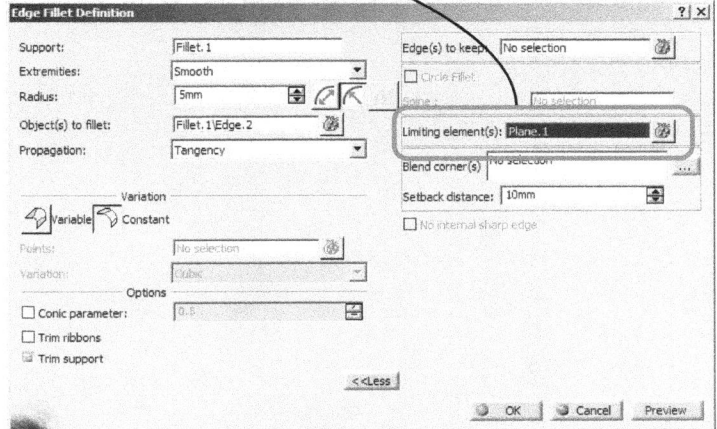

Edge Fillet Definition

Support:	Fillet.1	Edge(s) to keep:	No selection
Extremities:	Smooth	☐ Circle Fillet	
Radius:	5mm	Spine :	No selection
Object(s) to fillet:	Fillet.1\Edge.2	**Limiting element(s):**	**Plane.1**
Propagation:	Tangency	Blend corner(s)	No selection
		Setback distance:	10mm

Variation

Variable / Constant

Points: No selection

Variation: Cubic

Options

☐ Conic parameter: 0.5

☐ Trim ribbons

☑ Trim support

<<Less

OK | Cancel | Preview

Figure 8–36

9. Complete the fillet. The model displays as shown in Figure 8–37.

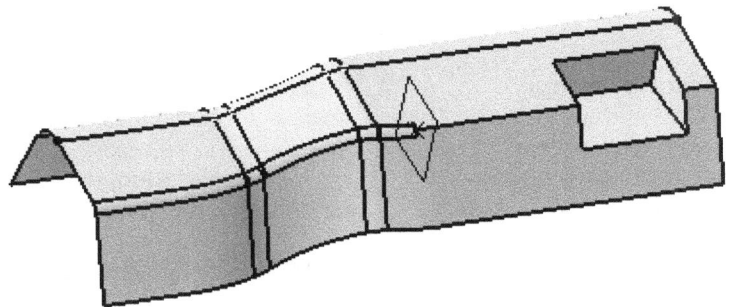

Figure 8–37

Task 5 - Create a fillet with blended corners.

1. Create an Edge Fillet. Select the five edges shown in Figure 8–38.

Note that you can select the edges individually, or select each vertex, and the system will select the adjacent edges automatically.

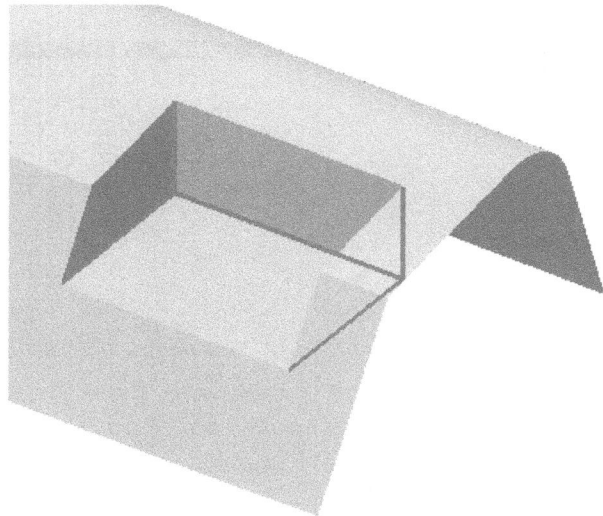

Figure 8–38

2. Enter a *Radius* value of **5mm**.

3. Click **More**.

*Depending on your installed surface pack, the right-click option might be **Create by edges or vertex**.*

4. Right-click in the *Blend corner(s)* field and select **Create by edges**. All corners formed from the selected edges are automatically selected. Two corners are added to the dialog box as shown in Figure 8–39. The name of the corners might be different in your model.

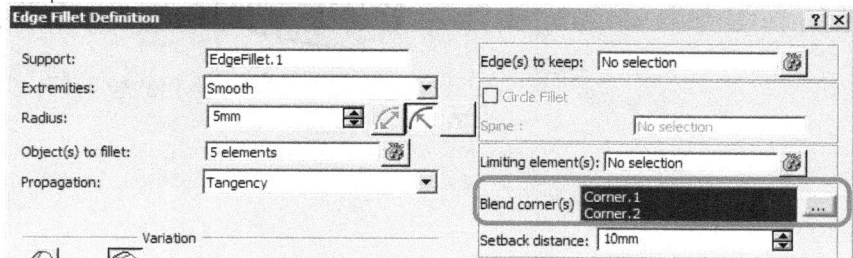

Figure 8–39

5. Complete the feature. The model displays as shown in Figure 8–40.

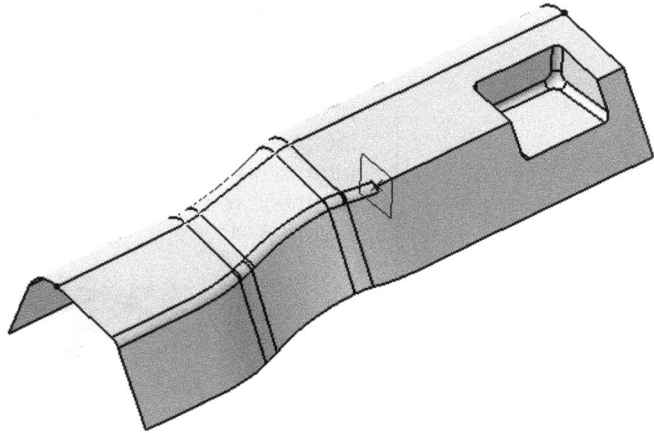

Figure 8–40

6. Save the model and close the file.

Practice 8b

Conic Fillets

Practice Objectives

- Create a conic sweep to act as fillet geometry.

In this practice, a conic sweep will be used to create the rounded look between two surfaces. This method is introduced as an alternative to using traditional **Fillet** tools and is often used for aesthetic reasons. The completed practice displays as shown in Figure 8–41.

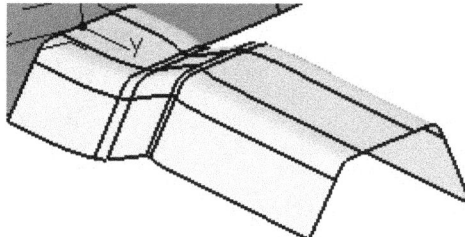

Figure 8–41

Task 1 - Open a part file.

1. Open **T_Bracket_Start.CATPart**. The part displays as shown in Figure 8–42.

2. A surface and two curves have been imported into the model as shown in the specification tree in Figure 8–42. The design intent of the model is to build a bracket that connects to the existing green surface. The two curves will be used to build the bracket.

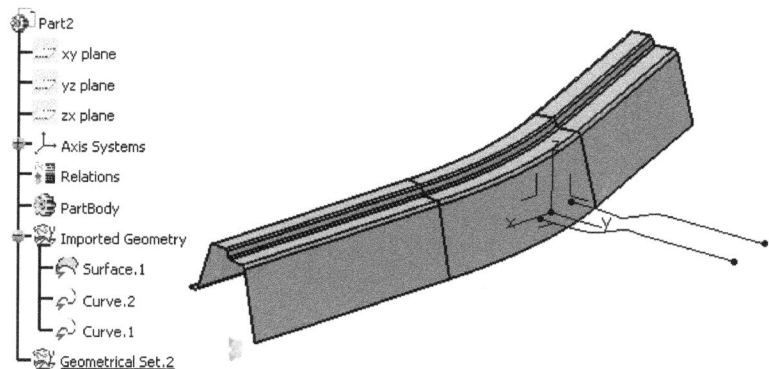

Figure 8–42

Task 2 - Create line sweeps.

1. Ensure that the **Swept Surfaces** geometrical set is the active Work Object.

2. Create a sweep using the following specifications:

   - *Profile type:* **Line**
   - *Sub-type:* **Two limits**
   - *Guide curve 1:* **Curve.1**
   - *Guide curve 2:* **Curve.2**
   - *Spine:* **Y-axis**
   - *Length 1:* **0mm**
   - *Length 2:* **0mm**

   The completed line sweep displays as shown in Figure 8–43.

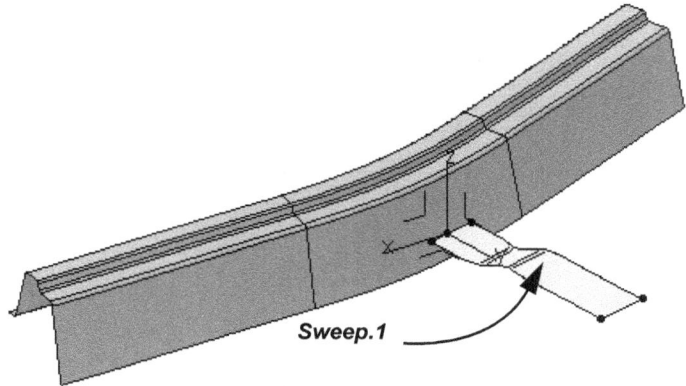

Sweep.1

Figure 8–43

The arrows representing the angular sector do not display on the screen until the Length 1 value has been entered.

3. Create a sweep using the following specifications:

   - *Profile type:* **Line**
   - *Sub-type:* **With reference surface**
   - *Guide curve 1:* **Curve.2**
   - *Reference surface:* **Sweep.1**
   - *Angle:* **50deg**
   - *Angular sector:* Select the one shown in Figure 8–44
   - *Length 1:* **65mm**
   - *Length 2:* **0mm**
   - *Spine:* **Y-axis**

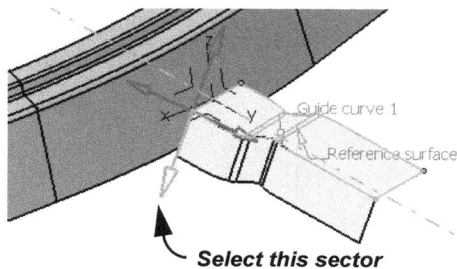

Figure 8–44

The completed line sweep displays as shown in Figure 8–45.

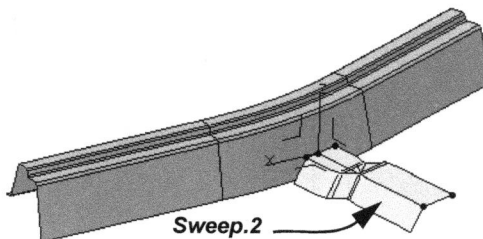

Figure 8–45

4. Create a sweep using the following specifications:

   - *Profile type:* **Line**
   - *Sub-type:* **With reference surface**
   - *Guide curve 1:* **Curve.1**
   - *Reference surface:* **Sweep.1**
   - *Angle:* **80deg**
   - *Angular sector:* Select the one shown in Figure 8–46
   - *Length 1:* **75mm**
   - *Length 2:* **0mm**
   - *Spine:* **Y-axis**

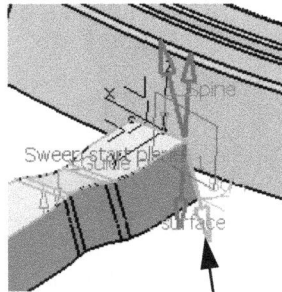

Select this sector

Figure 8–46

The completed line sweep displays as shown in Figure 8–47.

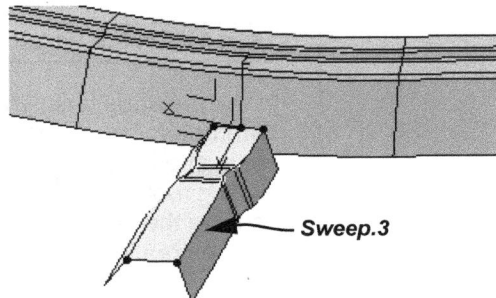

Sweep.3

Figure 8–47

5. Hide **Curve.2**.

Task 3 - Create a Conic fillet.

1. Click (Shape fillet).

2. Create the fillet using the following specifications:

   - *Support 1:* **Sweep.1**
   - *Trim support 1:* **Selected**
   - *Support 2:* **Sweep.2**
   - *Trim support 2:* **Selected**
   - *Radius:* **35 mm**
   - *Conic parameter:* **0.75**
   - *Spine:* **Y Axis**
   - Ensure that both direction arrows point toward the inside of the profile.

3. Complete the feature. The model displays as shown in Figure 8–48.

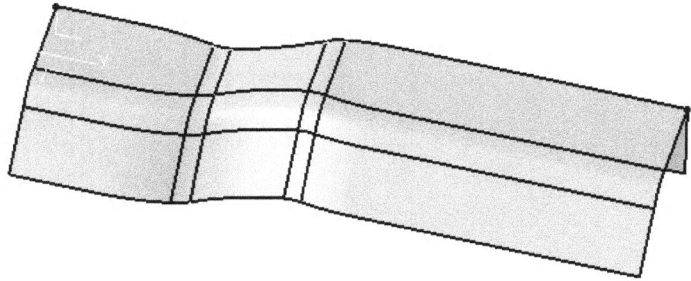

Figure 8–48

Task 4 - Create wireframe for the second conic fillet.

In the previous task, you created a shape fillet using the conic parameter. The other side of the model also needs to be a conic-shaped fillet. The design intent cannot be captured using a filleting tool. An alternative filleting technique needs to be used to achieve the design requirement; therefore, you will use a sweep. Before creating the conic sweep, you must create a wireframe.

1. Create a geometrical set named **Wireframe and Surfaces**.

2. Create a Parallel curve using the references shown in Figure 8–49.

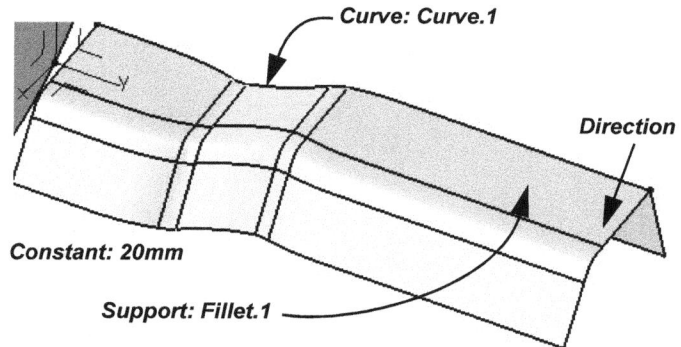

Figure 8–49

The completed Parallel curve displays as shown in Figure 8–50.

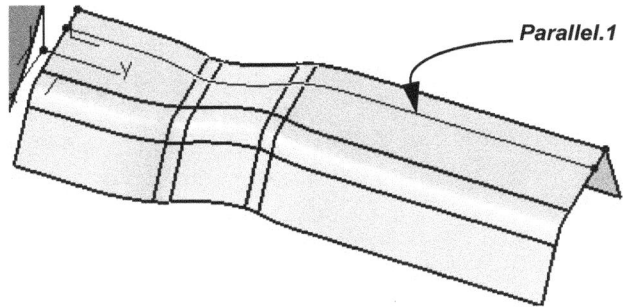

Figure 8–50

3. Create another Parallel curve using the references shown in Figure 8–51.

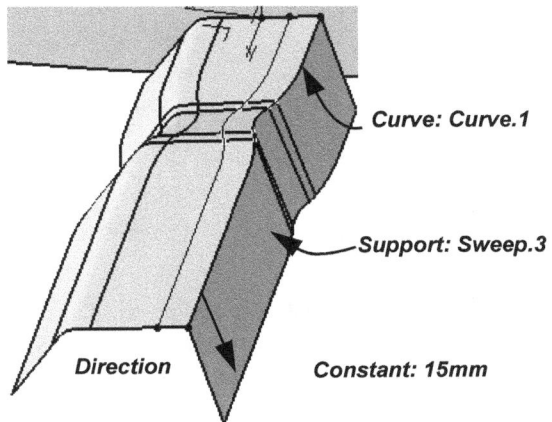

Figure 8–51

The completed parallel curve displays as shown in Figure 8–52.

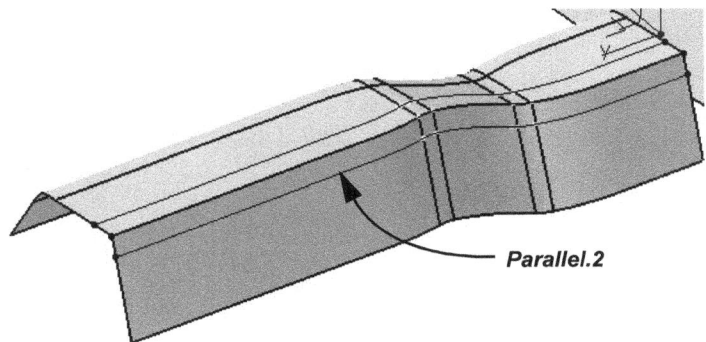

Figure 8–52

Task 5 - Curve Smooth wireframe.

1. Create a Curve Smooth using specifications shown in Figure 8–53. The curve smooth erases vertices from Parallel.1 that would otherwise create a lesser quality surface later in the design.

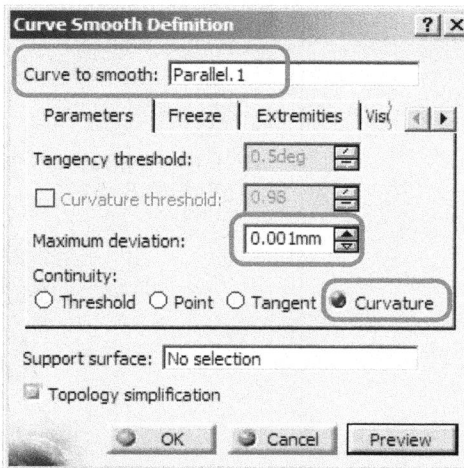

Figure 8–53

2. Complete the Curve Smooth. **Parallel.1** was consumed in the operation. **Curve Smooth.1** now acts as a guide curve in later operations.

3. **Curve Smooth** the other parallel curve using the same specifications as in Step 1.

4. Ensure that the name of the Curve Smooth features match the names shown in Figure 8–54.

5. Using the graphic properties, change the color of the two Curve Smooth features to blue.

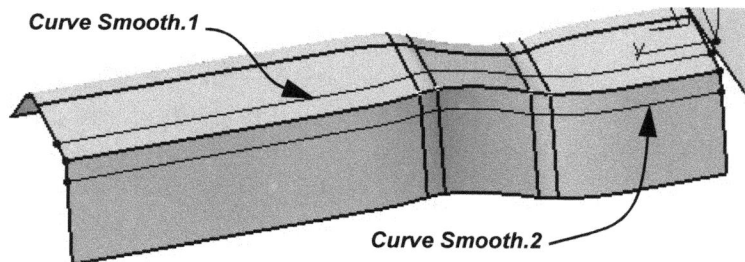

Figure 8–54

Task 6 - Create conic fillets.

1. Hide **Curve.1.**

2. Create a sweep using the following specifications:

   - *Profile type:* **Conic**
   - *Sub-type:* **Two guide curves**
   - *Guide curve 1:* **Curve smooth.1**
   - *Tangency:* **Fillet.1**
   - *Angle:* **0deg**
   - *Last guide curve:* **Curve smooth.2**
   - *Tangency:* **Sweep.3**
   - *Angle:* **0deg**
   - *Parameter:* **0.75**
   - *Spine:* **Y-axis**

   The completed conic sweep displays as shown in Figure 8–55.

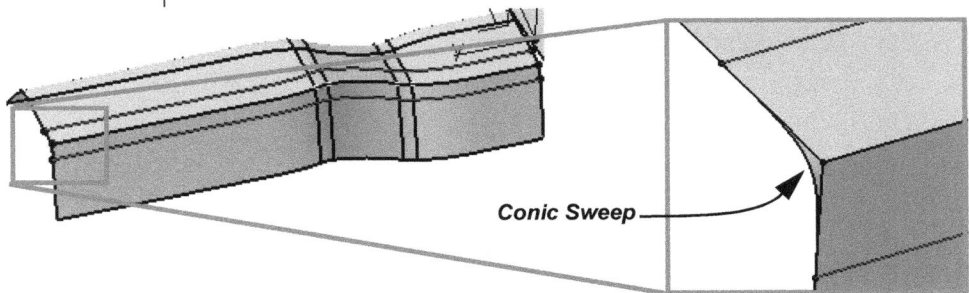

Figure 8–55

3. Ensure that the name of the newly created conic sweep is **Sweep.4**.

Task 7 - Perform surface operations.

The standard **Fillet** tools have the ability to trim the support surfaces. Sweeps do not have this ability. Because of this, the conic fillets from the last task will have to be manually split and joined.

1. Split the filleted and swept surfaces using the following curves:

   - **Curve Smooth.1**
   - **Curve Smooth.2**

2. Join the split surfaces and conic shaped swept surface.

3. Hide all of the curves. The completed model displays as shown in Figure 8–56.

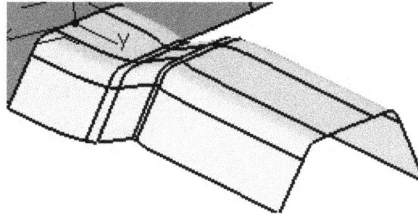

Figure 8–56

4. Save the file as **T_Bracket_ST-1.CATPart**.

Practice 8c

Curvature Continuous Fillet

Practice Objective

*   Create a curvature continuous fillet using the Blend tool.

In this practice, you create fillet geometry that is curvature continuous. The **Blend** tool will be used to complete the model. The completed part displays as shown in Figure 8–57.

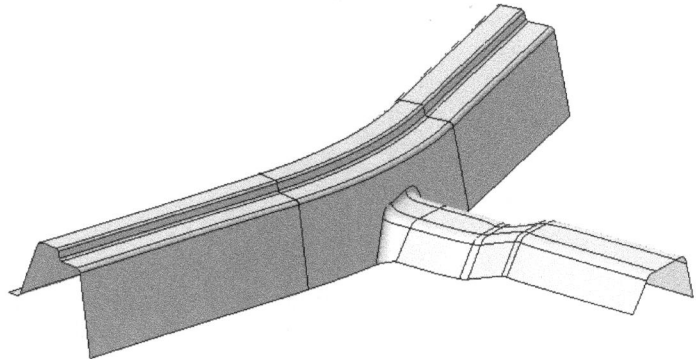

Figure 8–57

Task 1 - Open a part file.

1. Open **T_Bracket_2245.CATPart**. The part displays as shown in Figure 8–58.

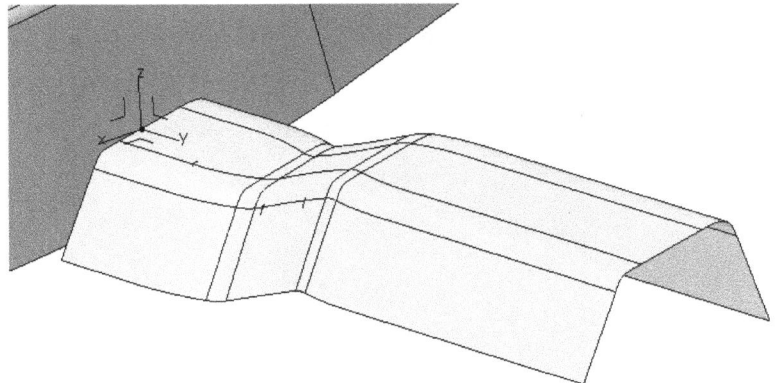

Figure 8–58

2. Create a geometrical set named **Blend Geometry**.

3. Extract the curve shown in Figure 8–59. Rename the curve as **Extracted Bracket Profile**. This curve is used as a reference in the Blend creation at the end of this practice.

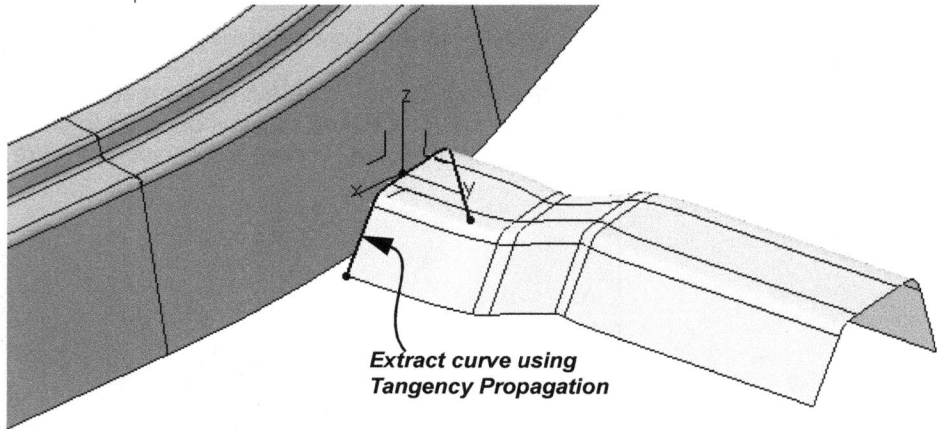

Extract curve using
Tangency Propagation

Figure 8–59

4. Extract the edge shown in Figure 8–60. Rename the curve as **Limit Curve Green Bracket**.

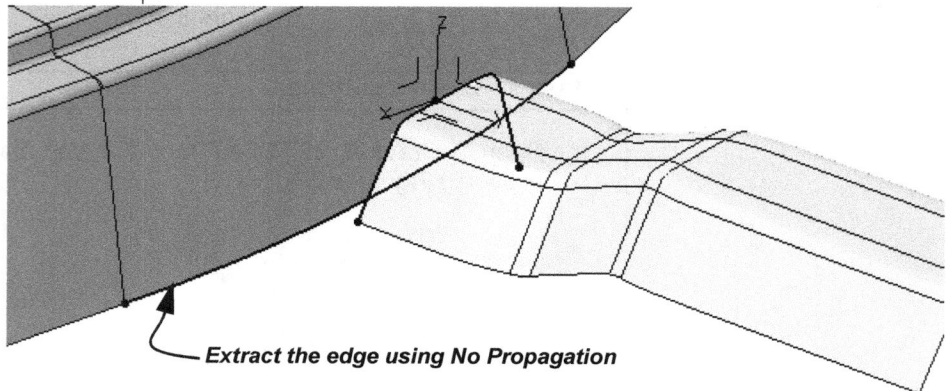

Extract the edge using No Propagation

Figure 8–60

Task 2 - Create green bracket profile.

1. Project Extracted Bracket Profile onto **Surface.1** using the **Along a direction** projection type. Specify the Y-axis as the direction reference. The completed project curve displays as shown in Figure 8–61.

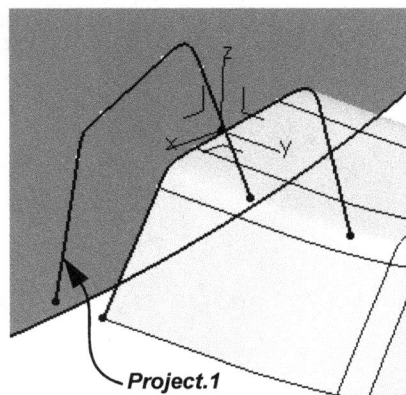

Figure 8–61

2. Create a parallel curve using the references shown in Figure 8–62.

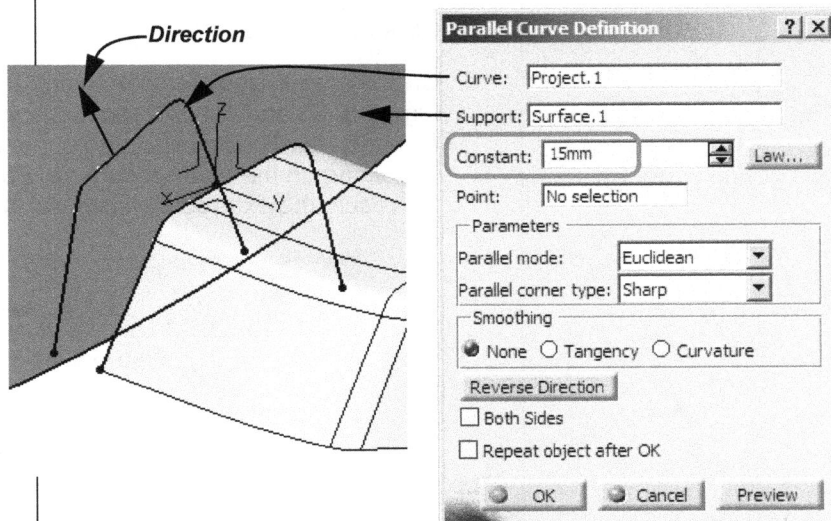

Figure 8–62

3. Ensure that the parallel feature is named **Parallel.1**.

4. Create points at the end points of Parallel.1 as shown in Figure 8–63. The points created in this step facilitate the extrapolate curves created in the next steps.

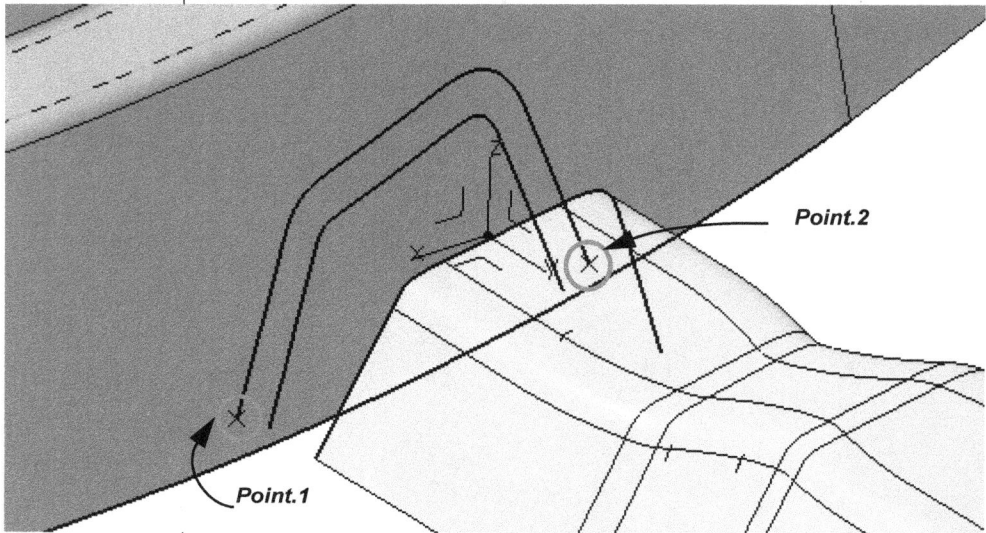

Point.2

Point.1

Figure 8–63

5. Click [icon] (Extrapolate).

6. Create the extrapolate curve using the references shown in Figure 8–65 and the Extrapolate icon as shown in Figure 8–64. The extrapolated curve extends Parallel.1 while remaining on the support surface, Surface.1. By assembling the result, the extrapolate is joined to Parallel.1.

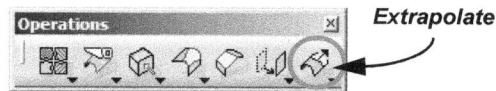

Extrapolate

Figure 8–64

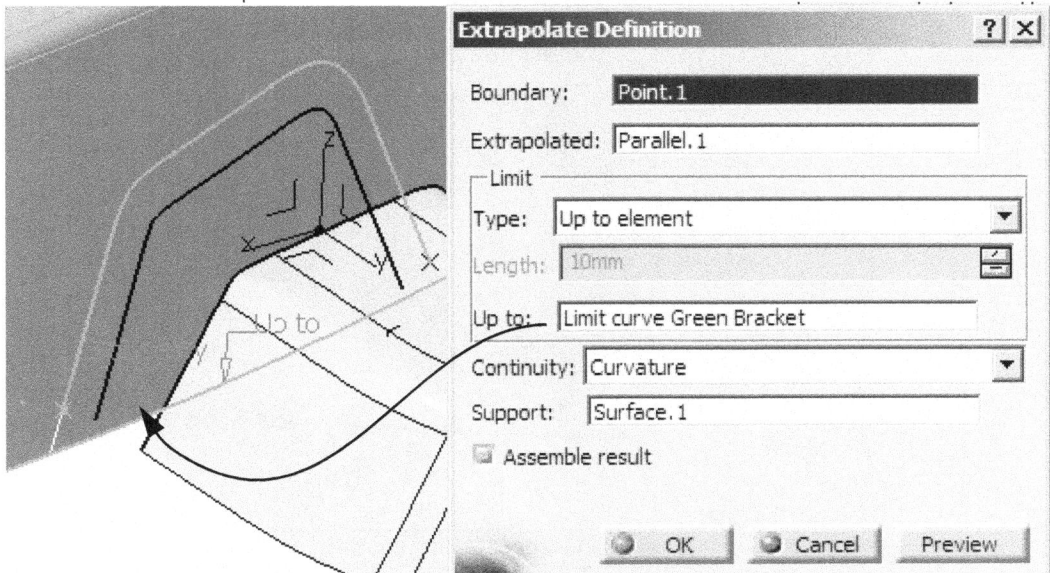

Figure 8–65

7. Create another Extrapolate curve using the following specifications and as shown in Figure 8–66.

- Boundary: **Point.2**
- Extrapolated: **Extrapol.1**
- Limit type: **Up to element**
- Up to: **Limit Curve Green Bracket**
- Continuity: **Curvature**
- Support: **Surface.1**

*Ensure that **Assemble result** is selected.*

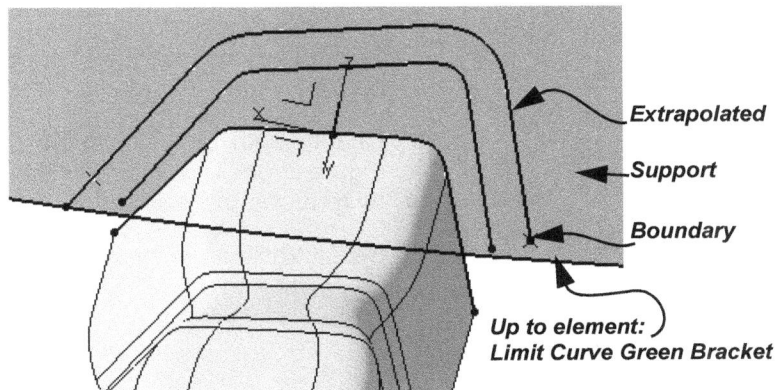

Figure 8–66

The completed Extrapolate curve displays as shown in Figure 8–67.

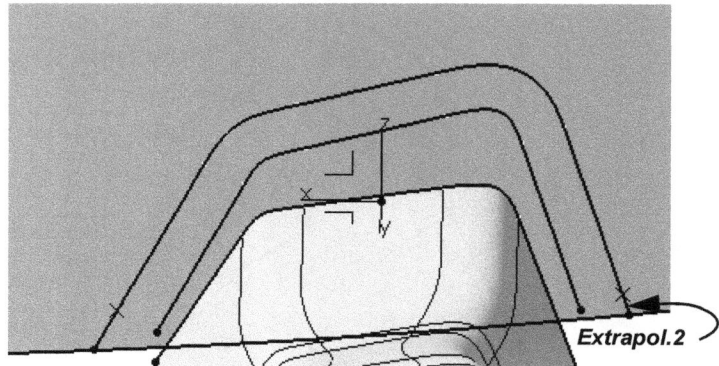

Extrapol.2

Figure 8–67

Task 3 - Complete the model.

1. Hide the following elements:

   - **Project.1**
   - **Point.1**
   - **Point.2**
   - **Absolute Axis System**
   - **Limit Curve Green Bracket**

2. Click (Blend). The Blend Definition dialog box opens.

3. Select the references shown in Figure 8–68.

4. Select **Curvature** in the First continuity and Second continuity drop-down lists.

5. Change both T1 values to **0.5** in the *Tension* tab, as shown in Figure 8–68. This improves the quality of the blend surface by reducing the tension.

6. Select **Vertices** in the drop-down list in the *Coupling/Spine* tab.

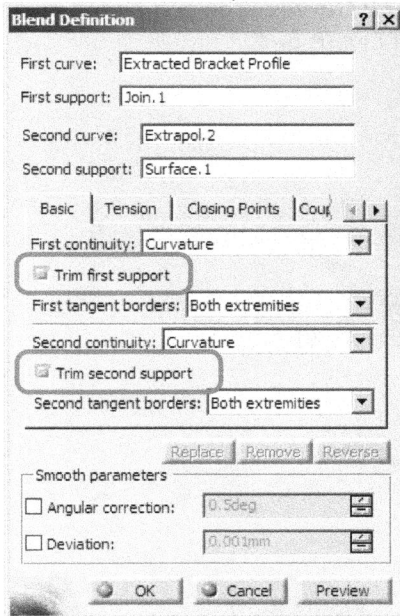

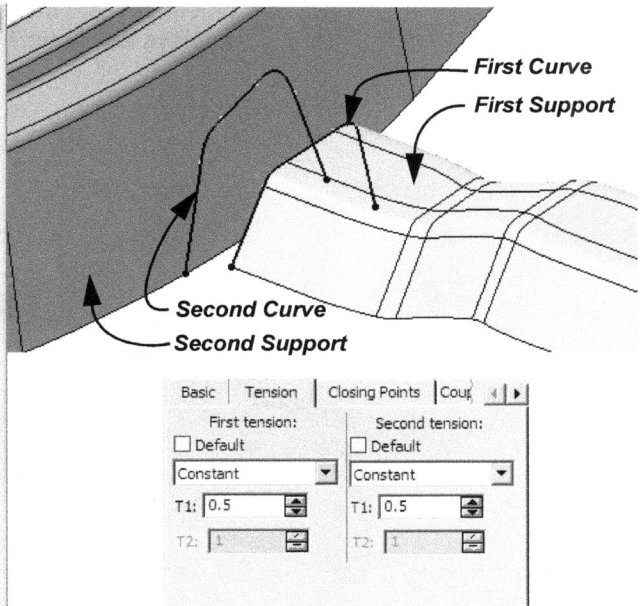

Blend Definition

First curve: Extracted Bracket Profile

First support: Join. 1

Second curve: Extrapol.2

Second support: Surface.1

Basic | Tension | Closing Points | Cour ◄ | ►

First continuity: Curvature

☐ Trim first support

First tangent borders: Both extremities

Second continuity: Curvature

☐ Trim second support

Second tangent borders: Both extremities

Replace | Remove | Reverse

Smooth parameters

☐ Angular correction: 0.5deg

☐ Deviation: 0.001mm

OK | Cancel | Preview

First Curve

First Support

Second Curve

Second Support

Basic | Tension | Closing Points | Cour ◄ | ►

First tension:
☐ Default
Constant
T1: 0.5
T2: 1

Second tension:
☐ Default
Constant
T1: 0.5
T2: 1

Figure 8–68

7. Complete the Blend feature. The model displays as shown in Figure 8–69.

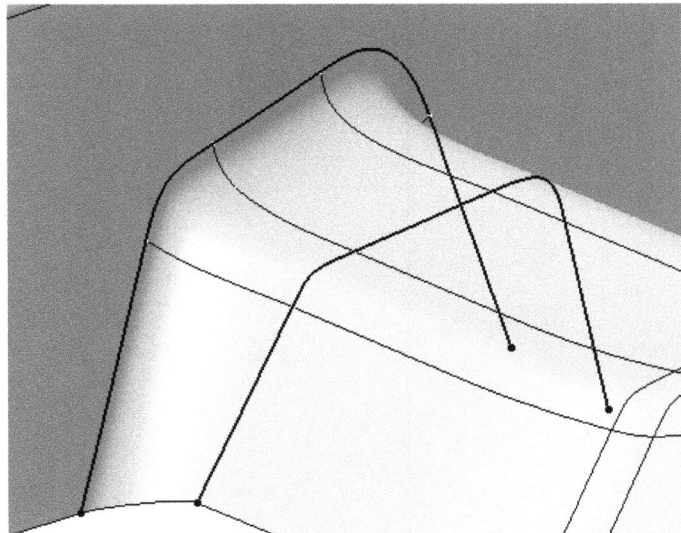

Figure 8–69

8. Select **Tools>Hide>All Curves**. The completed model displays as shown in Figure 8–70.

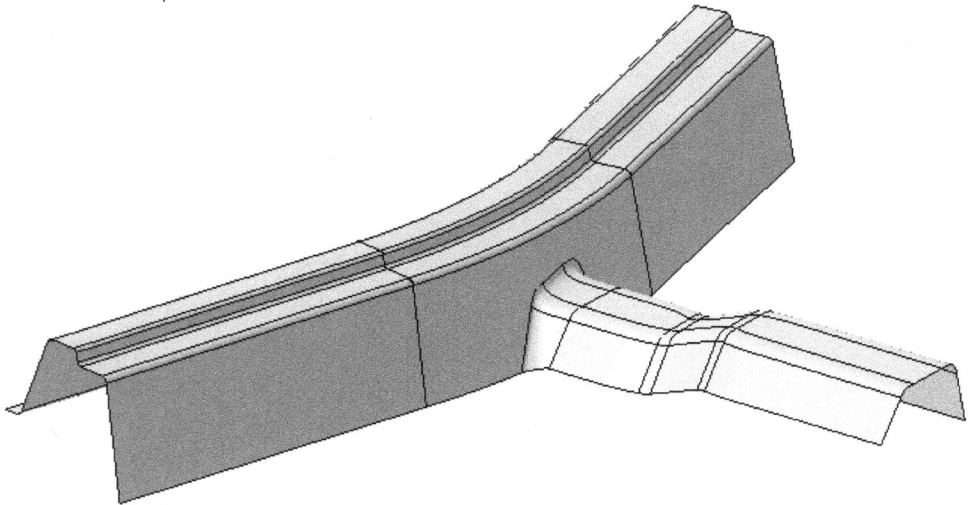

Figure 8–70

9. Save the file as **T_Bracket_ExB_ completed.CATPart**. Close the file.

Practice 8d | Complex Fillets

Practice Objective

- Rebuild a complex fillet using wireframe and surfaces.

Another alternative method of filleting involves creating a fill surface to represent the fillet geometry. In this practice, a fill surface will be created to represent a complex surface where multiple fillets join together. This model could successfully be created with a traditional fillet, but the shape is not desirable. Therefore, surfaces and curves will be extracted from the solid and rebuilt to suit the design intent. The completed model displays as shown in Figure 8–71.

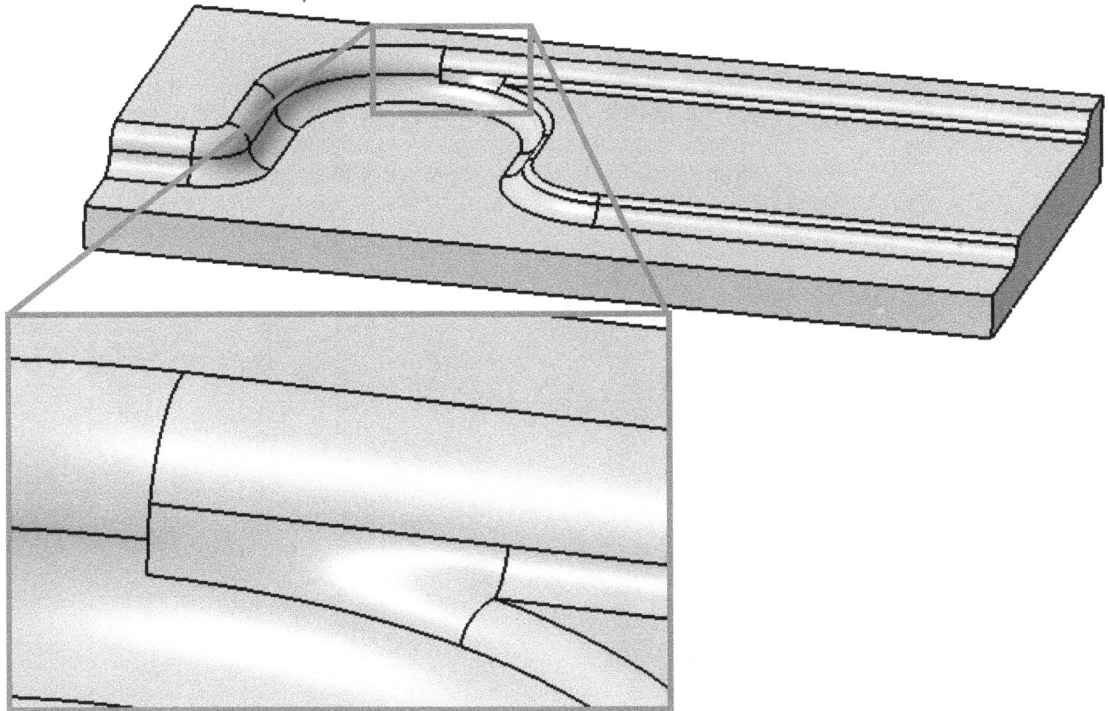

Figure 8–71

Task 1 - Open a part file.

1. Open **Complex_Fillet_Start.CATPart**. The part displays as shown in Figure 8–72. One fillet feature has been created on the solid.

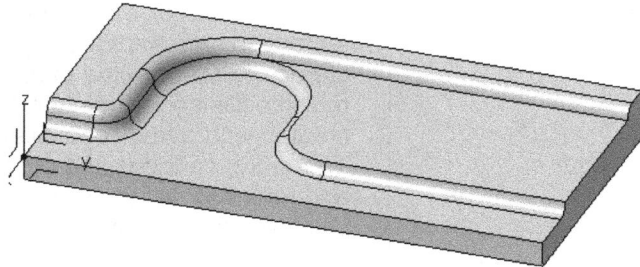

Figure 8–72

Design Considerations

The goal of the practice is to create fillets on the edges as shown in Figure 8–73. If the **Edge Fillet** tool in the Part Design workbench is used, the fillet would display as shown in Figure 8–74. However, this is not the required result.

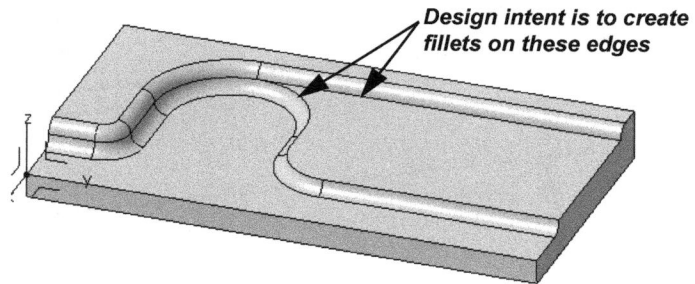

Design intent is to create fillets on these edges

Figure 8–73

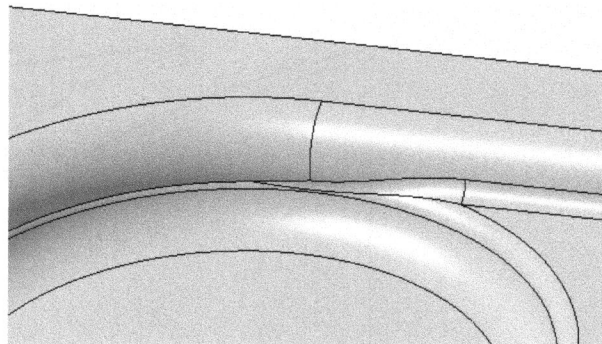

Figure 8–74

Task 2 - Create a solid fillet.

1. Enter the Part Design workbench.

2. Show the **Limiting Surface for Fillet** surface. It is located in the Pre-existing **Reference Geometry** geometrical set. The model displays as shown in Figure 8–75.

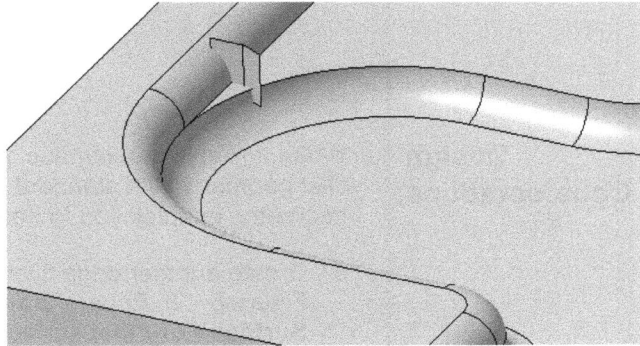

Figure 8–75

3. Create an Edge Fillet using the references shown in Figure 8–76. Enter a **2mm** radius value. The limiting element stops the fillet creation at the selected surface.

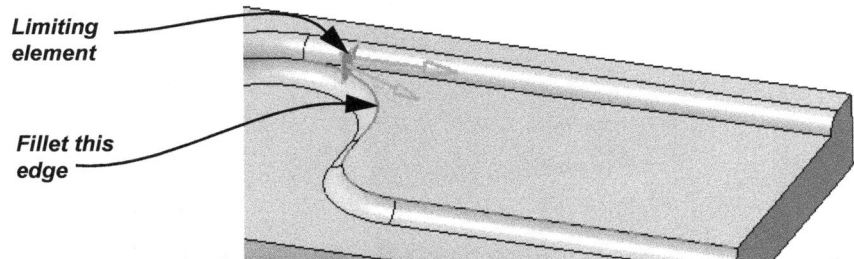

Limiting element

Fillet this edge

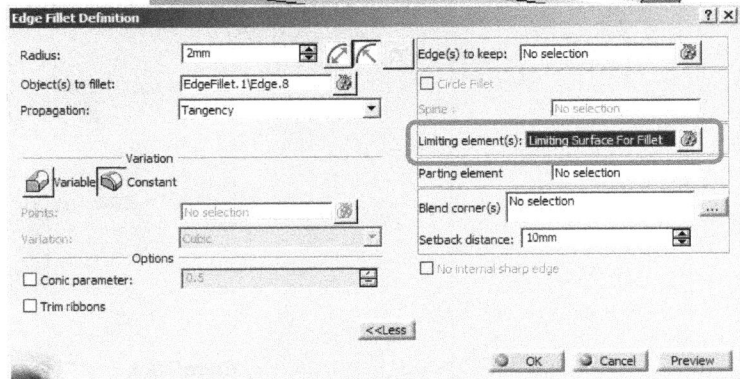

Figure 8–76

4. Complete the Edge fillet. The model displays as shown in Figure 8–77.

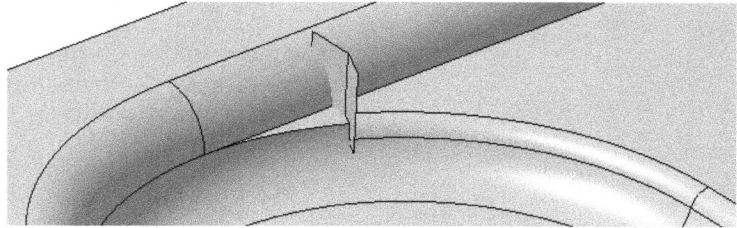

Figure 8–77

Design Considerations

When a fillet is problematic, attempt to create as much of the fillet geometry with standard **Fillet** tools. Creating some fillet geometry, enables you to have some geometry to build from.

5. Create another edge fillet using the edge shown in Figure 8–78. Enter a **2mm** radius value. Select the **Limiting Surface For Fillet** surface as the Limiting element reference.

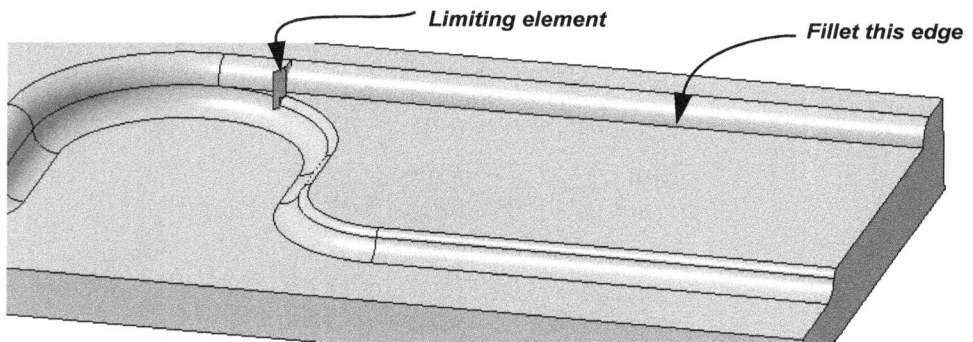

Figure 8–78

6. Complete the edge fillet. The model displays as shown in Figure 8–79.

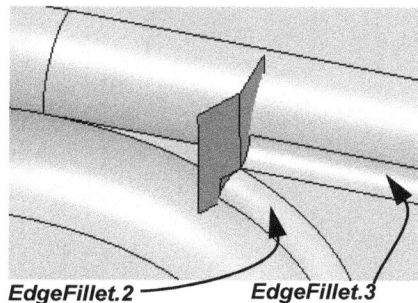

Figure 8–79

7. Hide the Limiting Surface For Fillet surface. This shows the limitation of the fillet features more clearly. The model displays as shown in Figure 8–80.

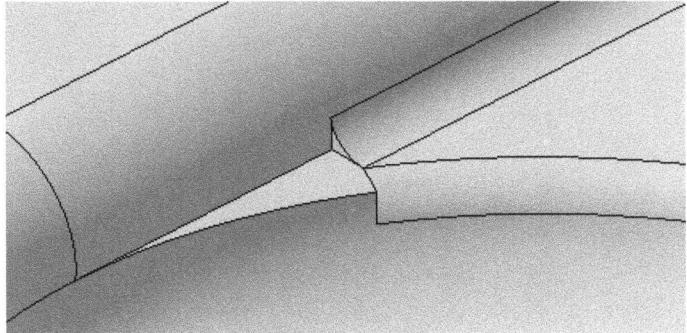

Figure 8–80

Task 3 - Extract reference geometry.

1. Enter the Generative Shape Design workbench.

2. Create a geometrical set named **Extract Geometry**.

3. Extract the seven surfaces shown in Figure 8–81.

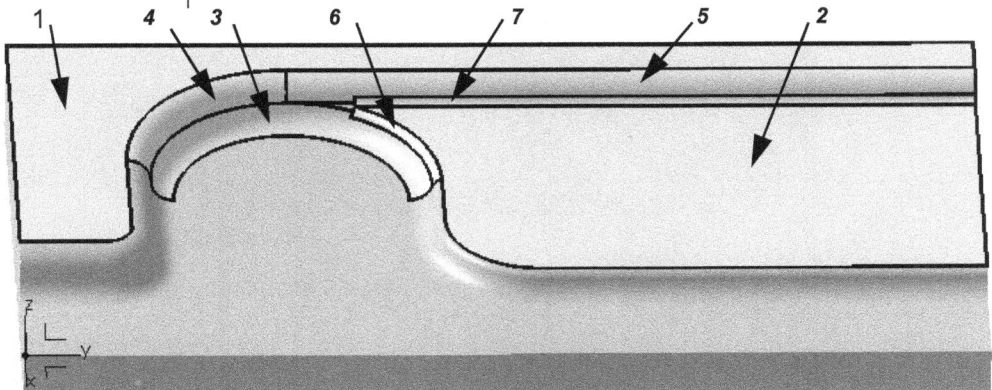

Figure 8–81

4. Rename each extract, as shown in Figure 8–82.

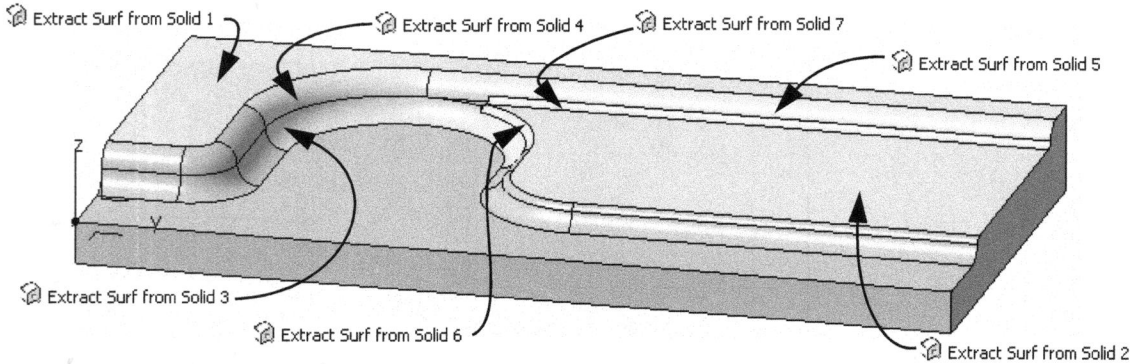

Extract Surf from Solid 1

Extract Surf from Solid 4

Extract Surf from Solid 7

Extract Surf from Solid 5

Extract Surf from Solid 3

Extract Surf from Solid 6

Extract Surf from Solid 2

Figure 8–82

5. Hide the seven extracted surfaces. If the surfaces are not hidden, it is easier to select the wrong reference in the next operation.

6. Extract the edges shown in Figure 8–83.

Extract these two edges

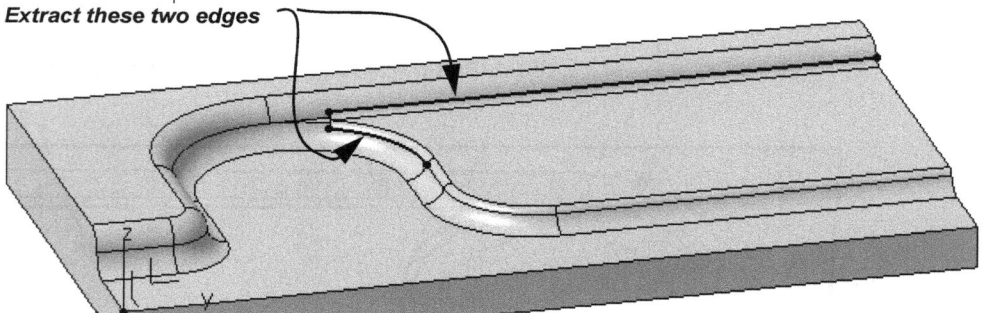

Figure 8–83

7. Rename the edges, as shown in Figure 8–84.

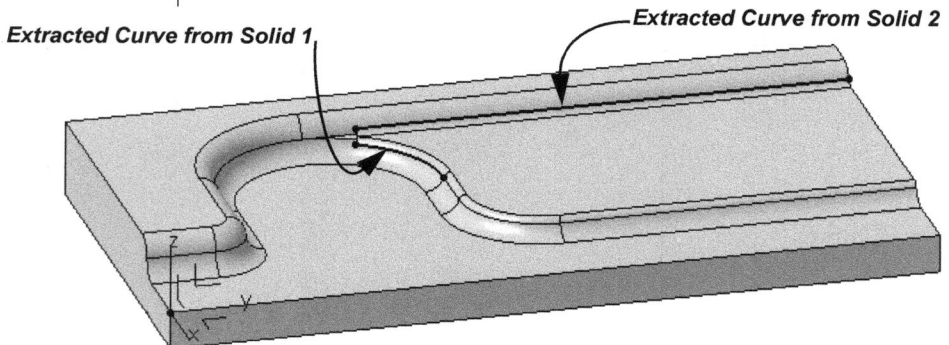

Extracted Curve from Solid 1

Extracted Curve from Solid 2

Figure 8–84

8. Show the seven extracted surfaces.

9. Join the following two surfaces:

   - **Extract Surf from Solid 3**
   - **Extract Surf from Solid 4**

10. Rename the Join feature as **Join 3+4**.

11. Join the following surfaces:

    - **Extract Surf from Solid 2**
    - **Extract Surf from Solid 6**
    - **Extract Surf from Solid 7**

12. Rename the Join feature as **Join 2+6+7**.

Task 4 - Create curves from extracted geometry.

1. Create a geometrical set named **Profile Geometry**.

2. Hide the **PartBody**.

3. Create a Multiple Extract feature, selecting the edges shown in Figure 8–85. The Multiple Extract feature joins the elements together.

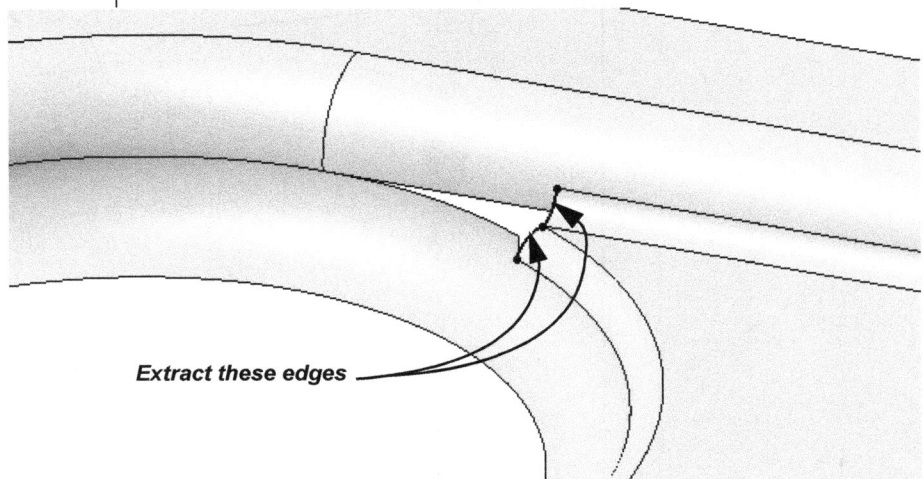

Extract these edges

Figure 8–85

4. Rename the Multiple Extract feature as **Profile1**.

5. Show **Circ Center Plane** in the Pre-existing **Reference Geometry** geometrical set.

6. Create an Intersection between Circ Center Plane and Extract Surf from Solid 3.

7. The completed Intersection curve displays as shown in Figure 8–86.

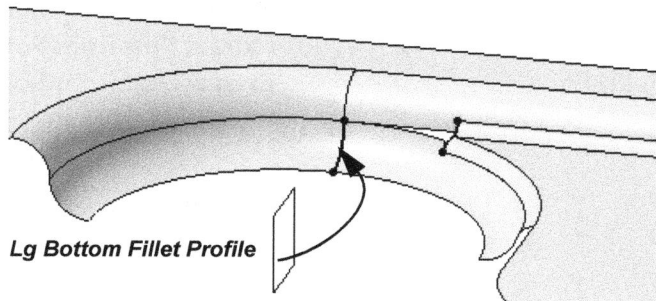

Figure 8–86

8. Rename the Intersect curve as **Lg Bottom Fillet Profile**.

9. Extract the edge shown in Figure 8–87.

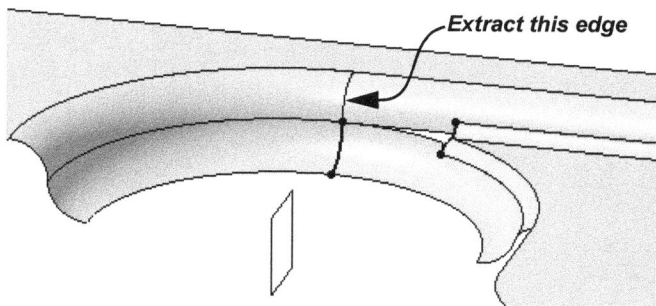

Figure 8–87

10. Rename the extracted curve as **Lg Top Fillet Profile**.

11. Join the following elements:

   * **Lg Bottom Fillet Profile**
   * **Lg Top Fillet Profile**

The completed Join displays as shown in Figure 8–88.

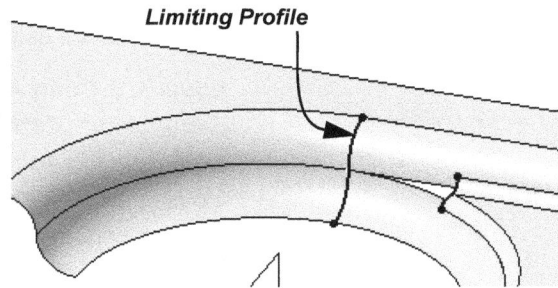

Figure 8–88

12. Rename the Join as **Limiting Profile**.

Task 5 - Extrapolate curves.

---

1. Create two points using **On Curve** as the point type. The points are located at the end points of **Profile1**, as shown in Figure 8–89.

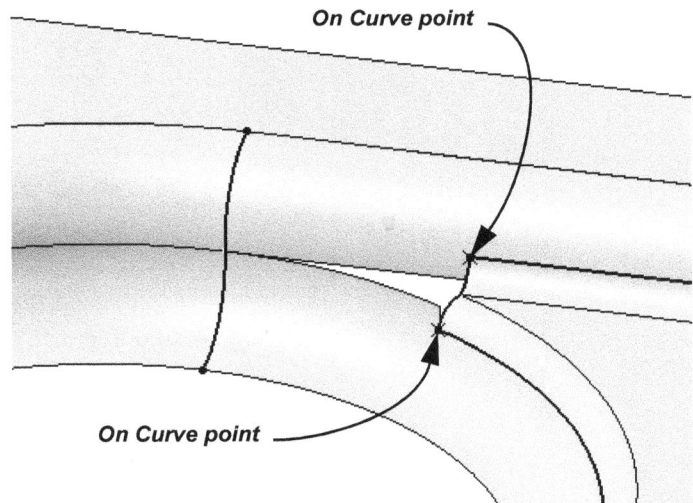

Figure 8–89

2. Rename the top end point as **Point A**.

3. Rename the bottom end point as **Point B**.

4. Click (Extrapolate) in the Operations toolbar. Create the Extrapolate curve using the following references:

- *Boundary:* **Point A**
- *Extrapolated:* **Extracted Curve from Solid 2**
- *Limit type:* **Up to element**
- *Up to:* **Limiting Profile**
- *Continuity:* **Curvature**
- *Support:* **Extract Surf from Solid 5**
- Deactivate the **Assemble result** option.

The Extrapolate Definition dialog box opens as shown in Figure 8–90.

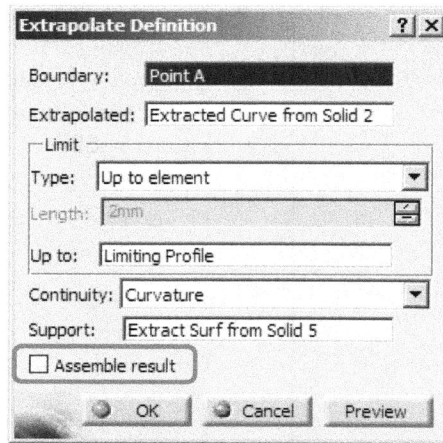

Figure 8–90

The completed curve displays as shown in Figure 8–91.

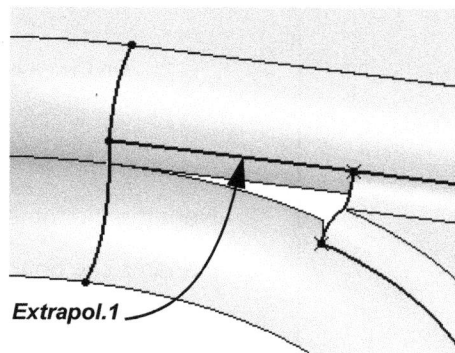

Figure 8–91

5. Create another Extrapolate curve using the following references:

- *Boundary:* **Point B**
- *Extrapolated:* **Extracted Curve from Solid 1**
- *Limit type:* **Up to element**
- *Up to:* **Limiting Profile**
- *Continuity:* **Curvature**
- *Support:* **Extract Surf from Solid 3**
- Deactivate the **Assemble result** option.

The completed curve displays as shown in Figure 8–92.

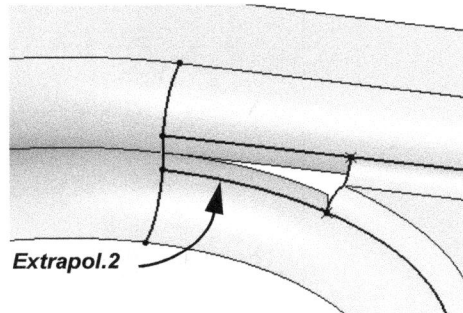

Extrapol.2

Figure 8–92

Design Considerations

Both extrapolate curves extend the extracted edges from the fillet and are located on a respective support surface. Other curve types could have been used, but this a faster method of extending the curves up to the Limiting Profile curve.

6. Create two points using **On Curve** as the point type, as shown in Figure 8–93.

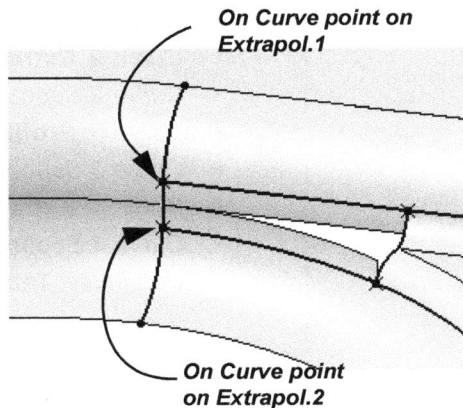

On Curve point on Extrapol.1

On Curve point on Extrapol.2

Figure 8–93

7. Use the two newly created points to split the Limiting Profile curve so that it displays as shown in Figure 8–94.

8. Rename the split feature as **Profile2**.

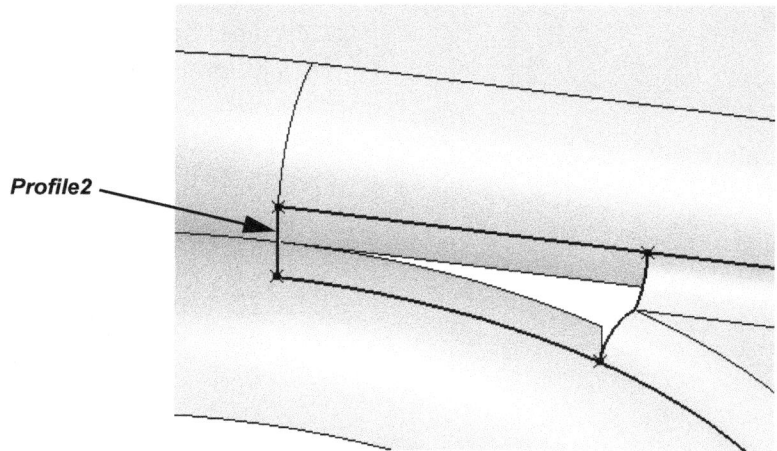

Profile2

Figure 8–94

9. Hide all points in the model.

Task 6 - Create a surface to represent the fillet.

In this task a fill surface will be created using the curves created in the last task. It will use the extracted surfaces as support references. That way continuity can be specified. When completed the fill will be sewn into the solid.

1. Create a fill feature the following references:

   - *Curve 1:* **Profile2**
   - *Curve 1 Support:* **Join 3+4**
   - *Curve 2:* **Extrapol.2**
   - *Curve 2 Support:* **Extract Surf from Solid 3**
   - *Curve 3:* **Profile1**
   - *Curve 3 Support:* **Join 2+6+7**
   - *Curve 4:* **Extrapol.1**
   - *Curve 4 Support:* **Extract Surf from Solid 5**
   - *Continuity:* **Tangent**

The Fill Definition dialog box opens as shown in Figure 8–95.

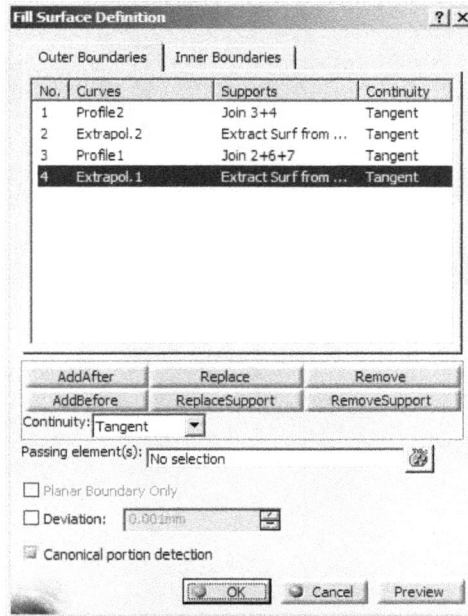

Figure 8–95

The completed Fill displays as shown in Figure 8–96.

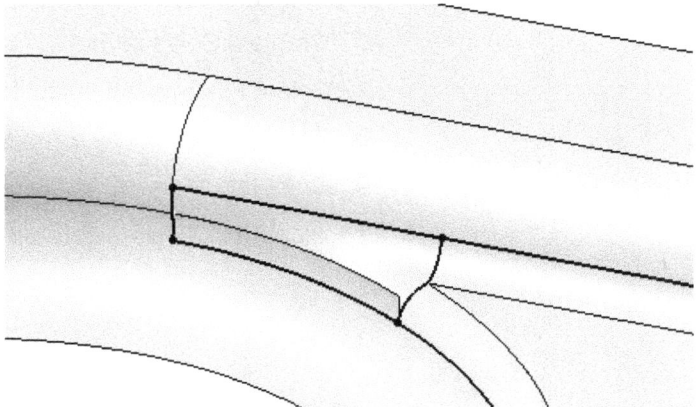

Figure 8–96

Design Considerations

The surrounding surfaces do not need to be trimmed or split. Only the Fill surface is required to complete the solid fillet. The surfaces helped you to build the references required to create the fill.

2. Hide all wireframe and surfaces except for Fill.1, as shown in Figure 8–97.

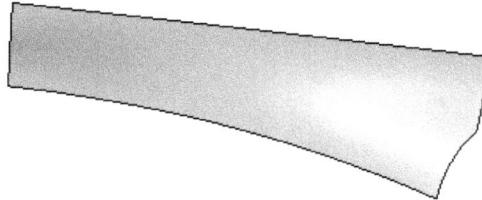

Figure 8–97

3. Enter the Part Design workbench.

4. Show the PartBody as shown in Figure 8–98.

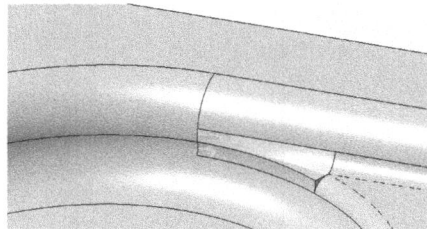

Figure 8–98

Surface Based Features toolbar.

5. Activate the PartBody.

6. Create a Sew feature.

7. Select **Fill.1** as the object to sew.

8. Ensure that the sew arrow is pointing into the solid.

9. Complete the sew.

10. Hide **Fill.1**. The model displays as shown in Figure 8–99.

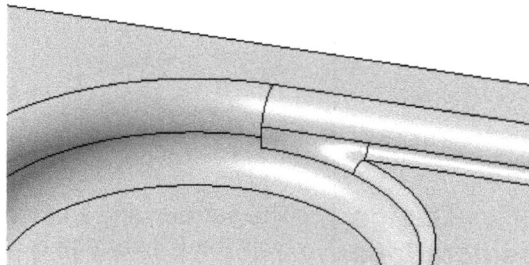

Figure 8–99

11. Save the model as **Complex Fillet Complete**.

12. Close the file.

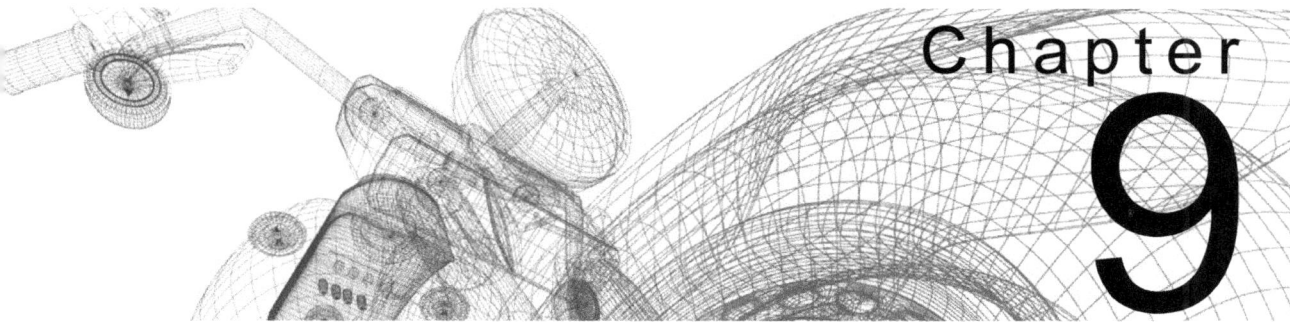

Chapter 9

Laws

Laws provide additional control over the creation of wireframe and surface geometry. They enable you to create complex shapes by varying the value of surface or wireframe parameters. Parameters can include angles, lengths, and radii.

Learning Objectives in this Chapter

- Define Laws.
- Create a Law feature.
- Understand when to use Laws.

9.1 Law Definition

Laws enable you to vary the value of a parameter, which can control wireframe or surface geometry. A law is a 2D graph plotting the value of the parameter. The following features enable a law to control feature parameters:

- Sweep surfaces

- Parallel curves

- Helix curves

- Shape Fillets

An example of a sweep is shown in Figure 9–1.

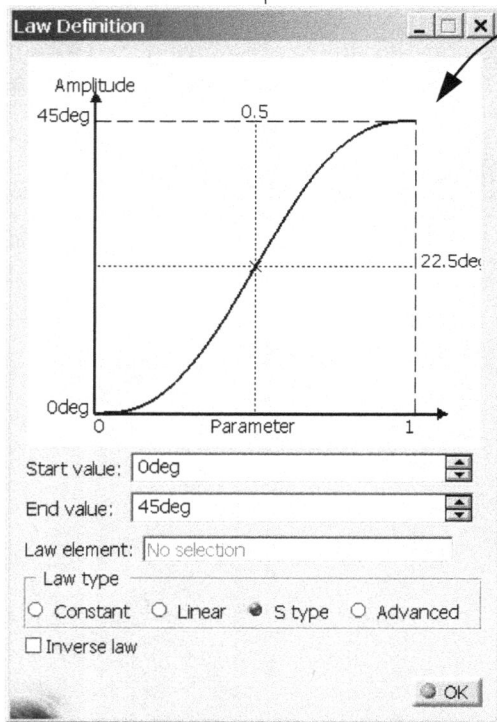

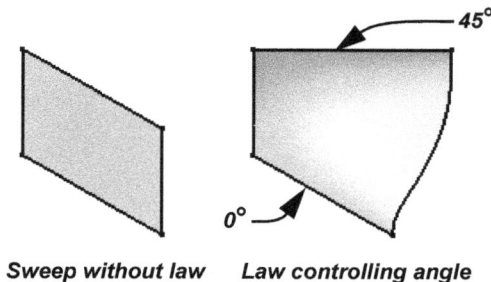

Sweep without law   Law controlling angle

Figure 9–1

General Steps

Use the following general steps to control the value of a parameter using a law:

1. Start the creation of a Law.
2. Select a type of Law.
3. Enter start and end values.
4. Apply the Law.

Step 1 - Start the creation of a Law.

Click **Law** next to the parameter to be controlled in the Feature dialog box. The Law Definition dialog box opens as shown in Figure 9–2.

Only one law can be defined at a time.

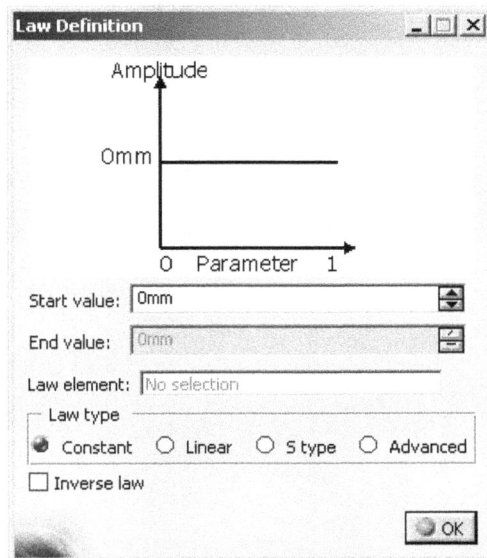

Figure 9–2

The X-axis of the graph indicates the position along the length of the guide curve, curve, or axis. (The curve type depends on the feature the law is used with.) The name of this position is known as the X-parameter. The X-parameter equals 0 at the start of the curve and 1 at the end of the curve. The Y-axis of the graph shows the Amplitude or value of the law at specific positions along the length of the guide curve.

Step 2 - Select a type of Law.

Four types of laws can be defined:

- Constant

- Linear

- S-type

- Advanced

Constant

The value of this type of law remains constant across the entire length of the X-parameter. Once any type of law is added, it cannot be deleted. This option can be used to clear a law-driven value. Once applied, the parameter value can be edited in the Swept Surface Definition dialog box.

Linear

The value of this law varies linearly from the start to the end of the X-parameter. The linear slope is defined by specifying start and end values, as shown in Figure 9–3.

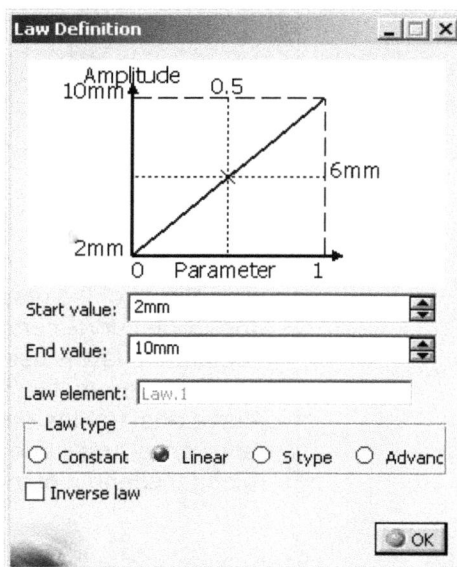

Figure 9–3

S-type

The value of the law is defined by an S-shaped curve specifying the start and end values, as shown in Figure 9–4.

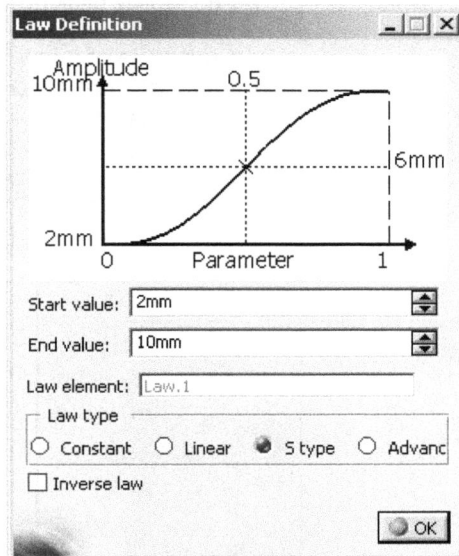

Figure 9–4

Advanced

An Advance law enables you to use an existing Law feature and apply it to the creation of the current surface feature.

Step 3 - Enter start and end values.

To identify values along the curve, move the mouse cross-hairs onto the graph.

If a Linear or S-type law is being defined, you must enter start and end values for the X-parameter. The values are interpolated to calculate results for all values of the X-parameter. The Law Definition dialog box updates to display a graph of the law. The graph can be panned and zoomed using the standard model orientation mouse methods.

The **Inverse law** option enables you to flip the law about the horizontal axis.

Step 4 - Apply the Law.

Click **OK** to apply the law to the selected parameter value. Once a law is defined, it becomes unavailable to select and can only be edited by clicking **Law**.

An example of a law is shown in Figure 9–5. The law varies the parameter from a start value of 0 degrees to an end value of 45 degrees using an S-shaped curve.

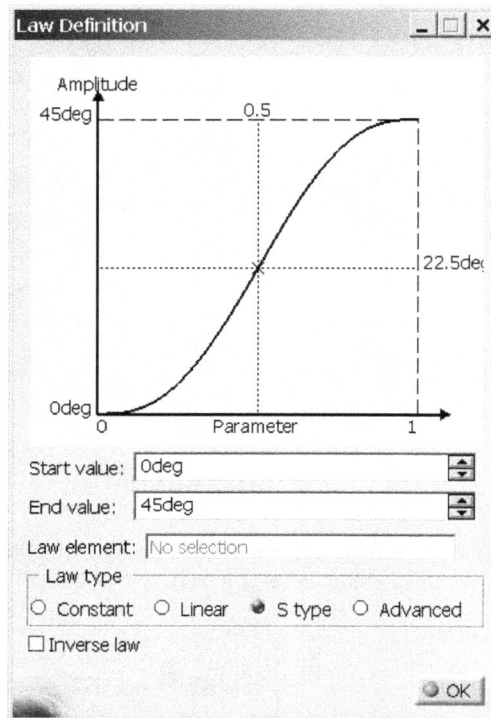

Figure 9–5

9.2 Creating a Law Feature

For very complex geometry definitions, a Law feature can be created to control the shape of an existing or future wireframe or surface entity. For example, you might want the shape of a turbine blade to follow a specific profile provided by a customer as shown in Figure 9–6.

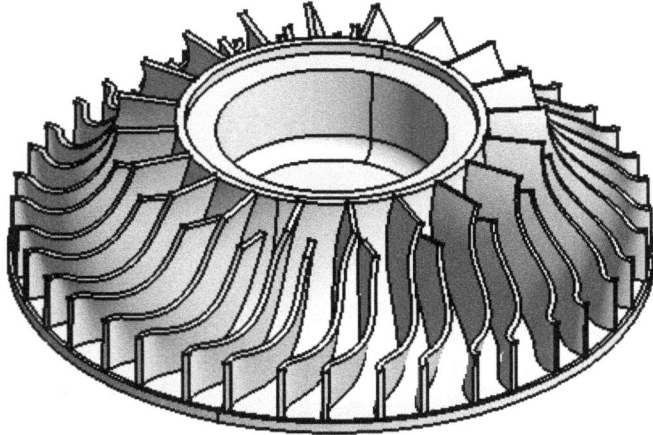

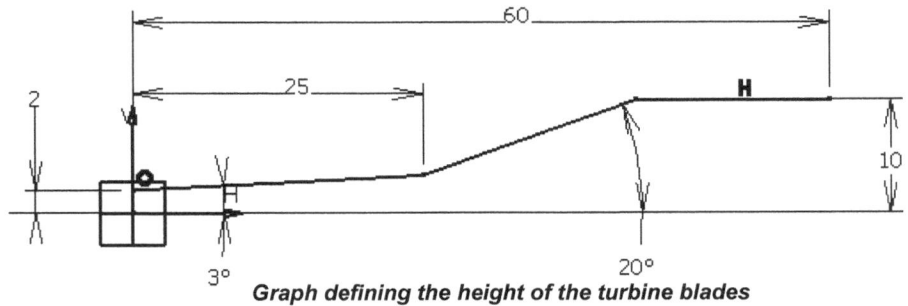

Graph defining the height of the turbine blades

Figure 9–6

The profile is defined by a curve whose shape can be mapped by a Law feature. The feature can then be applied to the creation of a swept surface to control its shape.

General Steps

Use the following steps to create a Law feature:

1. Start the creation of a Law feature.
2. Select a reference and definition.
3. Enter a scale.
4. Define the system of units.
5. Complete the feature.

Step 1 - Start the creation of a Law feature.

Click ▱ (Law) in the Law toolbar. The Law Definition dialog box opens as shown in Figure 9–7.

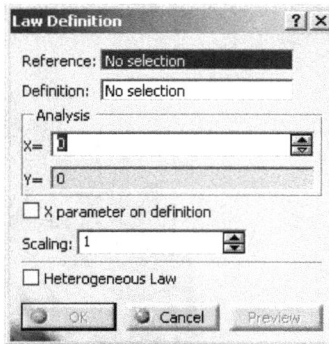

Figure 9–7

Step 2 - Select a reference and definition.

Reference

The reference element defines the X-axis for the law and must be a linear element. Model edges or line elements can be selected from the main window or specification tree.

Alternatively, you can select an element by right-clicking and selecting an option in the context menu, as shown in Figure 9–8.

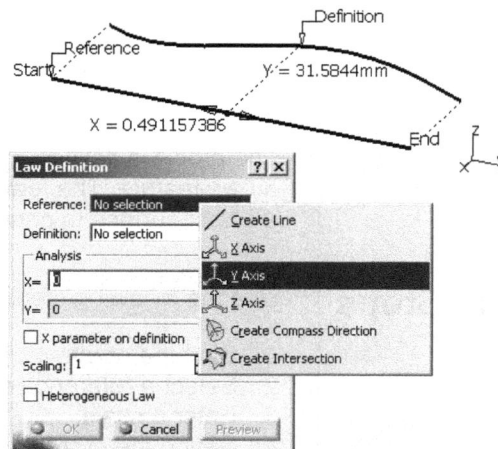

Figure 9–8

Definition

The reference element is normalized so that at the start of the selected element the X-parameter is 0, and at the end the X-parameter is 1.

The definition element defines the shape of the Law feature. The distance between the reference element and the definition element is measured along the length of the reference element. In the example in Figure 9–8, the distance between the definition element (spline) and the Y-axis is measured.

You can position the cursor over the arrows shown in Figure 9–9 and drag them along the reference element. The dialog box updates with the current X-position and the result of the law in the *Analysis* field.

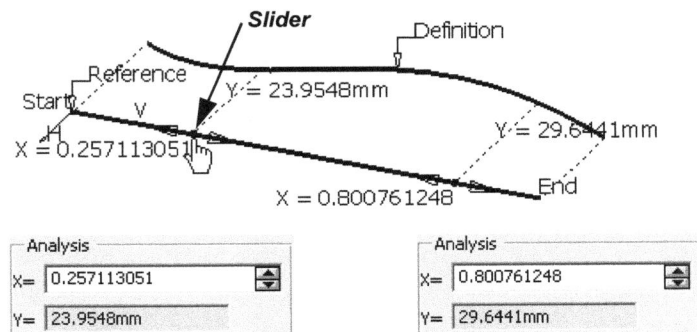

Figure 9–9

X-parameter on Definition

By default, the X-parameter displays along the length of the reference element. To track the X-parameter using the definition element, select **X-parameter on definition**. The slider arrows are moved to the definition element as shown in Figure 9–10.

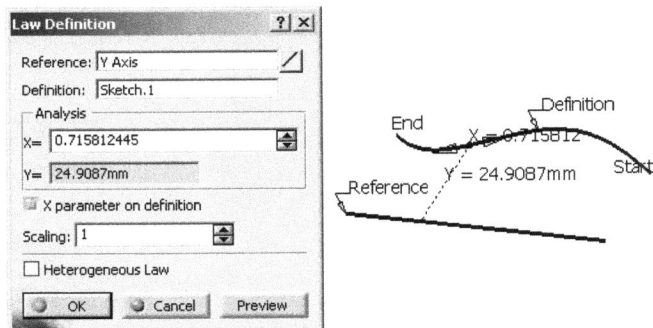

Figure 9–10

The values for the law are calculated by projecting the point on the definition element normal to the reference line.

Step 3 - Enter a scale.

Depending on the application of the Law feature, you might want to increase the results by applying a scale factor. The results are multiplied by the value entered when applied to downstream features.

The depth of the swept surface on the left side of Figure 9–11 is controlled by the spline using a scale of 1. The scale of the law is increased to 2 so that the surface has doubled in width, as shown on the right side.

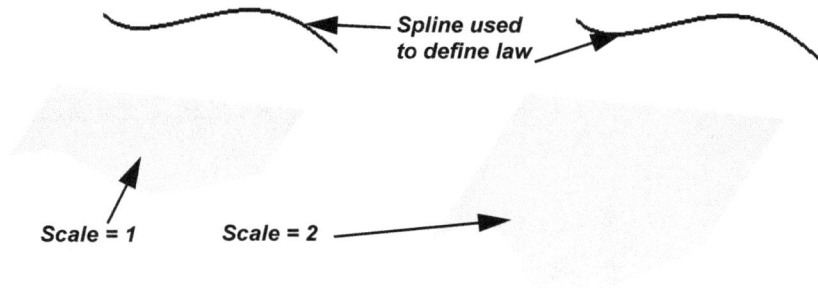

Spline used to define law

Scale = 1   *Scale = 2*

Figure 9–11

Step 4 - Define the system of units.

The system of units is defined by enabling the **Heterogeneous Law** option. The dialog box updates as shown in Figure 9–12.

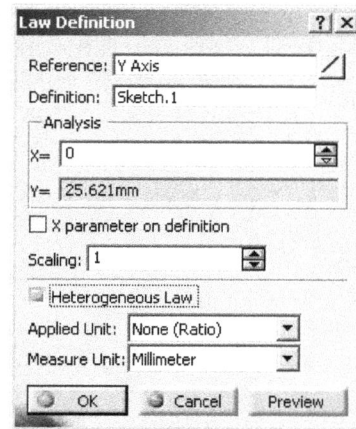

Figure 9–12

The options in the Applied Unit (also called Law Unit) drop-down list define the purpose of the law, as shown in Figure 9–13.

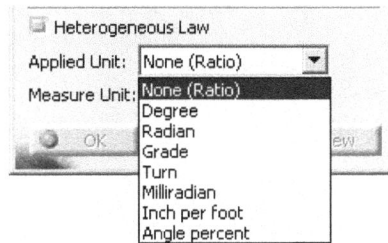

Figure 9–13

- **None** (default): Sets the units of the law to be the same as the units of the feature to which it is applied.

- **Degree**: Applies to the angles in the law. It interprets the results of the law in degrees.

- **Radian**: Applies to angles in the law. It interprets the results of the law in radians.

- **Grade**: Interprets the results of the law as a grade.

- **Turn**: Interprets the results of the law in turns.

- **Milliradian**: Interprets the results of the law in milliradians.

The options in the Measure Unit drop-down list define the units of the dimensions in the law calculation, as shown in Figure 9–14.

The default value is the current units.

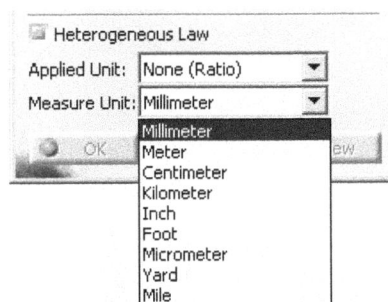

Figure 9–14

Step 5 - Complete the feature.

Click **OK** to complete the feature. The Law feature is added to the specification tree as shown in Figure 9–15.

*Law features are applied to the geometry using the **Advanced Law** option.*

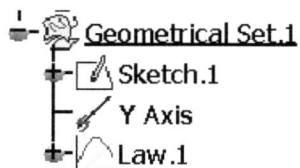

Figure 9–15

This feature can now be used to control downstream geometry.

9.3 Using Laws

Not all features enable a law to drive a parameter. In the Generative Shape Design workbench only Sweeps, Shape Fillets, Parallel curves, and Helix curves have the ability to use a Law feature.

Sweeps

One of the most common features to use with a law is the Sweep feature. Laws enable a more controlled definition of the sweep. Any sweep angle, length, radii, or conic parameter can be driven by a law as shown in Figure 9–16.

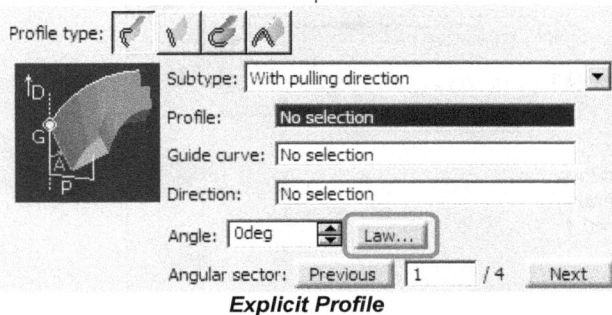

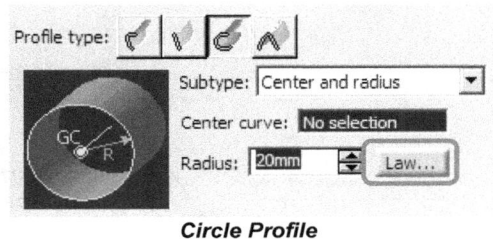

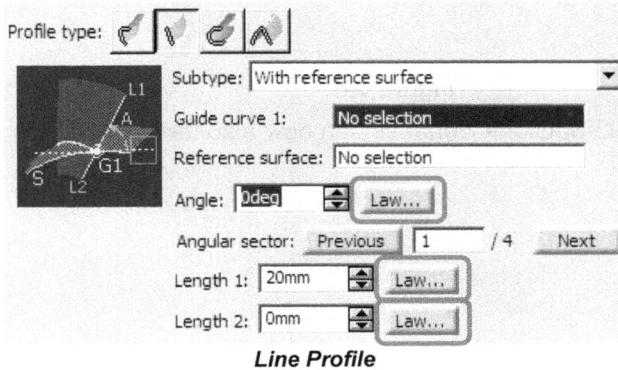

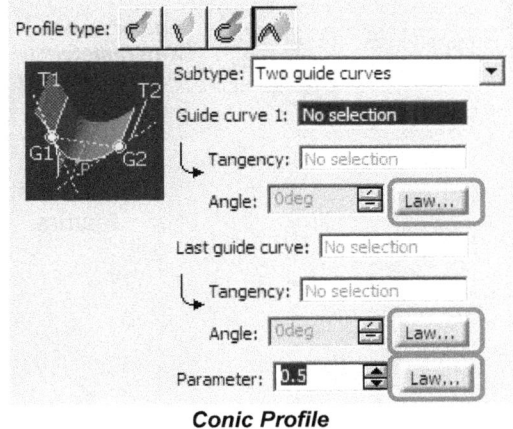

Explicit Profile

Circle Profile

Line Profile

Conic Profile

Figure 9–16

An X-parameter value of zero corresponds to the start of the sweep. A value of 1 corresponds to the end of the sweep. As the profile moves along the sweep the law dictates the parameter value.

A conic sweep has been created using a law to drive the conic parameter value as shown in Figure 9–17.

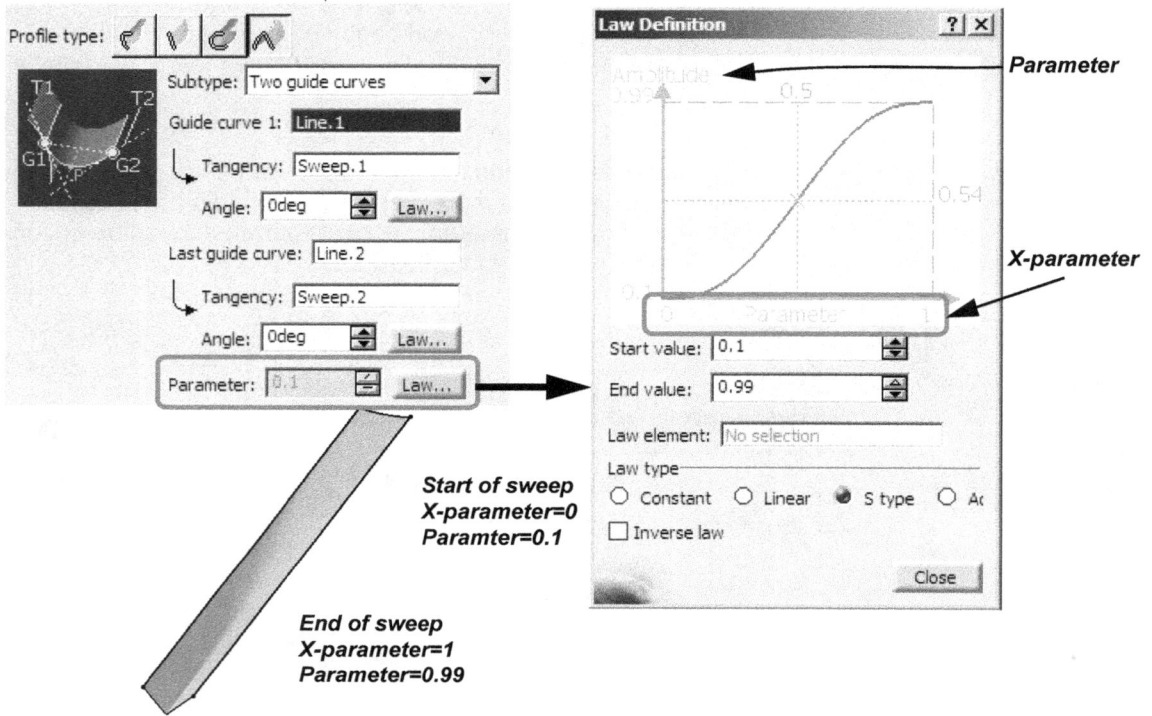

Profile type:

Subtype: Two guide curves

Guide curve 1: Line.1
  Tangency: Sweep.1
  Angle: 0deg   Law...

Last guide curve: Line.2
  Tangency: Sweep.2
  Angle: 0deg   Law...

Parameter: 0.1   Law...

Start of sweep
X-parameter=0
Paramter=0.1

End of sweep
X-parameter=1
Parameter=0.99

Law Definition

Amplitude

Parameter

X-parameter

Start value: 0.1
End value: 0.99
Law element: No selection

Law type
○ Constant ○ Linear ● S type ○ A(
☐ Inverse law

Close

Figure 9–17

Note that Multi-Sections Surfaces can now also use a Law feature.

Parallel Curves

The offset value for a Parallel curve can be driven by a law as shown in Figure 9–18.

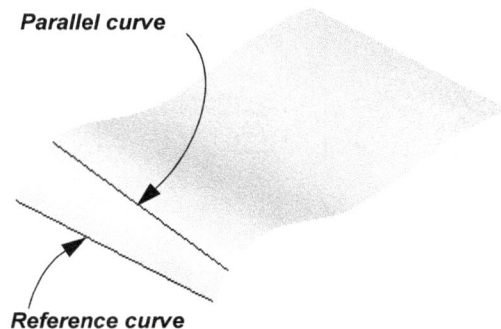

Parallel curve

Reference curve

Figure 9–18

The law definition displays as shown in Figure 9–19. The law types Constant, Linear, S-type, and Advanced are available when defining a law for a Parallel curve. The end value is indicated by the arrow direction. Select **Inverse law** to change the direction.

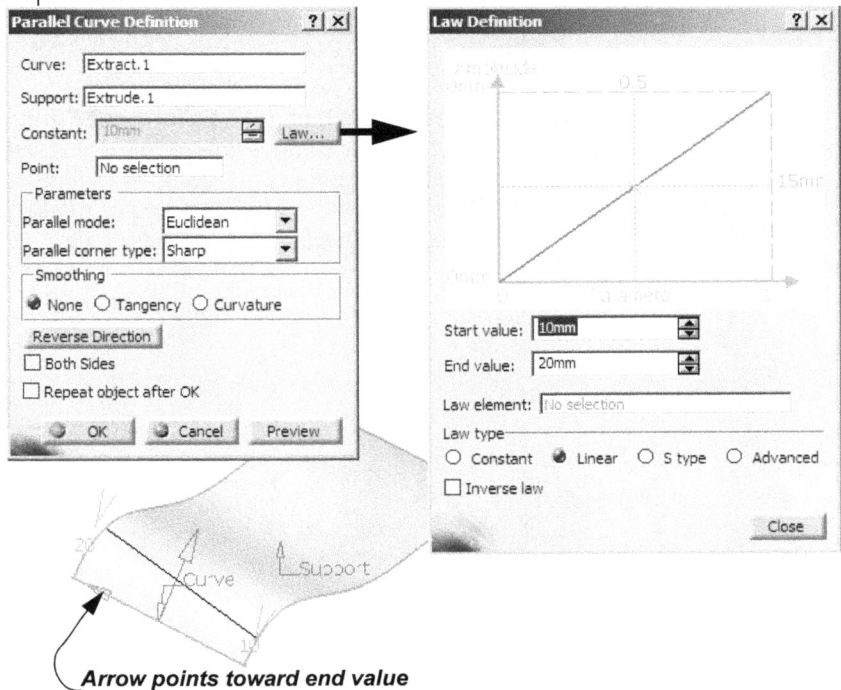

Arrow points toward end value

Figure 9–19

Helix

The pitch value for a Helix can be driven by a Law feature. The law defines the pitch or linear dimension between each revolution of the helix. In the example shown in Figure 9–20, the law changes the pitch from 5mm at the start of the helix to 20mm at the end of the helix.

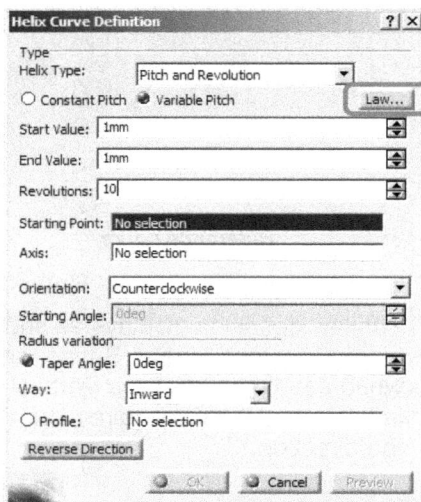

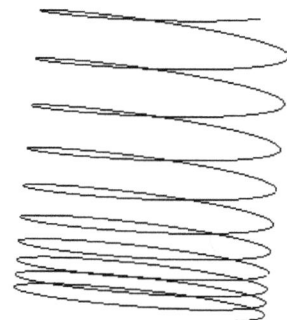

*Depending on your Service Pack, this option may display as **Create by edges or vertex**.*

Figure 9–20

Shape Fillets

Shape fillets using the **BiTangent Fillet** fillet type have the ability to use a law to drive the radius value. Before the law can be created, a spine curve must be defined as shown in Figure 9–21. This defines the start and end of the law. If a spine is not selected the **Law** icon is grayed out.

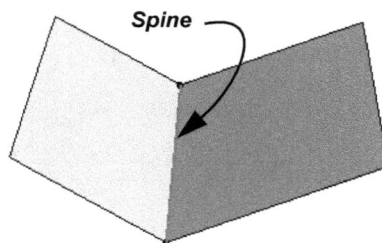

Figure 9–21

In addition to the law types Constant, Linear, S-type, and Advanced, a **Implicit** type exists for Shape Fillets as shown in Figure 9–22.

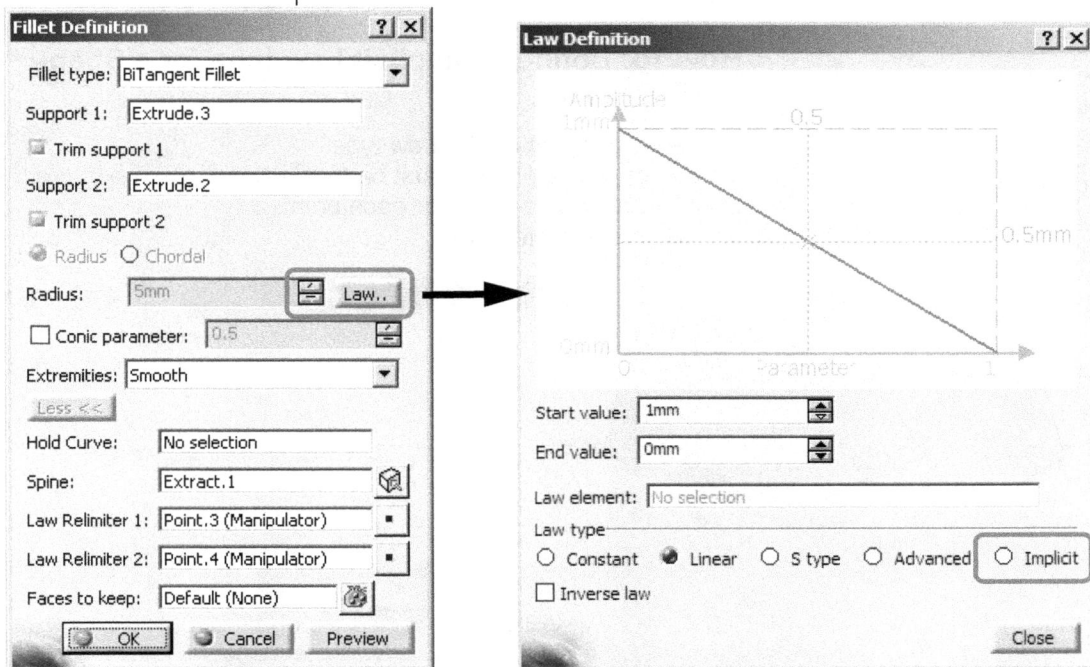

Figure 9–22

The Implicit law type enables points located on the spine to be selected. At each point, a radius value can be specified. The law graph is then generated from the input values as shown in Figure 9–23.

How To: Define an Implicit Law type for a Shape Fillet

1. Select **Implicit** as the Law type.
2. Select points. Points must be located on the spine curve.
3. Enter a Radius value for each point.
4. Complete the feature.

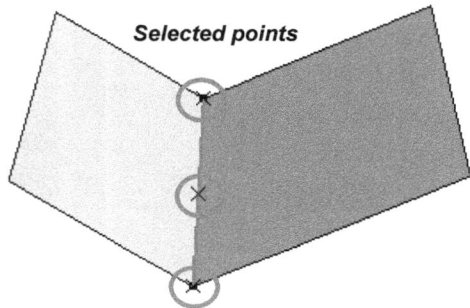

Selected points

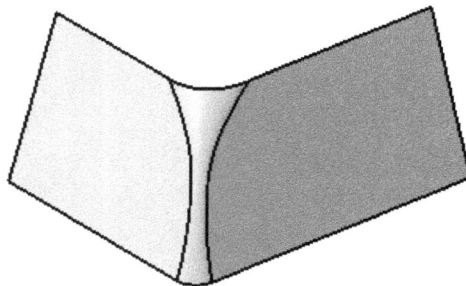

Completed fillet

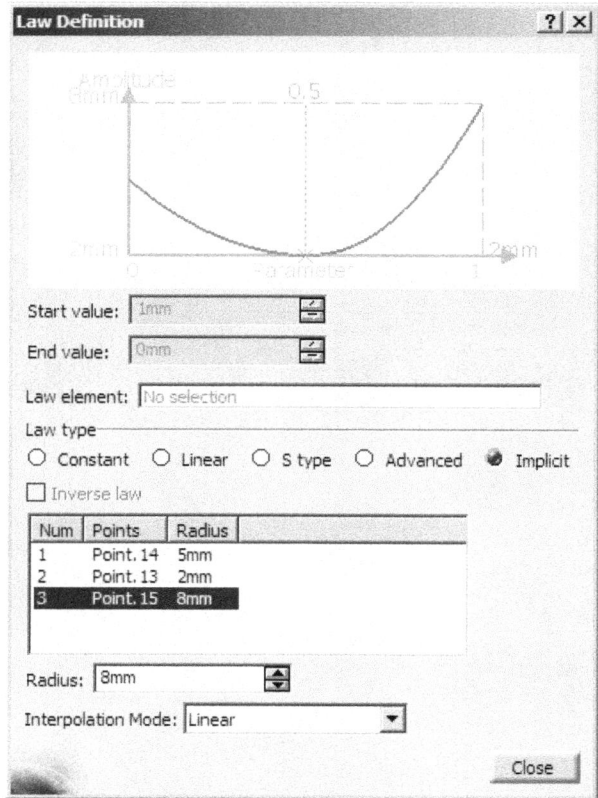

Figure 9–23

Practice 9a

Law Driven Shape Fillet

Practice Objectives

- Create a Law feature.
- Apply a Law feature to a shape fillet.
- Create an implicit law type.

In this practice, you will create a shape fillet driven by a law. There are a variety of law types that can define the fillet radius. An advanced law type and implicit law type will be created in this practice to demonstrate the process. The completed model displays as shown in Figure 9–24.

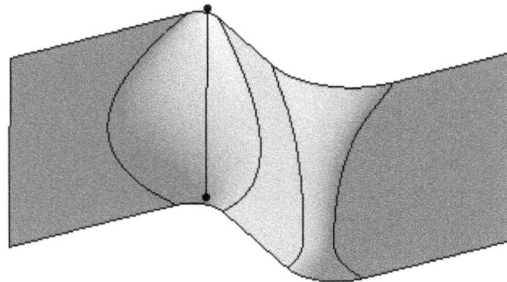

Figure 9–24

Task 1 - Open a part file.

1. Open **Shape Fillet_Laws_Start.CATPart**. The part displays as shown in Figure 9–25.

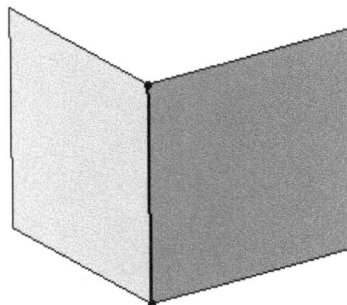

Figure 9–25

Task 2 - Create reference geometry.

1. Create an On Curve point using the following specifications:

   - *Curve:* **Line.1**
   - *Ratio:* **0.25**

2. Ensure that the name of the point is **Point.1**. The completed point displays as shown in Figure 9–26.

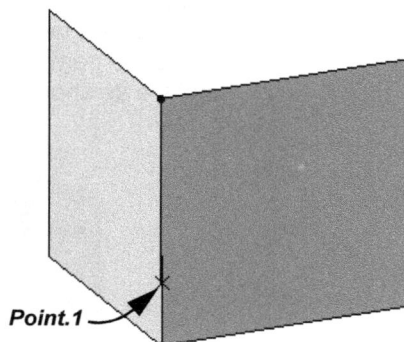

Figure 9–26

3. Create another On Curve point using **Line.1**. Use the ratio: 0.75. The completed points display as shown in Figure 9–27.

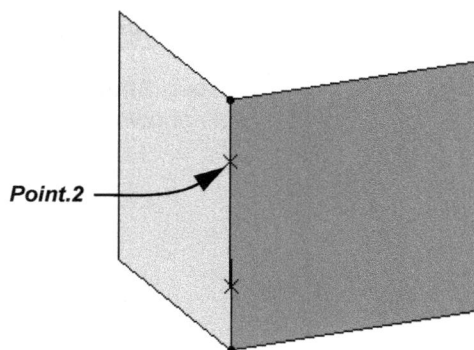

Figure 9–27

Task 3 - Create a law driven Shape Fillet.

1. Click (Shape Fillet).

2. Select **Extrude.1** as the *Support 1* reference.

3. Select **Extrude.2** as the *Support 2* reference.

4. Ensure that both arrows point in the directions shown in Figure 9–28.

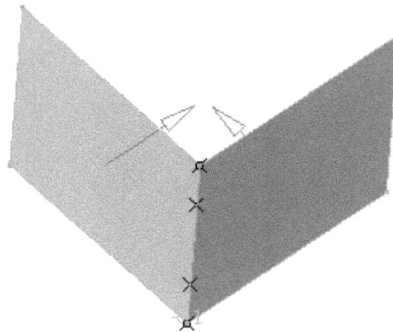

Figure 9–28

5. Click **More**.

6. Click in the *Spine* reference field, as shown in Figure 9–29.

*Ensure that **Trim support 1** and **Trim support 2** are selected.*

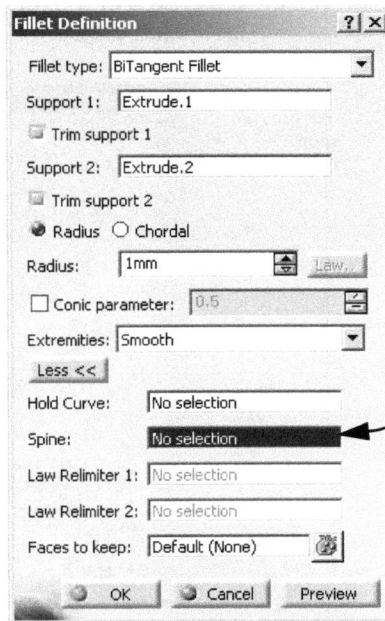

Figure 9–29

7. Select **Line.1** as the spine reference. The model updates to display the locations of Law Relimiter 1 and Law Relimiter 2 as shown in Figure 9–30. Law Relimiter 1 designates the start of the fillet, while Law Relimiter 2 shows the end. This is what the law will be based on.

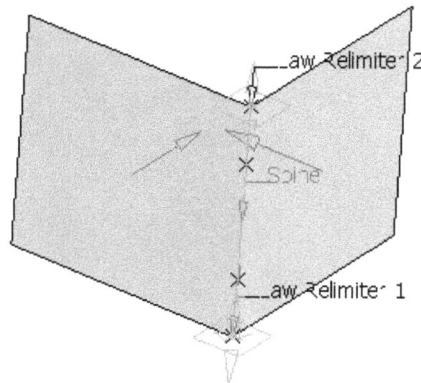

Figure 9–30

8. Click **Law** in the Fillet Definition dialog box. The Law Definition dialog box opens as shown in Figure 9–31.

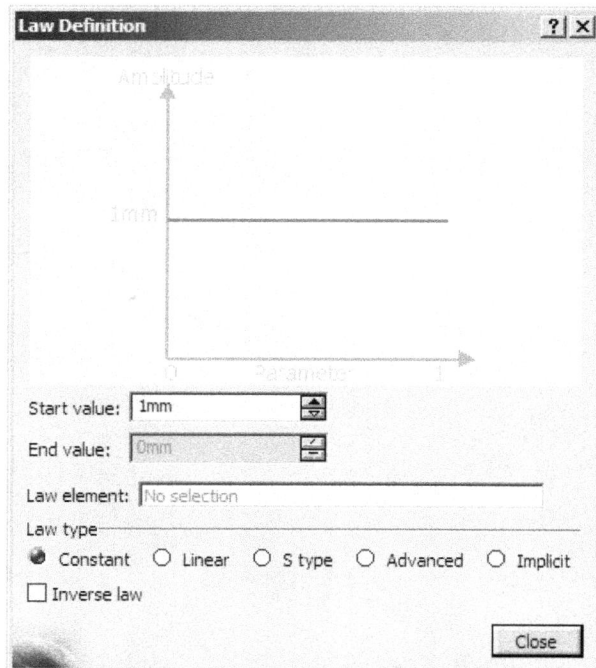

Figure 9–31

9. **Constant** is the default Law type. Change the type to **Implicit.** The dialog box updates as shown in Figure 9–32. Note that two points have been automatically added. These points represent the end points. CATIA created these points for you.

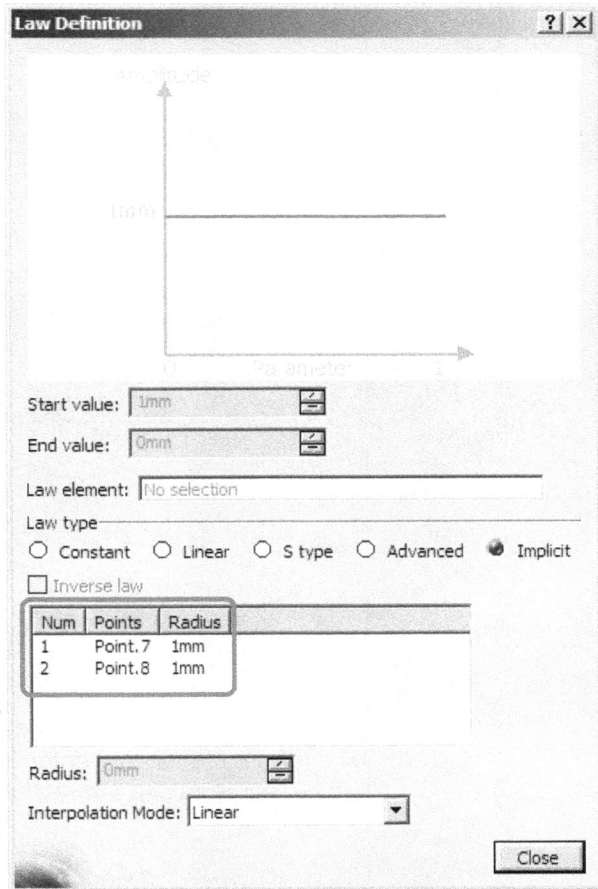

Figure 9–32

10. Select **Point.1**. This adds the point to the list. CATIA automatically adds **Point.1** as the **Number 2** point. This is because CATIA knows that the position of **Point.1** is between the other two points.

11. Select **Point.2**. CATIA again bases the order of points in the list on the points location on the selected spine curve. The Law Definition dialog box opens as shown in Figure 9–33.

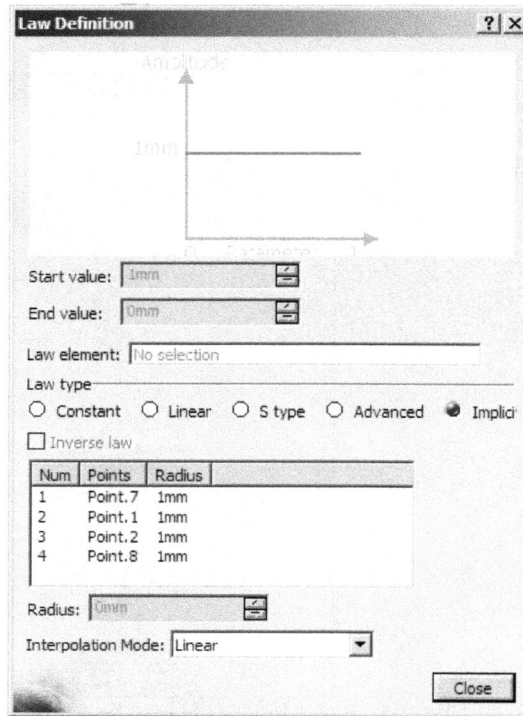

Figure 9–33

12. To change the radius value for each point, select the point from the list and enter a value in the radius field. Enter the radius values for each point as follows:

- *Num 1:* **5mm**
- *Num 2:* **2mm**
- *Num 3:* **4mm**
- *Num 4:* **8mm**

13. The Law Definition dialog box opens as shown in Figure 9–34. The Law graph has been generated.

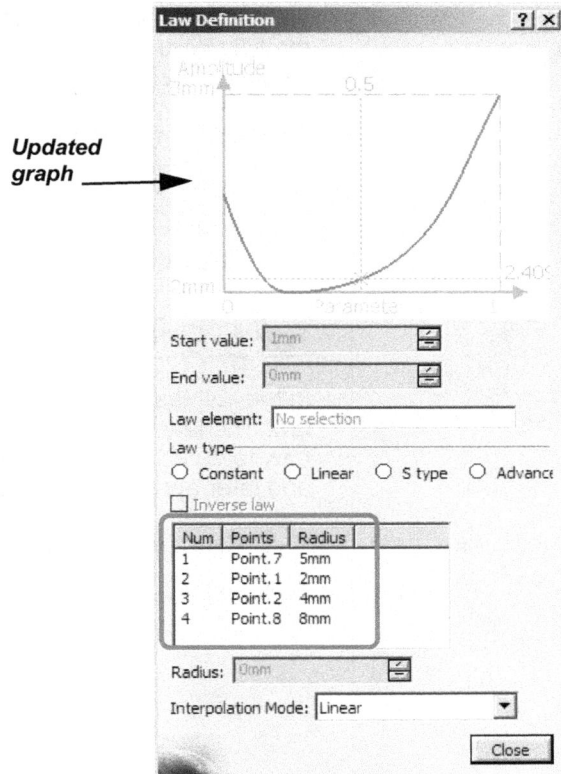

Updated graph

Figure 9–34

14. Close the Law Definition dialog box, and complete the Fillet. The model displays as shown in Figure 9–35.

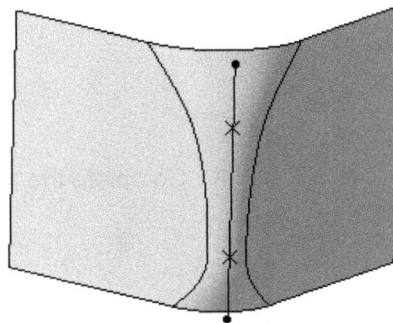

Figure 9–35

Design Considerations

All parameters driven by a law need a curve as a reference to determine what the X-parameter 0 (the start) and X-parameter 1 (the end) should be. In the case of the Shape Fillet, Line.1 was selected as the spine. The spine determines the start and end of the fillet. You can tell visually what the start of the law is by locating Law Relimiter 1.

15. Hide the following elements:

- **Line.1**
- **Point.1**
- **Point.2**

Task 4 - Create a Law feature.

In the last task, you created a fillet whose radius was driven by a law. The law used the Implicit type. In this task, you will create a Law feature. The information is stored in the specification tree, and later applied to drive a parameter of a feature.

1. Create a sketch on the xy plane.

2. Sketch and dimension the spline, as shown in Figure 9–36.

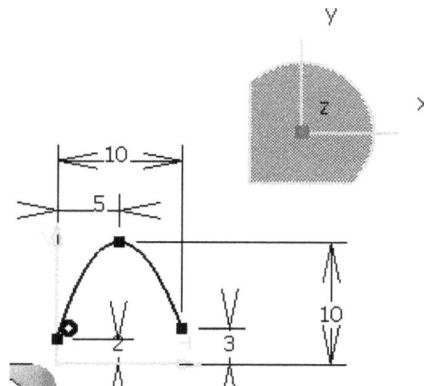

Figure 9–36

3. Complete the sketch.

4. Click (Law). The Law Definition dialog box opens as shown in Figure 9–37.

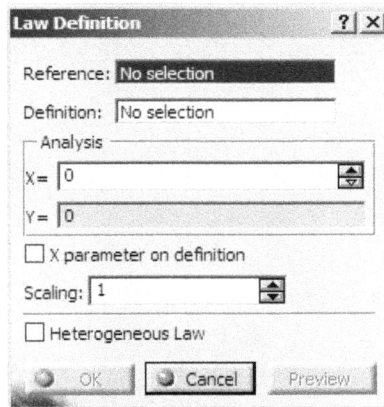

Figure 9–37

5. Select the **X-axis** as the Reference.

6. Select **Sketch.1** as the Definition. The model displays as shown in Figure 9–38.

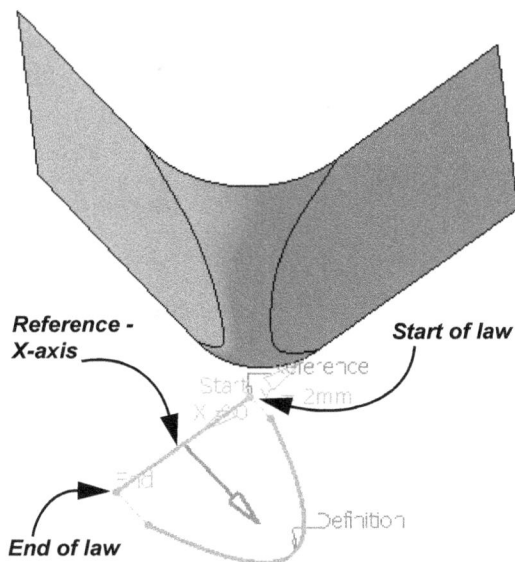

Reference - X-axis

Start of law

End of law

Figure 9–38

7. Complete the Law feature.

8. Hide **Sketch.1** as it is no longer required.

9. Show **Extrude.3** and **Extract.1**. The model displays as shown in Figure 9–39.

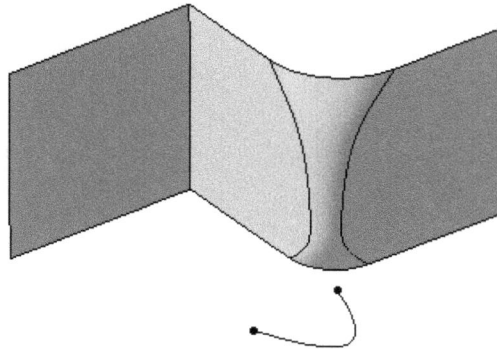

Figure 9–39

Task 5 - Create another shape fillet.

In this task, a shape fillet's radius will be driven by a law. The Law feature created from the sketch will define the radius value.

1. Create a shape fillet with the following specifications:

   * *Support 1:* **Extrude.3**
   * Select **Trim support 1**.
   * *Support 2:* **Fillet.1**
   * Select **Trim support 2**.
   * *Spine:* **Extract.1**

2. Click **Law** in the Fillet Definition dialog box.

3. Select **Advanced** as the Law type.

4. Select **Law.1** in the specification tree. The Law Definition dialog box updates to display as shown in Figure 9–40.

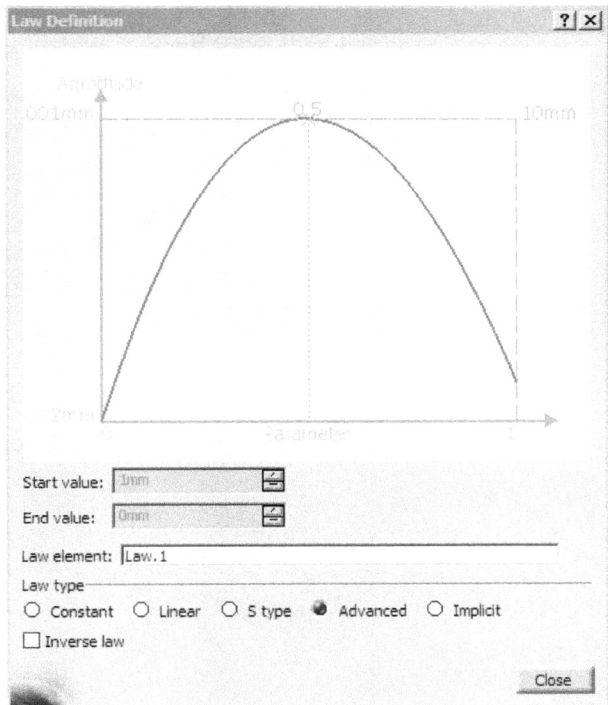

Figure 9–40

5. Close the Law Definition dialog box.

6. Preview the fillet. Ensure that the arrows point in the direction shown in Figure 9–41.

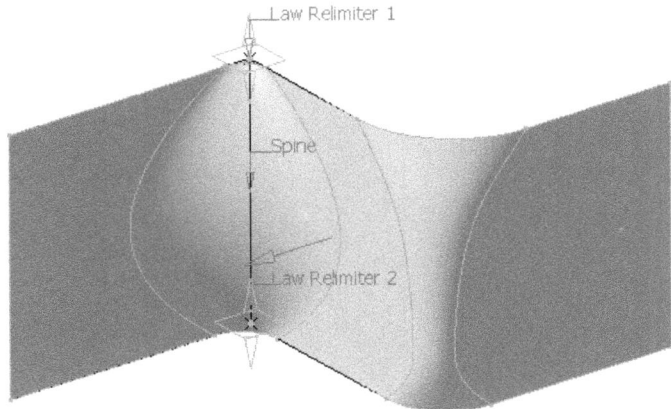

Figure 9–41

7. Complete the fillet. The model displays as shown in Figure 9–42.

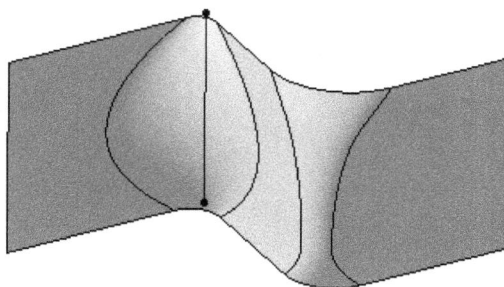

Figure 9–42

8. Save the model and close the file.

Practice 9b

Using Laws

Practice Objectives

* Define a Linear law.
* Define an S-type law.

In this practice, you will test a variety of types of laws on a simple swept surface. This practice will help you understand how you can use laws to control your design.

Task 1 - Open a part file.

1. Open **Law.CATPart**. The part displays as shown in Figure 9–43. It consists of two extruded surfaces connected with a line.

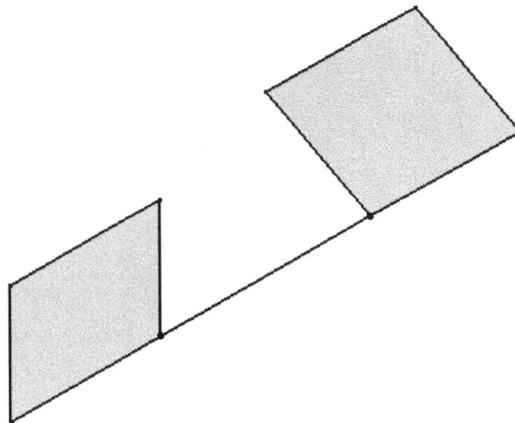

Figure 9–43

Task 2 - Create a swept surface to connect the existing surface geometry.

1. Click (Sweep) and select the **Line** profile type and **With reference surface** sub-type.

2. Select **ConnectCurve** as *Guide Curve 1* and zx **plane** as the Reference surface.

3. Enter an *Angle* of **0** and *Length 2* of **40mm**.

4. Click **Preview**. The model displays as shown in Figure 9–44.

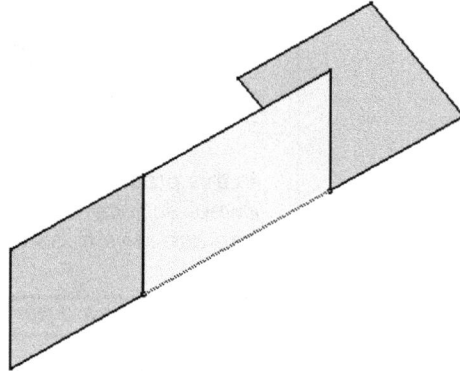

Figure 9–44

Task 3 - Control the swept surface angle with a law.

1. Click **Law** next to the *Angle* field. The Law Definition dialog box opens as shown in Figure 9–45.

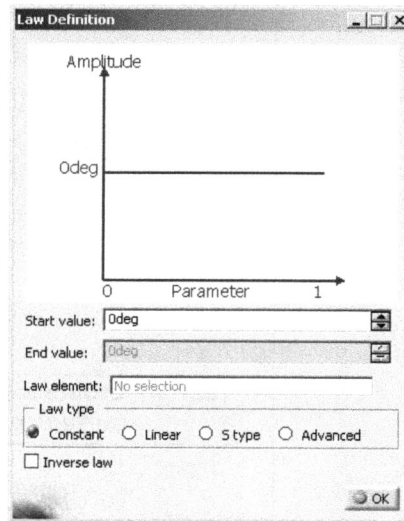

Figure 9–45

2. Select **Linear**.

3. Enter a *Start* value of **0** and an *End* value of **-45**. The angle is negative to follow the angle of the second extruded surface.

4. Click **Close** to complete the law definition and click **OK** to complete the swept surface. The model displays as shown in Figure 9–46.

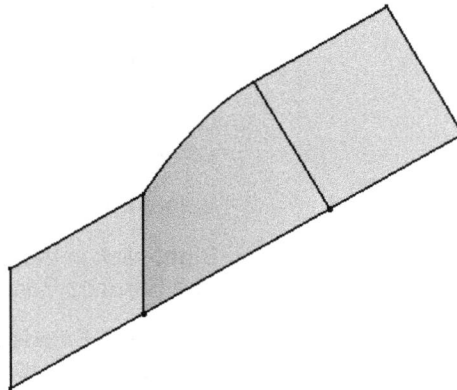

Figure 9–46

Task 4 - Edit the swept surface to use an S-type law.

1. Double-click on the swept surface and click **Law** next to the *Angle* field.

2. Select **S-type**.

3. Click **Close** and **OK**. The model updates as shown in Figure 9–47.

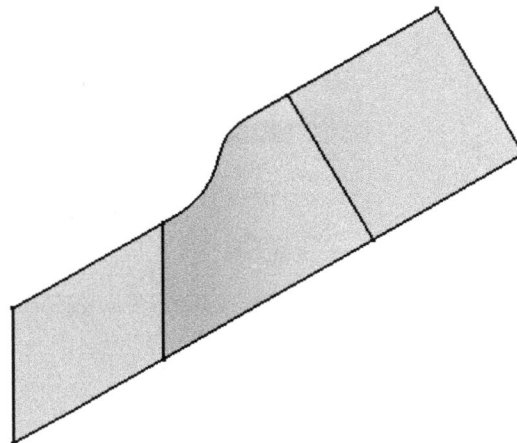

Figure 9–47

Task 5 - Use formulas to drive the design intent of the model.

Modify the angle of the second extruded surface to see how the model geometry updates. To do this you must relate the angle of the law to that of the extruded profile.

1. Double-click on the swept surface, and click **Law** next to the *Length 2* field.

2. Select **Linear**.

3. Right-click in the *Start value* field and select **Edit formula**. The Formula Editor dialog box opens.

4. Select the **Extrude1Profile** sketch in the specification tree and select the 40mm length dimension from the display (the one that does not have the Formula icon on it).

5. Repeat Steps 3. and 4. to relate the end length of the swept surface to the length of **Extrude2Profile**, as shown in Figure 9–48.

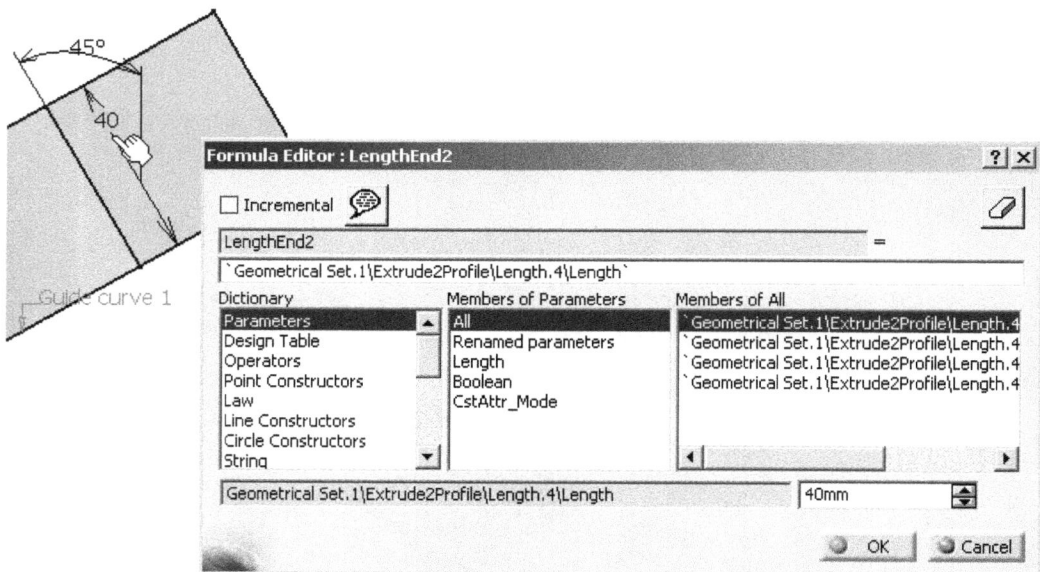

Figure 9–48

6. Click **Law** next to the *Angle* field, right-click in the *End value* field, and select **Edit formula**. The Formula Editor dialog box opens.

7. Enter a - sign to use the negative value of the selected parameter.

8. Select **Extrude2Profile** in the specification tree and select the 45 degree angle dimension.

9. Complete the feature. The model displays unchanged.

10. Modify **Extrude2Profile** by changing the length to **60** and the angle to **60**. The model updates as shown in Figure 9–49.

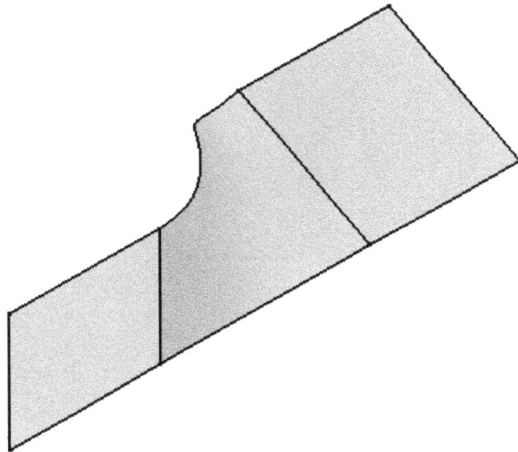

Figure 9–49

11. Save the model and close the file.

Practice 9c | Advanced Laws

Practice Objectives

- Create a Law feature.
- Use an Advanced Law to define a swept surface.

In this practice, you will design a rotational cam to be used in a cam-follower assembly. The path through which the follower must travel is shown in Figure 9–50. You will use this information to develop the shape of the cam part by using a Law feature to drive the shape of the cam's swept surface.

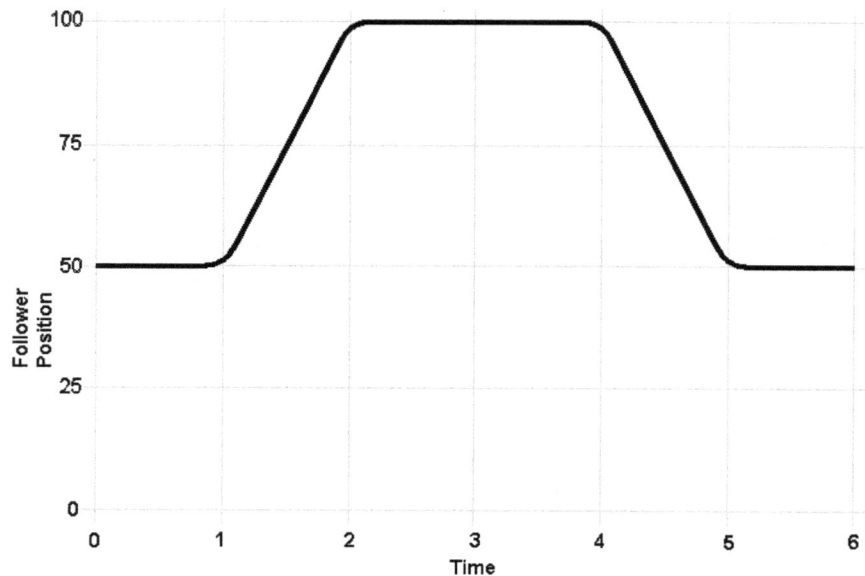

Figure 9–50

The completed cam model displays as shown in Figure 9–51.

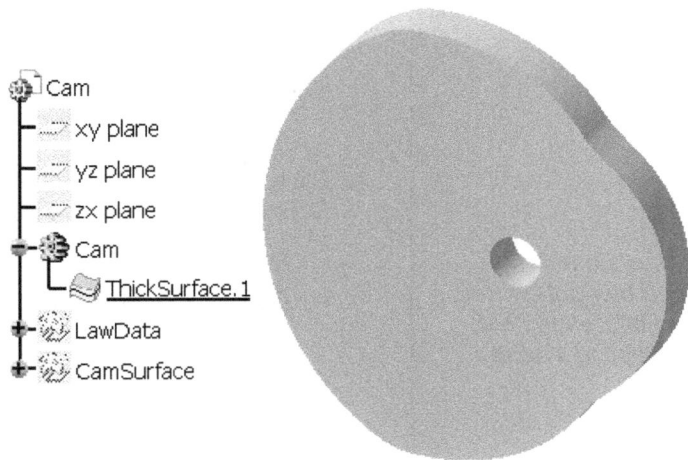

Figure 9–51

Task 1 - Open a part file.

1. Open **Cam.CATPart**. The part displays as shown in Figure 9–52.

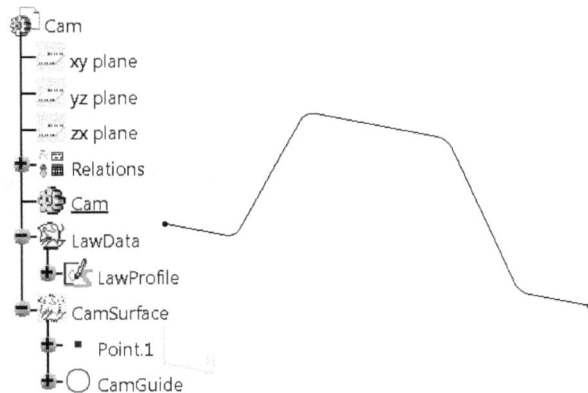

Figure 9–52

The model consists of the following two geometrical sets:

- The **LawData** geometrical set contains a sketched section, LawProfile, which defines the vertical position of the follower. This section is used to define a Law feature.

- The **CamSurface** geometrical set defines a swept surface whose external boundary is controlled by the Law feature. The surface is then used to define the solid cam geometry.

Task 2 - Create a Law feature.

1. Ensure that LawData is the active geometrical set.

2. Click [icon] (Law). Enter the following information in the Law Definition dialog box, as shown in Figure 9–53:

   • *Reference:* **Y-axis** (context menu)
   • *Definition:* **LawProfile**

*The Y-axis can be entered by right-clicking in the Reference field and selecting **Y-axis**.*

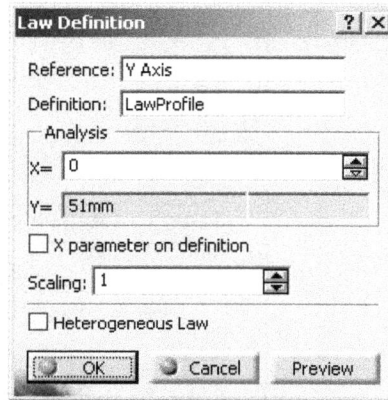

Figure 9–53

3. Select the arrows in the bottom left corner of the section and drag them across the reference axis. The system reports the value of the law at the specific location on the reference axis as shown in Figure 9–54.

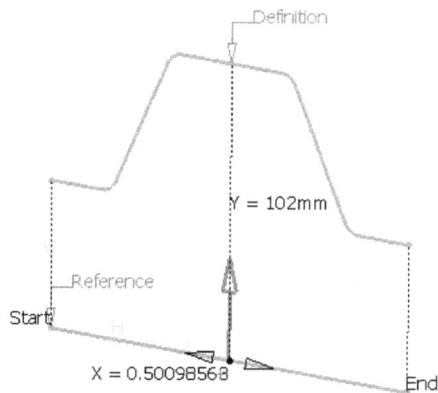

Figure 9–54

Using this technique, you can determine that the follower will start at an initial height of 51 millimeters. Once the cam starts rotating, the follower will move up to 102 millimeters and then return to its initial position.

4. Click **OK** to complete the Law feature.

5. Rename the Law feature as **CamLaw**.

Task 3 - Generate a planar surface for the cam.

In this task, you will define a planar surface using a Line Sweep feature. A circle curve is used to define the guide for the Line Sweep.

1. Hide the **LawData** geometrical set.

2. Define the **CamSurface** geometrical set as the active work object.

3. Click [icon] (Sweep) and specify the following:

   - *Profile type:* [icon] (Line)
   - *Sub-type:* **With reference surface**
   - *Guide curve 1:* **CamGuide**
   - *Reference surface:* **yz plane**
   - *Length 1:* **25**

4. Click **Preview**. The swept surface displays as shown in Figure 9–55.

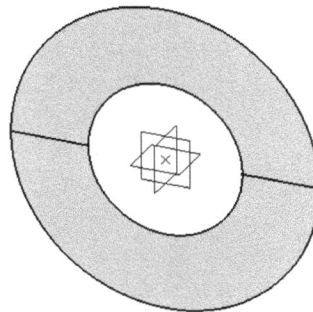

Figure 9–55

Task 4 - Apply the law to the swept surface.

In this task, the Law feature will be used to control *Length 1*.

1. Click **Law** next to *Length 1* and specify the following:

    *   *Law type:* **Advanced**
    *   *Law element:* **CamLaw** (Select in the specification tree.)

    The Law Definition dialog box opens as shown in Figure 9–56.

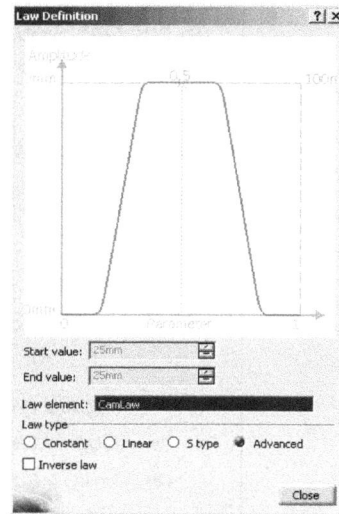

Figure 9–56

Design Considerations

The parameter value in the Law Definition dialog box varies between 0 and 1. These values actually indicate the beginning and end of the swept surface. In this application of the law, 0 denotes 0 degrees and 1 denotes a 360 degree rotation about the circular guide curve.

2. Click **Close**. The value of *Length 1* is grayed out in the Swept Surface Definition dialog box. This indicates that the *Length 1* value is controlled by a law.

3. Click **Preview**. The model displays as shown in Figure 9–57.

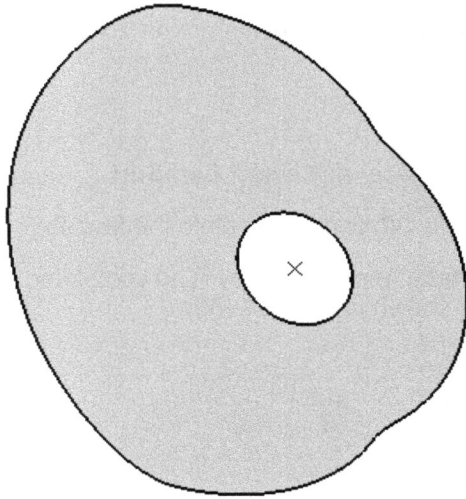

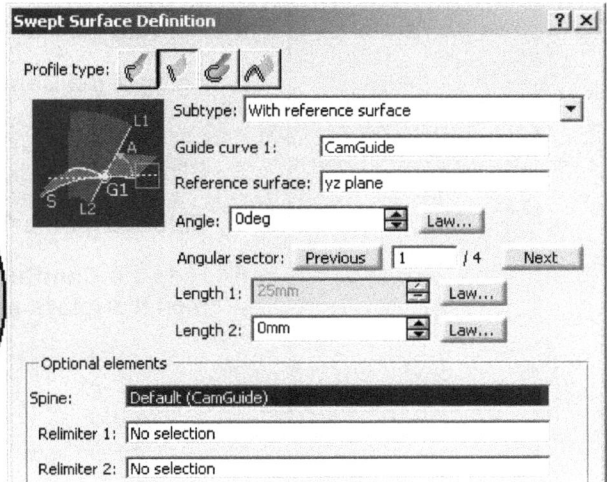

Figure 9–57

4. The cam will be inserted onto a 25 millimeter diameter shaft. Enter **13** for *Length 2* to reduce the hole in the surface to 25 millimeters.

5. Click **OK** to complete the feature and rename *Sweep.1* as **CamSurf**. The model displays as shown in Figure 9–58.

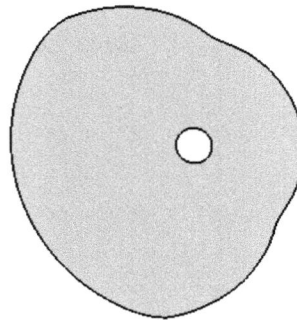

Figure 9–58

Task 5 - Create the solid cam geometry.

1. Activate the Part Design workbench.

2. Activate the **Cam** PartBody.

3. Click [icon] (Thick Surface) and select **CamSurf**.

4. Enter **25** for the *First Offset* and complete the feature.

5. Hide the **CamSurface** geometrical set. The completed cam model displays as shown in Figure 9–59.

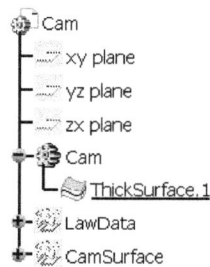

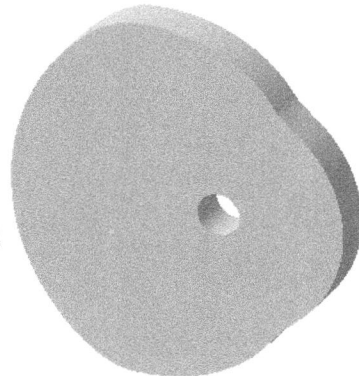

Figure 9–59

6. Save the model and close the file.

Practice 9d

Drill Auger

Practice Objective

- Create swept surface using laws without any instructional information.

Create the swept surface for an auger, as shown in Figure 9–60. To do so, use the Law function described in the chapter material.

Specifications:

   Overall height=100mm

   Width 1: 20mm

   Width 2: 1mm

   Total angle: 1080deg

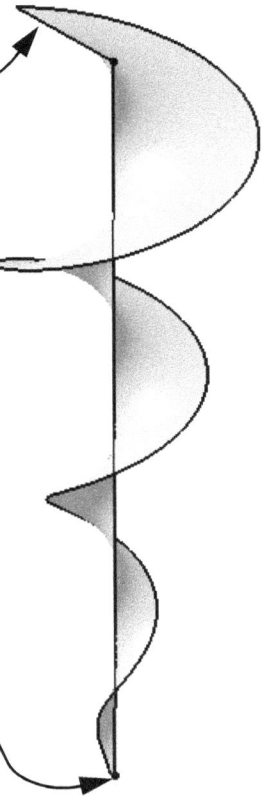

Figure 9–60

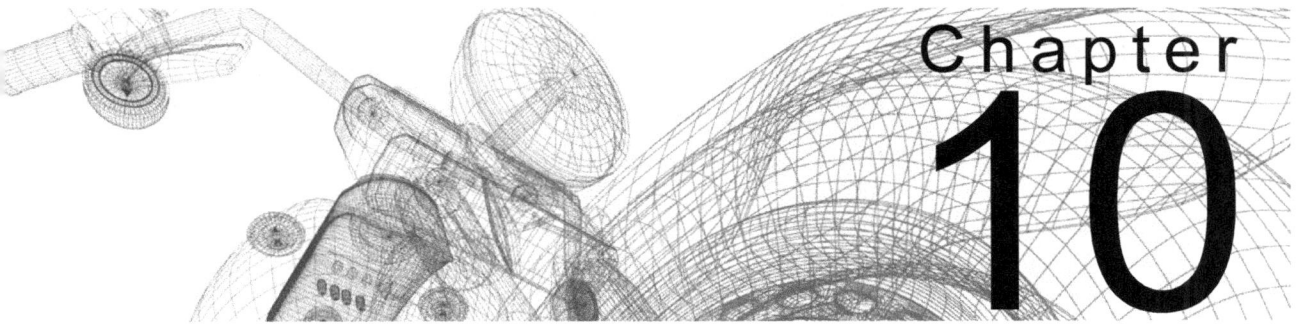

Duplication Tools

The GSD workbench provides access to duplication tools. These tools (common to the Part Design workbench) enable you to increase productivity by reusing data throughout the design. As a result, models maintain consistency during the design process.

Learning Objectives in this Chapter

- Review the Duplication Tools in the GSD workbench.
- Learn how to use the Repetition tools.
- Learn how to pattern surface features.
- Duplicate a Geometrical Set.

10.1 Duplication Tools

A number of tools can be used in the GSD workbench to increase performance during the creation of surface geometry.

The Replication toolbar options in the GSD workbench are shown in Figure 10–1. The following functions are discussed in this chapter:

- Repetition

- Patterns

- Duplicate Geometrical Sets

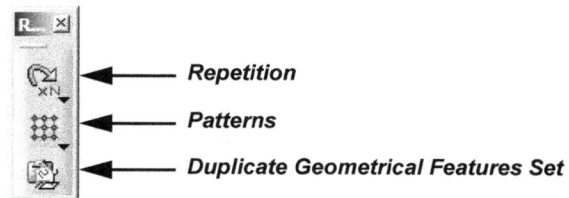

Figure 10–1

10.2 Repetition

The Repetition toolbar is accessed by clicking (Object Repetition) in the Replication toolbar. The toolbar options are used to duplicate wireframe elements in the model. The toolbar displays as shown in Figure 10–2.

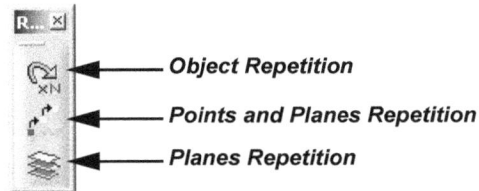

- Object Repetition
- Points and Planes Repetition
- Planes Repetition

Figure 10–2

Object Repetition

The **Object Repetition** tool repeats a curve or object in the model. The entity should be created to include a reference (to duplicate along) and an offset dimension (to determine the spacing between the repeated objects). For example, a point created On Curve at 20mm from the end of the curve can be repeated to positions at 40mm and 60mm, as shown in Figure 10–3.

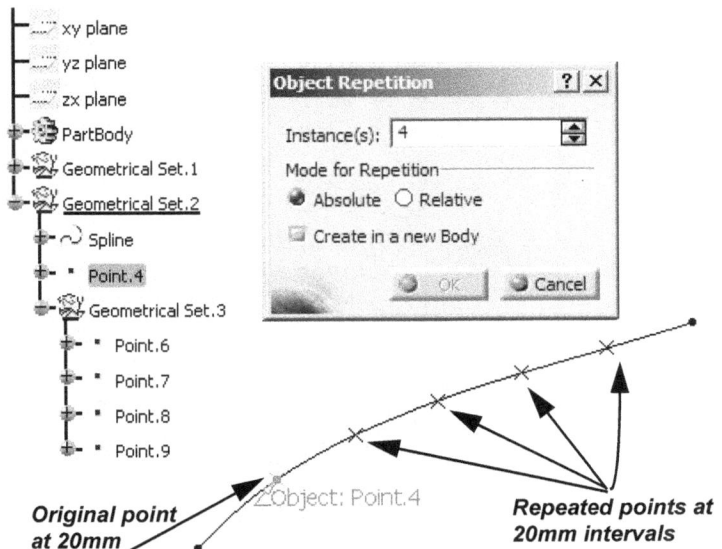

*The **Create in a new Body** option adds the repeated entities to a new geometrical set below the active geometrical set.*

Original point at 20mm

Repeated points at 20mm intervals

Figure 10–3

To repeat an object, select the entity and click [image: Object Repetition icon] (Object Repetition). Enter the number of instances to be repeated and click **OK**.

Points Repetition

The **Points Repetition** tool enables you to create a series of points along a curve, edge, or line. You can also add planes or axis systems at each point created. Planes are created normal to the curve. The Points Repetition dialog box is shown in Figure 10–4.

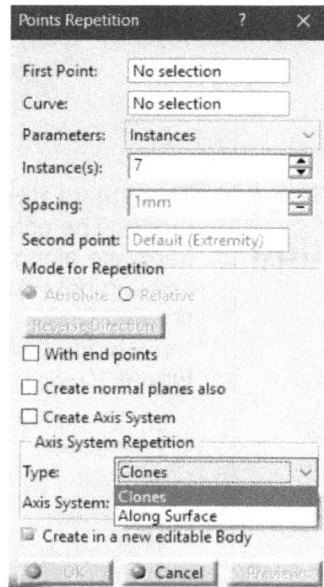

Figure 10–4

Axis Systems can be created at each point using two types. The **Clones** type copies a reference axis that you select at each point. The **Along Surface** type creates an axis system with the Y axis direction normal to the surface that you select at each point. At each point, this command creates a line tangent to the curve used to set the X direction of the axis. Then, a line is created normal to the surface that is used to set the Y direction of the axis and then repeated at each point. By default, all the instances are be created in a new editable Body. This body or set can be modified by double clicking on it in the specification tree.

In the example shown in Figure 10–5, six Axis Systems, with the Y axis normal to **Sweep.1**, are created at each point. The Axis System Repetition can then be used with the **User Pattern** command.

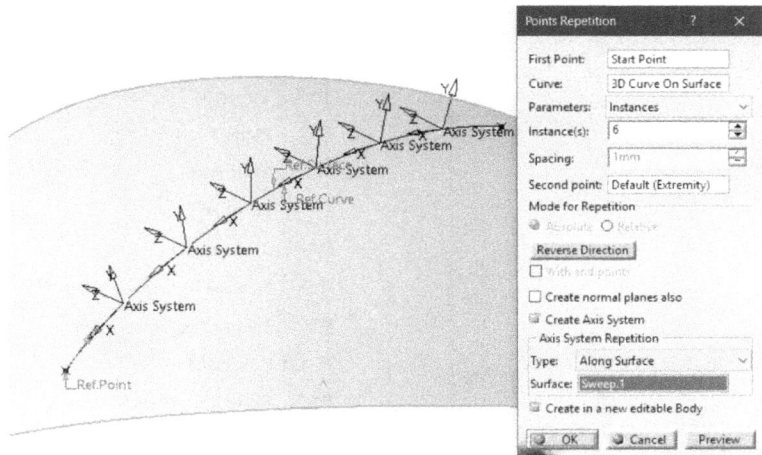

Figure 10–5

A User Pattern can use a Sketch, 3D Points, Axis Systems, and Axis System Repetition for Positions of all object to be Patterned. Additonally, the Anchor can be an Point or Axis System, as shown in Figure 10–6.

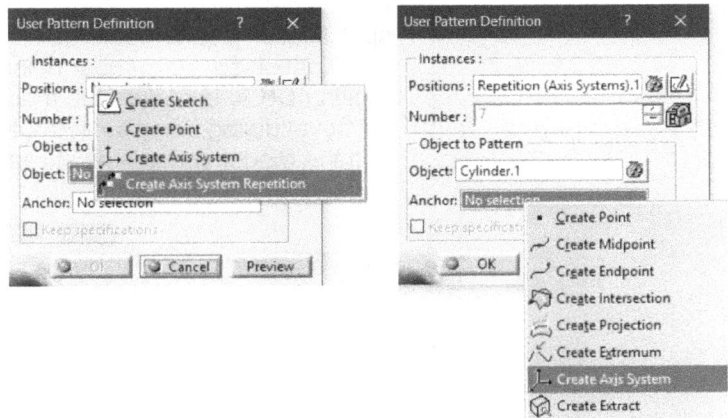

Figure 10–6

Figure 10–7 shows an example of a User Pattern used to duplicate the **Cylinder.1** surface to each position in the Repetition Axis system using an Anchor Axis to keep the **Cylinder.1** surface normal to the **Sweep.1** surface at each instance.

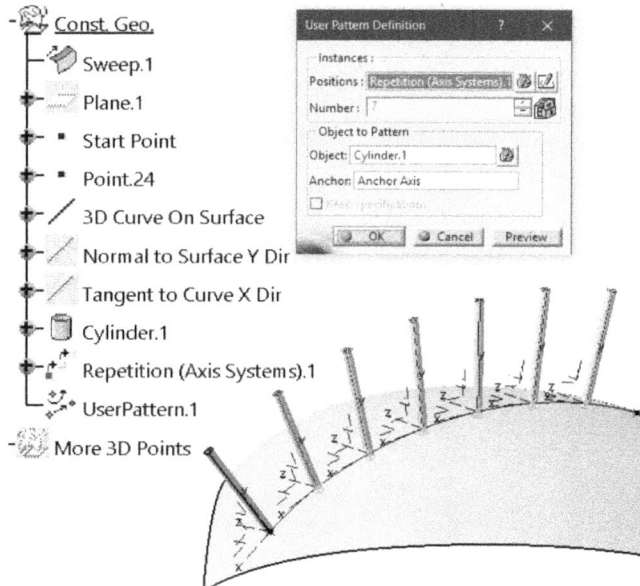

Figure 10–7

Double clicking on the Repetition (Axis Systems).1 in the specification tree to open the Points Repetition menu for modification so the number of instances are reduced. After clicking **OK** to complete the modification, a Repetition Feature Removal dialog box displays. Click **Yes** to update User Pattern and the model updates as shown in Figure 10–8.

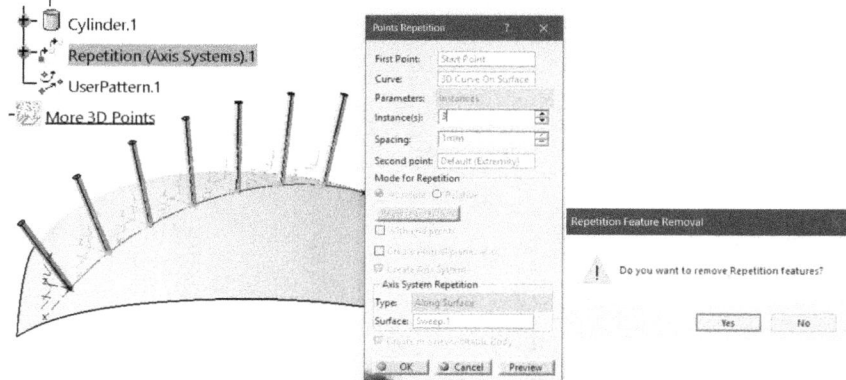

Figure 10–8

Modification of both Repetition (Axis Systems).1 and UserPattern.1 is complete as shown in Figure 10–9.

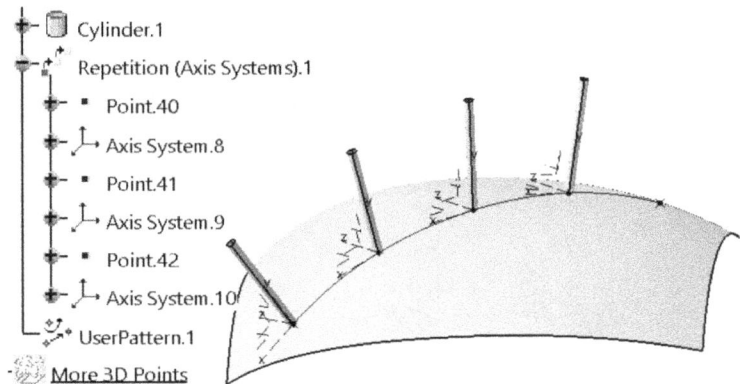

Figure 10–9

A User Pattern can be created using 3D points. By placing all the points under a Geometrical Set, select the *Positions* field in the User Pattern dialog box. Then, select the **More 3D Points** Geometrical Set from the specification tree. With one click, all 9 points are added to the *Positions* field, as shown in Figure 10–10. This shows the benefits of organizing or grouping points under Geometrical Sets to be used with a User Patterns.

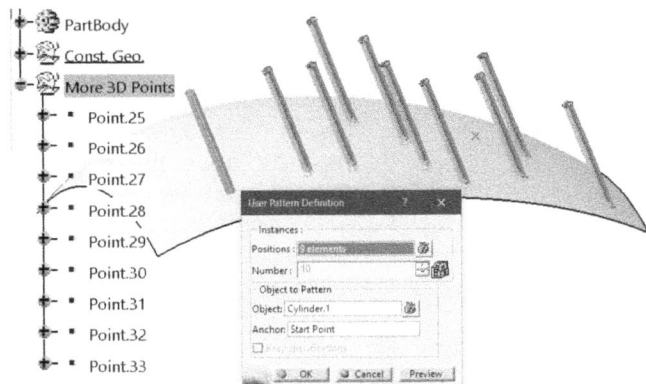

Figure 10–10

Planes Repetition

The **Planes Repetition** tool is used to create a series of equally spaced planes. The planes are located in the model between two selected reference planes as shown in Figure 10–11. Model and surface faces cannot be selected as a reference plane.

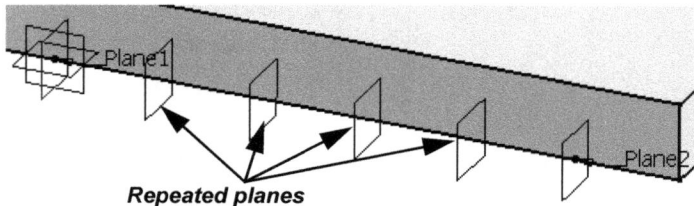

Figure 10–11

To repeat planes, click (Planes Repetition). The Planes Repetition dialog box opens as shown in Figure 10–12.

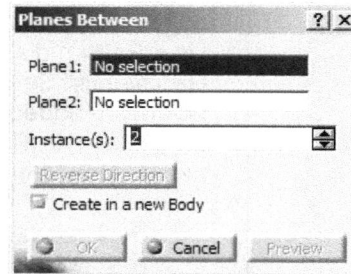

Figure 10–12

Select the two reference planes between which planes are repeated and enter the number of instances. You can also select **Create in a new Body** to create the planes in a new geometrical set beneath the geometrical set. Click **OK** to complete the operation.

10.3 Patterning Surface Features

Patterns are used to quickly duplicate geometry. Once the initial surface feature(s) is created, several instances of the same geometry can be patterned using a specified dimensional increment. The pattern can be created as a rectangular or circular pattern. If a dimension change occurs in the original feature, the instances update to reflect the change.

Surface patterns are created in the GSD workbench using the same process as the Part Design workbench.

When a surface feature is patterned, the resulting group of surface data can be selected as a single entity. The patterned surfaces do not need to be joined. This makes future operations, such as creating a split in a solid part or trimming the patterned surfaces, quick and easy.

It should be noted that the surface feature that was originally patterned is not included in this group of surface geometry. In the example in Figure 10–13, two split operations must be performed to cut all of the spokes from the base cylindrical pad.

Split 1: Original surfaces   *Split 2: Patterned surfaces*

Figure 10–13

10.4 Duplicate a Geometrical Set

Up to now, the tools used to duplicate wireframe and surface geometry have created associative copies. When the original geometry is modified, the duplicated geometry updates associatively.

The **Duplicate** option enables you to make a copy of a Geometrical Set and reposition the geometry in a new location of the model. The duplicate geometrical set can be manipulated independent of the original geometry. In the graphic on the left side of Figure 10–14, the surface geometry of a turbine blade contained within a geometrical set is copied to a new location. In the graphic on the right side, the copied geometry is modified to a new angular position, independent of the original blade.

Original Geometrical Set

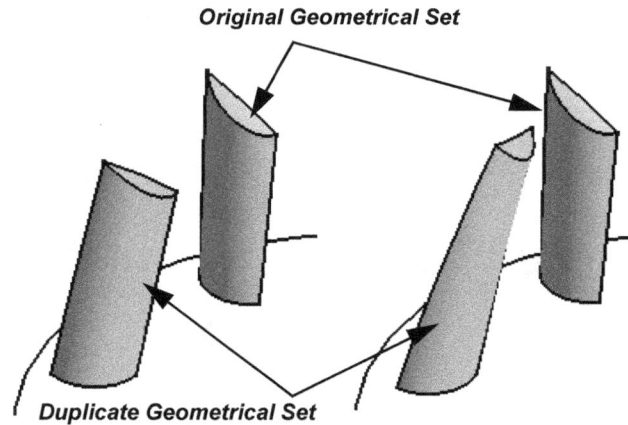

Duplicate Geometrical Set

Figure 10–14

Geometrical Sets gather wireframe and surface geometry into an organized location. When using the **Duplicate Geometrical Set** tool, it is important to ensure that the geometrical set contains all of the construction geometry for a specific item of solid geometry.

General Steps

Use the following general steps to make a copy of a Geometrical Set in your surface model:

1. Start the creation of the copy.
2. Select new references.
3. Complete the operation.

Step 1 - Start the creation of the copy.

Click ⬚ (Duplicate Geometrical Set) in the Replication toolbar and select the Geometrical Set to be copied. The Geometrical Set can be selected directly on the model or in the specification tree. The dialog box opens as shown in Figure 10–15.

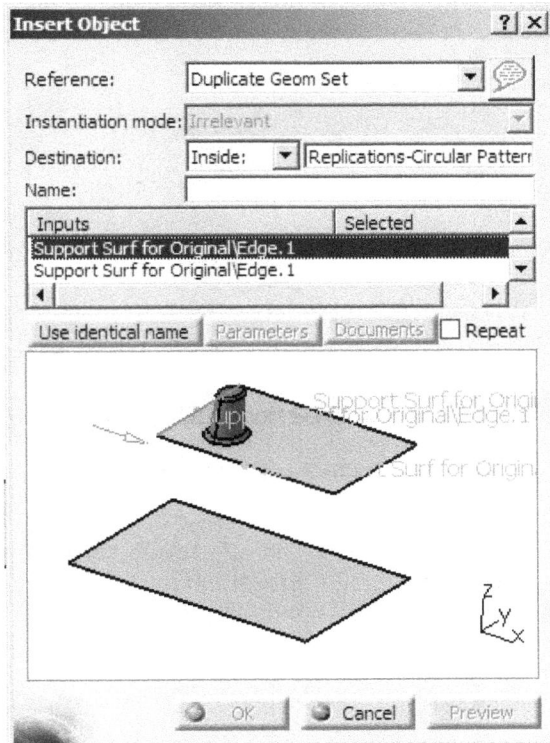

Figure 10–15

Enter a name for the geometrical set in the *Name* field in the Insert Object dialog box.

Step 2 - Select new references.

The duplicate geometrical set can be repositioned in the model by selecting new references. The Insert Object dialog box lists all references that were previously established when the original Geometrical Set geometry was created. To specify a new reference, select the old reference in the *Inputs* column and select a new reference on the model, as shown in Figure 10–16.

Old reference edge used to locate geometry

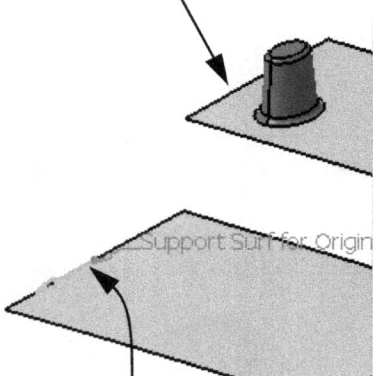

New reference edge

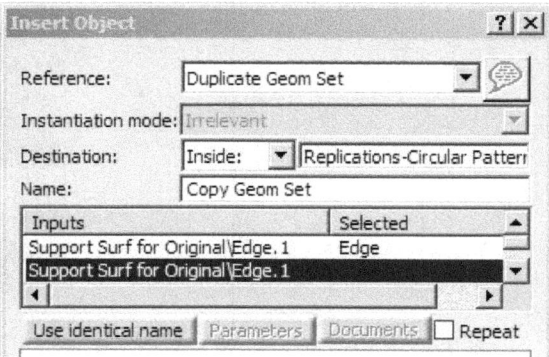

Figure 10–16

Try to use descriptive names for your references so they can be easily interpreted when performing this operation.

Old references can automatically be assigned by clicking **Use identical name**. To complete the duplication, all references must be defined.

Step 3 - Complete the operation.

Click **OK** to complete the operation. The new geometrical set is added to the model, as shown in Figure 10–17.

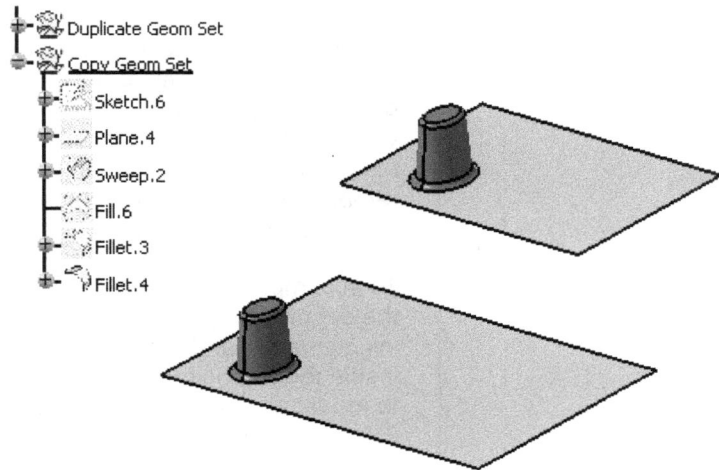

Figure 10–17

The new geometrical set contains the same set of features as the original geometrical set. Each of these features can be modified independent of the original geometry.

Practice 10a | Surface Patterns

Practice Objective

• Pattern surface geometry.

In this practice, you will model the spokes of a wheel rim. The model you begin with is designed with solid features. Instead of creating new geometry to create the spokes, you will use existing profile sketches and surface features to remove material from the solid. These cuts will be patterned in a circle and the remaining solid will represent the spokes. This method best captures the design intent.

To accomplish this task, you will use swept surfaces based on the cut profiles provided. These surfaces extend into the solid inside the rim and are used to remove any solid material that falls inside them. The cutting surfaces are copied in a circular pattern to model all cuts. The final model displays as shown in Figure 10–18.

Figure 10–18

Task 1 - Open a part file.

1. Open **WheelRim.CATPart**. The wheel displays as shown in Figure 10–19 and contains a **LargeCutOut** geometrical set. This geometrical set contains geometry used to define the geometry for material removal. The material removal defines the location and geometry of the spokes.

2. Set the **LargeCutOut** geometrical set as the Work Object.

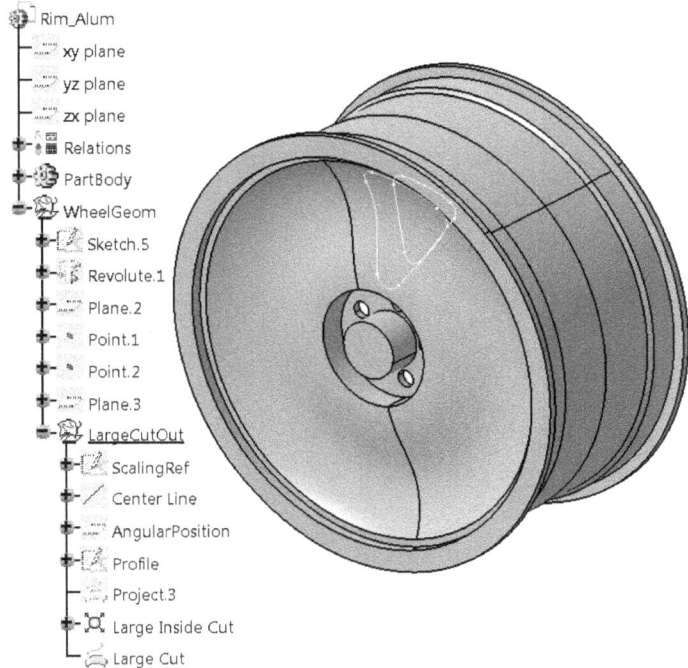

Figure 10–19

Task 2 - Create a swept surface.

In this task, you will create a Swept Surface feature with the Circle sub-type. This requires the selection of two guide curves to control the path, and a radius parameter to control the curvature of the implicit profile. This feature captures the design intent by following the projected curves as guides.

1. Click ![icon] (Sweep) and specify the following:

- *Profile type:* ![icon] (Circle)
- *Sub-type:* **Two guides and radius**
- *Guide curve 1:* **Large Inside Cut**
- *Guide curve 2:* **Large Cut**
- *Radius:* **50**

2. Click **Preview** and enter the following:

- *Solution:* **2**
- Close warning message

The dialog box opens as shown in Figure 10–20.

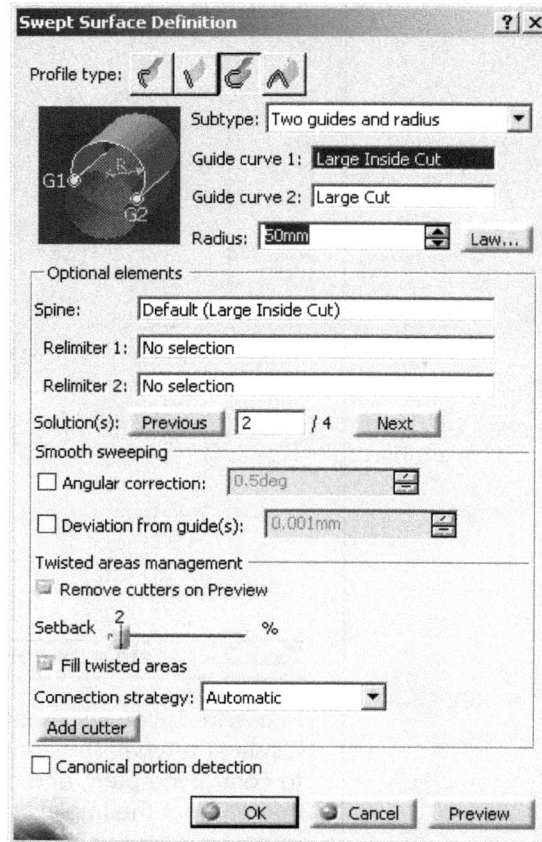

Figure 10–20

3. Click **OK**.

4. Hide **PartBody**. The Swept Surface feature displays as shown in Figure 10–21.

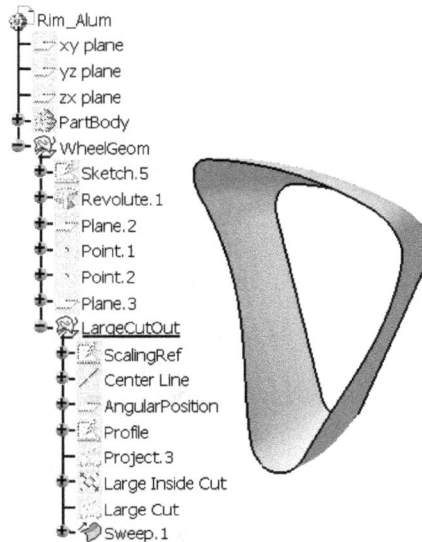

Figure 10–21

Task 3 - Pattern each swept surface in a full circular pattern.

1. Select **Sweep.1**, click [icon] (Circular Pattern), and specify the following:

   - *Parameters:* **Complete Crown**
   - *Instance(s):* **6**
   - *Reference element:* **Center Line** (Select in specification tree.)

2. Click **OK**. The model displays as shown in Figure 10–22.

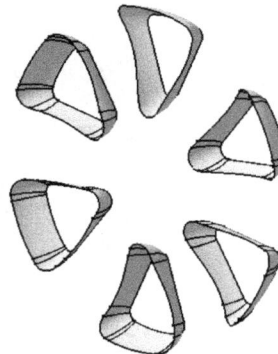

Figure 10–22

3. Zoom in on the Swept Surface feature, rotate the model, and view the geometry. This complex surface geometry is easily accomplished using the pattern process.

Design Considerations

A sketch was projected onto the surface of a solid rim and those projections were used as center curves for the Swept feature.

The Swept Surface feature effectively captures the design intent of the required cutout using the **Two guides and radius** sub-type.

Using the **Complete Crown** option to define the circular pattern maintains the intent by ensuring that the entered number of instances always remains equally spaced.

Task 4 - Remove solid material surface features.

In this task, you will use the surface features to cut away solid material.

1. Set PartBody to be the Work Object.

2. Activate the Part Design workbench.

(Split) is in the Surface-Based Features toolbar.

3. Click (Split).

4. Select **Sweep.1**. The arrows indicate the solid to keep. Ensure that they are pointing outwards, as shown in Figure 10–23.

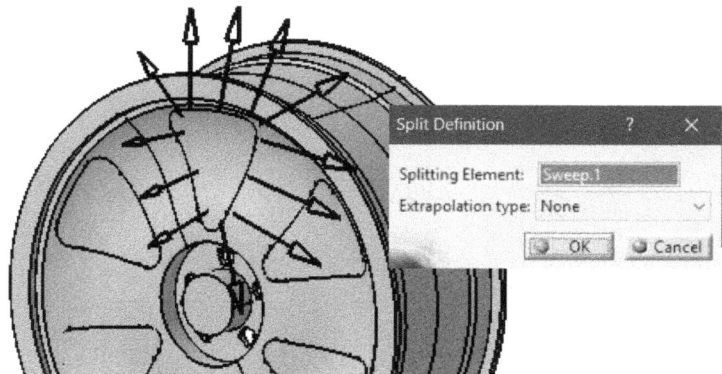

Figure 10–23

5. Click **OK**. The model displays as shown in Figure 10–24.

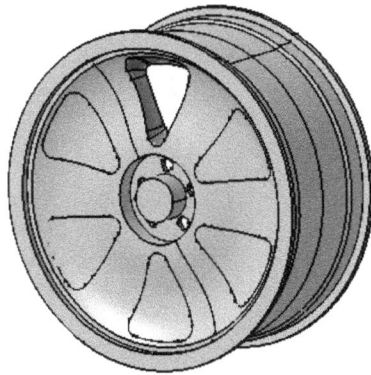

Figure 10–24

The Split feature is not patterned with the surfaces. To remove the solid inside the patterned surfaces, the pattern must be used to create a Split feature.

Task 5 - Remove solid using patterned cutting surfaces.

1. Click (Split).

2. Select **CircPattern.2**. Ensure that the arrows are pointing outward.

3. Click **OK**.

4. Hide the **LargeCutOut** geometrical set. The model displays as shown in Figure 10–25.

Figure 10–25

5. Save the model and close the file.

Practice 10b | Copying Geometrical Sets

Practice Objectives

- Copy a geometrical set.

In this practice, you will create a sketch and an Extrude Surface feature in a geometrical set. You will then copy the geometrical set. To place the copied geometrical set, you will use the same references used to create the original geometry.

Task 1 - Open a part file.

1. Open **CopyBody.CATPart**. The part displays as shown in Figure 10–26.

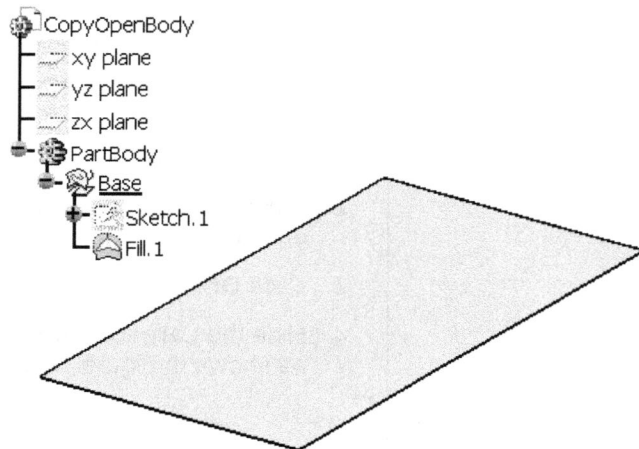

Figure 10–26

2. Ensure that the GSD workbench is active.

3. Insert a Geometrical set and specify the following:

- *Name:* **Object**
- *Father:* **Base**

The specification tree displays as shown in Figure 10–27.

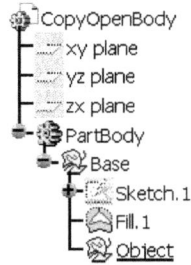

CopyOpenBody
- xy plane
- yz plane
- zx plane
- PartBody
  - Base
    - Sketch.1
    - Fill.1
    - Object

Figure 10–27

Task 2 - Create a sketch.

In this task, you will create a sketch that is used as a profile for an Extruded Surface feature. Keep a note of the references selected to fully define the sketch.

1. Select the **Fill.1** surface, as shown in Figure 10–28, and activate the Sketcher workbench.

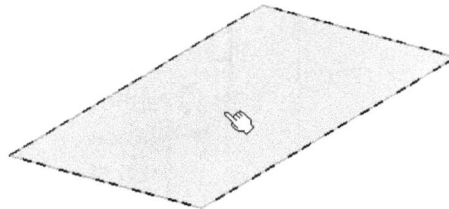

Figure 10–28

2. Sketch a circle in the upper right corner and dimension the diameter as **7**, as shown in Figure 10–29.

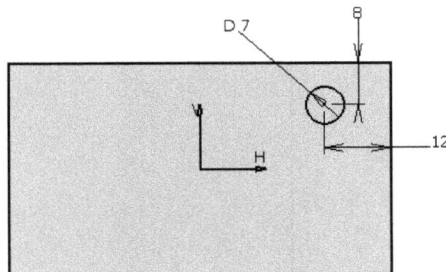

Figure 10–29

3. Dimension the center of the circle first to the upper edge, and then to the side edge, as shown above.

4. Exit the Sketcher workbench.

   To fully define the circle sketch, you have selected the following three references:

   • Sketch plane (**Fill.1** surface feature)
   • Dimensional reference (upper edge)
   • Dimensional reference (side edge)

   When you copy this geometrical set, three corresponding references must be selected to place the copied geometrical set.

Task 3 - Create an Extrude feature.

1. Select the circle sketch and create an Extrude feature with a limit of **20**. The Extrude feature displays as shown in Figure 10–30.

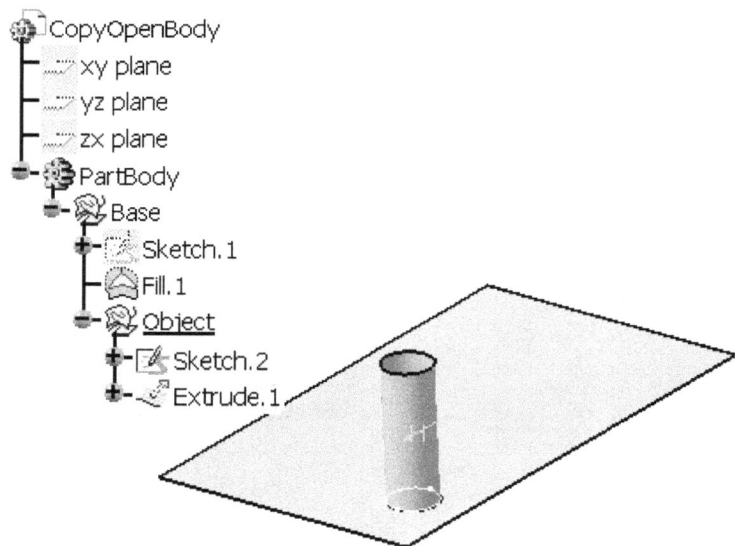

Figure 10–30

Task 4 - Duplicate a geometrical set.

In this task, you will step through the process of duplicating a geometrical set. When you have completed this task, the model displays as shown in Figure 10–31.

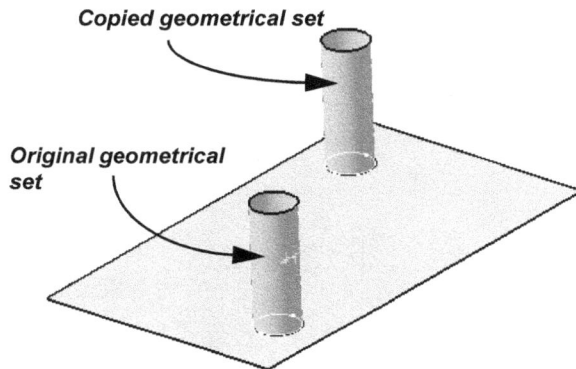

Copied geometrical set

Original geometrical set

Figure 10–31

1. Preselect the **Object** geometrical set and click

    (Duplicate geometrical set) in the Replication toolbar. The Insert Object dialog box opens as shown in Figure 10–32. Enter **Object2** in the *Name* field.

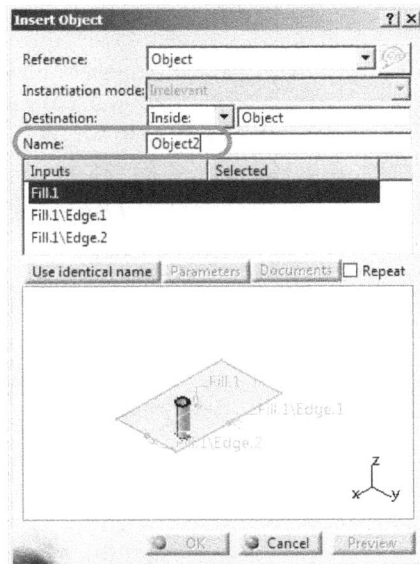

Figure 10–32

**Design
Considerations**

The system prompts you for all three references to fully place the copied geometrical set. The first reference you are prompted for is the sketch plane (**Fill.1**).

Since the two geometrical sets (**Object** and **Object2**) share the same sketch plane, the same feature name can be used. Therefore, no selection is required.

2. Click **Use identical name**, as shown in Figure 10–33.

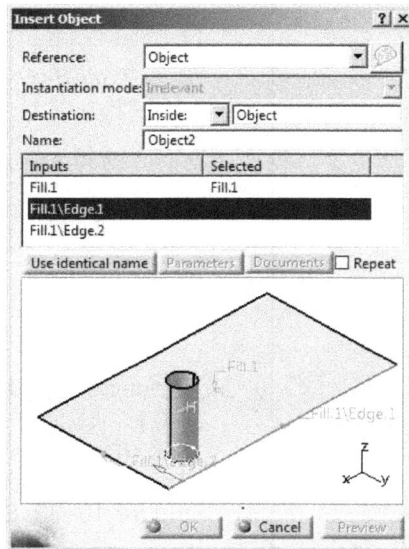

Figure 10–33

3. The system prompts you for the next reference (upper edge used to create the 8 dimension). Select the edge shown in Figure 10–34.

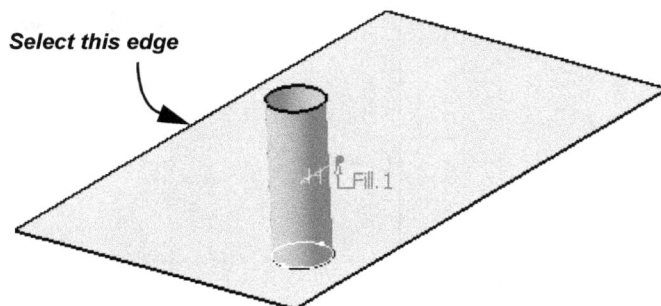

Figure 10–34

4. Select the edge shown in Figure 10–35 for the third reference.

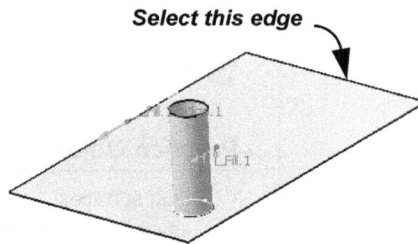

Select this edge

Figure 10–35

5. Click **OK**. The copied geometrical set geometry displays as shown in Figure 10–36.

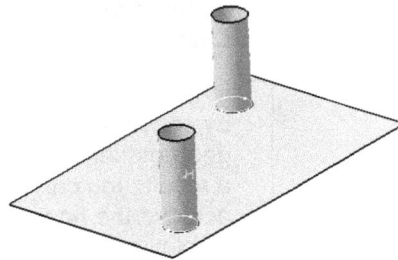

Figure 10–36

Task 5 - Investigate the copied geometrical set.

1. Edit the sketch (**Sketch.3**) of the copied geometrical set (**Object2**). The sketch is fully constrained to the new references with the same dimensional values that were used to define the original sketch, as shown in Figure 10–37.

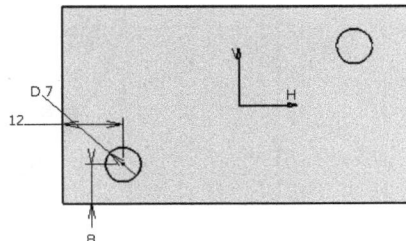

Figure 10–37

2. Exit the Sketcher workbench.

3. Save the model and close the file.

Practice 10c

(Optional) Duplicate Geometrical Set

Practice Objectives

- Offset surfaces.
- Remove erroneous faces from a surface to use in an offset.
- Rebuild surface geometry.

The cut-outs that form the spokes of the rim are all the same geometrical shape; however, the width varies so that every other spoke is the same size. In , you created the swept surface feature and split features to define the large cut-out. All of the features required to define the large cut-out were created in the **LargeCutOut** geometrical set.

In this practice, you will create a **SmallCutOut** geometrical set by copying the **LargeCutOut** geometrical set. The copied geometrical set inherits the design intent of the LargeCutOut. As a result, you can make simple dimensional changes to efficiently achieve the final geometry. The completed wheel rim model displays as shown in Figure 10–38.

Figure 10–38

Task 1 - Investigate surface geometry.

1. Open **WheelRim_DuplicateGset.CATPart**.

2. Hide **PartBody** and show the **LargeCutOut** geometrical set.

3. View the features listed under the **LargeCutOut** geometrical set in the specification tree. The specification tree is shown in Figure 10–39.

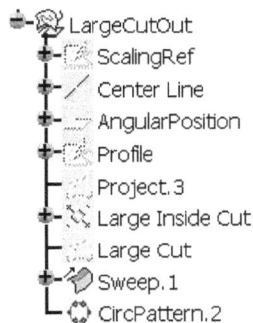

Figure 10–39

Design Considerations

Note the design intent of the following features:

* The AngularPosition reference plane is created using the Angle/Normal to plane type through CenterLine. The angular dimension used to place the plane can be modified to rotate the plane about the CenterLine axis of the rim.

* The Profile sketch defines the shape of the cut-out and is constrained to the AngularPosition plane so that an increase in the angle rotates the swept surfaces.

* Project.3 and Large Cut are projections of the Profile sketch; they are projected onto the surface of the rim geometry. The Large Inside Cut is a scaled version of Project.3. These features are developed to serve as guide curves for the swept surface.

The Profile sketch is shown in Figure 10–40 and is symmetrical about the vertical axis. The width of the section is driven by the 23 degree dimension.

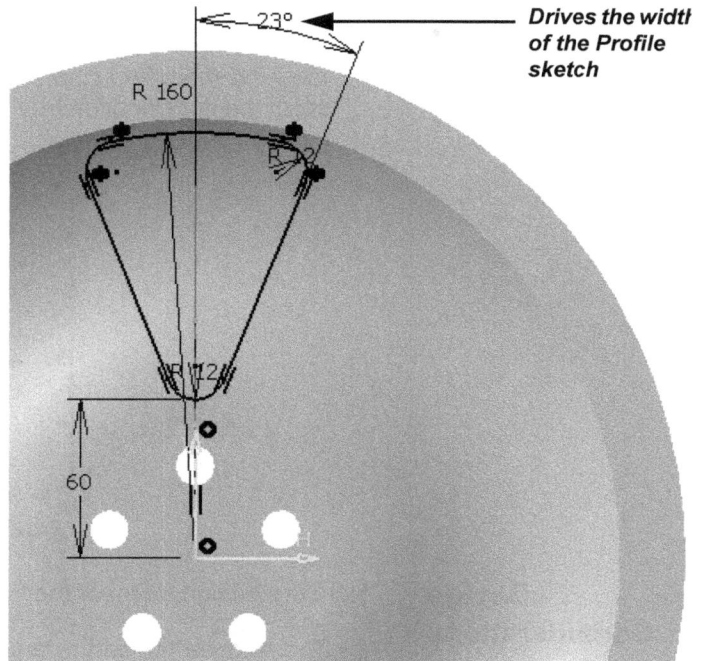

Figure 10–40

4. Set LargeCutOut to be the Work Object.

Task 2 - Create a copy of the geometrical set.

1. If not already highlighted, preselect the **LargeCutOut**

   geometrical set and click ![icon] (Duplicate Geometrical Set).
   The Insert Object dialog box opens as shown in
   Figure 10–41. Enter **SmallCutOut** as the name.

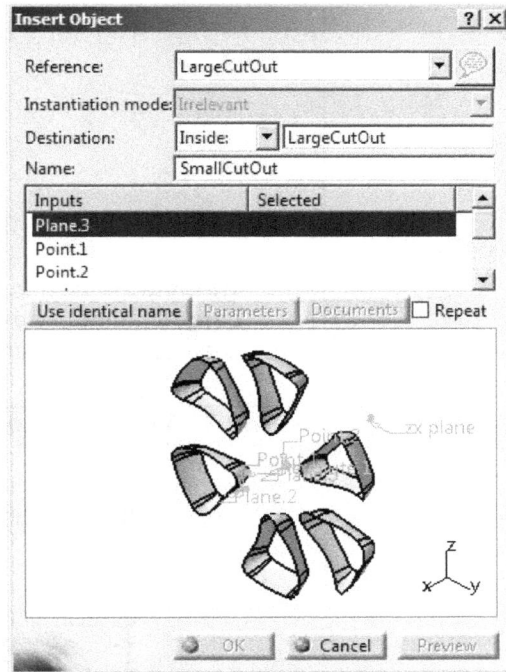

Figure 10–41

Design Considerations

The list of Inputs in this dialog box displays all references that
were selected when creating the geometry of LargeCutOut.

You will use the same references for the new geometrical set to
position the copied geometrical set on top of the original. **Use
identical name** can be used to facilitate these selections by
reusing all reference geometry such as points, lines, and planes.

2. Click **Use identical name**. The system automatically selects
   the references.

3. Click **OK**. The copied geometrical set is added to the specification tree and displays as shown in Figure 10–42.

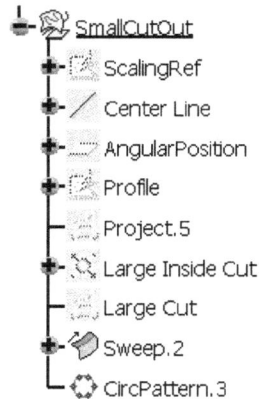

Figure 10–42

This new geometrical set is now a non-associative copy of **LargeCutOut** geometrical set. The geometry of the two geometrical sets can be modified independently.

Task 3 - Modify the copied geometry.

1. Modify the angular value of the AngularPosition plane under the **SmallCutOut** geometrical set to **30**, as shown in Figure 10–43.

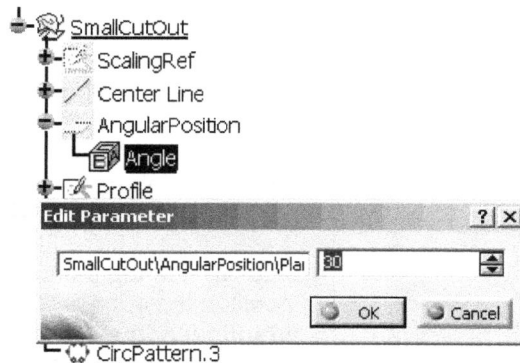

Figure 10–43

2. Edit the Profile sketch under the **SmallCutOut** geometrical set and change the 23 degree value to **10**, as shown in Figure 10–44.

Modify this dimension to 10 ⎯⎯⎯

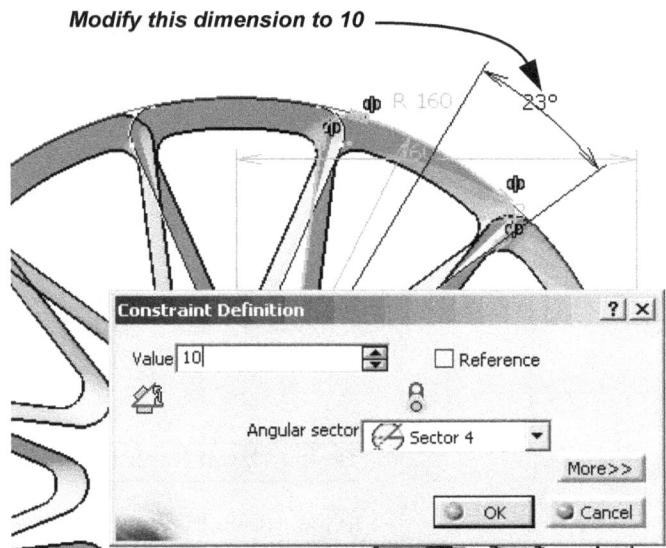

Figure 10–44

3. Exit the Sketcher workbench. The updated model displays as shown in Figure 10–45.

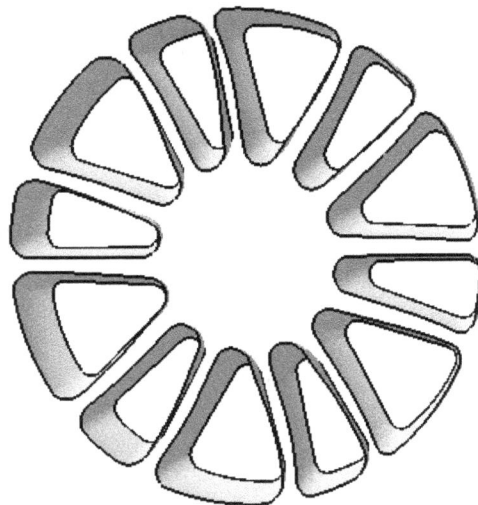

Figure 10–45

4. Show **PartBody**, as shown in Figure 10–46.

Figure 10–46

Task 4 - Split the surface geometry from the solid.

In the previous practice, the original swept surface and patterned surfaces were split from the solid part geometry using two Split features. In this task, you will join the swept surface and the pattern so that only one Split feature is required.

1. Click (Join) and specify the following, as shown in Figure 10–47.

    •   *Elements To Join:* **Sweep.2**, **CircPattern.3**
    •   Clear the **Check connexity** option.

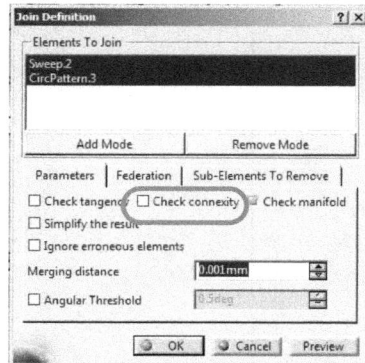

Figure 10–47

2. Click **OK**.

3. Activate the Part Design workbench, and set the PartBody as the work object.

4. Click ⬚ (Split).

5. Select **Join.1** in the specification tree.

6. Ensure that the arrows are pointing outward, as shown in Figure 10–48 and complete the feature.

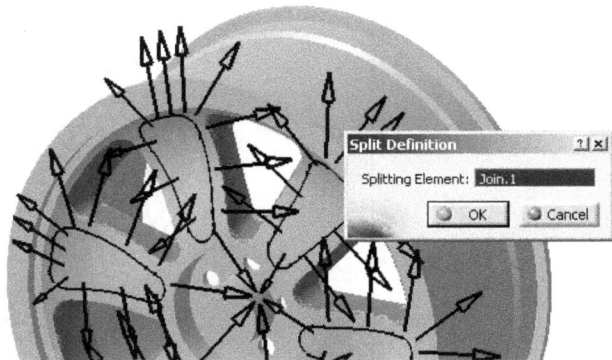

Figure 10–48

7. Select **Tools>Hide>All geometrical sets**. The completed model displays as shown in Figure 10–49.

Figure 10–49

8. Save the model and close the file.

Practice 10d | Speaker Cover 1

Practice Objective

* Create a pattern without any instructional steps.

Create the speaker cover as shown in Figure 10–50. The exact dimensions are not important.

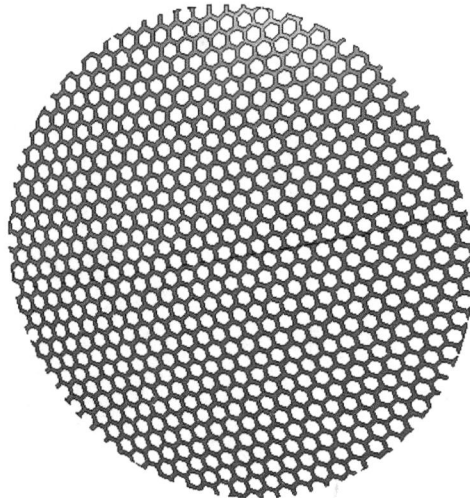

Figure 10–50

Open **Speaker_Cover1_Start.CATPart**. The model displays as shown in Figure 10–51.

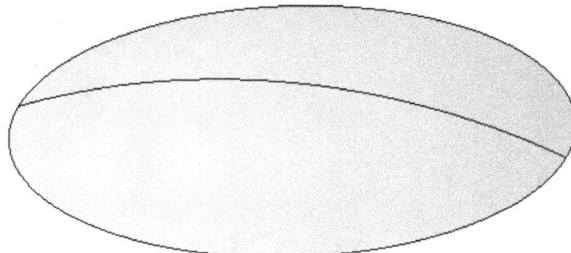

Figure 10–51

Chapter 11

Knowledge Templates

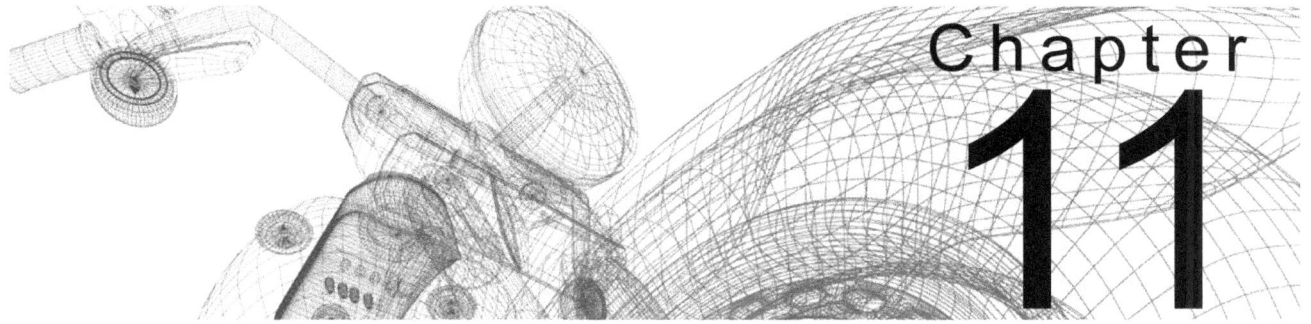

Reusing existing information saves time and ensures consistency. Two types of knowledge templates are available: PowerCopy and UserFeature. PowerCopy enables you to use features in other documents. This provides more control over the placement of data than simply copying and pasting. UserFeatures are similar in function, but result in a single representative feature (PowerCopy results in a group of features).

Learning Objectives in this Chapter

- Use Knowledge Templates.
- Create a PowerCopy.
- Instantiate a PowerCopy.
- Investigate Catalogs.

11.1 Knowledge Templates

A **Knowledge Template** is a replication tool that enables a sequence of features to be created automatically. Features must be able to locate new references to be successfully created; these references must correspond to those used when the geometry was originally created. This way, previously created geometry can be adapted to a new design that is similar in context.

Knowledge templates can be used for a variety of applications, including:

- Adding frequently created features to a part. These features can be modified to apply to the design intent and context of the new part.

- Adding a complete and validated sequence of features to a part. Once positioned in the new part, these features are ready to use and do not require modification.

- Creating a series of customized features for a specific field of activity.

This chapter introduces PowerCopy knowledge templates only. UserFeature knowledge templates are beyond the scope of this learning guide.

Two types of knowledge templates are available: PowerCopy and UserFeature. The templates are described as follows:

Knowledge Template	Description	Result	Applications
PowerCopy	Copies a selection of features and parameters from the source model into a template that can be applied to target part models.	Copies the entire list of features into the target model. Features act identically to the original features and can be modified.	Redundant creation of features that require modification in the target model.
UserFeature	Copies a selection of features and parameters from the source model into a template that can be applied to target part models. This type of knowledge template requires a Product Knowledge Template (PKT) license.	Places a single feature into the target model that contains the geometry of all selected features. Only published parameters can be modified.	Redundant creation of features that do not require modification in the target model.

11.2 Create a PowerCopy

PowerCopies can be very useful when a feature, or group of features, are required in several models. Rather than recreate the features in each model, you create them once and then use **PowerCopy** to copy the original feature(s) into another model. Unlike the **Paste** option, you can also control the referencing features and dimensions while placing the feature.

General Steps

Use the following general steps to create PowerCopy:

1. Start the creation of a PowerCopy.
2. Add features to the PowerCopy.
3. Rename the features.
4. Set variable parameters, as required.
5. Set an icon or preview for the PowerCopy.
6. Complete the PowerCopy.

Step 1 - Start the creation of a PowerCopy.

You cannot create a PowerCopy in a model with unsaved changes.

Save the model once all features for the PowerCopy have been created. Select **Insert>Knowledge Templates>PowerCopy**, as shown in Figure 11–1, to open the PowerCopy Definition dialog box.

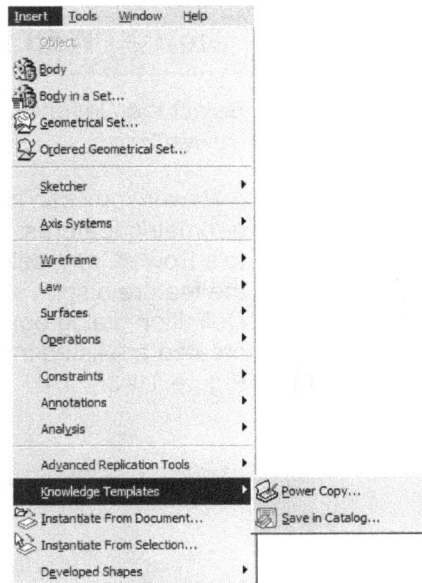

Figure 11–1

- Alternatively, click ⬚ (Create a Power Copy) in the Product Knowledge Template Toolbar.

The PowerCopy Definition dialog box opens as shown in Figure 11–2.

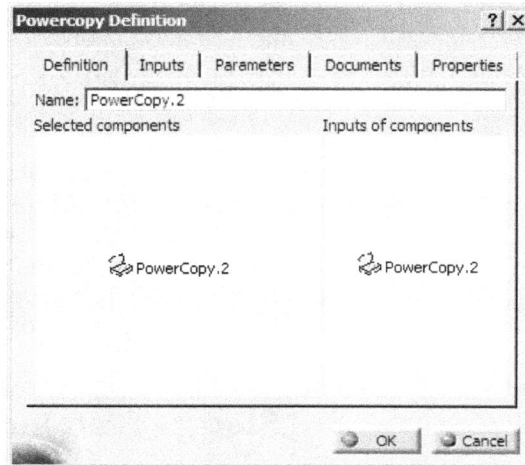

Figure 11–2

Enter a more descriptive name for the PowerCopy and press <Enter>.

Step 2 - Add features to the PowerCopy.

Select the *Definition* tab to begin adding features to the PowerCopy.

If you accidentally select a feature you do not want to be in the PowerCopy, select the feature again in the specification tree to remove it.

A PowerCopy can contain a variety of features, such as geometric features, formulas, and constraints. To add a feature to a PowerCopy, select it in the specification tree. Once selected, the feature displays in the Components area in the PowerCopy Definition dialog box. Any references used when the feature was created are listed in the Inputs of components area, as shown in Figure 11–3.

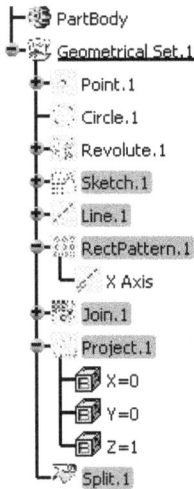

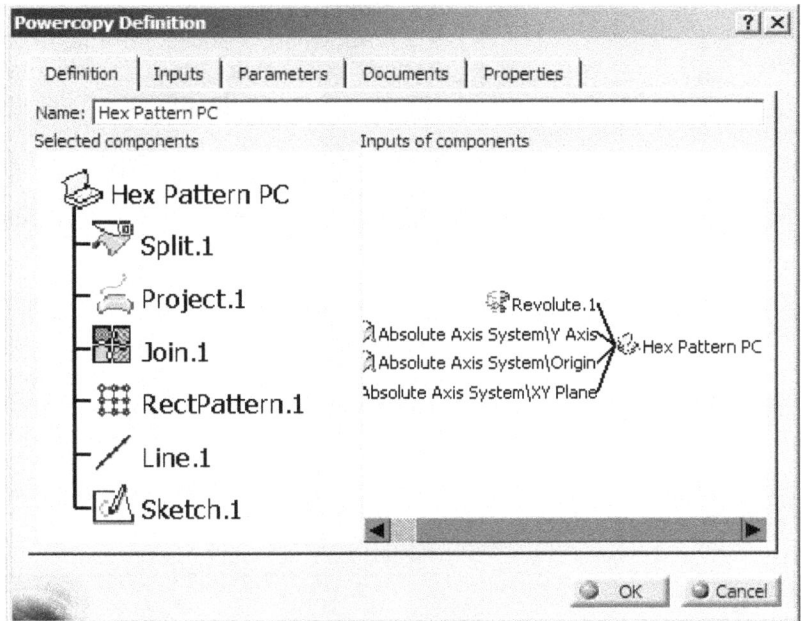

Figure 11–3

These references are used as inputs when the PowerCopy is placed in another model.

Try not to add a large number of features to the PowerCopy. Keeping the number of features to a minimum avoids making the PowerCopy complicated and avoids problems that could occur when placing the PowerCopy later.

Step 3 - Rename the features.

After you finish adding the features to the PowerCopy, it is a good idea to enter a more descriptive name for the features. This makes placing the PowerCopy easier.

To rename an input, select the *Input* tab. Select the feature from the Input window and enter a new name in the *Name* field at the bottom of the dialog box. The original name of the feature remains in brackets, as shown in Figure 11–4.

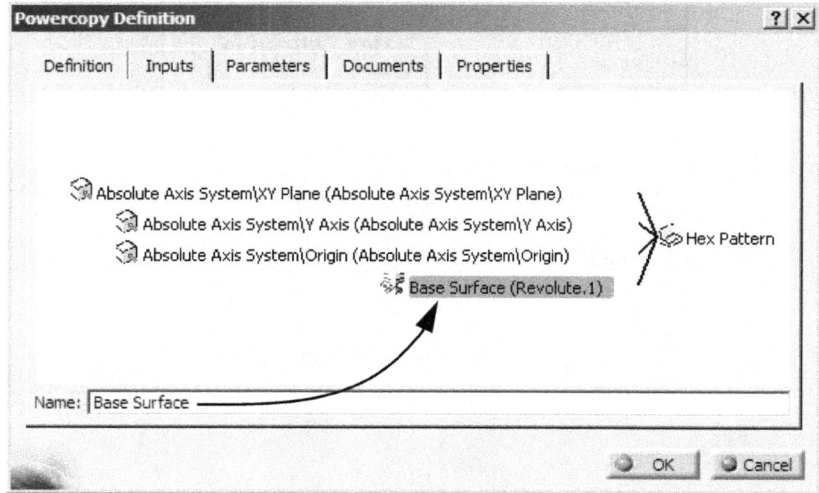

Figure 11–4

Step 4 - Set variable parameters, as required.

Select the *Parameters* tab to define the parameter values that you want to be variable when placing the PowerCopy feature. A variable parameter enables you to change its value to suit the model in which it is placed.

To create a modifiable parameter, select the parameter and select **Published**. The *Name* field displays. Enter a more descriptive name for the feature. The new name is used when the PowerCopy is placed in the new model.

For example, the parameter selected in Figure 11–5 is published and is now variable. The remaining values associated with the PowerCopy are not published; therefore, their values are not modifiable during placement.

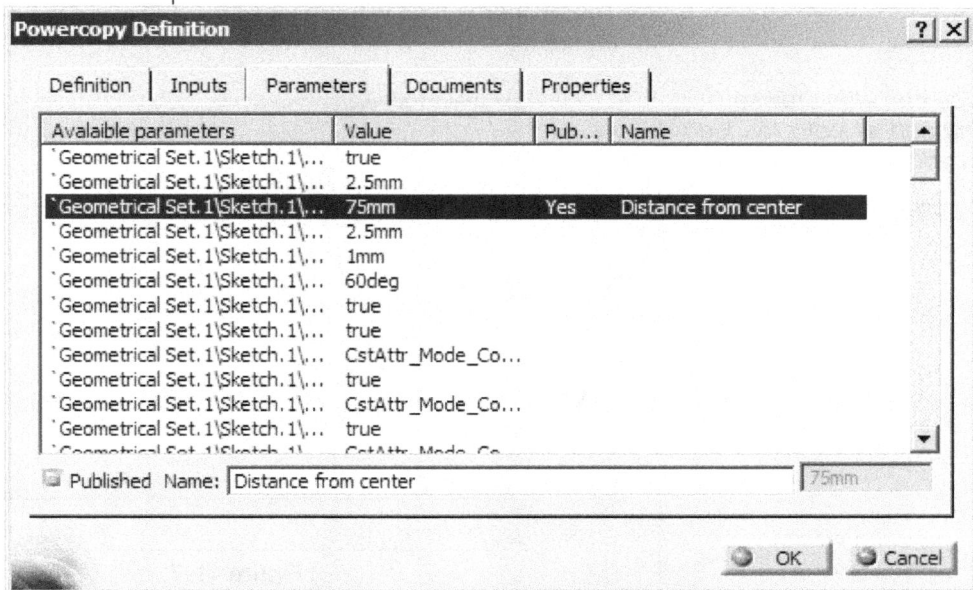

Figure 11–5

Step 5 - Set an icon or preview for the PowerCopy.

Select the *Properties* tab to select an icon to identify the

PowerCopy in the specification tree. Click [icon] to expand a list of commonly selected icons, as shown in Figure 11–6.

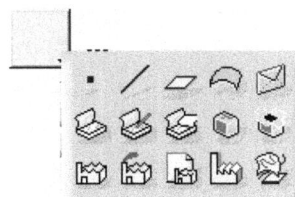

Figure 11–6

The *Properties* tab with an icon selected is shown in Figure 11–7.

You can also browse through all icons loaded in your CATIA session by clicking **...** .

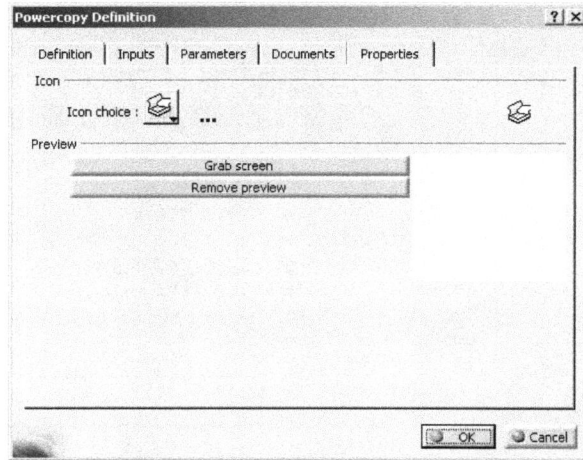

Figure 11–7

Preview

The *Properties* tab also enables you to create a preview that is stored with the PowerCopy Definition. To create a preview, set up the model display according to the way you want it to display in the preview. Select **View>Specifications** or **View>Compass** to clear the display of the specification tree and compass as required. Click **Grab screen** to take a screen shot. The screen shot is used as the preview, as shown in Figure 11–8.

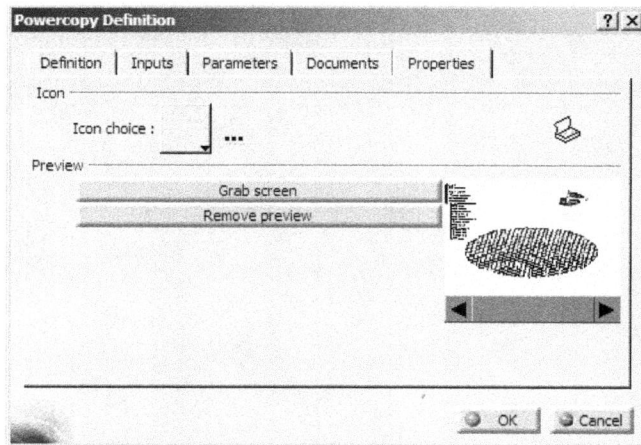

Figure 11–8

Click **Remove Preview** to remove the preview.

Step 6 - Complete the PowerCopy.

After you have completed the PowerCopy Definition, click **OK** to exit the dialog box.

11.3 Instantiate a PowerCopy

Once a PowerCopy has been created it is ready to use in other models. Any variable parameters that were created can be modified to suit the new model.

General Steps

Use the following steps to instantiate the PowerCopy.

1. Select the PowerCopy to be instantiated.
2. Place the PowerCopy.
3. Change the parameters and complete instantiation.

Step 1 - Select the PowerCopy to be instantiated.

The document containing the PowerCopy must be closed (i.e., not in session) when it is being inserted into another document.

Select **Insert>Instantiate From Document** from the target model (where you are placing the PowerCopy). Alternatively,

click (Instantiate From Document) in the Product Knowledge Template Toolbar.

Navigate to the document containing the PowerCopy in the File Selection dialog box and click **Open** to begin inserting the object.

Step 2 - Place the PowerCopy.

Once you select a document to open, the Insert Object dialog box opens as shown in Figure 11–9. Select the correct PowerCopy in the Reference drop-down list, if more than one exists in the source document.

The destination of the geometry can also be specified by selecting **Inside** or **After** in the Destination drop-down list. The reference field enables you to define the geometrical set where the features are going to be located.

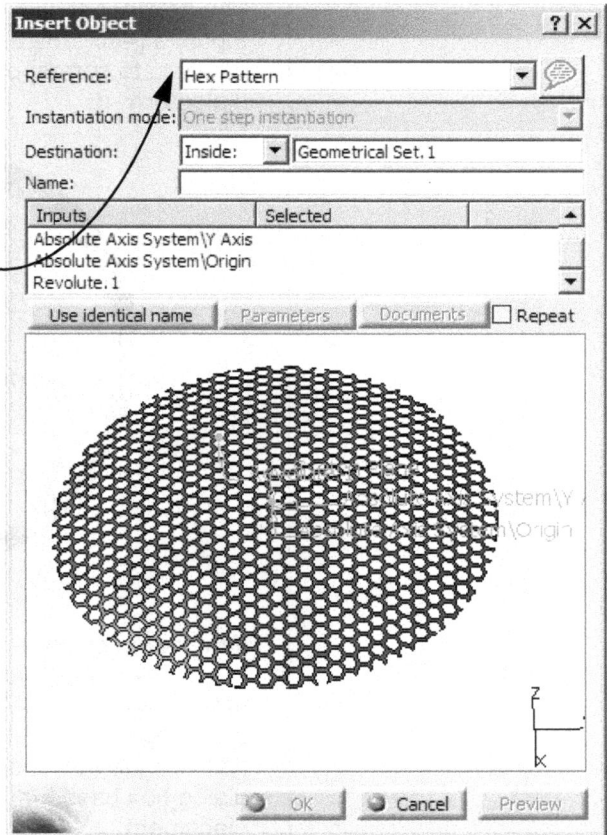

When multiple power copies exist in the document they are listed in the drop-down list.

Figure 11–9

Once you select the PowerCopy to reference, CATIA highlights a reference in the *Inputs* column in the dialog box and waits for you to select the corresponding feature in the new model. This selection process is repeated until all references are selected and the PowerCopy is successfully positioned.

At this point, you can view the PowerCopy with the model by clicking **Preview**.

The hexagonal cuts on a speaker cover are shown in Figure 11–10. The references indicated on the model are selected to correspond to the references listed as inputs in the dialog box.

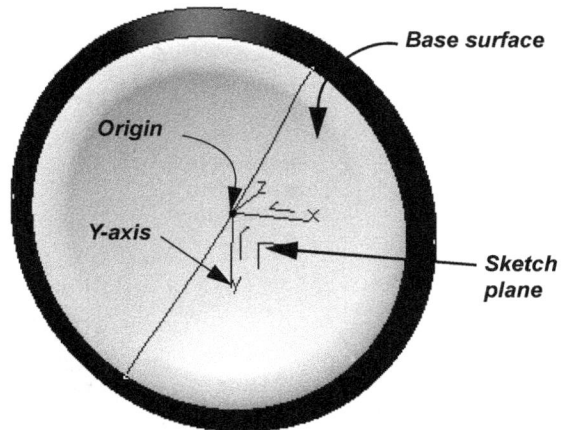

Figure 11–10

If the name of the reference in the target model is the same as in the source model, you can also place references by clicking **Use identical name**. CATIA automatically places the reference by matching the reference name in the PowerCopy to the reference name in the new model. For example, the XY-plane listed in the dialog box uses the XY-plane in the model as a reference for placement.

If you place more than one of the same object, you can select **Repeat** to save time. Once you finish placing the PowerCopy, the dialog box remains open enabling you to place another one.

Once instantiated, each feature of a PowerCopy becomes a separate feature and is no longer linked to the original PowerCopy.

Step 3 - Change the parameters and complete instantiation.

If any parameters have been published with the PowerCopy, **Parameters** is available. Click **Parameters** to open the Parameters dialog box. Any modifiable parameters are listed with the default values, as shown in Figure 11–11.

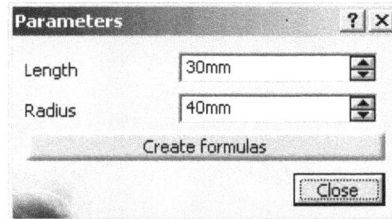

Figure 11–11

Click **Create formulas** to automatically create a formula for any parameter in the model with the same name as a parameter in the PowerCopy. When the PowerCopy is instantiated in a model with a parameter of the same name and **Create formulas** is used, the length of the rectangular box is automatically driven by the new value.

Once the PowerCopy is placed correctly in the model, click **OK** to complete the instantiation.

11.4 Catalogs

Similar to the Part Design workbench, Knowledge Templates can be saved to and instantiated from a catalog.

How To: Save a Knowledge Template to a Catalog

1. Save the target CATPart file. Knowledge Templates cannot be saved to a catalog if the file itself is not saved.
2. Select the Knowledge Template(s) in the specification tree that are going to be saved in the catalog as shown in Figure 11–12.

Select Knowledge Template

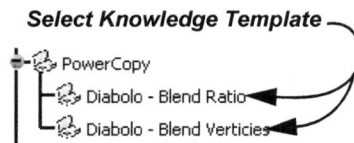

PowerCopy
Diabolo - Blend Ratio
Diabolo - Blend Verticies

Figure 11–12

3. Select **Insert>Knowledge Templates>Save in Catalog.**

   Alternatively, click ▨ (Save in Catalog) in the Product Knowledge Template Toolbar. The Catalog save dialog box opens as shown in Figure 11–13.
4. Specify whether a new catalog is to be created in which to save the Knowledge Templates, or if an existing catalog is to be used.

5. Click ▭ (Browse), as shown in Figure 11–13, in the Catalog save dialog box to:

   • Identify the existing catalog's location.

   • Identify the new catalog's location.

Select to browse

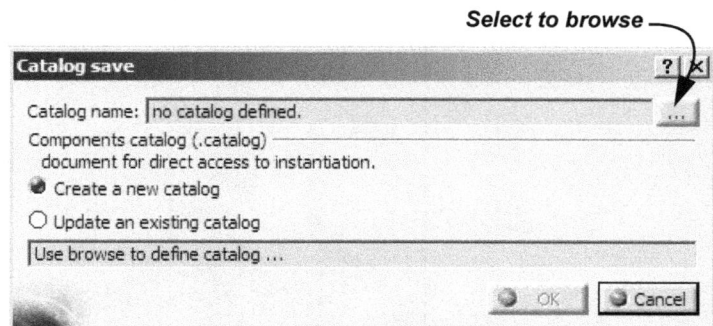

Catalog save

Catalog name: no catalog defined.

Components catalog (.catalog) document for direct access to instantiation.

◉ Create a new catalog

◯ Update an existing catalog

Use browse to define catalog ...

OK   Cancel

Figure 11–13

6. After the location is specified, click **OK** to complete the Catalog save operation.

How To: Instantiate a Knowledge Template from a Catalog

1. Open the source CATPart file.
2. Create any reference geometry required to support the Knowledge Template.
3. Click ⬦ (Catalog) in the Tools toolbar.
4. Browse for the catalog where the Knowledge Template is located, as shown in Figure 11–14.

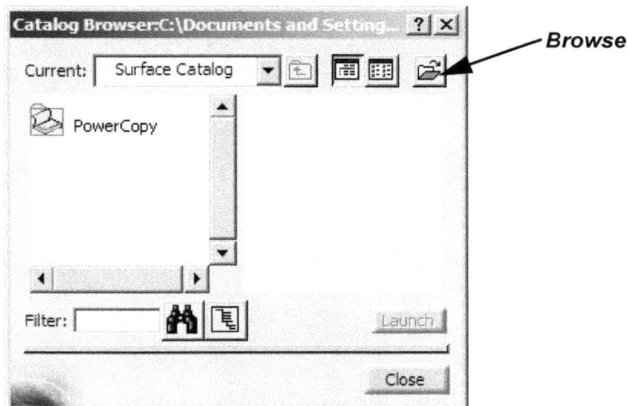

Figure 11–14

5. Locate the Knowledge Template in the catalog.
6. Double-click on the Knowledge Template to instantiate it into the document.

The Insert Object dialog box opens as shown in Figure 11–15.

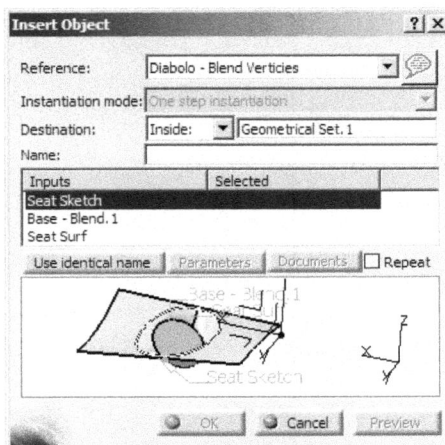

Figure 11–15

7. Similar to instantiating any Knowledge Template:
   - Select the Destination location.
   - Specify input references.
   - Specify any parameters values as required.
8. Complete the instantiation by clicking **OK**.

Practice 11a

PowerCopy Creation

Practice Objectives

- Create a PowerCopy.
- Save a PowerCopy to a catalog.
- Instantiate a PowerCopy from a catalog.

In this practice, you will create a PowerCopy from existing wireframe and surface geometry. The PowerCopy will then be saved to a catalog. Once saved, another model will be opened. The cataloged powercopy will then be instantiated into the target model. The completed geometry displays as shown in Figure 11–16.

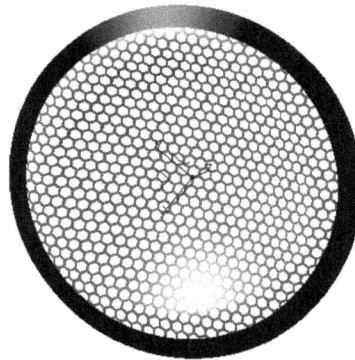

Figure 11–16

Task 1 - Open a part file.

1. A completed speaker cover has been created for you. Open **Speaker_Cover_Source.CATPart**. The part displays as shown in Figure 11–17.

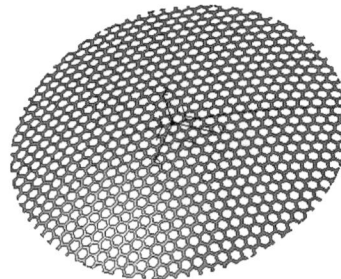

Figure 11–17

Task 2 - Create a PowerCopy.

The information to be stored in the PowerCopy is the hexagonal pattern geometry and the cut it creates on the curved surface. The design intent is for a future user to instantiate this hexagonal cut on their curved surface.

1. Select **Insert>Knowledge Templates>Power Copy**. The Powercopy Definition dialog box opens as shown in Figure 11–18.

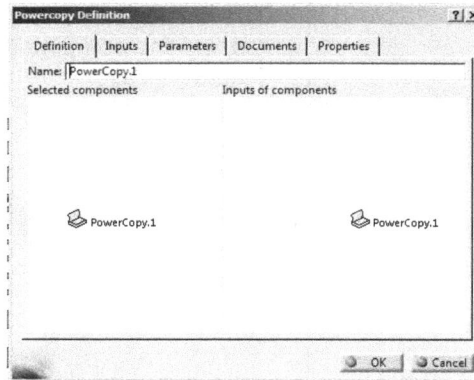

Figure 11–18

2. Enter **Hex Pattern** in the *Name* field. Press <Enter> to update the entered name.

3. Select the following features in the specification tree, as shown in Figure 11–19:

   - **Sketch.1**
   - **Line.1**
   - **Line.2**
   - **RectPattern.1**
   - **Join.1**
   - **Project.1**
   - **Split.1**

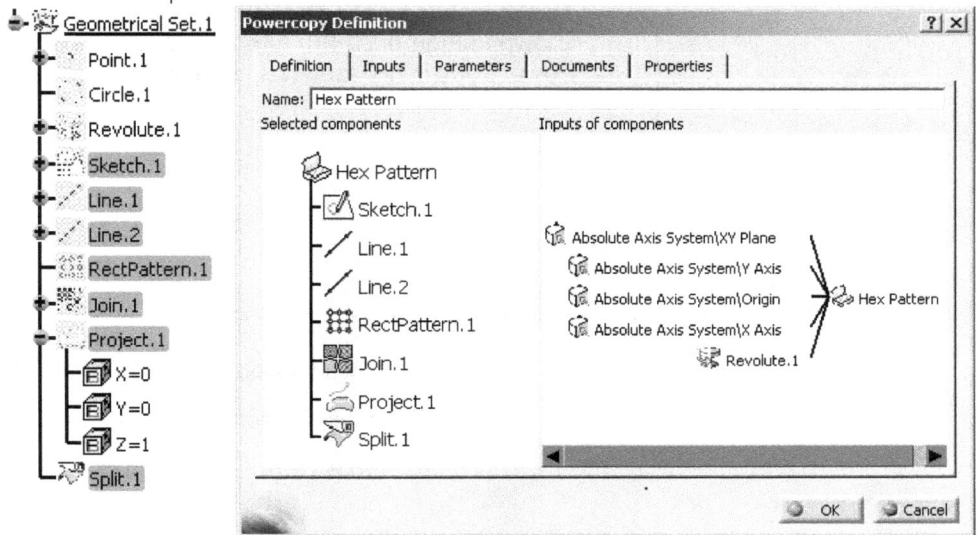

Figure 11–19

Design Considerations

These references were selected because they were features that were used to create the hexagonal cut. All features that helped build this geometry must be selected.

4. Select the *Inputs* tab. In this tab, each input reference required for the PowerCopy's placement can be given a more descriptive name.

5. Select **Absolute Axis System\XY Plane**.

6. Enter **Sketch Plane**.

7. Change the remaining input references to the following:

   - Y-axis
   - Origin
   - X-axis
   - Base Surface

The completed changes to the input references display as shown in Figure 11–20. Although this process in creating a PowerCopy is not required, it helps future users instantiate the PowerCopy.

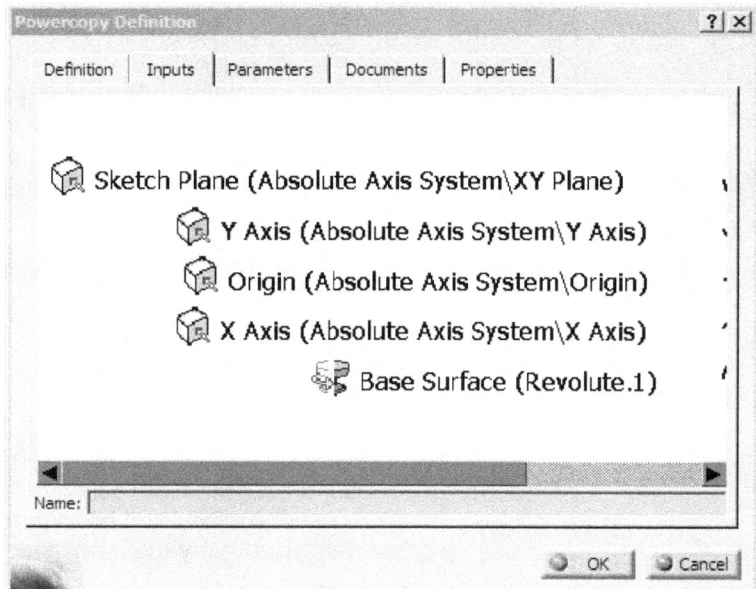

Figure 11–20

8. Click **OK** to complete the PowerCopy.

Task 3 - Save the PowerCopy to a catalog.

1. Save the model.

2. Select the **Hex Pattern** in the PowerCopy branch of the specification tree, as shown in Figure 11–21.

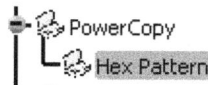

Figure 11–21

3. Select **Insert>Knowledge Templates>Save in Catalog**. The Catalog save dialog box opens as shown in Figure 11–22.

4. Select **Create a new catalog** in the dialog box, as shown in Figure 11–22.

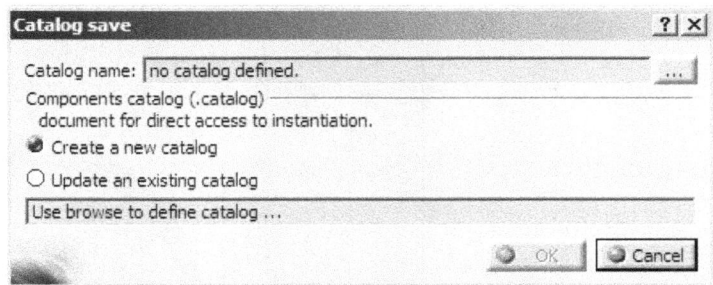

Figure 11–22

5. Click [...] (Browse) in the Catalog save dialog box.

6. Locate the directory where the training files are stored.

7. Enter the filename **AdvSurf_Catalog**. The file format has the catalog extension.

8. Press <Enter> to complete the operation. The Catalog save dialog box opens as shown in Figure 11–23.

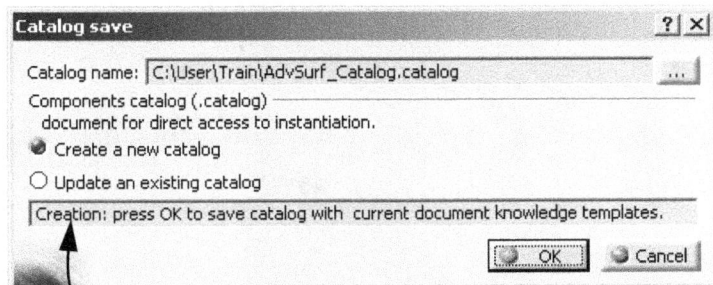

Status message has been updated

Figure 11–23

9. Click **OK** to complete the save to catalog operation.

Task 4 - Instantiate the PowerCopy.

1. Close the file. Save the file if it prompts you to do so.

2. Open **PC_Speaker_Cover_Target.CATPart**. The model displays as shown in Figure 11–24.

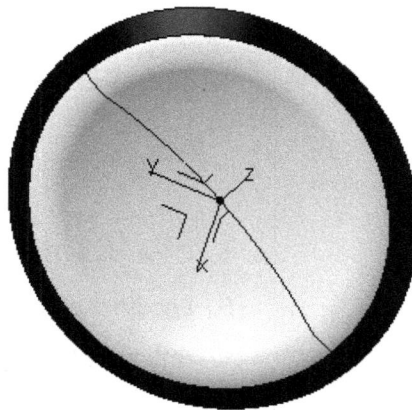

Figure 11–24

3. Click ⬛ (Catalog) in the Tools toolbar.

4. Browse for the catalog, as shown in Figure 11–25.

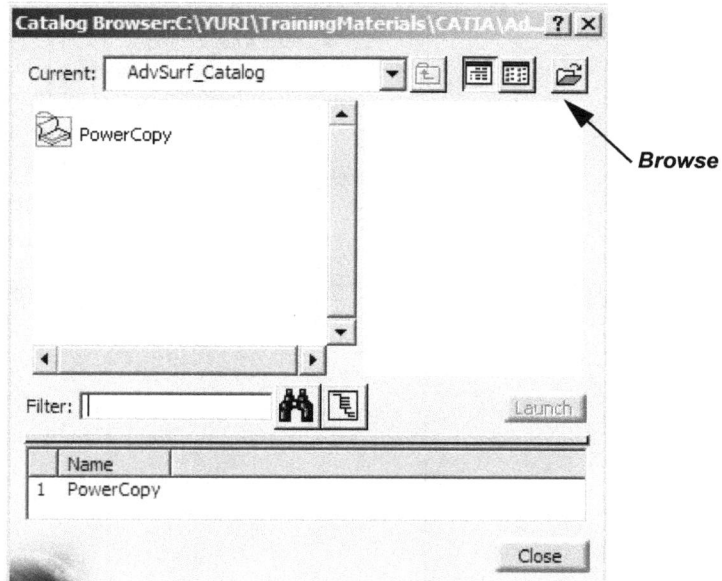

Figure 11–25

5. Locate the catalog named **AdvSurf Catalog.catalog**. This was the catalog saved in the last task. The dialog box updates as shown in Figure 11–26.

6. Double-click on **PowerCopy** to see PowerCopies saved in the catalog. PowerCopies are automatically organized in a catalog by how many inputs are required to instantiate the geometry.

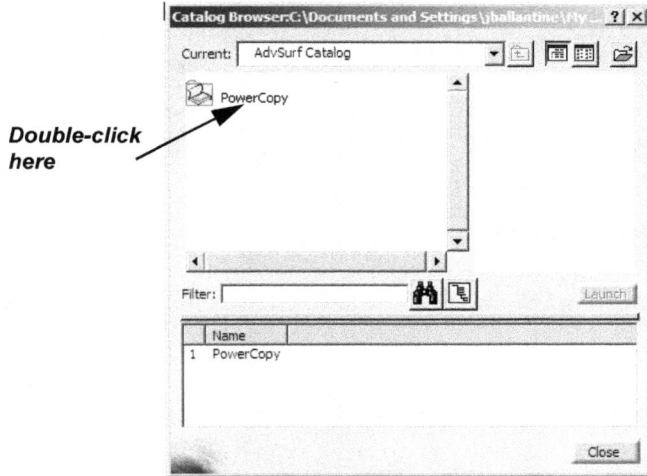

Double-click here

Figure 11–26

7. Double-click on **5 inputs**. The dialog box updates as shown in Figure 11–27.

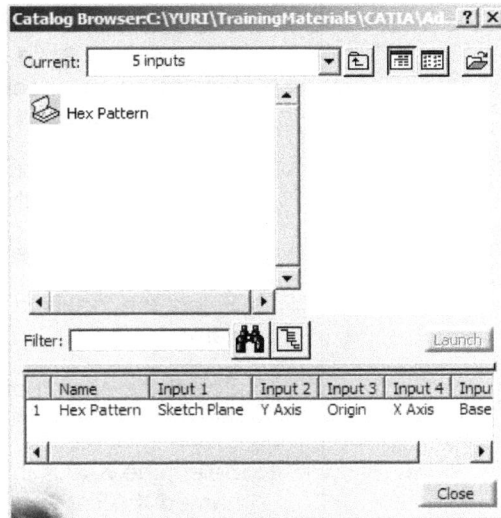

Figure 11–27

8. Double-click on **Hex Pattern** to instantiate the component. The Insert Object dialog box opens as shown in Figure 11–28.

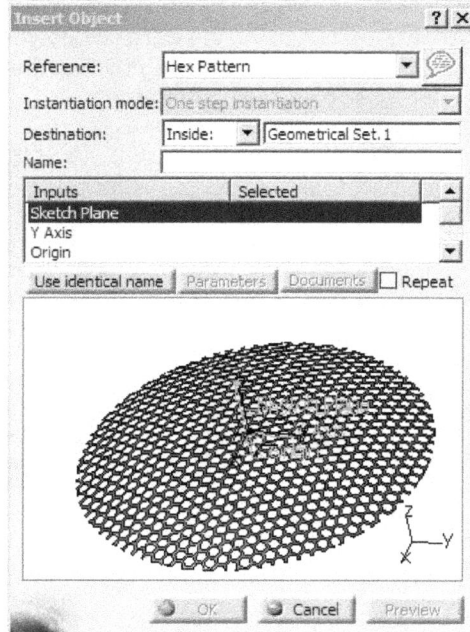

Figure 11–28

9. Ensure that Hex Pattern is the PowerCopy specified in the Reference drop-down list.

10. The default option to place the PowerCopy inside **Geometrical Set.1** is acceptable. If this is not what the dialog box indicates, specify the destination to be Inside: **Geometrical Set.1**.

11. To define each input reference, select the item in the list starting with Sketch Plane.

12. Select the xy plane from the model or specification tree.

13. Select the Y-axis in the Absolute Axis System for the input named Y Axis.

14. Select the origin point of the Absolute Axis System for the input named Origin.

15. Select the X-axis in the Absolute Axis System for the input named X Axis.

16. Select **Revolute.1** as the Base Surface input. The input references are labeled as shown in Figure 11–29.

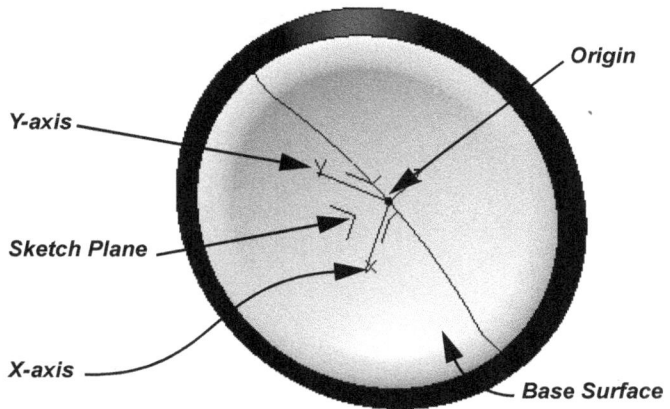

Figure 11–29

17. Click **OK** to complete the operation. Each individual feature that was included in the Hex Pattern PowerCopy is now located in the specification tree.

Instantiating the PowerCopy into the model might take a long time.

18. Hide **Revolute.1**. This surface was referenced for placing the PowerCopy, and is no longer required. The model displays as shown in Figure 11–30.

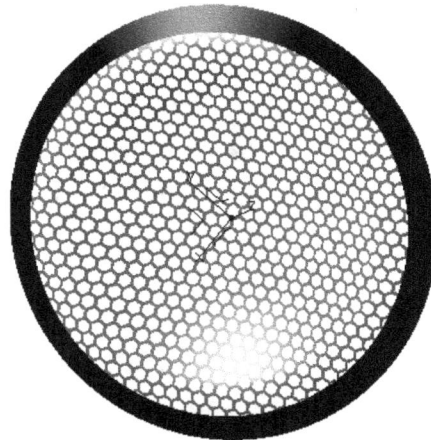

Figure 11–30

19. Save the model and close the file.

Practice 11b

Thread PowerCopy

Practice Objectives

- Create a PowerCopy without any instructions.
- Perform surface operations.
- Instantiate a PowerCopy without any instructions.

In this practice, you will create and instantiate a PowerCopy without any instructions. The finished model displays as shown in Figure 11–31.

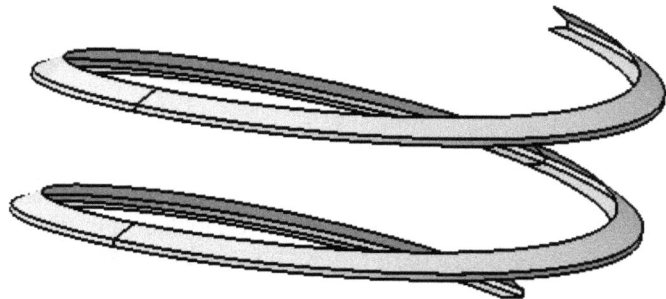

Figure 11–31

1. Create a new part called **Thread_Source.CATPart**.

2. Create wireframe and surface geometry for a thread. Exact dimensions are not required.

3. Save the PowerCopy.

4. Instantiate the PowerCopy into a new part.

Chapter
12

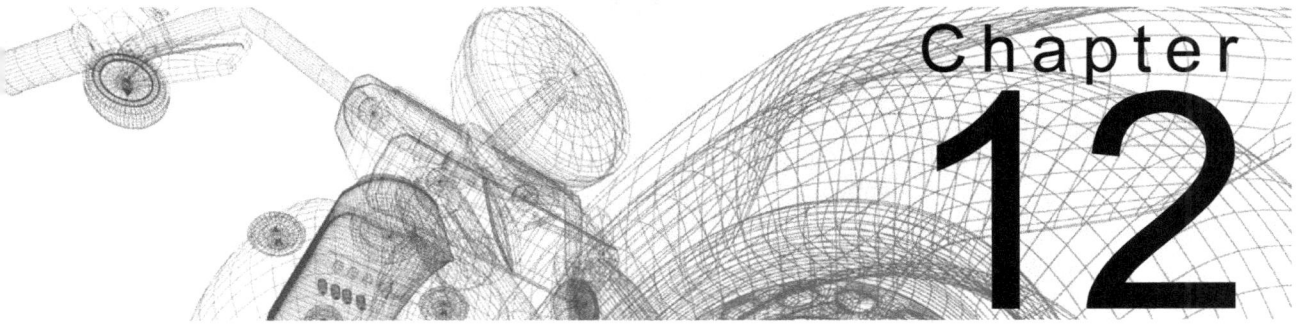

Surface Analysis and Repair

The quality of wireframe curve elements directly impacts the surface features that reference them. Understanding the errors and how to repair them is important for creating models that meet the design intent. This chapter discusses the tools available to identify and correct surface feature errors.

Learning Objectives in this Chapter

- Recognize the need for analysis and repair tools.
- Understand the options for surface error display.
- Understand the surface analysis process.
- Use Porcupine Curvature and Surfacic Curvature Analysis.
- Perform a temporary analysis of the resulting geometry during the creation of an Offset feature.
- Learn how to repair surface geometry.
- Understand the tools for controlling element direction.
- Review several tips for rebuilding geometry.

12.1 Analysis and Repair

The quality of wireframe curve elements has a direct correlation to the surface features that reference them.

The following types of errors can result in a surface feature as shown in Figure 12–1:

- Inflection
- Internal flaw
- Tangency discontinuity
- Curvature discontinuity

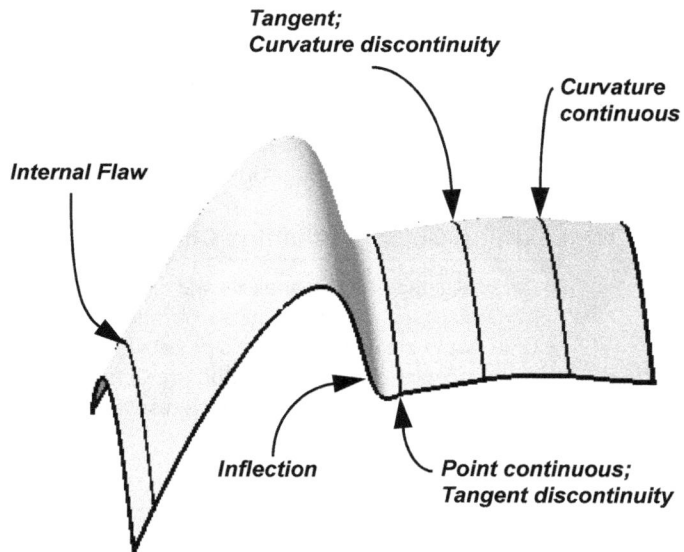

Figure 12–1

Various analysis tools are available to investigate surfaces.

12.2 Surface Error Display

Some errors might be difficult to see on the model. Before investigating surfaces, you might want to change the display of the model to view errors in the surface data more clearly. Use the following techniques to manipulate the display.

3D Accuracy

Set 3D accuracy by selecting **Tools>Options**, selecting **Display** in the tree on the left and selecting the *Performances* tab. Select **Fixed** and enter **0.01** as the value as shown in Figure 12–2. Setting the 3D accuracy increases the level of visual detail; however, the refresh rate slows as the level of detail increases.

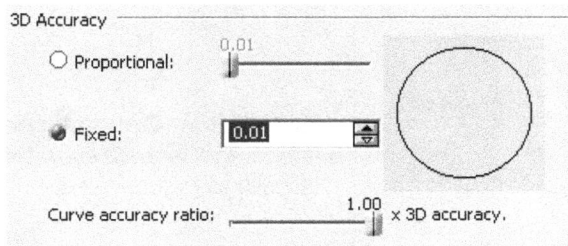

Figure 12–2

Display Mode

The surface model shown in Figure 12–3 is a single cohesive surface feature.

Figure 12–3

If the ▣ (Shaded with Edges) display mode is set, the model displays as shown in Figure 12–4. The model is made of four surface features.

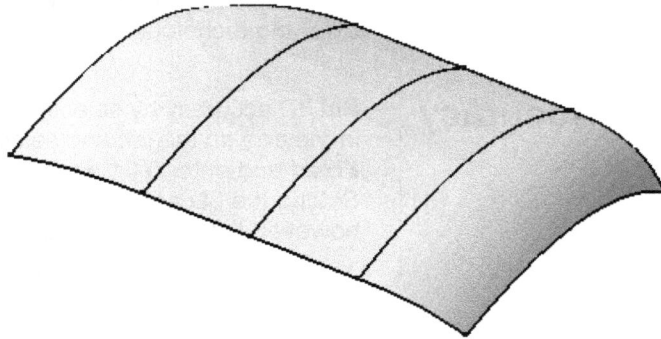

Figure 12–4

Click **Tools>Options**, select **Display** in the tree on the left and select the *Visualization* tab. Select **Surfaces' Boundaries**, as shown in Figure 12–5.

Figure 12–5

The color and thickness of the boundaries can be set, as well as the level of visibility.

Color

Changing the color of surface features helps define contrast between features. Right-click and select **Properties**. Specify a color, as shown in Figure 12–6.

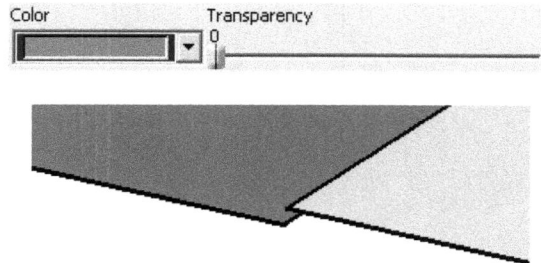

Figure 12–6

WYSIWYG Mode

Clicking 🔚 (WYSIWYG mode) switches the model display to What You See Is What You Get mode. This Visualization mode instantly reveals gaps between surfaces and wires that have been concealed by repair features, such as Heal or Merging Distance, and offers an accelerated alternative to Connect Check analysis. It reveals errors in surface integrity that could cause secondary features, such as Offset, Projection, and Thick Surface to fail. However, the representation is strictly graphical and should only be used on a feature-specific troubleshooting basis.

A Join feature is created with sufficient Merging distance to join two non-connex extruded surfaces. CATIA graphically represents a smooth, connected transition between the two joined surfaces, as shown in Figure 12–7.

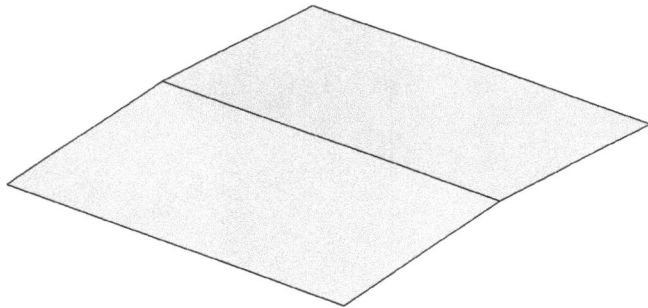

Figure 12–7

When 🔚 (WYSIWYG mode) is activated, the true distance between the two joined surfaces is revealed, as shown in Figure 12–8.

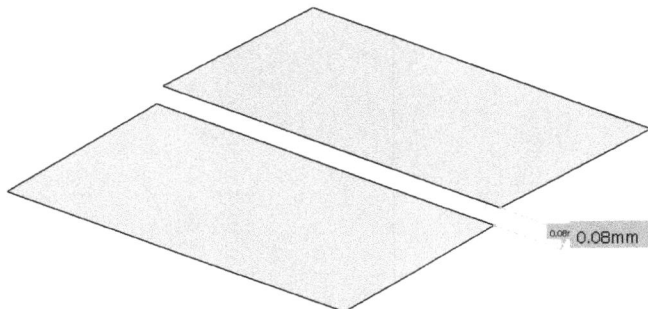

The Measure feature has been added for illustrative purposes.

0.08mm

Figure 12–8

To exit WYSIWYG mode, click 🔚 (WYSIWYG mode).

12.3 Analyzing Surfaces

Surfaces can be analyzed for overlap, gaps, tangency, and curvature discontinuity using the Connect Checker Analysis. When analyzing surfaces with this tool you can perform the following analyses:

- Surface - Surface Boundary

- Surface - Surface Projection

Surface - Surface Boundary Analysis

This type of analysis enables you to check the continuity type between surfaces. A G0 information for a Surface - Surface Boundary analysis is shown in Figure 12–9.

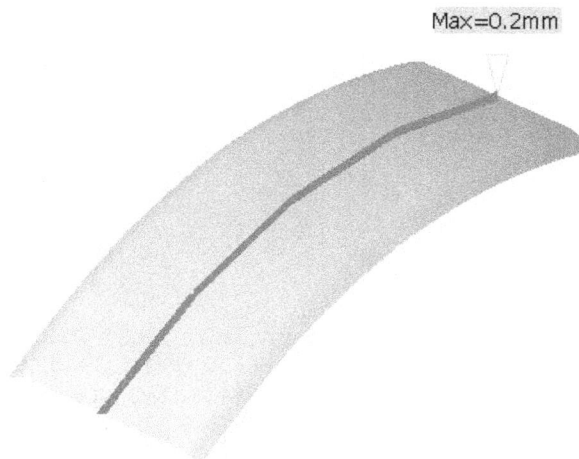

Figure 12–9

Surface - Surface Projection analysis

The border of the source surface is projected in the direction of the normal for the target surface. An example of a Projection on a surface analysis for G2 type is shown in Figure 12–10.

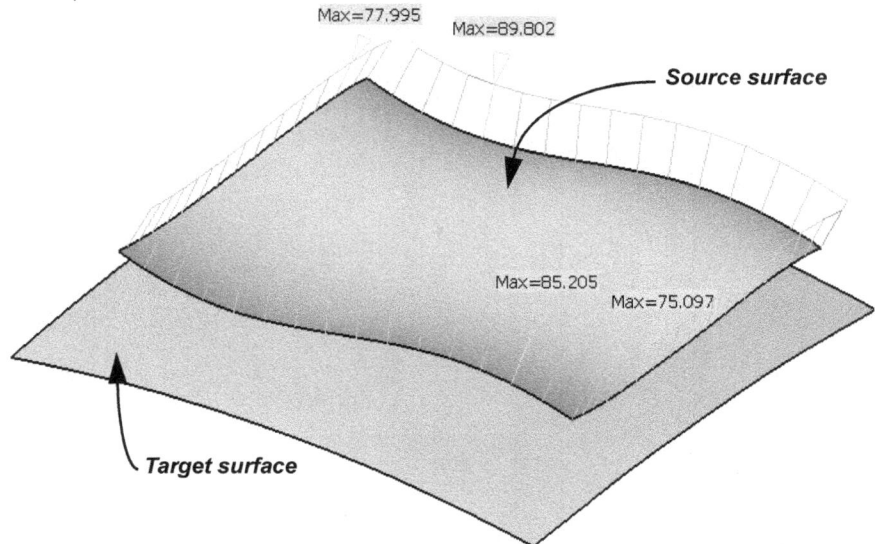

Figure 12–10

General Steps

Use the following general steps to analyze surfaces using the **Connect Checker**:

1. Start the Connect Checker.
2. Specify the type of analysis.
3. Specify the type of continuity.
4. Set the Display options.
5. Set the settings.
6. Complete the analysis.

Step 1 - Start the Connect Checker.

Click ![icon] (Connect Checker Analysis) in the Analysis toolbar.

Activate ![icon] (Surface-Surface Connection) in the Connect Checker dialog box as shown in Figure 12–11.

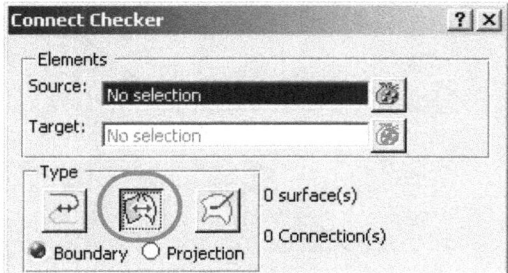

Figure 12–11

Step 2 - Specify the type of analysis.

Select **Boundary** to run a Connection between surfaces analysis, as shown in Figure 12–12.

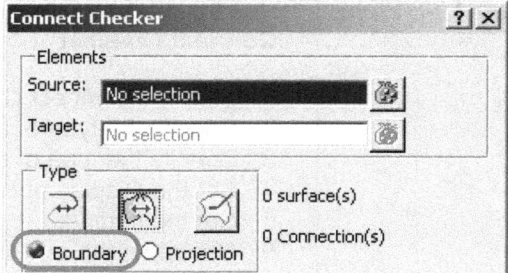

Figure 12–12

![icon] (Internal Edge) can be enabled when the internal edges of the surface(s) must be analyzed.

Connection between surfaces

In Boundary mode, only the Source field is activated.

Set the Maximum and Minimum Gap values, as shown in Figure 12–13. If the existing gap between the surfaces is not between the Maximum and Minimum Gap values, the analysis result does not display.

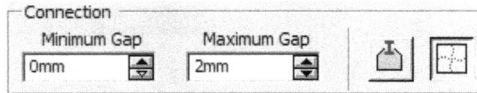

Figure 12–13

Select the surface(s) to analyze from the display, as shown in Figure 12–14, or specification tree. To select more than one surface, press and hold <Ctrl>, then select the surfaces.

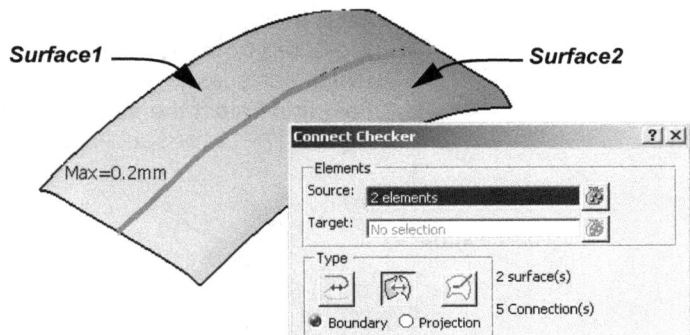

Figure 12–14

Projection on a surface

Select **Projection** to run a Projection on a surface analysis, as shown in Figure 12–15.

Figure 12–15

Set the Maximum Gap value greater than the current distance value between the surfaces, as shown in Figure 12–16.

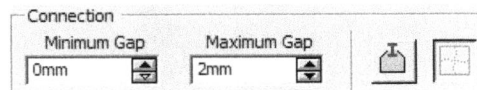

Figure 12–16

The Maximum Gap value should not be set larger than the smallest surface.

If the distance between the surfaces is greater than the Maximum Gap value, or the gap between the surfaces is smaller than the Minimum Gap value, an Information dialog box opens, as shown in Figure 12–17.

Use 🖱 *(Ignore Small Free Edges) to ignore the connections involving free edges of length less than the maximum gap specified.*

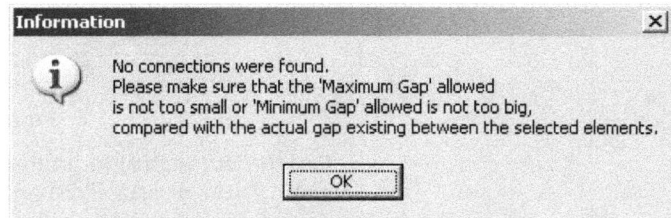

Figure 12–17

Click in the *Source* field, and select the surface(s) to be projected from the display or specification tree. To specify on which surfaces to project Source surface(s), click in the *Target* field and select the surface(s) from the display, as shown in Figure 12–18, or specification tree.

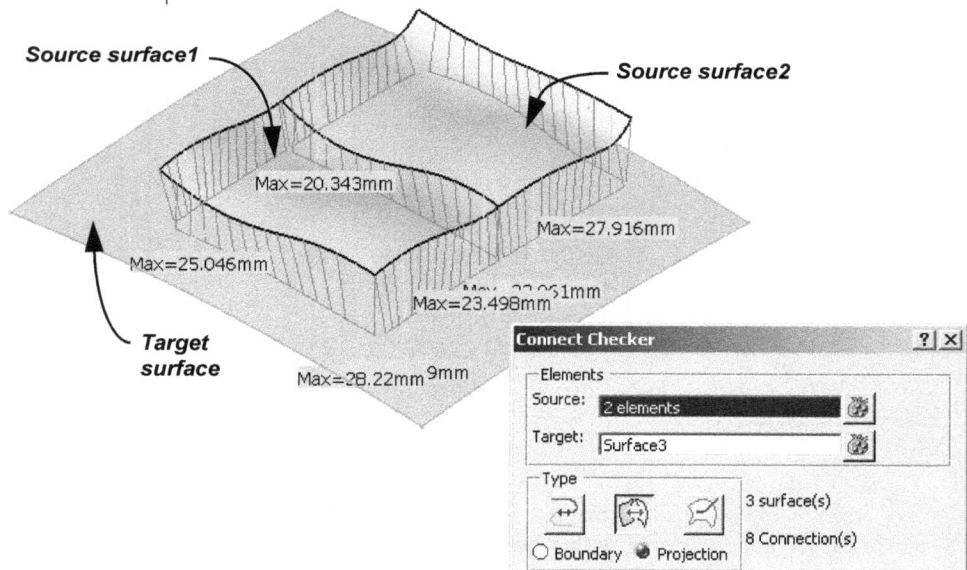

Figure 12–18

Step 3 - Specify the type of continuity.

You can check five different types of connections between
surfaces. The connection types are described in the table below.
You can check five different types of connections between
surfaces, as shown in Figure 12–19. The connection types are
described below. When a different type of connection is selected,
the display dynamically updates the analysis information on the
model.

Icon	Connection Type	
◈	Overlap Defect	
G0	G0 Continuity	
G1	G1 Continuity	Quick ∣ Full ∣ ◈ G0 > 0.1mm G2 > 0.5 G1 > 0.05deg G3 > 0.05deg
G2	G2 Continuity	
G3	G3 Continuity	

The analysis information is also displayed in the *Max Deviation*
area in the Connect Checker dialog box, as shown in
Figure 12–19.

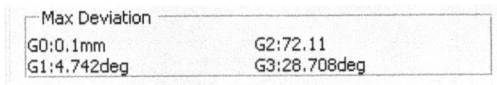

```
Max Deviation
G0:0.1mm          G2:72.11
G1:4.742deg       G3:28.708deg
```

Figure 12–19

Step 4 - Set the Display options.

The display options are described as follows:

Icon		Description
Display		Specify how to visualize the analysis result on the model.
Limited Color Scale		Displays the results on the model in up to four different colors.
Full Color Scale		Displays the results on the model in up to ten different colors.
Comb		Displays the continuity conditions using porcupines.
Envelope		Displays the inflection points of the curve.
Amplitude		Specify the size of the comb (porcupines) by entering a value.
Automatic		Automatically defines the density of the comb depending the size of the model.
Discretization		Specify the density of the comb.
Light		The number of spikes is **5**.
Coarse		The number of spikes is **15**.
Medium		The number of spikes is **30**.
Fine		The number of spikes is **45**.
Information		In the *Discretization* area, you can display the maximum and minimum analysis results on the model.

Minimum		Displays the minimum analysis result.
Maximum		Displays the maximum analysis result.

Step 5 - Complete the analysis.

Click **OK** to complete the analysis. A Connect Checker Analysis feature is added to the specification tree, as shown in Figure 12–20.

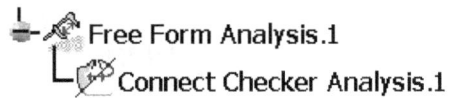

Figure 12–20

12.4 Porcupine Curvature

The Porcupine Curvature analysis is a valuable tool for determining the curvature condition or radius size of selected surface features. The most common display setting for this tool is **Comb**. An analysis using the Comb display gives you an idea of the surface condition very quickly.

General Steps

Use the following general steps to analyze surfaces using a Porcupine Curvature analysis:

1. Select surface feature(s).
2. Start the Porcupine Curvature.
3. Specify the type of analysis.
4. Set display options.
5. Complete the analysis.

Step 1 - Select surface feature(s).

Select a Join feature consisting of surface features or select two or more individual surface features using <Ctrl>.

Step 2 - Start the Porcupine Curvature.

Click ![icon] (Porcupine Curvature Analysis) in the Analysis toolbar. The Porcupine Curvature dialog box opens as shown in Figure 12–21.

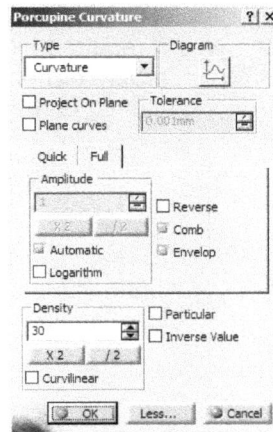

Figure 12–21

Step 3 - Specify the type of analysis.

The two types of analysis are **Curvature** and **Radius**. Select the type in the Type drop-down list, as shown in Figure 12–22.

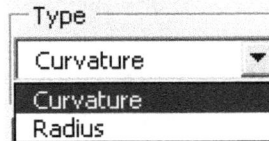

Figure 12–22

Step 4 - Set display options.

Various options to control Density and Amplitude can be selected in the Curvature Analysis dialog box, as shown in Figure 12–23.

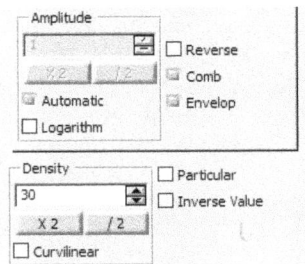

Figure 12–23

If required, you can click ⊞ (Diagram) to view each curve in a graph format, as shown in Figure 12–24. The cross-hair can be moved to report information at a specific point.

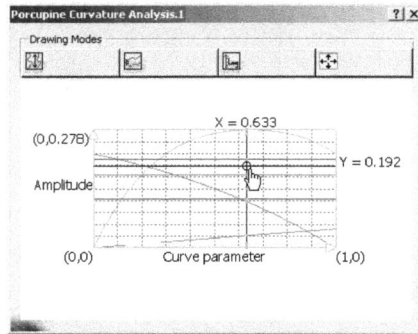

Figure 12–24

Step 5 - Complete the analysis.

Click **OK** to complete the analysis. A Porcupine Curvature analysis is shown in Figure 12–25. The visual display of the Comb display gives you information regarding the curvature condition of the selected surface.

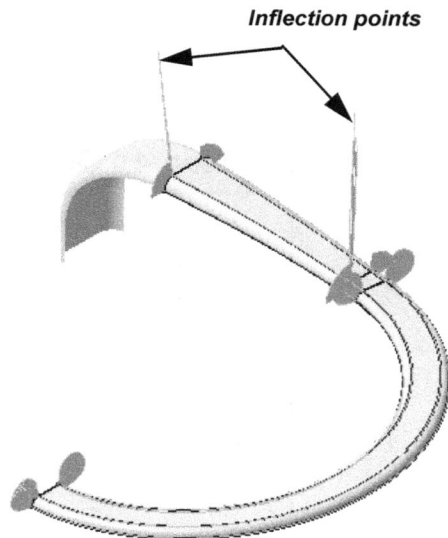

Figure 12–25

12.5 Surfacic Curvature Analysis

The Surfacic Curvature analysis analyzes the curvature of a surface feature. The analysis is based on color-coded areas, which indicate values of curvature within a specified range.

General Steps

Use the following general steps to analyze surface features using Surfacic Curvature analysis:

1. Set error display options.
2. Select surface feature(s).
3. Start the Surfacic Curvature analysis.
4. Specify the type of analysis.
5. Set Maximum and Minimum values.
6. Set display options.
7. Complete the analysis.

Step 1 - Set error display options.

Before starting the analysis, set 3D accuracy by clicking **Tools> Options**. Select **Display** in the tree on the right and select the *Performances* tab. Select **Fixed** and enter **0.01**, as shown in Figure 12–26.

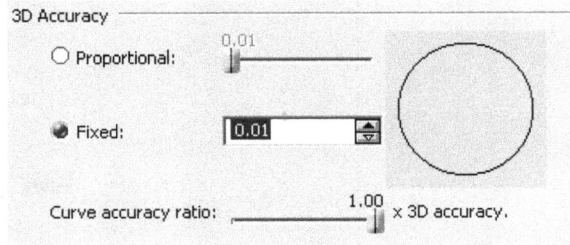

Figure 12–26

Select **View>Render Style>Customize view** and select **Material**, as shown in Figure 12–27.

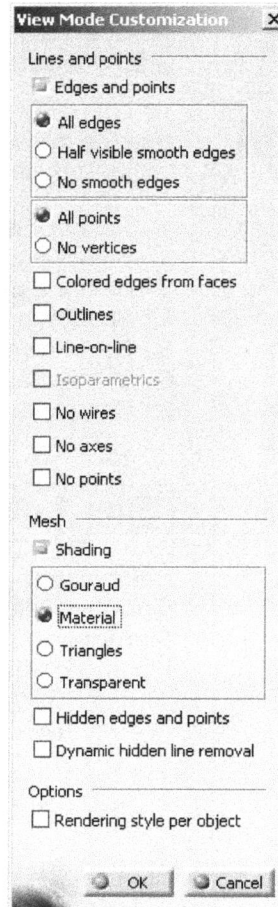

Figure 12–27

The **Material** view mode must be applied for the analysis results to be displayed.

Step 2 - Select surface feature(s).

Select a Join feature consisting of surface features or an individual surface feature. You can also select two or more surface features using <Ctrl>.

Step 3 - Start the Surfacic Curvature analysis.

Click ![icon] (Surfacic Curvature Analysis) in the Analysis toolbar. The Surfacic curvature dialog box opens as shown in Figure 12–28.

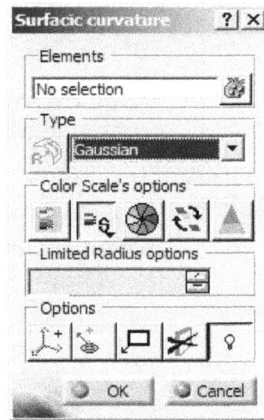

Figure 12–28

Step 4 - Specify the type of analysis.

Specify the type of curvature analysis by selecting an option in the drop-down list, as shown in Figure 12–29.

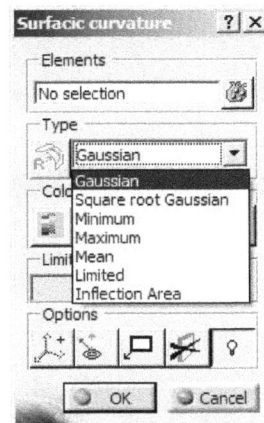

Figure 12–29

A **Gaussian** curvature analysis displays the maximum and minimum curvature for any given point on the surface, as shown in Figure 12–30.

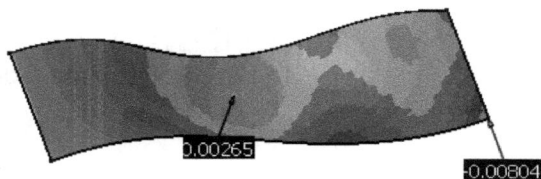

Figure 12–30

A **Square root Gaussian** curvature analysis displays the square root of the maximum and minimum curvature for any given point on the surface.

A **Minimum** curvature analysis displays the area where minimum curvature exists, as shown in Figure 12–31.

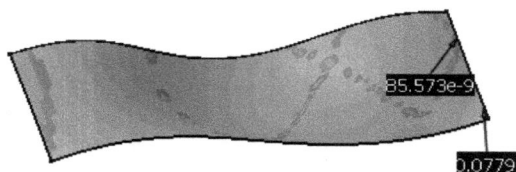

Figure 12–31

A **Maximum** curvature analysis displays the area where maximum curvature exists, as shown in Figure 12–32.

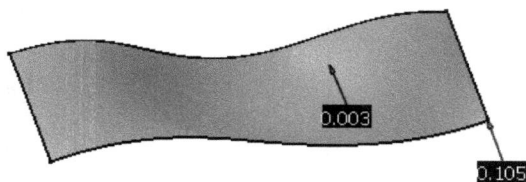

Figure 12–32

A **Mean** curvature analysis displays the value equal to (Minimum curvature + Maximum curvature) / 2. Both the mean curvature and radius values can be displayed.

A **Limited** curvature analysis uses a value entered in the *Limited Radius options* field to display the areas matching that value, as shown in Figure 12–33.

Figure 12–33

An Inflection Area curvature analysis identifies areas of curvature with the same orientation, as shown in Figure 12–34.

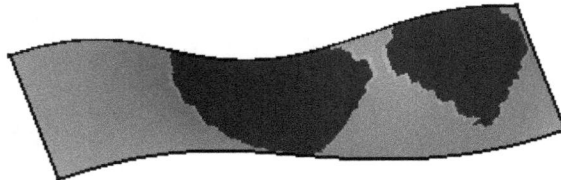

Figure 12–34

Step 5 - Set Maximum and Minimum values.

Unless otherwise specified, CATIA uses a range of system-defined values to analyze the surface. You can modify the range to use the maximum and minimum curvature values relative to the surface being analyzed. Setting the maximum and minimum values ensures that the range between these values correctly matches the degree of curvature of the model, producing an accurate analysis.

To set the maximum value, click **Use Min Max** or right-click on the Max value and select **Use Max**, as shown in Figure 12–35. Use the same procedure to set the Minimum value.

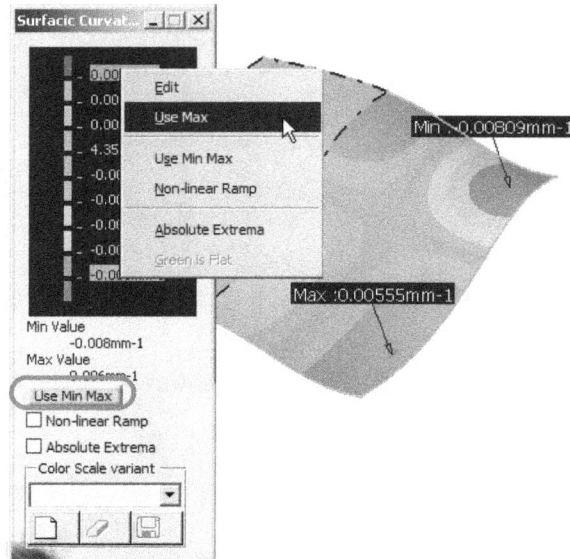

Figure 12–35

Linear interpolation enables the prediction of an unknown value between two particular values, assuming that the rate of change is constant.

Colors can also be changed by right-clicking and selecting **Edit**, as shown in Figure 12–36. A specific color specifies a specific curvature value. The **Unfreeze** option enables a linear interpolation to be performed between non-defined colors.

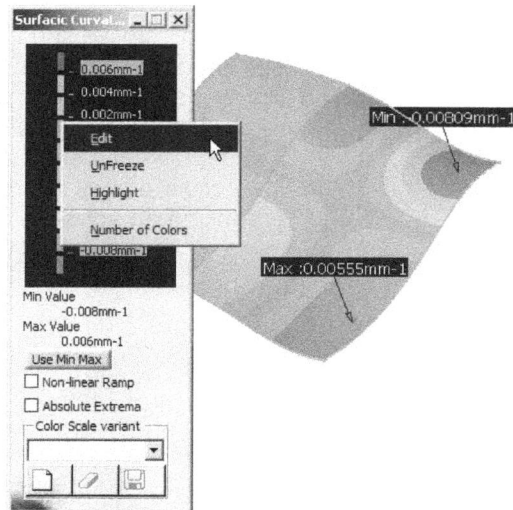

Figure 12–36

The color editor is shown in Figure 12–37.

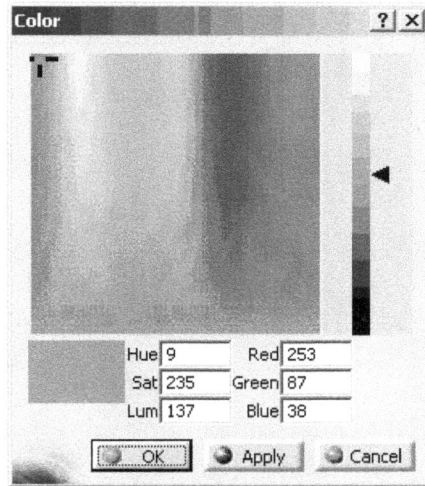

Figure 12–37

Step 6 - Set display options.

The *Color Scale's options* and *Options* areas in the Surfacic Curvature dialog box enables you to toggle off the color scale, show values on the fly, and display 3D minimum and maximum values. The options are described as follows:

Icon	Description
(Hide/Show color scale)	Enables you to display the Surfacic Curvature Analysis dialog box associated with the current analysis.
(Color Scale's size)	Enables you to change the scale of colors in the Surfacic Curvature Analysis dialog box.
(Reset colors)	Enables you to reset the colors of the color scale.
(Inverse colors)	Enables you to inverse the colors of the color scale.
(Sharp mode)	Enables to switch from the **Gradient** mode (default mode) to view the sharp interpolation of colors on the curvature of the surface.

(Positive only)	Enables you to get analysis values as positive values, available with **Gaussian**, **Minimum** and **Maximum** analysis types only.
(On the Fly)	The **On The Fly** option enables you to display the curvature value anywhere the cursor displays over the geometry. To create a point at the currently displayed value location, right-click (this locks the current value), then right-click again on the current value. You can then select one of the following options: **Keep Point, Keep Min Point, Keep Max Point**. For example, you might want to create a point at the minimum point of curvature, as shown below.

(Show Min/Max)	Enables you to locate the minimum and maximum values for the selected analysis type, except for **Inflection Area** analysis type.
(No Highlight)	Enables you to disable the **Highlight faces and edges** option in **Tools>Options>General> Display>Navigation** which highlight of the geometry selection.
(Light Source)	Enables you to turn the light source.

Step 7 - Complete the analysis.

Click **OK** to complete the analysis. A surface Surfacic Curvature Analysis feature is added to the specification tree, as shown in Figure 12–38.

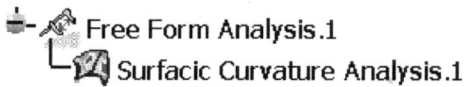

Figure 12–38

12.6 Temporary Analysis

You can perform a temporary analysis of the resulting geometry during the creation of an Offset feature. The system adds the Connect Checker or Curve Connect Checker analysis to the specification tree only while the Offset Surface Definition dialog box is open. Once closed, the Temporary Analysis node is removed.

How To: Run a Temporary Analysis During the Creation or Modification of an Offset Surface Feature

1. Define an offset surface and preview the result.

2. Click ![icon] (Temporary Analysis Mode) in the Tools toolbar to indicate that the analysis that is performed is temporary. If Temporary Analysis Mode is not enabled, the analysis remains in the specification tree after the offset surface is completed.

3. Click ![icon] (Connect Checker) in the Analysis toolbar. The system adds a Temporary Analysis node to the specification tree, as shown in Figure 12–39.

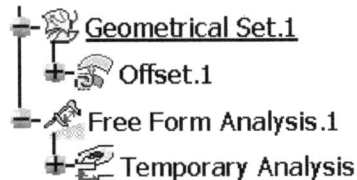

Figure 12–39

4. Complete the analysis and the Offset feature. The analysis is removed from the tree once the Offset Surface Definition dialog box is closed, as shown in Figure 12–40.

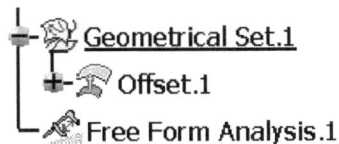

Figure 12–40

You can configure the system to automatically enable a temporary analysis during the creation of an Offset feature, so that you do not need to click 🔲 (Temporary Analysis mode) each time. Select **Tools>Options>Shape>Generative Shape Design**, select the *General* tab, and select **Stacked analysis default behavior set as temporary**, as shown in Figure 12–41.

Figure 12–41

12.7 Repairing Surface Geometry

The result of a Connect Checker analysis might indicate that a gap exists. The **Healing** tool can be used to repair the selected surface features.

Healing surfaces fill any gaps between selected surface geometry. This operation is useful when working with imported geometry, such as *.IGS files.

The ends of two swept surface features that do not match result in a gap, as shown in Figure 12–42.

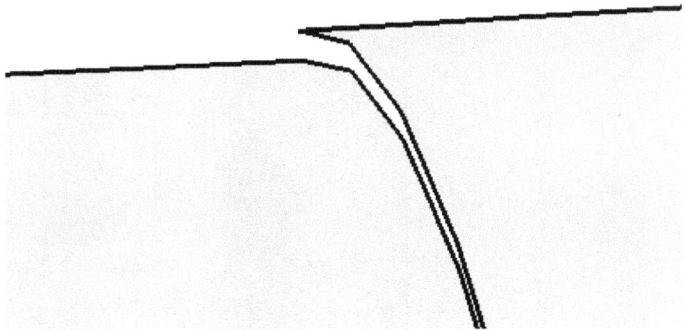

Figure 12–42

The **Healing** operation has been completed on the two surfaces, shown in Figure 12–43. The gap has been eliminated.

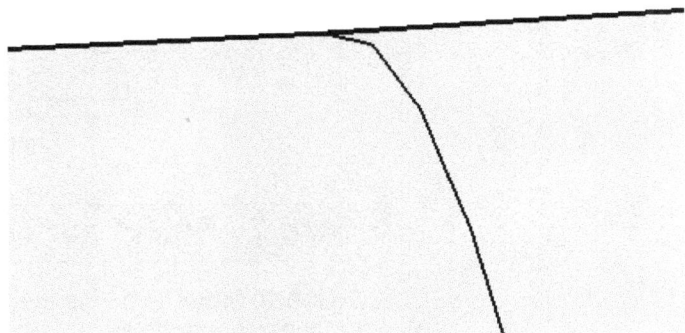

Figure 12–43

General Steps

Use the following general steps to repair gaps in geometry:

1. Start the Healing operation.
2. Select surface features to heal.
3. Specify parameters.
4. Define additional options, as required.
5. Complete the analysis.

Step 1 - Start the Healing operation.

Click (Healing) in the Operations or Join-Healing toolbar. The Healing Definition dialog box opens as shown in Figure 12–44.

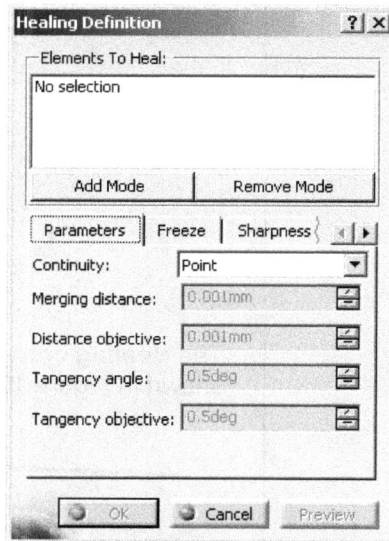

Figure 12–44

Step 2 - Select surface features to heal.

Click **Add Mode** to define the surfaces to heal and select the surfaces on the model.

Step 3 - Specify parameters.

The options in the *Parameters* tab enable you to assign specific criteria on how to heal the surfaces. The *Parameters* tab is shown in Figure 12–45.

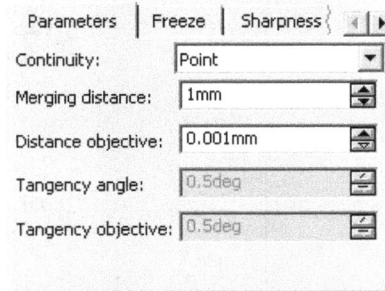

Figure 12–45

The Merging distance parameter identifies the maximum gap between two surfaces that the operation attempts to heal. The Distance objective parameter identifies the maximum allowable gap that the operation can leave between two healed surfaces. The Merging distance and Distance parameters are required values.

The Tangency angle becomes active depending on the selected geometry. The system corrects any deviation below the entered value. The Tangency objective parameter is similar to the Distance objective; it identifies the maximum allowed tangency deviation between healed surfaces. The default range is between 0.1 and 2.0 degrees.

Step 4 - Define additional options, as required.

Click **OK** to complete the operation. If the operation is successful, the two surfaces are joined and a feature is added to the specification tree, as shown in Figure 12–46.

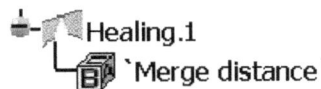

Figure 12–46

If the Merge Distance is set too small relative to the gaps, the system still creates a Healing feature; however, the Healing feature consists of two elements, as shown in Figure 12–47. To avoid a Multi-Result, increase the merge distance value.

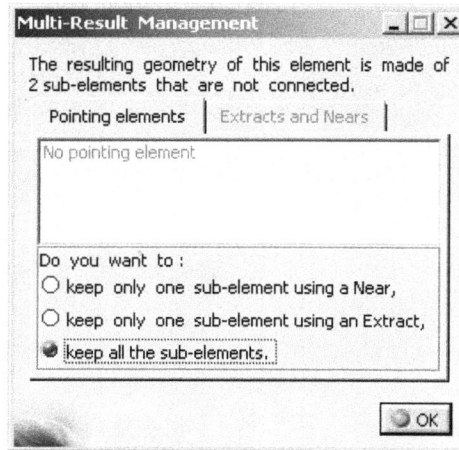

Figure 12–47

Step 5 - Complete the analysis.

Once you finish setting the parameters for the healed feature, you can use the remaining tabs to further define the resulting feature.

Freeze Tab

The *Freeze* tab enables you to freeze elements of a surface that is being healed. Frozen elements are not affected by the Healing operation; therefore, they remain unchanged. The *Freeze* tab displays as shown in Figure 12–48.

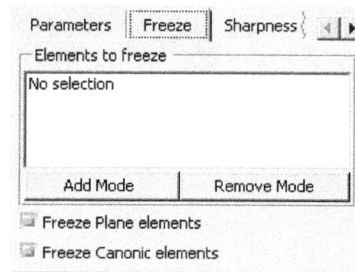

Figure 12–48

Sharpness Tab

If the Tangent mode is active, the *Sharpness* tab can be used to select one or more edges to remain sharp. The *Sharpness angle* field enables you to define an angle. Entering an angle is recommended if your intent is to create an offset surface from the resulting geometry. The angle controls the degree of tangency at a selected boundary. If the surface is offset, the angle might need to be changed to enable the offset geometry to be created. The *Sharpness* tab displays as shown in Figure 12–49.

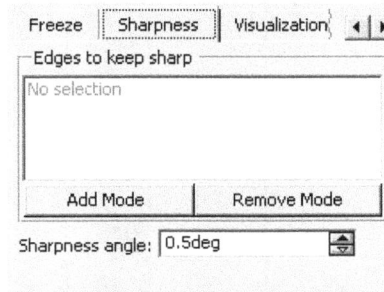

Figure 12–49

Visualization Tab

The *Visualization* tab enables you to simplify the display of information. This option is useful when a large number of messages display and only certain messages are required. If multiple solutions are possible, use the **Display information sequentially** option and toggle through the different solutions. The **Display information interactively** option enables you to display local information by holding the cursor over a particular area of the model. The *Visualization* tab displays as shown in Figure 12–50.

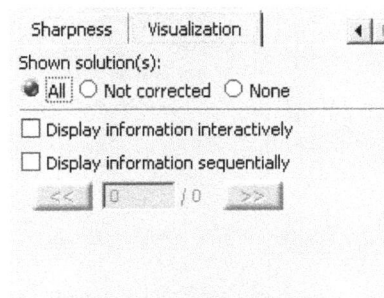

Figure 12–50

12.8 Element Direction and Inversion

Curve/Surface Orientation

Curves and surfaces have a geometric orientation. The orientation of a curve can be thought of as a flow direction. It is similar to fluid flow in a pipe or the flow of electrical current in a wire. The orientation of a surface is defined by the normal vector pointing in or out of the surface as shown in Figure 12–51.

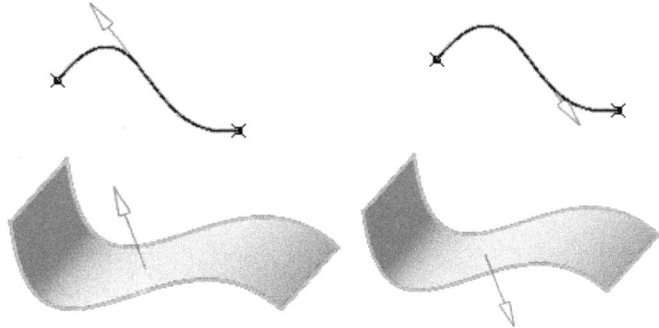

Figure 12–51

A curve or surface's orientation is sometimes used to define downstream features. Some features that are based on the orientation of its parent include: Pt on Curve, Parallel, Offset, and Shape Fillet. An example of Pt on Curve is shown in Figure 12–52.

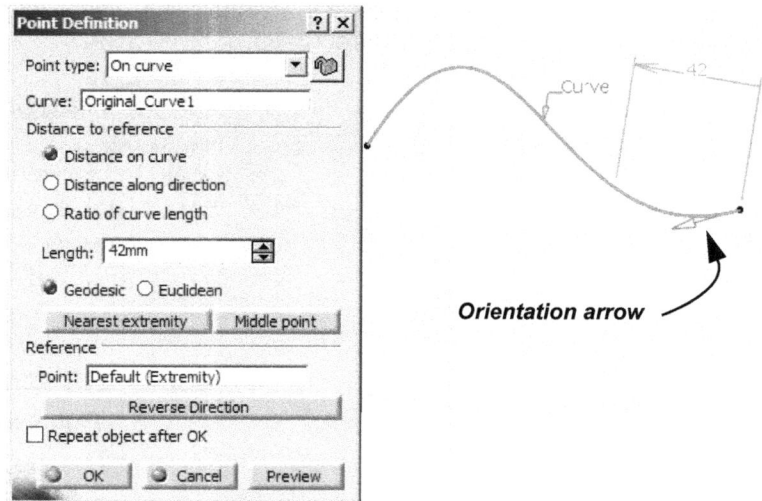

Figure 12–52

Identification

To identify the orientation of a feature, create a Join of the feature and edit it. The orientation of the feature is identified by a direction arrow. When editing the Join, you can also invert the orientation by selecting the arrow. An example of identifying a curve's orientation using a Join feature and its inverted orientation is shown in Figure 12–53.

Figure 12–53

Invert Orientation

Inverting a feature's orientation can occur automatically during a **Replace** operation, or an Inverse feature can be created independently by clicking **Insert>Operations>Invert Orientation**.

The result is the creation of an Inverse feature that is added to the specification tree, as shown in Figure 12–54.

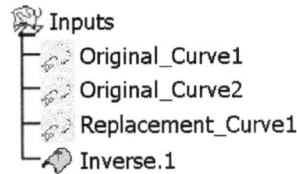

Inputs
- Original_Curve1
- Original_Curve2
- Replacement_Curve1
- Inverse.1

Figure 12–54

The Inverse feature can be modified, enabling the orientation to be reset to the original, by clicking **Reset Initial** in the Invert Definition dialog box, as shown in Figure 12–55.

Invert Definition ?|X|

To Invert: Replacement_Curve1

Reset Initial

OK   Cancel   Preview

Figure 12–55

Downstream Effects

If a feature's orientation is reversed from its originally design intent, downstream features can be affected. Surfaces can fold in on themselves and feature failure often occurs.

You can use an Inverse feature when designing a PowerCopy. This enables you to easily invert the orientation of an input after instantiation.

12.9 Tips for Rebuilding Geometry

Sometimes the healing operation cannot fix the geometry for various reasons. If the gap between the surfaces is larger than the merging distance, the Healing operation cannot repair and join the geometry. Also, if the surfaces are tangency discontinuous greater than the specified tangency angle, the Healing operation cannot fix the geometry. In this case, repairing the geometry is not effective. You have to rebuild the geometry manually.

Considerations when rebuilding geometry:

- Bad curve geometry creates bad surface geometry. Discontinuities in a curve display in the surface made from the curve.

- The Porcupine curvature analysis gives an in-depth visual display of the quality of the curve or surface.

  - Inflection points shown in a Porcupine curvature analysis show a direction change in curvature.
  - The presence of many inflection points in the analysis shows poor curve quality.

- Extract curves or points to use as references in rebuilding geometry.

- Determine the continuity required for the model.

Commonly used tools when rebuilding geometry:

- Extract

- Boundary

- Fill

- Blend

- Untrim

- Disassemble

- Invert Orientation

Practice 12a	# Distance Analysis

Practice Objectives

- Use Join operation to check surface continuity.
- Use analysis tool to check for surface gaps.

In this practice, you will work with a model that was imported into CATIA V5 from CATIA V4. The model displays as a number of individual surfaces in CATIA. It might contain gaps that prevent the application from creating a solid. You will use analysis techniques to locate these gaps and resolve them using the **Join** tool. The completed model is shown in Figure 12–56.

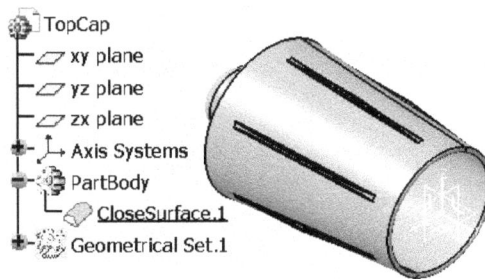

Figure 12–56

Task 1 - Open a part file.

1. Open **MarkerCap.CATPart**. The part displays as shown in Figure 12–57.

Figure 12–57

2. The PartBody does not contain any features. Expand **Geometrical Set.1**. The model consists of 130 separate isolated surfaces.

Task 2 - Join all surfaces.

In this task, you will use the **Join** tool to investigate the group of surfaces. You will first try to join all surfaces with the **Check connexity** option enabled to confirm whether or not the group of surfaces contains gaps.

1. Preselect all surface features by selecting **Geometrical Set.1** in the specification tree and clicking [icon]. The Join dialog box opens as shown in Figure 12–58.

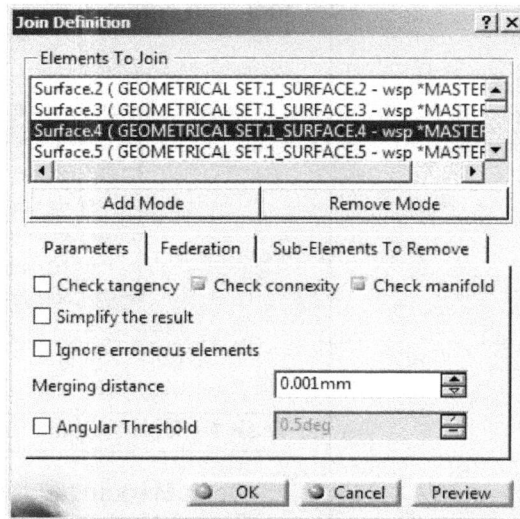

Figure 12–58

2. Click **Preview**. The Error message dialog box shown in Figure 12–59 displays, indicating that the join results in two separate domains. This confirms that a gap is present in the group of surfaces.

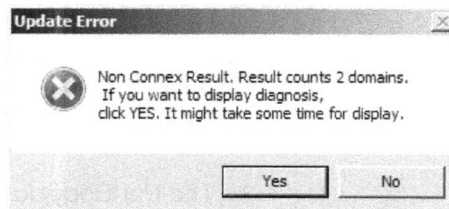

Figure 12–59

3. Click **Yes**. The Connexity error displays on the model as shown in Figure 12–60.

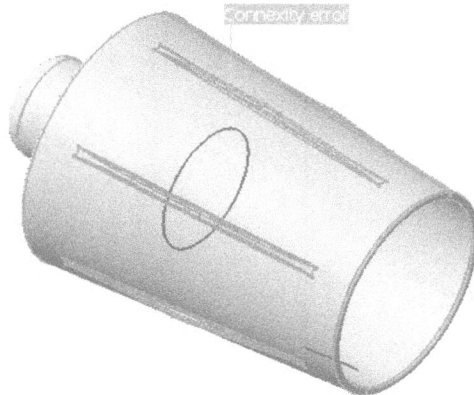

Figure 12–60

Task 3 - Change join parameters.

In this task, you will use the properties of the **Join** tool to locate the gap in the surfaces. By clearing the **Check connexity** option, the system will create the join regardless of any gaps. The **Join** tool will also highlight any boundaries of the join. This enables you to locate the gap in the surfaces.

1. Clear the **Check connexity** option in the Join dialog box, as shown in Figure 12–61.

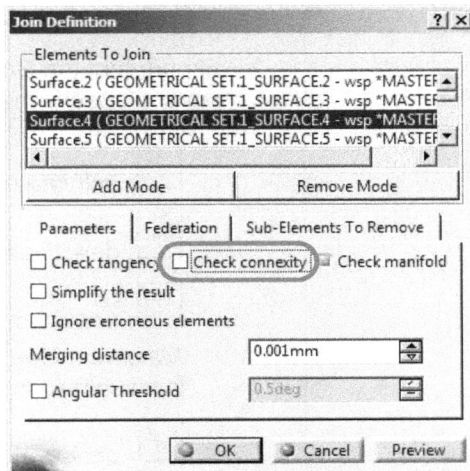

Figure 12–61

2. Click **Preview**. The preview displays as shown in Figure 12–62.

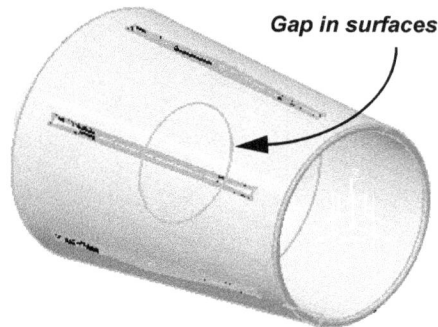

Gap in surfaces

Figure 12–62

Design Considerations

With default CATSettings, the boundary or gap is highlighted with a green edge, as indicated in Figure 12–62. You have located the gap in the surfaces. In the next task, you will use the **Analysis** tools to determine the size of the gap. For now, you do not need the **Join** operation and can cancel it.

3. Cancel the **Join** operation.

Task 4 - Perform a distance analysis.

1. Click [icon] (Connect Checker Analysis), and then click [icon] (Surface-Surface Connection).

2. Ensure that the **Boundary** option is activated. Select the *Full* tab and specify the following:

- [icon]: activated

- [icon]: deactivated

- [icon]: activated

- *Maximum Gap:* **0.05mm** (Any gap smaller than this value is visualized in the model.)

- [icon]: deactivated

- [icon]: deactivated

3. Select **Geometrical Set.1** from the specification tree. The model displays as shown in Figure 12–63.

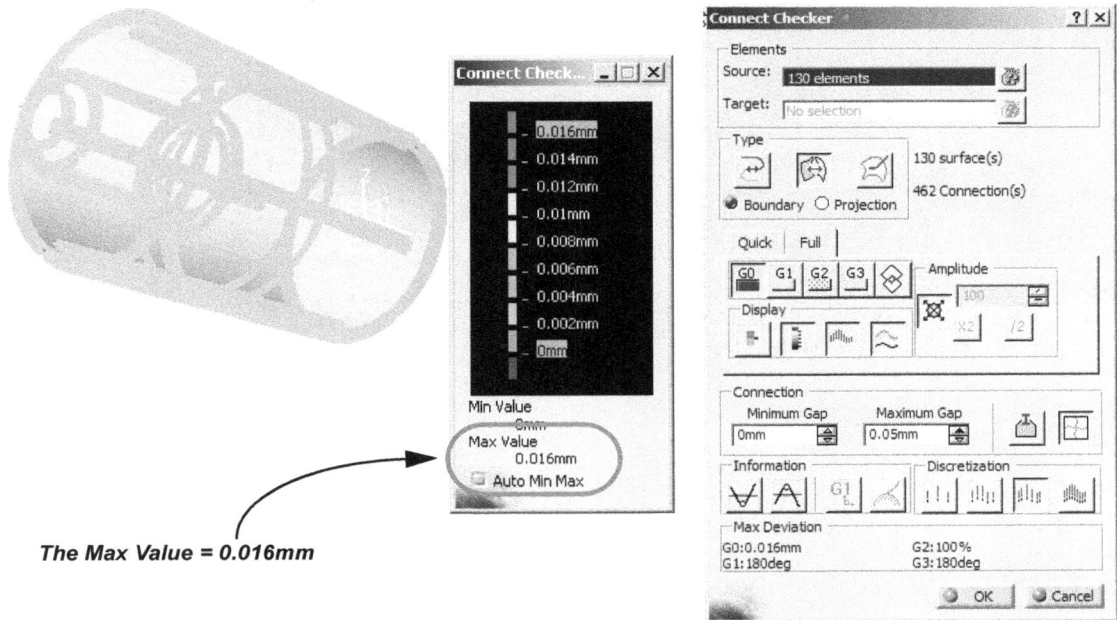

The Max Value = 0.016mm

Figure 12–63

4. Select **Auto Min Max**, as shown in Figure 12–63.

5. The G0 analysis reports a maximum gap of 0.016mm. Click Cancel from the Connect Checker dialog box.

Task 5 - Perform a Join operation.

In this task, you will perform a Join operation on the entire surface model. This time you will change the merging distance so that the join will heal gaps up to 0.02mm in size.

1. Select **Geometrical Set.1** and click .

2. Make the following change as shown in Figure 12–64:

- Merging distance: **0.02mm**

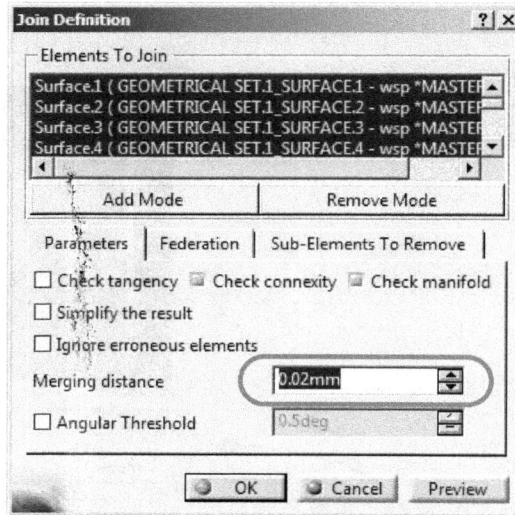

Figure 12–64

3. Click **Preview**. The **Join** operation does not result in two domains because the Merging distance parameter is set higher than the largest gap distance.

4. Click **OK** to complete the join.

Task 6 - Create solid geometry.

1. Activate the Part Design workbench.

2. Set PartBody to be the work object.

3. Click 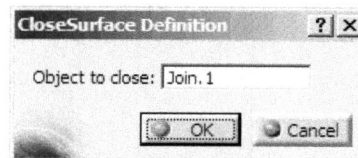 (Close) and select **Join.1**, as shown in Figure 12–65.

Figure 12–65

4. Click **OK**.

5. Hide **Geometrical Set.1**. The completed solid model displays as shown in Figure 12–66.

Figure 12–66

6. Save the model and close the file.

Practice 12b | Problem Pipe

Practice Objectives

- Use the Join operation to identify tangency errors.
- Use Connect Checker to analyze tangency conditions.

In this practice, you will use the Join operation to locate problems that prevent a solid from being created from a surface-based model. The errors that you encounter are shown in Figure 12–67.

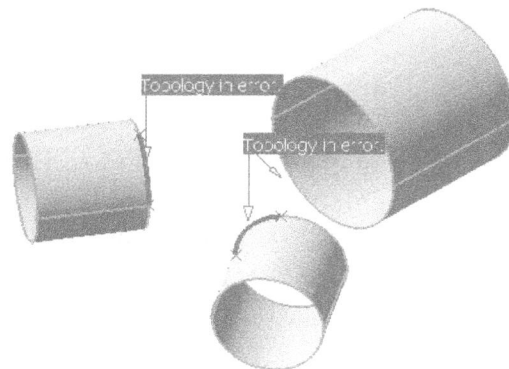

Figure 12–67

Task 1 - Open a part file.

1. Open **ProblemPipe.CATPart**. The part displays as shown in Figure 12–68.

Figure 12–68

2. Ensure that the Part Design workbench is active.

3. Click to create a thick surface with the following specifications, as shown in Figure 12–69:

- *First Offset:* **2mm**
- *Object to offset:* **Join.2**
- If required, click **Reverse Direction** to match the arrows in Figure 12–69.

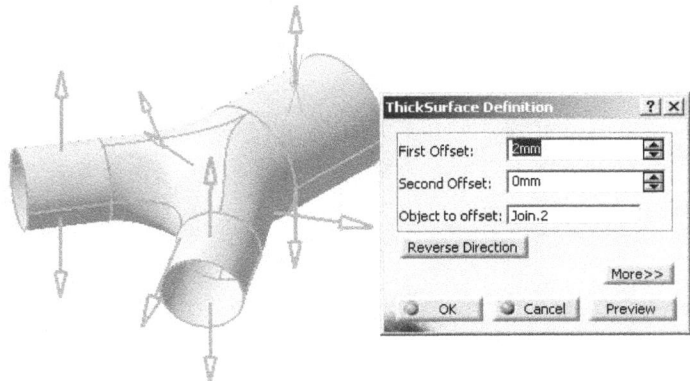

Figure 12–69

4. Click **Preview**. The Error message dialog box opens, as shown in Figure 12–70.

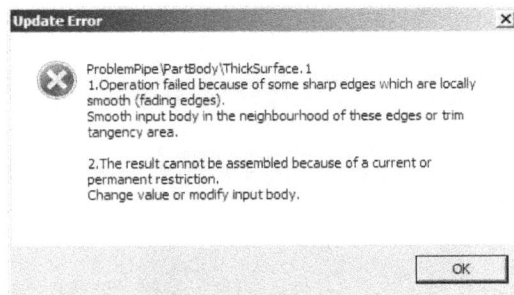

Figure 12–70

Design Considerations

The Error message dialog box opens because offsetting the join surface to generate the solid results in sharp edges in some of the geometry. This is because surface features are not tangent to each other at a shared boundary.

5. Click **OK**.

6. Click **No** in the Feature Definition Error dialog box.

7. Click **Cancel** to cancel the **ThickSurface** command.

Task 2 - Edit Join.2.

In this task, you will use join parameters to check for non-tangent conditions in the part.

1. Show the **OriginalSurfaces** geometrical set.

2. Edit Join.2 in the **JoinedSurfaces** geometrical set and make the following change, as shown in Figure 12–71:

   • Select **Check tangency**.

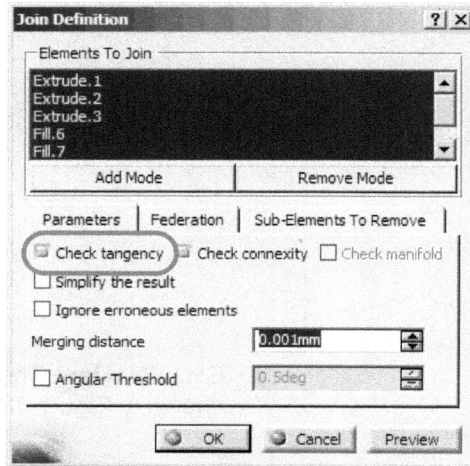

Figure 12–71

3. Click **Preview**.

Design Considerations

The Error message dialog box opens, indicating that a non-continuous tangent condition exists, as shown in Figure 12–72.

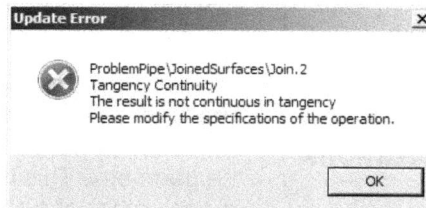

Figure 12–72

4. Click **OK**.

The application indicates the problem areas, as shown in Figure 12–73.

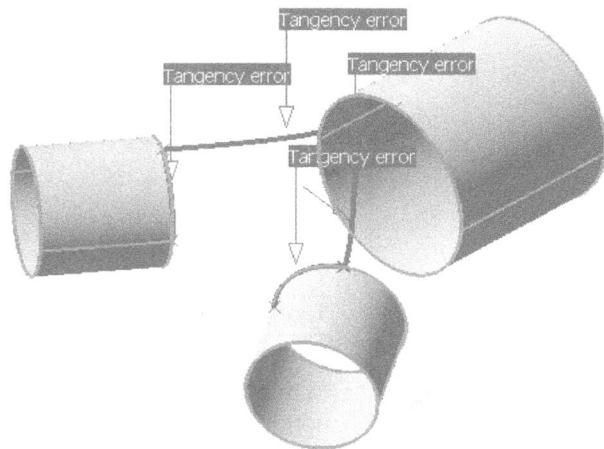

Figure 12–73

5. Click **Cancel** to cancel the join edit.

Task 3 - Edit the native geometry.

---

1. Hide the **JoinedSurfaces** and **OriginalSurfaces** geometrical sets.

2. Show the **NewSurfaces** geometrical set. The part displays as shown in Figure 12–74.

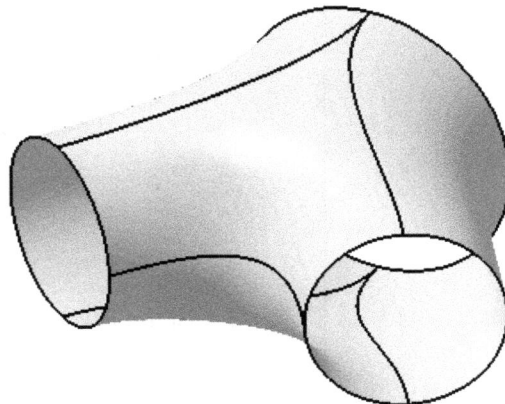

Figure 12–74

3. Show **OriginalSurfaces**. The part displays as shown in Figure 12–75.

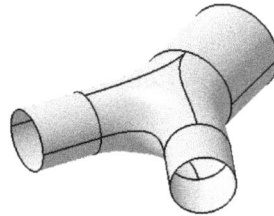

Figure 12–75

Task 4 - Analyze tangency conditions.

Design Considerations

In this task, you will use **Connect Checker** to analyze tangency conditions between selected surface features.

1. Activate the Generative Shape Design workbench.

2. Click (Connect Checker Analysis), and then click (Surface-Surface Connection).

3. Ensure that the **Boundary** option is activated. Select the faces shown in Figure 12–76.

Select these two surfaces

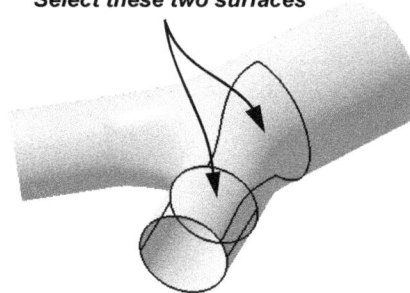

Figure 12–76

4. Select the *Full* tab and specify the following:

- : activated

- : deactivated

- : activated

5. Ensure that the **Auto Min Max** option is selected. The analysis result displays as shown in Figure 12–77.

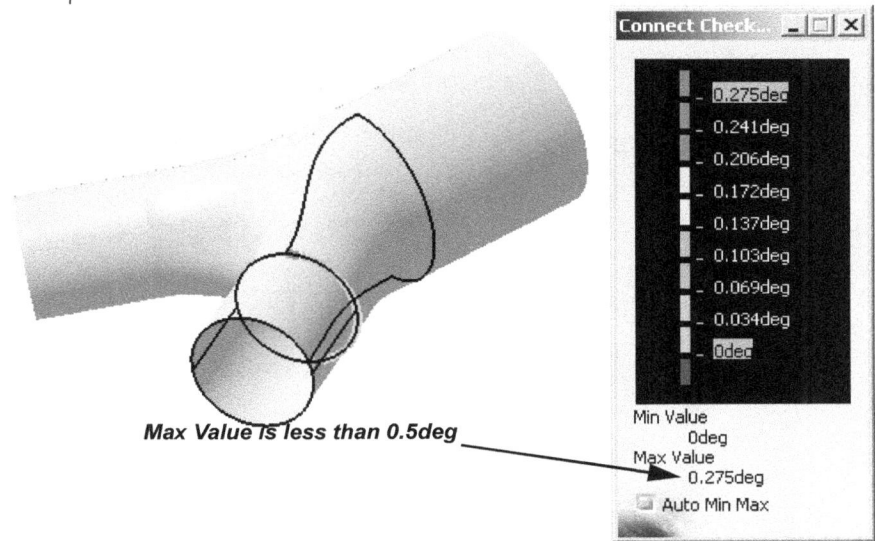

Max Value is less than 0.5deg

Figure 12–77

Design Considerations

Surfaces are considered tangent if the angle between them at a shared boundary is less then 0.5deg; therefore, the Tangency analysis shown in Figure 12–77 reports a tangent condition.

6. Select the two surfaces shown in Figure 12–78 and run a G1 analysis. The *Max Value* is **12.833deg**.

Select these two surfaces

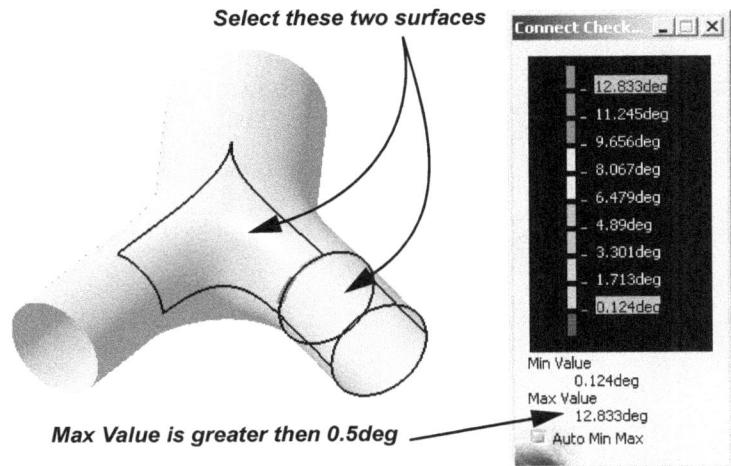

Max Value is greater then 0.5deg

Figure 12–78

7. Click **Cancel**.

Design Considerations

Task 5 - Add tangency support to a surface.

In this task, you will correct the non-tangent problems by editing the native surfaces (surfaces that the Join references) and add support references.

1. Edit **Fill.8** in the **NewSurfaces** geometrical set. The dialog box opens as shown in Figure 12–79.

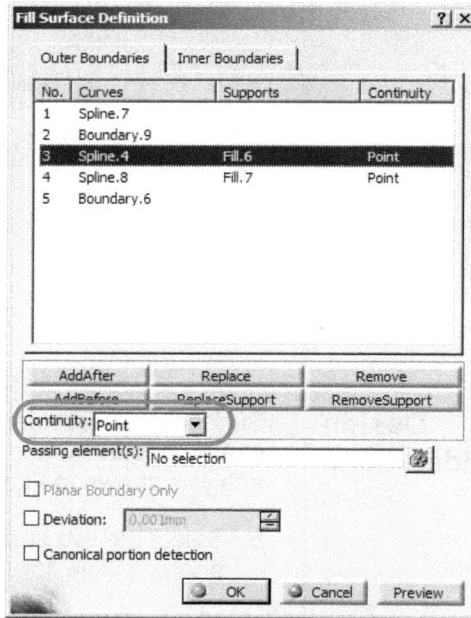

Figure 12–79

2. The Continuity for the supports of the fill surface is currently set to Point.

3. Change the two point continuities to **Tangent**.

4. Add tangency supports for the following curves, as follows:

No	Curve	Support
2	Boundary.9	Extrude.3
5	Boundary.6	Extrude.2

The dialog box should display as shown in Figure 12–80.

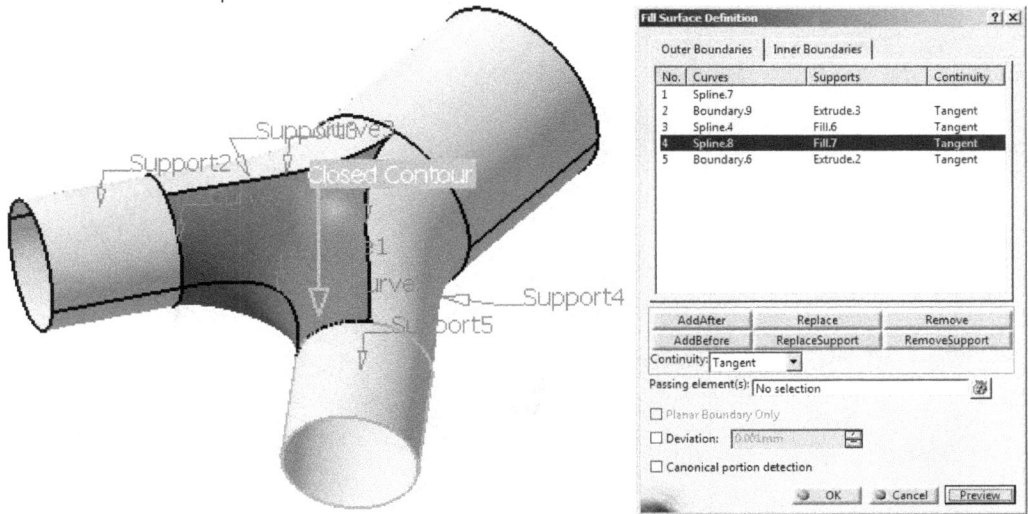

Figure 12–80

5. Click **OK**.

6. Edit **Join.2** and check for tangency, as shown in Figure 12–81.

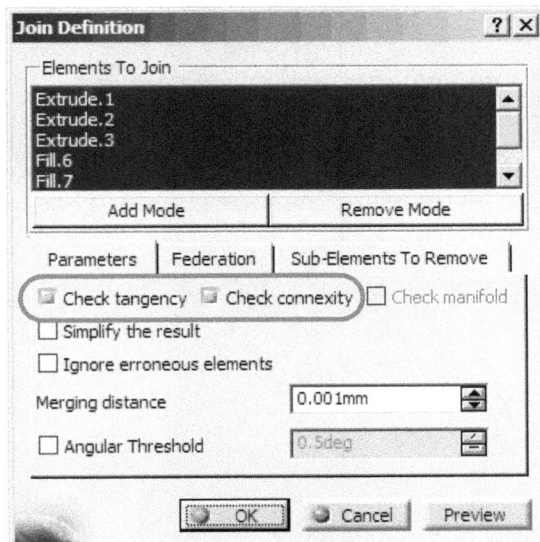

Figure 12–81

7. Show the **JoinedSurface** geometrical set.

8. Create a thick surface feature using the Join.2 surface with an *Offset* of **2mm**, as shown in Figure 12–82.

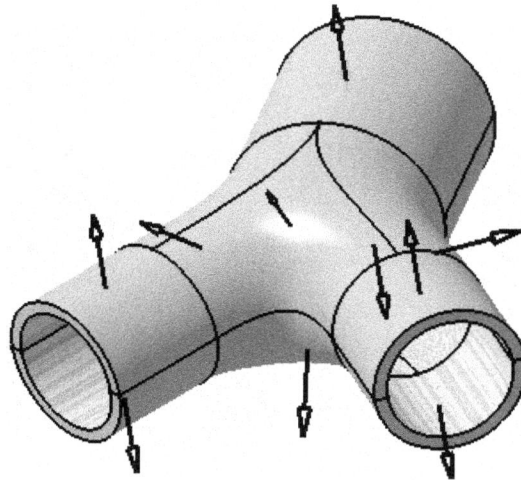

Figure 12–82

9. Save the model and close the file.

Practice 12c

Imported Surface

Practice Objectives

- Analyze imported geometry.
- Heal gaps in the surface model.
- Create solid geometry from an imported surface.

In this practice, you will analyze imported surface geometry to determine the surface quality, and use healing to heal any gaps in the imported data. You will also create a solid part from healed surface geometry. The completed model displays as shown in Figure 12–83.

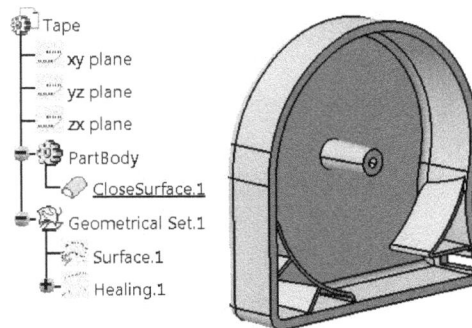

Figure 12–83

Task 1 - Open a part file.

1. Open **MeasureTape.CATPart** and activate the Generative Shape Design workbench. The part displays as shown in Figure 12–84.

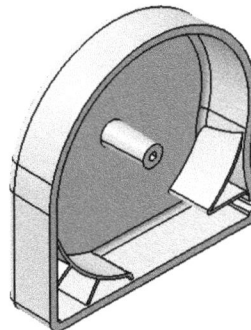

Figure 12–84

Task 2 - Analyze the imported data.

In this task, you investigate the imported geometry to find out the maximum gap in the model.

1. Click ⬚ (Connect Checker Analysis), and then click ⬚ (Surface-Surface Connection).

2. Ensure that the **Boundary** option is activated.

3. Select the *Quick* tab and specify the following:

    *   ⬚ : activated (enter **0.01mm**)
    *   *Minimum Gap:* **0.01mm**
    *   *Maximum Gap:* **0.05mm** (Any gap smaller than this value is visualized in the model.)
    *   ⬚ : activated
    *   ⬚ : activated

4. Select **Surface.1** in the specification tree. The model displays as shown in Figure 12–85.

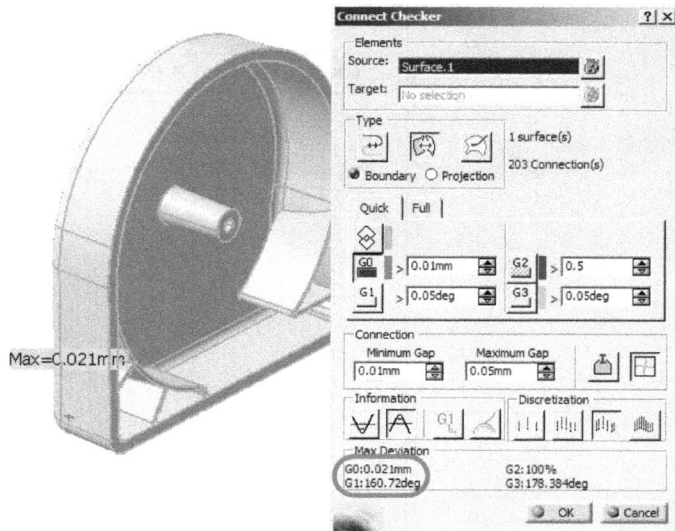

Figure 12–85

5. Click **Cancel**.

Task 3 - Perform a healing operation.

1. Highlight **Surface.1** and click (Healing). Enter **0.03mm** for the *Merging distance*, as shown in Figure 12–86.

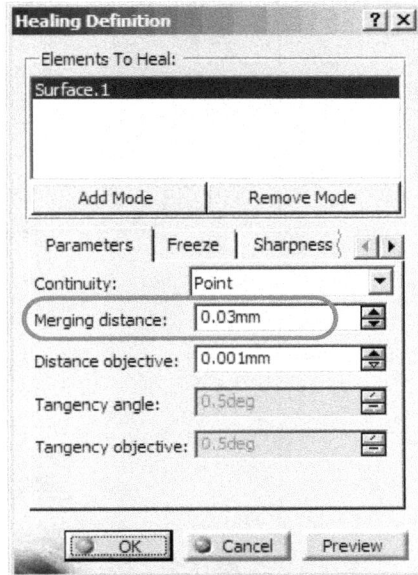

Figure 12–86

2. Click **Preview**. The Warning dialog box opens as shown in Figure 12–87.

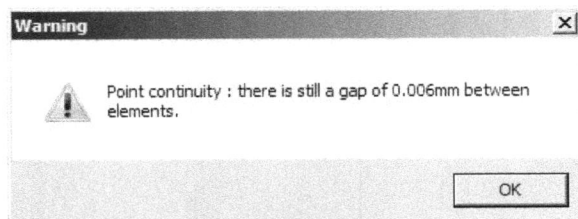

Figure 12–87

3. Click **OK**.

4. Enter the following as shown in Figure 12–88:

   • *Distance objective:* **0.006mm**

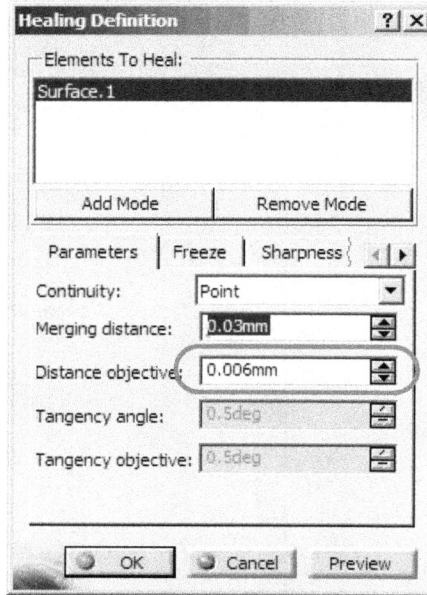

Figure 12–88

5. Click **Preview**. The model displays as shown in Figure 12–89.

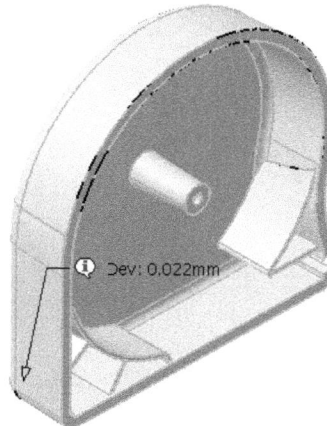

Figure 12–89

6. Click **OK**.

Task 4 - Create solid geometry.

1. Use the resulting healing to create a solid part. The completed part displays as shown in Figure 12–90.

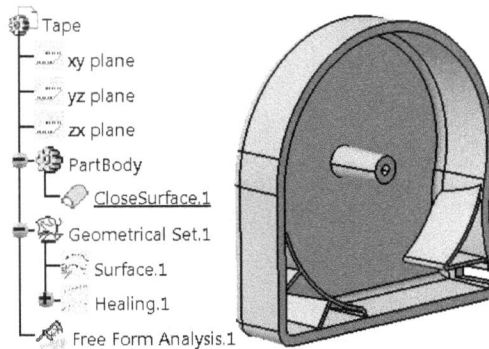

Figure 12–90

2. Save the model and close the file.

Practice 12d | Repairing Surfaces

Practice Objectives

- Analyze curves and surfaces for imperfections.
- Rebuild curves and surfaces.

In this practice, imported surfaces will be analyzed and repaired. This practice will demonstrate that CATIA's repair tools, such as **Curve Smooth** and **Healing**, are not always the best options for improving geometry. Recreating wireframe and surfaces can at times yield better results. The completed model is shown in Figure 12–91.

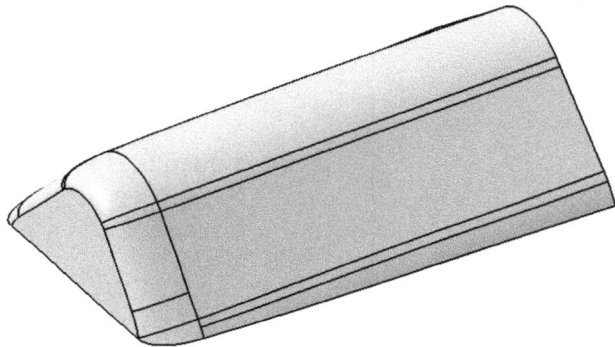

Figure 12–91

Task 1 - Open a part file.

1. Open **Surface-Quality-Start.CATPart**, and activate the GSD workbench. The part displays as shown in Figure 12–92.

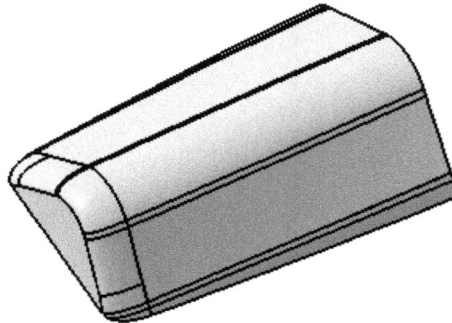

Figure 12–92

A geometrical set named **Iso Surfaces** contains surfaces that have been imported from another model, as shown in Figure 12–93. The red lightening bolt icon by each feature indicates that these surfaces are isolated.

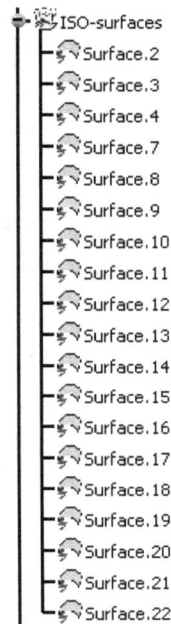

ISO-surfaces
— Surface.2
— Surface.3
— Surface.4
— Surface.7
— Surface.8
— Surface.9
— Surface.10
— Surface.11
— Surface.12
— Surface.13
— Surface.14
— Surface.15
— Surface.16
— Surface.17
— Surface.18
— Surface.19
— Surface.20
— Surface.21
— Surface.22

Figure 12–93

Task 2 - Analyze the surface geometry.

The intent of the model is to have a tangent group of surfaces to join together. The **Connect Checker** enables you to visualize whether the surfaces being analyzed have gaps, are tangent to one another, or posses curvature continuity. Once this information is determined, there are various courses of action to repair the geometry, as required.

1. Click (Connect Checker Analysis), and then click (Surface-Surface Connection).

2. Ensure that the **Boundary** option is activated.

3. Select the *Full* tab and specify the following:

- ▤ : activated

- ⬛ : deactivated

- 𝗚𝟢 : activated

- *Maximum Gap:* **0.5mm** (Any gap smaller than this value is visualized in the model.)

- ⊞ : activated

- ⩔ : deactivated

- ⌂ : deactivated

4. Select the **ISO-surfaces** geometrical set from the specification tree. The model displays as shown in Figure 12–94.

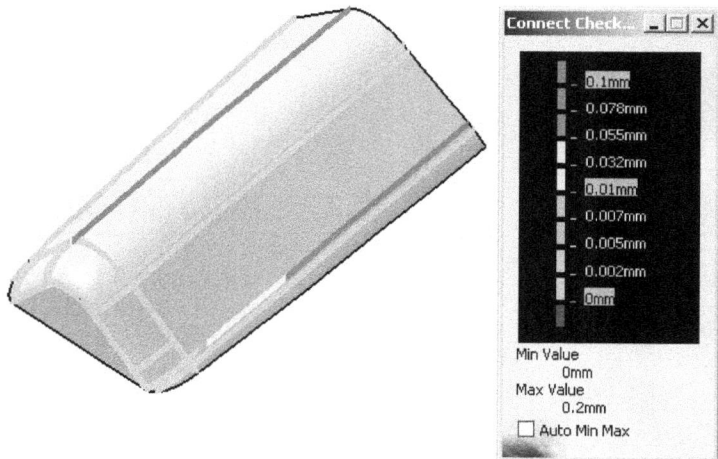

Figure 12–94

Design Considerations

The two areas of geometry that display in green, yellow, red, and pink represent geometry that has a large gap. These areas of geometry need to be repaired or rebuilt.

5. Complete the analysis. A new branch called **Free Form analysis.1** is added to the specification tree. Under this branch is the newly created analysis called **Connect Checker Analysis.1**.

6. Hide **Connect Checker Analysis.1**. You know where the problematic areas are based on the color coding from the analysis. Based on this, the surfaces and curves involved in this geometry are going to be repaired.

Task 3 - Repair geometry.

It is important to attempt different methods of fixing problematic geometry. You should compare the results from the **Heal and Curve smooth** tool to manually rebuilding geometry.

1. Select **Surface.2** and **Surface.21**.

2. Perform a Heal. The purpose of the **Heal** tool is to join and repair the selected surfaces.

3. Select **Tangent** in the Continuity drop-down list.

4. Click **OK** in the Healing Definition dialog box. The Multi-Result Management dialog box opens as shown in Figure 12–95.

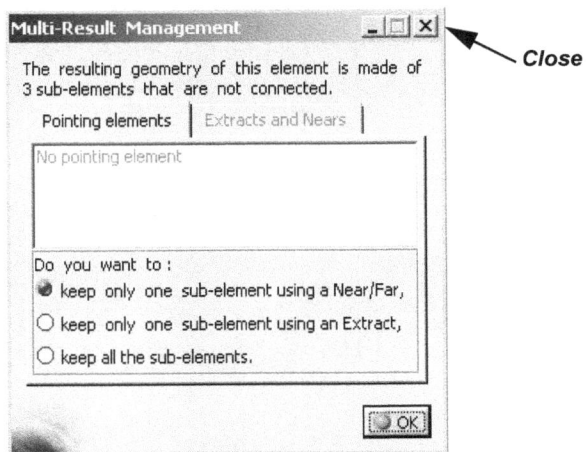

Figure 12–95

5. Close the dialog box.

This indicates that there are gaps larger than the Merging distance or that discontinuity was greater than the Tangency angle. Therefore, the **Healing** tool could not join the selected surfaces. The Multi-Result Management displays because multiple surfaces result from the feature. These multiple surfaces are the same surfaces that were originally selected in Step 1.

6. A Heal feature displays in the specification tree. Undo the Heal feature that was created. It is not the solution required for the problematic geometry. Because of the large gaps, the **Heal** tool cannot effectively fix the geometry.

Design Considerations

The **Heal** tool could be attempted on the other problematic surfaces displayed in the **Connect Checker**. If Healed these surfaces would give the results shown in this task. For this model, the **Healing** tool is not the most effective method for repairing geometry.

Task 4 - Disassemble geometry.

In this task, geometry will be manually rebuilt. This method has been selected because the **Healing** tool could not improve the geometry.

1. Rotate the model so that Surface.22 is more clearly visible as shown in Figure 12–96. Because the **Healing** tool was not effective in fixing the gaps in the model, the problematic geometry will be rebuilt.

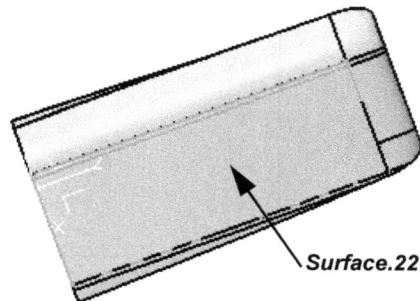

Surface.22

Figure 12–96

2. Create a Geometrical Set named **Rebuilt Geometry**.

3. Select **Surface.22**.

4. Click (Disassemble). The dialog box opens as shown in Figure 12–97. This tool breaks up **Surface.22** into smaller surfaces. You can then more easily work with the geometry once it has been disassembled.

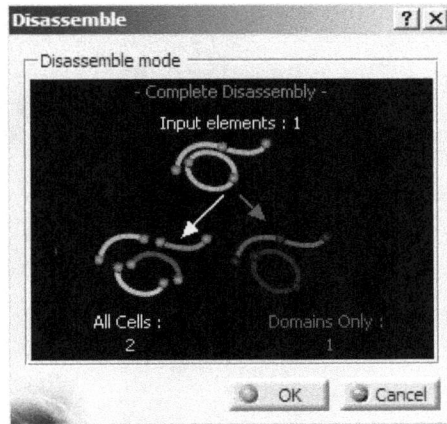

Figure 12–97

5. Complete the **Disassemble** operation. **Surface.23** and **Surface.24** were produced from the **Disassemble** operation.

6. Hide **Surface.22** and **Surface.24**. They are no longer required. The model displays as shown in Figure 12–98.

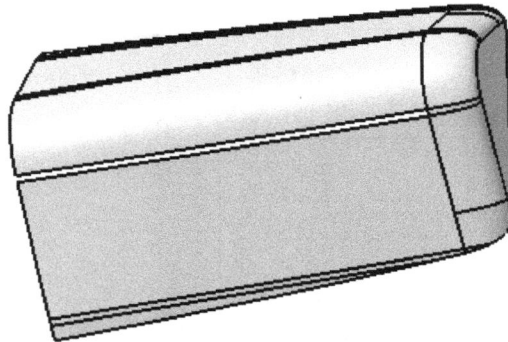

Figure 12–98

Task 5 - Rebuild a surface.

In this task, you will rebuild a surface to take the place of **Surface.24**. You will create a blend surface. This will enable continuity to be specified. To create the blend, curve geometry must first be created.

1. Extract the two edges shown in Figure 12–99. These will be used as the curves in the **Blend** operation later in this task.

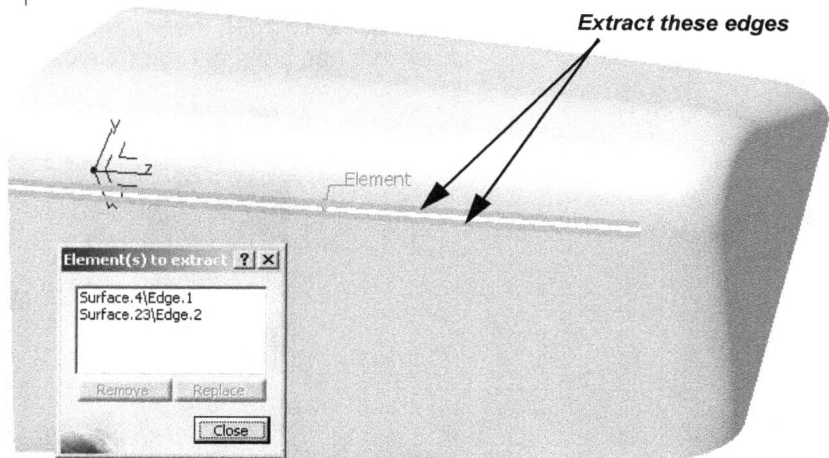

Extract these edges

Element

Element(s) to extract

Surface.4\Edge.1
Surface.23\Edge.2

Remove   Replace

Close

Figure 12–99

2. Complete the **Extract** operation.

3. Create a Blend surface using the references shown in Figure 12–100. Set the continuity to **Tangency**.

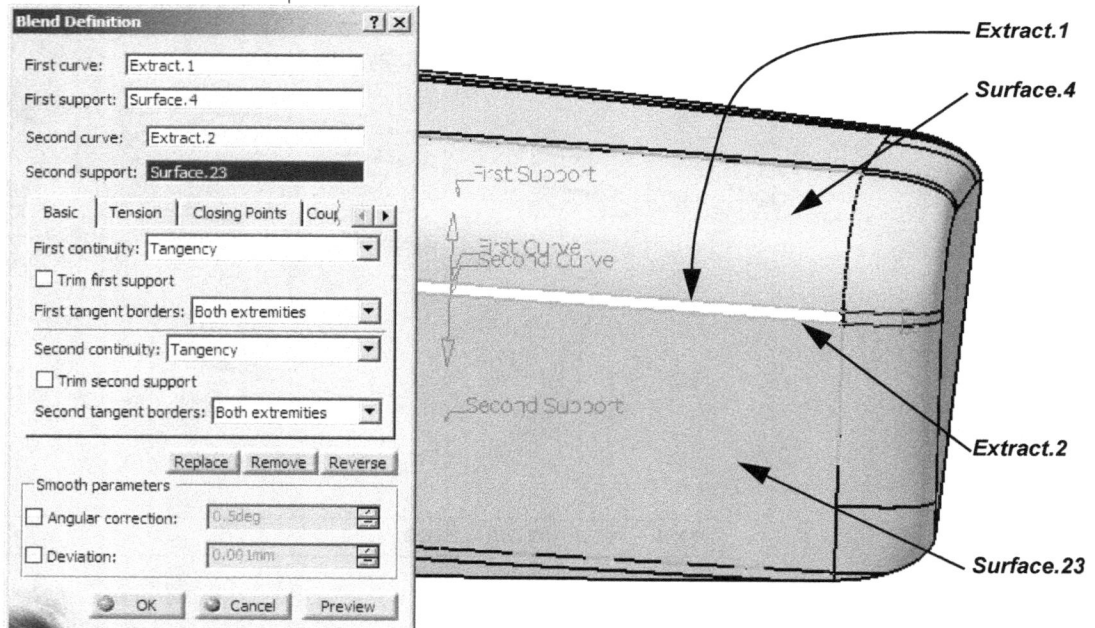

Blend Definition

First curve: Extract.1
First support: Surface.4
Second curve: Extract.2
Second support: Surface.23

Basic | Tension | Closing Points | Cou

First continuity: Tangency
☐ Trim first support
First tangent borders: Both extremities
Second continuity: Tangency
☐ Trim second support
Second tangent borders: Both extremities

Replace   Remove   Reverse

Smooth parameters
☐ Angular correction: 0.5deg
☐ Deviation: 0.001mm

OK   Cancel   Preview

Extract.1

Surface.4

First Support

First Curve
Second Curve

Second Support

Extract.2

Surface.23

Figure 12–100

The completed Blend surface displays as shown in
Figure 12–101.

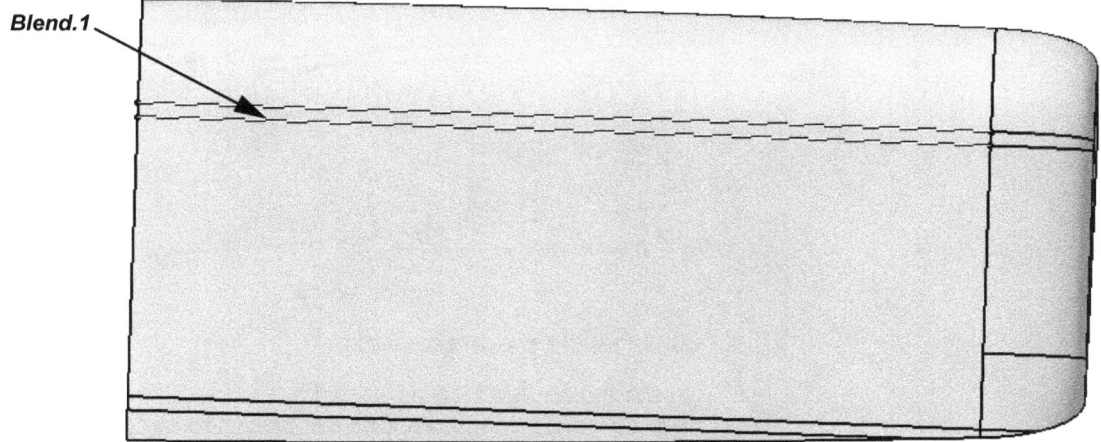

Blend.1

Figure 12–101

4. Hide the two curves extracted in this task.

Task 6 - Rebuilt another surface.

1. Hide **Surface.21**.

2. Rotate the model so that it displays as shown in
   Figure 12–102. This is the side of the part that will be edited
   in this task.

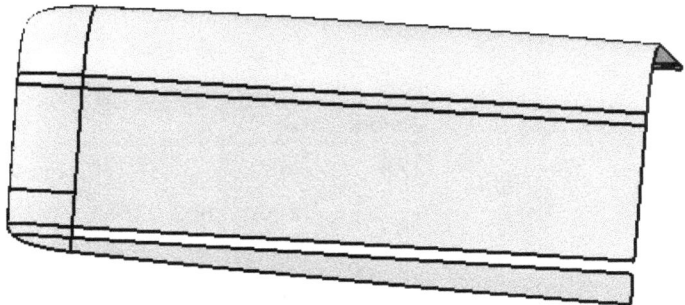

Figure 12–102

3. Extract the two curves shown in Figure 12–103.

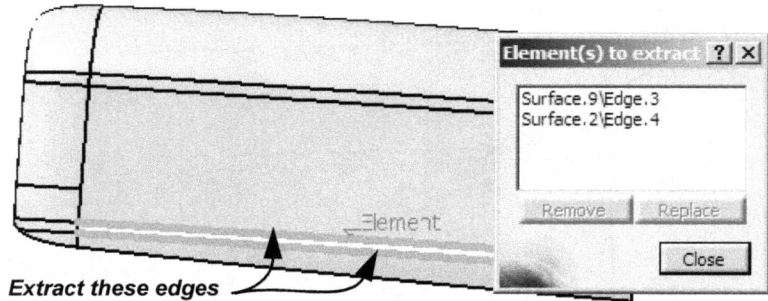

Figure 12–103

4. Complete the **Extract** operation.

5. Create a blend surface as shown in Figure 12–104. It must have tangency continuity. Use the extracted curves as the curve references. Use the adjacent surfaces and support references.

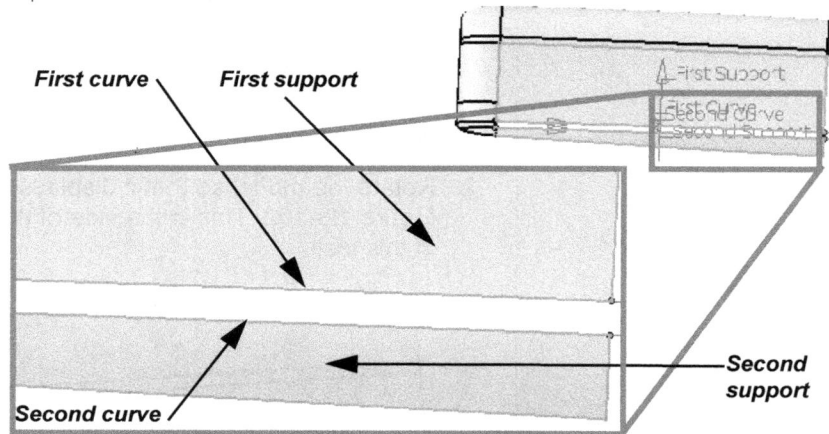

Figure 12–104

The completed blend will take the place of **Surface.21**. This was a surface that had gaps between itself and the adjacent surfaces. The blend surface used these adjacent surfaces as part of its definition.

6. The two completed Blend features display as shown in Figure 12–105. These surfaces have been colored to make them stand out in the figure. They do not display in this color on your model.

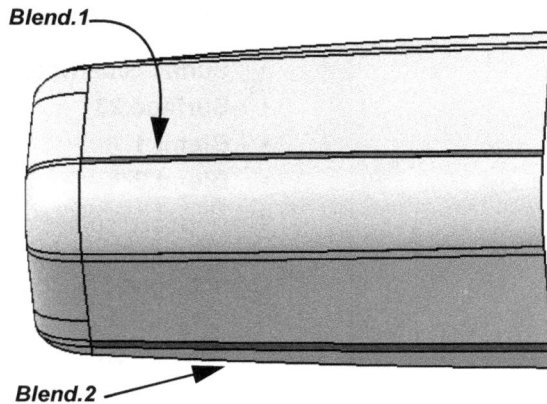

Blend.1

Blend.2

Figure 12–105

7. Hide the two curves extracted in this task.

Task 7 - Reanalyze the geometry.

1. Click ⬚ (Connect Checker Analysis), and then click ⬚ (Surface-Surface Connection).

2. Ensure that the **Boundary** option is activated.

3. Select the *Full* tab and specify the following:

   - ⬚: deactivated

   - ⬚: deactivated

   - ⬚: activated

   - *Maximum Gap:* **0.5mm** (Any gap smaller than this value is visualized in the model.)

   - ⬚: activated

   - ⬚: deactivated

   - ⬚: deactivated

4. Select the following surfaces:

- Surfaces between (2 - 20)
- **Surface.23**
- **Blend.1**
- **Blend.2**

The model displays as shown in Figure 12–106. The analysis shows that there are no gaps between any of the surfaces. Do not close the Connect Checker dialog box.

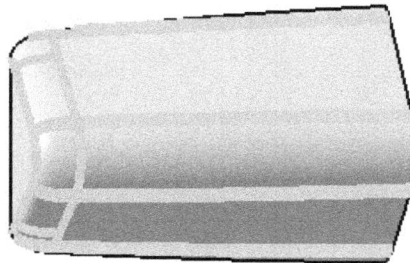

Figure 12–106

5. Select **G1** to check the tangency discontinuity. The model displays as shown in Figure 12–107. This shows that one area on the model exhibits tangency discontinuity.

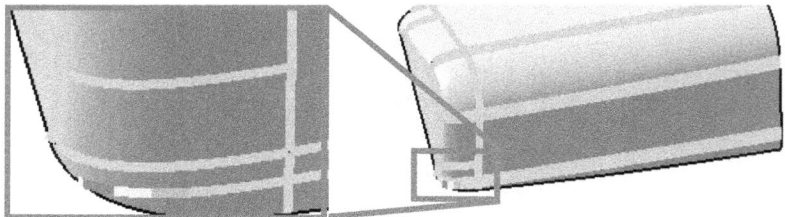

Figure 12–107

6. Click **Cancel** in the Connect Checker dialog box. In the following tasks, you rebuild the geometry displaying tangency discontinuity.

Task 8 - Create curve geometry.

In this task, you will create curves that will be used later to build a surface. By the end of the next two tasks, the model will display as shown on the right side of Figure 12–108. The left side of Figure 12–108 shows the geometry at the beginning of this task.

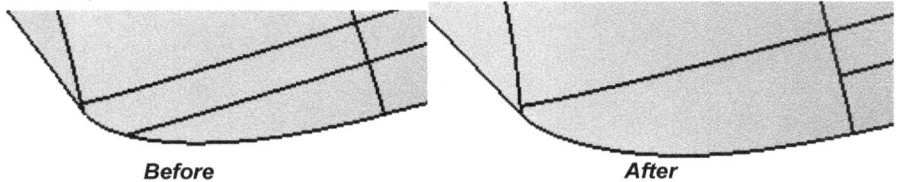

Before   *After*

Figure 12–108

1. Zoom in on the geometry shown in Figure 12–109.

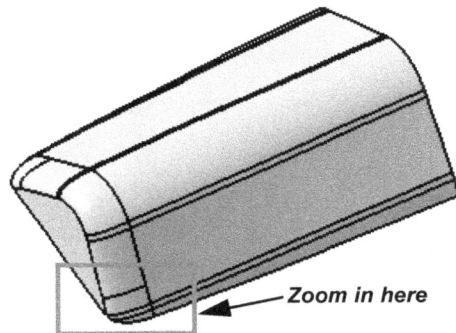

Zoom in here

Figure 12–109

2. Extract the five curves shown in Figure 12–110.

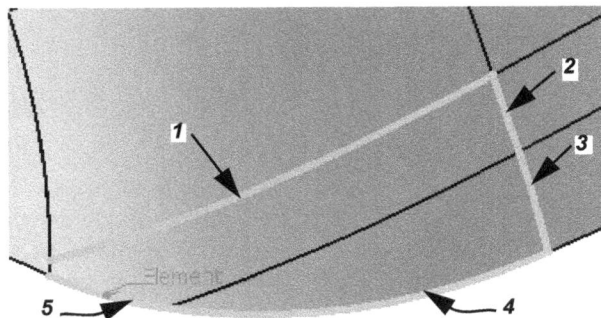

Figure 12–110

3. Click ⌒ (Boundary) to create a curve using the specifications shown in Figure 12–111. Both Limit1 and Limit2 use the extracted curves from the last step.

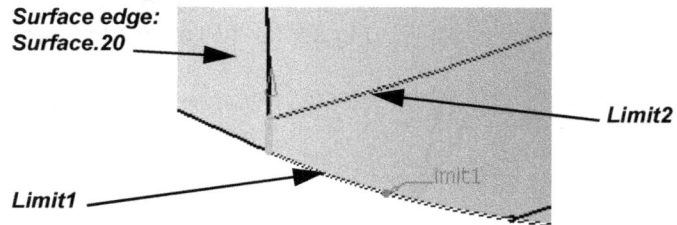

Figure 12–111

4. Join the extracted curves shown in Figure 12–112.

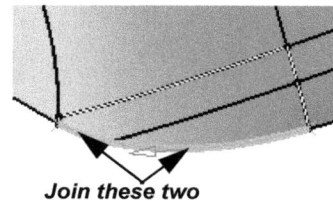

Figure 12–112

5. Use the **Connect Checker** to find out if the join created in the last step is Tangency continuous. Ensure that the **Curve-Curve Connection** type is used. The results display as shown in Figure 12–113.

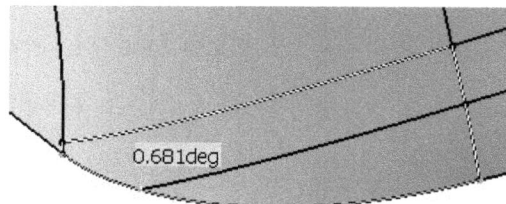

Figure 12–113

The Connect Checker Analysis result shows that the join curve is tangency discontinuous. You will improve the continuity of this curve. A good quality curve will produce a good quality surface.

6. Hide the join curve. This curve needs to be rebuilt because of the discontinuities discovered in the last step. Therefore, the join curve no longer needs to be displayed.

7. Extract the three points, as shown in Figure 12–114. By extracting these points, you can reference these locations in building a curve.

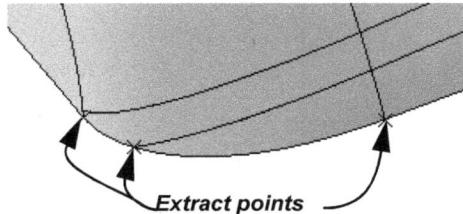

Figure 12–114

8. Create a plane using the **Through three points** type. Use the extracted points from the last step. The completed plane displays as shown in Figure 12–115.

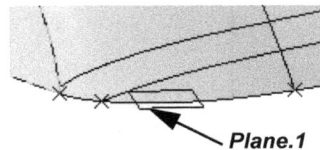

Figure 12–115

9. Extract the two curves shown in Figure 12–116. They are referenced when rebuilding a curve later in this task.

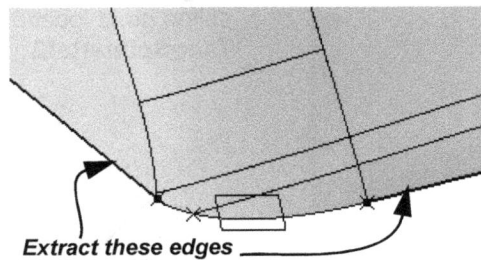

Figure 12–116

10. Rename the extract curves, as shown in Figure 12–117.

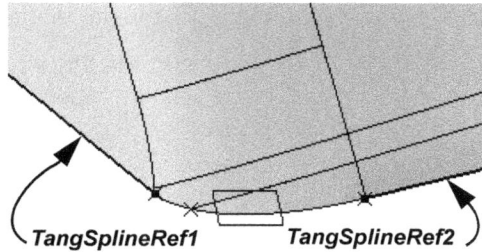

TangSplineRef1   *TangSplineRef2*

Figure 12–117

11. Hide **Surface.16** and **Surface.17**.

12. Create a spline. It goes through the three extracted points shown in Figure 12–118.

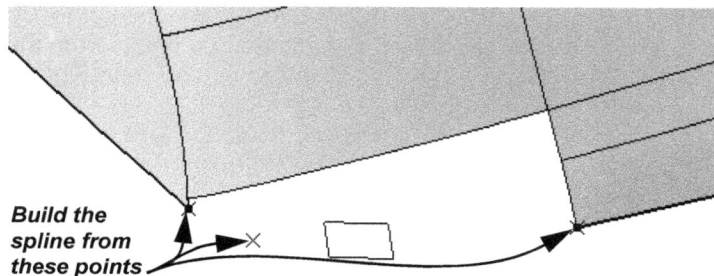

Build the spline from these points

Figure 12–118

13. At the spline point locations shown in Figure 12–119, use the tangency references noted. The tangent references for the spline point locations use **TangSplineRef1** and **TangSplineRef2**.

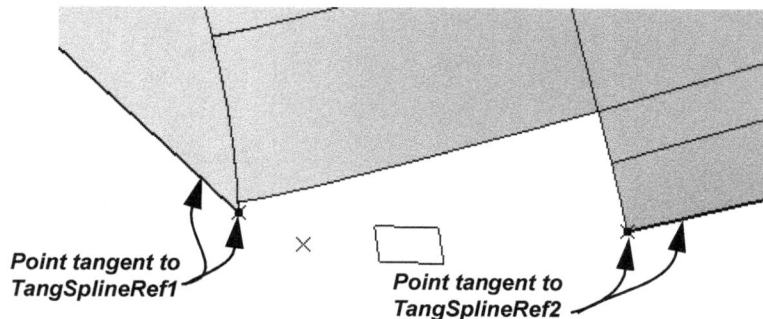

Point tangent to TangSplineRef1

Point tangent to TangSplineRef2

Figure 12–119

14. Activate **Geometry on support** and specify **Plane.1** as the support reference.

15. Complete the spline. The curve displays as shown in Figure 12–120. This spline will take the place of the join curve from step 5.

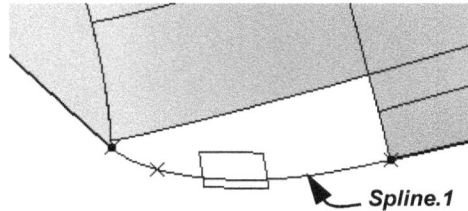

Figure 12–120

Task 9 - Create a fill surface.

At this point in the practice, curve geometry has been either extracted or created with a spline. The extracted curves and spline will be used to define a fill surface in this task.

1. Hide **Plane.1**.

2. Create a fill using the curve and support references shown in Figure 12–121. The curves are labeled in the order in which they will be selected. These names are not the feature's name in the specification tree.

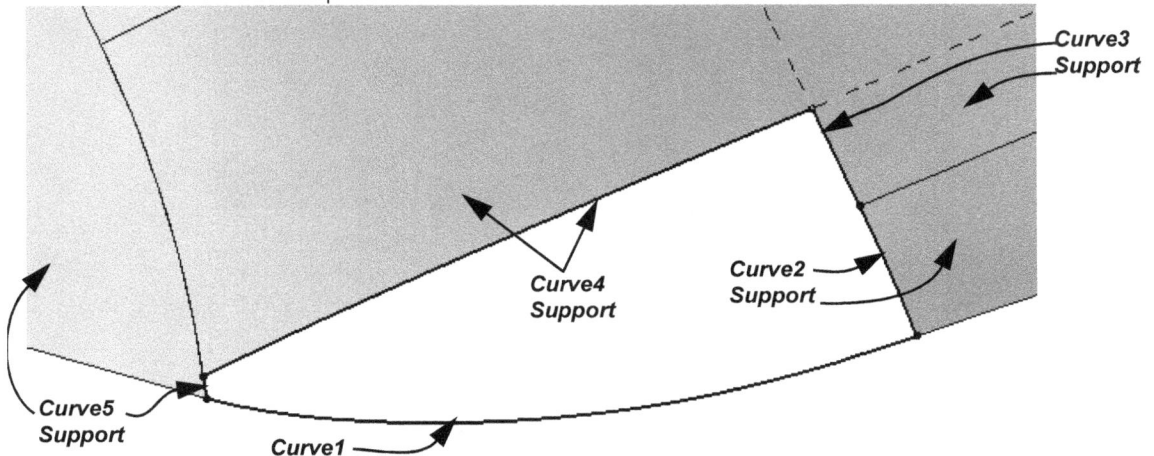

Figure 12–121

3. Select **Tangent** in the Continuity drop-down list.

4. Complete the Fill. The model displays as shown in Figure 12–122.

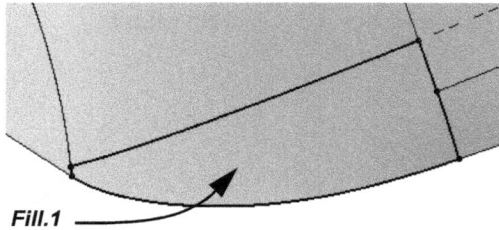

Figure 12–122

Task 10 - Join the surfaces.

In this practice, three surfaces were rebuilt. The two of them were rebuilt using blend surfaces. The last surface was created with a fill. These surfaces were rebuilt because the gaps and discontinuity of some of the imported surfaces were too great for the **Heal** tool to fix.

1. Join the surfaces shown in Figure 12–123.

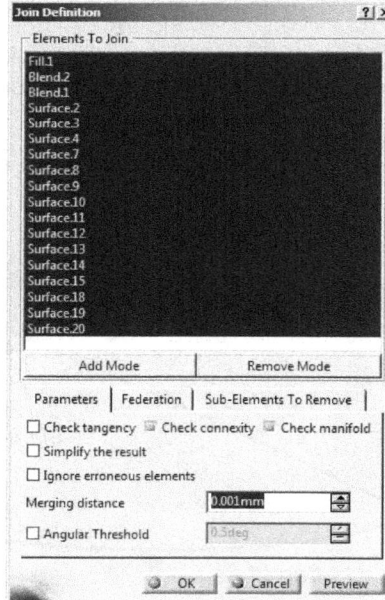

Figure 12–123

2. Complete the Join feature and rename it as **Join - All Surfs**. The model displays as shown in Figure 12–124.

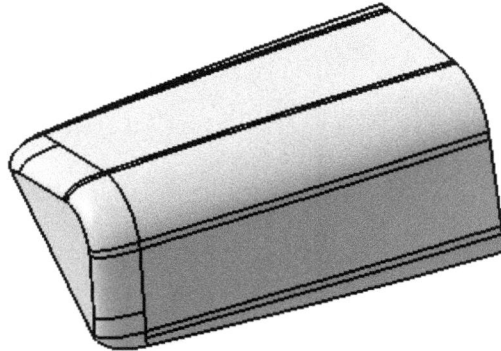

Figure 12–124

3. Perform a **Connect Checker** analysis on Join - All Surfs. Find out if all surfaces are tangency continuous and if there are still any gaps.

4. Save the model as **Surface-Quality-Rebuilt.CATPart**.

5. Close the file.

Offset Surfaces

The Offset tool is helpful in creating a copy of a surface that is translated normal to the surface by a specified linear value. It is common in complex models that the Offset tool cannot successfully offset the surface. In this chapter, more available options for the Offset tool are discussed. In addition, when the Offset tool is unsuccessful other methods of manually building the geometry are discussed.

Learning Objectives in this Chapter

- Understand the Offset tool.
- Learn how to smooth offsets.
- Understand options available for the Offset tool.

13.1 Offset Overview

An Offset surface creates a copy of the selected part surface, surface feature, or reference plane by a specified offset distance.

How To: Create an Offset Surface

1. Click ⟨image⟩ (Offset) to create an Offset surface.
2. Select the surface to offset. The Offset Surface Definition dialog box opens as shown in Figure 13–1.

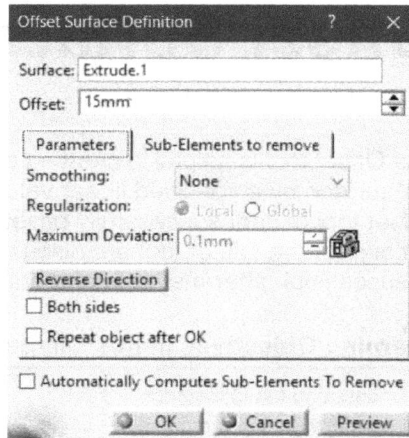

Figure 13–1

3. Enter an offset value. The resultant surface is measured from the reference surface's normal vectors as shown in Figure 13–2.

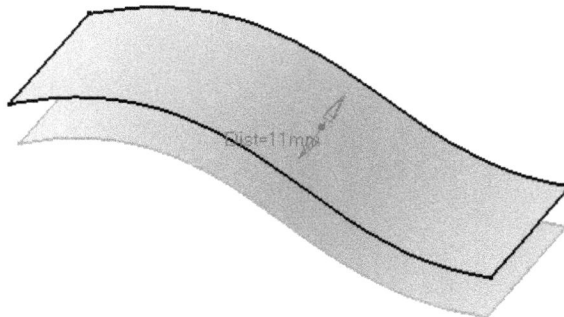

Figure 13–2

4. Set the **Smoothing Setting** in the Smoothing drop-down list.
5. If required, remove any sub-elements from the offset surface.
6. Complete the offset. The geometry displays as shown in Figure 13–3.

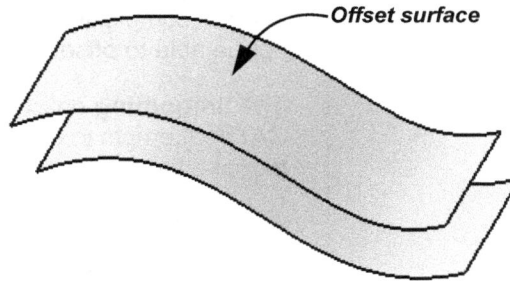

Figure 13–3

Reasons errors occur with offset surfaces

- The geometry referenced has too great a curvature.

- The faces cannot be offset by the specified value. Usually this is because the value is too large.

- Smoothing setting set to **None**.

Faces that cannot be offset highlight on the model. If you hover the mouse over any of the displayed annotations, an explanation for the offset error is provided as shown in Figure 13–4.

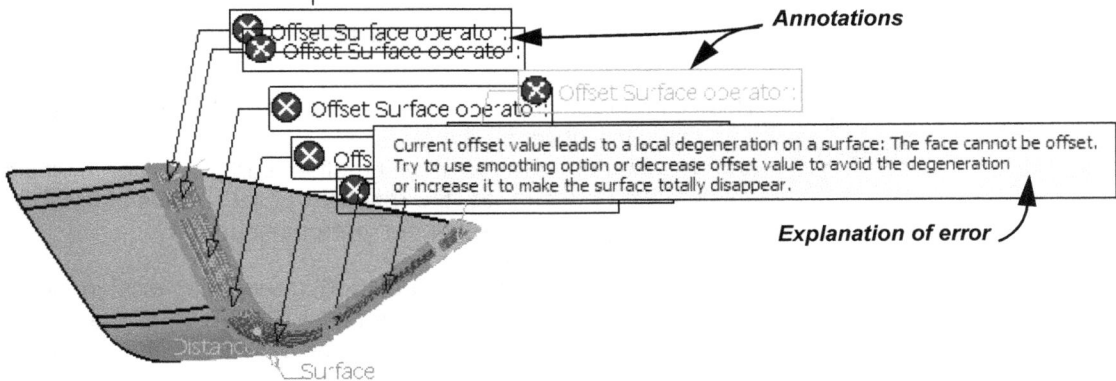

Figure 13–4

13.2 Offset Smoothing

The resultant surface is offset in the direction of the normal vector's of the referenced surface. Depending on the offset value and the complexity of the surface being offset, the feature might not be able to offset the surface(s).

The **Smoothing** options can aid in offsetting complex geometry. CATIA attempts to deviate or change the resulting offset surface to make the offset successful.

There are three smoothing options in the Offset Surface Definition dialog box as shown in Figure 13–5.

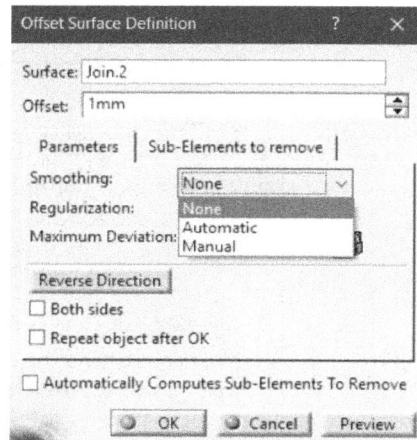

Figure 13–5

Smoothing-None

This is the default option when using the **Offset** tool. CATIA calculates the offset by the reference surface's normal vectors and does not change the resulting offset surface. When multiple faces make up a surface, the resultant offset surface maintains the continuity established in the reference surface.

In the example shown in Figure 13–6, three faces exist in the reference surface. However, due to the complexity of the geometry, only two of the faces can be offset. The middle face fails, and CATIA removes the face.

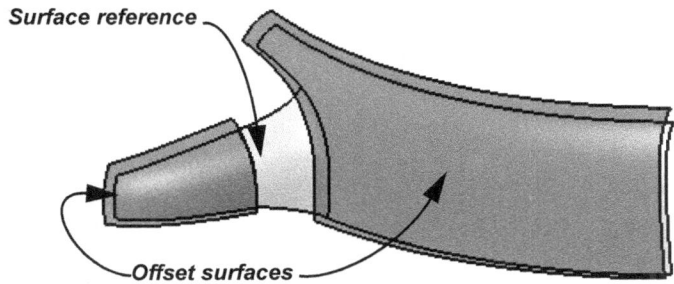

Figure 13–6

Smoothing-Automatic

The **Automatic Smoothing** option modifies the resulting surface to enable a successful offset.

This means that the resulting surface is skewed slightly in attempting to complete the offset. When multiple faces are involved in the offset, continuity between those faces is not always maintained.

In the example shown in Figure 13–7, three faces are offset using **Automatic Smoothing**. When the smoothing was set to **None**, the middle face could not successfully be offset. However, when the smoothing was set to **Automatic**, the face was successfully offset. The continuity is compromised in the smoothing process.

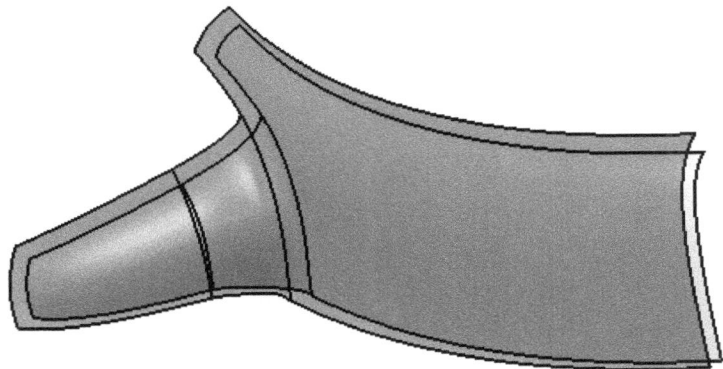

Figure 13–7

When the offset surface is analyzed, the discontinuities are revealed, as shown in Figure 13–8.

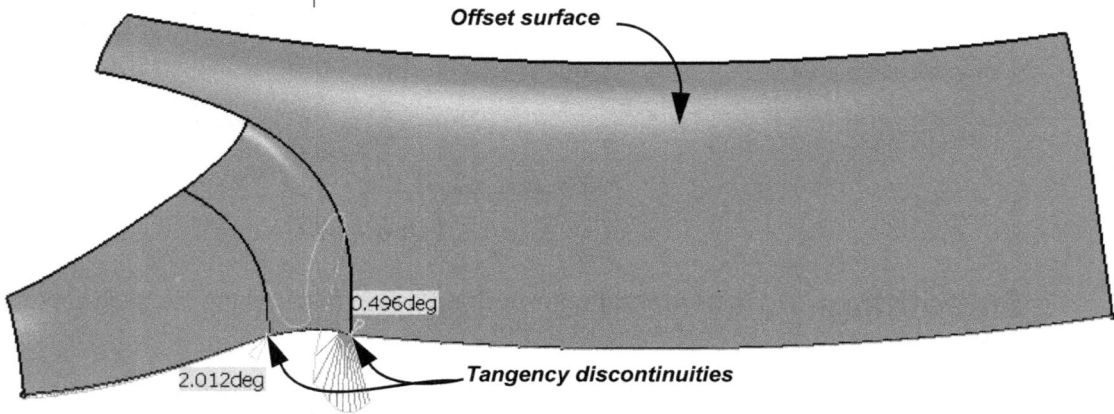

Figure 13–8

Smoothing-Manual

Manual smoothing enables you to enter a maximum deviation by which the resultant offset surface can be smoothed as shown in Figure 13–9. The maximum deviation value must be less than the entered offset value. Similar to **Automatic Smoothing**, continuity might not be maintained between faces in the offset surface.

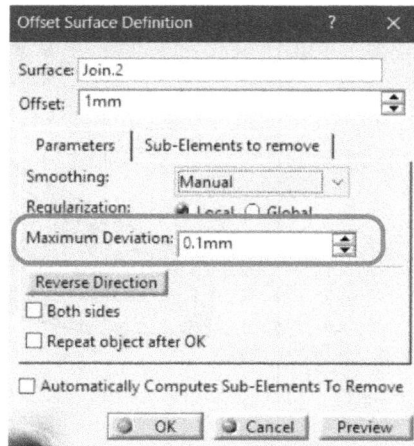

Figure 13–9

13.3 Sub-elements to Remove

*The Warning dialog box opens when you click **OK** or **Preview** in the Offset Surface Definition dialog box.*

When faces cannot be offset because of the offset value or the smoothing parameter set, CATIA displays the Warning dialog box shown in Figure 13–10.

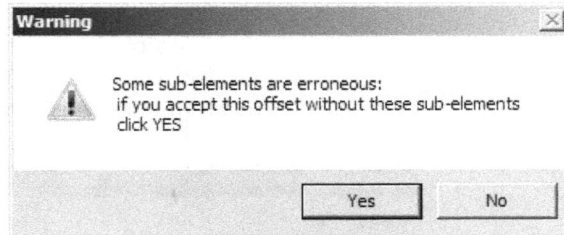

Figure 13–10

If you select **No**, the Error box opens as shown in Figure 13–11. This indicates that the Offset feature cannot be completed with the current offset value, smoothing parameter, or reference surface.

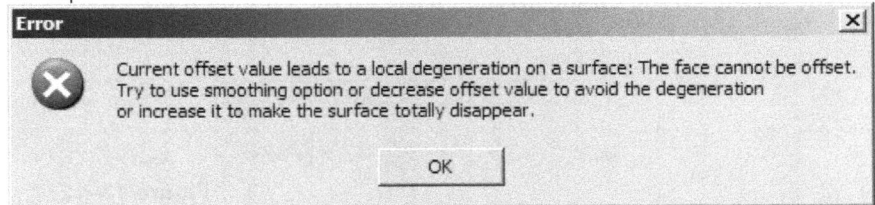

Figure 13–11

If you select **Yes** in the Warning dialog box, the erroneous faces are automatically added to the Sub-Elements to remove the list as shown in Figure 13–12.

The *Sub-Elements to remove* tab in the Offset Surface Definition dialog box enable sub-elements (faces) on the reference surface to be removed from the resulting offset surface.

It is also possible for you to manually add faces to this list. When faces are manually added to the Sub-Elements to remove list, the faces must be selected from the reference surface.

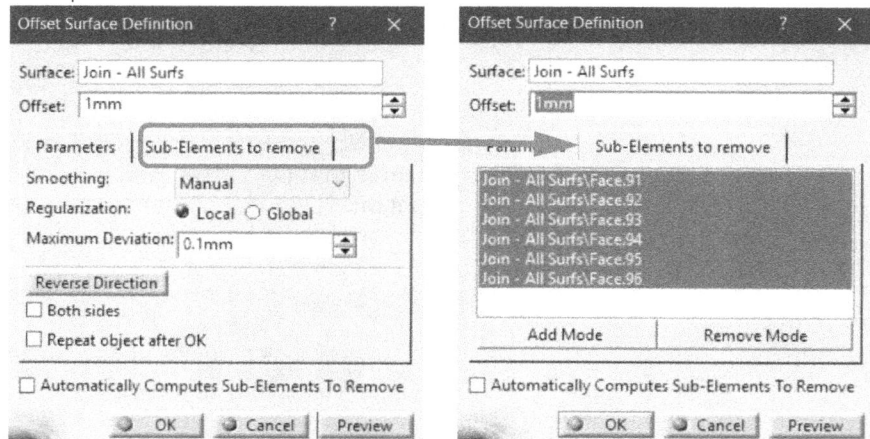

Figure 13–12

Use the **Automatically Computes Sub-elements To Remove** check box to automatically compute and remove sub-elements. Use this check box to obtain a better result after a modification of the offset parameter for the offset feature.

Note: With this option, the *Sub-elements to remove* list is not available for manually adding or removing the sub-elements.

In the example shown in Figure 13–13, the reference surface displays on the left. The resulting offset surface is shown on the right. Selected two faces from the reference surface to remove from the resulting Offset feature.

Reference surface

Offset surface

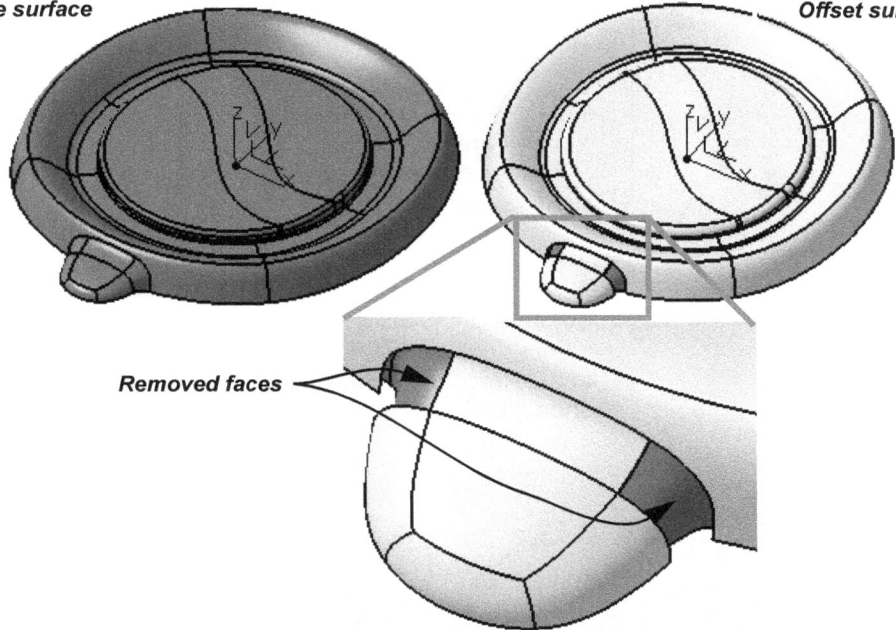

Removed faces

Figure 13–13

Faces are removed from the offset because either the user does not want those faces to be offset, or it is not possible to offset the faces. In that case, CATIA adds those faces to the list of Sub-Elements to remove.

After the Offset feature is created, you might have to rebuild the surfaces that were not offset. By extracting curves and points, a wireframe can be constructed. Fill surfaces can be created from the wireframe geometry surfaces as shown in Figure 13–14.

Fill surfaces

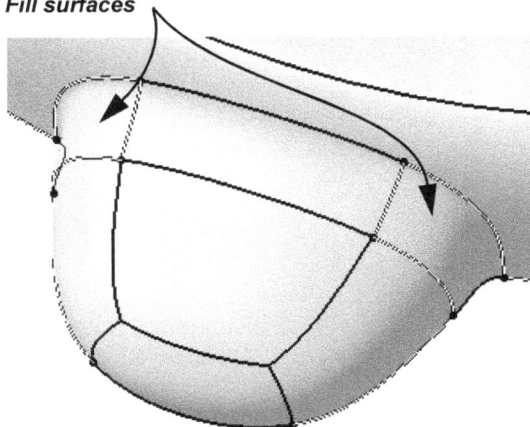

Figure 13–14

Practice 13a | # Plastic Top

Practice Objectives

- Offset surfaces.
- Remove erroneous faces from a surface to use in an offset.
- Rebuild surface geometry.

In this practice, complex geometry from a plastic top will be offset. Some of the faces will be unable to be offset and they will be rebuilt. The inside surfaces of the plastic top will be offset at different values. The final surfaces will be joined together for use in the Part Design workbench. The completed model displays as shown in Figure 13–15.

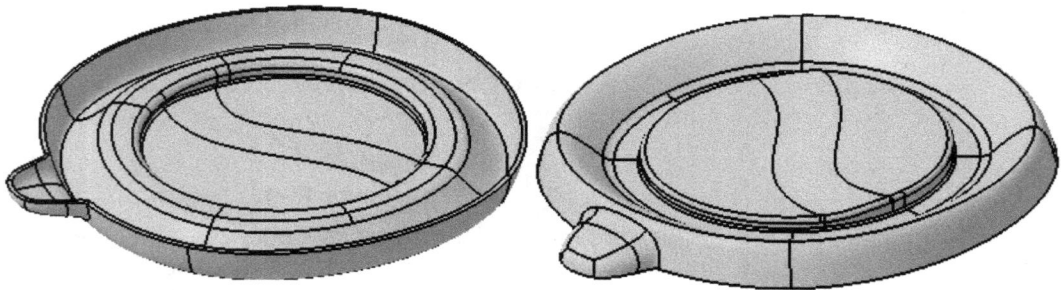

Figure 13–15

Task 1 - Open a part file.

1. Open **Plastic_Top_Start.CATPart**. The part displays as shown in Figure 13–16.

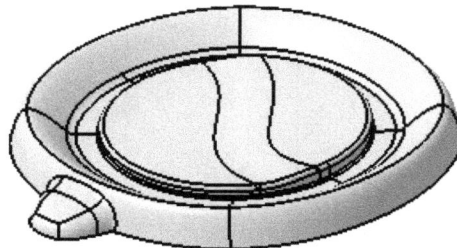

Figure 13–16

2. Define the active work object as the geometrical set named **Outside Surfaces**.

Task 2 - Create an offset surface.

1. Click (Offset) in the Surfaces toolbar. The Offset Surface Definition dialog box opens as shown in Figure 13–17.

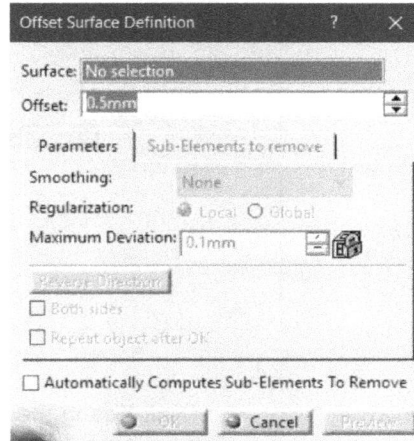

Figure 13–17

2. Select **Inside Surface Join** as the surface to offset.

3. Enter an *Offset* value of **1mm**.

4. Ensure that the direction of the offset displays as shown in Figure 13–18. Reverse the direction if required.

Offset direction arrow pointing to the outside of the surface.

Figure 13–18

5. Click **Preview** in the Offset Surface Definition dialog box. A Warning dialog box will open as shown in Figure 13–19. It states that with the current surface reference and offset value, there are faces that cannot successfully be offset. The highlighted faces cannot be offset on the model.

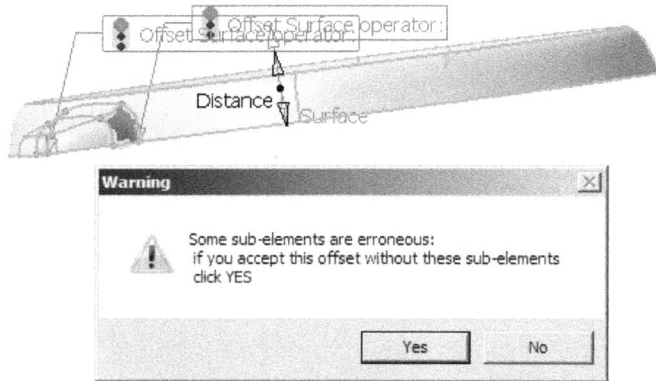

Figure 13–19

6. Click **Yes** in the Warning dialog box. This adds the highlighted faces to the list of sub-elements to remove as shown in Figure 13–20. The *Sub-Elements to remove* tab enables individual faces from the reference surface not to be offset.

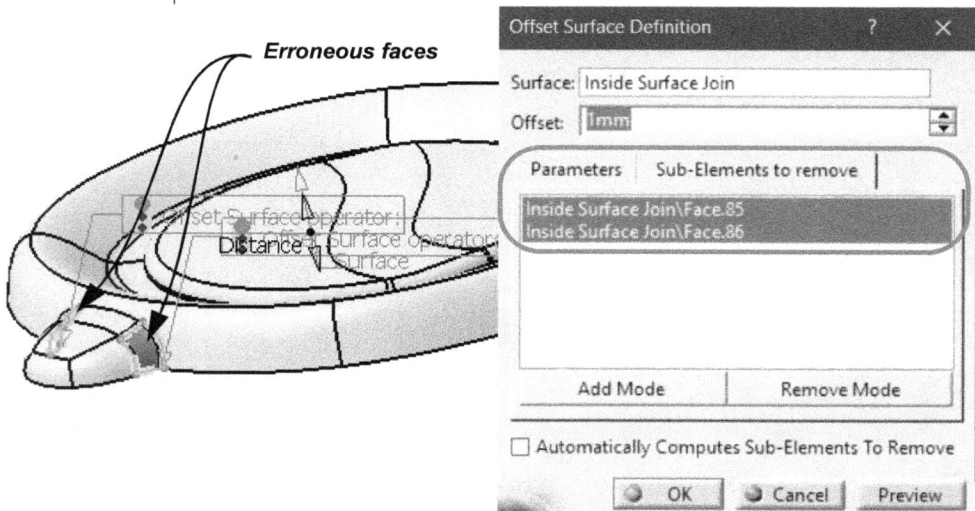

Figure 13–20

7. Complete the Offset. The model displays as shown in Figure 13–21. Note the faces that were not offset.

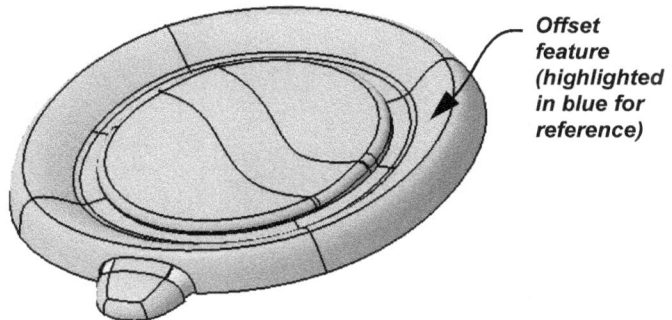

Offset feature (highlighted in blue for reference)

Figure 13–21

Task 3 - Edit Offset.1.

When the offset surface was created, erroneous faces were removed from the offset. In this task, you will edit the offset and manually add faces to the list of sub-elements to remove.

1. Edit the Offset feature.

2. Select the *Sub-Elements to remove* tab, as shown in Figure 13–22. A list of faces not included in the offset display.

Figure 13–22

3. Select the five faces shown in Figure 13–23. These faces are added to the list of *Sub-Elements to remove*. They are highlighted in blue in Figure 13–23, but do not display in this color on your model.

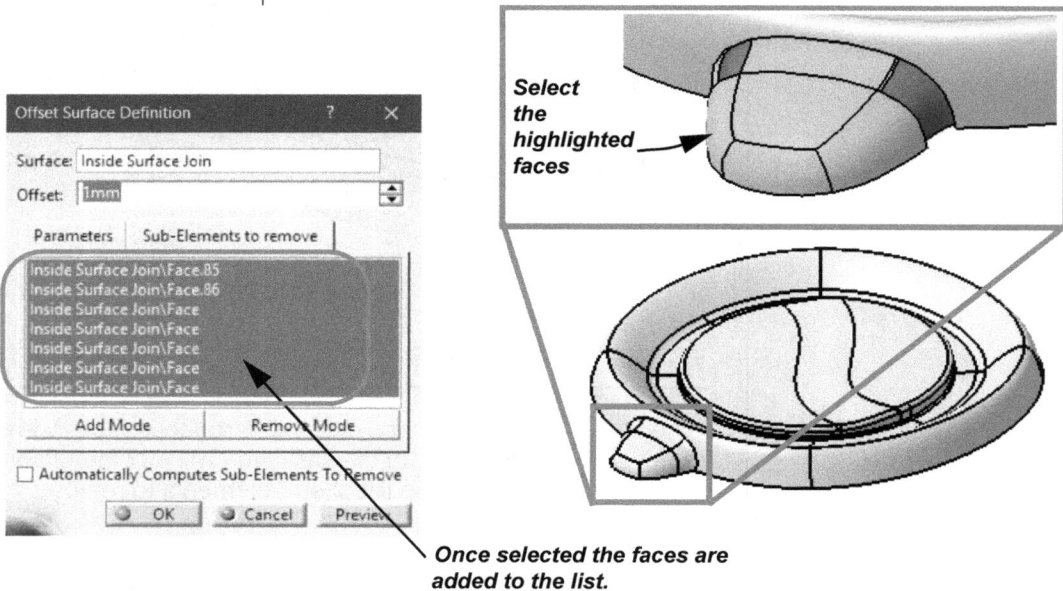

Offset Surface Definition

Surface: Inside Surface Join

Offset: 1mm

Parameters | Sub-Elements to remove

Inside Surface Join\Face.85
Inside Surface Join\Face.86
Inside Surface Join\Face
Inside Surface Join\Face
Inside Surface Join\Face
Inside Surface Join\Face
Inside Surface Join\Face

Add Mode | Remove Mode

☐ Automatically Computes Sub-Elements To Remove

OK | Cancel | Preview

Select the highlighted faces

Once selected the faces are added to the list.

Figure 13–23

4. Complete the offset.

5. Hide **Inside Surface Join**. The model displays as shown in Figure 13–24.

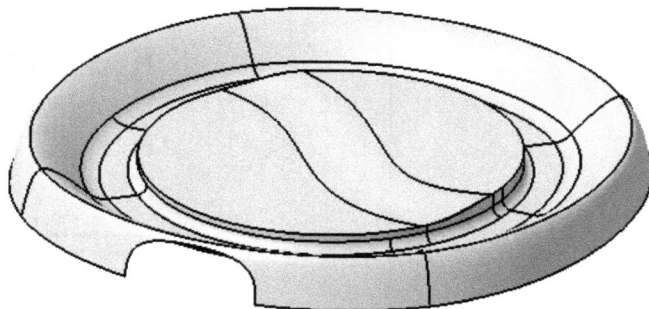

Figure 13–24

Task 4 - Create another offset surface.

1. Show **Multiple Extract - Tab** located in **Group-Geometrical Set.1**. The model displays as shown in Figure 13–25.

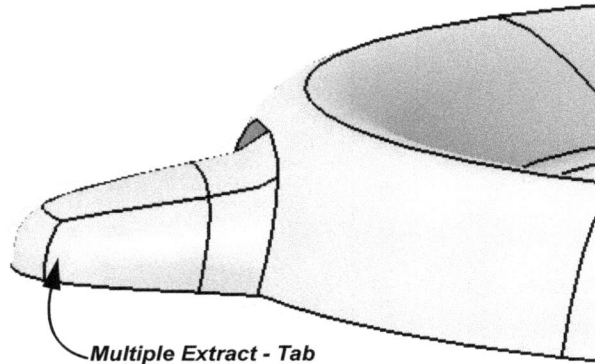

Multiple Extract - Tab

Figure 13–25

2. Create an offset surface using the following specifications:

   - *Surface:* **Multiple Extract - Tab**
   - *Offset:* **0.5mm**
   - *Direction:* Pointing to the outside of the reference surface.
   - Remove the three faces shown in Figure 13–26.

Remove these faces

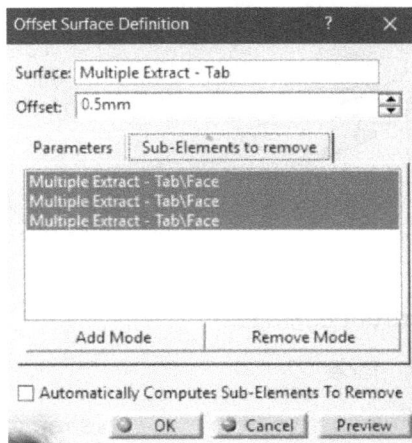

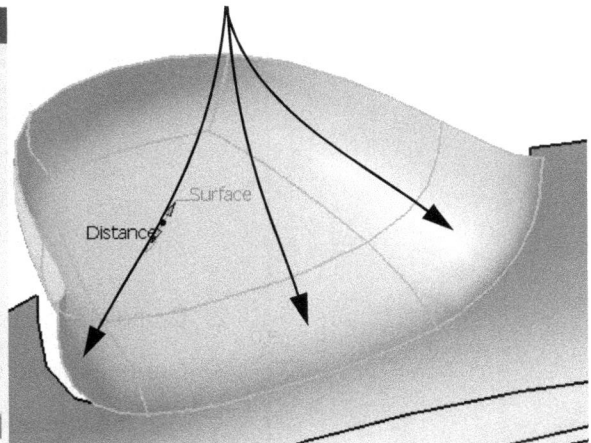

Figure 13–26

3. Preview the offset. The model displays as shown in Figure 13–27.

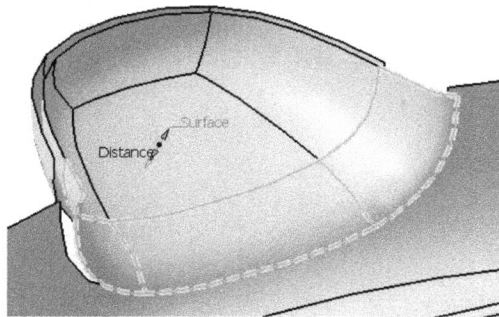

Figure 13–27

4. Complete the offset.

5. Hide **Multiple Extract - Tab**.

Task 5 - Create a blend surface.

---

1. Extract the two curves shown in Figure 13–28. Use the **Tangent continuity** option.

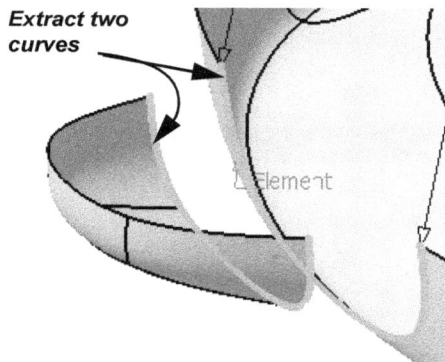

Figure 13–28

2. Complete the **Extract** operation.

3. Create a blend surface.

4. Use the extract curves from Step 1 as curve references.

5. Both offset surfaces created in earlier tasks will be used as support references.

6. Activate both **Trim Support** options.

7. Ensure tangency continuity is set for the Blend. The model and dialog box open as shown in Figure 13–29. Note that the entity names might vary slightly on your model.

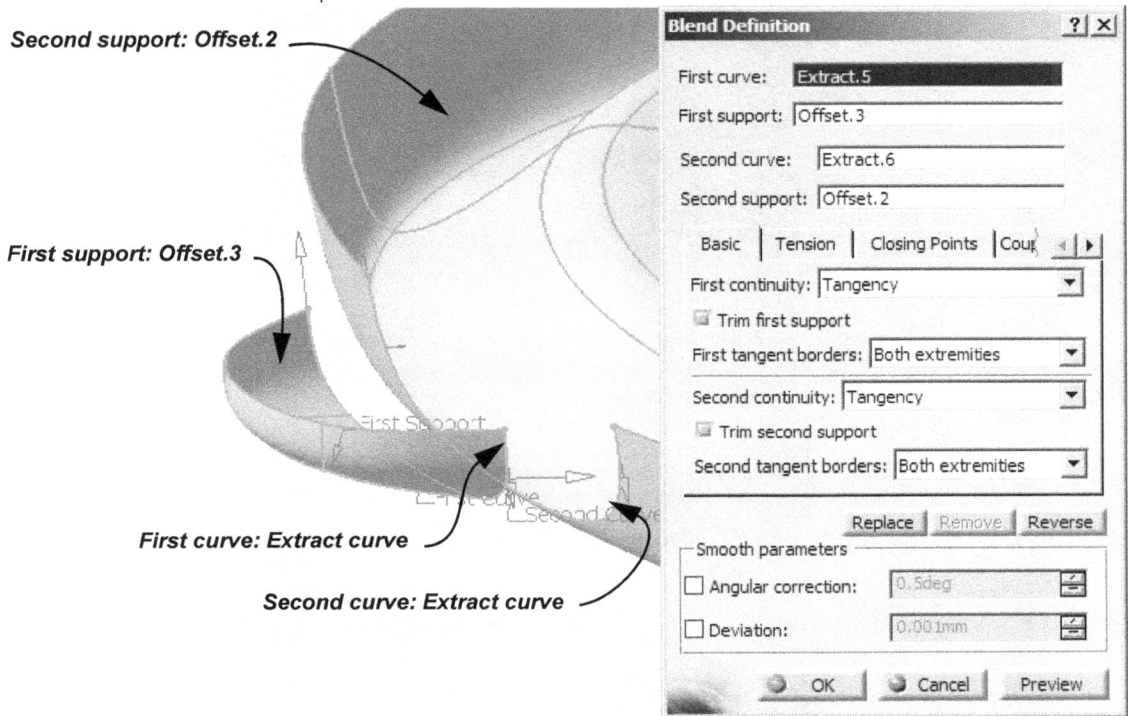

Second support: Offset.2

First support: Offset.3

First curve: Extract curve

Second curve: Extract curve

Blend Definition ? X

First curve: Extract.5

First support: Offset.3

Second curve: Extract.6

Second support: Offset.2

Basic | Tension | Closing Points | Cou ◄ ►

First continuity: Tangency ▼

☐ Trim first support

First tangent borders: Both extremities ▼

Second continuity: Tangency ▼

☐ Trim second support

Second tangent borders: Both extremities ▼

Replace | Remove | Reverse

Smooth parameters

☐ Angular correction: 0.5deg

☐ Deviation: 0.001mm

OK | Cancel | Preview

Figure 13–29

8. Select the *Coupling* tab, and select the **Vertices** coupling in the drop-down list.

9. Complete the blend. The model displays as shown in Figure 13–30.

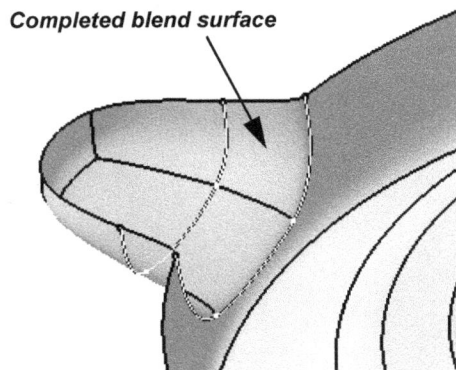

Completed blend surface

Figure 13–30

10. Hide both extract curves. The model displays as shown in Figure 13–31.

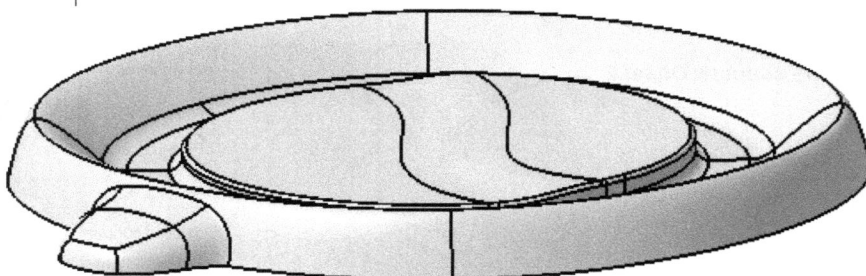

Figure 13–31

Design Considerations

The blend surface created a transition between the 1mm offset, and the 0.5mm offset. Tangency continuity was also maintained using a blend.

Task 6 - Complete the plastic top.

1. Show **Inside Surface Join**. The model displays as shown in Figure 13–32.

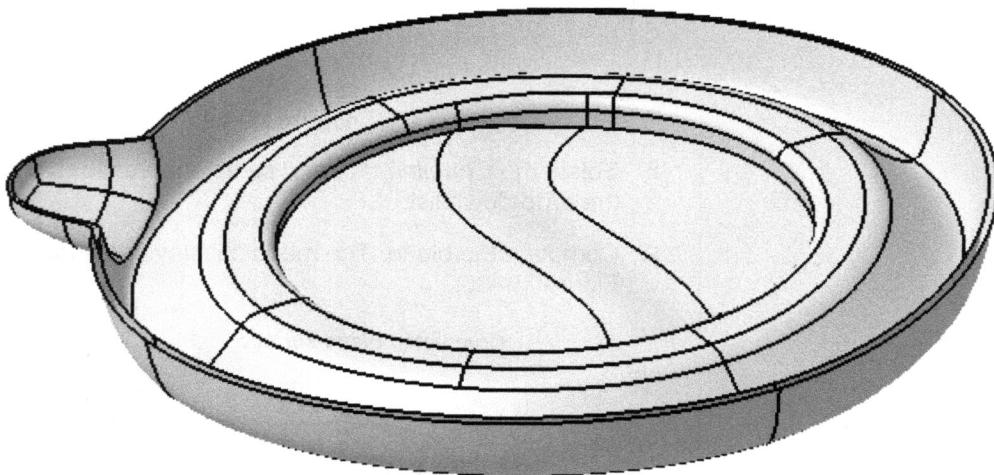

Figure 13–32

2. Create a swept surface to close the gap between the inside and outside surfaces as shown in Figure 13–33.

Completed swept surface

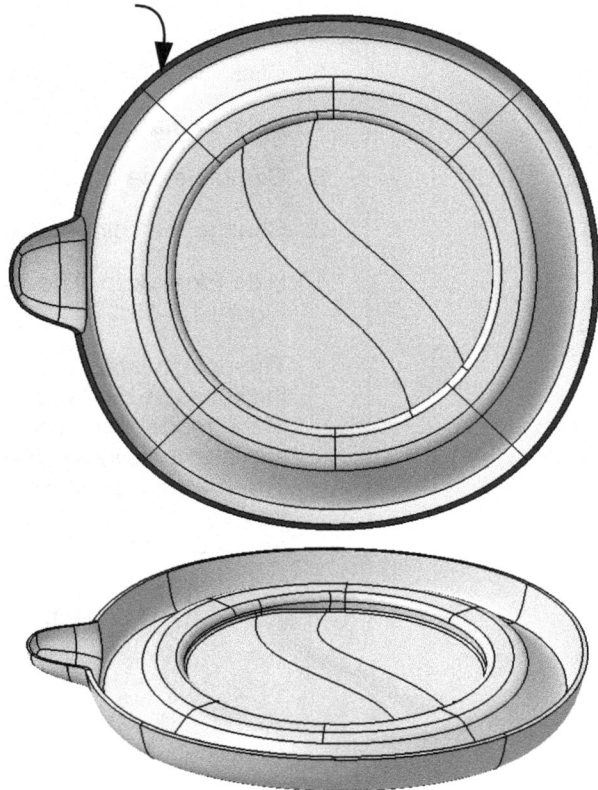

Figure 13–33

3. Join the following three elements:

 - **Blend surface**
 - **Swept surface**
 - **Inside Surface Join**

4. Rename the feature as **Final Join**, as shown in Figure 13–34.

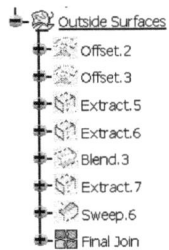

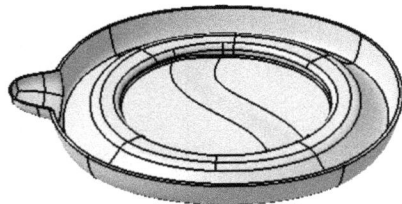

Outside Surfaces
Offset.2
Offset.3
Extract.5
Extract.6
Blend.3
Extract.7
Sweep.6
Final Join

Figure 13–34

5. Enter the Part Design workbench.

6. Click [⬛] (Close Surface).

7. Select **Final Join**.

8. Complete the Close Surface feature.

9. Change the color of **CloseSurface.1** to light blue.

10. Hide **Final Join**. The model displays as shown in Figure 13–35.

    The design intent of the plastic top was to have a different thickness on the tab geometry of the top compared to the rest of the model. By creating two Offset features and using the sub-elements to remove, this specification could be obtained. There were also faces on the model that had to be removed from the offset because they were wrong. These faces were rebuilt using the **Blend** tool.

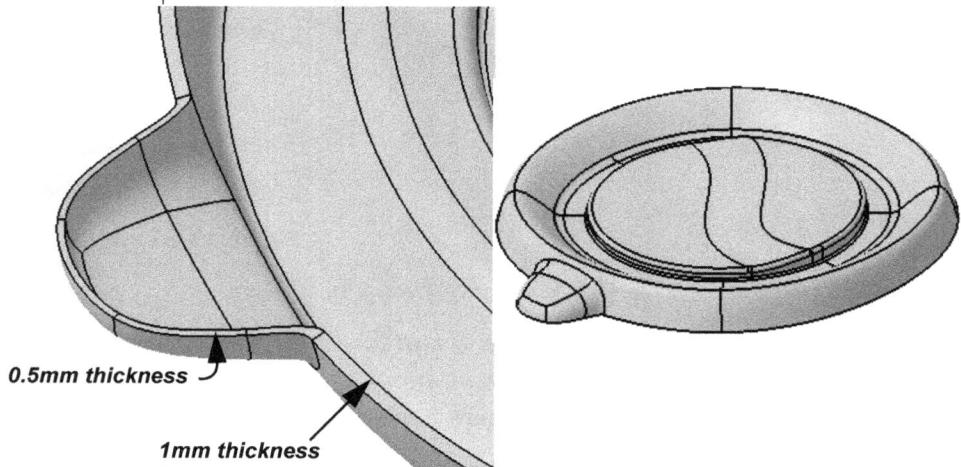

0.5mm thickness

1mm thickness

Figure 13–35

11. Save and close the file.

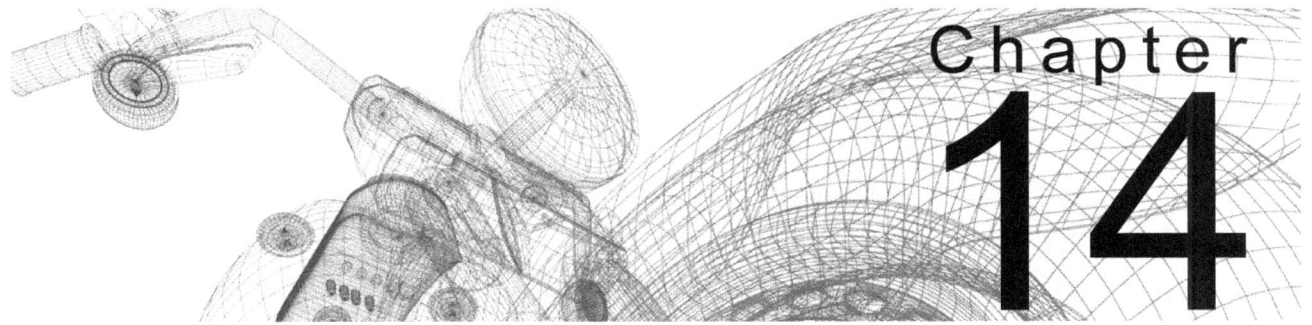

Advanced Surfacing Projects

In this chapter an overview of creating wireframe and surfaces is discussed. The design intent of the model guides the decisions made when creating it. Certain features do not meet the design intent, while others are better suited.

Learning Objectives in this Chapter

- Review the methods for creating curves and surfaces.
- Complete several projects with limited instruction.

14.1 Surfacing Overview

As there are multiple ways to create curves and surfaces, it is recognized that multiple solutions exist. However, one must rule out tools that do not meet the design intent. When working with a model, the design intent dictates the tools that are appropriate to use. Some tools are used to create or modify geometry, others to fix or aid in rebuilding imported geometry, while others are for analyzing geometry. The tools that can be used for these three purposes of modeling are shown in Figure 14–1. Also, the highest levels of continuity that can be enforced on curves or surfaces displays. These are not all of the tools available in the Generative Shape Design workbench.

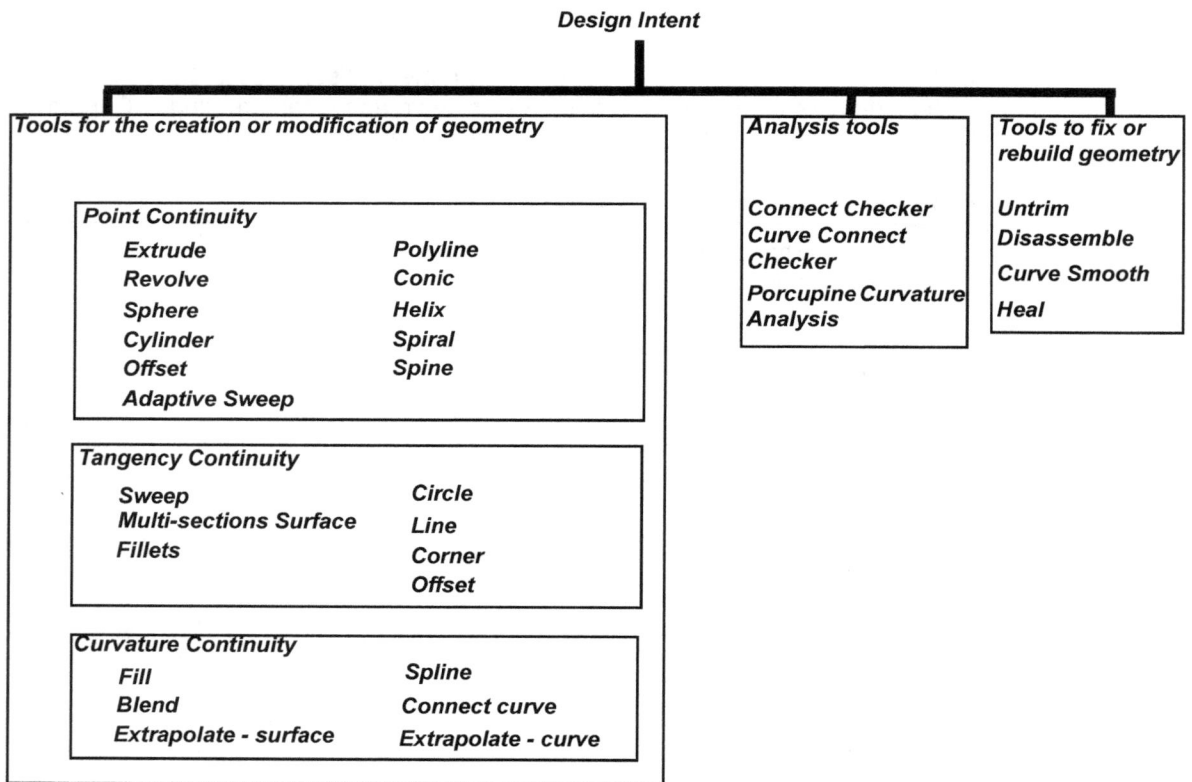

Design Intent

Tools for the creation or modification of geometry

Point Continuity

Extrude	Polyline
Revolve	Conic
Sphere	Helix
Cylinder	Spiral
Offset	Spine
Adaptive Sweep	

Tangency Continuity

Sweep	Circle
Multi-sections Surface	Line
Fillets	Corner
	Offset

Curvature Continuity

Fill	Spline
Blend	Connect curve
Extrapolate - surface	Extrapolate - curve

Analysis tools

Connect Checker
Curve Connect Checker
Porcupine Curvature Analysis

Tools to fix or rebuild geometry

Untrim
Disassemble
Curve Smooth
Heal

Figure 14–1

The tools in the Generative Shape Design workbench can be categorized in many different ways, not just as described above. For example, which tools enable you to define the profile of the resultant surface?

- Extrude

- Revolve

- Adaptive Sweep

- Sweep

- Fill

- Multi-sections surface

- Blend

Which tools can force the resultant curve to lie on a support surface?

- Line

- Reflect line

- Parallel curve

- Corner

- Circle

- Spline

- Spiral

- Isoparametric curve

- Project curve

- Sketch

Which tools are operational tools? These would be the tools that cause the resultant curve or surface to change in some way.

- Join

- Split

- Trim

- Heal

- Curve Smooth

- Untrim

- Disassemble

- Fillet tools

- Translate

- Rotate

- Scale

- Affinity

- Symmetry

- Extrapolate

In trying to avoid referencing sub-elements or boundary representations, which tools aid in the creation of an explicit element as a reference?

- Point

- Extract curves

- Extract points

- Extract surfaces

- Boundary curves

It is important to consider these basic questions when modeling curve and surface geometry.

Practice 14a

Exhaust Diffuser

Practice Objectives

- Create curvature continuous wireframe without instruction.
- Create surface geometry without instruction.

In this practice, the exhaust diffuser will be completed without any instruction. The completed part displays as shown in Figure 14–2. All splines and connect curves in the model need to be curvature continuous. All surfaces need to be tangency continuous.

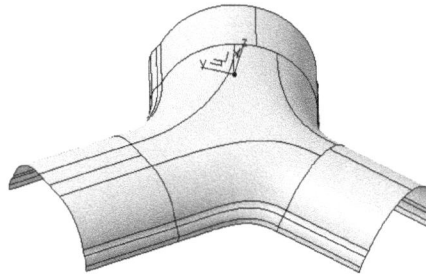

Figure 14–2

Task 1 - Open a part file.

1. Open **ProjectA_Start.CATPart**. The part displays as shown in Figure 14–3.

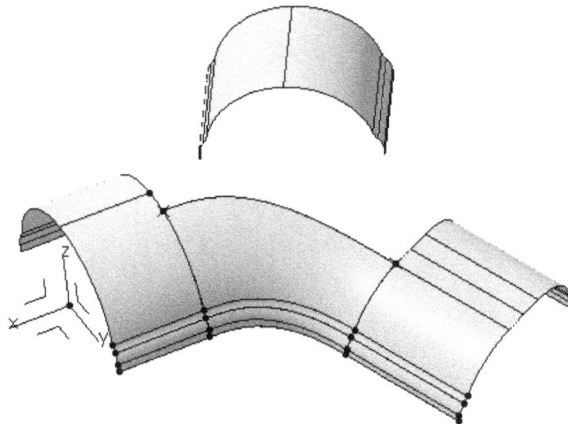

Figure 14–3

2. Extract the edges highlighted in Figure 14–4. The extracted curves aid in building the wireframe in the next step.

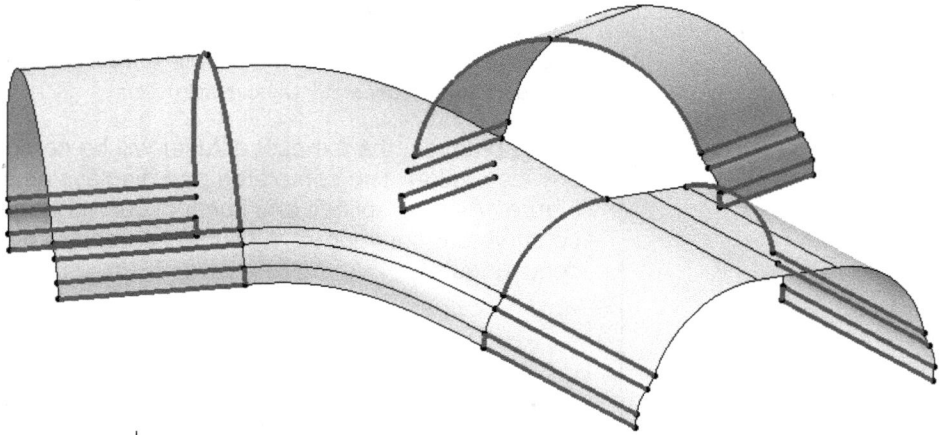

Figure 14–4

3. Create points at the locations highlighted in Figure 14–5. These points are located at the extremities of the respective extracted curves from Step 2.

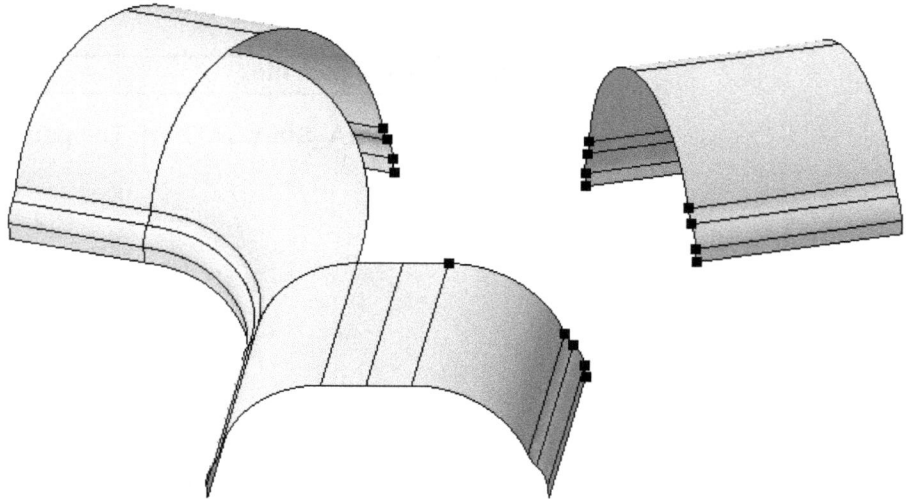

Figure 14–5

4. Create the points shown in Figure 14–6. The three points shown are **On curve** type points using a ratio of 0.8. The points are located on the respective extracted curves.

Ratio: 0.8

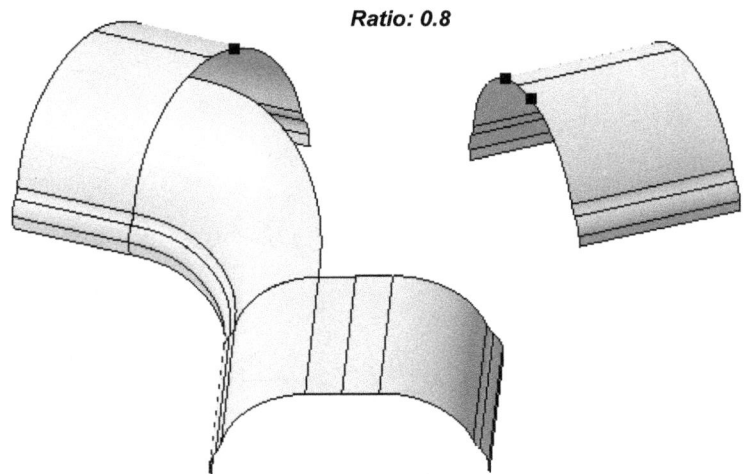

Figure 14–6

5. Create the splines and connect curves as shown in Figure 14–7. Use the points and extracted curves as references when creating the wireframe. Ensure that all of the splines and connect curves are curvature continuous.

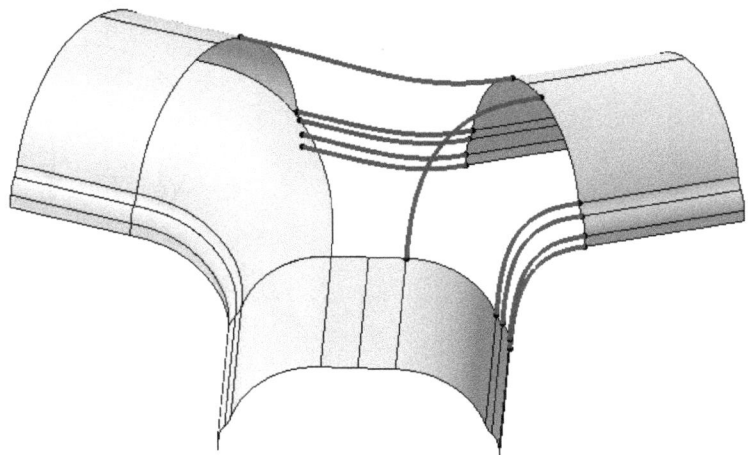

Figure 14–7

6. Create eight surfaces from the wireframe created in this project as shown in Figure 14–8. The model has been rotated to display different views. All surfaces must have tangency continuity.

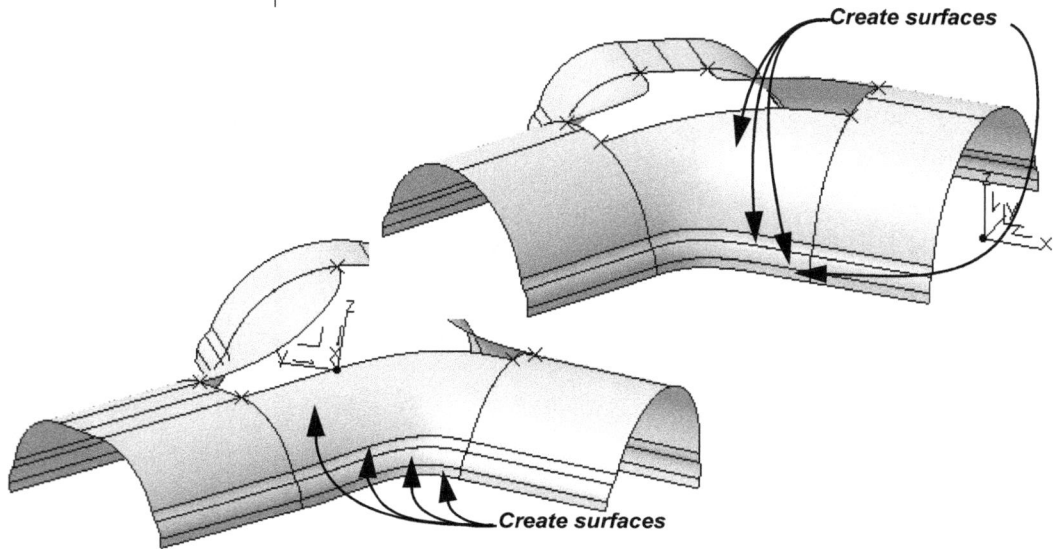

Create surfaces

Create surfaces

Figure 14–8

7. Create a surface to complete the top surfaces of the exhaust diffuser as shown in Figure 14–9.

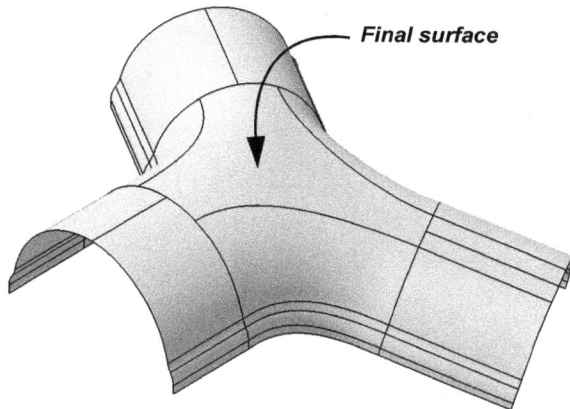

Final surface

Figure 14–9

8. Join all surfaces. The completed model displays as shown in Figure 14–10.

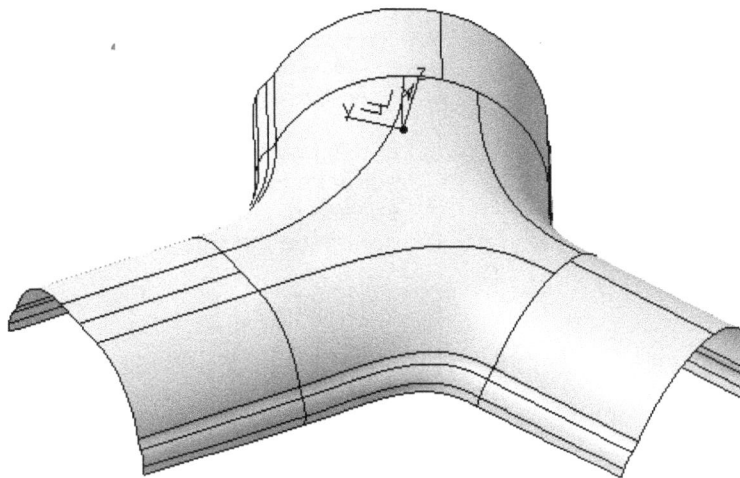

Figure 14–10

9. Save the model as **Exhaust_Diffuser_Final_ Completed.CATPart**.

10. Close the file.

Practice 14b | Offset Surface Project

Practice Objectives

- Create wireframe and surfaces without any instruction.
- Analyze surfaces without any instruction.

In this practice, you will use various tools to create the inside surfaces for the model shown in Figure 14–11. The inside surface must have tangency continuity. It is up to you to determine the wireframe and surface types to use.

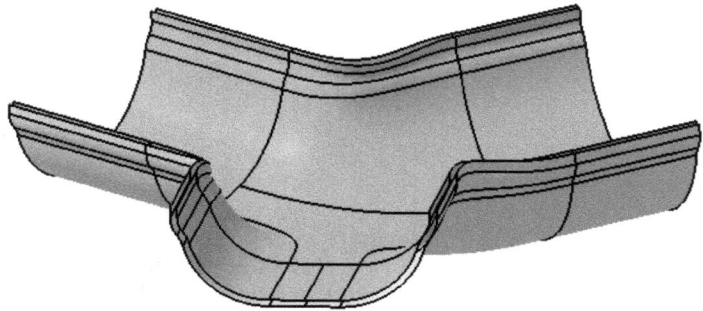

Figure 14–11

Task 1 - Open a part file.

1. Open **ProjectB_Start.CATPart**. The part displays as shown in Figure 14–12. Do not use the part from the last project.

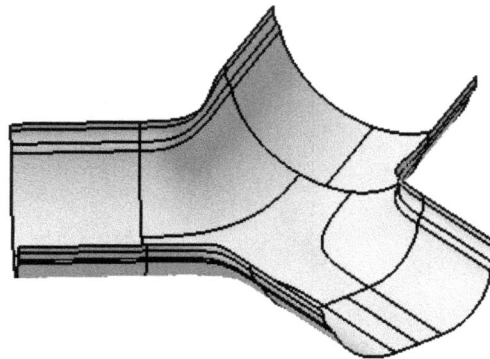

Figure 14–12

2. Create the inside surfaces shown in Figure 14–13. The inside surfaces are offset 2mm from the outside surfaces. All inside surfaces must have tangency continuity. If there are faces that cannot be offset, they must manually be rebuilt.

3. Use the **Connect Checker** to determine whether the surfaces are tangency continuous. If some inside surfaces do not meet this specification, they must be rebuilt. The completed model displays as shown in Figure 14–13.

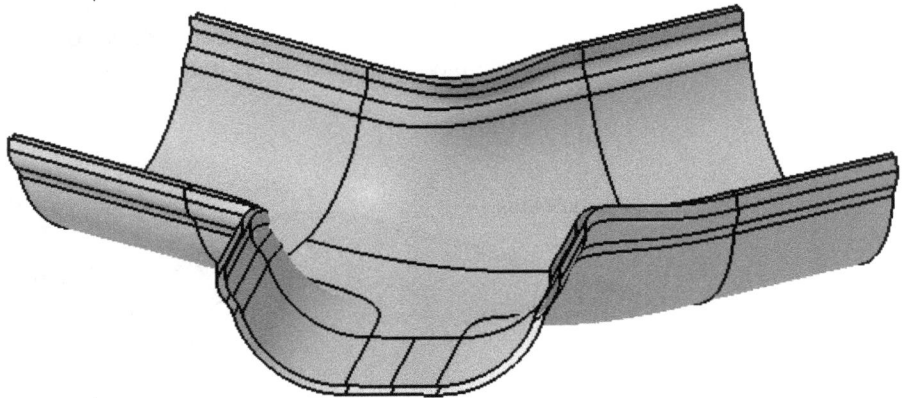

Figure 14–13

4. Save the completed model and close the file.

Practice 14c | Surfacing for Solids Project

Practice Objectives

• Create wireframe and surfaces without any instruction.
• Create solid geometry from surface without any instruction.

In this project, you will be given two surfaces to work with. You will build the appropriate wireframe and surface geometry so that the model can be solidified with a 10mm thickness. The wireframe and surfaces created need to have tangency continuity. The solid faces indicated in Figure 14–14 must be planar.

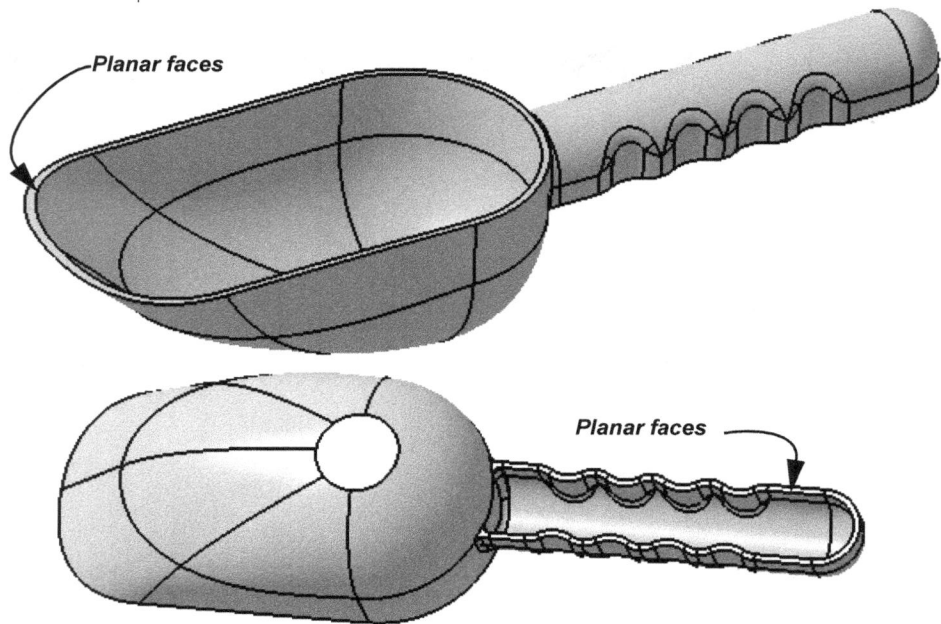

Figure 14–14

Task 1 - Open a part file.

1. Open **ProjectC_Start.CATPart**. The part displays as shown in Figure 14–15. The surfaces provided have tangency continuity and do not have any gaps.

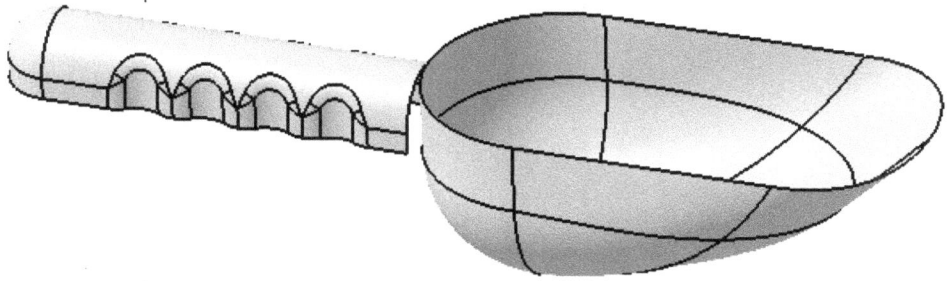

Figure 14–15

2. Create additional wireframe and surfaces so that the model can be solidified. The model must have a **10mm** inside thickness. The solid model must have planar faces, as shown in Figure 14–16.

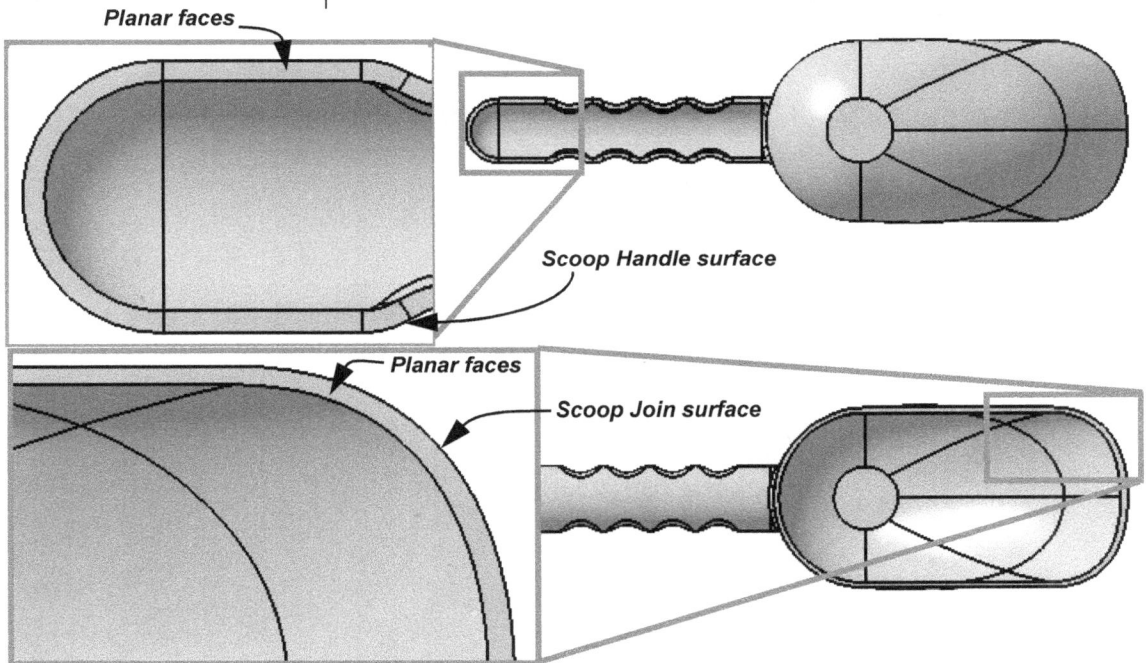

Planar faces

Scoop Handle surface

Planar faces

Scoop Join surface

Figure 14–16

3. Add a **10mm** fillet to the solid model on the edges shown in Figure 14–17.

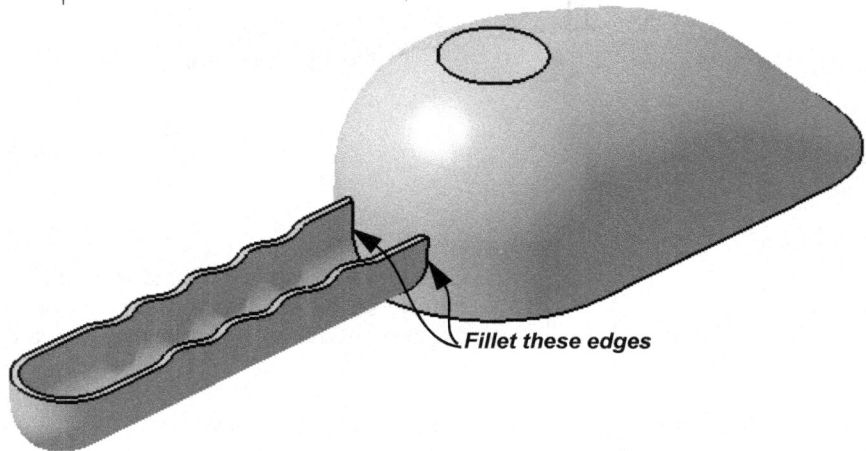

Fillet these edges

Figure 14–17

The completed fillet displays as shown in Figure 14–18.

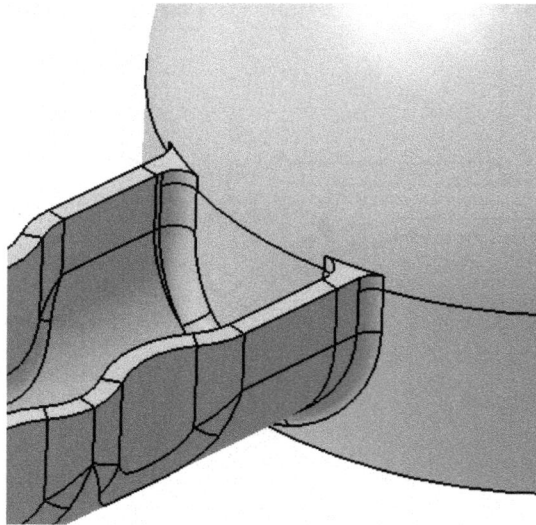

Figure 14–18

4. Save the model and close the file.

www.ingramcontent.com/pod-product-compliance
Lightning Source LLC
Chambersburg PA
CBHW082033230326
41598CB00081B/4664